2001 – ADAM TUER
2002 – Dave Topiwala
2002-3 – ~~Ed Delgado~~
2003 – Minz Guirges.

ONTARIO EDITION

Canada
A Nation Unfolding

Senior Author
Garfield Newman
Curriculum Consultant, York Region District School Board

Authors
Bob Aitken
OSSTF, and former History Consultant, Etobicoke Board of Education

Diane Eaton
Writer, Calgary, Alberta

Dick Holland
Pre-service Instructor, OISE, University of Toronto, Toronto, Ontario

John Montgomery
Former History Department Head, Eastview Secondary
School, Barrie, Ontario

Sonia Riddoch
Professor of History, Queen's University, Kingston, Ontario

McGraw-Hill Ryerson

Toronto Montréal New York Burr Ridge Bangkok
Bogotá Caracas Lisbon London Madrid Mexico City
Milan New Delhi Seoul Singapore Sydney Taipei

**McGraw-Hill
Ryerson Limited**

A Subsidiary of The McGraw·Hill Companies

ISBN 0-07-560903-7

http://www.mcgrawhill.ca

2 3 4 5 6 7 8 9 0 TCP 0 9 8 7 6 5 4 3 2 1 0

Printed and bound in Canada

Canadian Cataloguing in Publication Data

Newman, Garfield
   Canada: a nation unfolding

Ontario ed.
First ed. written by Diane Eaton and Garfield Newman.
For use in grade 10.
Includes index.
ISBN 0-07-560903-7

1. Canada – History – 20th century. I. Eaton, Diane F. Canada. II. Title.

FC170.N48 2000 971.06   C00-930774-5
F1026.N48 2000

Publisher: Patty Pappas
Associate Editor: Jennifer Burnell
Supervising Editor: Crystal Shortt
Copy Editor: John Eerkes
Permissions Editors: Jacqueline Donovan,
   Maria DeCambra
Production Supervisor: Yolanda Pigden
Production Co-Ordinator: Madeleine Harrington
Editorial Assistant: Joanne Murray
Interior Design: Dave Murphy/ArtPlus Ltd.
Page Layout and Formatting: Barb Neri/ArtPlus Ltd.
Technical Art: Donna Guilfoyle, Renné Benoit,
   Sarah Coviello, Ryan Koetstra/ArtPlus Ltd.
Cover Design: Dave Murphy/ArtPlus Ltd.

Reviewers

Michael Begley
Teacher, Collège catholique Samuel Genest,
Ottawa, Ontario.

Michael Butler
History Department Head, Weston Collegiate
Institute, Weston, Ontario

Colleen Chandler
History Department Head, Mother Theresa
Catholic Secondary School, Scarborough, Ontario

Halton Doyle
History Department Head, St. Matthew High
School, Orleans, Ontario

James Ellsworth
Assessment and Accountability Program
Coordinator, Grand Erie District School Board,
Brantford, Ontario

Robert Evans
Teacher, Dunbarton High School, Pickering,
Ontario

Murray Locke
History Department Head, Dr. Norman Bethune
Collegiate Institute, Agincourt, Ontario

McGraw-Hill Ryerson and the authors would like
to also extend special recognition to our content
specialists, Dr. Peter Seixas of The University of
British Columbia, and Dr. Veronica Strong-Boag of
The University of British Columbia.

Acknowledgements

To the team of authors whose research and expertise has filled these pages — thank you.

To Laura Gini-Newman, I want to express my undying love and admiration. Your help and insight into the material and your patience with the long nights and early mornings of work has been incredible.

To my children, Mathew, Geoffrey and Nikita who have tolerated my heavy work schedule over the past several months. The Canada of the twenty-first century will be their Canada. I hope this text will help to educate their generation about how the past has helped to determine the present and will shape their future as Canadians.

Garfield Newman

To my wife and family whose acceptance of my prolonged absences, both physical and mental, was essential, I extend my profound gratitude.

Bob Aitken

To Curtis, Brett, and Sarah Eaton, whose cheerful support made this venture possible.

Diane Eaton

To my compañera, Salma Latif, who is always there and always strong — bohut shukria.

Dick Holland

To Dad and Val – love you.

John Montgomery

To Marc Keirstead, Paulette Courchene, John Montgomery and John Fielding; our work preparing curriculum guidelines generated ideas and insights that have shaped my contribution to this text. I am also grateful for the encouragement and support I received from Elva and Bob McGaughey, two good friends and wonderful teachers.

Sonia Riddoch

This edition could never have been realized without the guidance of Patty Pappas who had the foresight to assemble a talented team and the courage to pursue new ideas and new approaches in text design.

Indispensable to the entire project was the indomitable spirit and superb talent of Jennifer Burnell. Jennifer deftly steered the project from the outset, working with the authors to produce a first-rate text.

Others among the supporting cast who helped breathe life into Canada: A Nation Unfolding were Crystal Shortt who oversaw production, John Eerkes who fine-tuned our writing, and Jacqueline Donovan and Maria De Cambra who performed super-human feats in the search for photo, illustration, and text permissions.

Bob Aitken
Diane Eaton
Dick Holland
John Montgomery
Garfield Newman
Sonia Riddoch

McGraw-Hill Ryerson and the authors would also like to extend recognition to Dr. Robert de Frece of the University of Alberta for writing the feature studies on Canadian music, Todd Mercer for writing the Humour in History feature studies, and all of our guest authors for sharing their stories and experiences.

Contents

Tour of the Textbook

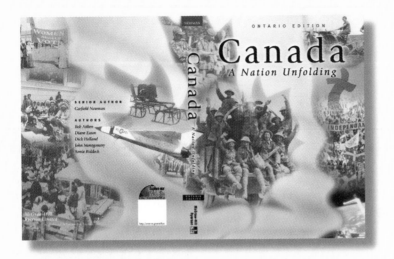

COVER

Organized to tell the story of Canada and Canadians. By moving from the international and national events which shaped Canada, to the challenges and triumphs of regions, groups, and individuals, *Canada: A Nation Unfolding* tells the story of all Canadians.

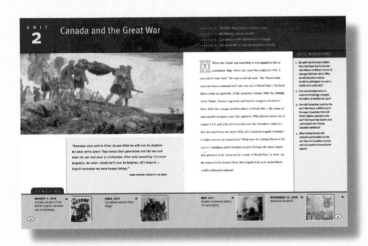

UNIT OPENER

• *Let's Investigate* Overall curriculum expectations for the unit appear in the form of diagnostic questions.
• A striking *painting, illustration*, or *photo* sets the stage, as each unit opens.
• A *quotation* helps frame the content to follow.
• A *unit timeline* sequences international, national, regional, and personal events from the unit era.

CHAPTER OPENER →

• Each chapter begins with an engaging illustration, photo, or painting, accompanied with a brief caption, which sets a visual stage for the chapter.
• *Inquiring Into the Past* questions, tied directly to the curriculum, will be answered within the chapter.
• The chapter *Timeline* sequences key events of the chapter.
• *Key Terms* are are always introduced in **bold** and defined in context.

Tour of the Textbook

DESIGNED AND WRITTEN TO MAKE CANADIAN HISTORY FASCINATING FOR TODAY'S YOUNG PEOPLE

Canada: A Nation Unfolding ensures that the study of Canadian history is fascinating for adolescent learners.

- **Feature Studies** are written to provide greater insight into 20th century Canada.

Humour in History

Each unit examines how comedy has been an important part in Canadian history, and highlights comedy as a major Canadian export.

Canadian Contributions

Highlights the various contributions that Canadians have made to technology, arts, and education.

Leisure

Allows students to catch a glimpse into the favourite past-time leisure activities of Canadians, during both times of war and peace.

Technology

Examines technological advances that dramatically changed the world, and specifically looks at Canadian technological invnovations.

Canadian Profiles

Highlights the lives of famous and no-so-famous Canadians who have made important contributions to Canadian society.

The Arts

Highlights Canadian artists, musicians, and authors. Paintings, musical scores, and literary excerpts help students to experience the arts in Canada.

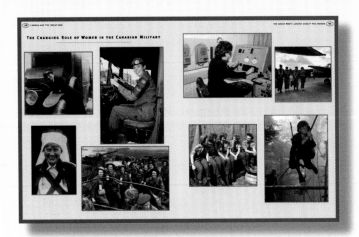

Web Connections – one per chapter – encourage students to explore topics further through the use of the Internet. McGraw-Hill Ryerson monitors these sites and adds new ones regularly.

Photo Essay –Each unit includes a visual look at an aspect of Canadian history such as transportation, fashion, Canadian symbols, etc. (With minimal narrative, the photo essays are ideal for ESL students, non-academic students, and visual learners.)

DEVELOPS HISTORICAL SKILLS

Canada: A Nation Unfolding provides the tools needed to allow students to "do history".

• *Methods of Historical Inquiry* features, appearing in each unit, allow students to learn and apply historical skills.

CHAPTER REVIEW →

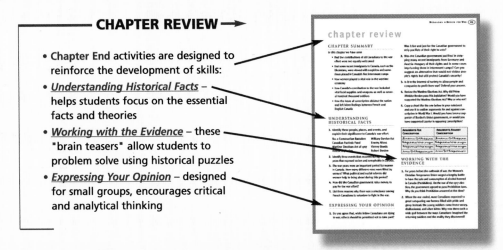

• Chapter End activities are designed to reinforce the development of skills:

• *Understanding Historical Facts* – helps students focus on the essential facts and theories

• *Working with the Evidence* – these "brain teasers" allow students to problem solve using historical puzzles

• *Expressing Your Opinion* – designed for small groups, encourages critical and analytical thinking

Tour of the Textbook

UNIT REVIEW →

"*Bringing the Past into Focus*" reviews the broader themes and issues in the unit, and can be used as assignments, group work, or presentations.

- *Reviewing the Facts* – ideal for individual homework, focuses on the content of the unit
- *Historically Speaking* – for group or individual work, requires synthesis and analytical skills
- *Making Connections* – helps students make connections between the past and the present
- *Perspectives* – helps students to consider the impact of events or decisions from different perspectives

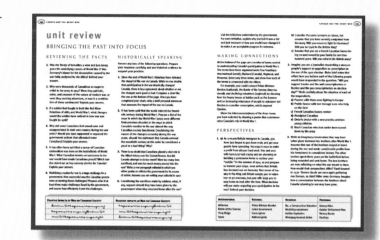

SUITED FOR STUDENTS IN BOTH ACADEMIC AND APPLIED COURSES

Maps

- Excellent detailed maps, following rules of geography

Visuals

- Photos, illustrations, paintings, and maps –
- always have captions,
- often suggest students explore further,
- located next to the relevant narrative.

Reading Cues

- Sufficient reading cues to assist non-academic students with the narrative

Laying the Foundations

Maps can be powerful tools for conveying a message. What message did this stamp attempt to send regarding Canada's place in the British Empire and the world?

RECONSTRUCTING THE PAST

Let's check your knowledge of Canadian history before 1900. The six events below represent important events in Canada between 1750 and 1900. In what order should these descriptions be placed to construct an accurate timeline? Provide a date for each event, and then create a new timeline. Good luck!

TIMELINE

| Rebellions erupt in Upper and Lower Canada | ▶ | Upper and Lower Canada are united as the Province of Canada | ▶ | Americans invade the Canadas to start the War of 1812 | ▶ | Wilfrid Laurier becomes Canada's first French-speaking Prime Minister | ▶ | British defeat French on the Plains of Abraham | ▶ | Confederation unites British North American colonies | ▶ |

Too often history is seen to be the study of dates, names, and facts. This can lead people to question the importance of what they are learning. When we realize that history continues to unfold all around us, the relevance of the past becomes apparent. The title of this textbook, *Canada: A Nation Unfolding*, was selected to convey a sense that the events that have occurred in the past century are a part of an ever-evolving time line in which we all participate. Canada in the nineteenth century was shaped by the legacy of previous centuries, just as the twentieth century will shape the Canada of the twenty-first century.

In her first address as Governor General, Adrienne Clarkson described Canada as a 450-year-old experiment that continues to unfold. She noted: "Our history demonstrates that we have the self-confidence to act and to act successfully. We can — when we trust ourselves — seize hold of the positive energy, flowing out of the choice we have made to be here and to continue what remains an unprecedented experiment." When the study of the history of Canada is seen as a means to understand the present and prepare for the future, its relevance to our lives on a personal and national level becomes clear.

In 1999 Adrienne Clarkson, who fled China with her family at the age of three, became the first Chinese Canadian Governor General.

The course **Canadian History in the Twentieth Century** examines the Canadian experiment from the dawn of the twentieth century, when Prime Minister Wilfrid Laurier proclaimed that the century would belong to Canada, to the end of the century, when the United Nations ranked Canada as the most livable country for six years in a row. Five distinct strands (themes) run throughout the course and this text. In learning about Canada in the twentieth century, you will explore:

- **Communities: Local, National, and Global** to become aware of the forces both inside and outside the country that have shaped Canadian society and Canada's place in the world.
- **Change and Continuity** to become aware of the forces of change that have shaped Canada and the aspects of Canadian society that have remained constant.
- **Citizenship and Heritage** to appreciate the various contributions made both by individuals and by groups of Canadians.
- **Social, Economic, and Political Structures** to become aware of government in Canadian society and the ways in which changing economic times have influenced the lives of Canadians.

Along with these themes, woven throughout *Canada: A Nation Unfolding* are **Methods of Historical Inquiry**. Through lessons, questions, and activities you will develop the historical skills necessary for "doing the discipline of history." You will become a strong, independent thinker, capable of tracking sources of information and drawing insightful conclusions based on available evidence. Armed with these skills, you will be able to participate in the Canada of the future as an active and informed citizen.

Communities: Local, National, and Global

Much like an onion is made up of several layers, Canadian history can also be understood on several levels. Also, like the onion, each layer on its own is only a part of a more complex whole. To understand

METHODS OF HISTORICAL INQUIRY

PREPARING TO WRITE A HISTORY ESSAY

Writing a history essay is perhaps the most complex task you will face during this course. It requires you to ask thoughtful questions, find relevant information, create and defend a clear thesis, organize your thoughts, and write in a clear and convincing manner. Following some key steps can make the challenge of writing a history essay much more manageable and help to ensure your success.

STEP ONE:
SELECTING YOUR TOPIC

Be sure to select a topic that interests you. Few people excel at researching and writing about something in which they have no interest. Spend some time in the library leafing through some books about Canada, or quickly glance through the pages of this book. What catches your attention?

STEP TWO:
PREPARING FOCUS QUESTIONS

Once you have selected a topic of interest, take the time to read something about your topic. You may want to read what is in this textbook on your topic, skim the pages of a magazine or book, or look into an encyclopedia on CD-ROM. Once you have some general ideas about your topic, prepare a list of three to five questions that you would like to attempt to answer. These questions must be analytical, not factual. For example, asking "When did the Great Depression start?" will lead to a brief and specific answer but will not provide a focus for an essay, whereas the question "Why were government actions ineffective in dealing with the Depression?" opens the door to insightful discussion, the basis of a sound essay. The focus question will help you narrow your research, making the writing of an essay much more manageable.

STEP THREE:
PREPARING YOUR BIBLIOGRAPHY

You now have a topic and several focus questions to guide your research. The next step is to locate a variety of sources from which you can gather information. This is a crucial step in the essay-writing process. Take time to prepare a list of five to seven resources that you will use. If you cannot locate more than a few sources, you may need to re-think your topic. Keep in mind that a sound history essay considers several sources of information. Using various sources will help you to detect their biases and to get a fuller picture of your topic. Also remember that there are many resources you can use in gathering your research, including books, videos, CD-ROMs, interviews, magazines, and Web sites. Once you have gathered five to seven sources, list them in alphabetical order by the author's last name, followed by the title of the source (underlined), the city where the source was published, the name of the publishing company, and the year the source was published.

Sample bibliography entry:

Newman, Garfield and Christine DeGeer. *Odyssey Through the Ages*, Toronto: McGraw-Hill Ryerson Limited, 1992

STEP FOUR:
GATHERING INFORMATION

Armed with your bibliography, you are ready to begin gathering the information you will use to construct your essay. Try to use four or five of the resources. When making research notes, indicate the title of the resource used and the page from which the information was taken. Always make point-form notes in words you understand. Making notes by "lifting" information directly from a resource provides no evidence that you understood what you read.

STEP FIVE:
CREATING A THESIS

Only when you have completed your research should you attempt to create a thesis. A thesis is a clear and concise statement that identifies the writer's point of view and what the essay will set out to prove. People who create a thesis before their research is complete run the risk of tailoring their evidence to fit their thesis. This produces biased history as the historian attempts to fit research into a pre-selected thesis.

To create your thesis, carefully review the notes you have made during your research. What trends emerge? Have some of your inquiry questions been answered? Can you formulate a clear thesis statement on a topic and defend this point of view with the research you have completed? If so, you are ready to begin organizing the sections of the essay. Remember, an effective thesis does not state the obvious, but expresses the argument to be developed throughout the essay.

STEP SIX:
CREATING AN ESSAY OUTLINE

With a clear thesis in hand and research notes to support your argument, you are nearly ready to begin writing a history essay. To ensure that your essay is coherent and makes sense to the reader, prepare an essay outline. The first section of the essay will be the introduction, which will contain your thesis. The final selection will be the conclusion. Arranging the middle sections so that the ideas flow naturally from topic to topic or from idea to idea is crucial to the success of any essay. Once you have sketched out an essay outline that seems to make sense, you can begin to connect your research to each section of the essay.

Weak Thesis: The Great Depression was a difficult period for many Canadians. (This is too obvious and there is no issue to be proven.)

Strong Thesis: The Great Depression exposed the weaknesses of the capitalist economy and forced governments to become more directly involved in managing the Canadian economy. (This thesis takes a stand on an issue which could be debated. The author now needs to provide evidence to support his/her claim.)

STEP SEVEN:
BEGIN WRITING!

Having invested considerable time in preparing to write your essay, you will now find that the writing will go quite smoothly. As you write, do not lose sight of your thesis. Each of the subsections of your essay must be connected to your thesis. If you have information that does nothing to support your thesis, it is probably not necessary for your essay. Including only information that relates to your thesis will help you to create a clear and focused essay.

WHAT DOES AN EFFECTIVE ESSAY LOOK LIKE?

Introduction
Broadly sets the context for the essay and identifies the issue to be discussed. The introduction ends with a clear statement of the thesis.

Introduction — general discussion of topic — clear statement of thesis

Body
The body is comprised of a series of arguments which support the thesis statement. Each argument should be dealt with in a separate paragraph. Be sure each paragraph has a clear topic sentence which clearly explains the argument. A minimum of three arguments should be developed to support the thesis statement.

Argument #1
Argument #2
Argument #3

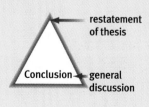

Conclusion
The conclusion restates the thesis you set out to prove, and then connects each of the arguments that have been developed to support the thesis. The introduction and conclusion act like bookends of the essay.

Conclusion — restatement of thesis — general discussion

your place in the Canadian experiment, it is important that you understand the forces that have shaped Canadian society and culture. These forces have operated at the local level (in communities, schools, and places of work), at the national level (such as in the building of transcontinental railways and a country-wide medicare system), and at the global level (such as in Canada's involvement in peacekeeping and international trade agreements). Both internal and external forces have influenced the development of Canada for several centuries.

External Forces That Shaped Canada

For thousands of years prior to the arrival of Europeans, Aboriginal people inhabited North, Central, and South America. Extensive trade routes criss-crossed the continents, clashes occurred between Aboriginal peoples, and complex societies developed. When Europeans first arrived in the Americas, they developed trading relationships with the Aboriginal peoples. Initially these relationships benefited both the Europeans, who received the furs

they valued, and the Aboriginal peoples, who received manufactured goods such as metal pots and metal axes. Eventually, weakened by the diseases brought by Europeans, the Aboriginal peoples were unable to resist the increasing pressures from land-hungry European colonists. By the eighteenth century, Aboriginal peoples were being pushed off their lands and to the margins of the developing colonial society. For the next two centuries, they faced racism and exploitation and became the poorest group in a country whose wealth attracted immigrants from all over the world.

During the first half of the twentieth century the harsh treatment of Aboriginal peoples in Canada reached extremes. Aboriginal children were forced into residential schools (away from their reserves), were denied the right to speak their original language or practise their cultural traditions, and were often abused. Once released from the residential schools they faced a life of poverty on the reserves, which offered little opportunity for them to either succeed in Canadian society or remain connected to their heritage. Some progress was made in the final

The painting *The Death of General Wolfe* served a purpose beyond recording a historical event. What evidence in the painting shows that the artist was not primarily interested in depicting historical truths? Speculate about what some of the artist's hidden purposes for the painting may have been.

decades of the twentieth century toward recognizing the place of Aboriginal peoples in Canada's past, present, and future. The story of Canada's Aboriginal peoples in the twentieth century will unfold throughout the text, leaving you to consider how fair and just treatment can be achieved in light of the past centuries of mistreatment.

French–English Relations

During the seventeenth and eighteenth centuries France laid claim to much of what is now known as Canada, while Britain developed colonies along the eastern seaboard of today's United States. Fierce competition between these two nations to be the dominant European state and to control the lucrative fur trade in North America often brought them into conflict. The final clash between Britain and France for control of North America occurred during the Seven Years War (1756–1763), during which New France fell to the British.

Since Britain's conquest of New France in 1759, the development of British North American society (and, later, Canadian society) has been partly defined by the coexistence of French and English cultures. In 1774, eleven years after New France became the British colony of Québec, Britain enacted the Quebec Act, which recognized the rights of French colonists to maintain their Roman Catholic religion and to protect their culture. The Quebec Act profoundly influenced the shaping of Confederation and Canadian history in the twentieth century. Today, Québec separatists often cite threats to their culture as the central reason why Québec should separate from Canada. As you learn about the rise of the separatist movement in the second half of the twentieth century, reflect back on the events and decisions made in the eighteenth century and consider the degree to which the past continues to influence and shape the present.

Resisting the Influence of the United States

The history of Canada is intertwined with the history of the United States. Shortly after New France was handed over to the British, the thirteen British colonies along the Atlantic seaboard erupted in revolution against Britain. As a result of that revolution, the United States of America was born. This new nation was unlike any other in the Western world at the time: it was to be a republic, in which the people ruled through a democratically elected president, and in which everyone, whether rich or poor, was to be protected by a constitution. Upper Canada (now Ontario) was created after ten thousand British Loyalists fled the newly created United States of America. They were loyal to the British King and fiercely resisted the values of the new republic.

In 1812, while Britain was preoccupied with the Napoleonic wars in Europe, the Americans saw their chance to invade the Canadas and expand the boundaries of their republic. Many Americans were convinced that Canada could be easily invaded because the citizens of both Upper and Lower Canada would welcome their American liberators. To their surprise, Canadians poured into the streets to drive out the unwanted Americans. It appeared that the United States government had forgotten that not even thirty years earlier, thousands of Loyalists had clearly chosen British values over the new American republicanism.

Even Confederation in 1867 was a clear rejection of American values and a symbol of support for strong ties to Britain. When the shape of the new Dominion government was debated, the Americans served as an inspiration — of what not to do. The bloody American Civil War, which had raged from 1861 to 1865 and claimed over 600 000 lives, was seen as evidence of the failure of the American political system. Too much power in the hands of the states had led to the tragedy that engulfed the United States. In Canada, it was believed a strong federal government would ensure that no such disaster would occur.

Resistance to American influence became increasingly difficult in the twentieth century. Television, American movies and magazines, and the increasing American economic power in Canada brought the two countries closer together. At the same time, as Canada's population became more culturally diverse, the close British ties weakened. Has Canada become a strong, independent country? Are Canadians as anti-American as they were in the past, or is there an emerging North

American culture that is shared by the two countries? Should the Canadian government actively promote a distinctive Canadian culture? These questions, as you will see, have run throughout the twentieth century and have provided fuel for heated debates over the past few decades.

A Canadian Identity

One of the questions most often asked by Canadians is how they should define themselves. Are there elements of Canadian culture that are common to most Canadians? Do Canadians share a unifying common past?

One possible answer to the riddle of Canadian identity lies in the relative harmony in which its citizens have come to live. The way in which Canadians from coast to coast have embraced the world within their borders may define the essence of Canada at the dawn of the new millennium.

The woman standing in this picture is Laura Secord. Who is she speaking to? In a few lines, capture the essence of what she was saying in this conversation, and the importance of this conversation in Canadian history.

Change and Continuity

A quick review of Canada in the years 1800, 1900, and 2000 reveals that few countries in the world have experienced as rapid a pace of change as Canada has. Less than forty years ago many Canadian school children were educated in rural, one-room school houses, and less than fifty years ago outhouses were common in rural areas. As recently as fifteen years ago, most television viewers in rural Ontario could choose programming from only three networks: the CBC, CTV, and Global.

Demographic Patterns

Over the past three hundred years, changes in population and settlement have profoundly shaped the development of Canadian society. The relative success of Canadian society in the last decades of the twentieth century has encouraged the myth that Canadians have always lived in harmony. But it is misleading to suggest that Canadian society has evolved through compromise and tolerance without conflict. To suggest that the history of Canada has been one of accommodating various cultures is misleading. As you will see throughout this course, the development of a cosmopolitan society tolerant of cultural and religious differences has been one of Canada's great accomplishments in the second half of the twentieth century.

Canada's Emerging International Status

When the United States successfully defeated the British in the Revolutionary War, it immediately severed ties with Britain and established clear and unquestionable independence. For Canada, however, the growth of autonomy has been a long, evolutionary process. In fact, it can be argued that Canada was not fully independent until its constitution was repatriated (brought home) in 1982, 115 years after Confederation! Although Canada's autonomy evolved over time, the move toward full independence was steady.

Following the Upper and Lower Canadian Rebellions of 1837, Robert Baldwin and Louis Lafontaine devised a made-in-Canada solution to the political strife that had plagued these colonies. Known as "responsible government," the new political system would lay the foundations for a

the arts

O CANADA

How does a new nation define itself with music? Patriotic national songs are often a way of identifying a country. That symbolism continues today at international sporting competitions when the national anthem of the gold-medal winner's country is played at the award ceremony.

One Canadian nationalistic song, "The Maple Leaf For Ever," composed in 1867 by Scottish-born Alexander Muir (1830–1906), a Toronto school teacher, was very popular at the time of Confederation. Because its words referred to the British victory over the French in 1759, it was never accepted as a national song by French Canadians.

In 1880, the Governor General asked the well-known British composer Sir Arthur Sullivan to compose music for "Dominion Hymn," a poem written by the Governor General himself. This would become Canada's national anthem.

The idea of Canada's national anthem being written by two Englishmen did not sit well with Québec's Société Saint-Jean-Baptiste. This organization was formed in 1834 to organize annual celebrations for June 24, the feast day of the patron saint of Québec, St. John the Baptist. They attempted to organize a songwriting competition for a true Canadian hymn. There was not enough time to organize the competition, so they asked Calixa Lavallée, a well-known composer, to write the music for a national song. Ernest Gagnon, president of the festival music committee, asked Judge Adolpe-B. Routhier to write the lyrics.

The premiere performance of "O Canada" was at a banquet in Québec City's Pavillon des Patineurs (Skaters' Pavilion) in 1880. Looking back, it seems appropriate that Canada's national anthem, which is heard at so many hockey games, should have had its first performance in a skating rink.

Many attempts were made at a suitable English translation for "O Canada." The words used today are based on those written by Judge Robert Stanley Weir in 1908. "O Canada" did not officially become the nation's anthem until 1980, and it is now often performed in a bilingual form, reflecting Canada's cultural diversity.

O Canada!
Our home and native land!
True patriot love in all thy sons command.
Car ton bras sait porter l'épée,
Il sait porter la croix!
Ton histoire est une épopée
Des plus brillants exploits.
God keep our land glorious and free!
O Canada, we stand on guard for thee.
O Canada, we stand on guard for thee.

highly effective parliamentary democracy that has served Canada well. In a few decades the Dominion of Canada would emerge from the collection of colonies in British North America. Although not a fully independent country, Canada had set out along the road to independence. Decisions concerning its future would increasingly be made by Canadians, as the role of Britain began to fade. Many of Canada's prime ministers in the twentieth century worked to bring about full independence for their nation. As you learn about the efforts of William Lyon Mackenzie King, John Diefenbaker, and Pierre Trudeau, you will come to see that the Canada of today is the product of a long and careful evolution of political and constitutional experiments and ideas.

Scientific and Technological Developments

As Canada began to mature as a nation, it also changed from a frontier and then rural society to an increasingly complex urban and rural mix. Underlying much of this change were significant scientific and technological changes. These changes were first influential on the farms, where new techniques and implements made farms increasingly profitable. Gasoline-driven tractors and steel ploughs, combined with new and hardier strains of wheat, made farming on the Canadian prairies profitable.

Scientific advances also transformed Canadian industry in the cities at the end of the nineteenth century. The steam-driven engine, electricity, and hydro-electric power fuelled an industrial boom. So did a whole spectrum of new inventions, including the refrigerator train car, the telephone, and the typewriter. But Canadians not only benefited from the many new inventions, they made valuable contributions. Reginald Fessenden, from East Bolton, Québec, is credited with inventing the forerunner to today's sonar, while Elijah McCoy, a Black Canadian from Colchester, Ontario, created a self-lubricating cup that kept machines oiled. The cup was in such demand that those who had the device began to boast about having "the Real McCoy," a phrase still common today.

Canadian inventor Elijah McCoy was the original "Real McCoy."

Throughout the twentieth century Canada continued to develop as a sophisticated urban nation. In this text you will learn much more about the significant contributions Canadians have made and are continuing to make in the fields of science and technology.

Social, Economic, and Political Structures

At the beginning of the nineteenth century the colonies of British North America consisted of a diminishing Aboriginal population and a sparse British and French population thinly scattered throughout the Maritimes, along the St. Lawrence River, and on the north shores of Lakes Erie and Ontario. Within a century this sparse, predominantly rural population would experience tremendous growth, leading to explosive growth in the cities. The rapid changes in technology and population would transform the Canadian landscape and create a need for a radical change in the role of government in Canada.

Economic Development

By the mid-nineteenth century the colonies of British North America had progressed from being largely self-sufficient clusters of farms and villages to participating in an increasingly complex economy. Shortly after Confederation, John A. Macdonald conceived of an economic strategy that he believed would ensure prosperity for Canada. **The National Policy** included three initiatives:

- high tariffs to protect Canadian manufactures,
- the settling of the West to serve as Canada's breadbasket and to provide markets for industries in Central Canada,
- a transnational railway to move settlers and manufactured goods to the West and to move wheat to the East.

Underlying Macdonald's strategy was a belief that by developing an agricultural West and an industrial East, and by encouraging East–West trade, the threat of American dominance in the Canadian economy could be avoided.

Since the time of Macdonald's National Policy, there has been much debate about its effectiveness. Did it block American expansion into Canada or merely promote the establishment of branch plants (American-owned plants operating in Canada) to avoid the tariffs? Did the attempt to develop an industrial East restrict the development of the West? Should trade have flowed north–south rather than east–west? Although these questions have their origins in the nineteenth century, they continued to play a critical role in Canada's political and economic debates as the twentieth century drew to a close. Throughout this text you will encounter the political and economic issues faced by Canadians and their governments in the past century and will come to understand the important issues that Canadians face in the new century.

The Changing Role of Government

Another issue of constant debate among Canadians concerns the role their government should play in the lives of citizens. In the years following Confederation, the government played an active role in the development of Canada geograph economically, and socially.

As Canada became an increasingly complex society, the role of government evolved. The growth of big business created a need for labour laws to protect workers; the shift from an agricultural economy to an industrial economy spawned the growth of cities and an expanded role for government in regulating housing and related services. As we head into the "information age," governments must play an increasingly critical role in the education and training of youth to maintain an internationally competitive workforce. Is the Canadian government playing an active enough role in society? Is it too involved in the day-to-day lives of Canadians? Keep these questions in mind as you learn about the emergence of modern Canada in the twentieth century.

Citizenship and Heritage

In studying the history of Canada, it is important to attempt an inclusive and balanced view. There is no doubt that political and economic elites played crucial roles in the development of the Canadian econ-

This photograph of Donald Smith symbolically driving in the "Last Spike" to finish the transcontinental railway was widely used to promote rail travel and became one of the most famous photographs in Canadian history.

This photograph of the workers who actually built the transcontinental railway and drove in the last spike was taken immediately after the dignitaries shown on the previous page went home. Few Canadians recognize this photograph. What does this tell us about who shapes historical memory?

omy and political system. Yet, it is the common people—those who are not among the economic, political, and social elites — who provide the soul of any country. In coming to understand the triumphs and failures of Canada, all those who contributed to the building of the country must have a place in its history.

Individual Canadians and Canadian Identity

Traditional histories of Canada tend to present a political and economic view of the development of the country in which the nation's elites receive most of the attention. Much is taught about political leaders, wealthy bankers and industrialists, and prominent scientists, inventors, and war heroes. Their contributions to the development of Canada must not be overlooked, but neither do they solely account for the history of Canada. Too often forgotten in the pages of Canadian history are the everyday heroes without whom Canada could not have been built. Although a politician may express a vision, the efforts of a whole society breathe life into that vision.

Throughout Canada there are fascinating stories of Canadians who worked in the mines and forests, fished the waters, built the cities, and struggled to improve the lives of other Canadians. Without these men and women, Canada would be little more than an unrealized ideal.

Canada Moves Confidently into the New Century

This chapter has introduced you to the strands that run through the course on Canadian history that you have embarked upon. It has also provided a brief review of the highlights of the two centuries preceding the twentieth century as they relate to the strands in this course. Clearly the events of the past several centuries exerted a powerful influence on the course of the twentieth century. So, too, the events of today will shape and influence the century to come. Approach your study of Canada in the twentieth century as a journey into the past that will shed light on the present and illuminate the path to the future.

chapter review

UNDERSTANDING HISTORICAL FACTS

The terms listed below are central to your understanding of Canadian history. If you are unfamiliar with any of these terms, spend some time reviewing them before tackling the history of Canada in the twentieth century.

The Conquest of New France

The Québec Act

The War of 1812

The Rebellions of 1837

Lord Durham's Report

Confederation

The Riel Rebellions

The National Policy

Western Settlement

SOLVING THE GREAT CANADIAN RIDDLE

Can you solve the riddle of Canadian identity? See if you can depict the essence of being Canadian in a song, a poem, a cartoon, a collage of images, a paragraph, or a collection of uniquely Canadian phrases. Select the medium that you feel you can best use to capture the essential elements of being Canadian. Reflect on the information in this chapter, and draw on past experiences in attempting to capture Canada. How do you think other people's depiction of being Canadian might differ from yours if they live in the North? On the East or West Coast? On the Prairies? In Québec?

"Canada has been modest in its history. In my estimation, it is only commencing. It is commencing in this century. As the nineteenth century was that of the United States, so, I think the twentieth century shall be filled by Canada."

WILFRID LAURIER, 1904

TIMELINE

1896
Wilfrid Laurier becomes
Prime Minister of Canada ▶

1899
Canadian contingents
leave for the Boer War ▶

Canada a century ago was a nation in the midst of great changes. During this time one of Canada's most respected leaders, Sir Wilfrid Laurier, served as Prime Minister for fifteen years (1896–1911). An economic boom swept the nation as immigration brought the population from about five million to over seven million and growth occurred in all industries and regions. With the opening of the railway and settlement in the Prairies, Canada truly became a nation from sea to sea and tried to take its place among the great powers — Britain and the United States. Beneath the image of prosperity, however, there lurked the reality of many Canadians who never shared fully in the economic boom.

LET'S INVESTIGATE

1. At the beginning of the twentieth century, was Canada truly a nation from sea to sea, or was it divided by language and the unequal distribution of prosperity?

2. Was immigration a cause or a consequence, or both, of Canada's economic boom?

3. How did Canada's international status change during the first decade of the twentieth century?

4. How did the effects of the economic boom lead to reactions from labour, women, and the reform movements?

1903
Henri Bourassa forms
La Ligue Nationaliste
Canadienne

1912
Nelly McClung helps
form the Political
Equality League

Eager to attract immigrants to settle the expanding West, the Canadian government placed posters in certain countries to tempt people to come to Canada. What features did they use in this poster to attract Dutch immigrants? Do the pictures tell the complete truth about pioneer life in Canada?

INQUIRING INTO THE PAST

- **What key elements made Canada a nation at the turn of the century?**
- **How were government policies designed to help the growth of Canada?**
- **How important was migration to Canada during the Laurier years?**
- **In what ways did the Canadian economy grow in this period?**

KEY TERMS

Compromise

Cultural Mosaic

Dominion

Free Trade

National Policy

Subsidies

Transcontinental Railways

TIMELINE

1896 ►
Wilfrid Laurier becomes Prime Minister

1896 ►
Clifford Sifton launches new immigration campaign

1905 ►
Autonomy Act comes into force (Alberta and Saskatchewan created)

1910 ►
Frank Oliver's Immigration Act comes into force

Imagine that you are a newspaper reporter from Paris or London and are visiting Canada at the beginning of the twentieth century. What would you notice? You land at St. John's, Newfoundland (not yet a part of Canada), and begin your journey west across a country bigger than any you had known. As you travel through Atlantic Canada, you see a sparse population spread out in small coastal communities that survive mainly by fishing.

As you move up the St. Lawrence River, you notice both similarities and differences between Québec and Ontario. Both provinces have a mix of rural farming and big industrial cities such as Montréal and Toronto. Most of the people in both provinces live within a 150 kilometers of Canada's border with the United States, but those who live in the Canadian Shield country are many days' journey from city life. The big differences are between the French Canadian culture of Québec, with its long, vibrant history and distinct language and traditions, and the "new" British manner of Ontario.

Moving west, you take the train and cross the Prairies, which are just beginning to change from an area of Aboriginal civilizations to one dominated by immigrants from many nations. You complete your journey by going through the many mountain ranges of British Columbia and stopping at the small but bustling port of Vancouver.

Most of the people you meet along the way are workers: women and men working six days a week as farmers, fishers, and factory workers. You encounter

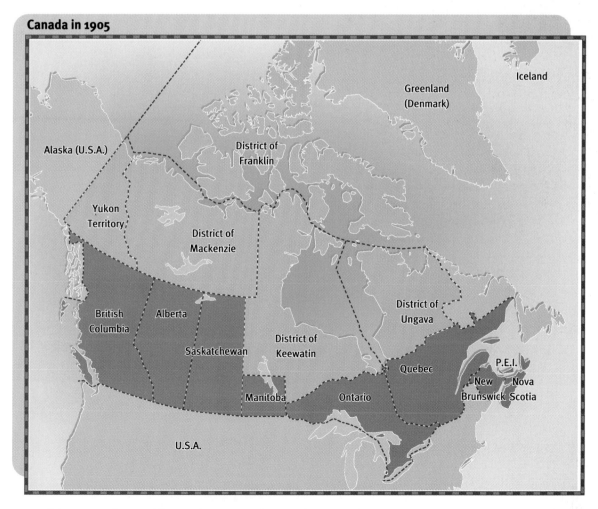

Canada in 1905

Canada in 1905. List the many differences between Canada's boundaries then and now.

Typical living conditions for many Canadian workers at the beginning of the twentieth century. What makes this house unsafe for children?

areas of different languages and ethnic origins; this is the most diverse country you have ever visited. Everywhere you go, people talk about growth. Towns are growing. Exports are growing. People act as if this will go on forever. What seems to unite Canadians is their optimism.

Wherever you go, you hear people talk about the man who seems to symbolize the national mood — Prime Minister Wilfrid Laurier. With his silver hair swept back and a warm and friendly voice, he fixes the crowd with his gaze as he proclaims: "The flood tide is upon us that leads to fortune; if we let it pass, it may never recur again. If we let it pass, the voyage of our national life, bright as it is today, will be arrested in the shallows. We cannot wait because time will not wait."

The National Mood

In 1900 Canada was less than forty years old as a nation, yet everywhere people felt the country had a promising future. Prime Minister Laurier put into words the mood of many Canadians when he proclaimed: "Canada has been modest in its history. In my estimation, it is only commencing. It is com-mencing in this century. As the nineteenth century was that of the United States, so, I think the twentieth century shall be filled by Canada." Although most Canadians were of British or French heritage, many felt a growing loyalty to their own young

Laurier's many years in office made him one of the symbols of Canada in the early 1900s.

country, and most newcomers from other parts of the world quickly took up this growing patriotic feeling.

Two travellers from England, Henry Morgan and Lawrence Burpee, seemed to reflect this optimistic outlook when they wrote about Canada:

> *Fate holds in store for this young **Dominion** a golden future. In her vast forests, her coast and inland fisheries, her exhaustless coal deposits, her gold and silver mines, iron, copper, nickel, and nearly every other known variety of mineral, and, above all, in the tremendous possibilities of her grain fields, Canada holds the promise of such commercial prosperity as the world has seldom seen.*

While the promise of good economic times meant that people were happy to be a part of Canada, the overall prosperity hid problems and divisions within the country. Not all regions would benefit from the economic boom. There would also be a growing gap between the rich and the poor. In fact, poverty among Aboriginal peoples and many of the new immigrants would become worse as Canada's industrial economy grew stronger.

A Leader for the Nation

As the young nation underwent economic changes, so too did the political face of Canada. When the Liberal Party came to power in 1896, its leader, Wilfrid Laurier, seemed "made to order" for leading the new country to maturity as a nation. His passion for Canada and his enthusiasm for the boom times received support everywhere. The fact that he was a French Canadian also meant that he appealed strongly to the French Canadians of Québec, who often felt overlooked by an English-Canadian–dominated government. Laurier seemed to be the ideal candidate for bridging the divide between English Canadians and French Canadians.

Laurier was respected as a good politician and a self-confident leader. He always seemed to have a sense of what the public needed and wanted. To people across Canada, his image was of a well-dressed modern gentleman with flowing hair, a strong face, and his identifying top hat. He was an excellent public speaker and a strong spokesperson for placing Canada in the global community.

Laurier on a "whistle stop" tour. Why was this a common way for politicians to campaign? What is the modern equivalent of the whistle stop tour?

Laurier's Spirit of Compromise

As Canada changed from a rural to an industrialized nation during the Laurier years, Canadians were often divided about what was best for the country. Laurier had to find a delicate balance among different interests and rival groups. It was no easy task; his success depended on drawing conflicting groups together in a spirit of tolerance and fair play. He summed up the process in the following statement.

In the settlement of political problems it is very seldom that a solution can be reached on pure abstract principles. When a conclusion is arrived at, it is reached by taking into consideration several points of view, and a common ground has to be found upon which the different shades of thought, the different prejudices and passions, and the different shades of public opinion can be united.

Laurier made **compromise** — finding an answer that would satisfy all sides — into a political art. His first challenge came during a disagreement between French-speaking and English-speaking Manitobans over funding for Roman Catholic schools. Manitoba's French-speaking Catholics had been guaranteed official bilingualism and separate Catholic schools when their province entered Confederation. In the Manitoba Act of 1870, Ottawa had made constitutional promises to take action if the rights of the French Catholic minority in the province were threatened. However, in 1890 Manitoba passed the Manitoba Schools Act, which cut off money for Roman Catholic schools in the province and made English the only language of instruction. Manitoba's Catholics appealed to the federal government for help.

Laurier looked for a way to give something to both French- and English-speaking Manitobans. Eventually he struck a compromise: Manitoba would not have to support Catholic separate schools, but the public system would provide a half hour at the end of each school day for religious instruction. Also, a French-speaking teacher would be provided wherever ten or more students spoke French. The compromise was accepted, but it did not satisfy everyone completely. It was less than Catholics had demanded and not all that the Manitoba government and Protestants had hoped for.

In Ontario another important group was suspicious of the Liberal Party. Business interests had always supported the Conservative Party, primarily because it had imposed the tariff, which was a tax on imports (items brought into Canada from other countries) to protect the young Canadian industries. The Liberals, on the other hand, had supported **free trade**. Laurier sensed that the tariff policy would have to change, and he passed very careful legislation that continued the tariff but freed up trade, especially with Britain (the "mother country" of most Ontarians).

Some historians say that Laurier sought short-term solutions and ignored long-term consequences. His famous compromises kept people happy, but compromises sometimes avoid or postpone dealing with the root cause of the problem. His government's support of growth helped Canada appear prosperous, but in some ways it delayed paying for the growth. It was hard to believe, for example, that Canada could sustain all the railways that it had built, the towns that had appeared, or the pace of forestry, fishing, and factory expansion. At the time, however, Laurier was loved by most people and came to symbolize what were later called the "Laurier Years."

Web Connections

http://www.school.mcgrawhill.ca/resources

Go to the Web site above to find out more about Sir Wilfrid Laurier. Go to *History Resources*, then to *Canada: A Nation Unfolding, Ontario Edition* to find out where to go next.

The National Economy

By 1900, major changes were taking place in Canada's economy. Growth in the natural-resources industries increased the need for transportation systems, especially railways. Foreign investment from Britain and

Prospectors climbing the treacherous Chilkoot Pass to reach the gold fields. Would you have been one of those people who came to the Yukon to take their chances?

the United States helped industry expand to meet the need for manufactured goods as the population expanded in the cities and as the West opened up. Factory workers and service industries became major employers. A worldwide economic boom was underway, and Canada rode into the twentieth century on this wave of prosperity.

Natural Resources

The Canadian economy was growing in the area of raw materials and natural resources. The northern areas of New Brunswick, Québec, Ontario, and British Columbia were important sources of timber, and the lumber industry was growing. Pulp and paper mills were being built to export newsprint to Europe and especially to the United States. Fishing on both the East and West Coasts remained strong.

Exciting discoveries were also being made under the ground. The discovery of gold in the Klondike area of the Yukon in 1898 made headlines around the world, and people rushed from as far away as Australia to make the dangerous trek that might make them rich. In the following decade, prospectors also helped find minerals in other places. Northern Ontario was rich in underground resources, and by 1910 Cobalt had grown up around silver deposits, the Timmins brothers had named a town after themselves near veins of gold, and Sudbury had become the nickel capital of the world.

The Opening of the West

The biggest boom in the economy was created by the opening of Western Canada. Manitoba, Saskatchewan, and Alberta had some of the best farmland in the world. Wheat and other cereal crops were vital to feeding the growing population of Canada's cities and for selling to other countries. The government encouraged settlement in these provinces by advertising all over the world and providing plots of land at low prices. In exchange, Canada developed a cheap labour force of farmers who did the extremely difficult work of ploughing the grasslands for the first time and growing the beneficial crops.

The Canadian economy was mature enough by 1900 that it did not have to rely completely on external trade with Britain. In fact, the United States was gradually becoming Canada's most important trading partner. Canadian resources like fish, wheat, lumber, and minerals were part of global trade, but they also were traded within Canada. The biggest internal trade was the movement of wheat from west to east and the movement of manufactured goods from east to west. This internal exchange of goods was the heart and soul of the **National Policy**, designed by Canada's first Prime Minister, John A. Macdonald.

The Business Community

Canada's major business leaders were also building a nation-wide business network, and with help from banks and other investment, big companies became even bigger. The beginning of the twentieth century was a time when many small companies merged together to survive or, more often, were taken over by bigger companies. In 1902 Canada had only a few consolidated companies, but ten years later there were sixty of them, which were made up of over 250 smaller companies. Some of these larger companies were so strong that they were able to expand abroad and invest in enterprises such as streetcar companies and power utilities as far away as Brazil, Argentina, Mexico, Jamaica, and Cuba.

Max Aitken, a New Brunswick financier, was an example of the businessman of the times. Known as the "merger king," he founded Canada Cement in 1909 (from eleven smaller cement companies in Alberta, Ontario, and Quebec) and Stelco (the Steel Company of Canada) the next year — when he was only thirty years old. He published a newspaper whose motto was "We lead, let those follow who can!" and went on to form a newspaper empire. In 1917 he was given a title (Lord Beaverbrook) by Britain's King George V and later became a strong supporter of universities and the arts.

The Railways

The most important symbol of the new country, crossing the land from sea to sea, was the system of railways. All over the world, railways were becoming the most efficient way to transport people, raw materials, and manufactured products. Highways and transport trucks were yet to be developed, and railways fuelled by coal could carry many tonnes of goods at a time. Governments everywhere helped companies to build railways that would link cities and service areas that they were trying to open up for settlement.

Canada experienced the same increase in railway construction. Railway growth was not new in 1900, but the first ten years of the century witnessed a boom in railway building. Every small settlement on the Prairies wanted a railway stop, and the future of these communities depended on the new rail companies putting a branch line and a station in their area. By World War I, many areas of Canada were crossed by more than one railway line. New towns also developed along the new railway lines.

The Canadian government had provided huge **subsidies** to the Canadian Pacific Railway by giving it tax breaks, loans, and extensive land grants. Now other railway companies wanted the same consideration. The Canadian Northern Railway had built up sections of line across the country and wanted to fill in the missing parts in order to become the second transcontinental line. It appealed to the federal and provincial governments for financial support and received guarantees of over $230 million.

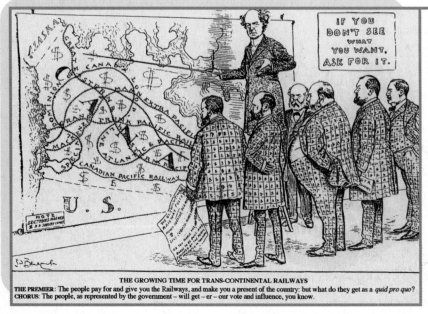

A cartoonist's view of railroad expansion in Canada. In your own words, summarize the artist's criticism of Wilfrid Laurier and his policy.

THE GROWING TIME FOR TRANS-CONTINENTAL RAILWAYS
THE PREMIER: The people pay for and give you the Railways, and make you a present of the country: but what do they get as a *quid pro quo*?
CHORUS: The people, as represented by the government – will get – er – our vote and influence, you know.

Laurier then convinced his Cabinet to give similar breaks to the Grand Trunk Pacific Railway, which received guarantees of $13 000 per mile in the Prairies and 75 percent of the cost of construction in the Rockies. The Canadian Northern and Grand Trunk were encouraged to co-operate, but they never did. Soon the overextended system of three **transcontinental railways** collapsed, and eventually the Canadian Northern and Grand Trunk became part of Canadian National Railways.

Immigration in the Early 1900s

With business, mining, and logging occurring in the East, farming in the West, and a drive to build railways across the country, Canada needed more labourers and farmers than were available. In 1896 Laurier had appointed the young, ambitious Clifford Sifton as minister of the interior, and Sifton decided on an aggressive "open door" immigration policy.

Sifton pinpointed what he considered "desirable" countries and then flooded them with pamphlets, posters, and advertisements promising free land in Canada's West. Notices went up in the post offices and railway stations of European cities and towns. Agents were hired to set up immigration offices so that they could process potential migrants faster. In countries where Canada's agents were unwelcome, Sifton used undercover agents operating as part of the North Atlantic Trading Company. To attract immigrants from the United States, advertisements were placed in American farm journals and rural newspapers.

With pamphlet titles like "Five Thousand Facts About Canada" and "The Wondrous West," Canada promoted the idea that it was the "last frontier" and the land of opportunity. This marketing campaign caught the hearts of many people in Europe. Most of the newcomers were fleeing bad conditions there. Cities were overcrowded, and farmland was expensive and owned by rich landlords who rented out the land and expected most of the crops in return. Many people in Eastern Europe and the Russian Empire were also being persecuted because of their religion. Canada must have seemed like a dream come true. Soon Germans, Americans, Swedes, British,

Humour in History

Stephen Leacock is recognized as one of Canada's and the world's great humourists. As well as being a humourist, Leacock was a political economist. He taught economics and political science at McGill University, in Montréal, from 1903 to 1936. In 1910, against the advice of a friend who felt his humorous writings would ruin his reputation as an economist, he wrote *Literary Lapses*. Luckily for Canada and the world, Leacock in 1912 went on to write *Sunshine Sketches of a Little Town*, a humorous look at the social, political, business, and religious life of a fictional small Canadian town.

In 1903 Wilfrid Laurier called for a second transcontinental railway, starting one of Canada's

greatest railway-spending sprees and a boom time for rail travel. In his "Hints to Travellers" in *Literary Lapses*, Leacock offers some tips for those about to travel by rail in Canada.

Sleeping in a Pullman car [a railway sleeping car] presents some difficulties to the novice. Care should be taken to allay all sense of danger. The frequent whistling of the engine during the night is apt to be a source of alarm. Find out, therefore, before travelling, the meaning of the various whistles. One means, "station," two, "railroad crossing," and so on. Five whistles, short and rapid, mean sudden danger.... Should they reach five, draw on your trousers over your pajamas and leave the train instantly. As further precaution against accident, sleep with the feet towards the engine if you prefer to have the feet crushed, or with the head towards the engine, if you think it best to have the head crushed. In making this decision try to be as unselfish as possible. If indifferent, sleep crosswise with the head hanging over into the aisle.

Ukrainians, Dutch, Icelanders, Norwegians, Russians, and more were coming by the thousands. Canada's population swelled by two million in the first decade of the twentieth century.

Mixed Reactions

Despite the crucial need for hard-working immigrants, they were received with mixed feelings by some Canadians. Many English-speaking Canadians wanted only settlers of British background, in order to keep Canada's ties with England strong. Many French-speaking Canadians were afraid that in a West of so many languages and cultures, their claims for French-language rights and separate Roman Catholic schools might be weakened.

A famous Canadian immigration poster. What advertising techniques did the artist and layout people use to make this poster convincing?

Sifton argued the opposite: the best worker was "a stalwart peasant in a sheep-skin coat, born on the soil, whose forefathers have been farmers for ten generations." Eastern Europeans were often escaping unfair conditions in their homeland and were more likely to be happy in the new country. They were also much less likely to come from a tradition of organized labour; workers who had been in unions back home were seen as troublemakers by the government.

A Policy of Exclusion

Frank Oliver, a strong critic of Sifton's policy, became minister of the interior in 1905. In 1910 he changed the Immigration Act to slow the tide of non–English-speaking settlers into Canada. Oliver compared his Immigration Act with Sifton's open-door policy and proudly proclaimed that his approach was "restrictive, exclusive, and selective." This was "not an Act to promote immigration," he said bluntly. For example, under section 37 of the 1910 Act, immigrants had to have a minimum sum of money, but the amount could "vary according to the race." Immigration officers could and did use such powerful restrictions to turn away members of certain groups — especially Asians and African Americans, Jews, Asiatic Indians, and southern Europeans.

The reality was that the waves of newcomers around the turn of the century were the vital fuel for the engine of Canada's fast-growing economy. In spite of Oliver's policies, non–English-speaking immigrants from many countries continued to flow into Canada until the outbreak of war in 1914. The Laurier years marked the real beginning of the Canadian **cultural mosaic**. Many newcomers stayed in the industrial centres, and most major Canadian cities had an Italian district, a Polish quarter, or a Chinatown. Other immigrants took up homesteads on the Prairies, and maps of the Canadian West are sprinkled with place names brought from the "old countries," such as Strasbourg, Esterhazy, Verigin, and Stettler.

BIRTHPLACES OF CANADA'S POPULATION, BY PROVINCE, 1911 (PERCENT)	Canadian - Born		Immigrants	
	Born in province	Born in another province	British-born	Foreign-born
Nova Scotia	90.2	2.5	5.1	2.2
New Brunswick	90.7	4.1	2.9	2.3
Prince Edward Island	95.4	1.8	1.8	1.0
Québec	91.1	1.6	3.6	3.7
Ontario	76.6	3.3	14.2	5.9
Manitoba	37.5	20.6	20.9	21.0
Saskatchewan	20.7	29.8	16.5	33.0
Alberta	19.7	23.6	18.6	38.1
British Columbia	21.5	21.6	30.1	26.8
CANADA	70.2	7.8	11.6	10.4

Source: *Canada Year Book*, 1913. Data rounded off.

The birthplaces of Canada's population, by province, 1911. What three conclusions can you draw from these numbers?

A Decade of Change

Canada at the beginning of the twentieth century was a country that felt for the first time that it could begin to live up to its motto and stretch "from sea to sea." The boundary with the United States had been settled in the 1800s and there had long been European settlement on both the Atlantic and Pacific coasts, but it was at this time that population growth occurred on the Prairies. In 1905 Saskatchewan and Alberta became provinces, and with regular rail traffic crossing Canada there was a feeling that it was a complete nation. Mining developments also meant increasing populations in the northern areas, and the boundaries of Québec and Ontario were extended to what they are today.

As that imaginary European reporter who crossed Canada, you might return home full of stories. You would be able to write about Canada during the Laurier years as a country undergoing many changes: forests that heard the sounds of mills and mining for the first time, new farms everywhere, and towns becoming cities; newcomers arriving from all over the world to start a new life in Canada.

You might read your fellow traveller J.A. Hobson exclaim that for Canada, "her day has come ... the poor relation has come into her fortune, a single decade has swept away all her diffidence, and has replaced it with a spirit of boundless confidence and booming enterprise."

METHODS OF HISTORICAL INQUIRY

TECHNOLOGY AND THE HISTORIAN

What image comes to mind when you think of a historian? A professor in a university, someone working in a museum, a researcher in a library, or possibly a high school history teacher? Are they reading books, looking at old documents, or teaching history? Does your image include microfilm, CD-ROMs, and the Internet? If not, you're missing some of the most important tools that historians now use to study the past.

In the past historians relied on material that they could physically handle, ranging from books, diaries, letters, and official documents to objects found in gravesites, shipwrecks, and abandoned villages. They communicated their research by writing books or articles for journals. The problem was that valuable documents and books are located all over the world. Some artifacts are too old and delicate to let historians and the public handle them. As a result, historians often could not get the documents they needed.

In the 1960s and 1970s technology began to change the way historians did research. The use of microfilm meant that students of history could see records that were located too far away or were too delicate and valuable. Microfilm contains microphotographs of the original document or artifact. By using microfilm readers, historians now had inexpensive and easy access to thousands of documents. For example, using microfilm, a historian in Regina could now go to the local library and look at the *Toronto Globe* newspaper from 1911.

As with many other disciplines, the technology that most changed the way historians do their research is the computer. The computer appeals to a basic needs in every historian — the ability to access and interpret information. Although historians may start their investigation by using books and journals, they may move on to historical CD-ROMs. One CD-ROM can store an entire set of encyclopedias or every issue of a newspaper printed for a whole year. CD-ROMs often have research tools built into their technology to help the historian quickly access the information they contain.

One of the most powerful sources of information the historian can use is the Internet. The Internet may be the first, middle, or last tool the

Microfilm allows the storage of a whole month's issues of newspapers on one roll of film. Why are documents much more accessible with microfilm? What disadvantages does this technology have?

Historians often use a computer first for research, before looking through books and journals. What sources do you think a historian should go to first? Why?

historian uses. Imagine being able to view the collection of artifacts at the Glenbow Museum in Calgary, read Sir Wilfrid Laurier's personal papers, or see a collection of turn-of-the-century photographs in the City of Toronto Archives, all without leaving your desk. Using a search engine to help narrow down the number of Web sites on a subject, the historian can look at several Web sites from around the world and chat with other people who have the same interests.

It is tempting to venture off of these Web sites, but beware of getting lost among interesting but unrelated or unreliable sites. Follow these tips as you proceed in your research.

1. Make sure the sites are reliable. Use sites that have been recommended or are produced by government or educational institutions. Use the URL (Web address) or opening page to check the source of the site.
2. Check that the Web site is current. Most reliable Web sites will tell you when they were last updated.
3. Keep track of everywhere you go, and bookmark good sites. Remember that Internet research needs to be documented in your bibliography as well.
4. Use multiple search engines that search more of the Internet, but remember that they do not cover everything.
5. Remember to use good search terminology; putting quotation marks around a phrase or proper name and a plus or minus sign in front of a search term to make sure that it either appears or does not appear. You might, for example, type the following: "Salvation Army" + Canada-Britain.

Finally, before starting their research for the day, historians check their e-mail. Thousands of scholars are on-line around the world, and they may be part of at least one Internet discussion group (or listserv) focused on the subject of their interest.

After historians complete their initial research, computers again become an important part of the process. Imagine doing an analysis of immigration numbers without the spreadsheet and charting capabilities of the computer. Finally, consider how slowly the numerous drafts would be prepared without a word processor.

For high school students, innovations in technology mean that they get an opportunity to practice some of the skills of actual historians. How do you use technology in your research?

chapter review

CHAPTER SUMMARY

In this chapter we have seen

- how many people in the young country called Canada felt that theirs was a nation from the Atlantic to the Pacific for the first time during the Laurier years

- how the development of the West (with productive farms and hundreds of thousands of newcomers) fuelled an economic boom that lasted more than ten years

- that the boom resulted in railroad expansion, greatly increased exports of crops and raw materials, and an expansion of the industrial economy

- that immigration was key to this growth and to the growing diversity of Canada

UNDERSTANDING HISTORICAL FACTS

1. Identify these people, places, and events, and explain their historical significance.

   Grand Trunk Pacific Railway   Cobalt, Ontario
   Clifford Sifton   Liberal Party
   Manitoba Schools Act   Immigration Posters
   Immigration Act of 1910   Max Aitken

2. Make a two-column comparison chart that lists Laurier's achievements in the first column and compares these to his shortcomings in the second column.

3. Create a web to indicate at least six ways in which immigration changed Canada.

4. How did Frank Oliver's Immigration Act differ from Clifford Sifton's?

5. Using a Canadian atlas, select ten Western communities. For each, do some research to determine the origin of the community's name. How many of the names you selected have European origins?

6. Make a two-column chart about immigration that compares the reasons why people left their countries (the "push" factors) with their reasons for choosing Canada (the "pull" factors).

EXPRESSING YOUR OPINION

1. Is it fair to call the years 1896 to 1911 "the Laurier years"? Support your answer with historical evidence.

2. Why did business owners benefit the most from the economic boom?

3. Drawing on the historical evidence presented in this chapter, write a two-paragraph critique of either Clifford Sifton's or Frank Oliver's immigration policy. In your critique, either defend or condemn the policy. Be very clear in expressing your opinion.

4. Economic boom times are often followed by a "bust." What were the weaknesses of the economy in Laurier's time?

WORKING WITH THE EVIDENCE

1. List at least five questions you would ask Wilfrid Laurier if you had a chance to have dinner with him in 1910.

2. The University of Victoria's Department of History has collected the facts surrounding a historical mystery on its Web site. Go to http://web.uvic.ca/history-robinson/ and try to solve the mystery.

Canada's Emerging Diversity

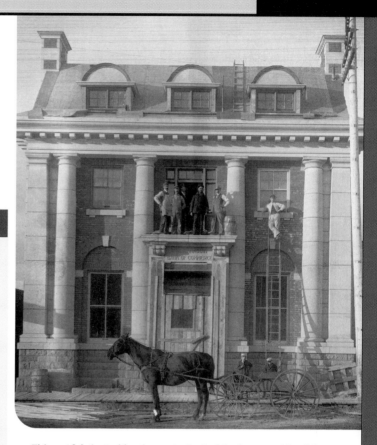

This prefabricated bank was typical of the boom spirit of the Laurier years. Twenty railroad cars shipped the whole bank building in pieces. This one was assembled in fast-growing Edmonton in 1902.

INQUIRING INTO THE PAST

- Why were the various regions of Canada at different points of development in 1900?
- How did the increasing immigration to Canada affect Aboriginal communities?
- Why did French Canadians feel that their culture was threatened?
- What barriers were faced by non-White newcomers to Canada?
- How did immigrant communities participate in and contribute to the development of Canada?

KEY TERMS

Discrimination

Industrialization

Nationaliste

Racism

Reserves

Sodbusters

TIMELINE

1903	1906	1907	1910
Henri Bourassa founds La Ligue Nationaliste Canadienne	Ontario Hydro is established	Anti-Asian riots occur in Vancouver	Amendments are made to the Indian Act

During the first decade of the twentieth century, Canada began to experience enormous growing pains. The country began to see that it was made up of regional economies that were not growing with equal rates of success. Also at this time, Canada experienced the largest wave of immigration in its history to that point. Depending on where they settled and the skills they brought with them, some newcomers prospered, while others faced poverty. Immigrants did not always find the better life that they were hoping for, and the Aboriginal peoples found themselves pushed to the margins of Canadian society. It was all these factors — the differing economies, the massive immigration to Canada, and its effect on the Aboriginal peoples — that changed Canada into a truly diverse country by 1900.

Prime Minister John A. Macdonald's National Policy had been developed in 1879 to integrate the economies of the various regions. The Western settlers were to sell their agricultural products to the Eastern provinces, and the Eastern provinces were to sell their manufactured goods to the Westerners. While it made sense in theory, the National Policy was far from completing its task. During the Laurier years, not all of Canada's regions shared in the growing prosperity of the young country.

The Prairie Economy

One of the fastest-growing areas of the economy during the Laurier years was the wheat boom on the Prairies. When Wilfrid Laurier became Prime Minister in 1896, Canada produced eight million bushels of wheat per year. At the end of his term in 1911, however, wheat production had reached 230 million bushels and totalled 42 percent of Canadian exports. Prosperity, however, did not come to the West simply because of the worldwide demand for its wheat. Dairy and mixed farming were important in some areas of Western Canada, and ranching spread quickly in southern Alberta and eastern British Columbia. Railway expansion helped the West develop more than any other region in Canada by reducing the time and cost of transporting its produce. The boom in the Western economy resulted from the hard work of the new settlers. It was backbreaking work, and not everyone could succeed.

The Sodbusters

Newcomers to the Prairies were sold a quarter section of land (160 acres, or 65 hectares) for only ten dollars. Once the land was located, the settlers would "bust the sod" (break the tough surface soil) and cut it into bricks to build a shelter, or "soddie," for the first

Kimberley, Saskatchewan, in October 1909 and thirty-five days later. Why was this town built so quickly, and what evidence do you see that it was a good site?

winter. The **sodbusters** would then try to raise at least one small crop. If they could harvest and sell the crop, the money earned could buy better tools and some of the food and staples that they could not grow. Often, members of a family would work on the railway or in lumber camps for part of the year to earn extra money so that the family could survive.

The sheer size and emptiness of the Prairies often impressed and sometimes shocked the settlers. One woman wrote in her diary: "I'll never forget the desolate feeling that came over me when we sat on a box and looked around, not a sign of any other human habitation.... If we wanted a house to cover us, a stable for our horses, a well for drinking water, it would all have to be the work of our own hands." Nearly 40 percent of families who claimed a section of land were eventually forced by nature to give up or sell their land. Those who had survived prairie life for even a year were called "old-timers." Families prayed that they could avoid wheat rust, grasshoppers, sawflies, or drought, and they constantly watched the horizon for lightning-fast grass fires, hail storms, and winter blizzards. Through the hard work of the immigrants, the prairie landscape slowly became settled, and rapidly growing towns became scattered across the West. The largest urban centre on the Prairies was the gateway city of Winnipeg.

The Growth of Winnipeg

Winnipeg was a city with one of the highest rates of growth in Canada. Its strategic position at the eastern edge of the Prairies meant that it acted as a two-way funnel. All the wheat and grain exports to Eastern Canada had to go through the city via the railroads, and all the manufactured goods and immigrants going to the West also had to pass through it. A Chicago writer in 1911 described the situation in this way:

> All roads lead to Winnipeg. It is the focal point of the three transcontinental lines of Canada, and nobody, neither manufacturer, capitalist, farmer, mechanic, lawyer, doctor, merchant, priest, nor labourer, can pass from one part of Canada to another without going through Winnipeg. It is a gateway through which all the commerce of the East and West, and the North and the South must flow.

Winnipeg's Main Street, 1904. What evidence can you find in the photograph that Winnipeg was a large, multicultural, commercial city by this time?

The Coastal Economies

The east–west trade fuelled by the establishment of factories in the cities of Eastern Canada and the great wheat boom on the Prairies meant that traditional resource industries such as fishing and small-scale forestry had to struggle to compete. The fisheries were one of Canada's oldest industries, and it seemed that the coastal regions could prosper forever with the endless bounty of the sea. But British Columbia and, especially, Atlantic Canada struggled for their share of Canada's boom-time benefits.

Atlantic Canada

Like other areas of Canada, the East Coast grew during the Laurier years. Compared with other regions of Canada, however, the economy of the Atlantic region did not prosper as much, and the region began to resent the success and domination of Ontario and Québec. Many factors contributed to this region lagging behind the others. Prized industries like shipbuilding, which had relied on wood and had been the backbone of the Atlantic economy, were being forced out of production by the manufacture of steel ships. Local fisherman could no longer compete with the freighter-size fishing boats that could fish farther away and for longer periods of time.

Also, if the fishing industry was to be able to continue, a huge investment was needed in recent inventions such as safe canning and cold storage. Investment in the Atlantic economy was the key to its survival, but local banks and businesspeople were putting their money into the booming industries of Québec and Ontario. Some success came with the diversification of the economy into areas such as iron and steel, but even these industries were largely owned by Ontario investors, and profits were not reinvested in the Atlantic economy. By the end of Laurier's years as Prime Minister, the prosperity of the Atlantic provinces lagged far behind that of the other regions of Canada.

British Columbia

The presence of outside investment meant that Canada's West Coast economy fared better than that of the East Coast. Various types of valuable salmon made the fishing industry attractive for investment, and by 1902 the industry was dominated by an American-owned firm, the British Columbia Packers' Association.

British Columbia was also expanding its economy by investing in its other primary industries. The province was the new frontier in forestry, and Canada was soon to become the world leader in the production of newsprint. Mining also benefited

from investment from Central Canada, Britain, and the United States. Less than a generation after the discovery of copper and gold deposits in the Kootenay region in 1887, the Cominco company was one of Canada's largest mining companies. In 1910, British Columbia was second only to Ontario in the value of its mining industry.

Industrial Canada

Central Canada was the economic powerhouse of Canada by 1900. While most of Canada's regions relied upon their primary industries, southern Ontario and Québec experienced an industrial revolution. In the second half of the 1800s the production of consumer goods such as clothing, textiles, and footwear helped to expand the factories and cities of southern Ontario and Quebec.

After 1900 these areas used Canadian and foreign investment to expand into the manufacturing of machinery and equipment that were needed to process the primary products from the other regions. Mining, forestry, farming, and even fishing needed new equipment to remain competitive. Related industries also grew up near the centres of production. Central Canada saw important growth in oil refining, chemical and fertilizer production, and the electric power industry.

Two views of Victoria harbour, 1886 and 1910. List the differences between the situations in Victoria depicted in these two photographs, and relate the differences to the signs of growth indicated in the text.

Ontario's Growth

Although the Laurier years were a boom time for much of Canada, most of the profits seemed to end up being invested in new industries in Ontario. Iron and steel production needed heavy investment to survive, so these profitable industries became concentrated in Ontario. The demand for iron and steel was tremendous because these metals were essential for the growth of the railroads and were used in a vast array of manufactured products, from screws and nuts, drills, and appliances to bicycles, carriages, and the new automobile. In the twenty years before 1900, iron and steel production increased sixfold and then grew another tenfold before World War I.

The establishment of the key industries of iron and steel production in Ontario led to the develop-

ment of secondary industries such as automobile, farm machinery, and appliance manufacturing there as well. For example, Massey-Harris, a farm equipment manufacturer, began business in Toronto in 1891 and soon became Canada's largest company. During the Laurier years, it alone accounted for 15 percent of Canada's exports of manufactured goods. The growth of primary and secondary industries in turn led to the rapid rise of the service sector in Ontario: grocery, clothing, and hardware stores were just a few of the types of stores that opened to serve the growing population. Perhaps the best-known Canadian store was started by Timothy Eaton, who transformed his small store on Yonge Street in Toronto into the major department-store chain of Eaton's. His country-wide success was assured when he introduced the mail-order catalogue. Through the catalogue, many rural families purchased items that they would never find at their local general store.

As southern Ontario continued to prosper, so too did its neighbour to the east. But the cultural differences of Québec would create a very different story from the one in Ontario.

Eaton's spring and summer catalogue, 1907. Why would families across Canada be excited to receive this catalogue? How did women's fashions at the time parallel the status of women in society?

Changes in Québec

The Québec economy grew in much the same way as Ontario's during the Laurier years. Hydro-electric power was expanded across the province, mining opened up the northern areas, and the cities of the St. Lawrence Valley grew by leaps and bounds in response to the development of factories. There were, however, key differences in Québec's growth. Many people felt that **industrialization** threatened the nature of French Canadian society. In 1913, Louis Hémon published his beautiful and moving tribute to habitant (Québec farmer) life, *Maria Chapdelaine*. But the life he celebrated in that novel was fast slipping away. Only half of French Canadians still lived in the countryside; many had been forced to leave their childhood villages to make a living in larger communities, including cities in the United States. Those who remained in Québec were afraid that their language and culture might not survive.

In addition, as economic growth transformed Québec, French Canadians realized that they were often being overlooked. Many factors contributed to this. While the Roman Catholic Church, the dominant church among francophones, encouraged industrialization in some areas, it did not want French Canadians to lose their old rural way of life. Also, as business-oriented Quebeckers tried to make it in the new economy they encountered language barriers. English was the language of business, and English speakers were most able to benefit from the network of English-language information about new inventions and business practices. Many Quebeckers felt trapped between fighting to save their culture and adopting English-speaking ways to get ahead in the business world.

The Growth of French Canadian Nationalism

The struggle to keep the Québec culture alive, and at the same time to counterbalance Imperialist sentiment and advance French Canadians in their own country, continued. A number of organizations emerged at the turn of the century to help mobilize this sentiment of cultural patriotism (or what was termed, in French, *nationalisme*). The most influential was La Ligue Nationaliste Canadienne, organized in 1903 by a group of ten young Québec intellectuals. Henri Bourassa, their unofficial leader, commented on Quebeckers' growing sense of isolation from the rest of the nation — their feeling that Canada was not "Canada for all Canadians." The people of Québec, Bourassa

Cornelius Krieghoff, *The Habitant Farm*, 1856. National Gallery of Canada.

The Habitant Farm, by Cornelius Krieghoff. What is being portrayed here, and why were paintings like this one popular in French Canada even after life there had changed?

the arts

THE WOODCARVERS OF SAINT-JEAN-PORT-JOLI

As home to some of the oldest European settlements in North America, Québec is a province rich in traditions spanning several centuries. The picturesque town of Saint-Jean-Port-Joli is one Québec village in which the past is preserved in cultural traditions. It is renowned for its woodcarvers, miniature boat builders, and weavers. In fact, this small town boasts the largest concentration of woodcarvers in North America

The long tradition of woodcarving can best be seen in the Church of Saint-Jean-Port-Joli, which was built in 1779. Inside are exquisite woodcarvings spanning the years 1740 to the present. The oldest piece, which predates the church, is the tabernacle, carved in 1740 and later covered in gold leaf. In 1937 one of the church's most famous pieces, the pulpit, with carved figures of saints, was completed by two of Saint-Jean-Port-Joli's best-known woodcarvers, Médard and Jean-Julien Bourgault.

Credit for the tremendous revival and growth of woodcarving in Saint-Jean-Port-Joli falls to the three Bourgault brothers, Médard, André, and Jean-Julien. These three men not only established Saint-Jean-Port-Joli as a major woodcarving centre but also established the first school of woodcarving in Québec, thereby ensuring that the tradition of woodcarving would continue to thrive.

Like the society of Québec, which has evolved and changed over the century, the woodcarvers of Saint-Jean-Port-Joli too have undergone significant change in their art. Religious themes, which initially dominated, gave way in the 1930s to habitant themes that reflected the traditional lifestyle of rural French Canada. While habitant scenes remain popular, the current generation of artists in Saint-Jean-Port-Joli are experimenting with interpretative ways to capture youthful personalities.

These three photos reflect very distinct phases in woodcarving in Saint-Jean-Port-Joli. The first is a modern piece, called *Près de l'étang*, by Pier Clautier. The second is a typical *paysan* or peasant scene, carved by André Bourgault, while the third is of the church, showing the influence of religion in early French Canadian society.

added, "are bound to come to the conclusion that Québec is our only country because we have no liberty elsewhere." Most French Canadians were deeply patriotic, but it was a patriotism rooted in Québec and the French language. **Nationaliste** leaders like Bourassa became more influential in Québec as French Canadians looked for leaders who would fight to protect their distinctive culture.

A *National* Policy?

Historians have argued over the years about whether the National Policy favoured Ontario. Some have said that the tariff system that was set up to protect business growth helped factories and corporations in Ontario and Québec but stunted any growth in the Maritimes. The policy of Western settlement opened up the Prairies but encouraged the domination of a single crop, and high freight costs left British Columbia always trying to catch up to Central Canada.

Other historians have claimed that real issue was the economic system. Expecting the Laurier government to intervene and change economic realities was too much to ask. Investment naturally flowed to the population centres and the places where it got its best return. Atlantic Canada simply could not attract enough investors. The Prairies continued to concentrate on the crops that made money. British Columbia was "too far away" to be able to establish a diverse and solid economic base. At the centre of it all, and near the industrial centres of the United States, were the booming towns of southern Ontario and Quebec. Whatever the cause, these regional economic differences created tensions among the provinces of Canada. But it wasn't just economics that was affecting the face of Canada. Millions of immigrants were about to transform the cultural make-up of Canadian society.

Whose Canada Is It?

Between 1900 and 1911, immigration to Canada was at its peak. In every region there was public debate about its impact on the country. Although the muscle-power of the immigrants fuelled the economic boom, the concept of a multicultural society was a new one for many Canadians. Even the progressive reformer J.S. Woodsworth, who worked hard for the rights of the working people, wrote a bestseller called *Strangers Within Our Gates*, in which he wrote: "English and Russians, French and Germans, Austrians and Italians, Japanese and Hindus — a mixed multitude, they are being dumped into a Canada by a kind of endless chain.... How shall we weld this heterogeneous mass into one people? That is our problem."

Some people believed that the answer lay with the social services provided by the churches. Others said that the newcomers must be educated and, above all, must speak English. Yet others took part in a backlash against the migrants that resulted in exclusionary immigration legislation, discriminatory hiring practices, and, sometimes, violence. However, the millions of immigrants did their best to adapt to a foreign, and often hostile, land. Together with those who settled before them, these peoples' impact on the Aboriginal peoples would forever change the cultural identity of Canada.

The Long Journey: Immigrant Experiences

Whatever country they came from, the newcomers began with high hopes for a better life in Canada. Most were leaving conditions of poverty, overcrowding, or religious or political persecution. After a crowded and dirty journey of about two weeks in the bottom of a ship across the Atlantic, they disembarked at Halifax or Quebec City and were inspected for diseases and "general suitability."

The next stage in the journey was a long train trip. The families rode in wooden boxcars with a cook stove in the middle. Many left the trains at cities like Montréal and Toronto to find jobs in the factories and mills and possibly find a place to live in neighbourhoods where they could speak their own language and make valuable contacts.

Thousands, however, stayed on the trains for a trip across a nation wider than Europe to find a job in fast-growing Western towns or to take their chances at farming a section of land.

Web Connections

http://www.school.mcgrawhill.ca/resources

Go to the above Web site to find out more about immigration to Canada during the Laurier years. Go to *History Resources*, then to *Canada: A Nation Unfolding, Ontario Edition* to find out where to go next.

Jewish Canadians

Jews have been a part of Canadian history since the 1750s, when they first arrived in British North America. Jewish immigration increased greatly during the Laurier years because of Russian pogroms, which were officially organized massacres of Jews that followed years of **discrimination** by the government in Russia. As a result, Russian Jews fled to Western Europe. With other refugees facing anti-Semitism (discrimination against Jews), they found their way to Canada and, in even greater numbers, to the United States. The Jewish population of Canada rose from 2500 in 1881 to over 75 000 by 1914. The largest Jewish community formed in Montréal, but other solid communities existed in Saint John, Quebec City, Toronto, Hamilton, and Winnipeg. Hoping for the promised land of freedom, however, they were sometimes disappointed. Canadian society often devised policies of **segregation** against Jews. They were limited in the jobs they could have and were sometimes allowed to live only in certain areas of cities.

Despite the barriers set up against them, the Jewish community was determined to survive as a distinct culture within Canada. Jews founded synagogues, schools, financial institutions, and newspapers. They kept Yiddish alive as the language they shared and preserved Judaism as their religion in a Christian-dominated society.

Black Canadians

The 1800s were a time of Black migration to Canada. Escaping slavery in the southern United States and racial discrimination in the northern U.S. cities, Black people came to Canada via the Underground Railway and established communities across Canada.

Although they had escaped from slavery, Blacks in Canada still faced **racism**. Many city councils actively encouraged them to return to the United States after the Civil War, and many Blacks took up the offer as land opened up and the long-delayed end of slavery finally occurred. By 1901 there were fewer than eighteen thousand Blacks in Canada. Those who stayed, however, formed strong communities in Nova Scotia, southwestern Ontario, British Columbia, and

Born as a slave, John Ware moved with his family from Texas to Alberta (then part of the North West Territories) in 1882. Ware is credited with bringing longhorn cattle to Canada and with developing the rodeo in Canada's West. What barriers would he and his wife have faced, living in the West? What education would they have wanted for their children?

Canadian Voices

AH SING'S WIFE[1] REMEMBERS

When I left my village in Taishan[2] in China twenty years ago, I was a sixteen-year-old pledged in marriage to Ah Sing who lived in Nanaimo in British Columbia, a man I had never laid eyes on.

The year was 1898. The trip across the huge ocean in the steamer took three months. Before that, the only bodies of water I had ever known were the fishponds in our village.

The marriage proposal came to my parents through *Min Baak*,[3] who made frequent trips between China and the Gold Mountain[4] to recruit and escort Chinese workers to various construction projects there. Ah Sing had asked Min Baak to propose marriage on his behalf to a hardworking young woman who would be willing to live in *Gum San* and help him run his recently acquired laundry.

Min Baak made it very clear to me and my parents that such an opportunity would never come again. According to rumours he had heard, the fifty-dollar Head Tax that each person had to pay upon arriving in *Ga Na Dai*[5] would soon be raised to over a hundred. "When that happens," he explained, "no one will be able to save enough money to bring another family member over to *Gum San*." We were told that it was most generous of Ah Sing, who had been saving up his daily wage of one dollar a day working on the railway in Canada to buy the laundry business, to offer to pay the fifty dollars in Head Tax for me.

From our village, I travelled to Hong Kong where I took the steamer to *Gum San*. The only thing that kept my spirits up during the long voyage was the hope that I might some day be able to save enough money to send for my brothers, so that, they, too, would have a chance of making a better life for themselves. In our family, we all knew that we could not pin our hopes on the tiny plot of farmland which never produced enough, even in a "good year"[6] when there were no natural disasters, to feed everybody in our family of ten.

Ah Sing went to Canada twenty years ago when he was fourteen to work on the railway. When that was completed, he made his way back to Chinatown in Nanaimo to work as a coolie[7] for Chinese-owned stores. Since Ah Sing did not speak English and was illiterate in Chinese, he had little choice when it came to employment. His determination and perseverance, however, had culminated in the little laundry that I was going to help him run.

Life in *Gum San* was not easy. Ah Sing and I lived in a small room in the back of the laundry. Because we could not afford to employ any workers, the two of us worked long hours. The air in the laundry was hot and damp any time of the year from the steam rising from the hot water we used, the charcoal stove on which we heated our irons, and the irons themselves. We ate our meals when we could find a moment in between tasks. Mostly, we ate standing at the basin or the ironing board, sweat pouring down our faces. Although the laundry closed at seven in the evening because of restrictions placed on Chinese businesses by the city, our day did not end until midnight. Ah Sing spent the evenings doing as much with the mountain of clothes as he could, while I mended or sewed on buttons — special services that we provided for our customers. We worked every day of the year, even on the first day of Chinese New Year. With Ah Sing's entire life's savings invested in our little store, we could not afford to lose money.

I never did manage to save enough money to send for my brothers. In 1900, two years after my arrival, the Head Tax was raised to one hundred dollars. Then, three years later, in 1903, it was raised to five hundred dollars. At that point, *Min Baak* decided to retire because no new worker would ever make enough money to pay the Head Tax. He returned with his family to his ancestral village in China. Many of our acquaintances in

Chinatown made the same decision because the prolonged separation from their families was just too hard to bear.

Communication with our families in China came to a halt shortly after that. Political unrest in China[8] made it hard for letters from overseas to reach the farming villages. We heard all kinds of rumours about bandits plundering villages and widespread famine. We could only pray that everyone at home was safe.

Do I regret coming to the Gold Mountain? A little. Life in the laundry is no less hard than tilling the tiny plot of land in our village in China. However, living in Gum San, we know that our hard work will bring us enough food. We are luckier than most because with our two sons, Ah Sing and I have created a family for ourselves in which we can support each other. I no longer think that I would ever see my ancestral village again. To harbour such hopes, I think, would be asking for too much from life.

CONTRIBUTED BY GLORIA FUNG. GLORIA FUNG IS A COMMUNITY LIASON TEACHER WITH THE YORK REGION DISTRICT SCHOOL BOARD IN ONTARIO.

Notes
1. Rather than referring to married women as "Mrs.," the Chinese preferred to use this form of address.
2. The majority of early Chinese immigrants were from the four prefectures, Taishan, San Wui, Yan Ping, and Hoi Ping, in the Pearl River Delta in the Province of Guangdong on the South China coast.
3. A respectful term for addressing older men.
4. Also *Gum San*. A term referring to North America, where many Chinese workers worked in the gold mines along the West Coast. In Chinese, even today, the city of San Francisco is sometimes still called the "Old Gold Mountain."
5. Canada.
6. Between 1851 and 1908 the Pearl River Delta, where Taishan is, suffered 14 floods, 7 typhoons, 4 earthquakes, 2 droughts, 4 plagues, and 5 famines.
7. Unskilled Asian labourer.
8. Major political events during this period include Boxer Rebellion in 1900; the Ching Dynasty was overthrown in 1911.

across the Prairies. Leaders arose among the Black communities, too: people like James Robinson Johnston (a Halifax lawyer and civil rights activist) and William Hubbard (a Toronto alderman who at one point was the acting mayor of the city). Prominent Black Canadians also made enormous contributions to Canadian society: Mary Ann Shadd became the first female newspaper editor, and Elijah McCoy, a lawyer, invented a cup to help machines stay oiled while running and gave us the expression "the real McCoy."

Chinese Canadians and Japanese Canadians

Chinese Canadians first came to Canada from San Francisco in search of gold. A Chinese community was established in Victoria, B.C., as early as 1858. In the generation that followed, thousands of Chinese male workers were lured from southern China to work on the construction of the western section of the Canadian Pacific Railway. They were given the most dangerous jobs — tunneling and setting explosives — and received much less pay than their fellow White workers. It is said that three Chinese men died for every kilometre of track that was laid.

A head tax certificate issued to Chinese people entering Canada. Why might a descendant of one of the early Chinese workers save one of these certificates, and what memories would it call to mind?

Chinese labour continued to be important to the Canadian economy, and many workers wanted to stay in Canada to avoid the turmoil and poverty of China at the time. British Columbians, however, were fearful that Chinese and Japanese immigrants would take their jobs. Suspicion and discrimination increased among Whites in British Columbia, and governments began to pass restrictive legislation. Non-Whites (including Japanese and South Asians) were not allowed to vote and were allowed to hold only certain jobs. A "head tax" was introduced that forced every immigrant to pay for the right to enter Canada. In 1885 the tax was a costly $50 per person; it was raised to $100 in 1902 and $500 in 1903. From 1907 onward, Chinese newcomers entering Victoria had to wait in a prison called "the Piggery" before being allowed into Canada. Sometimes they were held for up to six months. The Piggery was finally torn down in 1978, and this poem was found on one of its walls.

I have always yearned to go to Gold Mountain.
But instead it is hell, full of hardships.
I was detained in a prison and tears roll down my cheeks
My wife at home is longing for my letter,
Who can foretell when I will be able to return home?
I cannot sleep because my heart is filled with hate
When I think of the foreign barbarians, my anger will rise skyhigh.
They put me in jail and make me suffer this misery.
I moan until the early dawn,
But who will console me here?

In 1907 anti-Asian feeling reached such a frenzy that riots broke out in Chinese sections of Vancouver. Windows were smashed and shops were plundered, and Chinese and Japanese residents hid in fear. The federal government eventually granted compensation to those who made damage claims, but most rioters were never caught and the riot left a feeling of bitterness in the Asian communities.

A procession outside a Ukrainian Orthodox church in Vegreville, Alberta, in 1906. Compare this church with a religious building that you know. What does it tell you about the culture of the Ukrainians?

In an attempt to assimilate Aboriginal Peoples into the White Canadian culture, Aboriginal rituals such as the one pictured here, were banned by the Canadian government.

Ukrainian Canadians

The first major wave of Ukrainian immigration to Canada, in the late 1800s, was part of a huge migration out of the Austro-Hungarian Empire. Between 1870 and 1914 about one million Ukrainians left the Empire, and about 170 000 of them came to Canada. Ukrainians eventually migrated to all regions of Canada, but this first group went primarily to the Prairies. In the beginning, most of those who came were men. Without the comfort and help of their families, these men faced the difficult task of building a successful farm alone. Ukrainians had a reputation for being hard-working and loyal to Canada, but general suspicions about outsiders extended to them as well, and English and French Canadians criticized them for keeping to their traditions and wanting to express their culture in their architecture and ways of life.

Immigrant groups such as the ones discussed here were not the only victims of prejudice. Together with the earlier British and French immigrants, they inflicted their own prejudice on the original inhabitants of Canada: the Aboriginal peoples.

The Aboriginal Peoples in 1900

A century ago the original peoples of Canada, the Aboriginal nations, continued to be dominated by European settlers. In the years since the arrival of the Europeans, the pattern of contact seemed to repeat itself over and over. Trade with the Aboriginal peoples was followed by European settlement and ultimately led to the loss of Aboriginal land. In treaty after treaty, the Aboriginal peoples, who had towns, farms, and wide-ranging trade across what they called Turtle Island, were forced to give up their freedom and control over their lives. Many died from the diseases and epidemics that colonists and settlers brought from Europe. Others were forced to move away from the waterways where the White people settled and retreat to the forests of the North.

The Reserve System

By 1906 ten major treaties had forced tens of thousands of Aboriginal people onto **reserves**, which were small parcels of public land. The reserve system was set up to contain the various Aboriginal groups and to allow immigrants to use what was formerly Aboriginal land for farming, ranching, mining, and forestry. The racist attitudes toward Aboriginal people led many immigrants to believe they were doing something positive for these people by placing them on a reserve. They had no concept that Aboriginal societies were civilized and complex structures involving democratic decision-making, cross-continental trade routes, complex religions, and a sophisticated world view.

The basis of the reserve system was that Aboriginal people would become dependants of the federal government. Ottawa, however, often never delivered on the promises set out in the treaties. Schools were rarely built, agricultural tools were seldom given, and the small sums of money that had been promised were rarely received by the Aboriginal peoples. By 1910, settlers were even pressuring the government to take back some of the reserve land, and the Indian Act was amended by Frank Oliver, minister of the interior, to give the government power to do this. During the next year over half of Alberta's Blackfoot Reserve was taken in return for small compensation, and in 1912 a number of reserves were forced to exchange their land for slightly larger tracts of very poor territory. Meanwhile, more and more of the land was coming under cultivation from the flood of newcomers moving north from the United States or coming west from overseas. This disrespect for and discrimination against Aboriginal people would leave a permanent scar on Canada's history.

A Nation of Regions and Peoples

The Laurier years saw sweeping changes in the nature of Canada. United from sea to sea, with a string of nine provinces and a transcontinental railway system, Canada was still in some ways a collection of regions, each with its own cultural character and economy. Immigrants from many countries continued to make their mark on the social fabric of the country, and each made a distinctive contribution to Canada's growth and development.

chapter review

CHAPTER SUMMARY

In this chapter we have seen

- how the various regions of Canada developed differently during the Laurier years, with Ontario benefiting the most

- how French Canadian *nationalisme* grew strong as a result of changes in Québec

- how various immigrant groups were treated upon arriving in Canada

- how non-White newcomers and Aboriginal people faced racism and exclusion

UNDERSTANDING HISTORICAL FACTS

1. Identify these people, places, and events, and explain their historical significance.

   Reserve System   The Piggery
   Sodbusters   Head Tax
   Maria Chapdelaine   Timothy Eaton
   Henri Bourassa

2. Outline the weaknesses of an economy that relies on primary industries such as fisheries, forestry, mining, and farming.

3. Explain why Ontario was the wealthiest Canadian region during Laurier years.

4. The industrialization of Québec not only challenged the traditional lifestyle of French Canadians but also heightened French–English tensions. What evidence in this chapter supports this statement?

EXPRESSING YOUR OPINION

1. If the question "What is a Canadian?" were asked of people across Canada in 1900, would everyone provide the same answer? Explain your opinion.

2. Assume that you are an adviser on Aboriginal affairs to the Laurier government. Prepare a list of clearly explained recommendations on how the government can improve the treatment of Aboriginal people. Make at least five recommendations.

3. Is the National Policy to blame for the uneven development of Canada? Why or why not?

4. To what extent does the separatist movement in Québec today have its roots in the rising nationalist movement in the early part of the twentieth century? Explain your answer.

5. Was the discrimination and racism that many newcomers faced a result of government policy? Did the policy reflect the wishes of the public?

WORKING WITH THE EVIDENCE

1. During the Laurier years, many groups faced Canadian immigration restrictions. Yet, the Canadian government could not officially ban the immigration of Asiatic Indians to Canada. Why not?

2. If high-quality translation software had been available in Laurier's time and people could have communicated without language barriers, would newcomers to Canada have faced less discrimination? Explain your answer.

Canadian Life in 1900

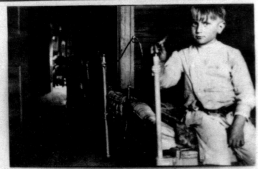

OUR TREATMENT OF THE IMMIGRANT

A RUSSIAN HOME IN HAMILTON

IT IS OUR DUTY *TO PREPARE FOR OUR GUESTS BY MAKING NEW SURVEYS AND CONSTRUCTING HOUSES AND SEWERS* **BUT WE HAVE FAILED** *AND HAVE LEFT THEM TO CREATE SLUMS BY CROWDING INTO THE DARK, UNSANITARY BUT HIGH RENT HOUSES "DOWN TOWN" WHERE WE REFUSE TO LIVE.*

Church groups circulated posters like this one to appeal to people's conscience and gain support for their reform efforts.

INQUIRING INTO THE PAST

- Why did all Canadians not share equally in the economic boom of the Laurier years?
- What types of reform movements would appear in the early 1900s?
- How did changes in technology transform the lives of Canadians?
- What was life like for Canadian families during the Laurier years?

KEY TERMS

Assimilation

Depopulation

Mass Production

Mechanization

Progress

Prohibition

Service Sector

Social Gospel

Suffrage

TIMELINE

1897 ▶
First Women's Institute founded

1899 ▶
Frontier College founded

1901 ▶
First Transatlantic wireless message sent

1909 ▶
First airplane flight in Canada completed

Over the centuries many people have asked the question: what is **progress**? For some, progress meant that they were accumulating more things — more money, more clothes, or more personal possessions. To others, it meant improving the health of the people and decreasing the number of deaths from disease. The social reformer J.S. Woodsworth proclaimed: "True prosperity cannot be measured by the volume of trade and bank clearings. It consists in the social and moral welfare of the people."

In 1900 Canada was a country of economic contrasts. The nation saw the creation of its first millionaires, but the cities also included huge unmappable slums, where more than a quarter of the babies died before they reached their first birthday. New appliances made life easier for some people, but most citizens could not afford such luxuries. As the differences between society's "haves" and "have-nots" grew, concerned people began to feel a moral obligation to help the poor. As changes affected the home, family, and workplace for better or worse, reform movements sprang up across the country to help the less fortunate.

In 1909 Eaton's offered this Chatham vacuum cleaner for $25. Whose labour did this new machine rely on? Who benefited from new appliances in the homes?

The Effects of Technology in the Home

The early twentieth century was a time of gadgets. Inventors came up with new devices every year, and many of these inventions made their way into wealthier homes. Bathrooms contained such items as the new safety razor for shaving. Housework was made easier by the electric iron and the vacuum cleaner, and the grass could now be cut with a push lawnmower. And, in a growing number of wealthier households, an automobile would sit in the driveway.

Time Off

The spread of new technology in the home meant saved time, and for the first time many people talked of leisure. Before the turn of the century in Canada, besides Sundays, the concept of a holiday was limited to perhaps two days a year: the Christian "holy days" of Good Friday and Christmas. Around 1900 the concept of spending a few "working days" away from work began to emerge. People used the term "weekend" for the first time and thought of other activities in addition to going to a place of worship; some even had a half day off on Saturday.

Some people also began to plan vacations. The middle class might have a week away from work once a year to visit family in other parts of their province, and wealthier people travelled across Canada to visit "cottage country" or the Canadian Rockies. The growth of towns and railways meant they could keep in touch with relatives in other towns and provinces.

Changes in the Family

For most families, however, fancy gadgets and vacations were only a dream. In many working-class and farm homes, the family often needed additional income to supplement what the husband brought in. Many wives took outside jobs in addition to their regular duties of housework and raising the children.

Canadian profiles

REGINALD FESSENDEN: CANADA'S FORGOTTEN INVENTOR

The late nineteenth century was a time of tremendous change in North America. Many innovative ideas that radically altered life in North America flowed back and forth between Canada and the United States. Alexander Graham Bell, Thomas Edison, and Guglielmo Marconi are all familiar names in the history of invention. But what about Reginald Fessenden? Despite his more than five hundred inventions and his profound contributions to the development of radio, sonar, and television, Fessenden remains an obscure character in Canadian history.

A tireless worker, Reginald Fessenden spent many hours working on his inventions.

Reginald Fessenden was born in East Bolton, Québec, on October 6, 1866, and was educated at Trinity College School in Port Hope, Ontario, and Bishop's College School in Québec. His life-long fascination with mathematics and science and his incredible inventiveness led to numerous achievements. He once stated, "An inventor is one who can see the applicability of the means to supplying demand five years before it is obvious to those skilled in the art."

Persistence was one of Fessenden's greatest attributes. At the age of twenty, having found teaching to be unstimulating, Fessenden moved to New York City, where he made numerous efforts to be hired by Thomas Edison, considered the leading inventor of the day. He was hired by Edison only after repeatedly knocking on his door. Impressed by Fessenden's ideas and abilities, Edison quickly promoted him to chief chemist after only three months. Following Edison's bankruptcy, Fessenden went on to work for Westinghouse, the United States Weather Service, and two American universities.

Fessenden's greatest efforts and achievements lie in the field of telegraphy, particularly in sending intelligible speech through air rather than wires. But he was a prolific inventor in many fields. For example, he invented a lamp that could be rolled up and down the inside of industrial chimney stacks so that workers could see the chimneys while repairing them. Following the sinking of the *Titanic*, Fessenden developed a system using electrical impulses to determine the location of icebergs. During World War I, he created a submarine-to-shore radio and the forerunner of today's sophisticated sonar.

Despite his numerous inventions and the respect he earned from his colleagues, Fessenden was snubbed by his own country. When McGill University established a department of electrical engineering, he was turned down for the position of chair of the department in favour of an American. Later, in 1909, when Fessenden and a group of Montreal businesspeople founded the Fessenden Wireless Telegraph Company of Canada to ensure that transatlantic communication remained in Canadian hands, the Laurier government granted sole wireless rights to the Marconi Wireless Telegraph Company of Canada.

Although Fessenden undoubtedly earned the respect of his colleagues and a reputation as a great inventor, his achievements are little-known by Canadians. He remains one of our obscure heroes.

Children were also often forced into the workplace, and the average child completed school only up to grade three. In 1896, 20 percent of women and 4 percent of children worked for pay, and these percentages rose dramatically through the Laurier years. The increasing number of children in the workforce troubled many people; J.S Woodsworth commented: "Often children are kept from school and set to work at a very young age. Frequently health is impaired, morals corrupted, and educational opportunities forever lost."

Living Conditions

City neighbourhoods were defined by wealth as they grew during the economic boom of the Laurier years. In the most desirable locations were the mansions of the rich — the owners of the factories and big businesses. Every city also had a growing middle-class district of family homes on small plots of land. But the biggest areas by far were the slums — large areas of substandard accommodation for workers and their families. These divisions were due in part to changes in technology. Traditionally, people walked to work, so factories and residential

areas were often side by side. The invention of the automobile and the increasing use of the streetcar meant that those who could afford to use these kinds of transportation lived away from the smoke and noise of factories and railways, leaving the poor to live in the noisiest and dirtiest areas.

Social reformers who investigated cities at the time were shocked at what they saw. In his 1897 book *A City Below the Hill*, Herbert Ames wrote about life in working-class Montréal. Families of five lived in two rooms, with no electricity and little ventilation. Toilets were outside and dangerously dirty, especially in summer. Unfiltered water and unpastuerized milk led to diseases, and everywhere smoke and garbage endangered health. The adult death rate in Montréal was twenty-five per thousand — higher than it was in Rome, Paris, or London — and among the poor it reached thirty-five per thousand. A shocking 26.8 percent of babies died before they reached their first birthday.

It was almost impossible for families to climb out of these conditions. The average worker in 1901 was paid about $425 per year (women and children made much less), but the cost of living was higher than that. A basement accommodation cost $12 per room per month, and the government's estimate of

The LaPrell home (*left*) was thought to be the finest in Edmonton in 1902. The one-room dwelling (*right*) was typical of what was affordable to the working class. People seldom travelled to other districts of their city. What would the LaPrells or the family on the right (whose names were not recorded) have thought if they had seen how the other families lived?

TAKE A SHOPPING TRIP TO YESTERYEAR

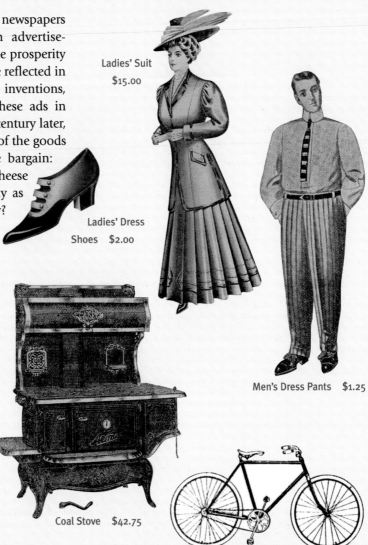

Ladies' Suit $15.00

Ladies' Dress Shoes $2.00

Men's Dress Pants $1.25

Coal Stove $42.75

Bicycle $25.00

Toaster $4.00

Ingersoll Cream Cheese 25¢

Ford Model T $775.00

In the early 1900s, the pages of newspapers and magazines abounded with advertisements for consumer products. The prosperity and optimism of the Laurier era were reflected in the many advertisements for recent inventions, such as the automobile. Reading these ads in newspapers and magazines nearly a century later, we may feel that the prices for most of the goods offered for sale were an incredible bargain: shoes for $2, cars for $800, and a cheese for 25¢. Yet, were these goods really as affordable as they appear to us today?

Take an imaginary shopping trip through this page. Decide on a variety of items you would like to purchase for your family (assume three children in the family), and add up the total cost. Now consider the average yearly wage for workers: at the turn of the century, women workers earned on average $182.50 per year while men earned $389. Allow 40 percent for food and housing expenses, and consider that you must still clothe your family. There are, however, no income taxes, and remember that very few married women worked outside the home.

Were most of the items listed on this page within reach of the average family? (Assume that only the husband has a paying job.) Were they within reach of a single mother raising three children? Were automobiles within reach of the average family? Have wages kept pace with the increase in the cost of goods over the century? Given that the average worker today earns $28 000 annually, are Canadians today economically better or worse off than those at the beginning of the twentieth century?

the minimum cost of a weekly family shopping basket (which only contained a small amount of meat and no fruits and vegetables) was $13.38. These expenses left little for clothing and other necessities.

Changes in the Workplace

The Canadian workplace in 1900 was in the midst of great changes. While many workers were still working in primary industries — fishing, farming, forestry, and mining — most were employed either in factories or in the fastest-growing area of the economy, the service sector.

Mass Production

The number of large companies was on the increase, and many small businesses had to combine to survive. The most efficient way to produce things was to have workers specialize in one aspect of the production and to do that part day after day. This approach fit well with the advances in **mass production**. A generation before, a woman might have worked with her husband in producing handmade shoes. Now it was much more common for her son to make shoes on an assembly line in a factory.

The Service Sector

The other growth area in the economy was the **service sector**, the group who serve other workers and the public. A whole range of jobs existed in the service sector, such as taxi driver, letter carrier, railroad porter, bank teller, accountant, salesperson, and cleaner. Clerical work emerged as one of the biggest growth areas in the service sector. General office workers and bookkeepers were replaced by telephone operators, filing clerks, stenographers, accountants, and secretaries. Office work was transformed by inventions such as the telephone, the typewriter, and a new filing system called the Hollerith punch-card machine.

Service-sector jobs were increasingly given to women as the economy expanded. At the time it

A stenographer's pool at the Canadian Pacific Railway offices in Calgary, 1915. Why were stenographers' jobs given almost exclusively to women?

was said that women were more suited to these tasks because they were better at handling detail and had nimble hands that were efficient in the constant use of the new machines. Behind these reasons, however, was a more important one: women could be paid much less than men.

Farm Mechanization

Canadian farms were also being changed by technology. Labour-saving machinery was adopted by many large farms, and when the new devices were too expensive for individual farmers to own, families banded together and rented machines or shared the purchase cost. Gasoline tractors were becoming more common, and motorized threshers, reapers, and hay mowers made productivity skyrocket. A farmer could mow forty times as much hay in a day as his father could have, and he could harvest a bushel of wheat in 1 percent of the time.

Factories were also now part of the farming process. A generation before, items like dairy products and fruit were processed on the farm, usually by women. After the nineteenth century, these products were increasingly sent off to factories for processing and canning. By 1901, for example, 40 percent of Canadian cheese came from factories.

Rural Depopulation

The consolidation and **mechanization** of farms also meant that fewer opportunities remained to make a living as a farmer. A farm might be passed on to the oldest son, leaving the other siblings to find work elsewhere. Labour-saving machinery also resulted in rural **depopulation**, because fewer farmhands were needed. Many young people left the farms with hopes of a better life in the city. Women also began to leave farming country. Technology eliminated many of the jobs that had been traditionally been done by women on the farm. The law discriminated against women owning and inheriting property, and the work that most women did was never paid for. For many, there was no alternative but to seek employment in the city.

These changes caused great worry among the writers of the day. The rhythm of rural life was seen as pure and more healthy than the stress and strains of city life. But romanticizing life on the farm overlooked the hard work, long hours, uncertainty of income, and the truth that at times rural life was lonely and tedious.

Women at Work

Most women worked in the home. The expectation in Canada's male-dominated society at that time was that women might try their hand at some delicate jobs from the time they left school at the age of about fifteen until they married. Marriage was the goal (as quickly as possible, after the age of twenty) and the ideal was that women would serve their families by cooking, sewing, cleaning, and, of course, raising children.

For many women, however, this ideal was impossible to achieve. They needed to supplement their income, either because they lived on their own or because their families needed more than one income to survive. Many women took in work such as sewing and laundry and were paid a small amount for every piece they completed. Others took jobs outside the home.

The most common paid occupation for women at the turn of the century was as a domestic, a job that was often done by daughters from rural areas or immigrant families. They cleaned, cooked, and, as servants, were expected to do whatever the family asked them to do.

How does this painting "Harvesting" by Clarence Gagnon reflect the idea of rural Canada in the early twentieth century? Is it an accurate portrayal of rural life at this time? Why or why not?

Women worked in various other jobs as well. Many women were forced into factory work, where employers considered them cheap labour. Their smaller size meant that women (and children) were sought after because they could manipulate some machines more easily. Other occupations, such as office work, teaching, and nursing, were acceptable because they fit the stereotype that society had of women as caring and detail-oriented people.

Working Conditions

In the early 1900s most jobs involved hard labour, long hours, and low pay. It was common to work ten to twelve hours a day for six days a week. While mechanization had changed some aspects of these industries, much of the work still needed to be done by hand. To save money, companies often tried to employ women or children where possible. In Cumberland County, Nova Scotia, nearly 16 percent of the workforce consisted of children, who fit into the small spaces in the mines. This was some of the hardest and dangerous labour in Canada, and there were many mine accidents. The worst occurred at the Hillcrest Mine in the Rockies, on June 9, 1914, when a methane gas explosion killed 189 workers.

Factory work was also gruelling. To save money, lighting and ventilation in most factories were poor, the work area was noisy and dirty, and the machinery was extremely dangerous. There were no laws regulating the levels of chemicals like zinc and asbestos, and coal miners and textile workers were forced to retire young because they were unable to breathe properly after inhaling coal dust or fabric fibres for years.

Providing job security was not part of the employers' commitment, and unemployment was common. If a worker was injured or killed on the job, there was usually little or no compensation. On the streets of Canada one hundred years ago, it was very common to see a disabled person; if an amputation or other physical disability caused the person to be unable to work, then unemployment was inevitable. Workers' Compensation Acts were just beginning to be introduced, but they were underfunded and seldom applied.

In the early 1900s, health and safety conditions in industries were poor. What dangers does this drawing show?

The Unstable Labour Market

Workers' struggle to survive in their poor working conditions was made more difficult by the instability of jobs. Many of the jobs were seasonal, and the movement of workers meant that there were occasional labour shortages, but most of the time there were more people than jobs available. This situation made employers happy, because it allowed them to pay low wages and threaten workers that if they did not do a good job or "behave," they could be fired — there was always another person waiting to work.

Job instability was further complicated by the huge inflow of immigrants. Although the symbol of the Laurier years was the settler staking a claim to a section of land in the newly opened Prairies, more than 70 percent of the newcomers ended up working in industry or transportation. This created friction because the immigrants were seen as an exploitable labour source, which employers were able to pay lower wages and use as strikebreakers when convenient. Businesses liked the free-flowing supply of labour and actively worked with the government to ensure that an increasing number of healthy workers entered Canada every year. They also lobbied the government about the type of immigrant they wanted. Thomas Shaughnessy, a president of the CPR, asserted that he did not want any more "men who came here expecting to get high wages, a feather bed, and a bath tub."

The Rise of Reform Movements

As working and living conditions worsened, especially for the new industrial poor, Laurier's government did little to remedy the growing urban problems of worker exploitation, poverty, crime, and disease. Private charities were left to help the poor and sick, and social reformers swept into action.

The Social Gospel

At the heart of the social-reform movement was a religious revival that helped people see that working with and for others was a necessity for Christians in a time of great social change. Protestant reformers preached the **social gospel**, which maintained that it was everyone's duty to help improve the lot of less fortunate people. Church groups such as the Women's Christian Temperance Union (WCTU), the Young Men's Christian Association (YMCA), and the Salvation Army played an important role in this reform movement. The WCTU was one of the strongest voices campaigning for **Prohibition**, the banning of alcoholic beverages. They blamed the consumption of alcohol for violence at home, the moral corruption of youth, and inefficiency at work.

Urban Reform

As thousands of immigrants arrived in urban centres hoping for work, major Canadian cities such as Montreal, Toronto, Edmonton, and Calgary experienced explosive growth. As the cities grew, little thought was given to proper housing, schools, parks, water supply, or sanitation systems. This lack of planning led to unsanitary conditions such as impure drinking water and the spread of disease. Since no public-health programs were in place, the mortality rate among young children skyrocketed. The plight of the working class became the focus of middle-class reformers, who realized that if society as a whole were to be bettered, they would have to improve the living conditions of the working class and the poor. Soon, water and gas lines were laid, and sewage-treatment plants were built. Telephone and electrical wires leaped from corner to corner across the cities. Public-transportation systems such as the Toronto Transit Commission were established.

Reformers were also worried about homeless street children. John Kelso, a police reporter for the Toronto *World*, was convinced that the only way to help these children was to establish an organization that would care for them until they could be adopted into stable families. As a result, in 1892 the first Children's Aid Society shelter opened in Toronto.

Education

The education system also became the focus of many reform movements. By 1905 most provinces had legislation providing for free schooling and for compulsory attendance for children aged seven to twelve. Two innovative programs were introduced for those who were not served by the regular public-school system. The first public-school kindergarten in Canada was established in Toronto to provide preschool classes with "reverent love for the child, profound respect for his individuality ...

A typical Canadian classroom at the beginning of the twentieth century. What evidence is there in the picture of the purposes of the educational system, as stated in the text?

Canadian profiles

DR. LEONORA HOWARD KING

Ask most Canadians to create a list of fifty great Canadians and few, if any, will include the name of Dr. Lenora Howard King. Born Leonora Howard on a farm near Farmersville, Ontario (in the Kingston area) in 1851, Leonora dreamed of becoming a doctor but faced many obstacles in Canada because medical schools would not admit women in the 1870s. Not easily hindered, she applied and was accepted into the University of Michigan's Women's Medical College. Upon graduating with honours (making her one of the first Canadian women to earn a medical degree), Dr. Howard applied to serve with the Women's Foreign Missionary Society and was posted to China. At the age of twenty-six, Dr. Howard sailed for China, where she would spend most of her life.

Two years after arriving in the Chinese province of Chihli, Dr. Howard was summoned to treat Lady Li, the wife of the provincial ruler. For curing Lady Li, Howard was given part of the Tseng Kuo-fan's memorial temple, which she used to open China's first hospital for women and children. She went on to open China's first Government Medical School for Women after marrying Alex King. The contributions of Dr. Leonora Howard King to Chinese society were recognized by the Empress Dowager, who made her the first Western woman to become a mandarin (an official member of the Chinese elite). In 1895 she also received the Order of the Double Dragon, which elevated her to the status of Chinese royalty.

Dr. Leonora Howard King continued her medical and missionary work through war and revolution until 1916, when she retired. On June 30, 1925, forty-seven years after arriving in China, Dr. Howard King died from a virus, at the age of seventy-four. Her work continues to live on, as the Hospital for Women and Children is now the Ophthalmologist Hospital of Tianjin, and the medical and nursing school she founded continues as the Tianjin Nursing School. Dr. Leonora Howard King is one of the unsung heroes of Canadian history, a woman whose dedication and concern helped the lives of countless others.

Web Connections

http://www.school.mcgrawhill.ca/resources

Go to the above Web site to find out more about the history and present activities of Frontier College. Go to *History Resources*, and then to *Canada: A Nation Unfolding, Ontario Edition* to find out where to go next.

and freedom and self-activity as the condition of most perfect growth physically, intellectually, and spiritually." Also, a Nova Scotia minister, Alfred Fitzpatrick, saw the need for educating workers who were labouring in camps far from the cities. To help them, in 1899 he began Frontier College on Georgian Bay in Ontario. The college's teacher-labourers were hired from money raised by donation to go out to lumber and railway camps. They worked alongside the other men by day and helped them with basic literacy skills at night.

Education was also viewed as a way to "Canadianize" immigrants through **assimilation** by teaching them the values and customs of Canada. The intent was not that Canada would be a nation of immigrants, in which each group kept its own heritage, but that newcomers should be assimilated into the new culture. They should, eventually, speak and act like Canadians.

The movement to educate rural women was another reform that occurred at this time. Founded by Adelaide Hoodless, whose child died after drinking impure milk, the Women's Institute was started in rural Ontario. With campaigns to support legislation and education concerning cleanliness and nutrition, women's institutes spread across rural Canada and overseas.

The Struggle for Equality: The Women's Movement in Canada

Many female reformers were especially concerned with women's issues, and many groups made headlines in their fight for women's rights. The campaign for women's **suffrage** — the right to vote — was launched in Ontario by the Toronto Women's Literary Club. The club was led by Emily Stowe, a doctor who had been denied access to university in Canada and then, after training in the United States, was denied entry to the College of Physicians and Surgeons. As the popularity of women's suffrage spread across the country, the club changed its name to the Canadian Women's Suffrage Association. Women's organizations took up the cause on the Prairies with a particular vigour. Leaders like Nellie McClung, Emily Murphy, and Henrietta Edwards crusaded tirelessly with speeches, meetings, and petitions.

By the outbreak of war in 1914, women were still denied the right to vote or hold office (except in some municipalities), but reformers had raised the awareness of Canadians in many ways.

The Growth of the Labour Movement

Alongside the social-reform movements that were springing up in many areas, workers realized that to get better working conditions they would also have to fight for themselves. In various ways, men and women of the working class banded together to demand better treatment in the workplace.

Organized labour initially consisted of societies of workers whose donations helped the families of workers who were killed or injured on the job. As they gained strength, they evolved into unions —

One view of women and their campaign for the vote. What is the cartoonist saying about the effects of the suffragette movement?

organizations that argued for better wages, hours, and working conditions. Immigration brought experienced unionists to Canada from Europe, and in the late 1880s the American-based Knights of Labor mobilized thousands of workers, especially in Ontario and Québec.

Another American organization, the International Workers of the World (IWW), was founded in 1905 and went even further to try to organize all workers into one giant union. The IWW wanted the one giant union to call a strike and use the only weapon that workers had at their disposal: withdrawing their labour. The problem with this approach was that strikers could easily be replaced by other workers. There was no law against this practice, and employers actively brought in strikebreakers (or "scabs") whenever they needed them.

In contrast, the newly formed Trades and Labour Council (TLC) moved much more cautiously. It believed that the only way to deal with the superior power of employers and business organizations was

Canadian voices

NELLIE McCLUNG'S STRUGGLE TO WIN THE VOTE

The early 1900s were a time of tremendous change in Canada. The rapid increase in industrialization, the growth of cities, and the numerous inventions that changed the way people lived gave many reasons for optimism. Unfortunately, many Canadian women were unable to participate fully in society because they had neither political nor legal equality. Before 1917, an eligible voter in Canada was defined as "a male person, including an Indian and excluding a person of Mongolian or Chinese race…. No woman, idiot, lunatic, or criminal shall vote."

Besides lacking political rights, women also had very little economic security. They were paid less than men, and the money married women earned was legally the property of their husbands. Husbands also had control of their children and were legally entitled to physically abuse their wives.

By the time of the Laurier era, several women had become active in the struggle for women's rights. Central to the struggle was winning the right to vote, for with the vote would come the opportunity to influence political decision-making. One of the leading supporters of women's right to vote was Nellie McClung, who began her campaign for women's suffrage in Manitoba in 1911. In 1912, she helped to form the Political Equality League.

One of the barriers McClung had to face was the attitude of the government of Manitoba at the time. Premier Rodmond Roblin once commented, "I don't want a hyena in petticoats talking politics at me. I want a nice gentle creature to bring me my slippers." When a delegation led by McClung presented its case for the right of women to vote to the Manitoba legislature, Roblin responded:

Let it be known that it is the opinion of the Roblin government that women's suffrage is illogical and absurd as far as Manitoba is concerned. Placing women on a political equality with men would cause domestic strife…it will break up the home; it will throw the children into the arms of servant girls…. The majority of women are emotional and very often guided by misdirected enthusiasms, and if possessed of the franchise would be a menace rather than an aid.

McClung seized upon Roblin's remarks as an opportunity to make a mockery of the arguments against female suffrage. The day following Roblin's remarks, the Political Equality League held a "mock parliament," during which Nellie McClung turned the male arguments inside out:

The trouble is that if men start to vote, they will vote too much. Politics unsettles men, and unsettled men means unsettled bills, broken furniture, broken vows, and — divorce…. If men were to get into the habit of voting — who knows what might happen — it's hard enough to keep them home now. History is full of unhappy examples of men in politic life — Nero — Herod — King John….

By making the most of her opportunities to speak out publicly, Nellie McClung was able to build a solid base of support for women's suffrage. Success finally came for the women of Manitoba on January 27, 1916, when the Enfranchisement of Women Act was passed, giving women the right to vote. Over the next few years the work of Nellie McClung and several other suffragettes proved fruitful; eventually all Canadian women won full political rights.

The English suffragist Emmeline Pankhurst (*left*) and Canada's Nellie McClung were leaders in the struggle to win political and legal equality for women. Although they were successful, the struggle for social and economic equality continues. What changes need to be made in our society to further guarantee the equality of men and women?

to argue for a better deal, but not demand radical changes to the system. If companies were able to call out the militia and police to end strikes, the best option was to bargain peacefully. Other unions were also started at this time: the United Mine Workers, the Fishermen's Protective Union, and farm organizations spread across Ontario and the Prairies. For all the reformers' efforts, the government did little to respond to the unions' struggles for the plight of the workers.

The efforts of middle- and working-class Canadians to make changes in response to the changing econ-omy seemed to end in frustration. The standard of living of the country as a whole had risen, and some Canadians were enjoying new consumer goods and benefiting from modern technology for the first time. Others, however, felt left out, and most of soci-ety recognized the disruptions that the economic boom had brought about — industrial expansion often was being paid for in terms of the environment and the lives of workers and their families. At the outbreak of World War I, many small victories had been won; but bigger advances and fundamental changes were yet to come.

A strike in Saint John, New Brunswick, in 1914. Imagine being one of the demonstrators in this photo and meeting a friend a couple of hours later. How would you describe the scene?

chapter review

CHAPTER SUMMARY

In this chapter we have seen

- that Canada's standard of living rose during the Laurier years, but not all Canadians shared equally in the economic boom

- how broad and varied reform movements responded to changing living and working conditions in Canada

- how the spread of new technologies to the home and the workplace, both in the cities and in rural areas, significantly changed Canada

- how many of the economic and technological changes resulted in changes in the pattern of family life

UNDERSTANDING HISTORICAL FACTS

1. Identify these people, places, and events, and explain their historical significance.

   Nellie McClung
   Children's Aid Society
   Hay Mower
   Frontier College

   Trades and Labour Council
   J.S. Woodsworth
   Temperance Movement

2. Write a paragraph that compares rural Canada in the late 1800s with rural Canada in 1910. In your comparison, draw on evidence that is presented in this chapter.

3. The beginning of the twentieth century is generally seen as a prosperous time. Was it a prosperous time for all Canadians? Explain your answer.

4. Why were public services such as hydro-electricity and public transit considered important developments?

5. Create a crest or banner for a typical turn-of-the-century Canadian school that reflects the goals of education in the early 1900s.

EXPRESSING YOUR OPINION

1. Draw a mind-map in your notes that investigates the various answers to the question "What is progress?"

2. Assume that you are a reporter for the *Toronto Daily Star* in 1908. Your assignment is to investigate the myth of "the good life" on the farm at that time. Write a 200–300-word news story that captures the reality of life in rural Canada at the turn of the twentieth century.

3. Do schools still follow the factory-like model of the early twentieth century? What would need to change if schools were to de designed with the twenty-first century in mind?

4. Labour unions became a permanent part of Canadian society in the late nineteenth and early twentieth centuries. Did they play a positive or negative role? Would business leaders and workers agree on business an labour issues? Explain your answer.

5. The urban-reform movement at the turn of the twentieth century believed that cities could be made into better places to live. Did the reformers have a lasting and positive effect on Canadian society? Support your answer with specific examples.

WORKING WITH THE EVIDENCE

1. Try to imagine what would happen if women had been given the vote at the time of Confederation. How would Canadian politics have been different? List five laws that you think women would have advocated.

Canada in the World

ONE FLAG, ONE ARMY, ONE COUNTRY.

This image, which appeared at the top of the front page of the Toronto *Globe* in 1900, illustrated Canada's commitment to a united British Empire.

INQUIRING INTO THE PAST

- **Why did Canada feel caught between the power of Britain and that of the United States?**
- **What support did Canada provide to Britain during the Boer War and the Naval Crisis?**
- **How would Canada's support for Britain during the Boer War and the Naval Crisis create friction between English Canadians and French Canadians?**
- **What were the key characteristics of Canadian–American relations during the Laurier years?**

KEY TERMS

Expansionism

Imperialism

Nationalism

Reciprocity

Sovereignty

TIMELINE

1899–1902 ▶	**1903** ▶	**1910** ▶	**1911** ▶
Boer War is fought in South Africa	Alaska boundary dispute occurs between Canada and the United States	Naval Service Bill passed	Robert Borden becomes Prime Minister after Canadian general election

One hundred years ago Victoria Day was a big celebration of Canada's British heritage in many cities and towns. British flags (Union Jacks) were waved, people marched in parades, and bands played familiar British songs. In 1897, Empire Day had been established to celebrate Queen Victoria's sixtieth year as the Queen of England.

Empire Day became the school day before Victoria Day, when students, whatever their heritage, would recite and parade together to celebrate the glory of the British Empire. The Department of Education in Ontario sent out instructions about how schools should honour the day. Part of the memo read: "The aim of the teacher in all of his references to Canada and the Empire should be, to make Canadian patriotism intelligent, comprehensive, and strong."

The front page of the Toronto *Globe*, January 23, 1901. What did Queen Victoria and the British monarchy mean to Canadians at the beginning of the twentieth century?

Victoria Day and Empire Day were two of Canada's largest non-religious celebrations in the year. These holidays did not, however, accurately reflect Canada's population, which consisted of many cultures other than British. Canada had originally been the home of many Aboriginal nations. French Canadians, too, had been here much longer than the British, and they found an alternative holiday to celebrate. Every June 24, French Canadians celebrated the patron saint of Québec on St-Jean-Baptiste Day, which also marked the summer solstice. Additionally, in the Laurier years, many of the two million newcomers did not speak French or English at all. Although Canada was a nation with many people of either British or French heritage, it was increasingly becoming a multiracial and multicultural country.

A Time of Nationalism

Victoria Day was more than just many Canadians celebrating their Queen. They were celebrating Canada's part in the great British Empire. The celebrations of Victoria Day and Empire Day reflected a trend occurring in countries around the world — **nationalism**, the love of one's country. Many Canadians at the turn of the century believed that Canada was destined to become one of the most powerful nations in the world. A group of business and academic leaders came together to promote such ideas in what they called the British Empire League. They believed that the huge economic growth generated by the growth of cities and the settlement of the West could make Canada one of the great powers of the new century. Agnes Laut, a political commentator at the turn of the century, ended her book *The Canadian Commonwealth* by boasting that "unless history reverse itself and fate make of facts dice tossed to ruin by malignant furies, then Canada's destiny can only be one — a Greater Britain Overseas."

In a land of so many cultures, however, not all people shared the same vision and spirit of nationalism. Those who disapproved of the British Empire League felt that a true nationalist would want

Canada to become as independent as possible. It was time, they thought, for Canada to break its ties with Britain. Canada was a maturing country and could now leave the mother country. To them, nationalism also meant not living in the shadow of the United States. The optimism that accompanied Canada's growing economy encouraged some to say that the nation could survive on its own.

Most French Canadians believed in a strong Canada and respected the language and civil rights that had been guaranteed at Confederation. What they did not agree with was English Canadians' continuing emotional tie to Britain, which constantly ignored the reality of the Canadian population. They were deeply patriotic, but it was a patriotism rooted in Québec and the French language. In Québec and the Western provinces, especially, a majority of the people had no special tie to Britain and the royal family. These different visions would create trouble for the young Canada.

A Time of Imperialism

Another very important force was at work in the world at the turn of the century — imperialism, the policy of extending a nation's authority by taking control of the territory or economy of other nations and creating an empire of colonies under the control of the parent country.

At the beginning of the twentieth century, much of the world was influenced by **imperialism**. Huge areas of Africa and Asia had been colonized by European countries, including Britain, France, Germany, and Belgium. Old European rivals were becoming dangerous contestants in a race to own the most colonies. Even the United States, which itself had been a colony and had now been independent for over a century, was establishing an empire of strategic bases and trading areas around the world.

Many Canadians in 1900 benefited from being a part of the British Empire. Settlers in Canada received protection, and Britain was Canada's biggest economic partners in trade and investment. Britain wanted to strengthen its ties with all the colonies of its empire and hoped that Canada would provide it with money, weapons, and increased trade.

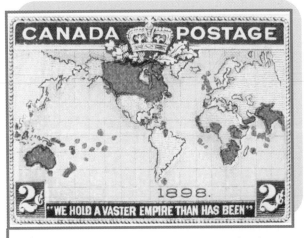

This stamp, issued on December 7, 1898, reproduced a map that was placed in many classrooms in Canada. What was the message of this image, and why was it put on a stamp?

Caught in the Middle

Canada was caught in the middle of these nationalist and imperialist trends. Both geographically and emotionally, it was situated between the British and the Americans. However, although Canada had economic ties with both nations and relied on them for its prosperity, Prime Minister Laurier did not want it to be dominated by either of the major powers.

The other challenge facing Laurier and Canada in its international relations was **sovereignty**, or political freedom. Canada had moved from being a colony to becoming a nation in 1867. Confederation made Canada a self-governing Dominion: it could make its own laws and pursue its own policies. Being a Dominion, however, meant that control over foreign affairs, such as international trade, was still in the hands of Britain. Although many Canadians believed that Britain should remain in control of Canada's foreign affairs, a growing number felt that their country should make its own decisions.

Laurier's government had to balance these different interests in Canada. The movement for imperial unity and strengthening British ties within Ontario and the Maritimes was strongest among businesspeople and descendants of the United Empire Loyalists. Many farmers and other workers, however, came from places other than the British

Isles, and the stronger the Canadian economy became, the more they thought that Canada should increase its trading relations with the United States. French Canadians, too, wanted to ensure that the nation did not lose its identity by allying too closely with any other country.

During the colonial conference held in London as part of the Queen's jubilee celebrations, and in the conferences that followed in 1902, 1903, and 1907, Laurier maintained his usual style of compromise, hoping to please everyone in Canada. He pledged allegiance to the Empire and expressed hope for independence in the future. In his speeches he claimed that Canada would always support the Empire. The best way for Canadians to strengthen the Empire, he asserted, was to strengthen Canada and make it prosperous. The only change needed was for the Dominions (Canada, Australia, and New Zealand) to become independent over time. This compromise approach would eventually lead to conflicts between the people of the young country.

The Boer War

The first real test of Canada's position in world affairs came with the Boer War. The conflicting imperialist goals of empires often led to territorial disagreements, and southern Africa in 1899 was a prime example of conflicts over land.

Starting in the seventeenth century, Dutch settlers (Boers) had come to the southern tip of Africa and forced the original African inhabitants to retreat to poorer land. British and Indian immigration followed, and Britain annexed the Cape Province in 1806. But the fiercely self-reliant Boers dominated in southern Africa, especially in two republics, the Transvaal and the Orange Free State. They clashed with Uitlanders (mostly British immigrants) over the Uitlanders' migration to the newly discovered gold fields in Boer territory. They also fought over the question of Uitlander civil rights under Boer rule. Tensions mounted between the Boers and the British. In 1899, under the leadership of Transvaal President Paul Kruger, the Boers declared war on Britain. Britain informed Canada that it expected Canadian troops to go to South Africa to help defeat the Boers.

Canadian troops at the Paardeburg field hospital, February 19, 1900. What does this photograph tell you about the conditions faced by Canadians in the Boer War?

This demand split Canadians along imperialist and nationalist lines. What made the situation worse was that this division was largely between French Canadians and English Canadians. Imperialists and most of the English-language press saw the war as a perfect chance for Canada to show its support for the Empire and to flex its new muscle on the world stage. To the imperialists, the Uitlanders were a politically oppressed group who needed rescuing.

Most French Canadians, led by Henri Bourassa and his newly formed pro-Québec group, La Ligue Nationaliste Canadienne, were against Canada's participation. They were joined by some farm groups who shared Bourassa's view that Canada should not have to fight a British war in a far-off continent. Canada had enough troubles at home without entering into Britain's imperial adventuring abroad. Canadians who opposed sending troops to South Africa were also worried that the action would set a precedent. In future, they believed, Canada would be obliged to take part in every new British conflict around the world.

Canadian Contributions to the Boer War

Prime Minister Laurier was determined to steer a cautious middle course and find a compromise acceptable to both sides. He feared that otherwise the country would rupture along French and English lines. "A greater calamity could never take place in

PHOTO ESSAY

A NATION ON THE MOVE

A carriage going to the Banff Springs Hotel in Alberta.

Women on bicycles.

A Royal Mail sleigh, 1908.

A train on a trestle bridge, around 1900.

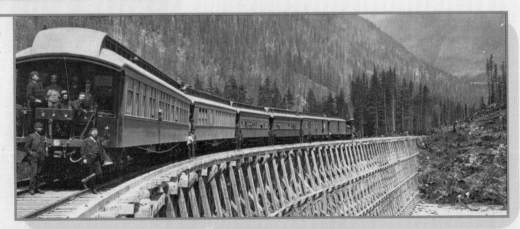

A view of 8th Avenue, Calgary, in 1908.

A passenger ferry.

Members of the Aerial Experimental Association with the "Baddeck I" aircraft, Petawawa, Ontario, 1909.

A car rally.

Henri Bourassa, founding editor of *Le Devoir*, became the leading opponent of Canadian involvement in the Boer War. Suggest some differences in how French Canadian and English Canadian newspapers may have covered the war.

Canada," he warned. The situation reached a crisis point when it was discovered that the British commander of Canadian troops had already promised Canadian involvement. Convinced that the English Canadian majority would not be satisfied without at least token Canadian support in South Africa, Laurier decided to outfit a voluntary force of one thousand infantry and send them to South Africa. Once Canadian troops reached Cape Town, however, it was up to Britain to pay for their keep.

About 7300 Canadian soldiers and nurses took part in the three-year Boer War. Eighty-eight Canadians died in action, 252 were wounded, and a further 136 died of illness or accident. Although Laurier's compromise was grudgingly accepted, it satisfied few Canadians. Bourassa nicknamed his former ally and friend "Waffley Wilfy" because Laurier refused to take a clear stand on Canada's role in the British Empire. Some English Canadians called him "Sir Won'tfrid" because he refused to provide more than token support to Britain. Laurier's art of compromising would be further tested later in the Naval Crisis.

The Naval Crisis

Britain and Germany were two of the strongest economies in Europe in the early twentieth century. They began a deadly arms race in which they especially tried to outdo each other in creating the most powerful navy. In 1906 things suddenly changed when Britain's Royal Navy launched a new super battleship, H.M.S. *Dreadnought*. This ship gave its name to a whole new class of ships: it was as long as a football field, ran on turbine engines, and was armed with ten thirty-centimetre guns. Because of its supiority to all the old battleships, the *Dreadnought* caused a new escalation in a naval arms race.

In 1909 the naval arms race in Europe took a new turn. British spies discovered that Germany was secretly building four dreadnought-class battleships. The cry for more British battleships rang out across the British Isles, and Britain turned to its Dominions for help. Australia and New Zealand responded immediately, and Canada was put in an awkward position.

Since Canada was a Dominion, the Laurier government was committed to a naval policy and the protection of Canada as part of the Empire. It did not, however, want to be forced into handing over to Britain large sums of government funds. Again Laurier offered a compromise; this time, it was the Naval Service Bill. Canada would not contribute to the British navy, but it would build a small navy of its own that could be placed under British control with the consent of Canada's Parliament. Pro-British Canadians sneered at what they considered another instance of token Canadian support. They

THE GREAT CONTINGENT JUGGLER, OR TRYING TO PLEASE EVERYONE.

Wilfrid Laurier, the great juggler. What does this cartoon say about Laurier's leadership of Canada during the Boer War?

called the proposed fleet of five cruisers and six destroyers a "tin pot navy" and accused Laurier of giving Britain too little, too late.

Labour and farm groups believed that Canada was too hasty in its support for an arms race that might bring Europe closer to war. French Canadian nationalists were outraged that Canada was prepared to help Britain at all. They still felt that the rest of the British Empire should look after itself.

Henri Bourassa founded the daily newspaper *Le Devoir* in 1910 partly to defeat Laurier's naval plans. He and his followers believed that Canada would now be drawn automatically into every fight Britain that became involved in around the world. They argued that conscription — involuntary military service in wartime — would soon follow.

Laurier's art of compromise had once again left a division among the people of Canada. But Britain's demands on Canada were not the only crisis that Laurier had to deal with during this time. Canada's relationship with its southern neighbour was also quickly changing.

American Expansion

Throughout the Laurier years Canada had to juggle its relations with Great Britain and the United States. Living immediately north of the United States had always posed a dilemma for Canadians. On the one hand, there were natural ties of heritage and migration that brought the countries together. Year after year, trade and American investment in Canada increased. Canadians, however, were always nervous about the size and military power of the United States.

Canada's southern neighbour had never hidden its strong leaning toward **expansionism**, a policy that aimed to extend the United States across North America. American expansionists talked about America's "Manifest Destiny," its duty to form a continental nation that included Mexico and Canada. The United States had already acquired sizable portions of the North American continent. The British Empire League's Colonel G.T. Denison angrily stated that the Americans "wanted Florida, and they took it; Louisiana and Alaska they annexed; California and Mexico they conquered; Texas they stole."

In the years since Confederation, the United States had seemed more interested in taking Canadian territory through politics and diplomacy than through open warfare, but Canadians remembered the War of 1812 and did not rule out the possibility of yet another American invasion. In 1898 a joint commission was established between Canada and the United States to solve minor disputes between the two countries. The two governments appointed officials to investigate complaints and issues. The Klondike Gold Rush, however, turned an old disagreement about a border into an emotional war of words.

The Alaska Boundary Dispute

In 1825 a poorly worded treaty had created a vague boundary between Canada and the United States in the thousand-kilometre stretch of land down the northern coast of British Columbia, commonly called the Alaska Panhandle because of its shape on the map. During the Klondike Gold Rush of the late 1890s, Canadian and American merchants became

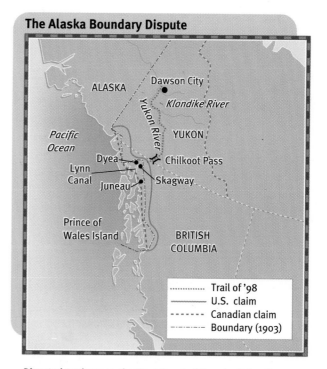

The Alaska Boundary Dispute

Disputed territory on the West Coast of Canada. Using the map, explain why the difference of a few kilometres either way made such a difference to the Americans and Canadians.

rivals in selling supplies to the miners. These supplies had to be brought by ship and then taken inland. The key question was, who owned the coastal ports? The Americans claimed that they owned the Panhandle, including all the coastal inlets. If the United States' claim was accepted, Canada's convenient water access to the Yukon through the Lynn Canal would be cut off and American traders would benefit. The Canadians wanted a different boundary line, much closer to the coast.

Who actually owned the territory was an open question. In 1903 the dispute was referred to a joint commission of six officials — three from the United States, two from Canada, and one from Britain. Canada had stood by Britain during the Boer War; surely, Laurier thought, the British Foreign Office, which still handled Canada's foreign affairs, could be counted on to support Canada in the boundary dispute. But American President Theodore Roosevelt was known for his bullying. He appointed three pushy, expansionist U.S. commissioners and put pressure on Britain to settle in favour of the United States.

American goodwill was important to Britain, so at the end of the deliberations the British appointee on the tribunal voted with the Americans. Most of the Alaska Panhandle was awarded to the United States. Canadians were left fuming at both the Americans and the British. One newspaper claimed that Britain had led Canada "like a lamb to slaughter," and a theatre crowd in Vancouver booed when "God Save the King" was played. The incident confirmed Canadian suspicions, both about American aggression and about Britain's willingness to put its diplomatic interests before Canada's. Many Canadians became determined to take their nation's destiny into their own hands.

Web Connections

http://www.school.mcgrawhill.ca/resources

Go to the Web site above to find out more about the Alaska boundary dispute. Go to *History Resources*, then to *Canada: A Nation Unfolding, Ontario Edition* to find out where to go next.

Canadian–American Relations Settle Down

As the Laurier years progressed, relations between Canada and the United States improved and the bad feelings generated by the Alaska Panhandle decision were overshadowed by the growing storm clouds in Europe. As tensions rose between the great imperial powers in Europe, the north Atlantic triangle of Britain, Canada, and the United States drew closer together.

In 1909 Canada established the Department of External Affairs. This was not only another small step toward autonomy from Britain, but an important step in working with the United States. Instead of having diplomatic messages go from Ottawa to London to Washington and from there to return to Ottawa through London, Canada and the United States could now negotiate directly for the first time.

The Reciprocity Agreement

The next major step in Canada's relations with the United States came when Washington unexpectedly brought up the idea of a new **Reciprocity** treaty, in which the two nations would negotiate a mutual exchange of trade privileges and formalize them in an agreement. Reciprocity would provide for free trade in the natural products supplied by Canadian farms, fisheries, and forests, but leave most of the protective tariffs on manufactured goods untouched. This seemed perfect for Canada's healthy farming community and industrial areas, and the Laurier government pursued the idea quickly.

The wisdom of Laurier's decision to pursue a free-trade agreement seemed to be confirmed during his tour of Western Canada in 1910. He was surprised at the depth of farmers' resentment toward the big-business interests of Central Canada, including banks, railways, grain elevator companies, milling companies, and manufacturers. Reciprocity was meant to make peace with Western farmers by giving them easier access to the vital United States grain market — and, of course, to secure their votes for the Liberals in the upcoming election.

Laurier was convinced that Reciprocity would be welcomed in the West and easily accepted in other regions of the country. The Conservatives thought so, too, and were in despair. It looked as if Laurier and his Liberals were destined to win the 1911 election. But the Conservatives were not about to give up. They raised the fear that other tariffs on manufactured goods would be stripped away and argued that Canadian industries needed tariff protection to remain prosperous.

The anti-Reciprocity forces were led by a group of unhappy Central Canadian manufacturers, bankers, and businesspeople. Under the leadership of the Canadian Manufacturers' Association, the anti-Reciprocity campaign argued that the protective tariffs that had been in place allowed for a heavy flow of American direct investment into Canada in the form of branch factories. If Reciprocity were to go through, its opponents argued, Canada would lose this huge amount of American money, which was crucial to its economic growth.

Many other anti-Reciprocity activists were, surprisingly, prominent members of the Liberal Party, including Laurier's former Cabinet minister, Clifford Sifton. Other important Canadian businesspeople included J.C. Eaton, president of T. Eaton Co., R.J. Christie of the milling and biscuit company Christie and Co., and William Van Horne of the Canadian Pacific Railway. Van Horne was afraid that new north–south trade relations might ruin his east–west railway. He came out of retirement, he declared, just to "bust" the Reciprocity agreement.

Reciprocity had many defenders, however, especially farmers and many working people who were paying the price for high tariffs on imported food, clothing, and household items. They soon counterattacked. Under the slogan "Laurier and Larger Markets," they argued that Canadian industries needed access to the huge American market to survive and prosper. They also said that the trade deal would mean cheaper goods for ordinary people.

The 1911 General Election

There was no radio or television campaigning in 1911, and although the political-party leaders crossed the country by train, much of the campaign was carried out in newspapers. Most of these papers supported one party or the other. The Liberal newspaper, the *Toronto Star*, and the Conservative

A political cartoon about Reciprocity. Explain the artist's message. What do the different images in this cartoon represent?

newspaper, the *Toronto News*, even plastered their windows with banners about the benefits or harm that would result from Reciprocity. The anti-Reciprocity forces were so organized that they were able to distribute pamphlets and other literature to more than three hundred daily and weekly papers across the country.

Canadian continentalists counterattacked. They said that the only way to save the young country was to vote for Reciprocity, because it would make Canada's economic future brighter without endangering its political independence. Once Canada's economy was strong, they said, the Canadian nation would be better able to keep Americans at bay.

Comments by American politicians, however, did not help the defenders of Reciprocity. An American member of Congress, Champ Clark, remarked that he was for the Reciprocity bill because he hoped "to see the day when the American flag will fly over every square foot of the British North American possessions clear to the North Pole." U.S. Senator Porter McCumber proclaimed: "Canadian annexation is the logical conclusion of Reciprocity with Canada." That was enough to convince many nervous Canadians that although America might seem to

The windows of the *Toronto Star* offices and the *Toronto News* offices before the 1911 election. Summarize the arguments being made for and against free trade.

smile on Canada and offer economic favours, its real aim was to draw Canada into an economic union and then annex it.

The debate that began on economic issues soon expanded to include emotional appeals to Canadian patriotism and national survival. Canadian nationalists argued that, sooner or later, a trade deal would lead to a political takeover by the United States: Canada would be swallowed up. Meanwhile, in Québec, the election was fought mostly over the Naval Service Bill, and anglophone nationalists and francophone *nationalistes* began to sway opinion against the Liberals.

On election day, September 21, 1911, almost a million and a half men voted for their parliamentary representatives — women could not yet cast a ballot. The Conservative Party won. The popular vote was close; Borden's Conservatives received only 52 percent of the votes cast. Laurier's Liberals

won in Alberta, Saskatchewan, and the Maritimes, and they squeaked by in Québec. The party, however, crumbled under a landslide Conservative vote in Ontario. Robert Borden became the new Prime Minister of Canada.

The Picnic Ends

When Borden took office, Canada had grown in maturity and was more politically independent than when Laurier took power. It held a more prominent place on the world stage. But Canada had paid a price for its new role. The Boer War had cost many lives, the Alaska boundary dispute had spread disenchantment about Britain, and most of all, Canada found itself an inevitable part of the moves toward war that were taking place in Europe and around the world.

chapter review

CHAPTER SUMMARY

In this chapter we have seen

- how the Laurier years were a time when optimistic growth at home was sometimes overshadowed by events abroad

- how Canada attempted to become more independent of Britain in foreign affairs without becoming entangled in the growing American empire, but was not ready to "go it alone" completely

- that Canada had to realize that if Britain was at war, it was at war; and when economic issues were at stake, the United States would use political muscle to get its way

UNDERSTANDING HISTORICAL FACTS

1. Identify these people, places, and events, and explain their historical significance.

Manifest Destiny	*Le Devoir*
Victoria Day	Alaska Panhandle
Uitlanders	"Sir Won'tfrid"
British Empire League	H.M.S. *Dreadnought*

2. Make a two-column chart comparing the pressures on Canada from Britain with those from the United States.

3. Explain how the invention of the dreadnought class of battleship contributed to an arms race.

4. Construct a two-column chart comparing arguments for and against the Reciprocity proposal.

5. Why are natural resources (such as the gold in Transvaal) sometimes the cause of international conflict?

6. What were Laurier's strengths and weaknesses in international affairs?

EXPRESSING YOUR OPINION

1. Was it reasonable or egotistical for Canada to imagine that it could have become the "Greater Britain Overseas?"

2. Create a political cartoon or write a 200–300–word column that might have appeared in a Canadian newspaper in 1910. The theme of the cartoon or column is Canadian–American relations at the beginning of the century.

3. Would you side with Bourassa or Laurier in the Naval Crisis, and why?

4. How would you have voted in 1911, and why?

WORKING WITH THE EVIDENCE

1. John A. Macdonald's National Policy tried to protect Canada's industries by raising tariffs (import taxes) on manufactured goods from the United States. In many cases this led to American ownership of Canadian industries. Why was this a side effect of the National Policy?

2. Concentration camps were first used by the British during the Boer War to hold Afrikaner (Boer) civilians. The Afrikaners were fighting a guerrilla-style, hit-and-run type of warfare. Why did the British think it was necessary to place civilians in concentration camps to combat this type of warfare?

unit review

BRINGING THE PAST INTO FOCUS

REVIEWING THE FACTS

1. Construct a chart that compares the ways in which Canada at the turn of the century was *united* and the ways in which it was *divided*.

2. How would the attitudes that people today have toward immigration and newcomers compare with what you have learned in this unit?

3. Draw a picture or diagram that summarizes Canada's position in foreign affairs, compared with that of Britain and the United States.

4. The reform movements at the beginning of the twentieth century set the stage for key advances in social policy. Explain.

MAKING CONNECTIONS

1. Draw a web diagram that illustrates connections between the concepts explored in this unit. Use at least one concept from each column of the following table.

HISTORICALLY SPEAKING

1. Which person would be happier: a teenager now or a teenager at the beginning of the twentieth century? Use at least five criteria to make your comparison.

2. Evaluate the effectiveness of the Laurier government in three of the following areas: immigration policy, labour issues, international affairs, and economic development.

3. Choose a symbol that might represent Canada in the Laurier years, and defend your choice with historical evidence.

NATIONAL	INTERNATIONAL	REGIONAL	PERSONAL
Dominion	imperialism	discrimination	mechanization
federal system	militarism	racism	depopulation
nationalism	Reciprocity	*nationaliste*	assimilation
immigration	political autonomy	National Policy	reform

PERSPECTIVES

1. The following song, "The Maple Leaf For Ever," was composed by Alexander Muir. It was regarded as Canada's unofficial national anthem in Laurier's time.

The Maple Leaf For Ever
(Alexander Muir)
In days of yore, from Britain's shore,
Wolfe the dauntless hero came,
And planted firm Britannia's flag,
On Canada's fair domain.
Here may it wave, our boast, our pride,
And joined in love together,
The thistle, shamrock, rose entwine,
The Maple Leaf for ever!
Chorus:
The Maple Leaf, our emblem dear,
The Maple Leaf for ever!
God save our King, and Heaven bless,
The Maple Leaf for ever!

How might the following four Canadians react differently to the playing of this song?
a) Québécois *nationaliste*
b) Ojibwa elder
c) Boer War veteran
d) Ukrainian farmer

2. Write a list of notes for Colonel G.T. Denison and for Henri Bourassa including points that they might make in preparing for a debate on Canada's participation in the Boer War.

3. Choose one of the ethnic groups discussed in this unit. Put yourself in the shoes of one of these people, and write a letter home one month after your arrival in Canada.

4. Imagine you are a woman who is a social reformer in 1900. Write a diary entry including information about the movements you support (labour rights, Prohibition, or women's suffrage) and your views on the status of women at this time.

"Someone once said to Clive: do you think we will ever be forgiven for what we've done? They meant their generation and the war and what the war had done to civilization. Clive said something I've never forgotten. He said: I doubt we'll ever be forgiven. All I hope is — they'll remember we were human beings."

FROM TIMOTHY FINDLEY'S *THE WARS*

TIMELINE

AUGUST 4, 1914
Canada, as part of the British Empire, declares war on Germany

APRIL 1917
Canadians capture Vimy Ridge

When the *Titanic* was launched, it was reputed to be an unsinkable ship. When the Great War ended in 1918, it was said to have been "the war to end all wars." The *Titanic* sank, and wars have continued well after the end of World War I. Yet both these events are symbolic of the twentieth century. With the sinking of the *Titanic*, human ingenuity and human arrogance received a blow. With the carnage and bloodshed of World War I, the sense of unstoppable progress came into question. Why did war break out in August 1914, and why did it escalate into the bloodiest confrontation the world had ever seen? Why did Canadians eagerly volunteer to fight a war so far from home? What were the lasting effects of the war on Canadians and Canadian society? Perhaps the most important question to be answered by a study of World War I is, how can the lessons to be learned from this tragedy help us to avoid future conflicts between nations?

LET'S INVESTIGATE

1. By 1918 over fourteen million lives had been lost in the war and billions of dollars' worth of damage had been done. Why would European nations decide to participate in such a deadly and costly war?

2. How had developments in modern technology changed the nature of warfare by 1918?

3. How did Canadians react to the war? Was there a difference in the ways Canadians from different regions reacted to the war? Did mounting deaths and a prolonged war change Canadian attitudes?

4. What lasting impact did Canada's participation in the war have on Canadian society and on Canada's international status?

MAY 1917 ▶
Borden announces policy
of conscription

NOVEMBER 11, 1918 ▶
Armistice declared

▶

Canada's Response to a Global Crisis

When war was declared, thousands of young Canadians rushed to enlist in the army. This group is preparing to leave from Valcartier, Quebec, where they will receive their first military training.

INQUIRING INTO THE PAST

- **What major factors led to the outbreak of war in 1914?**
- **Why was Canada drawn into a European war?**
- **Why did some Canadians enthusiastically enlist to fight a war in Europe?**
- **How had modern technology changed the nature of warfare by 1914?**

KEY TERMS

Alliances

Assassination

Diplomacy

Imperialism

Militarism

Nationalism

Neutrality

Patriotism

Ross rifle

Shrapnel

TIMELINE

JUNE 1914 ▶
Assassination of Archduke Francis Ferdinand in Sarajevo

AUGUST 1914 ▶
Canada, as part of the British Empire, declares war on Germany

SEPTEMBER 1914 ▶
Canadian troops board ships bound for England

APRIL 1915 ▶
Canadians see first action at the Battle of Ypres

When Prime Minister Robert Borden came to power on September 21, 1911, Canada was riding a wave of prosperity and optimism. The optimism that characterized the pre-war years would be dashed by events that were soon to unfold. The economic boom that Canada had enjoyed throughout the Laurier era came to a crashing halt in the fall of 1913, when British investors suddenly withdrew much of their capital from Canada in anticipation of a major European war. By the spring of 1914, tens of thousands of Canadian workers were unemployed and the labour movement was calling for a halt to immigration to protect the jobs in Canada for Canadian labourers.

For years prior to 1914, storm clouds had been gathering over Europe. Few people, however, were prepared for the almost unthinkable events of the summer of 1914 that led Europe into a devastating war. Certainly, Prime Minister Borden had no idea of the bloodbath and turmoil he was about to lead Canada into.

Canada's Place in the British Empire

Britain declared war on Germany on August 4, 1914. News of the declaration reached Ottawa that evening. As a part of the British Empire, Canada was automatically at war with Germany; only the nation's level of participation was to be determined by the Canadian government. Yet, in 1914 being a part of the British Empire was far more than a legal technicality to most Canadians. When the war began, many Canadians either had been born in Britain or were of British descent. Loyalty to the King and the Empire was widespread in Canada. As well, Canada's economy was still closely tied to Britain's. A healthy and secure British Empire was critical to Canada's future economic success.

When Laurier had declared that the twentieth century belonged to Canada, he imagined the nation enjoying an economic boom as "the jewel in the crown" of the British Empire. It was, therefore, not surprising that news of the outbreak of war was greeted by cheering Canadians who demonstrated their **patriotism** by pouring out into the night, jubilantly waving their handkerchiefs and hats. Military experts planned on a quick victory, in which the loser — Germany — would pay the costs. Almost everyone expected a short war and thought the troops would be home by Christmas. Some soldiers would be killed, they knew, and others would suffer severe wounds; but most would have a glorious adventure to talk about for the rest of their lives.

In 1914 Canada was a young, pioneering nation of 7.5 million people. Almost two million immigrants had arrived in the past few decades, and they were still working hard to earn a living from land that had to be

Try to imagine how a conversation between Prime Minister Robert Borden and one of these Canadian soldiers might have sounded in 1918, after four years of war.

cleared and prepared for farming. How much should a small, young nation like Canada be expected to contribute to a European war? Given Canada's British heritage and economic ties, did its citizens have an obligation to support the war effort? Some argued that Canada should be able to contribute fifty thousand soldiers to the war effort. Should all regions be expected to contribute equally? If not, from where should the soldiers be drawn?

When word of war reached Canada, eager young men stood for hours in the heat of an unexpectedly hot August, waiting for their chance to sign up. Some of them worried that the war would be over before they reached the front. But not until Christmas 1918 — four brutal and bloody years later — did Canadian troops finally come home again. More than 60 000 Canadians never returned from battle at all; another 250 000 returned home battle-scarred. By the time the war had ended, Canada had sent over 650 000 men and women overseas to serve in the army, navy, and air force. This represented an astonishing 8 percent of the nation's population. Had Canada tried to do too much? Conscription (the forced enlistment of civilians in the army) would cause a rift that would never heal between Quebec and the rest of Canada. Had the country sacrificed national unity to meet the incredibly high demands of the first modern war?

The Birth of Industrial Warfare

During the Laurier years, technology had brought economic growth and new prosperity. In World War I, however, technology was used to create new weapons of mass destruction. In the four long years between 1914 and 1918, the world would witness the painful birth of modern warfare. In 1914, soldiers mounted on horses led the charge into battle; by 1918, soldiers marched behind tanks, which were initially known as "iron horses." Prior to 1914, the use of such horrific weapons as poisonous gas would have been considered uncivilized, as would dropping bombs from the air on unsuspecting victims. What had been heralded as great technological progress in the nineteenth century would prove to be the angel of death for millions of soldiers in what would come to be known as the Great War.

The terrible efficiency of modern weaponry resulted in a dramatic increase in the number of casualties suffered during war. Heavy artillery dropped hundreds of kilograms of explosives on troops, blasting the ground out from under them. Machine guns brought down a dozen soldiers in the blink of an eye. Fast-firing field artillery guns spat out shells that burst into showers of deadly **shrapnel**. Mustard and chlorine gas rolled over the battlefield, inflicting slow, agonizing death on thousands of soldiers at a time. Later in the war, tanks, airplanes, and submarines added to the reign of terror. Only a few military technicians had fully anticipated the destructive powers of twentieth-century weapons of war.

Massive Canadian casualties were just part of the terrible price that Canada paid in World War I. Canadians were asked to dedicate everything, including their lives, to the war effort. By the end of the war,

New technology made the battlefield more deadly than ever before. How many kinds of weapons can you identify in this painting?

Canada was bleeding badly on both the battlefield and the home front. In 1914, Canadians had willingly entered the war as a part of the British Empire. By 1918, the sacrifices made by all Canadians — from the battlefields to the wheat fields and from the diplomatic tables to the operating tables — had earned Canada the right to stand as a nation on its own.

What Caused World War I?

Throughout the nineteenth century the *Industrial Revolution*, which brought about a manufacturing shift from small, independent shops to large factories, changed the economies of Europe. It also reshaped European politics and **diplomacy**. The new factories that sprang up across Europe required stable sources of raw materials and secure markets to which the manufactured goods could be sold. These needs led to the economic control of foreign lands by countries such as Britain. For much of the nineteenth century, Britain was the undisputed ruler of the high seas and controlled a colonial empire that covered one quarter of the earth's land mass. By the latter part of the century, however, Britain's naval and economic dominance faced a stiff challenge from efficient German factories, and German goods began to outsell British goods.

Accompanying Germany's rapid rise as an industrial superpower was the nation's attempt to forge a colonial empire and to strengthen its ties with other countries. This was to be achieved partly through expanding its naval force, a direct threat to Britain's naval supremacy. Despite the economic prosperity and general optimism throughout Europe and North America at the turn of the century, many keen observers of international politics wondered how long war could be avoided.

By 1914 the European powers had squared off against each other in two camps. France, Russia, and Britain stood together on one side; Germany, Austria–Hungary, and Italy stood against them on the other side. Both sides attempted to portray themselves as morally superior. Yet, in reality, World War I, like many wars before and since, resulted from clashing economic interests and the failure of governments and diplomats to arrive at a peaceful compromise. How did other forces, such as nationalism, imperialism, and militarism, create a situation that required only a small event to trigger a world war?

Imperialism

Imperialism is the extension of one nation's authority or control over other lands by economic, political, or military means. As a result, these other lands become colonies. At the beginning of the twentieth century, imperialism was driven largely by economics. The European nations were arguing over their possession of faraway colonies because these colonies were economically important. In these places European countries could both secure raw materials for their industries and sell their industries' manufactured goods. By acquiring colonies, nations were able to build empires that spanned the globe. France occupied parts of northwest Africa and the Far East. Russia held a vast stretch of land across northern Europe and Asia. The United States pushed across the Pacific Ocean to claim the Hawaiian Islands and the Philippines.

Britain had the world's largest empire, which included Canada, New Zealand, Australia, Burma, Malaya, India, parts of the East and West Indies, South Africa, and a number of other colonies in Africa and the Pacific Ocean. Its navy gave Britain an important advantage in retaining its existing colonies and seizing new ones. But Germany was a relative newcomer as a European power; it had become a unified nation only in the past century and had only a few colonies. If it was to be a world player, it needed its own empire.

Germany looked to the Balkans and the Middle East to feed its growing appetite for raw materials and new markets. It built a railway from its capital city of Berlin to Baghdad and planned lines deep into Egypt and other parts of Africa. Britain, however, was against the German plans because it felt threatened by Germany's aggressiveness. Russia feared that a German railway through the Balkans (an area that includes Greece, Turkey, and the former Yugoslavia) might prevent its access to the Mediterranean Sea. These and many other quarrels over access to distant resources and markets created tension between the dominant European nations.

Colonial Empires, About 1900

AMERICAN	FRENCH	DUTCH	GERMAN	PORTUGUESE	ITALIAN	BRITISH		JAPANESE
United States	French Guiana	Netherlands	German Empire	Portugal	Italy	British Guiana	New Zealand	Empire of Japan
Alaska	France	Dutch Guiana	German E. Africa	Angola	Italian Somalia	Dominion of	Tasmania	Formosa
Hawaii	Algeria	New Guinea	German S.W.	Port. E. Africa	Sardinia	Canada	Gold Coast	
Puerto Rico	French Somalia	Sumatra	Africa	Port. Guinea	Sicily	Britain	Bahamas	RUSSIAN
Philippines	French Indo-	Java	Kamerun	Goa		Ireland	Malta	Russian Empire
	China	Borneo	German New			Egypt	Barbados	
	Madagascar	Celebes	Guinea	SPANISH	TURKISH	Sudan	Trinidad	BELGIAN
	Guadeloupe		Togoland	Spain	Turkish Empire	Rhodesia	Bermuda	Belgium
	Martinique		New Pomerania	Rio de Oro	Tripoli	British Somalia	Scotland	Congo Free State
			Crete			Guatemala	Straits Settlements	
						Jamaica	Sarawak	
						Niger	British New Guinea	
						British Indian	Sierra Leone	
						Empire		
						Commonwealth		
						of Australia		

How did the colonial empires existing at the beginning of the twentieth century contribute to the outbreak of World War I?

Nationalism

Nationalism results from a shared sense of cultural heritage and is often reflected in a strong sense of pride in one's country. Imperialism often went hand in hand with nationalism because many nations believed that expanding their empire would help to strengthen their economy by providing access to markets and resources. The late nineteenth and early twentieth centuries were an era of rising nationalism. When carried to the extreme, nationalism can lead to a belief that a certain nation should be the exclusive domain of a certain group of people.

In the decades prior to World War I, the great European powers competed to have the largest armies and navies. Nationalist sentiments also fuelled the drive for overseas colonies. Each time a European nation seized new lands, it stepped up the ladder toward economic domination. Ruling over a vast overseas empire was also a symbol of national pride; the European powers were always eager for new territory, both on their continent and beyond to enhance the glory of the homeland.

Militarism

In an age of nationalism and imperialism, **militarism** seemed necessary. Militarism is the policy of building up military forces and weaponry and of threatening armed aggression. To challenge other nations for new territories or to protect existing empires, countries created larger and more expensive militaries. In Britain and Germany, militarism began when these two nations spent millions of dollars to build up their armies and navies and to equip them with the latest weapons of war.

The size and power of the dreadnoughts elevated naval warfare to a new level. Why was a powerful navy essential to maintaining an empire at the beginning of the twentieth century?

At the turn of the century, Germany had the most powerful army in Europe but Britain "ruled the waves." Britain pushed hard to keep its naval advantage over Germany. In 1906, British shipyards began building a new class of sophisticated warships known as dreadnoughts — big, fast ships with devastating firepower that was concentrated in ten giant guns mounted in heavy enclosures known as turrets. The British dreadnought could outrun and outgun any ship in the German navy.

Germany challenged Britain's supremacy at sea in 1908 by launching its own huge naval expansion. Britain replied to the German challenge by building four more dreadnoughts. By 1914, Germany had built a navy of seventeen warships and seven dreadnoughts, and the British navy boasted twenty-nine battle-ready dreadnoughts.

The Alliance System

As military tensions rose in Europe, many countries began to form **alliances** to help ensure their safety. Britain and its allies — "the Allies" — were known as the Triple Entente. Germany and its allies — "the

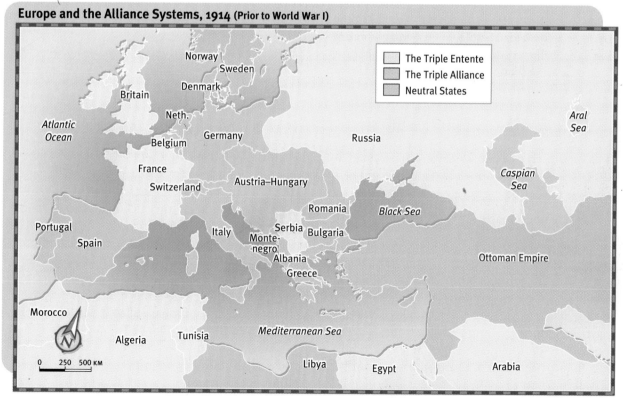

Europe and the Alliance Systems, 1914 (Prior to World War I)

Legend:
- The Triple Entente
- The Triple Alliance
- Neutral States

By the early twentieth century much of Europe was divided into two opposing camps, known as the Triple Alliance and Triple Entente. What alternative methods might a nation have used to ensure the safety of its borders?

Central Powers" — were called the Triple Alliance. These systems of alliances, or treaties between governments, were intended to keep peace in Europe. War with any allied nation meant war with the whole alliance, a threat that was intended to tame aggressive nations. But the alliances were dangerous. If war did break out anywhere in the "powder keg of Europe," as the region was called, it was sure to flame right across the continent.

The Events That Triggered World War I

Small nations are often overrun by their more powerful neighbours. The Austro-Hungarian Empire included many nationalities, mainly Austrians, Hungarians, and Slavs. Austria and Hungary had agreed to form two separate kingdoms under one crown in 1867. Then, in 1908, Austria–Hungary captured the provinces of Bosnia and Herzegovina. However, many Slavs in the two provinces resented their Austro-Hungarian rulers and wished to join the small new state of Serbia. Many Serbians shared Bosnia's dislike of Austro-Hungarian dominance. One radical Serbian, Gavrillo Princip, would fire the shots that started World War I.

The Granger Collection, New York

The murder of Archduke Francis Ferdinand has been called **"the shot that was heard around the world."** Why has this phrase been used?

Assassination at Sarajevo

It happened on a bright Sunday morning, June 28, 1914. The archduke of Austria, Francis Ferdinand, who was the heir to the throne of Austria–Hungary, was being welcomed to Sarajevo, the capital city of the province of Bosnia. As his motorcade drove along the parade route, the archduke and his wife, Sophia, waved to the well-wishers. Meanwhile, seven Serbian terrorists from a group called the Black Hand took up positions among the cheering crowds. Their target was the archduke. Suddenly, Gavrillo Princip, a nineteen-year-old Serbian, stepped forward, aimed a pistol at the archduke, and fired twice. Soon a coded message from the Black Hand flashed across the border to the Serbian capital: "Excellent sale of both horses." The archduke and his wife had died.

War Spreads to Western Europe

The two shots fired in a remote corner of Europe ignited a powder keg that would quickly engulf much of Europe in war. Austria blamed Serbia for the **assassination** of the archduke and declared war on the little Slavic kingdom. Russia, itself a Slavic nation, mobilized its army to support Serbia. Then the alliances began to take effect. Germany, supporting Austria–Hungary, declared war on Russia, while France declared war on Germany. Germany then declared war on France and moved to attack France by way of Belgium. When Germany invaded Belgium — a nation that Britain had promised to protect in a treaty signed almost a century before — Britain declared war on Germany. Canada was not a fully independent country but part of the British Empire, so Britain's declaration of war meant that Canada was at war, too. World War I had begun.

The Schlieffen Plan

Germany's first target was France. The German general Alfred von Schlieffen had planned an attack on France nine years earlier, and he now also knew that Germany would have to fight both France and Russia. The Russian army was large but badly trained, poorly equipped, and scattered across a huge country. It would take time for Russia to prepare its armed forces for full-scale war. Schlieffen's plan was to defeat France while Russia was struggling to get its army in order. Then Germany could turn its full firepower on Russia.

Since France had heavily fortified its border with Germany, a direct frontal attack across the French–German border would take too long. Schlieffen planned an attack on France through the "back door" of Belgium, despite that country's **neutrality**. According to his plan, a small force would be sent straight across the French–German border to attract French troops. The German force would then retreat, pulling the French army after it into the mountains of Lorraine. Meanwhile, a much larger

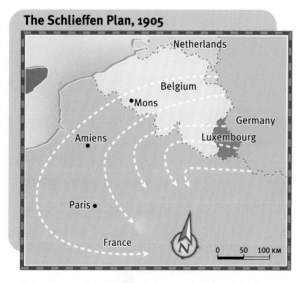

The Schlieffen Plan, 1905

According to Schlieffen's plan, conceived in 1905, Germany would strike France by sweeping south through neutral Belgium (each arrow represents a separate German army). The key to the plan's success would be the speed with which it was carried out. Why was this a risky plan?

German force would march across neutral Belgium and into France. Once on French soil, it would swing wide to the west and then circle back toward Paris to catch the French army in a giant trap.

Schlieffen realized that invading Belgium would bring other nations, especially Britain, into the war. He believed that invading Belgium was worth the risk if Germany was able to score a quick victory over France. But his plan failed; the French troops rallied and stopped the German army on the River Marne in France. Although the Germans had captured France's rich industrial region and had almost reached the gates of Paris before they were halted, they failed to score a decisive victory. The chance for a short war was gone.

After the Battle of Marne, the armies bogged down. Both sides began to dig in for the winter. Soon, two thick systems of trenches twisted across Europe: from the English Channel through a corner of Belgium, and across France to Switzerland. Enemy troops stood in the trenches and faced each other across a wasteland of mud and tangled wire called "no-man's land." By Christmas 1914, the war had ground to a halt. Neither side was able to make any significant progress along the Western Front. It was the beginning of a new kind of warfare — trench warfare.

Canada Prepares For War

Although Canada was automatically at war with Germany, as a part of the British Empire it could decide how far to support Britain's war effort. In the early days of the war, Canada's support was more than whole-hearted; it was overwhelming. When the call went out for volunteers to fight in Europe, recruiting stations across the country were mobbed by people wanting to enlist for duty. By September 1914, more than 30 000 Canadians had signed up.

Canada was better prepared for war than many Canadians had expected it to be. Defence spending was already six times higher than it had been at the turn of the century. Since 1909, most provinces had made military training a requirement for male high-school students. Military plans for keeping bridges, canals, and ports safe from "sneak attack" were in

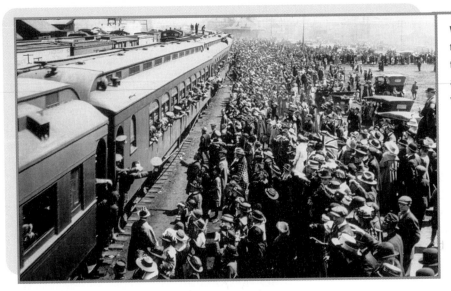

When war was declared in 1914, volunteers such as these troops boarding trains in St. Thomas, Ontario, were anxious to enlist. Why did the rush of volunteers slow to a trickle by 1917?

place, as was a detailed plan for mobilizing 25 000 volunteers as a Canadian expeditionary force.

When the minister of militia, Sam Hughes, ordered a huge training camp to be built at Valcartier, Quebec, an army of workers was assembled on the sandy plain outside Quebec City. They began laying out roadways, mess halls, latrines, drill fields, and the biggest rifle range in the world. Thirty days later, the huge tent city — complete with a power plant, a chlorinated water supply, and a rail link to Quebec City — was ready. By early September 1914, more than 30 000 soldiers and 8000 horses had poured into Valcartier Camp. The volunteers were issued equipment, and training began.

The soldiers' equipment, however, was often badly designed and poorly made. On one occasion a load of boots arrived, all for the right foot.

Hughes insisted on using the **Ross rifle**, a personal favourite of his because it was excellent for sharpshooting and it was manufactured in Canada. Unfortunately, it was useless in trench warfare. It was long and heavy and easily jammed by dirt. When it was fired rapidly, the firing mechanism overheated and seized up. On the battlefield, Canadian troops unofficially re-equipped themselves with Lee-Enfield rifles they had stripped from dead British soldiers or had stolen in raids on British arms depots, even at the risk of possible court martial. But a British War Office investigation had to be undertaken before Canadian forces were officially outfitted with Lee-Enfields in 1916. The Ross rifle was just one example of Canadian equipment that failed the test of warfare.

Sam Hughes created a mini–tent city at Valcartier to train raw recruits before they were sent overseas.

The Valcartier Camp was not equipped for the Canadian cold. Hughes wanted to get the training over and have the men packed off to war before winter set in. Prime Minister Borden, like most other Canadians, was impressed with Hughes's efforts. He gave permission for all 32 000 volunteers to ship out. On September 23, the soldiers were ready to board their ships for England. But the disorder in loading men, horses, and equipment on thirty ships was beyond description. As the convoy was about to leave, Hughes ordered leaflets to be handed out that read, "Men, the world regards you as a marvel." Many of the men crumpled the leaflets up and threw them to the ground.

Training for battle, Canadian troops march past Stonehenge on Salisbury Plain. Would the conditions that the soldiers encountered in England have changed their views on the war?

Web Connections

http://www.school.mcgrawhill.ca/resources

Go to the above Web site to find out more about Canada and World War I. Go to *History Resources*, then to *Canada: A Nation Unfolding, Ontario Edition* to find out where to go next.

The Canadian forces spent the winter of 1914 in tents on the windswept Salisbury Plain in southern England. It was the wettest winter in memory, and the plain was a sea of mud. Every morning, soldiers hung their blankets up in the rain to wash out the caked mud. They were always wet, cold, and hungry, and rations were short. The soldiers were lucky to get porridge and tea for breakfast, and leftover porridge and a bit of meat stew for supper. However, a few things changed for the better. Some of the Canadian equipment was replaced by sturdier British-made equipment. One Canadian soldier wrote, "We have been given new black boots, magnificent things, huge, heavy 'ammunition' boots, and the wonderful thing is they don't let water in. They are very big, and they look like punts, but it's dry feet now."

At this point in the war, Canadian officers were not yet ready to take command of a full division. The Canadian troops were placed under the command of the British general, Sir Edwin Alderson. Alderson weeded out the least well prepared of Hughes's recruits. Now the real training began. The Canadian troops drilled and marched, fired rifles, dug trenches, and practised with bayonets in the hard winter rains of England. But they would learn the reality of battle only in the trenches of France. By February 1915, the Canadian Division was ready for the Western Front. It took up its position near the small Belgian town of Ypres (pronounced ee-preh). There, Canadians would learn first-hand the horror of trench warfare.

The optimism so characteristic of the first decade of the twentieth century was shattered by the war some called "the war to end all wars." All of the supposed progress of the nineteenth century seemed to have suddenly been conscripted to wreak havoc and devastation on Europe. Technology that had held out so much promise for better lives now turned the battlefields of Europe into a deadly killing ground. Neither the soldiers who eagerly volunteered in 1914 nor the politicians who sent young Canadians off to war could have imagined what lay in store for the young nation. Unquestionably the events of the next four years would profoundly shape the destiny of Canada for years to come.

the arts

WORLD WAR I MUSIC

During World War I (1914-1919), a number of Canadian songwriters produced songs with a wartime theme that were Canadian favourites. The majority of the lyrics were written to raise morale among the troops, to show Canada's support for Britain, and to show the hardships that the young soldiers faced. Among these were "We'll Never Let the Old Flag Fall" and "Good Luck to the Boys of the Allies." Although these songs enjoyed great success within the country, they never became popular outside Canada. The one exception was "K-K-K-Katy," a Canadian song that became known throughout the English-speaking world during "The Great War." The words and music were written by Geoffrey O-Hara (1882-1966), who lived in Kingston, Ontario. "K-K-K-Katy" tells the story of a young soldier who tries to stammer out his affection to his girlfriend before he leaves to fight in France.

chapter review

CHAPTER SUMMARY

In this chapter we have seen

- how several factors, including imperialism, nationalism, and the alliance system, contributed to the outbreak of war

- how changes in technology radically altered the nature of modern warfare

- how many Canadians quickly rallied to support Britain in the war effort

- how the war, which was to be brief and glorious, became bogged down in the trenches

UNDERSTANDING HISTORICAL FACTS

1. Identify these people, places, and events, and explain their historical significance.

Imperialism	Triple Alliance/Triple Entente
Schlieffen Plan	Sam Hughes
Valcartier Camp	Salisbury Plain

2. Why did many European nations consider it important to acquire vast empires?

3. Explain the motive behind the assassination of Archduke Francis Ferdinand. How did the subsequent actions of several European nations lead to the outbreak of a world war?

4. Describe Alfred von Schlieffen's plan for the invasion of France, and explain why the defeat of France was Germany's primary objective.

5. Create a fictional time line that describes events in the life of a Canadian volunteer from the day war is declared in August 1914 to the day Canadian troops arrive on a European battlefield in April 1915.

EXPRESSING YOUR OPINION

1. Was the assassination of Archduke Francis Ferdinand a trigger to a tragic chain of events or was it a convenient excuse for a war that many wanted and expected? Support your answer with historical evidence.

2. Can any country or group of countries be blamed for the outbreak of World War I, or should blame for the war be placed several factors, including the aggressive competition resulting from the Industrial Revolution?

3. When the war started in 1914, Canada was a nation of 7.5 million people. Given that only males between the ages of eighteen and forty-five were accepted for combat roles, how large a fighting force was it reasonable for Canada to commit to the war effort?

4. World War I saw the introduction of deadly new weapons. As a result, the casualties suffered during this war were greater in number and more horrific than those in any previous war. Should a nation at war use all the weapons at its disposal to win? Is it possible to wage a moral war? Develop a set of guidelines for military leaders to follow in waging war.

WORKING WITH THE EVIDENCE

1. Revisit Sarajevo on June 28, 1914. Imagine that as Gavrillo Princip steps forward to fire his fatal shots, his arm is bumped and the bullets lodge harmlessly in a nearby tree. Shaken but unharmed, the archduke and his wife complete the procession. Describe the events that may have occurred over the next several months. Consider the existing tensions between nations as you construct a hypothetical chain of events.

2. When war began in 1914, British soldiers wore brown cloth caps instead of helmets. When the British War Office received reports of alarmingly high numbers of head injuries, it issued metal helmets to all soldiers. To its surprise and dismay, the number of head injuries increased, although the intensity of battle remained unchanged. Explain the increase in head injuries.

Mobilizing a Nation for War

This bronze relief is titled "Noonhour in a Munitions Factory." In Canada, the war created thousands of jobs in munitions factories and opportunities for women in roles traditionally filled by men.

INQUIRING INTO THE PAST

- Why were the contributions of some Canadians to the war effort not as welcome as the contributions of others?
- Why were some Canadians declared "enemy aliens"? How were they treated?
- How did the war create new types of industry in Canada?
- What new roles did women take on during the war?
- Why did the issue of conscription divide English and French Canada?

KEY TERMS

Battalions

Convoys

Enemy Alien

Internment Camps

Munitions

Pacifists

Suffragists

Xenophobia

TIMELINE

SPRING 1915 ▶
Canada opens its first internment camps

FALL 1916 ▶
No. 2 Construction Battalion (Canada's Black battalion) is created

MAY 1917 ▶
Borden announces policy of conscription

SEPTEMBER 1917 ▶
Wartime Elections Act is passed

By the winter of 1914, war in all its glory and ugliness had engulfed Canada. During the next four years Canada's war effort would yield heroic efforts and noble sacrifices from thousands, both on the battlefield and on the home front. Yet, at the same time the war would expose the racism and **xenophobia** that many Canadians were forced to endure. As well, while thousands died horrific deaths or suffered crippling wounds, a few used the war as an opportunity to make huge profits. In the end, the war years seem to have served as Canada's adolescence, an awkward age during which many blemishes appeared and mistakes were made. Nonetheless, it was an age during which Canada learned a great deal about itself and made huge steps toward national maturity.

Gearing Up for War

At the outset of the war, Canadians knew little about the horrors that their relatives and neighbours were facing in the trenches. A government press censor banned all news stories that were considered harmful to the war effort. Government propaganda posters appeared on street corners all over the country, and some artists were commissioned to paint pictures glorifying the "Great War."

In 1914, Canadians from coast to coast rallied for the war effort. Although not everyone supported Canada's participation in what some saw as a European war, support was generally widespread. Hundreds of church groups, women's organizations, and charities sprang into action. A Canadian Patriotic Fund, created by an Act of Parliament and staffed largely by volunteers, began to collect money for soldiers' families, many of whom were struggling to survive on a private's pay of $1.10 a day. Within three months the fund had raised $6 million in donations and was providing families in need with up to $50 a month. As well as providing monthly cheques, the Canadian Patriotic Fund also set up small co-operative stores, where families could buy food and fuel at the lowest possible prices. A military hospitals commission set up hospitals and health-care units in Canada to care for sick and wounded soldiers. Another organization

How effective would a poster such as this have been in persuading you to donate to the Canadian Patriotic Fund?

founded and equipped a Red Cross hospital in London, England. Women's voluntary societies provided food, clothing, medical supplies, and ambulances for returning troops. The Young Men's Christian Association (YMCA) and other groups set up clubs and canteens for soldiers on leave in England and Canada.

As the war dragged on, food and fuel became increasingly difficult to find. To support the war effort, families voluntarily changed their eating habits so that more butter, meat, sugar, wheat, and other foods could be sent to troops overseas. With hundreds of thousands of young men fighting overseas, women and children in Canada were left to harvest vital farm crops. Almost twelve thousand boys became "Soldiers of the Soil" to help out on Canadian farms. Even young children pitched in; they went without their favourite foods at home and bought 25¢ "thrift stamps" to help the government pay for the war. When they had pasted $4 worth of stamps into their stamp books, they received a government war savings stamp worth about $5 after the war. School rallies and variety shows were held to raise money for the personal items that Canadian soldiers appreciated, such as candy and soap, as well as army equipment. Children even scavenged along the railway lines for coal to burn in furnaces at home when the fuel shortage hit.

A White's Man's War: Racism in the Canadian Military

While Canadians from coast to coast were eager to do their part in the war, not all contributions were equally welcomed. Visible minorities, including Black, Asian, and Aboriginal Canadians, often found their efforts to enlist thwarted by racist attitudes. Gordon Wilson, a Black Canadian from Halifax, recalled, "Black people refused to accept the attitude that it was a White man's war. As loyal citizens we wanted to serve our country. It was our duty, our responsibility." Although only Aboriginal Canadians were directly denied admission to the army at the beginning of the war, other visible minorities were rejected for a variety of reasons, despite the official declaration that there was no "colour line" in the Canadian army. Some officials attempted to argue that Aboriginal Canadians might not be given civilized treatment if captured by the enemy, while others claimed that visible minorities would upset the delicate balance of the

Canadian voices

ABORIGINAL INVOLVEMENT IN WORLD WAR I

Canadian Aboriginal peoples were involved in all aspects of the war, including active duty at the front on land and in the air, as well as serving as railway troops and in forestry units.

Initially the minister of the militia, Sam Hughes, decided not to accept Aboriginal recruits, claiming: "While British troops would be proud to be associated with their fellow subjects, yet Germans might refuse to extend to them the privileges of civilized warfare." However, many Aboriginals had already enlisted and were being readied for active duty overseas. In 1915, as the need for more recruits increased, Hughes reversed his decision. By the end of war, over 3500 Aboriginals from all of Canada's provinces had enlisted.

Private David Kisek, a member of the Shoal Lake Band in Ontario, was awarded the Distinguished Conduct Medal for his bravery. The citation that accompanied the medal read:

He displayed marked courage and intelligence during the attack on enemy positions at Tilloy on 1st October 1918. When his company was held up by heavy fire, he on his own initiative ran into the open, and, with his Lewis gun at the hip, fired four pans into the enemy machine guns. His fire was so effective that a party of the company on the right were able to advance and capture four machine guns together with about 70 prisoners....

Two other Aboriginal Canadians who distinguished themselves on the battlefield were Henry Norwest and Francis Pegahmagabow. Norwest, a Cree from Alberta, has been described as one of the most successful snipers on the Western Front. At the time of his death on August 18, 1918, Norwest was officially credited with 115 hits. Pegahmagabow, an Ojibwa from the Parry Island Band in Ontario, was also an excellent sniper, whose bravery earned him the Military Medal three times: at Mount Sorrel in 1916, at Passchendaele in 1917, and at Amiens in 1918. Pegahmagabow, Norwest, and Kisek were only three of the many Aboriginal soldiers who made valuable contributions to Canada's war effort.

Private David Kisek.

military units. One recruitment officer even went so far as to tell fifty Black Canadians from Sydney, Nova Scotia, "This is not for you fellows, this is a White man's war." Underlying the weak excuses were racist assumptions, which were all too prevalent at the time. Some of the excuses expressed a sense of paranoia, a fear that giving non-Whites the experience of killing Whites on the battlefield might lead to problems at home after the war.

As the war dragged on and casualties mounted, the reluctance to admit non-Whites to the army was lessened. In the fall of 1915 the ban on Aboriginal Canadian enlistment was lifted, and by the summer of 1916 Japanese and Chinese Canadian men were reluctantly admitted into several **battalions**. Black Canadians were also allowed into the army, although most were restricted to a Black-only, non-combat battalion. Despite these changes, visible minorities remained on the fringe of the military. Having cleared the many hurdles placed before them, visible-minority Canadians who served overseas were often kept separate from White soldiers on ships and in camps; they even received their evening entertainment from a separate "coloured" YMCA. By the end of the war, 3500 Aboriginal Canadians, over 1000 Black Canadians, and several hundred Asian Canadians had served overseas in the Canadian army.

The No. 2 Construction Battalion

When war was declared in 1914, it soon became apparent that Black Canadians were considered second-class citizens. Brigadier General W.E. Hodgins stated in October 1915: "There are no regulations or restrictions which prohibit or discriminate against the enlistment and enrolment of Coloured men who possess the necessary qualifications. The final approval of any man, regardless of colour or other distinction, must of course rest with the officer commanding the particular unit in which the man in question is desirous of joining." This effectively allowed commanding officers to set recruitment policy. It was at this level that the racist attitudes were disturbingly apparent. Colonel Ogilvie, the officer commanding District Eleven, Victoria, B.C., stated: "Several cases of Coloured applicants for enlistment have been reported on by officers commanding units, and the universal opinion is that if this were allowed, it would do much harm, as White men here will not serve in the same ranks with Negroes or Coloured persons."

Despite the willingness of Black Canadians to serve in the military in defence of Canada, it was obvious that Canadian officials were not prepared to encourage their participation in combat battalions. As a result of Hodgins's memorandum, a separate Black Canadian battalion was formed. The No. 2 Construction

The No. 2 Construction Battalion was an entirely Black Canadian battalion of volunteers from across Canada. What does the existence of a segregated battalion say about racial tolerance in Canada during the first few decades of the twentieth century?

Battalion, unlike other battalions, was granted permission to recruit from across Canada. Despite earlier rejections, Black Canadians from across Canada eagerly enlisted. By December 1916, 575 Black Canadians had joined the No. 2 Construction Battalion.

When the battalion reached France, it consisted of 624 young men. It was attached to the Canadian Forestry Corps, where its members dug trenches, built bridges, and defused land mines. A few members were eventually transferred to front-line units, where they experienced trench combat, but the wartime experience of the vast majority of the No. 2 Battalion was limited to non-combat activities. Facing the same horrors of war, including mustard and chlorine gas attacks, many Black Canadians died serving their country. They received little recognition for their sacrifices. The song *Black Soldier's Lament*, by Captain George Borden, captured the Black Canadians' loyalty to Canada and their dismay at the lack of recognition.

With deep lament we did our job
Despite the shame our manhood robbed
We built and fixed and fixed again
To prove our worth as proud black men
And hasten sure the Kaiser's end

From Scotia port to Seaford Square
Across to France the conflict there
At Villa La Joux and Place Peronne
For God and King to right the wrong
The number two six hundred strong

Stripped to the waist and sweated chest
Mid-day's reprieve much needed rest
We dug and hauled and lifted high
From trenches deep toward the sky
Non-fighting troops and yet we die

The peace restored the battle won
Black sweat and toil had beat the hun
Black blood was spilled black bodies maimed
For medals brave no black was named
Yet proud were we our pride unshamed

But time will bring forth other wars
Then give to us more daring chores
That we might prove our courage strong
Preserve the right repel the wrong
And proud we'll sing the battle song.

Opponents of Canada's War Effort

Not all Canadians shared in the general enthusiasm for war. Small minorities of Canadians either opposed the war for religious reasons or were sympathetic toward Germany or the Austro-Hungarian Empire. For these people, the war years brought conflict and discomfort because fellow Canadians often viewed them with suspicion.

Pacifists

Before 1914, many Canadians had been against war on principle. Once Britain declared war, however, many former **pacifists** (those who oppose war on moral grounds) became staunch war supporters. The few Canadian pacifists who continued to speak out against war, such as the well-known social reformer J.S. Woodsworth, often lost their jobs. Some Canadian farmers, while not opposed to the war in principle, resisted participation on the basis that they were needed on the farm to plant and harvest badly needed crops. When the government cancelled the farmers' exemption from the draft in 1918, many reconsidered their support for the war.

Pacifist religious groups that had been welcomed to Canada before the war — Doukhobors, Mennonites, and Hutterites — were now treated with suspicion and hostility. Many Canadians believed that defeating the Germans was Canada's moral duty. Some even believed that Canadians who opposed the war were as dangerous as the enemy across the Atlantic. As a result, pacifist religious sects endured much anxiety throughout the war. Some of them saw their freedom of education abolished by an Act prohibiting teaching in the German language. As well, the Military Service Act, passed in 1917, extended the right to vote to all soldiers while taking away the right to vote from all who, due to their religious beliefs, opposed the war.

Prior to 1914 many religious sects were granted military exemptions, but in 1917 these exemptions were reconsidered. After a hearing that considered the continued exemption of Mennonites from military duty, a commanding officer concluded: "I am granting this exemption, but I think that you are wrong in your attitudes. You are living under the protection of the best government on the face of the earth, and you are doing nothing to show your appreciation." These words obviously caused much soul-searching within the Mennonite community. As a result, Ontario Mennonites formed the Non-Resistant Relief Organization to raise funds "which shall be donated as a memorial of appreciation for the privileges of religious liberty and freedom from military service." The goal of the organization was to raise $100 for each Mennonite youth exempted from war. The only stipulation attached to the donation was that the money would not be used for military purposes. Mennonites have continued to this day to raise money to support those whose lives have been disrupted by war or other disasters.

Why would someone throw this bust of Kaiser Wilhelm into a pond in Kitchener, Ontario, during World War I?

German Canadians

The war placed Canadians of German ancestry in a difficult situation. Some openly expressed support for Germany, while many were reluctant to enlist in a war against their former homeland. For Canadians who fervently supported the war effort, this reluctance was viewed as a betrayal of Canada and the British Empire. Some Canadians came to hate anything German. They pressured the government to fire German and Austrian immigrants who held government jobs. They put a stop to the teaching of the German language in Canadian schools and universities and objected to symphony orchestras playing the music of Beethoven and other German composers. Anti-German gatherings stormed through the streets in several Canadian cities. In Calgary, a mob of soldiers and civilians rampaged through the city's large German-speaking community, smashing windows and looting stores, while frightened families barricaded themselves inside their homes.

In Berlin, a small industrial city in southern Ontario, the divisions created by the war were most obvious. Populated largely by German immigrants, Berlin proudly displayed its German language and culture. When the call to arms came, enlistments from Berlin lagged far behind those in most other communities. Embarrassed and angered by the city's poor response, a group of citizens decided to take action. During the first few months of the war a statue of Germany's Kaiser Wilhelm was thrown into a pond, a German social club was raided, and a Lutheran pastor who continued to preach in German was assaulted and dragged through the streets. When the anti-German sentiment began to affect the orders being received by Berlin factories, a vote was held to rename the city. By a narrow margin it was decided to replace the name of Berlin (a connection to the city's German heritage) with its present name of Kitchener (after Lord Kitchener, a British war hero).

Canada's "Enemy Aliens"

The dark side of Canadian patriotism was again evident in the treatment of Ukrainians. During the Laurier era, Canada had actively and successfully sought immigrants from Eastern Europe to populate the west. By 1914, 170 000 Ukrainians lived in Canada. Many of them had fled the economic exploitation and political domination of the Austro-Hungarian Empire. When war was declared against Austria–Hungary, recent immigrants from there were viewed with increased suspicion and an anti-foreigner sentiment gripped Canada. Anyone who had not yet gained Canadian citizenship and who was a former citizen of a country at war with Canada was labelled an **enemy alien**. There is no doubt that the existence of pro-German organizations and the actions of some German Canadians and recent immigrants from the Austro-Hungarian Empire gave Canadians some reason to be concerned. The resulting paranoia, however, prompted the Canadian government to take action against thousands of recent immigrants.

The vast majority of the 95 000 immigrants from Austria–Hungary who were labelled enemy aliens were Ukrainian. An enemy alien was required to carry identification papers and report regularly to the police. By April 1915, feelings against enemy aliens were running so high that the federal government ordered nearly 9000 people — most of them recent immigrants, including more than 5000 from Ukraine — to be rounded up and taken to twenty-four remote **internment camps**. Internees were forced to do difficult physical labour such as clearing forests, draining land, and building roads. Life in the camps was difficult, and attempts to escape were discouraged by the threat of death. By the end of the war 107 internees had died in the camps and six had been shot and killed while trying to escape. After six hard years in the camps, the internees were released. But their properties and valuables, which had been seized when they were interned, were never returned to them. Wartime

Must Canadians' civil rights (such as free speech and freedom of association) always exist, or can they be suspended during times of crisis such as war? These men in the Castle Mountain Internment Camp near Banff, Alberta, had their freedoms taken away during the war because they were from countries with which Canada was at war.

hysteria and an anti-alien climate had led to the denial of civil rights of several thousand Canadians. This would not be the last time that Canadians would be interned for a threat that was often more imaginary than real.

French–English Conflict and the Conscription Crisis

Conflict between French and English Canada was also beginning to look like a permanent problem. Canada entered the war united, but it was soon torn by the worst French–English crisis since the hanging of Louis Riel.

The Decline in Voluntary Enlistments

In 1914, Canadian volunteers had flooded into recruiting offices. Prime Minister Borden declared that conscription would never be necessary in Canada, but by 1916 the flood of volunteers had slowed to a trickle. From July 1916 to October 1917, only 2810 men volunteered for the Canadian infantry. There were good reasons for the drop in volunteers. Already, by early 1917, one sixth of Canadian men between fifteen and forty-four years of age had joined the infantry. Thousands more had joined other branches, such as the artillery, forestry, and railway units, engineers or medical corps, and the Royal Flying Corps. Some Canadians felt that enough Canadian soldiers had been sent to Europe. Canada had already given more soldiers in proportion to its population than had either Britain or France. A further loss of men, they argued, would only undercut Canada's ability to supply vital foods and war materials.

On a visit to England, however, Borden became convinced that more Canadian soldiers were needed in Europe. He spent as much time as possible in British military hospitals, walking the long rows of beds and talking with wounded soldiers. Borden learned that many of them might be returned to the trenches if replacements were not found. He was deeply moved by their plight. In his New Year's message of 1916, Borden pledged 500 000 soldiers for the war — even though Canada's population totalled only about 7.5 million people.

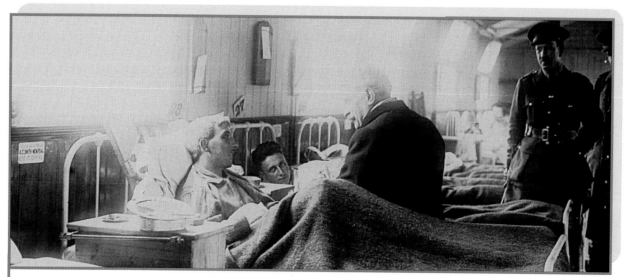

A visit to Europe, where he saw the devastation and suffering of the wounded, helped convince Prime Minister Borden that more soldiers needed to be sent to support the soldiers at the front. Propose an argument against sending more soldiers that takes into consideration the high casualty rate.

TABLE 7-1: VOLUNTARY ENLISTMENTS BY PROVINCES AND NATIONALITIES, AUGUST 1914 TO OCTOBER 31, 1917

Enlistments by Province	Population 1916†		Voluntary Enlistments
Ontario	2 713 000	—	191 632
Quebec	2 154 000	—	48 934
Nova Scotia and Prince Edward Island*	597 000	—	23 436
New Brunswick	368 000	—	18 022
Manitoba	554 000	—	52 784
Saskatchewan	648 000	—	26 111
Alberta	496 000	—	36 279
British Columbia and Yukon*	463 000	—	42 608
			439 806
Enlistments by Nationalities			
Canadian-born			197 473
British-born			215 769
Other Nationalities			26 564
			439 806

† Population figures are estimates derived from *Canada Year Book,* 1938, p. xxxi.

* The fact that Nova Scotia and Prince Edward Island, and British Columbia and the Yukon are bracketed together suggests that this table was based on statistics complied by Military Districts, since these areas comprised respectively Military Districts 6 and 11. This being the case, enlistments in four relatively thinly populated western counties of Quebec, which formed part of M.D. 3 (H.Q., Kingston) would be credited to Ontario, and those in a similarly thinly populated area of Ontario forming part of M.D. 10 (HH.Q., Winnipeg) would be credited to Manitoba.

Working with the data in this chart, calculate the percentage of enlistments for each province and rank them in order of highest to lowest. What reasons can you suggest for how the provinces rank?

Where could the new recruits be found? Voluntary enlistments in Quebec (and the Maritimes) were fewer than elsewhere in the country. Charges were common in English Canada that Quebec had not pulled its weight in the war effort. Many English Canadians pointed to Quebec as the place to find able-bodied Canadians who had not yet volunteered for war.

There were a number of reasons for Quebec's lagging enlistments. Many Quebec (and Maritime) couples married young, and it was harder for married men to volunteer. Also, Quebec was an agricultural province, and farm workers were needed at home. Historians sometimes blame Sam Hughes for failing to give French Canadians a stake in the war; while most other provinces had their own fighting units, Quebec did not. Instead, French-speaking volunteers were distributed among English-speaking units, where no consideration was given to language differences. Commands, instructions, and manuals were only given in English. As a result, French Canadians felt that they were being treated as second-class citizens. An attempt was made to repair the damage by creating the French Canadian 22nd Battalion in the Second Contingent. Known as the Van Doos (after the French *vingt-deux*, or twenty-two), the 22nd Battalion was one of the war's most distinguished units, winning over 150 medals.

Conscription: The Military Service Act

To many English Canadians, anything less than complete commitment to the war was unthinkable and unacceptable. They believed that if able-bodied Canadian men did not volunteer for service, they should be forced to serve. Borden knew that bringing in military conscription would touch off an outcry in Quebec. Since many Quebeckers had refused to volunteer, what would happen if they were forced to join the armed forces? Borden was convinced, however, of the need for more Canadian soldiers. On May 18, 1917, he stood up in the House of Commons to announce a new policy of conscription. "All citizens are liable for the defence of their country," he said, "and I conceive that the battle for Canadian liberty and autonomy is being fought on the plains of France

and Belgium." The Military Service Bill was introduced a month later in the House of Commons. It made military service compulsory for all men between twenty and forty-five years of age.

Almost half of all Canadians opposed Borden's conscription bill. Farmers were irate that their remaining sons and hired hands might now be taken away. Labour leaders considered calling a national general strike to protest conscription. But the reaction in French Canada was angriest of all; the day after the bill was introduced, riots broke out in Montreal. Peace was restored, but bitter opposition to conscription remained.

Henri Bourassa spoke out against the Military Service Bill. The Liberal leader, Sir Wilfrid Laurier, joined Bourassa in opposing conscription. "If this military service bill is passed," he warned, "we will

This poster was designed to appeal to Quebec's French heritage in order to encourage the province's young men to enlist in the army. How many symbols or references to their French heritage can you detect?

the arts

POSTERS, PATRIOTISM, AND GOVERNMENT PROPAGANDA

During World War I the federal government worked very hard to enlist the support of all Canadians in the war effort. Whether at home or in active duty on the Western Front, Canadians were urged to do their part to help ensure victory. In an age before television or the widespread use of radio, posters and full-page advertisements in newspapers were among the most effective means for the government to elicit support for its cause.

Most posters produced by the government in World War I served one of four purposes: (i) to encourage young men to enlist; (ii) to convince Canadians to buy Victory Bonds to help finance the war; (iii) to encourage Canadians to be thrifty and conserve food; and (iv) to urge Canadians to contribute to the Patriotic Fund, which provided assistance to the families of men fighting overseas.

Carefully study each of the accompanying posters from World War I before reflecting on the following questions:

1. What is the purpose of each of the posters?

2. How are Germans portrayed in the posters? How did this portrayal help the government gather support for the war effort? What are the dangers of using such propaganda?

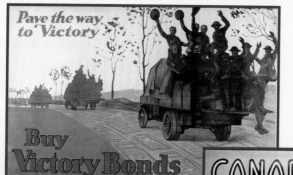

3. Identify the recruiting posters aimed at French Canadians and at English Canadians. How are the posters different? Speculate about why the government used a different approach for each group.

4. One of the posters suggests that men should not be at home playing sports while others are fighting overseas. How does it use emotion?

face a cleavage which may rend and tear this Canada of ours down to the roots."

After a summer of debate, the conscription bill was passed in late August 1917. Borden formed a new Union government — a coalition of Conservatives and Liberals outside Quebec — and fought the election of 1917 on the conscription issue. It was the most bitter election campaign in Canadian history. As Laurier predicted, Canada was torn apart by the bitter debate over conscription. The new Union government won the election, but Borden was now the leader of a deeply divided nation.

The Military Service Act was enforced after the election. When the first group of 404 395 conscripts was called, 380 510 appealed for an exemption. Many who did not win exemptions simply disappeared, and ultimately only 20 000 men reported for training. On the Easter weekend of 1918, military police in Quebec City grabbed a young man who had no exemption papers. Soon a mob gathered and attacked a military service registry office. They hurled office records out of windows and then turned to smashing and looting businesses owned by English Canadians. When local police refused to act, Ottawa sent soldiers from Ontario to restore order. On Easter Monday, an angry crowd surrounded soldiers in a city square and began pelting them with bricks and snowballs. The soldiers opened fire. Before the rioting ended, four people were killed and many more were injured. In the end, only 24 000 conscripts saw action in Europe. Some Canadians wondered if conscription had been worth the price of national discord.

Women During the War Years

Women's lives were dramatically changed by the war. Many watched in fear as their fathers, husbands, brothers, and sons trooped off to fight. They stayed behind to shoulder the responsibilities of family life alone. Many also suffered the pain of loved ones dying in battle. While full of hardship and sacrifice, however, the war years also brought women new successes.

Women played a key role in Canada's industrial achievements. They had worked in textile factories and other industries as long ago as 1880, but they had been kept out of jobs in heavy industry. By late 1915, however, so many men had gone to war that Canadian industries were crying out for workers. About thirty thousand women stepped in to take up jobs in machine shops, metal factories, **munitions** plants, aircraft factories, and shipyards across Canada. They also worked on streetcars and buses, in the police forces and the civil service, for banks and insurance companies, and on the farms.

Many Canadian women also crossed the Atlantic to make important contributions overseas. In all, 2400 Canadian women took jobs as nurses in military hospitals to care for Allied soldiers. Some nurses lost their lives, and some were decorated for valour and awarded Red Cross medals. Other Canadian women signed up to drive ambulances and to run clubs and canteens for soldiers on leave. Yet others staffed armed forces offices. Women in Canada and abroad shouldered their fair share of war work, but wartime labour was not a simple matter. At first, labour unions fought hard against hiring women, and in the factories women often worked side by side with men but were paid half the men's wages.

Working conditions in the factories were sometimes dangerous and unhealthy. In munitions plants, for example, acid fumes from high explosives damaged workers' lungs and turned their skins bright yellow, and accidental explosions killed and injured others. No effort was made to ease the women's move from the home to the workplace. Few employers thought to provide child care for working mothers or even to provide separate toilets for female workers. The message was clear: once the men were back from Europe, women were expected to return home to their traditional roles as wives, mothers, and domestic workers.

Early in the war a small number of women joined quasi-military organizations, in which they participated in shooting drills. Should women have been prepared for combat roles, or should they have restricted their activities to other types of patriotic work?

Women hard at work in a munitions factory. How did their participation in the workplace change women's roles in Canadian society?

Women, Social Reform, and the Vote

Despite opposition, women were taking on a stronger role in public life. They were increasingly active in fields such as social work, journalism, teaching, and public health. They were pushing open the doors into medicine and law and continued working for political and social reforms. In the cities, women campaigned for better working conditions, improved housing, and health inspection. The Halifax Local Council of Women, for example, created a women's employment bureau to give women better career training and opportunities for job advancement.

On the Prairies, women worked for new laws about women's ownership of property. Reformers such as Emily Murphy persuaded Alberta legislators to pass the Married Women's Relief Act, which entitled widows to a portion of their husband's estate. Other prairie women worked to change laws that prevented unmarried women and some wives from getting free legal title to lands under the Homestead Act.

In British Columbia, reformers tackled the plight of female workers who suffered from low wages, long hours, and miserable working conditions. Labour activist Helena Rose Gutteridge, for example, helped organize unions for city laundry and garment workers. A law passed in 1918 that restricted hours of work for women was, in part, a result of Gutteridge's efforts. Reformers in other provinces also demanded protection for female workers, and by 1920 laws had been passed in the Maritimes, Ontario, Quebec, and the Prairies.

In 1914, however, women were still denied the vote. Many **suffragists** continued to campaign hard for women's right to vote in provincial and federal elections. The first big breakthrough in Canada occurred in the West on January 26, 1916. A group of women journalists, including Nellie McClung, Cora Hind, and Francis Beynon, won for Manitoba women the right to vote in provincial elections. Within months, Saskatchewan and Alberta followed Manitoba's lead, and by 1917, women in British Columbia and Ontario could also vote in their provinces. By 1925, women were able to vote in New Brunswick, Nova Scotia, and Prince Edward Island. Only Quebec stubbornly resisted; not until April 1940 could the women of Quebec cast ballots in provincial elections.

In 1917, Robert Borden sought re-election on the issue of conscription. Realizing that he would need as much support as possible, his government passed the Wartime Elections Act, which gave Canadian nurses serving with the armed forces as

With the passing of the Wartime Elections Act in 1917, many women received the right to vote. These Canadian sisters are voting for their first time while stationed at a hospital in France in 1917.

well as the wives, sisters, and mothers of Canadian soldiers a vote in the upcoming federal election. During the campaign, Borden pledged to extend the vote to all women if he were re-elected. His strategy resulted in a victory for the pro-conscriptionists, and as promised, all women over the age of twenty-one were given the right to vote in federal elections following the war.

Canada's Contribution to the War Effort

Canada's main contributions to the war — besides providing thousands of soldiers — were food and munitions. When war broke out, Russian wheat exports to Europe abruptly stopped. Soon after, the German army rolled across France, and much of France's rich farmland fell into German hands. The Allies were desperate to obtain food for their soldiers and citizens alike. They needed all the food that Canadian farmers could produce.

Web Connections

http://www.school.mcgrawhill.ca/resources

Go to the above Web site to find out more about Canada's contributions to World War I. Go to *History Resources*, then to *Canada: A Nation Unfolding, Ontario Edition* to find out where to go next.

Food for the War Effort

Fortunately, 1915 had a perfect growing season for prairie wheat, and Western Canada's farmers that year harvested the biggest cash crop in their history. Wheat prices shot up, and thousands of people who had never farmed in their lives rushed to buy or rent prairie farmland and reap the profits from growing wheat. Between 1914 and 1918, more than sixteen million hectares of soil were brought into wheat production.

During the war years, Canadian farmers supplied millions of tonnes of food to Britain and France. Foodstuffs, including meat and dairy products, were one of the nation's most important contributions to the war effort. Even when crop yields dropped by half in 1917, skyrocketing wheat prices meant that the smaller crop earned farmers even more than the bumper crop of 1915 had. But intensive wheat farming was ruining the prairie soil. Farmers in the West were beginning to create the soil conditions that were to have disastrous results in the 1930s.

Canada's Munitions Industry

Munitions were another of Canada's significant contributions to the war effort. By 1917, Canada had shipped millions of dollars' worth of shells and explosives from over six hundred munitions factories. More than 250 000 Canadians worked in the thriving munitions industry. At the outbreak of war, however, Canada had just one small government factory outside Quebec City that produced only seventy-five shells a day. Assembling the machinery and labour required for munitions production was not easy; making munitions required precision tools and highly trained workers. A faulty shell could blow a gun apart and kill the soldier firing it. But in 1914 there were few precision instruments in Canada and very few skilled workers.

Britain was desperate for munitions and was willing to pay well for them. Canadian industrialists quickly realized that they could make large profits in the war munitions business. Friends of the minister of the militia, Sam Hughes, soon got his support to form a "shell committee." Its job was to bid for British artillery-shell contracts and find Canadian manufacturers to fill the orders. Hughes's Shell Committee was given $170 million in British contracts, and Canadian manufacturers with experience in metal work, such as bedspring makers, farm machinery factories, railway shops, and structural iron works, switched their operations to making munitions.

The Shell Committee, however, was plagued with problems. By 1915, evidence revealed that Hughes's friends on the committee were making huge profits from dishonest contract deals. At the same time, the committee was able to deliver on only $5.5 million of the $170 million worth of British contracts, and most of those deliveries were late. Britain's new minister of munitions, David Lloyd George, told Canadian Prime Minister Robert Borden that Canada would not receive another British order until the Canadian munitions industry was completely overhauled.

Borden agreed to disband the Shell Committee and set up the Imperial Munitions Board (IMB), which answered directly to the British government. A self-made millionaire in the bacon-exporting business, Joseph Flavelle, was chosen to head the new board. He put together a team of experienced business managers who had risen to the top during the Laurier boom years. Flavelle and his new team completely overhauled the Canadian shell-producing industry. Some greedy war contractors were charging far too much, and Flavelle forced them to roll back their prices. Others were making inferior products; a few even

Humour in History

With the horrors of war surrounding soldiers day and night, a chance to relax and laugh behind the front lines was something to look forward to. One of the most popular comedy and entertainment events was organized by the YMCA (Young Men's Christian Association). The Dumbells Concert Party was an entertaining mix of songs, comedy, and impersonations featuring soldiers from Canada's Third Division. They would delight soldiers with songs such as "The Dumbell Rag" and "Oh It's a Lovely War." The highlight of their show was the female impersonations with costumes, which originally were made from bandages.

The Dumbells enjoyed such success that after the war the musical comedy troupe became a hit in London and on Broadway in New York.

The Dumbells Concert Party in 1916. Soldiers often relied on humour to help ease the tension from the danger that surrounded them constantly. If you were in charge of entertaining the troops, what kind of event would you organize?

faked inspection stamps and filled holes in metal shell casings with paint. Flavelle and the IMB worked hard to make sure that Canadian-made munitions were up to standard.

By 1917 the Canadian munitions industry was setting records for both the quantity and the variety of its products. When the United States entered the war and needed to buy a whole range of new weapons, the Canadian munitions industry blossomed. By 1918, Canada was manufacturing airplanes and airplane engines, guns, cargo ships, chemicals, and many other weapons of war. Fifteen hundred factories in ninety Canadian cities employed more than 300 000 people.

Disaster Strikes Halifax: The Explosion of 1917

Many Canadian cities enjoyed an economic boom during the war years. In Halifax, Nova Scotia, the boom would come with a high price. During the war years Halifax became the chief Canadian port of the British Royal Navy. From here, vital war supplies, including munitions from the newly built factories, were shipped to Europe and guarded from German submarines by **convoys**. Unfortunately, disaster would accompany the prosperity. As a major wartime port, Halifax hosted ships from many countries and carrying a wide range of cargoes. Two such ships were the *Imo* from Norway and the *Mont Blanc* from France.

The morning of December 6, 1917, began like any other. Soldiers in the garrison had begun their duties for the day, labourers were going about their work, businesspeople were heading to their offices, and children were preparing to begin classes for the day. Meanwhile, in Halifax harbour, the *Mont Blanc*, a cargo steamer that had been loaded with 2400 tonnes of high explosives, was heading toward the Narrows while the *Imo* was also heading out of the harbour, beginning its journey across the Atlantic Ocean to Europe.

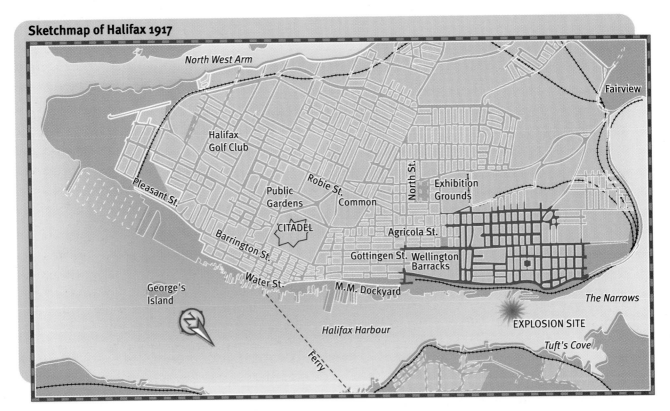

Sketchmap of Halifax 1917

The collision between the ships *Mont Blanc* and *Imo*, which led to the Halifax Explosion, occurred as the ships approached the Narrows. The darkened area of the map indicates the area of Halifax that was completely destroyed.

Levelled by a massive explosion, Halifax was the only Canadian city to suffer from the destructive power of modern technology. Would the explosion change the way Canadians viewed the war?

What happened next is not entirely clear, but the two ships collided.

Many who witnessed the events in the harbour that morning knew immediately of the danger of a burning munitions ship. Vincent Coleman, a Halifax train dispatcher, hurriedly sent this message to the station at Truro to warn a train scheduled to arrive in Halifax to stop its journey: "Munition ship on fire, making for Pier 6, Goodbye." It was the last message he would ever send. At 8:55 a.m. the *Mont Blanc* blew up. The explosion was reported to have been heard more than three hundred kilometres away and destroyed a large part of Halifax. In its wake the explosion left two thousand people dead, nine thousand injured, and thousands more homeless. An eyewitness provided the following description of the devastation.

> When one observed the destructive effects of the explosion on the glass all over the city and Dartmouth, their number is not surprising, as there must have been a lightning-like hail of millions of particles of flying glass, much of it travelling with terrific velocity.

The Halifax explosion brought the horrors of war to Canada's doorstep. It served as a reminder of the death and destruction that had plagued Europe for three years and would continue unabated for nearly another full year.

Profiteering and Scandal in the War

The story of Canada's involvement in World War I is tainted at some times by racism and prejudice and at other times by greed and corruption. These occasions stood in stark contrast to the many efforts of Canadians who had made substantial personal sacrifices for the war. As food and fuel became scarcer, many people tightened their belts and shivered through the winter. So they were stunned and disillusioned to see some millionaire industrialists growing richer from dishonest dealings in war contracts. Angry voices across the nation called for the government to do something about "food pirates and price manipulators." There was a public outcry to "conscript wealth" for the war. Some people even wanted the government to nationalize (take over) the nation's banks and industries until the war's end.

Despite his promise in 1914 not to interfere with business, Borden did make a small concession in 1916 by appointing a fuel controller, who had the power to imprison dealers who hoarded coal, and a food controller to oversee rising food prices. But instead of rolling back food price increases, as many Canadians had expected, the food controller asked citizens to stop eating so much and to change their tastes. No serious attempt was made to curb the corrupt practices of private enterprise during World War I.

Paying for War

Plagued by corruption and inefficiencies and a war that dragged on far longer than anyone imagined possible, the cost of Canada's involvement in World War I skyrocketed. By 1918, it had reached a staggering $1 million a day. Borden's government hurried to find new ways to pay for the war. At first, Canadians believed the war would be short and that Germany would be made to pay for the costs of the war. But as the war dragged on, huge sums of money were spent. In 1914, the federal government spent about $72 million on defence. Four years later, government spending had shot up to $439 million per year.

How could the government raise so much money? One idea was to create new taxes. Borden's government reluctantly introduced two new income taxes, intended only as temporary measures in a time of desperation. The tax on business income was announced in 1916, and the tax on personal income was introduced in 1917. But together these taxes brought in just over $50 million, so more money had to be found. Another strategy was to borrow money and let future generations of Canadians help repay the loan. The finance minister, Thomas White, explained that coming generations should pay part of the cost of World War I since the war was waged "in the interests of human freedom and [for] their benefit."

For the first time in history, Ottawa offered government bonds for sale, at a 5 percent interest rate. Canadians responded enthusiastically to "Victory Bonds." Although the finance minister hoped to raise $50 million by selling the bonds in 1915, more than $100 million worth were sold. In 1917, a special issue of Victory Bonds was offered. This time, the government hoped to sell $150 million worth; instead it raised almost $500 million. Although bonds and income taxes were brought in as temporary measures at a time of crisis, they were so successful that this source of government revenue became a permanent part of Canadian life.

In an effort to raise money to pay for the war, the government encouraged people to buy Victory Bonds by using posters like this one. Why do you think these posters were so effective?

A Changed Nation

When the soldiers would finally return from Europe, they would come home to a Canada deeply divided over conscription. The bitterness was to last long after the war ended, but Canada was also a more confident nation. Although the war on the home front had been marred by profiteering scandals, many Canadians had worked hard in the war effort. Canada's extraordinary successes in agriculture and industry were a source of national pride. Women had also taken a step forward on the road toward equality. They made important contributions to the war effort in the home and took on new roles in the workplace. They were active in social reforms, and they were winning the battle for the vote.

chapter review

CHAPTER SUMMARY

In this chapter we have seen

- that the contributions of all Canadians to the war effort were not equally welcomed

- that some recent immigrants to Canada, such as the Ukrainians, were viewed with suspicion and sometimes placed in Canada's first internment camps

- how women played a vital role in the wartime economy

- how Canada's contribution to the war included vital food supplies and weapons as well as several hundred thousand soldiers

- how the issue of conscription divided the nation and left bitter feelings between French and English Canada

UNDERSTANDING HISTORICAL FACTS

1. Identify these people, places, and events, and explain their significance to Canada's war effort.

No. 2 Construction Battalion	Military Service Act
Canadian Patriotic Fund	Enemy Aliens
Wartime Elections Act of 1917	Victory Bonds
Halifax Explosion	Robert Borden

2. Identify three events that occurred during the war years that exposed racism and xenophobia in Canada.

3. The war years were an important period for women in Canada. How many different roles were filled by women? What political and social reforms did women help to bring about during this period?

4. How did the Canadian government raise money to pay for the war effort?

5. List three reasons why there was a reluctance among French Canadians to volunteer to fight in the war.

EXPRESSING YOUR OPINION

1. Do you agree that, while fellow Canadians are dying in war, others should be permitted not to take part?

Was it fair and just for the Canadian government to strip pacifists of their right to vote?

2. Was the Canadian government justified in stripping many recent immigrants from Germany and Austria–Hungary of their rights and in some cases imprisoning them in internment camps? Can you suggest an alternative that would not violate people's rights but still protect Canada's security?

3. Is it in the interest of society to allow people and companies to profit from war? Defend your answer.

4. Review the Wartime Elections Act. Why did Prime Minister Borden pass this legislation? Would you have supported the Wartime Elections Act? Why or why not?

5. Copy a chart like the one below in your notebook and use it to outline arguments for and against conscription in World War I. Would you have been a supporter of Borden's Union government, or would you have supported Laurier in opposing conscription?

ARGUMENTS FOR CONSCRIPTION	ARGUMENTS AGAINST CONSCRIPTION

WORKING WITH THE EVIDENCE

1. For years before the outbreak of war, the Women's Christian Temperance Union waged a lengthy battle to have the sale and consumption of alcohol banned in Canada (Prohibition). On the eve of the 1917 election, the government agreed to pass Prohibition laws. Why do you think Prohibition occurred at this time?

2. When the war ended, most Canadians expected to greet conquering war heroes filled with pride and glory. Instead, the young soldiers came home weary, disillusioned, and often bitter. Why was there such a wide gulf between the ways Canadians imagined the returning soldiers and the reality they discovered?

Canadians on the Battlefields of Europe

Richard Jack's painting *The Second Battle of Ypres* captures what has been referred to as "Canada's baptism in fire".

INQUIRING INTO THE PAST

- Why were many young men eager to become pilots despite the high casualty rate?
- How did Canadian heroics on the battlefield contribute to a sense of Canadian nationalism?
- What was life like in the trenches for soldiers serving at the front?
- How did the withdrawal of Russia and the entry of the United States alter the course of the war?

KEY TERMS

Armistice

Artillery Barrage

Communism

Naval Blockade

No-Man's Land

Parapets

Reconnaissance

Shell Shock

Storm Troops

Trench Foot

Trench Warfare

U-Boats

Victoria Cross

TIMELINE

APRIL 1915 ▶
Canadians experience first combat at the Battle of Ypres

APRIL 1917 ▶
United States declares war on Germany

APRIL 1917 ▶
Canadians capture Vimy Ridge

NOVEMBER 1918 ▶
Armistice ends war

It has been said that the twentieth century truly arrived with the outbreak of war in 1914. When the war began, soldiers on horseback charged across the battlefield; four years later, armoured tanks were rolling across the battlefields, airplanes were dropping bombs from the sky, poisonous gas had been used by both sides, and submarines terrorized merchant ships crossing the Atlantic Ocean. Never before had nations committed so many resources to the destruction of military and civilian populations; and never before had war been so impersonal that thousands of people were killed by poisonous gases or bombs dropped from the sky on unsuspecting victims. The myth of honourable warfare was one of the casualties of World War I. It was killed by the new technology of war.

The Canadian soldiers received their "baptism in fire" at Ypres, in April 1915. Can you explain this term in relation to this painting of Ypres after the battle?

Technology and Modern Warfare

The Industrial Revolution, which had transformed the economies and daily lives of Europeans and North Americans during the nineteenth century, was about to have an equally profound effect on the nature of warfare. Writing in 1897, I.S. Bloch, a Polish banker and economist, warned that industrialization would radically alter the nature of warfare. His description of how the next war would unfold was strikingly accurate.

> At first there will be increased slaughter on so terrible scale as to render it impossible to get troops to push the battle to a decisive issue.... The war, instead of being a hand-to-hand contest in which the combatants measure their physical and moral superiority, will become a kind of stalemate.... Everybody will be entrenched in the next war; the spade will be as indispensable to the soldier as his rifle.

The newly built factories could produce one hundred times the quantity of metal that had been available a century earlier, and most scientists, convinced that they were contributing to a just cause, worked to develop increasingly deadly weapons. The result was a nearly inexhaustible supply of bullets and bombs

The new technology could be seen in all areas of war, on land, in the air, and on the sea. The side that best adapted to the new realities of twentieth-century war would have a decided advantage over its opponents. Initially, Germany held this advantage. Many British military commanders underestimated the potential of new weapons such as the machine gun and attempted to fight a nineteenth-century war against twentieth-century weapons. It would be the Germans who first made deadly effective use of the new weaponry.

Canadians Face the Horrors of Poisonous Gas at the Battle of Ypres

The First Canadian Division reached the Western Front in February 1915, where it joined French–Algerian troops in the trenches near the town of Ypres, Belgium. Two months later, the German army decided to unleash a new and terrible weapon — chlorine gas. It chose Ypres as the site for the first gas attack in history. The new Canadian troops had just joined the battle; it was considered an honour to defend the last scrap of Belgian soil under Allied control.

Their position was surrounded on three sides by German trenches. The Germans quietly carried 5730 cylinders of chlorine gas to the front line and set them in place. In the early evening of April 22,

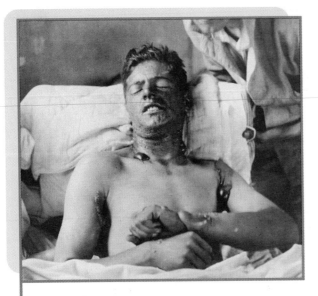

This soldier's wounds show the effect of chlorine gas. In a war that used a variety of efficient killing machines, ranging from the machine gun to the tank, was chlorine gas a less acceptable weapon of war?

they released the gas. Allied High Command had been warned about a possible German gas attack, but it failed to tell the soldiers on the front lines about it or to provide any instructions or means of defence. When the French–Algerian troops saw the cloud of strange, green gas rolling toward them, they panicked and ran. The Germans then smashed through the gap left by the panicking troops.

Soon a wall of deadly gas about three metres high began to drift over Canadian positions. Soldiers all over the battlefield gasped and cried as they breathed in the chlorine gas, and they began to suffocate.

The Canadian troops held their position for three more days, under repeated artillery and gas attacks, until they were relieved by British reinforcements. A British soldier described what he witnessed when he reached the front: "There were about 200 to 300 men lying in a ditch. Some were clawing their throats. Their brass buttons were green. Their bodies were swelled. Some of them were still alive. Some were still writhing on the ground, their tongues hanging out."

When the Canadian troops withdrew from the battlefield four days later, fewer than half of the soldiers had survived. Although Canadian casualties

totalled 6037, the soldiers had stood their ground. The Canadians won high praise as courageous fighters. Their first major battle was a harsh lesson in the heroism and hardship of days to come.

In the Trenches

When the war began, both sides on the conflict had planned to rapidly advance against their enemies. Battles such as Ypres prevented any such breakthrough for either side. Instead, as I.S. Bloch had predicted, the new technology of war quickly bogged down both sides as they dug in for a long and bitter battle. Realizing the need to construct continuous lines of defence to prevent being outflanked by the enemy, each side worked throughout the winter of 1915–1916 to create an unbroken line of trenches stretching 640 kilometres. By 1916, opposing trenches had been carved into Europe from the English Channel to the Swiss Alps.

The armies' defence systems were a maze of trenches zigzagging across mud, shell craters, minefields, and barbed wire. The front-line trenches closest to enemy guns were the firing lines. Machine guns were placed at key positions to rake enemy lines with bullets. Three or more lines of support trenches at the rear served as command and supply posts. Running at right angles between them were communication trenches. Sometimes, small trenches called "saps" snaked out to lookout posts or machine-gun nests in **no-man's land**. There were also blind alleys to confuse the enemy if the trenches were captured.

Duty on the front-line trenches usually lasted six days. Soldiers then fell back to the support trenches for six more days, where their job was to ferry ammunition and food rations up to the front. Then they were taken out of the trenches altogether for

Web Connections

http://www.school.mcgrawhill.ca/resources

Go to the above Web site to see how well you would do in the trenches. Go to *History Resources*, then to *Canada: A Nation Unfolding, Ontario Edition*, to find out where to go next.

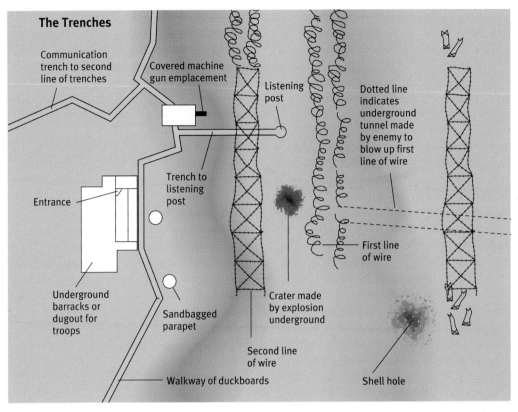

The Trenches

Communication trench to second line of trenches

Covered machine gun emplacement

Listening post

Dotted line indicates underground tunnel made by enemy to blow up first line of wire

Trench to listening post

Entrance

First line of wire

Underground barracks or dugout for troops

Sandbagged parapet

Crater made by explosion underground

Second line of wire

Walkway of duckboards

Shell hole

Trenches evolved into a complex system of tunnels, trenches, barbed wire, and makeshift command posts. Who would trench warfare have favoured — the attackers or the defenders? Why?

twelve days to rest in tarpaper barracks, barns, or abandoned villages at the rear of the battlefield.

On their tours of duty, soldiers ate, fought, and slept in the trenches. In the front line, days were spent standing sentry duty and repairing collapsing trench walls. The front-line trenches were usually about two metres deep by two metres wide and were dug down until water began to seep in. In wet weather, the men on patrol often stumbled through thick mud and slimy water up to their knees. One soldier described his first trip through a communications trench to the front line: "The trench was about three feet deep and wound across a swamp and every step squelched as one stepped on one of the bodies that floored the trench. The walls were part sandbags and part more bodies — some stiff with rigor mortis and others far gone with decay."

The soldiers often went for weeks without washing or changing their clothes, and most were infested with body lice. Others got **trench foot** from days spent knee-deep in water: their feet swelled up to

two or three times their normal size and went numb. When the swelling went down, the pain was agonizing. If gangrene set in, the soldiers' feet and legs were amputated. Conditions were so wet and filthy that even small sores became badly infected.

Miserable conditions were only one part of the horror of **trench warfare**. Daytime at the front was dangerous. Front-line trenches were sometimes within twenty-five metres of enemy lines, and soldiers moved carefully with their heads down. A head above the trench line was an easy target for German sharpshooters.

Nighttime was worse. Soldiers had to climb out of the trenches for patrols in no-man's land and to repair the **parapets** (low walls in front of the trenches) and string barbed wire along the trenches. Night was also the time for surprise attacks. Raiding parties would creep across no-man's land, using wire cutters to cut their way through the barbed wire. Then they would descend on enemy troops with grenades and bayonets.

leisure

REST AND RELAXATION IN THE MIDST OF WAR

After enduring days of relentless shelling while living in filthy trenches, soldiers looked forward to a few days of rest behind the lines. The opportunity to escape the front lines, for even a few days, allowed soldiers the opportunities to bathe, get a clean set of clothes, and to engage in some sports or have a few laughs.

GETTING A BATH

The greatest luxury most soldiers could imagine was a hot bath. Each of the rest areas along the front had improvised bath houses. When they entered they would set their clothes aside to be washed and repaired by local women. The soldiers then went into another room, where they were allowed ten minutes to soak and relax in a tub of hot, soapy water.

A VISIT TO THE YMCA

Bathed and in a clean set of clothes, soldiers on leave from the front welcomed some light entertainment. In each of the rest areas the YMCA (Young Men's Christian Association) set up huts or tents. Here soldiers could write letters, read a variety of newspapers, magazines, and books, and visit a canteen that sold coffee, sweets, and soft drinks. The YMCA also arranged lectures on a variety of topics, ranging from law and philosophy to English literature

FROM THE BATTLEFIELD TO THE SPORT FIELD

During their brief respite from the war, soldiers would engage in healthy forms of competition on the sports field. Field days were often organized at the rest area, during which teams would compete in games of soccer, boxing, sprinting, and water sports such as diving, underwater swimming, and tub races. These games not only were an opportunity for soldiers to enjoy themselves in sport, but also provided them with a chance to meet and talk with fellow Canadians. These opportunities to play, laugh, and relax were vital for soldiers who would spend much of their time staring out of trenches into the face of death.

The Canadian Championship Athletic Meet in France, 1917.

ACTIVITY

If you were among the soldiers at the front during World War I and were given the challenge of providing entertainment for the troops, what would you do? Make a contribution to the life of the soldiers by doing one of the following:

- writing a funny song about the war
- preparing a humorous skit
- creating a story to be told to the troops
- creating a sporting activity (invent a game or activity) or
- creating a poster to advertise an upcoming event at a rest area

Dawn was the worst time of all because it was the favoured hour for major attacks. The attacking troops were cut down by machine guns and artillery shells, or they were tangled in barbed wire as they scrambled out of the trenches and charged across no-man's land. Only a few made it to enemy lines. Soldiers who lay wounded in no-man's land could not be rescued. Sometimes it took days before they died, and their companions had to endure their agonized cries for help.

The miseries and danger of trench warfare were too much for some soldiers, who suffered nervous breakdowns. Victims of battle fatigue or **shell shock** (a serious nervous disorder resulting from prolonged exposure to sustained artillery fire) were unfit for fighting and sent away to asylums in England and Canada. Many never recovered. Some soldiers hoped for a "blighty" — a wound serious enough to cause the injured soldier to be sent back to England. At some time during the war, almost every soldier must have wondered what he was doing at the front.

The Battle of the Somme

The Battle of the Somme highlighted the deadly effectiveness of modern artillery and of the machine gun. Of all of the new weapons introduced during World War I, artillery claimed by far the most lives. Almost 50 percent of all the wounds suffered by soldiers were caused by either flying shell fragments or shrapnel-balls. Wounds caused by shrapnel and shell fragments were always more gruesome and often more deadly than a bullet wound, which cleanly pierced the body. Often artillery shells would be packed with nails or scrap pieces of metal. When the shell exploded, red-hot chunks of metal tore through the bodies of nearby soldiers.

The other weapon that showed its lethal power during the Battle of the Somme was the machine gun. At the outset of World War I, the German army understood the potential of the machine gun much more than any other army did. In 1914 it had 2500 Maxim guns and was receiving 200 new guns each month. By 1917 the army was being supplied with 14 400 new Maxim machine guns each month. During the winter of 1915–1916 Germany created and trained new machine-gun units called MG Scharfshutzentrupps (machine-gun marksmen sections). The British, by contrast, believed that the machine gun was an over-rated weapon. When war began in 1914, the British allocated only two machine guns to each infantry battalion and gave no special training to the soldiers who were to operate them.

In 1916 the German army began pressing the French troops hard at Verdun. The British commander in chief, Douglas Haig, decided to go on the offensive and smash through the German lines in what came to be known as the Battle of the Somme. Haig was slow to adjust to the new demands of trench warfare. By the time he had adjusted, count-

After major battles such as the Somme, the landscape was left scarred. What challenges would farmers have to overcome after the war if they wished to make land like that depicted in this photograph productive again?

less Allied lives were lost in a series of badly planned and poorly executed battles along the Somme.

For five days before the Allied attack, the British and French bombarded the German lines with 1.5 million rounds of ammunition. Haig hoped that the shelling would wipe out the German front lines and break the barbed-wire defences. But the Germans withdrew into trenches protected by massive concrete walls and nine-metre-wide rolls of barbed wire until the bombardment ended. As a result, the German casualties were much lower than Haig had expected and the Germans' barbed wire remained in place. Massive craters from the shelling made it hard for Allied infantry and cavalry units to charge the German line. The craters also were ideal as machine-gun nests for German gunners.

When the Allied shelling stopped, the Germans knew that an attack was coming. Haig had overesti-

mated the effectiveness of the **artillery barrage**. This miscalculation would have deadly results. One hundred German machine guns were waiting to sweep the Allied attackers with a hail of bullets. The first battle in the Somme campaign began under a cloudless blue sky on July 1, 1916. A British officer scrambled out of the trenches and waved his troops forward. The soldiers went over the top that day to meet the most ferocious artillery barrage they had ever faced.

One German soldier described the fighting from a machine-gunner's point of view: "When we started firing we just had to load and reload. They went down in the hundreds. You didn't have to aim, we just fired into them." When the first wave of English, Welsh, and Scottish soldiers was sent across no-man's land, it was broad daylight. It took only a few minutes for the German machine gunners to eliminate the entire first wave of soldiers from the battlefield.

Major Canadian Battles of World War I

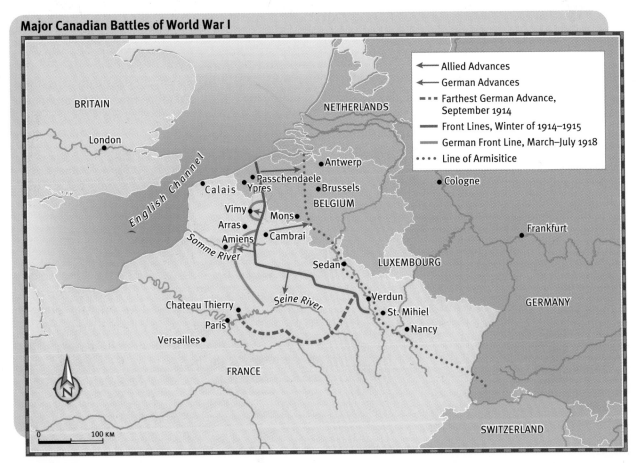

Using an atlas, try to determine how the course of the war was influenced by geographic features. For example, why did the Germans swing through neutral Belgium rather than attack France directly?

After battles such as the Somme, the surviving soldiers had little to smile about. What lasting impact would the high loss of soldiers have on Canada after the war?

Upon hearing of the failure of the first wave to capture enemy territory, Haig ordered the second wave, the Newfoundland Regiment, to go over the top. Burdened with packs weighing up to seventy-five kilograms, the soldiers were instructed to walk across no-man's land. The Newfoundlanders, marching into a steady stream of machine-gun fire, were then forced to funnel through a single gap in the barbed wire. This allowed the German machine gunners to focus their sights on a single spot. In twenty-two minutes it was over; the Newfoundland Regiment was destroyed. One witness described the actions of the Newfoundlanders as "a splendid example of disciplined valour which failed because dead men can advance no further."

That dreadful first day on the Somme did nothing to stop the Allied pursuit of victory. Haig insisted that the Somme campaign go forward, despite alarming casualty rates. During the next three months of fighting, the French and British endured losses of more than 600 000 dead and wounded soldiers. The Canadians were spared until September 15, 1916, when a Canadian battalion — the French Canadians of the 25th — captured the town of Courcelette and held it despite repeated and savage German attack. "If hell is as bad as what I have seen at Courcelette," a French Canadian colonel wrote in his diary, "I would not wish my worst enemy to go there."

Canadian troops fought battle after battle in the Somme campaign, including Flers-Courcelette, the Sugar Factory, Pozieres Ridge, Fabeck Graben, and Regina Trench. They gained most of their objectives but lost nearly 24 000 men. After 141 days, heavy winter rains forced Haig to call a halt. The Allied troops were utterly exhausted, as were the Germans. A total of 1.25 million men had been killed or wounded during the five-month Battle of the Somme. But after it was all over, the British army had advanced less than a dozen kilometres and the stalemate continued. By the end of 1916, the mood of Canadians both on the battlefield and on the home front had swung from hope to despair. It seemed as though the war might go on forever.

the arts

CHARLES YALE HARRISON'S *GENERALS DIE IN BED*

The novel *Generals Die in Bed* provides a shockingly vivid portrayal of the experiences of several Canadian soldiers on the Western Front. Throughout the novel, Charles Yale Harrison, who fought with the Canadian Corps, exposes the brutalizing effects of the war and debunks the myth of civilized war. The following extract describes the horrors faced by soldiers in the trenches.

Over in the German lines I hear quick, sharp reports. Then the red-tailed comets of the minenwerfer sail high in the air, making parabolas of red light as they come towards us. They look pretty, like the fireworks when we left Montreal. The sergeant rushes into the bay of the trench, breathless. "Minnies," he shouts and dashes on.

In that instant there is a terrific roar directly behind us.

The night whistles and flashes red.

The trench rocks and sways.

Mud and earth leap into the air, come down upon us in heaps.

We throw ourselves upon our faces, clawing our nails into the soft earth in the bottom of the trench.

Another!

This one crashes to splinters about twenty feet in front of the bay.

Part of the parapet caves in.

We try to burrow into the ground like frightened rats.

The shattering explosions splinter the air in a million fragments. I taste salty liquid on my lips. My nose is bleeding from the force of the detonations.

SOS flares go up along our front calling for help from our artillery. The signals sail into the air and explode, giving forth showers of red, white and blue lights held aloft by a silken parachute.

The sky is lit by hundreds of fancy fireworks like a night carnival.

The air shrieks and cat-calls.

Still they come.

I am terrified. I hug the earth, digging my fingers into every crevice, every hole.

A blinding flash and an exploding howl a few feet in front of the trench.

My bowels liquefy.

Acrid smoke bites the throat, parches the mouth. I am beyond mere fright. I am frozen with an insane fear that keeps me cowering in the bottom of the trench. I lie flat on my belly, waiting....

Suddenly it stops.

The fire lifts and passes over us to the trenches in the rear.

We lie still, unable to move. Fear has robbed us of the power to act. I hear Fry whimpering near me. I crawl over to him with great effort. He is half covered with earth and debris. We begin to dig him out....

The air screams and howls like an insane woman.

We are getting it in earnest now. Again we throw ourselves face downward on the bottom of the trench and grovel like savages before this demoniac frenzy.

The concussion of the explosions batters against us.

I am knocked breathless. I recover and hear the roar of the bombardment.

It screams and rages and boils like an angry sea.

I feel a prickly sensation behind my eyeballs.

A shell lands with a monster shriek in the next bay. The concussion rolls me over on my back. I see the stars shining serenely above us. Another lands in the same place. Suddenly the stars revolve. I land on my shoulder. I have been tossed into the air.

I begin to pray.

"God — God — please..."

I begin to cough. The smoke is thick. It rolls in heavy clouds over the trench, blurring the stabbing lights of the explosions.

A shell bursts near the parapet.

Fragments smack the sandbags like a merciless shower of steel hail.

A piece of mud flies into my mouth. It is cool and refreshing. It tastes earthy.

Suddenly it stops again.

I bury my face in the cool, damp earth. I want to weep. But I am too weak and shaken for tears.

We lie still, waiting....

EXCERPTED FROM CHARLES YALE HARRISON, *Generals Die in Bed* (WATERDOWN: POTLATCH PUBLICATIONS, 1999, 1974).

A German attack on the Canadian hospital complex at Etaples, France, left the nurses' quarters destroyed as well as three nurses dead and several severely wounded. Should all sites be considered legitimate targets during war? Make a list of sites that you think should not be attacked.

Life-Saving Efforts in the Midst of Battle

When we think of heroism during wartime, we often think of soldiers on the front lines. A few kilometres behind the front, however, another kind of heroics was being performed: life-saving efforts were carried out in the most primitive and challenging conditions. During World War I, thousands of doctors and nurses served in field hospitals, where wounded soldiers arrived fresh from the field of battle. The work performed by these men and women was miraculous, considering the conditions under which they worked and the severity of the wounds suffered by the soldiers. A Canadian nurse who served at the front throughout the war recorded these impressions in her letters home.

I thought I had seen a good many wonderful things, but I did not believe it possible to make any thing human out of some of the pieces of faces that were left, and in some of the cases they even get rid of the scars. Photos are taken when they first come in, and then in the various stages of recovery. One of the worst cases I saw the last day I was out. He has to have one more operation to fill a small hole in one side of his nose and then he will be all right.

Nurses in the field hospitals endured long days, often working from 7 a.m. to 9 p.m. During the day they provided care for up to eighteen patients, many of whom could not get out of bed. The workload of the nurses was compounded even further when soldiers suffered from wounds caused by gas attacks. These soldiers required constant care until they were out of danger.

On September 28, 1918, Frederick Banting, who served in the Canadian Medical Corps, advanced through intense shellfire to reach a Canadian battalion where several men had been wounded. While the battalion was under heavy fire, Banting tended to the wounded for seventeen hours, despite being wounded himself. For his bravery, he was awarded the Military Cross. Do you know Frederick Banting's other claim to fame?

Deadly Seas and Skies

Airplanes as Weapons of War

In 1914 airplane technology was still in its infancy. Although the first successful flight had taken place only eleven years earlier, both sides in the war sought every possible advantage and tried to maximize their use of modern technology. At first, airplanes were used only to scout enemy territory. On August 19, 1914, both sides made their first **reconnaissance** flights across enemy lines. The value of air reconnaissance struck home when British and French flyers reported in September 1914 that the German army had overextended itself. This information enabled the Allies to stop the German advance in the Battle of the Marne. From then on, airplanes were a serious part of the war strategy.

Later, pilots began smuggling aboard pistols, rifles, light machine guns, and even bricks to attack enemy aircraft. But soon more sophisticated weapons were developed for the war in the air. New German Fokker airplanes were mounted with a synchronizing device that let machine guns fire straight ahead without hitting the propeller blades. Soon the new device was copied by the Allies, and Allied pilots were firing at German Fokkers with their own synchronized machine guns.

The War in the Air

German and Allied air "aces" became the new knights of battle on the Western Front. Pilots did not suffer the mud and filth of the trenches. They had clean beds and good food. They did not die the impersonal deaths of foot soldiers or cavalry troops, who were killed by faceless enemies in poison gas attacks or artillery barrages. Instead, they fought in single combat, high in the sky. Their names and exploits were known and individually recorded.

The feats of pilots such as Billy Bishop, Raymond Collishaw, "Wop" May, and Roy Brown were a source of consolation and national pride in Canada. Their names appeared in newspapers around the world, and their stories were told by a whole generation of Canadians. Stories such as how Roy Brown came out of the clouds to surprise Germany's famous "Red Baron" (Manfred von Richthofen) just as he was about to fire on Wop May became legendary. After crashing his damaged plane, the Red Baron was killed by Australian ground troops. Billy Bishop's flying career also yielded many stories of heroism. During his flying career, Bishop took part in more than 170 air battles and shot down a record-breaking seventy-two enemy aircraft. But he was one of the few who survived to enjoy his celebrity. Flying was perhaps the most dangerous job of all: over a span of just two weeks, thirteen Allied pilots were shot down by German flying squadrons under the command of the Red Baron.

This Nieuport 17 is seen here with Canadian flying ace Billy Bishop. How would you have felt soaring above enemy lines in this airplane?

Ruling the Seas: German U-Boats

At the beginning of World War I, Britain still had the world's largest navy and continued to rule the waves. But Germany's new ships were big and efficient, and, unlike most British ships, had steel hulls. Despite their smaller fleet, the Germans felt

Canadian pilot Roy Brown is credited with shooting down the famous "Red Baron."

ready to challenge the British at sea. They also had a revolutionary new weapon of war — a fleet of deadly submarines called **U-boats** (for *Unterseebooten*, "undersea boats"). German U-boats carried twelve torpedoes. By the end of 1914, the U-boats had sent two hundred British supply ships to the ocean floor.

Germany knew that controlling the seas was the key to defeating Britain. Britain was an island nation and depended for its survival on supplies brought from abroad by merchant ships. So Germany decided to starve England into submission by cutting off all war materials and personnel, raw and manufactured goods, and foodstuffs. The U-boats went after British merchant ships with a vengeance.

Even civilian passenger ships were at risk from U-boat attacks. The German government had announced that passenger ships would be sunk on sight. On May 2, 1915, the British ocean liner *Lusitania*, sailing from New York City to Liverpool, was sunk by a German torpedo off the coast of Ireland. Nearly 1200 people went to a watery grave. Among the dead were 128 American civilians, most of whom were women and children. Americans seethed with rage at the attack on U.S. civilians. The U.S. government had so far been officially neutral in the war, and until the attack many American citizens had been actively pro-German. Germany insisted that it had sunk the *Lusitania* because the

The British luxury liner *Lusitania*, suspected by Germany of carrying arms, was sunk near Ireland and prompted the United States to enter the war. Should vessels carrying civilians and weapons be considered fair targets in wartime? How accountable for shipping disasters are those who use civilian vessels to transport arms?

ship was armed and carrying explosives, although it apparently had only a small amount of rifle ammunition on board. American sentiment shifted sharply, and everything German was despised. The sinking of the *Lusitania* prepared the way for the American declaration of war on Germany in 1917.

The British Naval Blockade of Germany

Britain countered Germany's blockade of shipping with its own **naval blockade** of Germany, which was so successful that by the winter of 1916–1917 Germany had been almost drained of resources by its war effort. The few meat and dairy products that were still available were sent to German soldiers at the front. Old men, women, and children behind the German lines had nothing to eat but the turnips grown as food for animals. As a result, that winter became known as the "turnip winter."

The outlook in Germany was so bleak by February 1917 that Kaiser Wilhelm II, the German monarch, was desperate for a quick victory. The Germans could still win the war if they cut off all supplies to Allied countries. The U-boats were unleashed again, with orders to attack ships of any nationality in British waters, a policy called "unrestricted submarine warfare." By the end of 1917, six billion tonnes of cargo bound for Britain had been destroyed by German U-boats.

The War at Sea

Canada provided crucial support to Great Britain in the war at sea. Perhaps Canada's greatest contribution came from its shipyards; it produced more than sixty steel anti-submarine ships and more than five hundred anti-submarine motor launches. But the nation's navy was also transformed. In 1914 Canada's navy consisted of two ships and 350 personnel. By 1918 it had 112 war vessels and 5500 officers and enlisted men under the command of a British Royal Navy officer.

The Battle of Jutland

Both sides in the war knew how important it was to rule the seas, and they were reluctant to risk their fleets in open sea battles. In fact, the two fleets met in just one major sea battle, on May 31, 1916, at Jutland, off the coast of Denmark. When the battle was over, the British had lost yet more ships and more lives. Six thousand British sailors died in the icy northern waters of Jutland — more than double

German U-boats sank over 200 British supply ships within the first year of World War I. Why did Germany believe that controlling the seas was key to defeating Britain?

the German losses. But the British fleet was still large enough to maintain its defence of the British Isles against the Germans. The German navy returned to port and never sailed out again. Thereafter, the Germans concentrated on fielding ever-larger numbers of U-boats.

The Shifting Tides of War: The Western Front, 1917–1918

The year 1917 was pivotal in World War I. Russia's withdrawal from and the United States' entry into the war altered the balance of power on the Western Front. Everyone believed that the bloody stalemate would come to an end at last. But no one could predict whether Germany or the Allies would emerge triumphant. In 1917, victory still hung in the balance. Two long, desperate years of fighting lay ahead.

The United States Declares War on Germany

Ironically, the success of German U-boat attacks helped bring about Germany's defeat. The U.S. president, Woodrow Wilson, was so angry at Germany's policy of unrestricted submarine warfare that he broke off diplomatic relations with

Germany. Then the American ships *City of Memphis* and *Illinois* were torpedoed. On April 6, 1917, the U.S. Congress declared war on Germany. The declaration marked a turning point in the war. Just when nations on both sides of the battlefield had almost exhausted their personnel and resources, the entry of the United States changed the balance of power.

The Americans, however, were not yet ready to join the fighting. Their army had fewer than 200 000 soldiers, and most of its weapons were badly outdated. It would take months for the Americans to gear up for war. The Germans began a race against time. They hoped to win a decisive victory before the Americans were ready to fight. Germany's chance for a quick success suddenly looked promising: its war with Russia on the Eastern Front was coming to an end, and Russia was ready to make peace with Germany.

Russia Makes Peace with Germany

On the same day in March 1917 that U-boats torpedoed two American ships, a revolutionary government toppled the Russian monarchy and came to power. Soon the new Russian government was overthrown by communist revolutionaries, led by Vladimir Lenin. Only days after taking power, Lenin announced that Russia wanted to discuss terms of peace with Germany. The country was exhausted by the war, its people were starving, and the new government was intent on building a state founded on **communism**. Russia was ready to accept defeat. With the Russians out of the war, Germany could now concentrate its full attention — and firepower — on the Western Front.

The Battle of Vimy Ridge

In the brutal trench warfare of the Western Front, Canadian troops were steadily gaining a reputation as tough, effective, and courageous fighters. The Battle of Vimy Ridge, a major turning point in the war, was the high point of Canadian military achievement in World War I. Vimy Ridge was a long, whale-shaped hump of land that rose sixty metres above the Douai Plain in France. It gave German soldiers a commanding view of the British

technology

TECHNOLOGY AND THE ART OF WAR

As the first truly modern war, World War I saw the application of new industrial technology to the killing grounds of Europe. A new age of warfare had been born, one in which the effective use of technology would most often determine the course of a battle. Led by military commanders who had risen through the ranks in the nineteenth century, the British would only grudgingly come to accept that the days of honourable warfare, when soldiers advanced in an orderly fashion across the battlefield, had been replaced by mechanized warfare. In the new age of war, an orderly march across the battlefield was a death sentence for vast numbers of soldiers.

When the war began in 1914, the British considered the machine gun an overrated weapon and refused to accept that a European nation would resort to the use of poisonous gas. The reluctance of British generals such as Douglas Haig to respond to the new technologies of war would lead to horrendous losses at battles such as Ypres and the Somme. Too often, Canadian soldiers were among the troops slaughtered by a German army that used vastly superior technology.

However, by applying ingenuity and inventiveness, Canadians would find their own ways to adapt to the new realities of war. By altering weapons or developing new tactics, Canadians were able to make a valuable contribution to the defeat of a well-trained and highly effective German army.

During the first two years of the war it was common for Canadian casualties to range from 30 to 40 percent. In contrast, the casualty rate in the last two years of the war dropped to 15 to 20 percent. Why did the significant drop occur? Canadians began to adapt to industrial warfare and to develop effective tactics of their own. The inventiveness of Canadian soldiers was largely a survival strategy in the face of constant shelling and machine-gun fire.

Machine guns changed the face of warfare.

ACTIVITY

If you were a commander given the challenge of driving the German army from a strategic hill, what strategy would you use? Assume that the German army has several machine-gun nests, rows of barbed wire, and heavy artillery to bombard the area in front of the hill. You must devise a strategy to provide artillery cover for your advancing troops, break through the barbed wire, and silence the deathly fire of the machine guns. Remember, you want to achieve maximum success with minimum casualties. Review the earlier section of this chapter to get a clear sense of the weapons available to you. Assume that the attack is to occur in the spring of 1918.

army and protected a vital area of occupied France, where mines and factories churned out supplies for Germany. The Germans had dug a maze of deep trenches and dugouts in the ridge and had carved out huge underground chambers, some large enough to shelter whole German battalions from Allied barrages. They had also built machine-gun positions that were footed in thick concrete and wrapped in hedges of thick barbed wire. Although French and British troops had made several attempts to capture the heavily defended ridge, they had been stopped and turned back by German artillery. The German army was confident that nobody could force it off Vimy Ridge.

The taking of Vimy Ridge now fell to the Canadian Corps under the command of the British general, Julian Byng. Under Byng's command was Major-General Arthur Currie, the Canadian-born commander of the First Canadian Division. Currie once said, "Thorough preparation must lead to success. Neglect nothing." Unlike earlier Allied attempts on Vimy Ridge, the Canadian assault left nothing to chance. Every stage of the attack was rehearsed to the last detail.

Currie and Byng agreed that the strategy at the Somme had failed. When the artillery fire had stopped just before the assault, German troops knew what to expect. The advantage of a surprise

attack was lost. The new strategy was to keep up a "creeping barrage" during the assault that would lay a curtain of gunfire just in front of the advancing troops. The assault plan worked because of detailed planning and the courage and discipline of Canadian soldiers. By noon, the Canadians were looking down from Vimy Ridge at the grey backs of thousand of German soldiers in full retreat.

The Vimy victory cost Canadians dearly. More than 3500 lives were lost. The German lines had been broken, however, and an important strategic position was now in Allied hands. Vimy showed the world that Canadians were capable of devising and carrying out a well-planned and successful attack. Currie was promoted to commander of the Canadian Corps in June 1917. It was no longer necessary for British officers to command Canadian soldiers. For the first time, Canada had its own officers in command of the Canadian Corps.

The Battle of Passchendaele

Unfortunately, Vimy was not the last battle of the war. Against all advice the British general, Douglas Haig, was determined to break through the German front. He launched a disastrous drive across Belgium in 1917, and in early October the Canadian Corps were ordered to prepare for the capture of Passchendaele. It was the same front that Canada had defended in the Battle of Ypres. Four million shells had destroyed dams and drainage systems, and as a result the battlefield was a nightmare of marshes and swamps. The Germans were on high ground above the battlefield. From their commanding position, they had the advancing Allied forces at their mercy. Currie estimated that it would cost sixteen thousand Canadian lives to take Passchendaele. He could not believe the military objective was worth the waste of lives, but Haig insisted on the offensive.

Beginning in late October, the Canadians made a series of attacks. They crawled forward, often waist-deep in mud and under a deadly hail of German shells. At last they reached the outskirts of the ruined village of Passchendaele and held on grimly for five days. By the time reinforcements finally came, the Canadians had been torn apart;

In preparation for their attack on Vimy Ridge, Canadians built light railways as a central part of the "creeping barrage."

Canadian profiles

LIFE AT THE FRONT: A SOLDIER'S VIEW

It is difficult to imagine the horror of the conditions faced by the soldiers who served on the Western Front during World War I. Although photographs and paintings give us visual images, they cannot convey the thoughts and feelings of the individuals who endured countless shellings in muddy trenches. Fortunately, many of the letters sent home by soldiers during World War I have been preserved. These letters, although censored by the army, provide invaluable insights into what it was like to serve on the front lines during the war.

The following letters were written by Roy Macfie to members of his family. Macfie was from a farm near Parry Sound, Ontario. He served with the 1st Canadian Infantry Battalion, 1st Brigade, and saw action in virtually all of the battles in which Canadians participated, including Ypres, the Somme, Vimy Ridge, and Passchendaele.

Roy to Muriel   Camblain l'Abbe, France
                                    April 14, 1917

Another little short letter tonight[.] I know you will be geting tired of these short notes of mine, but it can't be helped now. You people at home are the only ones that I have time to write to at all, you will likely have seen a good spiel in the papers by this time, and you know why we are so busy. We are glad to sleep any time we are not on the go, and the weather is still beyond discription, it has rained or snowed every day this month I think and we wade in mud here the same as you do in snow[.] My clothes are yellow and stiff with mud from head to foot[.]

Arthur was certianly lucky to get away as he did, but its funny he does'nt drop me a line, and tell me where he is, and John he never writes at all. And I never write to him because I dont know where he is[.] I dont know how the other fellows made out this time, I havnt had a chance to see them for a long time, Henry Payette was wounded the same time as Arthur.

No we havn't even a barn to sleep in now. A good barn would be a treat I'll tell you, we have a dug out with a leaky old canvass over the top, the only way to get dried at night is to sleep with all your clothes on, but it does'nt seem to do us any harm. If the horses were feeling as fit as we are I'd be contented but they are all playing out at once, and we have a big job to keep things moving....

I have none of my old pals now at all, Sgt Murphy is L[i]eut. Murphy now, and that cuts me out as long as the war lasts and I don't feel as contented as I used to when the old bunch was here. This is where a good chum or two counts too I'll tell you[.] Well I'd better stop or you will think I am getting melancholy; I'll pull through alright don't you fret, when they havnt killed me so far surely they wont do it now, Good Night Molly[.]

Roy to Muriel   France
                                           Jan. 8, 1918

... So I have a sister a munition worker eh? That sounds fine, (in a way) but I wish every body in the world would stop making munitions altogether. If I thought you had a hand in making the noise that we had to go through in the last place we were in, I would give you a talking to when I get home. ...

Roy to Muriel   Buxton
                                           Feb. 15, 1918

... I have been expecting for over two weeks that every days as it came would be my last here. And still I am sticking around. My name isnt on the orders tonight either so thats another day. ...

So the censor was taking liberties with one of my letters, eh? I guess I'll have to be carefull or I'll find myself in a bad fix. I can't remember what it could be that offended him so I guess you'll never know what that part of it was.

Well I must close, I can't write letters any more. I'll soon have to get home I guess. There is a possibility of us getting leave this spring too, but don't count on it till you see me.

SOURCE: FROM *LETTERS HOME* BY JOHN MACFIE © 1990.

only one fifth of the attack force was still alive. When the fighting stopped on November 15, the British had gained just six kilometres and Canadian casualties stood at 15 654. Despite the casualties, Canadian soldiers performed admirably. Nine Canadian soldiers at Passchendaele were awarded the **Victoria Cross**, the British Commonwealth's highest military honour.

The Last Battles

In the spring of 1918, Germany decided to strike hard before the United States could enter the war. On March 21, German forces began a renewed assault on the Western Front. Using new tactics based on mobility and surprise, the German army smashed through Allied defences and began to advance rapidly toward Paris.

The German offensive nearly succeeded. The German army overran Allied forward positions and cut off Allied supply and communications lines. Using airplanes, trucks, and mobile machine guns, they advanced within seventy kilometres of Paris. Although exhausted Allied troops reeled back and retreated under the massive assault, the Allied front did not collapse. Germany's last desperate bid for victory had failed.

Even though both sides suffered heavy losses in the German offensive, Germany suffered more. The success of the British naval blockade cut off food supplies to Germany, and German morale both at home and at the front was slipping badly. Germany was finding it almost impossible to replace the thousands of soldiers it had lost in the war. At the same time, American troops had arrived in force to fill out the Allied ranks. Now the Allied army had the superior forces. The tables were turned; it was time to mount a final Allied offensive.

Canada's Hundred Days

Using all the new techniques of mobile warfare, the Allied troops rolled forward to recapture French and Belgian territory that had been taken by Germany in the first months of the war. By now, the Canadian Corps were regarded as outstanding soldiers and were used as **storm troops**. They spearheaded the thrust through the German defences. August 8 to November 11, 1918, came to be known as Canada's Hundred Days. The Canadians advanced 130 kilometres and captured 31 537 prisoners, 623 guns, 2842 machine guns, and 336 mortars.

With German armies on the edge of collapse, Kaiser Wilhelm II gave up the throne and fled to the Netherlands, a neutral country during World

The mud was so deep at Passchendaele that Canadian troops had to lay trench-mats, also known as "duckboards," to advance across the battlefield. Why do you think the trenchmats earned the name "duckboards"?

War I. The new republican government that took power in Germany asked for an **armistice** (an agreement by opposing sides to stop hostilities). The Germans were exhausted and ready to talk terms of peace. On the same day that the armistice ended World War I, Canadian troops entered the Belgian city of Mons. Mons had been the scene of the first battle between British and German troops in 1914. Now it was the end of the road; the soldiers could come home.

The Guns Fall Silent

After four bloody years, the world's first modern war had finally come to an end. The new technology of the Industrial Revolution had initially held out great promise of improving the quality of life through labour-saving devices. Now, a lengthy war that had claimed more than fourteen million lives had shown that the new technology of the industrial age also had the potential to wreak havoc on the lives of millions of people. Little had actually been won when the war finally ended, but much had been lost. Lives, cities, and farmland had been destroyed at an alarming rate.

For Canadians, the war marked an important turning point in the maturing of their nation. They had entered the war as British subjects, fighting in the British army to defend primarily British interests. By the end of the war, however, people from a variety of homelands were looking at each other as Canadians. This sense of pride and patriotism would carry over in the post-war years as Canadian politicians came to demand a place for Canada on the international stage. An enormous step toward independence had been taken.

It was common for Canadians to label shells before firing them at the Germans.

chapter review

CHAPTER SUMMARY

In this chapter we have seen

- how technology changed the nature of modern warfare

- how Canadian heroics at battles such as Ypres, the Somme, and Vimy Ridge were vital to the eventual outcome of the war

- the horrible conditions that soldiers were forced to endure in the trenches, and the importance of their occasional rest behind the front lines

- the importance of the medical corps, including nurses and doctors, in tending the wounded at the front

- how Russia's withdrawal from the war and the United States' entry into the war in 1917 shifted the balance of power in favour of the Allies

UNDERSTANDING HISTORICAL FACTS

1. Identify these people, places, and events, and explain their significance to Canada's war effort on the battlefield.

Trench Warfare	Chlorine Gas
Battle of the Somme	Ypres
Douglas Haig	Billy Bishop
U-boats	Vimy Ridge
Creeping Barrage	Arthur Currie
Passchendaele	

2. Describe the events that happened at Ypres. What new weapon was used here for the first time? Why did Canadians earn high praise at this battle?

3. Outline the series of events that led the United States to enter the war in 1917.

4. Planning was an essential ingredient of the Canadians' success at Vimy Ridge. Outline the measure taken by Canadians in their preparation for the assault on Vimy Ridge.

5. Passchendaele has long been remembered as one of the most difficult battles fought by Canadians during the war. Describe the conditions faced by soldiers at Passchendaele.

6. For four years, the war's combatants were trapped in trench warfare because both sides failed to win decisive victories. What events eventually tipped the balance in favour of the Allies? To which event would you attach the most significance?

EXPRESSING YOUR OPINION

1. Select any three of the new weapons used in World War I, and explain how each altered the nature of warfare.

2. Reflect on what you know about the British officer Douglas Haig and his leadership at the Battle of the Somme. If you were in a position of authority, would you have promoted Haig to field marshal following the Battle of the Somme? Explain your answer.

3. Is a country justified in using all means available to win a war, including blocking trade, attacking civilian ships, and bombing cities? Why or why not?

4. What factors would you consider if you were deciding if you would apply to serve in the air force in World War I. What key factors would have influenced your decision?

WORKING WITH THE EVIDENCE

1. Before World War I, nightclubs were virtually unknown in London, England. During the war years, hundreds of nightclubs opened up and attracted both men and women, who danced the night away. Why did the rapid growth of nightclubs in London accompany the war?

2. Throughout this chapter, the importance of new weapons has been stressed. Create a web illustrating the profound effect of the machine gun on warfare between 1914 and 1918.

The Great War's Lasting Legacy for Canada

The return of wounded and disabled soldiers raised questions about government responsibility to war veterans. Stanley F. Turner's painting *A War Record* captures a scene that became common in many Canadian cities and towns.

INQUIRING INTO THE PAST

- **The Great War ended in November 1918. Why did most soldiers not see their families until a year later?**
- **What challenges did soldiers face in adjusting to civilian life after the war?**
- **How was the role of women in Canadian society affected by the end of the war?**
- **How had Canada's international status changed as a result of the nation's participation in the war?**

KEY TERMS

Autonomy

Demobilization

Labour Unions

Pandemic

Pensions

Reparations

Repatriation

Sanatoriums

TIMELINE

NOVEMBER 11, 1918 ▶
Armistice declared

JANUARY 1919 ▶
Veterans adopt the Calgary Resolution

MAY 1919 ▶
Winnipeg General Strike erupts

JUNE 28, 1919 ▶
Treaty of Versailles signed; League of Nations created

Each Remembrance Day, on November 11, at 11 a.m., Canadians from coast to coast pause and reflect on the sacrifices made by hundreds of thousands of men and women during the wars of the twentieth century. On the eleventh hour of the eleventh day in the eleventh month of 1918, the bloody confrontation that came to be known as World War I officially ended. The war's impact on many Canadians, however, would be felt for several more years. Canada's wartime experience would be a defining period in its history.

Web Connections

http://www.school.mcgrawhill.ca/resources

Go to the above Web site to find out more about John McCrae, author of "In Flanders Fields," which is recited in many countries on Remembrance Day. Go to History Resources, then to *Canada: A Nation Unfolding, Ontario Edition*, to find out where to go next.

Canada Steps onto the International Stage

In 1914 Canada had responded to Britain's call to war with a spirited and innocent "Ready, aye, ready." As part of the British Empire, Canada's duty was to stand by Britain — even though Canada had had no voice in the decisions that led to war. Once Canada was at war, its soldiers were placed under British officers and British control. The Canadian government was told little about Britain's war policy, so Prime Minister Robert Borden had to piece together information from newspapers and from rumours and speculations by unofficial observers. He complained about the lack of consultation between London and Ottawa, and insisted that Canada should have some say in the war effort. But Borden's complaints were politely ignored by British authorities.

On the morning of December 9, 1916, Borden's demands were finally met. The newly elected British Prime Minister, David Lloyd George, decided to ask the prime ministers of the British colonies to join in a new Imperial War Cabinet. Lloyd George invited Canada and the other colonies "to discuss how best they could co-operate in the direction of the war." After all, he said to his aide, "they were fighting not for us but with us."

Before returning home, several thousand Canadian soldiers were sent to Russia to oppose communist forces, as shown in the painting *Canadians Outside Depot, Russia* by Louis Keene. If you were a Canadian soldier serving on the Western Front, how would you have reacted to the news that you were not being sent home, even though the war had ended?

METHODS OF HISTORICAL INQUIRY

RECOGNIZING AND RESPONDING TO BIAS IN HISTORY

The essential goal of a historian is to understand the past on the basis of available evidence. This often requires sifting through mounds of information, much of which will be discarded. In the end, historians attempt to piece together the past by interpreting the data they have gathered. While reading the documents of the past, they must watch for biases that can distort their conclusions. Detecting and understanding bias is one of the most important tasks in reconstructing the past.

Bias is a slanted or prejudiced attitude that can prevent people from presenting evidence clearly and truthfully. Although people's perspectives or opinions on an issue may differ, they need not be biased if the conclusions they draw are based on the evidence rather than on preconceived beliefs or prejudices.

Recognizing and responding to bias provides protection from having the personal opinions of others being presented as fact. Everyone's viewpoints are shaped by their personal circumstances, such as where they live, their cultural and religious background, and their socio-economic situation. For example, it is likely that French Canadians and English Canadians will have conflicting views about whether or not Quebec should be granted special constitutional rights. These conflicting points of view are common in the study of history.

Recognizing bias in writing can shed light on past events, on the individual recording of the past, and on the time period itself. The following editorial from *Maclean's* magazine, January 1919, makes a strong case for Germany being required to pay for the costs of World War I. Is this a sound argument, based on available evidence, or does the author display biases? Use the following questions to assist

you in detecting and responding to bias in writing. This is a general list of questions that you can use to assess sources of information. Remember that not all questions will fit every source.

1. Who is the author, and what is his or her background?
2. What was the author's intent in writing the piece? Did this influence his or her point of view?
3. Who is the intended audience? How might this have biased the writing?
4. How might the period in which the author was writing have shaped his or her view of the events or issues being discussed?
5. Are the writer's statements based on solid factual evidence or speculation?
6. Do other sources on the same topic support or challenge the view presented?
7. Are sufficient facts presented to provide a firm basis for the argument?
8. Which words or phrases in the article reflect the author's bias?

Germany Can and Must Pay

The German People Are Responsible and Must Themselves Pay the Penalty

A fear lest the German people should escape the consequence of their own infamy is voiced by H.F. Wyatt in the Nineteenth Century. *No other course than that she be made to pay in full for their crime will establish the proposed League of Nations on a sound footing.*

Is it not time, and more than time, to put aside the miserable rubbish talked about our not being at war with the German people? There is hardly a soldier in France, Britain, American or French; there is hardly a live man or woman anywhere in the Entente countries, possessed of ordinary sense, who is not aware that such a statement is utterly false. If we, the Allies, are not at war with the German people, no nation has ever been truly at war with another since the world began. That German people with its whole brutal heart and its whole bestial soul has supported those who planned and prepared for the war from the moment and before the moment of its inception and up to the hour when defeat became imminent. In the vernacular, the whole German people "has been in it up to the neck." There has not been an infamy anywhere which, when known to it, it has not applauded. It yelled with delight over the idea that London was being blasted out of existence by zeppelins and aeroplanes. It roared with joy over the sinking of the Lusitania. Murder, rape, arson, torture have been clasped to its foul bosom from the beginning of the huge world-outrage even up to now. These are people with whom we are "not at war." These are they against whom we must not nourish "a spirit of revenge." These are the living emanations from hell who are not to be held responsible for the deeds which the Kaiser and the military chiefs (whom, while these were victories, they acclaimed and glorified in) have chosen to perform.

Must we live in ever in a mist of lies? Can the real truth never be spoken even at a moment when mankind's fate is hanging in the balance and the souls of the nobly dead might be thought to be heard speaking to the living? Perish this, foul fiction of the irresponsibility of the German people. By all that is sacred to man, they are responsible and they shall be held responsible.

The righteous punishment of Germany is that she should be made to pay — pay for the whole cost of the war, pay for all the devastated lands and the ruined towns, pay for every house she has bombed in London, in England, or in Europe, pay, by the enforced surrender of every merchant ship and by further outlay for any balance still due, for the shipping which she has sent to the bottom of the sea, pay for the arrest of the industries of peace and for the expenditure which she has compelled on those of war. This would be justice. This would prove the League of Nations to be something more than a phrase or a pious aspiration. This would establish it, as no other course could, on the firm basis of right and at once make world-law operative amongst men.

But how, it will be asked, is this to be done?…How can an exhausted and bankrupt Germany find the vast sum requisite to make good the economic mischief she has wrought? By payment in kind spread over a long series of years. Other pens have already pointed out the possibilities. The Westphalian coalfields alone have been estimated to be worth $400,000,000,000. The German supplies of potash offer another source of payment. By the efforts of a generation of German workers a great part of that wealth might be extracted for the benefit of Germany's creditors. Let the whole labor of Hunland for thirty years at least to come be devoted to the discharge of her debt to mankind, reserving only for them the means necessary to their existence. Had Germany conquered Britain, she intended, according to some of her writers, to make us pay an indemnity of $100,000,000,000 and to force our whole population to work under the lash until this sum had been obtained. Her actual treatment of the inhabitants of the conquered districts of France and Italy and Rumania and Serbia and Southern Russia and elsewhere also, lends not merely credibility but actual certainty to the forecast of the kind of treatment which in her own mind she reserved for us. For us she hated not less but more than she hated those others, and with us she would have dealt, had the heavens permitted us to come under her power, in modes of sustained and deliberate cruelty surpassing our imagination. Not so, the way in which we should deal with them. Outrage of women, torture of men, mutilation of children, wilful infliction of starvation, are not numbered amongst the methods of an Englishman. But "what is sauce for the goose is sauce for the gander." As the Huns intended to treat us, so with those crucial differences let us treat them.

SOME FINAL REFLECTIONS

Of what value is this primary document in studying World War I? Does it provide sound factual evidence? Does the tone of the writing shed light on the mood of the time? Do the author's biases make the document invalid, or are they also important in our understanding of the past? How did bias, as opposed to factual evidence, shape the author's point of view?

The implied promise of "**autonomy** within the Empire" — Borden's cherished dream — was not enough. Borden wanted to see that promise in writing, and he got it in the War Cabinet's Resolution IX. South Africa's General Jan Smuts was generally credited with producing the resolution, but it was really the handiwork of Robert Borden, even its phrasing. In the words of Resolution IX, Canada and the other colonies were given "full recognition as autonomous nations." The details remained to be worked out after the war, but in principle Britain now recognized Canada as a full partner in the British Empire.

The Paris Peace Conference

As the war was ending, Lloyd George called Borden to Paris, where the Allied leaders were gathering to set the terms of peace. They would dispose of their enemies and shape the new Europe. Lloyd George assumed that Borden would be pleased to represent Canada, Australia, and the other British dominions as one of Britain's five delegates at the Paris Peace Conference. Borden flatly refused. Canada, he insisted, would sit at the peace conference in its own right. Sacrifice in war was the bloody price Canada had paid for equal nationhood, and Borden meant to have it.

The Treaty of Versailles and the New Face of Europe

After strong resistance, especially from the United States, Canada was given two seats at the Paris Peace Conference. The Canadian delegates had no votes, and the peace treaties were written by the major powers. But Canada won a symbolic victory. It signed the Treaty of Versailles, which applied to Germany, and the four other treaties applying to the other losing nations, in its own right as an independent country.

Participation in the peace conference also guaranteed Canada a seat — and this time a vote, too — in the new League of Nations, which had been created by the Treaty of Versailles. The league's role was to guarantee the peace and to punish aggressive nations. The Treaty of Versailles was meant to

Do you think Prime Minister Borden's attendance at the Paris Peace Conference was of real or symbolic significance to Canada?

ensure that World War I would indeed be "the war to end all wars" and that Europe would enjoy a lasting peace. In 1918, Canada stepped onto the world stage as a mature nation both in its own eyes and in the eyes of the world.

A new Europe emerged from the ashes of World War I. The old Russian, German, and Austrian empires disappeared. Britain, France, and the United States — "the Big Three" — took their pencils to the map of Europe and redrew its nations' borders. They left Germany a crippled nation, stripped of its wealth and most of its armed forces. They also made sure that Germany was humbled; in signing the Treaty of Versailles, it was forced to accept all blame for the war.

The Conditions of the Treaty of Versailles

Among the key clauses of the Treaty of Versailles were the surrender of all German overseas investments to the Allied powers and a requirement to pay heavy war **reparations** to France, Britain, and Russia, as well as other nations affected by the war. Furthermore, Germany was forced to surrender rich coal mines in the Saar Basin to France. To prevent Germany from becoming a military power in the future, it was to be denied a naval and air force and was required to greatly reduce its military forces. As well, Germany was ordered to acknowledge the independence of Austria and Czechoslovakia and was prohibited from joining in any alliance. Being utterly exhausted by 1918, Germany had no option but to accept the harsh conditions of the treaty.

Article 231 of the Treaty of Versailles was perhaps the bitterest pill of all for Germans to swallow. Germany was forced to accept sole blame for World War I, even though many Germans believed that they had fought to protect themselves from the military aggression of Britain and France. On the basis of the "war guilt" clause, Germany was also forced to pay reparations for damage done during the war. German payments for war damages poisoned the atmosphere in Europe for years to come. The exact amount of German reparations was not spelled out in the peace treaty, but France and Britain were determined that Germany should be forced to pay for all the devastation it had caused.

The harshness of the Treaty of Versailles created an unstable peace in Europe because Germans were not content with the settlement. What did the future hold for this new Europe? On Armistice Day, Borden wrote in his diary, "The world has drifted from its old anchorage and [no one] can with certainty prophesy what the outcome will be." In 1918, no one realized that the Treaty of Versailles had sowed the bitter seeds of World War II. Twenty years later, the world would reap a harvest of destruction.

Europe 1919

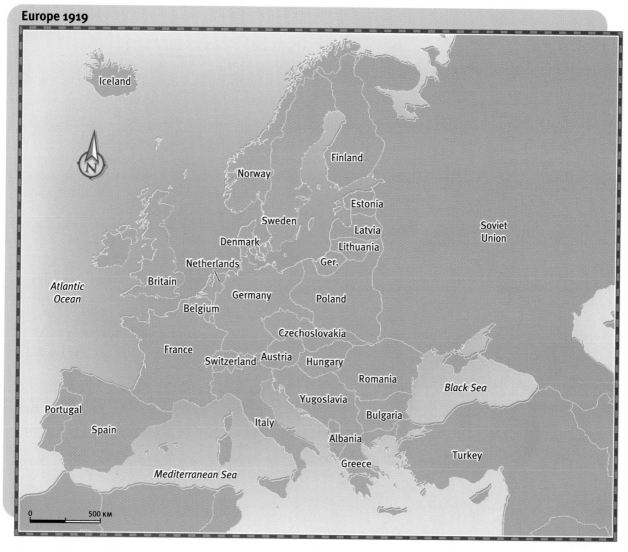

Compare this map with the map on page 79, of Europe in 1914. What major boundary changes resulted from the Treaty of Versailles? Which countries appear to be the major losers? Judging by the territorial changes, does the treaty appear to have been fair?

The Long Road Back to Normal

Although the armistice that came into effect on November 11, 1918, silenced the guns on the Western Front, most Canadians serving in Europe would not see their families for at least another six months. For some, further combat in Russia was yet to come. For others, crowded **demobilization** camps in England and a rough voyage home would have to be endured.

Once they arrived home, Canadian veterans faced new battles. Adjusting to civilian life was often made more difficult by government policies that did little to repay soldiers for their sacrifices and often left disabled veterans and their families in poverty. The government itself struggled to adjust to its role in the post-war Canada. Women too would be forced to re-examine their roles in Canadian society. November 11 brought an end to war and began a new era in Canadian history.

Spanish Flu

The final months of the war witnessed a disaster on a scale the world had never seen. While countries attempted to deal with the chaos brought by four years of warfare, another global crisis erupted in a **pandemic**. The spring of 1918 brought a strain of influenza that came to be known as the Spanish flu, which differed from other strains of the flu by being deadly. Often its victims died within a few days of becoming sick. Four years and hundreds of tonnes of munitions had just left fourteen million people dead from the bloodiest war in human history.

Within a few months the Spanish flu, whose effect was felt worldwide, killed up to 100 million people.

It must have seemed like the final injustice to the young men who had volunteered to fight for their country so far from home. Some had survived the horrors of life at the front since early 1915, only to face death as they were about to return home. One Canadian soldier, against all odds, survived four years on the battlefields of Europe. Eager finally to be reunited with his family in Montreal, he was stunned to find all seven of his siblings had died of the Spanish flu. Few Canadians, whether civilian or military, had the good fortune not to lose a friend or family member to the Spanish flu.

Demobilization and the Return to Civilian Life

In mobilizing for war, Canada had prepared healthy young men and women to go overseas over a period of four years. With war at an end, the Canadian government faced the monumental task of preparing over 600 000 Canadians, many of them sick or wounded, for a return to civilian life.

Homeward Bound

As welcome as peace was in 1918, the government was caught off guard by the November armistice. Rather than immediately beginning to transport troops home, the process of demobilization had to wait until spring. With winter fast approaching, ports would freeze up, opportunities for employment

After enduring the horrors of war, soldiers were anxious to return home. Here, soldiers sit and wait through the long process of demobilization. How could the government have made the wait shorter or more tolerable?

Canadian contributions

CANADIAN WAR MEMORIALS IN EUROPE

Each year, on November 11, Canadians from coast to coast pause to remember the gallant efforts of Canadian soldiers and the supreme sacrifice made by thousands of young Canadians in battles fought far from home. The memories of their brave deeds and of Canada's contribution to world peace are preserved by a number of solemn war memorials on the battlefields where Canadians fought and died.

THE NEWFOUNDLAND BEAUMONT HAMEL MEMORIAL

Newfoundland did not join Canada until 1949. In 1914, Newfoundland was an independently governed colony of Britain. When the call to arms came, more than six thousand officers and soldiers joined the Royal Newfoundland Regiment and fought heroically at Gallipoli, Turkey, before being sent to France and Belgium, where they would take part in the Battle of the Somme. Whereas the Canadian Corps did not arrive at the Somme until October 1916, the Royal Newfoundland Regiment was among the British troops that began the assault on July 1, 1916.

The assault began under the bright sun of the early morning. The heavily fortified Germans were well prepared for the attack. As 100 000 troops, including the Royal Newfoundland Regiment, advanced shoulder to shoulder, the German machine guns opened fire. Within a half hour the first wave had been decimated. Of the 801 Newfoundlanders who went over the top that morning, only 68 survived. Every officer was either killed or wounded.

Following the war, the women of Newfoundland collected money to buy the land where so many of their sons, husbands, and brothers had fallen. Today on the sixteen-hectare site stands a massive bronze caribou and spruce, fir, dogberry, and juniper trees, which were brought from Newfoundland and planted in the same earth in which many young Newfoundlanders were buried.

THE VIMY RIDGE MEMORIAL

The Battle of Vimy Ridge is one of the most famous events in Canadian history. It has often been said that a true sense of Canadian nationalism was born on the battlefield at Vimy. It is therefore fitting that the most impressive Canadian memorial is the one at Vimy Ridge. The memorial stands majestically overlooking the Douai Plains on land donated by "the French nation to people of Canada." The massive structure required eleven years to assemble; it includes 11 000 tonnes of concrete for the base and 5500 tonnes of "trau" stone. The "trau" stone, from which the central pylons and the sculptured figures are made, was imported from Yugoslavia. On the base of the memorial is this inscription, in both French and English:

TO THE VALOUR OF THEIR COUNTRYMEN IN THE GREAT WAR

AND IN MEMORY OF THEIR SIXTY THOUSAND DEAD

THIS MONUMENT IS RAISED BY THE PEOPLE OF CANADA

Newfoundland Beaumont Hamel Memorial

The names of the 11 285 Canadians listed as "missing and presumed dead" in France are listed on the ramparts of the memorial. This impressive monument is a fitting tribute to the gallantry of Canadian soldiers whose valiant sacrifices helped to ensure the Allied victory in World War I.

DESIGN YOUR OWN MEMORIAL

Select one of the other battles in which Canadians participated in World War I, and design a monument to commemorate it. In designing your monument, try to use shapes, images, or materials that reflect Canada. Include on your memorial a fitting inscription. Your model can be constructed of any material; consider clay, papier mâché, or Lego, for example. Also, to assist the view, prepare a brief "viewer's guide" that explains the memorial and the highlights of the battle.

Vimy Ridge Memorial

would decrease, and bad weather on the Atlantic would make transporting troops hazardous. Further complicating demobilization was the fact that the railways were worn out from heavy wartime use, the high demand for ships limited the number available for transporting troops, and one of Canada's main Atlantic ports, Halifax, had not yet recovered from the explosion of 1917. Even businesses and unions urged the government to delay demobilizing the army until the spring. They hoped an improved economy would help to absorb the thousands of returning soldiers.

The day the armistice came into effect, Canadian soldiers threw their helmets in the air and shouted with joy at the prospects of going home. A few weeks later, several Canadian brigades were ordered to march in full gear as they began a long, difficult march through Belgium and Germany. Canadian soldiers would serve for a number of months as part of an occupation force in Germany. To some, this was the breaking point. War was over. Why, many wondered, were they not going home?

Finally, in mid-January 1919, demobilization began. For soldiers, getting out of the army was nearly as difficult as the training they endured to get in; and it was certainly more tedious. The route home first took them from Europe to England. There they had to undergo several medical examinations, attend briefings on "civil re-establishment," and fill out many forms in quadruplicate before boarding the ships bound for Halifax.

Frustrated by the delays, suffering from a flu epidemic that hit soldiers in army camps particularly hard, and shivering through one of the coldest winters in years, Canadian troops lost their patience. Riots occurred at several **repatriation** camps throughout the spring of 1919. Spurred by the riots, the government managed to bring almost all troops home by the end of the summer — much sooner than many experts had expected.

The long wait was over, and soldiers were able once again to set foot on Canadian soil. Many were welcomed home by a parade through the streets and ending at city hall, where they were given one final order to "Dismiss." The next day, the soldiers turned in their

When news of the war's end reached Canada, people spilled out into the streets in celebration. How would you celebrate Canada's victory in a war?

rifles and equipment and were given a discharge pin, a transport warrant, $35 for civilian clothing, and a War Service Gratuity that averaged about $240 per person. They were once again civilians.

Adjusting to Civilian Life

Returning to civilian life was not merely a matter of shedding an army uniform for civilian clothing. Young people who had served at the front had witnessed more carnage and endured more stress than most people face in a lifetime. Several thousand returned home with battle scars they would carry for life. Some were missing limbs, others had damaged lungs from gas attacks, and many had hideous scars from their wounds. Still many others came home with pneumonia or a myriad of other illnesses.

Several Canadian soldiers suffered from shell shock. In 1919, veterans with shell shock received

no sympathy and certainly no support. Shell shock was believed to be "a manifestation of childishness and femininity," and ignoring the ailment was considered the best treatment. No **pensions** were offered to the victims, and no medical record of their condition was kept.

The returning soldiers' adjustment to civilian life was often made more difficult by their friends and families. Upon returning home, veterans who had faced death in the trenches had to listen to those who had stayed home complain about "Meatless Fridays" and "Fuelless Mondays." Compared with the battlefield experience, these hardships seemed trivial. During the war, soldiers' wages and the money provided for their families had not kept pace with inflation. By the end of the war, those who had gone overseas to fight for Canada came home to see their families facing poverty. As a result, many veterans were disillusioned when they came home, and government policies did nothing to change their mood.

Returning soldiers were often given a parade by their home towns. Why would so many of these soldiers face a difficult time when they returned to being civilians?

During the 1917 election, the Borden government had promised "full re-establishment." It had set up a new Department of Soldiers' Civil Re-establishment in February 1918 to carry out that promise. Unfortunately, as with many political promises, it was ambitious but vague. In fact, when war ended the government made it clear that "full re-establishment" meant the right to earn a living. In the months immediately following the war, many prominent Canadians pressured the government to resist providing excessive support for veterans. Returning soldiers must once again learn to depend on themselves; a veteran must not, as Lord Atholstan, owner of the *Montreal Star*, warned, "be allowed to consider himself an unlimited creditor of the State to be supported in idleness." There was to be little or no compensation for the soldiers' loss of earnings while serving overseas, even though their wages were kept very low while prices and wages at home soared.

Approaching the government on the basis of a moral right, veterans' groups joined forces to win fair compensation from the Canadian government. On a cold Sunday in January 1919, at Calgary's Allen Theatre, veterans adopted the "Calgary Resolution," which demanded a $2000 bonus for each veteran as compensation for lost wages during the war. Borden's Conservative Party steadfastly rejected the veterans' demand, considering it a "grab" for $2 billion. Despite some initial support, the Calgary Resolution failed to sway the government.

The government made some efforts to assist veterans to either return to their former jobs or find suitable new employment. A Soldier Settlement Plan made low-cost loans available to veterans who wished to purchase land and equipment. This was not a land grant but a scheme to help veterans to borrow money. The loans were made available only to veterans who could prove that they were physically and mentally strong and would be likely to succeed. Although businesses were encouraged to hire war veterans, which many did out of a sense of patriotic duty, this sense of duty passed and soon veterans were no longer given preferential treatment.

Those suffering from mental or physical disabilities as a result of the war were at a distinct disadvantage in the job market. By the end of 1921, 20 percent of all veterans, including the vast majority of disabled veterans, were unemployed. By 1939, only one third of the former soldiers who had purchased land through the Soldiers' Settlement Plan remained on the land. Most of the others had abandoned their farms, either having paid too much or having purchased unproductive land.

Canadian Victims of War: The Disabled, Widows, and Orphans

In 1917 Robert Borden's government had promised soldiers "full re-establishment" after their "holocaust of blood." But veterans' demands for fair treatment were turned down flat. Many veterans were angry and desperate, especially those who had returned to Canada disabled by the war.

Regardless of a veteran's earning potential prior to the war, government policies did little to prevent

Thousands of Canadians returned home disabled from wounds suffered in the war. Would you have supported the veterans' organizations that sought financial support for the disabled? What level of support should the government have provided?

disabled veterans and their families from living in poverty. Disability pensions for veterans were based on the wage rates for unskilled workers. It was argued by some members of the government that, although the government of Canada had a moral obligation to help support disabled veterans and their families, "Everyone must understand that armless, legless men can become self-supporting." Some officials even argued that, after spending months in hospital, the disabled soldiers "become accustomed to having everything done for them, they lose all ambition and have no desire to help themselves." By keeping pensions low, the government felt it would provide an incentive for disabled veterans to seek suitable employment.

Canada's pension rates were low compared with wages, but they were the most generous in the world at the time for those entitled to a full pension. One cynic suggested that the key to having the world's highest pension for disabled veterans was in making it available to very few. The vast majority of veterans who qualified for pensions received no more than 25 percent of a full pension. For example, a soldier hit by a bus during a London blackout did not qualify because, the government argued, pensions were not insurance. The families of soldiers who died overseas were often at the whim of the government. The family of a Toronto soldier killed in action received no pension because the Toronto police chief claimed the surviving wife was morally unfit. To qualify for a survivor's pension, widows had to demonstrate need, remain unmarried, and prove themselves worthy.

Labour in the Aftermath of World War I

Just after the war, prices soared and the cost of living shot up in Canada. At the same time, munitions plants closed down and few new factories opened up. Jobs were hard to come by. When thousands of veterans returned home and began looking for jobs, unemployment rose even higher. Women were often forced out of work so that men returning from the war could take their jobs. But there were still not enough jobs for the returning soldiers.

Canadian war workers were also angry with government and business. During the war, the Borden government had passed legislation denying workers the right to strike for better pay and working conditions. At the same time, Borden had only gently prodded employers to pay fair wages and negotiate with their employees. Most employers had simply ignored the government's directions.

Worker unrest did not end with the war. Rising prices for food and clothing meant that paycheques bought less. Some workers began to join **labour unions** in order to bargain for more pay. Whole new groups of workers joined the union movement, including police, municipal employees, West Coast loggers, and workers in meat-packing houses and garment shops in Toronto and Montreal. At a Western Labour Conference held in Calgary in March 1919, delegates called for a six-hour working day and proposed One Big Union, which would serve as an umbrella organization for all organized labour. The One Big Union organization was barely started before it collapsed, partly because of the opposition it faced from veterans' organizations, factory owners, and city councils, who strongly opposed new unions. But in the post-war labour turmoil, nothing could stop the union movement. By 1919 more than 420 strikes had occurred in Canada, and many working people outside the unions marched in support of worker demands.

The Winnipeg General Strike

Labour unrest climaxed in the Winnipeg General Strike of May 1919. Metal-trades workers, supported by more than thirty thousand working people, tied up the city for six weeks. The Winnipeg strike sparked dozens of sympathetic strikes from Vancouver Island to Nova Scotia. Many government and business leaders panicked at the worker revolt sweeping across Canada. They feared a "red (communist) menace." A communist revolution of Russian workers had toppled the government of the Russian czar in 1917, and some Canadians were afraid that a communist-style revolution was about to be repeated in Canada.

The Winnipeg General Strike turned violent on "Bloody Saturday" — June 21, 1919. A crowd of

Chaos swept through the streets of Winnipeg in June 1919. Did the police respond appropriately, or did they act with excessive force?

demonstrators had gathered on Winnipeg's Main Street to protest the pre-dawn arrest of ten strike leaders. They were also angry about strike-breaking Winnipeg streetcar drivers returning to work. Some of the demonstrators stopped a streetcar near City Hall and set it on fire. Winnipeg's mayor called out the troops. Royal North-West Mounted Police charged the demonstrators on horseback while the crowd hurled bricks and bottles. Eventually the police began to fire revolvers. By the end of the day, two people were dead, dozens more were injured, and scores were arrested.

The general strike had been broken, and the labour movement was left in disarray. Soon after, Canadian business, with the support of government troops and police, began a strong anti-labour campaign. Labour organizers were blacklisted and fired, strikes were put down by armies of strike-breakers, and union membership dropped off sharply in the 1920s. The Winnipeg General Strike did, however, mark the beginning of a new working-class awareness and a new political involvement. Over the next few years, labour leaders were elected to all levels of government. In the 1920 Manitoba provincial election, for example, eleven labour representatives were elected — including three people who were serving jail terms for their roles in the Winnipeg General Strike. And in the 1921 federal election, another activist in the strike — social reformer J.S. Woodsworth — became a member of Parliament.

Women in Post-War Canadian Society

As the post-war era began, conflicting views of the future role of women in Canadian society emerged. Marjory MacMurchy, a widely read journalist at the time, wrote: "It is only through the help of women that the future can be made secure. The co-operation of Canadian women in industrial life and reconstruction is indispensable." Like many other feminists in 1919, MacMurchy was inspired by the advances women had made in the past few years. The vital contribution of women to the labour force during the war years had helped to secure the vote and had ushered in a new era of social reform. Surely, many women believed, the period of reconstruction following the war would be an age in which society would become more equal.

Many other Canadians held a very different view of the reconstruction period. It was assumed by most men that when the war ended and the soldiers returned home, women would happily leave their paid jobs and return to their duties as homemakers. Through a poster campaign, the federal government actively encouraged women to leave their jobs. One poster read: "Do you feel justified in holding a job which could be filled by a man who has not only himself to support but a wife and family as well? Think it over." The Women's Department of the Canadian Reconstruction Association published a booklet titled "What Shall I Do Now? How to Work for Canada in Peace." In this booklet, women were reminded: "No other work that a woman can do is as important to Canada as making a home and taking care of children." Many women lost or gave up their jobs they had held during the war. By late 1918, female unemployment had skyrocketed. Those who did manage to keep their jobs saw their wages cut despite rising inflation.

The post-war years did bring about a wider acceptance of single women in the paid workforce and an increased emphasis on job training and higher education for young women. Employment was understood, however, to be a temporary phase in a woman's life that would be surrendered once she was married. While in the workforce, women were encouraged to seek jobs that were "feminine" and that would not be a threat to their woman-hood. Work in fields such as journalism, social work, sales, and nutrition were viewed as suitable for well-educated single women.

The dawning of a new age, hoped for by women such as Marjory MacMurchy and Nellie McClung, had yet to occur. The struggle for full social, legal, and economic equality for women continues to this day. Yet, women did make significant advances throughout the war years. With the vote women had gained some political clout to back their demands. And the widespread participation of women in the workforce during the war increased Canadians' acceptance of women in the workplace. By 1921 women made up 15 percent of the paid workforce in Canada. Feminists may not have witnessed the building of a perfect society, but neither did they see a complete return to pre-war conditions.

Technology and Post-War Society

War and technological developments seem to go hand in hand. When war erupted, many of the tech-nological developments of the past half-century were adapted for military use. The demands of war led to numerous technological advances, which, in turn, were adapted for use in civilian society in the post-war era. For example, the labour shortages and huge demands for supplies created by World War I led many factories to use the latest industrial tech-

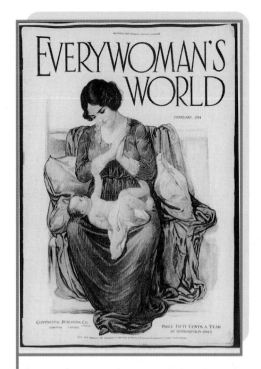

What does the cover of this 1914 magazine sug-gest about the role women were expected to play in Canadian society prior to the war? Did the war bring about any significant change?

nology and electrical equipment. War not only spawned new munitions factories; it began to change the way factories operated.

The demands of war led to rapid improvements in airplane technology, so that by 1919 there was a virtual explosion in airplane construction and development. Nowhere was the impact of this new technology more noticeable than in Canada's remote regions. When the war ended, surplus mili-tary aircraft were adapted for use in peacetime. Many of the Canadian pilots who had distin-guished themselves during the war became bush pilots when they returned to Canada. Using the sur-plus airplanes, these pilots were able to make remote areas of Canada's north less isolated and were able to play a vital role in developing the min-ing and lumber industries in northern areas. To encourage further aeronautical research, the gov-ernment created the Associate Air Research Committee in 1919.

PHOTO ESSAY

THE CHANGING ROLE OF WOMEN IN THE CANADIAN MILITARY

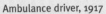

Ambulance driver, 1917

Nursing sister, 1916

Canadian Women's Army Corps, 1942

Nursing sisters, 1944

Royal Canadian Air Force Woman's
Division Photographers, 1944

Naval officer, 1965

Canadian Armed Forces, 1999

Peacekeeper, 1998

Redefining the Role of Government in the Post-War Years

When at first gearing up Canada for war, Prime Minister Borden had attempted to keep the role of government to a minimum. As the scale of the war and Canada's contribution escalated, however, it became clear that the government would need to become more actively involved. By the early 1920s government's direct role in the lives of Canadians was greater than ever before. From conscription to income tax, Canada's wartime experience led to a dramatic change in the role government played in Canadian society. In 1919 the Department of Health was created in response to the Spanish flu epidemic. The federal government was creating new pensions for disabled veterans, arranging loans for veterans, and collecting taxes to pay down a debt that was approaching $2 billion. In addition to these necessary functions, the government also branched out into distributing grants for the building of homes and highways, promoting technical education, and building **sanatoriums**, hospitals, and training schools.

The New Decade: A Time of Adjustment

By the early 1920s a sense of normalcy had returned to Canadian society. In many ways, it was merely a façade: too many emotionally charged issues had arisen during the past several years. The conscription crisis had left a lingering rift between Quebec and English Canada, and those who had been treated as "enemy aliens" felt isolated from Canadian society. Perhaps the most profound effect of the war was its psychological effect on Canadian society. War crushed the innocence and optimism that had characterized the Laurier era. Canadians' unbounded sense of potential had been shattered by a war that had used many modern technologies to cause the gruesome deaths of millions of young men and women. Although the 1920s would be characterized by a carefree party mood, this party attempted to escape the modern world, not celebrate it.

Surplus World War I planes such as this Curtis Canuck played a vital role in the mining and forest industries after 1919.

chapter review

CHAPTER SUMMARY

In this chapter we have seen

- how, despite the armistice in November 1918, most Canadian soldiers would not see their families for nearly a year

- that the devastation caused by war was followed by the worst pandemic in human history

- how demobilizing a force of nearly 600 000 soldiers was a monumental task for the Canadian government

- that soldiers faced many challenges in adjusting to civilian life after the war

- how Canada's contribution to the Allied war effort earned the nation international status and a seat at the Paris Peace Conference

UNDERSTANDING HISTORICAL FACTS

1. Identify these people, places, and events, and explain their historical significance.

Department of Soldiers' Civil Re-establishment

Spanish Flu

Soldier Settlement Plan

Treaty of Versailles

Calgary Resolution

Winnipeg General Strike

League of Nations

2. Prepare a bar graph that compares the total number of deaths resulting from World War I with the deaths resulting from Spanish flu.

3. Prepare a chart that lists and explains various government initiatives to support returning soldiers.

4. How did the views of feminists such as Marjory MacMurchy differ from those of many other Canadians, including most government officials?

5. Explain the causes and results of the Winnipeg General Strike.

6. How did technological advances during the war affect post-war Canadian society and industry?

EXPRESSING YOUR OPINION

1. World War I cost Canada over sixty thousand lives and billions of dollars. At the same time, women won the right to vote, Canada won greater autonomy from Great Britain, and Canadian industries expanded. In the end, was Canada's World War I experience good or bad for the nation? Defend your answer.

2. What obligations do you believe the government had toward war veterans? Were the government initiatives adequate, excessive, or insufficient?

3. When a war ends, what should the purpose of a treaty be: to impose the will of the victor, to punish the loser, or to establish a lasting peace? Explain why you think the Treaty of Versailles was or was not a fair and just treaty.

4. One of the lasting impacts of World War I was a dramatic increase in the role of government in the daily lives of Canadians. Explain why you believe the expansion of the government's role was a good or bad development for Canada.

WORKING WITH THE EVIDENCE

1. Try to imagine how the war may have unfolded if the United States had chosen to remain on the sidelines. Would Germany have won the war? What would the treaty have looked like after the war? How would the map of Europe have differed in 1919? Using "counter-factual" history, construct a hypothetical end to the war if the United States had remained neutral.

2. In November 1918, Canadian troops recaptured the city of Mons, France, from the Germans with virtually no casualties. Despite a relatively easy victory, several Canadian soldiers were very upset after the battle. Why?

unit review

BRINGING THE PAST INTO FOCUS

REVIEWING THE FACTS

1. Was the Treaty of Versailles a wise and just treaty, given the underlying causes of World War I? Was Germany's blame for the devastation caused by the war fairly assigned by the Allies? Defend your answer.

2. Why were thousands of Canadians so eager to enlist in the army in 1914? Were they patriotic, naïve, and unaware of the nature of modern war, or were they seeking adventure, or was it a combination of these sentiments? Explain your answer.

3. If a soldier had fought in both the Red River Rebellion of 1885 and World War I, what changes would the soldier have noticed in how war was fought by 1918?

4. Why did some Canadians feel unwelcome and unappreciated in their own country during the war years? Would you have supported or opposed the government actions that alienated some Canadians? Explain your answer.

5. It has often been said that a sense of Canadian nationalism was born on the battlefields of World War I. What Canadian heroics or successes in the war would have made Canadians proud? Which battles stand out as key success stories for Canada? Explain your answer.

6. Mobilizing a nation for war is a huge challenge for a government. How successful was the Canadian government at meeting these challenges? Prepare a list of at least three major challenges faced by the government, and assess how effectively it met the challenges.

HISTORICALLY SPEAKING

Answer any two of the following questions. Prepare your response carefully, and use historical evidence to support your position.

1. Since the end of World War I, historians have debated the impact of the war on Canada. While no one doubts that participation in the war drastically changed Canada, there is less agreement about whether or not the changes were good or bad. Complete a chart like the one at the bottom of the page. Once you have completed your chart, write a brief personal statement that assesses the impact of the war on Canada.

2. It has been said that the world entered the twentieth century during World War I. Prepare a list of the ways in which the World War I years were different from previous decades or the ways in which Canada's reaction to the war altered the way Canadian society functioned. Considering the nature of the changes occurring during the war years, should the statement that Canada entered the twentieth century at this point be considered a good or a bad thing? Why?

3. There is no doubt that Canadians played a vital role in the Allied victory over the Central Powers. But did Canada attempt to do too much? Were too many lives sacrificed, and was too much money poured into the war? Write a one-paragraph editorial in which you either praise or criticize the government for its course of action. Assume you are writing your editorial in 1917.

4. Considering the sacrifices made by soldiers, what, if any, support should they have been given by the government when they returned home after the war?

POSITIVE IMPACTS OF WAR ON CANADIAN SOCIETY	NEGATIVE IMPACTS OF WAR ON CANADIAN SOCIETY
(handwriting)	*(handwriting)*
(handwriting)	*(handwriting)*
(handwriting)	*(handwriting)*

List the initiatives undertaken by the government. For each initiative, explain why you feel it was a fair and just measure or how you would have changed it to make it an acceptable program for veterans.

MAKING CONNECTIONS

At the bottom of the page are a number of terms central to understanding Canada's participation in World War I. The terms have been organized under four headings: International (world), National (Canada), Regional, and Personal. Select any three terms, and show how each of the terms is connected with the others.

For example, you could connect Prime Minister Borden (national), the Battle of the Somme (international), and declining volunteers (regional) by showing how the heavy losses at battles such as the Somme and an increasing reluctance of people to volunteer led Borden to consider conscription, which angered Quebec.

Show the interconnectedness of the three terms you have selected by drawing a poster that commemorates Canada's role in World War I.

PERSPECTIVES

1. **a)** As a recent British immigrant in Canada, you have just begun to put down roots and get your prairie farm operating. You expect soon to make a profit from all your hard work. You and your wife have just had a baby and are planning on building a permanent home to replace your "soddie." In the summer of 1914, as you prepare to harvest your crops, news arrives that Britain has declared war on Germany. Your sense of loyalty to the King and Britain tempts you to volunteer to go overseas, but your wife begs you to stay home to look after the farm. What decision will you make regarding your participation in the war? Defend your decision.

   b) Consider the same scenario as above, but assume that you have recently emigrated from Germany. Will you return to fight for Germany? Will you be loyal to the British King?

   c) Assume that you are a French Canadian farmer living on land owned by your family for over two hundred years. Will you enlist in the British army?

2. Imagine you are a journalist researching a story on people's support or opposition to conscription on the eve of the 1917 election. Make brief notes that reflect how you believe each of the following people would have responded to the question: "Will you support Laurier and the anti-conscriptionists or Borden and the pro-conscriptionists on election day?" Think carefully about the situation of each of the respondents.

   a) Parents with three sons fighting in Europe

   b) Prairie farmer with two teenage sons who help on the farm

   c) French Canadian factory worker

   d) Aboriginal Canadian

   e) Ontario doctor with a new practice and two young children

   f) Black Canadian who had earlier been turned down by the army

3. Write an imaginary conversation that may have taken place between two brothers after World War I. Assume that one of the brothers stayed at home during the war and made considerable profits from his investment in a munitions factory. The other brother spent three years on the battlefield before being wounded and sent home. The two brothers are now reflecting on what the war meant to them. How would their perspectives differ? Flash forward to 1937. Storms clouds are once again gathering over Europe, as Adolf Hitler arms Germany. Imagine how a conversation between the brothers about Canada returning to war may have gone.

INTERNATIONAL	NATIONAL	REGIONAL	PERSONAL
Alliances	Prime Minister Borden	No. 2 Construction Battalion	Enemy Alien
Battle of the Somme	Union Government	Declining volunteers	Soldier Settlement Plan
Vimy Ridge	Conscription	Halifax Explosion	Victory Bonds
Ypres	National pride	Winnipeg General Strike	Pacifists

From Boom to Bust: Canada in the 1920s and 1930s

"Canadians were a cocky lot in the twenties. We were a nation. We had come of age. The twentieth century belonged to us. Oddly, and ironically, the proud process of nation building contributed to the economic disaster that followed. Greed and over-optimism cost Canada dear."

—FROM PIERRE BERTON'S *THE GREAT DEPRESSION*

TIMELINE

1921
William Lyon Mackenzie King becomes Prime Minister of Canada

1929
The stock market crashes

In the twenty years between the end of World War I and the beginning of World War II, Canadians experienced both unprecedented wealth in the Roaring Twenties and dreadful poverty in the Great Depression. As a result of these wide swings in the economy, the Canadian government came to play a far more active role in society. New political parties such as the Co-operative Commonwealth Federation and the Social Credit Party also emerged to broaden the Canadian political spectrum. In many ways, the two decades were formative years for Canada. Airplanes and automobiles made transportation easier, the world of entertainment was revolutionized by the development of the radio and film industry, and Canada made enormous strides toward establishing independence from Britain. But did all Canadians share in the prosperity of the 1920s? Was Canadian culture being threatened and influenced by the United States? Did the government do enough to help Canadians during the worst economic downturn in history?

LET'S INVESTIGATE

1. What impact did economic conditions have on the lives of Canadians in the 1920s and the 1930s? Was the impact the same for all regions and all Canadians?

2. How did Canadian governments at various levels react to the economic conditions of the Great Depression?

3. What technological developments occurred during the 1920s and 1930s, and how did they change the lives of Canadians?

4. How did American popular culture affect Canadians in these two decades?

1929
Women are declared "persons" under Canadian law

▶

1936
The Canadian Broadcasting Corporation is created

▶

▶

Many Canadians enjoyed good economic times in the 1920s. In 1929, however, the good times came to an end.

INQUIRING INTO THE PAST

- If not all regions of Canada prospered during the 1920s, which regions were likely to be less well off?
- How would technological advances help fuel the Canadian economy in the 1920s?
- What would cause thousands of people to begin investing in the stock market?
- What could cause a terrible economic depression to begin suddenly in the midst of prosperous times?

KEY TERMS

Drought

Great Depression

Handpick Mining

Market Value

Secondary Manufacturing

Spinoff Industries

Stock Market

TIMELINE

1922 ▶	**1925** ▶	**1929** ▶	**1933** ▶
The Canadian Tire Corporation is founded	Cape Breton coal miners strike	The stock-market crash occurs	Newfoundland is forced to give up its independence because of debt

Aroller coaster ride, with its ups and downs and combination of excitement and fear, aptly describes the Canadian economic experience in the years between the end of the Great War in 1918 and the beginning of World War II in 1939. An economic recession dominated the early part of the 1920s, but by the middle of the decade there was a global economic recovery and the world began to buy more Canadian goods. The last half of the 1920s were boom years for many Canadians. In fact, some were convinced that good times were here to stay. Then, in late 1929, the stock market suddenly crashed and the wild ride ended. Ever since, the 1930s have been known simply as years of the **Great Depression**.

The Growth of the National Economy

Until 1924 the effects of the Great War continued to depress Canadian economic activity. Because of the huge war debts of European countries, export markets for Canadian products fell dramatically. This, combined with near-drought conditions in the southern Prairies, hurt Western farmers badly. Higher tariffs in the United States also made it difficult for Canada, whose economy depended on foreign trade. There was simply no market for Canadian goods. The result was high unemployment and increased bankruptcies, which led many Canadians to abandon their country for the United States, where the negative effects of the war had not been as great. In the 1920s nearly a million Canadians moved to the United States from the rural areas of Eastern Canada.

Exports

By 1924, however, conditions were much improved. Britain and Europe were again able to buy Canadian produce, partly because loans from the United States were helping them to rebuild their economies. Because the United States, like Canada, had escaped the war without suffering from any destruction, its strong economy allowed it to lend funds to the ravaged European countries.

Recovering European economies would then create a demand for American and Canadian products. The value of wheat exports climbed from $45.5 million in 1911 to $353.1 million in 1928. At the same time, industries such as pulp and paper, hydro-electricity, and mining were developed and expanded as demand for their products grew in the United States and other countries. American investment in Canada soared, and people once again immigrated to Canada to take advantage of the new opportunities.

The demand for newsprint, especially in the United States, was incredible. Investment in Canadian paper mills increased by more than 350 percent between 1918 and 1928, as did production. By the end of the 1920s Canada was the world's leading maker of paper. Pulp and paper mills were soon built in British Columbia, Manitoba, Ontario, Québec, New Brunswick, and Nova Scotia. The 1920s saw greatly increased competition among the leading newsprint companies, such as the American-based International Paper Company and Abitibi Power and Paper.

If the hunger for newsprint was rapidly changing the surface of the land, the search for wealth under the surface was equally intense. Much of that wealth was found in the Canadian Shield. The discovery of

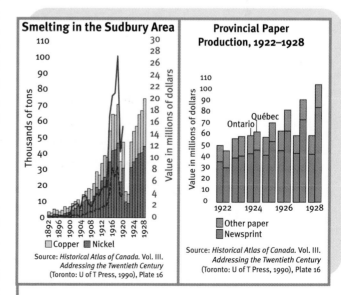

Source: *Historical Atlas of Canada.* Vol. III. *Addressing the Twentieth Century* (Toronto: U of T Press, 1990), Plate 16

Mining and paper production increased dramatically in the 1920s.

new uses for nickel, especially in auto parts, meant a 200 percent increase in production at the International Nickel Company (Inco) in Sudbury, Ontario. Huge copper finds led to the creation, almost overnight, of Noranda, in northern Québec. Aluminum production using bauxite ore imported from the West Indies also expanded, contributing to the growth of towns such as Shawinigan, Québec. The Aluminum Company of Canada (Alcan), an offshoot of the Aluminum Company of America (Alcoa), became the world's second-largest producer. Mining communities such as Kirkland Lake, Flin Flon, and Trail began to flourish. But other industries began to prosper as well.

The Growth of the Automobile Industries

By 1926 Canada was second only to the United States in its number of privately owned automobiles.

Twelve thousand workers made 200 000 cars in eleven Canadian auto plants every year. By the end of the decade there were more than 1.25 million motorized vehicles in the country. Automobile manufacturing boosted the production of leather, rubber, glass, steel, tin, lead, aluminum, and nickel, as well as intensifying the search for petroleum. It also encouraged "**spinoff**" **industries** like road construction, tire and auto-parts plants, service stations, and auto-supply dealers. In 1922 the Billes brothers, John William (J.W.) and Alfred Jackson (A.J.), went into the auto-supply business to form a company that became known as Canadian Tire. In 1934 they began franchising their concept and products through an "associate" store, and by 1939 there were seventy-one associated Canadian Tire Corporation stores.

However, Canadian entrepreneurs who aimed at the automobile market itself met with mixed

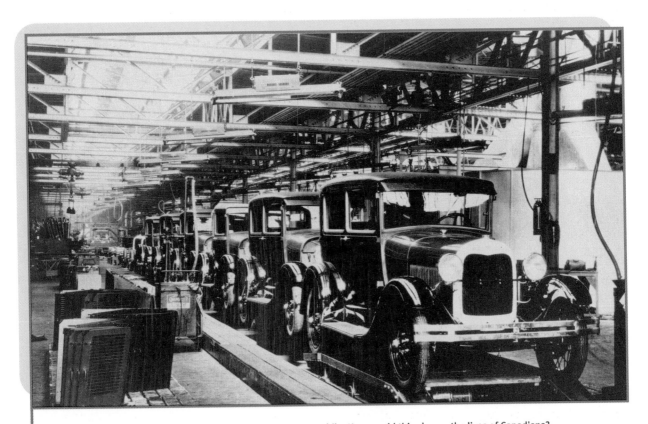

By 1928, one out of every two Canadian homes had an automobile. How would this change the lives of Canadians?

Road construction and tire stores were just two of the "spinoff" industries from the automobile. What other types of spinoff industries can you think of?

results. In 1927, when the American Ford Model T was selling for under $500, the last distinctively Canadian car, the Brooks Steamer (made in Stratford, Ontario), was selling for $3885. With such a difference in price, Canadian automobile manufacturers could not compete, and by the end of the decade they were forced to make and sell American models. In 1926, however, a more lasting and distinctive Canadian vehicle made its appearance in Québec's Eastern Townships. Armand Bombardier, a twenty-year-old garage owner in the village of Valcourt, sold his first snowmobile.

Regional Disparities in a Land of Plenty

The country's economy seemed to be firing on all cylinders, although prosperity was more evident in some regions than in others. Prosperity was concentrated in Central Canada and the urban centres, but even Canadian cities were populated by both rich and poor. Rising prices meant a lower standard of living. Many jobs in Canada still paid poorly. Women and new immigrants suffered most of all from low wages and often-deplorable working editions. Fewer than 5 percent of all workers earned an annual income of $2500, so

many Canadians could only read the advertisements about the new electric appliances. In 1931 only one Canadian farm out of ten had electricity and one in fifty had running water. Even as late as 1948, less than a third of Canadian houses had a mechanical refrigerator.

Canadian Farmers

Prosperity was also hit-and-miss on the Prairies. The price of wheat determined whether times were

Armand Bombardier's first snowmobile was built from his family sleigh, an automobile engine, and an airplane propeller. How would the invention of the snowmobile help northern communities?

good or bad. Between 1920 and 1924 the incomes of wheat farmers dropped by 40 percent. But after 1924 the price of wheat and world demand began edging steadily upward. By 1927 the incomes of Alberta farmers totalled almost $170 million. Some farmers splurged and built themselves big new farmhouses. They also bought up-to-date farm equipment to work their larger and more mechanized farms. Cars and trucks began to replace horses in farm yards, and more tractors and threshers lumbered across the prairie landscape.

But buying larger farms and more farm equipment often meant going heavily into debt. Later on, many farm families would find themselves burdened with debts they could not repay. Even in the good years of the mid-1920s, many other Canadian farmers lived drab and uncertain lives. Every week, people left their farms to seek a better life in the cities.

Glace Bay by Lawren Harris, 1925. This painting of a woman and children in Nova Scotia shows that not all Canadians shared in the prosperity. If you had been Prime Minister, how would you have reacted to the hard times faced by Maritimers?

The Maritimes

Much of the Maritime economy was based on its natural resources and its production of coal, steel, fish, and agricultural goods. During World War I most Maritimers had a taste of economic prosperity, but several events would force the decline of the Maritime economy. After World War I, railway construction in Canada slowed down and the demand for Maritime steel dropped sharply. In addition, the coal that Maritime miners produced not only fuelled the region's industries but was a major export to Central Canada. However, the demand for Nova Scotia coal declined as the use of oil and electricity in Québec and Ontario grew. Also, low tariffs allowed cheaper American coal and steel to dominate whatever demand was still left. If miners and workers weren't laid off, they had to face huge cuts to their already small wages. For example, the British Empire Steel Company (BESCO) was made up of many Nova Scotia steel, coal, and shipbuilding companies. As the companies faced hard times, BESCO's response was to reduce the miners' wage by a third.

In his newspaper, the *Maritime Labour Herald*, union leader J.B. McLachlan translated this wage cut in terms of its effects on miners and their families. Day labourers in the mines would now make an annual wage of only $707.60, less than half the

minimum that the Department of Labour would later say was necessary. McLachlan went further in an article entitled, "How Can They Live?" The following table shows McLachlan's calculation of how a family of five distributed this annual wage.

NECESSITY	COST
Clothing	$125.00
Rent for company house	$100.00
Utilities/taxes: coal, water, sanitation	$120.50
Deductions: doctor, hospital, church, trade union, insurance	$136.40
Food	$225.70
TOTAL	**$707.60**

All that was left for a family of five was $225.70 a year for food — about 13¢ per person per day. To earn this pitiful amount, miners, some as young as nine years old, did some of the toughest, dirtiest, and most dangerous work there was. It was a time when most of the work was done with hand tools — **handpick mining** — and workers were paid for what they produced. Two men worked a coal "room" by "tumbling" the coal from the face of the wall after they had "undercut" the wall by digging along its base in the fashion described by one handpick miner:

> You'd lay on your side after putting a little soft coal under your shoulder ... and you'd get in so far. Course when you had the undercut opening out wider, you'd be on your knees. Then you'd get so far in, you'd have to get down on your side again, underneath the wall of coal, picking away ... you'd go in about five feet I guess, just as far as you could reach in. Then you'd back out, bore and shoot [an explosive] ... blow it all down.

Mining was also very dangerous. The explosives consisted of loose blasting powder, which was placed in hand-bored holes. Too much powder or improperly bored holes was a death sentence. And, of course, there was constant threat of setting off a huge explosion caused by methane gas.

Considering all these factors, it is not surprising that the miners refused to accept the wage cut ordered by BESCO. As a result, between 1921 and 1925, Cape Breton, Nova Scotia, experienced a series of vicious strikes. When the company cut off essential services such as electricity and water to force the miners into submission, the miners, with the support of their families, responded by rioting and taking over the Glace Bay area. The government sent for the army. So many militia were sent to end

Miners often worked in cramped conditions like these.

outbreaks of violence that, at one point, half of Canada's army was on duty in Cape Breton.

The slow Maritime economy was further weakened by other factors. Most Maritime **secondary manufacturing** industries (companies that made finished products from raw materials) were controlled by owners based in Montréal or Toronto, such as Roy Wolvin, who operated BESCO out of Montreal. These owners had no ties to the Maritimes, and their response to the economic crisis of the early 1920s was to close up business and relocate to Central Canada. Between 1921 and 1925, in Nova Scotia and New Brunswick, 42 percent of skilled jobs disappeared. The goods that were still produced in the Maritimes were hit again by an increase in railway freight rates. Between 1917 and 1923, freight rates in the Maritimes increased between 140 and 216 percent. The added shipping costs made Maritime goods more expensive to buy in Central Canada and gave Ontario's and Québec's products an advantage over those of Maritime producers.

A further blow came when the United States raised tariffs on fish and farm goods, keeping Nova Scotia apples and Prince Edward Island and New Brunswick potatoes off American dinner tables. New U.S. regulations also thwarted the Maritime fishing industry. About the only exports the United States accepted freely from the Maritimes were their sons and daughters, as over 100 000 of them emigrated during the 1920s to the northeastern states.

Newfoundland in the 1920s and 1930s

Newfoundland became part of Canada in 1949, but the events that led to that decision began with World War I. Newfoundland's contributions to the war were very costly: her volunteer and casualty rates were among the highest in the entire British Empire. The war had also left Newfoundland with a national debt of $13 million. In addition, the thousands of wounded and disabled veterans, widows, and orphans of those killed in action were now Newfoundland's responsibility. By 1923 the debt had reached $60 million. Added to all of this came the collapse of one of Newfoundland's main industries in the 1920s and 1930s — the cod fisheries.

News of the stock market crash on October 29, 1929, made headlines around the world.

In the early 1920s the value of cod exports dropped by almost 50 percent. Then, in 1930, disaster struck as the prices for cod dropped to a twenty-year low and traditional markets put up high tariffs to protect their own fisheries. The debt reached $100 million, and paying the interest on it ate up 65 percent of Newfoundland's annual revenue. As a result, in 1933 Newfoundland was forced to give up its independent position in the Empire and submit to a government controlled by Britain. The decision Newfoundlanders made sixteen years later, to join Canada, was a direct result of the catastrophes of these years.

The Beginning of the Great Depression

Many Canadians thought that there was simply no limit to Canada's economic potential. In addition to the booming mining, pulp and paper, and hydro-electric industries, good times had returned to Western wheat farmers, who by the end of the decade supplied 40 percent of the world's export market. Public confidence was generally high in Canada in the late 1920s, but the prosperity of the Roaring Twenties was coming to an end.

Making "Easy Money" on the Stock Market

In the late 1920s, the **stock market** itself became "a new frontier for money-making." Increasingly, the value of stocks was not based on the real assets of the companies but on the **market value** of the stock. That value was being established by investors' demand for it. As the value of stocks increased through 1926, 1927, and 1928, it seemed there was no surer, or faster, way of making money. Investment was made easier because almost anyone could borrow money to buy stocks. As long as stock prices were rising, investors could sell their stocks, pay off their debts, and still make a profit.

Of course, the more money that people invested, the greater the market value of stocks increased. The shares of Canadian Marconi, a radio company that had not been very profitable, should have sold at $1 each, but market value inflated them to $28 each. Although Marconi had real assets of only $5 million, the New York Stock Exchange valued the company at nearly $130 million. One Canadian investment company, which bought and sold stocks of all kinds for investors, went from having two employees, one office, and $17 000 in capital in the mid-1920s to a huge forty-office business with fifteen hundred employees and thousands of kilometres of wire linking them to the important stock exchanges by the end of the decade.

Not only were individual Canadians investing in these highly inflated stocks, but big corporations were, too. The leaders of these corporations began to believe that the worth of their companies was what the stock market said it was, and they frequently borrowed money to expand their companies' production on the basis of this belief. Banks got into the act, too: they not only lent money to individuals and companies to invest, they invested their depositors' money as well.

The Balloon Bursts: The Stock-Market Crash of 1929

The economy that was being set up in the industrialized nations was a huge, linked network increasingly tied to the "value" of the stocks on the markets. On Tuesday, October 29, 1929 — "Black Tuesday" — stock holders, who over the previous weeks had been growing more nervous as stock prices climbed ever higher, finally decided that the stocks were overvalued. The result was as if a pin had been stuck into an overinflated balloon. Just as the air would rush out of the balloon, so did the "value" disappear from the overinflated stocks. As people rushed to convert their stocks into real money, panic selling took over. But now there were few buyers, and the prices continued to plunge. It devastated even the most solid of companies, as the following table of stock values reveals.

Thousands of investors, big and small, were wiped out because they could not sell their shares for a fraction of what they had paid for them. Banks began to demand payment for the loans that many investors had made in order to buy the stocks, but many borrowers could not repay their loans. Even worse, many banks had used their customers' deposits to buy stocks. Now the value of the stocks had fallen so low that the banks were unable to recover their depositors' money.

As well, many companies had borrowed money to finance the expansion of their production and were now unable to pay these loans. They were forced either to shut down or to severely cut back their production. Workers who had not even invested in the stock market lost their savings because of the banks' investment of their deposits. Now they were losing their jobs as well, when the companies shut down. When people lost their jobs and their paycheques, the businesses from which they purchased food, clothes, and other merchandise went bankrupt and put yet more people out of work.

SHARE VALUES, 1929 AND 1932			
Company	1929 high ($)	1932 low ($)	Decline (%)
Abitibi Power	57.75	1	98.3
Canadian Pacific Railway	67.5	8.5	87.4
Ford Canada	70	5.75	91.4
Imperial Oil	41.25	7.375	82.5
International Nickel	72.5	4.125	94.3
Massey-Harris	99.5	2.5	97.4
Stelco	69.25	11	84.1
Winnipeg Electric	109.5	2	98.1

The fifty leading stocks on Canadian exchanges lost 85.9 percent of their value between the highest price paid for them in October 1929 and the lowest price stockholders could get for them in May 1932. This table shows what happened to eight large firms.

"Black Tuesday" started a downward spiral that continued for years: people could not buy goods because of their debts and lower income; businesses cut back or shut down because of the resulting lower demand for their goods; more people lost their jobs; the demand for goods dropped further; more businesses shut down; and on it went. Canada had entered the Great Depression, the worst economic downturn in history.

From Boom to Bust in Canada's Regions

Statistics can give us a general idea of the impact of the "Dirty Thirties," but the real story can only be told by going beyond the numbers. As the following table indicates, the Depression affected the various provinces unevenly.

Residents of the Maritime provinces experienced a less severe drop in income than did Canadians in the other provinces, but since they had not shared in the earlier prosperity they had, in a sense, less to lose. British Columbia, like most of Canada, depended on exporting its resources, and that dependency created large numbers of unemployed miners, fishers, and forestry workers when those markets dried up. Central Canadian manufacturers could not sell their products, and this lack of a market resulted in thousands of laid-off employees.

The Prairie provinces suffered the most in the Depression. Prairie farmers had enjoyed prosperity in the second half of the 1920s: crops had been good, and European markets had improved. This had led farmers to put more land under cultivation, to invest in more expensive machinery, and to focus on wheat as the primary crop. All of these actions made the effects of the Depression more devastating for them.

Prices for wheat began to drop as a result of a huge crop of 1928, but the real impact came in the years that followed. By 1931 a bushel of wheat, which had earned a farmer $1.63 in 1928, dropped

CANADIAN PER CAPITA INCOME, BY PROVINCE, 1928–1929 AND 1933			
Province	1928–29 average per capita income ($)	1933 average per capita income ($)	Decrease (%)
British Columbia	594	314	47
Ontario	549	310	44
Alberta	548	212	61
Saskatchewan	478	135	72
Manitoba	466	240	49
Québec	391	220	44
Nova Scotia	322	207	36
New Brunswick	292	180	39
Prince Edward Island	278	154	45

Average incomes in each province had dropped significantly by 1933. Why did the Prairie provinces experience the highest percentage increase and the Maritime provinces experience the lowest?

below $0.30. Between 1931 and 1934 the farmers' costs of producing wheat were greater than any money they made from selling it. Then, **drought** struck southern Alberta and Saskatchewan year after year, and the topsoil turned to fine dust. Almost nothing could grow in these conditions. Grasshoppers and plant diseases destroyed the few crops that had managed to survive. On some farms, not a stalk of wheat was left standing. In 1928 the average Saskatchewan farmer had a net income of $1614, but by 1933 the same farmer earned only $66. Not surprisingly, between 1931 and 1941 almost 200 000 people left the Prairie provinces.

A Collapse Beyond Canada's Control

The Great Depression, which began at the end of the 1920s, demonstrated the limitations of Canada's independence. The nation's economy was closely tied to world conditions, especially those in Europe and the United States. Much of the prosperity of the 1920s was based on the production and sale of primary products, especially wheat, wood products like lumber and newsprint, and minerals. Eighty percent of this production was sold in international markets.

But Canada was not the only nation to suffer. The Great Depression was a worldwide economic disaster that affected countries as diverse as Germany, Chile, Japan, Australia, and the United States. The loss of these foreign markets would affect not only the agricultural, forest, and mineral sectors of the Canadian economy, but everything that was linked to these key industries as well.

Even before the stock-market crash in October 1929, there were signs that Canada and other countries were producing more goods than the markets could absorb. The production of newsprint, for example, had increased by 350 percent in Canada in the 1920s. However, prices for newsprint crashed in 1927, an indication that more newsprint was being made than could be sold. The same could be said for the production of automobiles and wheat.

In addition to overproduction, several other factors helped close off the international trade on which Canada depended for a third of its national income. Many countries raised their tariffs to protect their domestic markets from foreign competition. The result was a decline in international trade, and Canada which depended on trade, was especially hard-hit.

Duststorms like this one blew the topsoil off many prairie farms in the 1930s. Drought and Depression made the 1930s a decade of despair in the West.

Canadian contributions

REMEMBERING HARD TIMES

One of the richest resources available to historians writing about Canadian history in the twentieth century is the memories of those who lived it. Recorded memories are called oral history. To find out more about oral history, see "Methods of Historical Inquiry" in Unit 5. Following is one woman's memoir of life on the Prairies during the Great Depression.

I remember the year 1936, the year I got married, and how it was, the feeling we all had that as we'd gone for about five years in the Depression then, it soon had to end, because it was just crazy. The drought and the grasshoppers and the pain and the sorrow of it could not go on much longer. It didn't seem right that God should punish us that way, that farmers for miles and miles and miles around who were all God-fearing and honest men would be subject to such conditions — and their wives and their families.

Young people, we saw no hope. Young men thought they were a burden on their families and that's why so many left. Riding the rods, they called it. You know, travelling back and forth in box-cars across the country looking for work. There was nothing in the towns around, nothing, because the towns and villages, they all depended on the farmers for their money and living, and the farmers had no money. There was barter, too, of course. You'd take in a case of eggs or six pounds of butter and barter it for things you really needed. I mean really needed. There was no frivolity then.

At Christmas a child was lucky to get a fifty-cent toy and a bag of candy and an orange, and that was about it. It would be all right for a small child, say eight or nine, because they really hadn't known what it was like before the Depression.

So, we had no money. My husband and I knew that. We decided we can't wait forever. When you're farming dry land, good times may never come, and so we decided to get married. May 23, 1936, smack dab right in the middle of the Depression. A Saturday, and

it was a beautiful day. The wedding was in Coaldale and the reception was at the farm, and everybody came. Even the local Hutterites, and that is something. Well, the elders, the bosses. Not the people themselves. My father was very popular. A big party, wedding, at ten in the morning, and then the party, and have you ever heard of anyone going on a honeymoon in a truck? Well, John and I did. A 1928 Ford with the back cut off and made into a truck, and about three we headed off to Waterton....

When nobody has any money you fall back on other things, like yourselves, your family, the neighbours, and I guess just the community spirit. You helped each other out. It was amazing how you could survive and eat well and feel good. I think we all knew things had to get better.

They did, of course. The rains came about 1938, at the right time. That year the district got a good crop. Then the war, of course. We didn't lose many of our boys, but a lot of them joined up. That was the end of the Depression. By 1941, I'd say, everybody was back on their feet and doing just fine. In a few years everybody had forgotten about the Dirty Thirties. It was just something you talked about, once in a while.

EXCERPTED FROM BARRY BROADFOOT, *NEXT-YEAR COUNTRY: VOICES OF PRAIRIE PEOPLE* (TORONTO: MCCLELLAND & STEWART, 1994), PP. 89–91.

ACTIVITY

Imagine you have been invited to the wedding described in this passage. The Depression is at its worst, so money is scarce, but you want to take a suitable gift for the bride and groom. What will you do? Describe the solution to your dilemma and the gift you will take to the wedding.

As the United States tried to keep its own economy healthy, Americans stopped investing in places like Canada and focused on the home market. American bankers also demanded payment on loans that had helped rebuild the European economies that had been devastated by World War I. Many European countries found it difficult or impossible to repay the loans. The result was that they could no longer afford to purchase Canada's products.

In most countries, including Canada and the United States, there was another basic problem that was largely ignored during the 1920s. The average wage in Canada in 1929 was $1200. The Department of Labour's 1929 estimate of the amount required to maintain an average Canadian family at a "minimum standard of health and decency" was $1430. Since average Canadians were earning wages almost 20 percent beneath the poverty line, they were unable to purchase much of what the nation's businesses were producing in such large quantities.

The stock-market crash of October 1929 was not the only cause of the Great Depression, but it resulted in a loss of confidence among the business class and revealed the underlying problems that had lain hidden through most of the 1920s. In Canada the loss of both domestic and foreign markets for wheat, lumber, pulp, and paper, fish, and minerals set off a shock wave that affected all other parts of the economy.

Although the attention of most Canadians in the 1930s was naturally focused on their own difficulties, it must be remembered that the Great Depression was a global disaster. Perhaps even more significantly, its effects and its almost ten-year duration have left such an impression on our collective memory that even the possibility of a recurrence of an economic depression starts alarm bells ringing around the world.

Web Connections

http://www.school.mcgrawhill.ca/resources

Go to the Web site above to find out more about how the Great Depression affected life in Vancouver. Go to *History Resources*, then to *Canada: A Nation Unfolding, Ontario Edition* to find out where to go to next..

Canadian voices

THE BEST OF TIMES?

I am a seventeen-year-old Jewish female living in Toronto, and like many other young people I have never really been familiar with my own religion. Although I celebrate all the Jewish holidays and go to synagogue now and then, I never really knew about the roots of my family. By exploring the history of my ancestors, I have succeeded in answering many of my questions about the cultural gap that has existed between my grandparents' era and my own. What was it like being Jewish in Toronto during the 1930s? Where did Jews live? What did they do for a living? How did they deal with anti-Semitism (hostility or prejudice toward Jews)? One of the biggest challenges that our generation faces is to be aware of these historical events, for it is these events of the past that have shaped our present lives.

In 1931 there were 45 305 Jews in Toronto, and this was only 7.2 percent of the total population of the city. Many Jews found residence in the downtown areas. Many worked either in manufacturing or merchandising in the small shops and factories along Spadina Avenue. In the early 1930s Toronto entered the worst years of the Great Depression, and during this time the Jews, being an ethnic minority, were tolerated but always treated as outsiders.

As conditions worsened, many anti-Jewish newspapers would write disturbing comments stereotyping the Jew as a danger to Toronto's society. Jews were discriminated against ethnically, religiously, linguistically, culturally, and economically. They were not allowed to hold many occupations, such as medicine and teaching, and were not only made to feel unwelcome in many places but were often refused entry. Many eager tourists vacationing at summer resorts in Toronto were greeted with signs stating "No Jews or dogs allowed."

Although anti-Semitism was a danger to all Jews in the city, teenagers in public schools and high schools were subjected to discrimination more often than their parents were. Young people often faced discrimination by their teachers and classmates on a daily basis. Many Jewish children were allowed and even encouraged to leave school before the age of sixteen. Jewish youths were forced to learn what territories were their own — places where they could enter and not fear the attacks that plagued most Jewish people at that time.

Jews struggled through numerous forms of discrimination in their attempts to make a home and a living within Toronto. Should they endure the horrible conditions in Toronto, or try to find comfort in a more accepting city? Although many did leave, most remained and endured the hatred from others for years to come. If it weren't for these brave people, like my grandparents, who remained even through the worst of times, Toronto would not be what it is today — a multicultural city where Jews have the freedom to live, work, and believe whatever they desire.

Anti-Semitism existed throughout Canada, as this 1939 poster in Sainte-Agathe (a resort in the Laurentians north of Montréal) shows.

Fellow teens, remember that we are now living in a time of opportunity. But never forget the way it used to be — the life our grandparents lived, that time when many have said, "It was both the best of times and the worst of times." I have trouble seeing it as the best of times. Don't you?

CONTRIBUTED BY JENNIFER FINK. JENNIFER IS A MEMBER OF THE JEWISH COMMUNITY IN THORNHILL, ONTARIO, AND A STUDENT OF VAUGHAN SECONDARY SCHOOL.

chapter review

CHAPTER SUMMARY

In this chapter we have seen

- how some regions of Canada experienced economic boom and bust in the 1920s and 1930s, while others went from recession to depression

- how new industries, especially newsprint manufacturing, mineral production, and consumer-based manufacturing, created a new national economy in Canada in the 1920s

- how unrestrained optimism led to a massive stock-market speculation that ended with a resounding crash

- how several factors, including overproduction, high tariffs, and low wages, contributed to the coming of the Great Depression

UNDERSTANDING HISTORICAL FACTS

1. Identify these people, places, and events, and explain their historical significance:

   The Billes Brothers   Armand Bombardier
   BESCO   "Easy Money"
   "Black Tuesday"

2. Create a web, with the automobile at the centre, that shows the new industries that were either begun or stimulated by the great popularity of cars in the 1920s.

3. People have used the phrase "domino effect" to describe what happens when an important event or development sets off a chain of consequences. Using the stock-market crash of 1929 as the important event, explain how the crash helped bring about each of the following consequences:

   - increased debt and even failure among corporations

   - the closing and near-bankruptcy of many banks

   - the tremendous rise in unemployment

- the loss of savings by individuals who did not invest in the stock market

- the collapse or near-failure of hundreds of regular stores

4. List the main reasons for the Great Depression. Rank these reasons in order of importance. Be prepared to support and explain your decisions.

EXPRESSING YOUR OPINION

1. What suggestions would you have given to Canadian workers in the 1920s to help them improve their working conditions and wages?

2. How appropriate is the term "Roaring Twenties" in describing the Canadian Prairies and the Maritimes? How could the federal government have acted to better ensure economic prosperity for all regions in Canada?

3. In a group, create the front page of your local newspaper for October 29, 1929. Be sure to include headlines and articles about what is happening nationally and locally.

WORKING WITH THE EVIDENCE

1. The first half of the twentieth century was not kind to Newfoundland. In July 1916 many of Newfoundland's best and brightest young men died at the Battle of the Somme. Less than twenty years later a financial crisis forced Newfoundland to submit to control by Britain and eventually to join Canada in 1949. What is the connection between the Battle of the Somme and Newfoundland's crisis in the 1930s?

It would be up to Prime Ministers Mackenzie King and R.B. Bennett to guide Canada through the Depression.

INQUIRING INTO THE PAST

- **What special qualities would make Mackenzie King so successful as a Prime Minister?**
- **How would the federal government respond to a national crisis like an economic depression?**
- **What kinds of political responses to the Great Depression would come from Canada's regions?**
- **Would the contributions made by women during World War I lead to further successes in the years that followed?**

KEY TERMS

Business Cycle

Laissez-faire

On-to-Ottawa Trek

Pogey

Privy Council

Red Menace

Regina Manifesto

Social Credit

Social Welfare

Transients

Union Nationale

TIMELINE

1921 ▶
Mackenzie King becomes Prime Minister for the first time

1928 ▶
The Persons Case decision declares women to be legally "persons"

1930 ▶
R.B. Bennett defeats Mackenzie King and becomes Prime Minister as the Depression begins

1935 ▶
Mackenzie King returns as Prime Minister

The decades between the two world wars would bring numerous challenges to Canada's political system. Often, the response to these challenges would be in the form of a new political party or force the main parties of the Liberals and Conservatives to adopt new policies to address Canada's new realities. A new generation of political-party leaders had to deal not only with the ups and downs of economic recession, recovery, and depression, but they were also faced with regional economic inequalities that were becoming a characteristic of Canada's economic development. Complicating matters further were the social effects of these economic swings and growing demands for recognition on the part of women. Finally, the seemingly never-ending Great Depression of the 1930s brought forth new political ideas and programs to challenge traditional approaches. Through most of these years the nation would look to one leader: William Lyon Mackenzie King.

Politics in the Age of Mackenzie King

The previous leader of the federal Liberal Party, Sir Wilfrid Laurier, died soon after the end of World War I. Forty-five-year-old Mackenzie King became the new Liberal leader in 1919. King was proud of being the grandson of William Lyon Mackenzie, the fiery reformer who sparked the 1837 Rebellion in Upper Canada. But William Lyon Mackenzie King was a very different sort of man. Cautious and moderate, King was a successful civil servant and expert labour negotiator. Like Laurier, he was skilled at using compromise to hold the nation together. And, like Laurier, King put Canadian unity ahead of every other political goal.

Mackenzie King would become Canada's longest-serving Prime Minister. First serving as Prime Minister in 1921, he went on to win elections in 1925, 1926, 1935, 1940, and 1945. He was out of power only briefly, in the summer of 1926 and for the five years from 1930 to 1935. King surrounded himself with capable Cabinet ministers who reflected the interests of the country's different regions. For example, because he could not speak French, King relied on the excellent advice of Ernest Lapointe to retain support in Québec. The advice King received from his "lieutenants" in the provinces and his own sense of what Canadians wanted, or did not want, were such that he constantly outmanoeuvred his chief political opponent in the 1920s, the Conservative Party leader, Arthur Meighen.

Mackenzie King: A Man of Contradictions

The private life of Mackenzie King was not seen by many, nor was his personal life the subject of constant inspection, unlike those of today's political leaders. As an avid diarist, King painstakingly recorded his actions, thoughts and feelings on a daily basis. His diaries were opened to the public thirty years after his death. What the diaries contained shocked many historians and forced a re-evaluation of Mackenzie King. The public Mackenzie King was seen as a cautious life-long bachelor who was devoted to his mother. The private Mackenzie King suggests a very different kind of person. He appears to have been very involved in mysticism, often attending seances, consulting fortune-tellers, and even using a crystal ball to contact the spiritual world. Throughout his tenure as Prime Minister, King often sought the advice of his mother, Isabel, who had died in 1917, and his dog, Pat, who had also died.

One of Mackenzie King's contradictions is revealed in a diary entry in which he relates the following incident. On a winter evening, he assisted an elderly man who had fallen on the ice. This man was a Russian Jew who had immigrated to Canada and became wealthy. King noted in his diary how proud he was that a Russian Jew could flee from persecution and find prosperity in Canada. He then concluded by noting how troubling it was that Jews were beginning to move into the Sandy Hill area of Ottawa. There was much more to the Prime Minister than the general public ever saw.

Regional Protest in the 1920s

For those living outside of Central Canada, the "Roar" of the Twenties was often little more than distant rumblings. Whether they were Maritime fishers or rural farmers, it was becoming increasingly evident that the business interests of Ontario and Québec were directing the national agenda. From the beginning of the twentieth century, party policy for both the Liberals and the Conservatives was being shaped by increasingly wealthier and more powerful business leaders. From this growing sense of political alienation would arise protest movements in the West and the Maritimes. This would be the beginning of a history of regional protest parties in Canada that have come to include the Social Credit Party, the Union Nationale, and, most recently, the Reform Party.

The Progressive Party

The free-trade election of 1911, which pitted the interests of business against farm interests, had been a sign of the changing times. Laurier, who had decided to pursue the free-trade agreement after listening to the concerns of Prairie farmers, had underestimated the political clout business had come to enjoy in Canada. By the early 1920s many provinces had farm organizations and in some cases provincial political parties, such as the United Farmers of Alberta and the United Farmers of Ontario.

The surprise of the 1921 election was the success of the new Progressive Party. The Progressive Party had emerged as a national party representing the interests of farmers. Seizing on the frustration farmers felt with the Liberal and Conservative parties, the Progressive Party became the official opposition in the House of Commons by winning sixty-four seats, fourteen more than the Conservatives. Despite its early and stunning success, the Progressive Party would not be able to continue to build a solid national party. While there was universal support among farmers for the rapid elimination of tariffs, the party was divided on many other issues, such as public control of railways and utilities and the marketing of grain.

Women's sections of farm organizations were particularly supportive of co-operative measures, arguing that rural communities could only be strong if they worked together. In many rural communities in the West, women took the initiative to establish hospitals, clinics, community centres, and theatres and to improve rural schools. Some of the women's farm organizations, such as the United Farm Women of Alberta (UFWA), attempted to extend the spirit of co-operation beyond the community to the world at large in an effort to end war. Uniting with other women's peace groups, the UFWA pressured schools to develop curriculum that emphasized tolerance and peaceful resolution rather than violence and bigotry.

Ironically, the responsiveness of the Progressive MPs to the voters of their particular riding was both the appeal and the undoing of the party. The grass-roots nature of the Progressive Party prevented it from building a national organization with control over the local constituencies. Since the Progressive Party lacked a unified platform, Mackenzie King was able to lure many of the Progressives to the Liberal Party by lowering tariffs on farm machinery and equipment and by restoring the Crow Rate (a reduction on freight costs for grain shipments, which had been suspended during World War I). Many of those defecting to the Liberal Party claimed the movement had been a success. Regardless, by the end of the decade the Progressive Party was running out of momentum. In the 1930 election it won a mere twelve seats. In 1932 the few remaining Progressives joined with labour and farm groups to form the Co-operative Commonwealth Federation (CCF).

The Maritime Rights Movement

A.P. Paterson, a grocer from Saint John, New Brunswick, led a group of influential businessmen and professionals to launch the Maritimes Rights Movement in 1920. Believing they could have a strong voice if they banded together, the movement's members felt that all of Canada was responsible for any region that was economically disadvantaged by its geographic location.

Therefore, they demanded increased federal subsidies for the Maritime provinces, more international trade through the ports of Halifax and Saint John, and higher tariffs to protect the region's steel and coal industries.

Due to the depopulation of the Maritime provinces caused by residents leaving to find work elsewhere, Maritime representation in the federal House of Commons fell by one quarter. This decline in representatives meant that the Maritimes' demands were crowded out by the increasing representation of the Western provinces, who were demanding a lower tariff. Prime Minister Mackenzie King could not afford to lose the support of the Western provinces, so the higher tariff was not granted to the Maritimes. This allowed cheaper American coal, iron, and steel to flood the Canadian market. Maritime resources could not compete, so King set up a royal commission (the Duncan Commission) to look into the group's complaints. The commission recommended several major changes, including reduced rail rates and increased federal subsidies. King's Liberals, however, agreed to only a few minor changes. Discouraged and disillusioned, the Maritime Rights Movement disbanded in 1926.

Government Responses to the Depression

When the stock market crashed, King told Canadians that "business was never better, nor faith in Canada's future more justified." He was not alone in thinking that the crash was temporary. It was normal for an upswing of economic prosperity to be followed by a downturn toward recession and then rebound toward economic prosperity again. It was all part of what is sometimes called the **business cycle** of alternating economic upswings and downturns. Many people, including leading bankers and the Prime Minister, believed that the worst was over by the end of 1929. But as the Depression deepened, poverty and hardship spread across the nation.

During the winter of 1929–1930, many provincial governments (a number of which were led by the Conservative Party) asked the federal government for assistance in dealing with rising unemployment. King said that his Liberal federal government would not give them "a five-cent piece" — a remark that became known as his "five-cent speech." The opposition leader, R.B. Bennett, accused King of being unwilling and unable to deal with the Depression, and Canadians agreed. In the election of July 1930, King's Liberals lost to the Conservatives. It fell to Bennett to lead Canada through the worst years of the Depression.

Rising unemployment across Canada became a national problem by 1930. If you were unable to find work, how would you have reacted to Mackenzie King's "five-cent speech?"

Bennett Comes to Power

For most of his five years as Prime Minister, Bennett, a businessman, believed that if he could help businesses survive and grow, they, in turn, would provide jobs for workers. The workers' wages would then allow them to buy goods, thereby stimulating more business growth and more employment. The result would be an upward spiral of employment and production to replace the terrible downward spiral that Canada was in. Bennett tried to accomplish this by raising the tariff to protect Canadian businesses from foreign competition. These businesses, assured of being able to sell to the Canadian market, would begin the upward spiral.

But industries that depended on exporting their products, such as wheat farming, forestry, mining, and fishing, were not helped by these high tariffs. Bennett and his advisers mistakenly believed high tariffs would force foreign countries to lower their tariffs because of their need for these basic products. By 1935, only Britain had agreed to lower tariffs for Canadian products. International trade remained stagnant, while in Canada even the existence of lower prices for goods was not sufficient to restart the economy. Unemployed and underemployed people could not afford to buy even cheaply priced goods.

As a result of this disaster, many people began to believe that governments, as representatives of the citizens, had an important role to play in the well-being of the country. Bennett's government did spend money to help the unemployed — $20 million in 1930 — but many Canadians began to demand a broader range of imaginative government involvement, and some concluded that the existing political parties lacked the required imagination or the willingness to get involved.

Relief Camps

Bennett created relief camps for the thousands of **transients** — single, homeless men who roamed the country in search of work. These drifters were widely feared as a danger to the peace and safety of many communities. To move them away from towns and cities, the federal government built relief camps deep in the Canadian wilderness. The camps were run on a tiny budget by the Department of National Defence. Men in the camps were given food, shelter, army-style clothing, and twenty cents a day. In

Although relief camps gave unemployed men three meals a day and a roof over their head, workers complained about the small wages for hard work and the lack of recreational activities. Did the Bennett government do enough to help these workers by creating the camps, or were the relief workers being exploited?

return, they built bridges and roads, cut trees, dug ditches, and worked on other projects. But many men rebelled against life in relief camps, which gave them no hope for the future. How could they save for anything by making twenty cents a day?

Bennett's New Deal

Prime Minister Bennett realized that if he was going to win the 1935 election, his government had to make a change. On January 3, 1935, he made a coast-to-coast radio speech that shocked many Canadians. "I am for reform," he told listeners, "and, to my mind, reform means government intervention, it means government control and regulation, it means the end of **laissez-faire**." In several more radio addresses, he introduced what became known as his "New Deal." Bennett's promises were patterned on the new economic program of U.S. President Franklin Roosevelt, who had promised "a new deal for the American People." Bennett's New Deal included promises and laws to regulate hours of work, to provide a minimum wage, to improve working conditions, and to provide insurance against sickness, industrial accidents, and unemployment.

These measures, however, did little to help the thousands of Canadians who were already unemployed. Others believed Bennett's New Deal was a desperate effort to win votes in the upcoming election. Many of Bennett's proposals were passed by Parliament, but they were later struck down by the courts, which decided that **social welfare** (such as unemployment insurance), was an area under exclusive provincial control. Bennett's last-minute reforms did little to win his party the support of Canadians.

"Living on the Pogey"

The slang term for getting government vouchers for food, boots, clothing, coal, and shelter was "living on the **pogey**." It was a terrible experience for many hardworking people to ask for relief. Relief payments were purposely kept lower than the lowest-paying job to discourage people from applying for relief. Many Canadian families lived close to starvation. Malnutrition and disease, especially among children, were common.

The On-to-Ottawa Trek

While Bennett tried to capture public interest with his New Deal, conditions in the relief camps worsened. The camps were overcrowded with unemployed men who felt that the government was not doing enough to help their situation. In the summer of 1935, the relief-camp workers organized the **On-to-Ottawa Trek** to demand "work with wages." Thousands of young men from British Columbia poured out of relief camps, climbed onto railway boxcars, and headed east. But Bennett had no sympathy for the marchers and ordered the Royal Canadian Mounted Police to turn them back. They were stopped in Regina and warned to go no further.

On July 1, 1935, the Regina Riot broke out between the police and the protesters, leaving one officer dead and numerous protesters and officers injured. Only one strike leader was permitted to carry on to Ottawa to meet with an unfriendly Prime Minister. No changes to the relief camps came from the meeting, but Bennett's decision to make use of the police in Regina helped to turn many Canadians against his government. In the federal election that year, Canadians voted to return Mackenzie King to office.

About 1800 unemployed workers "rode the rails" en route to Ottawa to protest government inaction. Here, the march has stopped in Regina, where riots broke out. Why do you think Prime Minister Bennett stopped the On-to-Ottawa Trek in Regina?

Mackenzie King Again

Mackenzie King led Canada through the last years of the Great Depression. His government continued Bennett's policy of financial aid to Prairie farmers and passed the Prairie Farm Rehabilitation Act (PFRA). The PFRA gave money to develop new farming methods, seed vacant land, and relocate some families to better farming areas further north. King also introduced lower tariffs and signed a new trade agreement with the United States. But his main goal was to slash government spending and balance the federal budget. Overall, the Prime Minister was "waiting out" the Depression.

Regional Political Responses to the Depression

The two major political parties seemed to be giving Canadians the same old answer: "Wait and see." Both the Liberal and Conservative parties supported "hands-off" or laissez-faire ("let it be") economic policies, and neither wanted to tamper with the economic system in any major way. Meanwhile, tens of thousands of Canadians were in desperate economic circumstances. A sign of growing Canadian frustration was the practice of naming many make-do measures after Prime Minister Bennett. People with no money for gasoline and oil

Many families found creative ways to make ends meet during the Depression. "Bennett buggies," automobiles with their engines removed and drawn by horses or oxen, were one way people managed to survive on little money.

lifted the engines out of their automobiles and hitched horses to the bumpers. The resulting horse-drawn cars were called "Bennett buggies." There were also Bennett blankets (newspapers), Bennett barnyards (abandoned Prairie farms), Bennett coffee (roasted wheat, brewed like coffee), and Bennettburghs ("hobo jungles," where homeless drifters camped out).

The nation was restless for answers different from those the main political parties seemed to be offering. Disgust with these parties caused many people to turn away from them. As a result, Canada saw the rise of some new political parties, especially in those regions that had suffered the most.

The Co-operative Commonwealth Federation

In Saskatchewan in 1933, perhaps the worst year of the Depression, a regional political party was created. The founders of the Co-operative Commonwealth Federation (CCF), the forerunner of today's New Democratic Party, believed there were ways of avoiding the "boom" and "bust" cycles that seemed to be built into the capitalist free-market system. Members of socialist farm and labour groups met in Regina to hammer out a political platform, the **Regina Manifesto**, which set out the aims of the CCF's program. Farmers, one of the party's key founding groups, had been using co-operatives for years to pool their efforts and market their crops. Some farmers thought this approach should be used on a wider scale to benefit all citizens.

Others, including the new leader of the party, J.S. Woodsworth, believed that governments, as representatives of all citizens, should be more involved on their behalf in the economy. They wanted governments to provide, at a reasonable price, such necessities as water, hydro-electricity, transportation, and banking. Labour groups, another of the party's founding groups, wanted governments to ensure more protection for workers in difficult times. Workers' experiences in the previous years had taught them the need for laws regarding minimum wages, maximum hours, unemployment insurance, and workers' compensation for those injured on the job.

J.S. Woodsworth (sitting, at front, centre) was a church minister, social reformer, and labour leader. The party he led, the Co-operative Commonwealth Federation (CCF), pictured here, would eventually become the New Democratic Party (NDP).

Some employers labelled the CCF as communist and argued that its leaders should be arrested. Although some CCF leaders, like Woodsworth, did believe in getting rid of the capitalist system, they insisted that it must be done democratically by electing supporters to Parliament. Woodsworth, a former Methodist minister, had been a prominent member of Parliament since the early 1920s, so even his enemies could not accuse him of advocating the overthrow of government by violence. The CCF also operated democratically as a political party, giving local CCF organizations the power to select candidates for elections.

The CCF did not form a government during the 1930s, but it was the number two party in both British Columbia and Saskatchewan by 1934. It also was strong enough across the country to force Ottawa to consider the need for reform. (One of the strengths of both the CCF and its successor the NDP has been their ability to force the parties in power to adopt some of their policies.)

Social Credit

Just as the desperate conditions in Saskatchewan were partly responsible for the founding of the CCF, similar conditions in neighbouring Alberta gave birth to a new political party that became an amazing success story. **Social Credit** did not even exist as a formal political party until 1934; yet in the 1935 Alberta provincial election it won 56 of the province's 63 seats. Social Credit's incredible victory — gaining almost 90 percent of the legislature seats — was the result of three elements coming together at just the right time: a very popular, charismatic leader; a simple "solution" to the Depression that had tremendous appeal for ordinary Albertans; and the ongoing economic crisis that was driving many people to despair.

Alberta's Social Credit Party was the brainchild of a Calgary high school principal and radio preacher named William Aberhart. Aberhart's popular Sunday-afternoon radio sermons had a quarter of a million Alberta listeners. At first Aberhart preached only Christianity, but then he became convinced that the originally British economic theory of Social Credit was the answer to the Depression, and he began to preach that message. The idea behind Social Credit was that there were plenty of goods for sale in Canada but not enough money or credit in people's pockets to buy them. It was a situation of "poverty in the midst of plenty."

Aberhart proposed that the government give out "social credits" — dividends of twenty-five dollars a month for every Albertan — so that people could afford to buy. "Where does all the money come

the arts

WHY SHOOT THE TEACHER?

Despite the economic despair and the drought that ravaged crops on the Prairies, Canadians living in the West managed to survive the 1930s by relying on their own resourcefulness and the support of their neighbours. Max Braithwaite, one of Canada's best-known writers of humour, tells a story of life on the Prairies that is sometimes grim and sometimes hilarious, but always honest. The story is that of a young school teacher who accepts an ill-paid teaching assignment in an isolated school in Saskatchewan during the Great Depression.

In the following excerpts, the young teacher describes his first day on the Prairies and his experience at a community dance. As you read these excerpts, try to imagine how you would have reacted under similar circumstances. Continue the story by adding one or two paragraphs to either of the excerpts.

A HOME WHERE THE BUFFALO OUGHT TO ROAM

I didn't sleep well that first night in Willowgreen School District. The McDougall house was small and cold. There was no insulation in walls or ceiling and the house was heated, as were many prairie homes, by the kitchen range and a round ornate heater in the living room. Neither was kept burning all night. It just wasn't practical. McDougall had no coal to burn, and he couldn't be expected to stay up all night to shove wood into a stove.

Besides, who needs a fire at night? McDougall and his wife could certainly keep each other warm. The children slept together in their long, fleece-lined underwear and cuddled spoon style, generating enough heat for them. No provision was made for a visiting school-teacher. Why should there be? He was something foreign in the body of this culture.

When I awoke in the morning, it was pitch dark. I heard somebody in the kitchen clanging stove lids. Then I heard the kitchen door open and the sound of stamping feet. I knew it must be time to get up.

I slid my feet out from under the covers and onto the floor. Then I quickly slid them back again. The floor was like a block of ice. By fishing around on the floor I found my socks, wiggled into them, and made another try at the floor. This time I made it.

I found my pants, got a match from a pocket, and lit the coal-oil lamp. In the pale yellow light I could see frost clinging to the inside of the wall. Hurriedly I scrambled into my underwear and pants and picked up the big white pitcher to pour out some water. None came. A quarter of an inch of ice covered the surface. It was the first, but not the last, wash and shave I ever had in ice water.

THE DANCE

Over the course of the years I've attended dances in posh wardrooms, army messes, and ballrooms twenty times as big as Willowgreen School. I've waltzed, rhumba'd and cha cha'd to small combos and big bands whose members are world-renowned musicians. But the dance that sticks in my mind for all time is the one in Willowgreen School when Orville Jackson played the fiddle and Grandma Wilson chorded on the organ. I first got wind of it after school on Friday when, instead of slouching down the aisles making desultory passes at dust, Charlie McDougall and his band of helpers began by energetically pushing all the desks to the sides, back and front of the room.

"What's the idea?" I asked.

"Dance tonight."

"Here?"

"Yep."

"Who's coming?"

"Just about everybody in the district, I guess."

"Nobody said anything to me about it."

He merely shrugged at this and then, as an afterthought, "Oh yeah, Dad said to tell you they'll need your bed for the babies."

So they came, the old and the young, each with their bundles, many with babies. Some had come from as far as twelve miles, a three-hour journey over a winding snow trail. In the bottoms of their sleigh boxes they'd put stones, heated in the stove and wrapped in newspaper, for footwarmers. Some of the sleigh boxes were half filled with straw so that the children could snuggle down out of the wind like mice in a stack.

Why did they come? It was a break in the dreary drag of the winter months. They were sick to death of playing rummy and cribbage and the sound of each other's voices. They'd had a bellyfull of togetherness, babies, grandmothers, old-maid aunts, grown-up sons with no place to go, huddled in a few draughty rooms

like foxes in a den, satiated with the sight and sound and smell of each other. This was their chance to break out for a few hours, see different faces, hear some gossip. Find out about that cow of Mark Brownlee's that was due to calf, the vicissitudes of fate, the shortage of feed, the uselessness of the Bennett nickel — a five-cent bonus on every bushel of wheat paid through the good offices of a prime minister who, like everyone else, was rendered confused and inept by the magnitude of the depression.

EXCERPTED FROM MAX BRAITHWAITE, *WHY SHOOT THE TEACHER?* (TORONTO: MCCLELLAND AND STEWART, 1979), PP. 12-13, 51-52, 54-55.

from?" he asked his radio listeners. "We don't use money. Then where does all the credit come from? Why, out of the end of a fountain pen." Although most economists attacked Aberhart's ideas, his message appealed to the many Albertans frightened by poverty and debt. Aberhart swept into power in Alberta in 1935, but no social dividends were ever paid. Once in office, Aberhart gave Albertans a fiscally conservative government that was not too different from that of the federal Conservatives. Social Credit governments stayed in power in Alberta until 1971, and in British Columbia the party dominated almost continuously from 1952 until 1992.

Former teacher and preacher William "Bible Bill" Aberhart used radio broadcasts to get his Social Credit message to audiences across Alberta.

The Union Nationale

In Québec, Maurice Duplessis used the widespread demand for improved working conditions, aid to farmers, and an end to corruption in government to form a new party called the **Union Nationale**, which won power in 1936. Once he was in power, however, Duplessis made very few reforms. His main goal was a defence of Québec's national pride against the federal government's intrusion into provincial affairs. Although he was not a separatist, Duplessis pushed for more provincial self-government, or autonomy.

Duplessis' recipe for political success also included supporting Québec farmers with cheap loans, roads, and electrification programs. He also attacked those he considered to have communist connections. The Padlock Law of 1937 gave the Québec government power to lock the doors of and close down any organization suspected of having communist ties. This move won him support from the Roman Catholic Church in Québec because the Soviet Union, a communist country, had officially denied the existence of God.

Duplessis maintained the support of employers with his strong stand against unions and used provincial police on more than one occasion to break up strikes. There is ample evidence that he

Maurice Duplessis (centre) and the Union Nationale attracted large crowds in Québec. The main goals of the Union Nationale were to preserve French Canadian culture, gain provincial self-government, and limit the control of Québec business by English-speaking Canadians.

intimidated those who opposed him by threatening their jobs and the loss of government contracts. The Union Nationale also influenced elections by using faulty electoral lists, stuffed ballot boxes, and engaging in a variety of other illegal practices. But with the exception of the war years from 1939 to 1944, Duplessis remained in power until his death in 1959.

The Communist Party of Canada

The small but active Communist Party of Canada, under the leadership of Tim Buck, was busy staging rallies and organizing both workers and the unemployed. It wanted to begin a revolution that would completely change Canada's economic system. This threat of revolution, often referred to as the **"red menace"** (red was associated with revolution and was the colour of the flag of the communist Soviet Union) was feared by the Canadian government. The Communist Party of Canada was outlawed,

and Buck was jailed from 1932 until 1934. However, there was never a real danger of a revolution overthrowing the Canadian government.

Women and Politics in the 1920s

Many women continued to work hard for their right to vote. They believed that getting the vote would bring greater equality for women and allow them to have a more active role in public life. After some initial success, however, they too were disappointed. By 1920, women had won the right to vote in federal elections and in provincial elections in all provinces except Québec. The 1921 federal election was the first one in which women over the age of twenty-one could vote and run for political office. But of the five women who ran for Parliament, only one — Agnes Macphail, of Ontario — was elected.

Macphail, who was re-elected four times, was the only woman to sit as a member of Parliament until 1935. During that time she dealt with every kind of gender discrimination from her male colleagues. She gave as good as, and better than, she got. Treated condescendingly as a "lady," she retorted: "I'm not a lady, I'm an MP. This old-fashioned chivalry is all

Agnes Macphail: "I want for myself what I want for every woman — absolute equality."

hollow. It means nothing except that men think women inferior. I'm no gulf stream in the cold ocean of political life." At the other end of the spectrum, she endured vicious heckling such as, "Don't you wish you were a man?" She replied, "Don't you?"

Macphail advocated an organized national welfare system, including unemployment insurance and old-age pensions. In 1930, women students at the University of Toronto voted Agnes Macphail the woman they most wanted to be like. She was a peace supporter and spoke out passionately in favour of equal rights for women, equal pay, financial support for deserted wives, divorce, day care, and income-tax deductions for working wives — and she spoke alone.

Although Macphail won the admiration of many women, she was criticized by those who held traditional beliefs about the roles of women. Her response was, "If women are exclusively interested in private life and not in a place in the world, then they are not worthy of the franchise." Tired prematurely by her pursuit of justice, Agnes Macphail died on February 11, 1954, at the age of sixty-three. Canadian women are still acting on her simple advice: "A woman's place is any place she wants to be."

The Persons Case

When women were finally constitutionally recognized as "persons" in Canada in 1929, Agnes Macphail had already been a member of Parliament for seven years. Section 24 of the British North America Act declared that "qualified persons" could become senators, and other laws concerning government appointments contained similar declarations. But did women qualify as "persons" under the law? For years, government officials argued that women did not qualify, while women's groups argued that women were "persons." The debate became a see-saw legal battle spanning more than a decade. Five Alberta women reformers — The Famous Five — led the challenge: Emily Murphy, the first woman judge in the British Empire; Irene Parlby, the first woman Cabinet minister in Canada; Nellie McClung, a member of the Alberta legislature; and Henrietta Edwards and Louise McKinney, two suffragists and prohibitionists.

Emily Murphy (bottom right) led the battle to ensure that women were recognized as "persons" under the law.

Judge Emily Murphy led the fight. Lawyers appearing in Judge Murphy's court repeatedly objected that she was not a judge because she was not a "person" under the law for appointing judges. Day after day, Murphy noted the lawyers' objections, overruled them, and went on with the cases. Finally, in 1920, a lawyer tried to use the "persons" argument to get his bootlegger client — found guilty in Murphy's court — freed on the grounds of improper procedures. He appealed the case to the Supreme Court of Alberta, which ruled in Judge Murphy's favour: she was a "person" and therefore qualified to sit as a judge.

Murphy decided, however, that the provincial decision was not enough. She wanted to set a national precedent by asking the Supreme Court of Canada to state whether women qualified as "persons" in order to be named to the Senate. The Supreme Court of Canada decided in 1928 that women were not "persons," so Murphy and her supporters carried the battle all the way to the British **Privy Council**, the highest appeal court for Canadians at the time. The Privy Council ruled in favour of their claim in 1929, declaring that the "exclusion of women from all public offices is a relic of days more barbarous than ours." The court decision was a triumph for Canadian women, but after the "Persons Case" the women's movement lost momentum. It would not regain that momentum until the 1960s.

Web Connections

http://www.school.mcgrawhill.ca/resources

Go to the Web site above to find out more about The Famous Five and other Canadian women activists. Go to *History Resources*, then to *Canada: A Nation Unfolding, Ontario Edition* to find out where to go next.

Old Problems, New Solutions

In many ways, the 1920s and 1930s were formative political years for Canada. As a result of wide swings in the economy, the Canadian government came to play a far more active role in society. As poverty spread across the country, many Canadians believed that the traditional political parties were not doing enough to help their condition and began to support new parties such as the Co-operative Commonwealth Federation and the Social Credit Party. Other new parties, like the Union Nationale, fought to protect French culture in Québec. Nationally, after a long battle, women were officially recognized as persons in Canada. Canadians increasingly believed that governments should take an active role in securing the basic necessities of life for them — a role that would increase in years to come.

chapter review

CHAPTER SUMMARY

In this chapter we have seen

- how Mackenzie King remained Prime Minister for most of the 1920s and 1930s

- how R.B. Bennett attempted and failed to end the Depression, first through higher tariffs and then through a belated series of reforms that included minimum wages, better working conditions, unemployment insurance, and maximum hours

- how regional political parties, including the Co-operative Commonwealth Federation, the Union Nationale, and the Social Credit Party, emerged in response to the Depression

- how women finally achieved legal equality by winning the Persons Case in 1929

UNDERSTANDING HISTORICAL FACTS

1. Identify these people and events, and explain their historical significance.

   Agnes Macphail
   The Persons Case
   Bennett Buggy
   "Five-Cent Speech"
   Bennett's New Deal

   Co-operative Commonwealth Federation
   Union Nationale
   Social Credit Party
   Relief Camps

2. Identify some of Mackenzie King's strengths as Prime Minister.

3. Explain how R.B. Bennett would answer the criticism that up until 1935 his government had done nothing to try to end the Depression.

4. For each of the following party leaders, write one sentence that explains what that leader would say was the best way to end the Depression:

   a) J.S. Woodsworth (CCF)
   b) Maurice Duplessis (Union Nationale)
   c) William Aberhart (Social Credit)
   d) Tim Buck (Communist)

5. In your own words, explain the meaning and significance of the Persons Case decision.

EXPRESSING YOUR OPINION

1. How would each of the following have evaluated R.B. Bennett's efforts to end the Depression? In each case, explain your response:

   a) an unemployed worker
   b) a wheat farmer
   c) an Ontario manufacturer

2. Explain why you think Canadian voters defeated R.B. Bennett's Conservative government in 1935 and re-elected Mackenzie King's Liberals.

3. Which of the approaches to ending the Depression that was put forward by the regional political parties appeals to you the most? Why?

4. It is February 12, 1954, and Agnes Macphail has just died. Write an editorial for the newspaper to describe her place in Canadian history.

WORKING WITH THE EVIDENCE

1. Many economists attacked William Aberhart's plan to print and distribute money to end the Depression. At the time, the value of the Canadian dollar was tied to the country's gold reserves. What would have happened to the value of the Canadian dollar had the "social credit" been given but the gold reserves not expanded? Explain your answer.

2. P.L. Robertson invented a tool that was a vast improvement over its American counterpart. This tool is standard equipment in most Canadian garages but is virtually unknown to Americans. What is it?

Playing sports remained a popular leisure activity for both Canadian children and adults, despite the changing economic conditions.

INQUIRING INTO THE PAST

- **What were some of the ways in which Canadians would express the distinctiveness of the Canadian experience?**
- **How would technological changes in transportation and communication change the ways in which Canadians lived?**
- **How did Aboriginal and Black Canadians respond to the conditions they faced in the 1920s and 1930s?**
- **How were immigrants affected by the "Roaring Twenties" and the "Dirty Thirties"?**

KEY TERMS

Blind Pig

Bootlegging

Culture

Jazz Age

Potlatch

Residential Schools

Sun Dance

TIMELINE

1919
XWA, the world's first commercial radio station, begins broadcasting in Montreal

▶

1928
Pier 21 opens in Halifax

▶

1931
Maple Leaf Gardens is opened in Toronto

▶

1936
The Canadian Broadcasting Corporation is created in Ottawa

▶

In 1920 Canadians stood at the threshold of great national developments. In addition to moving toward increasing political independence and creating a more dynamic national economy, they were ready to expand the country's cultural horizons and to embrace the technological advances that had first appeared earlier in the century. As well, women emerged from World War I with greater expectations, having won the vote as a result of their contributions both at home and on the battlefields. Aboriginal and Black Canadians, along with immigrants arriving with dreams of starting new lives, would contribute to the increasing richness and diversity of Canadian life in the 1920s and 1930s. All of these changes would take place against the backdrop of economic recession, boom, and bust.

An Emerging Canadian Cultural Identity

In one sense, **culture** is simply the customs and way of life of people, especially particular groups of people. In the 1920s Canadian artists began to focus on the distinctive varieties of Canadian culture and to express these experiences to Canadians through their art. This was the case especially in literature and in painting.

The Arts

Nostalgia, the sentimental looking back at the past, was just as strong in the 1920s as it is now. The rural life that was quickly fading away became the focus of authors such as Ralph Connor, Sir Gilbert Parker, and Mazo De la Roche, whose *Jalna* and *Whiteoaks of Jalna* were romantic portrayals of rural Ontario life. Many French Canadian novels of the period, such as Ringuet's *Trente Arpents*, portrayed an ideal habitant life of small farms and a family-oriented, church-centred world at a time when Quebeckers were increasingly living in cities.

By contrast, other writers provided a more bleak portrayal of both urban and rural life in Canada. These included Germaine Guèvrement, Frederick Philip Grove, Martha Ostenso, and Morley Callaghan. Guèvrement's *Le survenant* tried to show

that many rural dwellers lived in a kind of cocoon, suspicious of anything that was not familiar.

In painting, the Group of Seven held that "an Art must grow and flower in the land before the country will be a real home for its people." The Seven, excluding Tom Thomson, who drowned tragically in 1917, originally included Lawren Harris, J.E.H. MacDonald, A.Y. Jackson, Arthur Lismer, Franklin Carmichael, Frank Johnston, and Fred Varley. They first painted scenes from Algonquin Park, the Algoma region, and Georgian Bay in Ontario's Canadian Shield. They then reached out to the Prairies, the Rocky Mountains, and the Arctic, as well as to Québec and Nova Scotia. They filled their canvases with brilliant, heavily layered colour and strong, sweeping forms to create a bold, new style of painting that celebrated Canada as a northern nation. Their work inspired others such as the Canadian Group of Painters, Montreal's Beaver Hall Group, and individual artists such as Emily Carr, Yvonne McKague Housser, Paraskeva Clark, Carl Shaefer, and David Milne. All these artists continued to experiment and to expand the body of distingushed Canadian art.

Tom Thomson drowned while on a canoe trip in Algonquin Park in 1917. His early paintings, like this one, *Afternoon, Algonquin Park*, helped to inspire the bold new style and spirit of Canadian painting.

the arts

ARTISTS OF THE 1920s AND 1930s

SOURCE: EMILY CARR, *BIG RAVEN*, 1931. CANVAS 87.3 x 114.4 CM.
COLLECTION VANCOUVER ART GALLERY, EMILY CARR TRUST

EMILY CARR

Born in Victoria, British Columbia, in 1871, Emily Carr became one of Canada's best-known painters. After studying art in San Francisco and making trips to England and France, Carr returned to Victoria, where her style began to take shape. By the late 1920s, Carr's paintings were becoming very popular. Influenced by the Group of Seven, Carr captured the wilderness and the way of life of Aboriginal people in the Queen Charlotte Islands.

PARASKEVA CLARK

Like Emily Carr, Paraskeva Clark was a Canadian woman who became well-known for her paintings; but here the similarities end. Clark, born in St. Petersburg, Russia, in 1898, moved to Canada with her Canadian-born husband in 1931. Clark's painting reflected the influence of Cubism, learned in Soviet studies, and contrasted sharply with the style of the Group of Seven. In her work, she focused on Toronto during the 1930s and 1940s, often reflecting the social distress of the Depression.

SOURCE: PARASKEVA CLARK, *PETROUSHKA*, 1937. COLLECTION OF THE NATIONAL GALLERY OF CANADA.
REPRODUCED WITH PERMISSION OF THE ESTATE OF PARASKEVA CLARK.

Technology and Society

In the 1920s radios, telephones, automobiles, airplanes, motion pictures, and many other modern conveniences became part of everyday life. The spread of new technologies and inventions in the 1920s and 1930s helped draw together a sprawling and sparsely populated country. The barriers of time and distance that had separated Canadians began to crumble.

Radio

In 1901 Canadian inventor Reginald Fessenden had become the first person to make a wireless transmission of the human voice when the joking message, "Is it snowing where you are, Mr. Thiessen?" crackled out to an assistant stationed 1600 metres away. The Italian physicist Guglielmo Marconi, however, is usually credited with inventing the radio. Marconi also set up the first commercial radio station in the world — XWA in Montréal. It hit the airwaves in 1919 with a medley of news, weather, and recorded music, and it still operates in Montreal today as the English-language station CFCF.

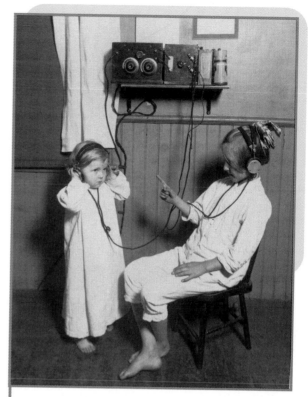

Imagine the excitement for these children as they get their first opportunity to listen to a new radio!

XWA, Montréal became the world's first commercial radio station. How would radio change the lives of Canadians in the 1920s?

Three years later, on July 22, 1922, radio station CKCK in Regina, owned and operated by *The Leader* newspaper, made its first broadcast. To understand the significance of radio in the lives of the people of Saskatchewan, consider that, according to the 1921 census, over 70 percent of the province's population lived on farms that were often great distances from their neighbours. Only a few farms had telephones or automobiles, and during the long prairie winters most families were housebound. Newspapers were already a few days old when they arrived, so the news and weather reports were out of date before they were read. Radio quickly began to break down this isolation.

From the mid-1920s on, radio became easier to use as a result of the efforts of Ted Rogers, a brilliant young electronics engineer in Toronto. His invention allowed the radio to be plugged directly into household electrical current, freeing it from dependence on batteries. Rogers's radio station was called CFRB. The "CF" indicated a Canadian station, and

"RB" stood for "Rogers Batteryless." From having fewer than ten thousand radios in 1923, Canadians owned an astounding 297 000 radios by 1929.

By 1924 there were fifty-one radio stations across Canada. The first national radio network began in 1923, when Canadian National Railways (CNR) installed radio receivers on its trains as a promotion to gain more passengers. By combining its own stations with those that it picked up from towns along the rail line, the CNR created the first coast-to-coast radio network. However, most of the programs that people listened to were provided by American broadcast networks such as the Columbia Broadcasting System (CBS) and the National Broadcasting Corporation (NBC). They featured early soap operas, crime and western dramas, comedy, and coverage of major sports events. One exception was the new Canadian sports show called "Hockey Night in Canada."

On March 22, 1923, a twenty-year-old reporter for *The Toronto Star*, Foster Hewitt, sat in a cramped glassed-in box in Toronto's Mutual Street arena and provided the first play-by-play broadcast of a Toronto Maple Leafs' hockey game. Generations of hockey fans across the country grew up hearing the sounds of Hewitt's distinctive, "He shoots! He scores!" and he became known as "the voice of hockey."

This experimental national network did not ease the serious concerns about the effects of the inflow of American culture on Canada. The Aird Commission, established in 1928 to review the broadcasting situation, made recommendations that led to the creation of the Canadian Radio Broadcasting Commission in 1932. In 1936 this commission was reorganized as the Canadian Broadcasting Corporation — the CBC — which provided quality programming that focused on national, educational, and non-commercial purposes. The creation of the CBC began the process of developing and focusing on Canadian content in the electronic media.

In the Depression years of the 1930s, radio became a central feature in the lives of many Canadian families. It brought drama, real and imagined, that cut into the daily gloom of unemployment, wage cuts, poor farm crops, and even

Hockey Night in Canada started in 1923, when Foster Hewitt gave play-by-play commentary for the Toronto Maple Leafs. Why would Hewitt's broadcasts help make hockey a national sport?

poorer prices for crops. Light-hearted shows like *The Happy Gang* not only entertained, but were "interactive" by responding to thousands of audience requests and making use of their jokes. At the same time, CBC radio offered Canadian programs as alternatives to American shows and provided radio service to remote areas in Canada. It helped to end regional isolation and to foster a sense of Canadian national unity.

Telephones and Automobiles

Few Canadians had telephones in 1920, but by 1929 three out of four families had one. Telephone networks made long-distance calls faster and more reliable. The early telephone networks linked a number of customers to the same telephone line (a "party-line"), so it was possible to listen in or eavesdrop on someone else's conversation. Canadians enthusiastically embraced another way to overcome the country's vast distances from inside their homes at the same time that the automobile began to make travel more convenient.

By 1930 over a million automobiles were registered in Canada. In Toronto the number of cars registered increased 800 percent, to over 80 000,

Humour in History

THE HAPPY GANG!

Here we are: the Happy Gang's here
Here we are: How do you do?
Here we are to chase away your troubles
With a song, a melody or two
So gather 'round, come on, let's get together
And we'll start our program with a bang!
For it's time to laugh and sing and shout out
With the Hap, Hap, Happy Gang!

If you were a CBC radio listener in the late 1930s, you probably would have heard this opening theme song for *The Happy Gang* radio program. This popular Canadian-made show ran from June 1937 to 1958 and could be heard from Monday to Friday. *The Happy Gang* was a response to a major CBC goal — to create Canadian-produced content.

Happy Gang fan Robert Just, originally from Nova Scotia, vividly remembers some of the skits from the Happy Gang. One of the cast members, Bobby Gimby, impersonated a grumpy old lady named Aunt Frieda. Aunt Frieda had a thick European accent and always complained about her ailments. One day, Robert Just recalls, Aunt Frieda was complaining to her friend about her new doctor:

"Oh that doctor! He's so fresh. The last time I saw him, I had to slap his face."
"Why?" the friend asked.
"He told me I had a-cute appendicitis," replied Aunt Frieda.

"It was very corny humour," Robert Just fondly remembers. "But it was a welcome relief from the troubles of the day — especially later, during the war years."

---

between 1916 and 1928. By 1930 the country's 128 000 kilometres of surfaced roads were literally laying the foundation of a revolution. Cities spread as "suburbs" began to develop, and the surrounding countryside became more accessible as well. Cars made visits to family, friends, and other social events easier.

But automobiles were anything but reliable. Headlights, clutches, and brakes were apt to fail. It was not unusual to have ten flat tires in a two-hundred-kilometre trip. By the end of the 1930s, however, the boxy-looking black Model Ts had given way to sleek, colourful, and elegant automobile designs. Car interiors became spacious and comfortable, and the automatic transmission was revolutionizing driving.

New Technology on the Farm

In the countryside, too, trucks were being increasingly used to make the trip from farm to grain elevator, and the improvements of both cars and roads made marketing easier for farm families. But trucks

Many Canadians were buying motor cars in the 1920s. Closed cars and better roads paved the way for luxury motoring.

and cars were not the only technological changes reshaping farm life in the 1920s and 1930s.

The number of horses on Canadian farms reached its peak in 1926 and then declined in the face of the new and improved machinery that took over more and more of the workload. By the early 1920s a standard form of the tractor had begun to emerge. Perhaps the most significant technological change in the 1920s, especially for wheat production on the Prairies, was the new combine, so named because it "combined" reaping and threshing. This harvester and thresher not only shortened the harvest period in an area with a short growing season, it replaced nearly a dozen men in the threshing crew as well as all of the hand labour previously involved in harvesting.

Air Travel and Transport

Travel in the 1920s and 1930s was mostly done by automobile, railway, and ship. There was only one scheduled air-passenger service in Canada until 1927, when a few more city-to-city links were started. Although there were many Canadian aviation companies in the 1930s, Canada did not have an official national airline system until the federal government established Trans-Canada Air Lines (TCA) in 1937.

When Trans-Canada Air Lines began commercial service in 1937, passengers flew in these luxury ten-seat Lockheed Electras.

By 1939, TCA had fifteen American-made ten-passenger Lockheed planes, since there was no Canadian airplane manufacturing industry. On April 1, 1939, TCA's first passenger flight took off from Vancouver for Montreal. The trip, including several stops, took fifteen hours — compared with three days and four nights by train — but the one-way fare was $130.90, a price only the well-off could afford.

Motion Pictures

Motion pictures, already known as "movies," had been showing to paying customers since 1896. By the 1920s, big American producers were emerging, and their control of the distribution of films through "chains" of movie theatres squeezed out both Canadian film production and the fledgling made-in-Canada chains. One Canadian company, the Allen chain, began in 1906 in Brantford, Ontario, and by 1919 owned forty-five movie theatres. By 1923, however, it had been overtaken by the American distribution network Famous Players Canadian Corp.

Canadians loved Hollywood movies and idolized American film stars like Charlie Chaplin,

The combine reaped and threshed wheat in one operation. What negative results would occur because of this technological marvel?

Rudolph Valentino, and Greta Garbo. Many talented Canadians headed for Hollywood, seeking — and sometimes finding — fame and fortune. Mary Pickford, known and loved across North America as "America's Sweetheart," was born Gladys May Smith in Toronto in 1893. She became the most popular film actress of the 1920s. With her husband, Douglas Fairbanks, and Charlie Chaplin, Mary Pickford founded the motion-picture studio United Artists in 1919.

In an effort to encourage a Canadian film industry, the federal government funded agencies to make Canadian films, but most of the resulting movies were expensive failures like the movie *Fishing Just for Fun*. Major success for the Canadian film industry did not come until the National Film Board (NFB), a crown corporation, was founded to produce Canadian films in 1939.

Canadian-born Mary Pickford became a major film star in the United States, where she was regarded as "America's Sweetheart" in the 1920s.

The Jazz Age

The term **Jazz Age** is often used to describe the culture of the United States in the 1920s. One of the reasons is that jazz, as a revolutionary form of music, became tremendously popular during these years. A blending of European and West African musical traditions, it originated among Black

American artists in New Orleans in the 1800s and had evolved into a variety of forms by the early twentieth century, including the blues and ragtime. Jazz artists like Louis Armstrong, Bessie Smith, and Duke Ellington became famous and, with the help of radio, helped the Jazz Age to spill over into Canada. The first Canadian jazz recording, "St. Louis Blues," was made by the Gilbert Watson Orchestra of Toronto in 1926. Although the musical jazz age ended around this time, its rhythms continued to emerge in popular music.

Jazz music took the 1920s by storm. Originating in New Orleans, jazz's innovative use of brass instruments, drums, bass, and piano made it popular in nightclubs throughout North America and Europe. Groups like the Elks Jazz Band, seen in this photograph, brought the sound of jazz to Canadian cities in the 1920s.

Canadian Chautauqua

The Jazz Age was generally an urban middle-class phenomenon. In the countryside, the "big show in town" was more likely to be a kind of travelling variety show called Chautauqua. Under a big brown tent, one might find a lecturer showing off the latest wonder of the world — the radio — or magic acts, puppets, and live theatre. Taking its name from the lake in New York state where it began, Chautauqua was brought to Canada in 1916 by John Erickson. Speakers were the core of the program, and their topics ranged from the new technologies to talks on war, peace, exploration, women's suffrage, and poli-

PHOTO ESSAY

"WHAT WE WERE WEARING"

High-society fashion à la Mayfair. The "smart young man" (paying a
much attention) sports a new, short dinner jacket combination – the T

tics. Music, an important part of the program, ranged from classical to popular numbers and from Swiss bell-ringers and Hawaiian groups to Scottish bagpipers. From the last years of the Great War until the mid-1930s, these three- to six-day shows were an important part of rural Canadian culture, especially in the West.

The Great Depression was partly responsible for the decline of Chautauqua, as fewer towns could afford the show. Radios and the movies also took their toll; people turned to these new forms of entertainment. Although Chautauqua disappeared, it left a legacy of having entertained, informed, uplifted, and distracted its audiences during a time when there were few other forms of entertainment.

Football was a popular spectator sport in Canada in the 1920s.

The Explosion of Spectator Sports

In the 1920s larger cities, more leisure time, the return of a measure of prosperity, and the creation of mass markets through radio and newspapers provided the context for a virtual explosion of professional sport, both in the United States and in Canada. In the United States, fans in the thousands watched as George Herman "Babe" Ruth hit home run after home run for the New York Yankess.

By 1927 the National Hockey League (NHL) was big business in the growing cities. It began with ten teams: two in New York, two in Montréal, and one each in Ottawa, Toronto, Detroit, Boston, Pittsburgh, and Chicago. Football, lacrosse, baseball, and track and field were also very popular in Canada in the 1920s.

Although high unemployment during the Depression had a negative impact on all spectator sports, enthusiasm for them was kept alive through extensive newspaper reporting and live radio broadcasts.

Women in Sport

The 1920s and early 1930s have been called the "Golden Age of Sports" for women. Many youth groups, especially the Young Women's Christian Association (YWCA), encouraged organized physical activities and games for young women. The biggest change was in the growth of women's amateur sports and athletic clubs. Basketball and baseball were among the popular sports. The Canadian women's basketball team the Edmonton Grads were the most successful team in competitive basketball. Over their twenty-year history, the Edmonton Grads won an astounding 502 out of 522 games, as well as winning four Olympic gold medals.

Women also made their mark in other sports. Gladys Robinsen won a speed skating title at Lake Placid in 1921, while Lela Brooks set six world records in speed skating in 1926. Ethel Smith won gold in Amsterdam at the 1928 Olympics in the 4 x 100 metre relay, while "the Saskatoon Lily," Ethel Catherwood, took gold in the high jump. Fanny "Bobbie" Rosenfeld, an all-round athlete, set Canadian records in the broad jump (now called the long jump). A magnificent athlete, Rosenfeld also set records in discus throwing and long-jumping and was a star tennis and hockey player. She was named to Canada's Sports Hall of Fame as an all-round athlete. In 1934, swimmer Phyllis Dewar of Moose Jaw, Saskatchewan, won four gold medals

The Edmonton Grads were the most successful basketball team in history. Why do you think interest in women's sports such as basketball declined during the 1930s?

at the British Empire Games.

In the depths of the depressed 1930s and later, women were pushed back into more traditional roles. By the mid-1930s doctors and educators were arguing that women were too delicate for competitive sports like baseball, and "girls' rules" were introduced to restrict physical contact, limit exertion, and keep women's sports "feminine." After that, women's sports went into an eclipse until the 1960s.

Fanny "Bobbie" Rosenfeld was the only woman to be named to Canada's Sports Hall of Fame as an all-around athelete.

Prohibition

One topic that dominated conversation during the 1920s and 1930s was Prohibition. Canada had introduced anti-liquor legislation during World War I, and by 1918 every province except Québec had followed suit. Prohibition brought benefits at first; once saloons and bars shut down, there was less public drunkenness and domestic violence. But even though Prohibition was created to end social ills, it created a new set of problems.

Much of the Canadian criminal activity in the 1920s and early 1930s resulted from American Prohibition, which was in effect in the United States from 1919 to 1933. By law, the United States was a "dry" country. But many "dry" Americans were thirsty and willing to pay for illegal alcohol. Even during Prohibition, Canadian liquor laws allowed distilleries on the Prairies to make liquor for "non-drinking" purposes, such as medical uses. Much of this alcohol was sold illegally to the "dry" Americans.

Profits from **bootlegging** (the illegal sale of alcoholic beverages) were enormous. A case of twelve bottles of liquor could be bought in Saskatchewan for about $50 and sold for $300 south of the border. Smuggling Canadian bootleg liquor into the United States — sometimes called

Many "rum-runners" looked for creative ways to smuggle liquor into the United States. How many bottles of liquor do you think this man could smuggle while wearing a large overcoat?

rum-running — became big business. "**Blind pigs**" — places where liquor could be bought illegally — popped up across Canada. Some of Canada's wealthiest families got their start by selling illegal alcohol during American Prohibition.

The attraction of huge profits from the illegal trade quickly drew machine-gun-toting American mobsters, and they brought with them gang warfare, murder, and the corruption of police, judges, and government officials. The lawlessness spilled across the Canadian border. Prohibition began to look like as much of a social evil as the drunkenness it tried to stop.

The determination of the American government to stop the smuggling peaked in 1929, when the Nova Scotia schooner *I'm Alone* attempted to sneak alcohol into the United States. As long as the schooner remained outside the territorial waters of the United States, it could not be arrested by the U.S. Coast Guard. After being pursued for two days, and despite being well out in international waters, the *I'm Alone* was captured and sunk by cannon fire. Despite the controversy created by this incident, Canadians continued to smuggle alcohol into the United States until Prohibition ended in 1933.

Fighting for a Voice

Some groups of Canadians experienced the worst of both decades. They did not share in the prosperity of the Roaring Twenties, and they suffered even worse than most people during the Great Depression. Limited in the jobs they could obtain, restricted by government policies, and discriminated against by fellow Canadians, groups such as the Aboriginal peoples, Black Canadians, and women faced harsh conditions throughout the 1920s and 1930s. But each group found its own ways to resist being swept under the carpets by the rest of Canadian society.

Aboriginal Peoples

Canada's Aboriginal peoples continued to suffer discrimination and poverty in the years after World War I. Since the Canadian government had taken over responsibility for Aboriginal peoples in 1867, it was official government policy to try and assimilate them — to make them a part of White culture. Efforts were made to take away every sign of tribal life. Bans on traditional ceremonies like the **sun dance** of some prairie tribes and the **potlatch** of the Northwest Coast peoples were enforced in the early 1920s.

One of the easiest ways to assimilate the Aboriginal peoples was to take their children from reserves to government-established **residential schools**, where the children would be far from their cultures. This approach was part of a policy of "aggressive civilization." Anything that connected students to their Aboriginal heritage was excluded in residential schools. Traditional religious practices were forbidden, and if the children spoke their own language, they were severely punished. They were dressed in European clothes and groomed to become English-speaking Canadians.

Although this system continued for several decades, Aboriginal people tried to resist these efforts of containment and assimilation. In the 1920s some of them emerged to lead the struggle for economic and cultural survival. Mohawk Chief F.O. Loft of Ontario had fought in World War I. On returning to Canada after the war, he

Despite government efforts to assimilate them into White culture, Aboriginal people organized themselves into groups to fight for their rights. Here, a delegation meets with Manitoba Premier John Bracken in 1929 to negotiate resource rights.

tried to draw public attention to the plight of his people. Frustrated by the lack of concern, Loft organized a national group called the League of Indians. He wanted Aboriginal people to have the right to vote without having to give up their special status and to have greater control over their reserves and funds. Aboriginal leaders elsewhere also organized groups such as the Native Brotherhood of British Columbia, founded by Haida and Tsimshian chiefs to represent Aboriginal fishers. These new organizations marked the beginning of Aboriginal activism that would blossom in the 1960s.

Black Canadians

By the 1920s most Black Canadians lived in cities, especially Halifax, Montréal, Toronto, and Vancouver. They faced discrimination in all areas of life, including employment. For example, in the 1920s and 1930s, although Black men worked as general labourers, janitors, waiters, barbers, and porters, the job of security guard was closed to them. Black women were even more restricted in the jobs they could obtain. At the outbreak of World War I, at least 80 percent of Black women in Canadian cities worked as domestic servants.

In 1919 a Black man from Montréal sued a local theatre for forcing him to sit in the balcony. The theatre was found not guilty of any offence. In 1924 an Ontario court handed down a judgment that said refusing to serve Black people in restaurants and bars or only in segregated seating areas was legal because there was no law saying it was illegal. Until the federal and provincial governments passed laws making these actions illegal, the courts were actually put into the position of defending racial discrimination, which is the practice of treating people differently, usually unfairly, because of their race. Until the larger Canadian public refused to accept these practices and forced governments to pass anti-discrimination and human-rights laws, this discrimination continued.

Working in the sleeping cars of Canada's railways, many Black Canadian men formed the Canadian Brotherhood of Sleeping Car Porters. What kind of support would this offer to Black Canadian men?

It is not surprising that in these conditions Black Canadians looked to themselves for encouragement and support. Everywhere in Canada, as well as in the United States, Black people found relief and comfort in their churches. Black women were the driving force behind the church-sponsored social services that kept the community together. Church leaders were also often the spokespersons who worked for change in the larger community.

Black men often worked the sleeping cars on Canada's railways, setting up and taking down the beds on the long runs across Canada's great distances. They formed the Canadian Brotherhood of Sleeping Car Porters and won union status within the Canadian Brotherhood of Railway Workers. Their job allowed them to keep in touch with Black communities across the country. It's no accident that Black advocates of civil rights, like Harry Gairey, emerged from this group. Gairey later wrote a memoir called *A Black Man's Toronto, 1914–1980.* Anti-discrimination laws were not passed in Canada until the 1940s and later, but the groundwork was laid earlier by the Black men and women who built the sense of community and raised Canadians' awareness of discrimination.

Women

Frequently people who have examined the terrible years of the Great Depression have focused on the desperate efforts of single — and some married — men to find work by "riding the rods" across Canada. But women also faced horrendous circumstances. The 1930s showed clearly that deeply rooted ideas about the place of women in society had not changed, in spite of women gaining the vote after World War I. When jobs became scarce after 1929, many people believed the remaining jobs should go to men and that women, especially married women, should return to their "natural" place — the home. As Mederic Martin, former mayor of Montréal, put it:

Wouldn't national life be happier, saner, safer if a great many of these men [the unemployed] could be given work now being done by women, even if it meant that these women would have to sacrifice their financial independence, go home to be supported by father, husband, or brother as they were in the old pre-feministic days?

In the workplace, women faced still more problems. Of the twenty-five work categories listed at the time, over 70 percent of working women were concentrated in only six: textiles and clothing (sewing and repetitious needlework); retail and wholesale trade (typists and sales clerks); education, health, and welfare services (teachers, nurses, and case workers); food and lodging (maids and cleaners); and personal and recreational services (domestic servants). This meant that there was always an oversupply of workers for the available jobs. The result was frequent lay-offs and the workers' inability to refuse poor working conditions.

After their contributions in the workplace during World War I and the winning of the vote shortly after it, many women expected to see the dawning of "a new day" of freedom from the old stereotypes and restrictions. Although many achieved personal victories and made significant contributions, the "new day" did not dawn in the workplace for most women in the 1920s and 1930s.

Immigration in the 1920s

There was much debate about immigration in Canada in the 1920s. During World War I immigration had dropped to a trickle, compared with the flood during the boom years after the turn of the century. It was not until the last years of the 1920s, with the short-lived return of prosperity, that annual immigration figures topped 150 000. The argument in favour of more immigration was that more settlers would mean more revenue and larger markets.

At the same time, there was a focus on the types of immigrants that were coming to Canada. The questions asked included: Had too many non-British been allowed in? Could they be "absorbed" into British "civilization"? As the premier of British Columbia put it in 1923, "We are anxious to keep this a British country. We want British and nothing else." His beliefs were supported by many others, including Conservative

Party leader R.B. Bennett, many leading doctors, politicians, educators, and journalists.

French Canadians also were concerned about how immigration would affect their position in the country. They recognized that wherever the immigrants came from, they were not coming from French-speaking countries. They were therefore not likely to adopt the French language and French culture. Some French Canadians believed this could lead to francophones becoming an increasingly smaller minority in the nation. They were worried about how this might affect their position in Canada.

The Gateway to Canada: Pier 21

Almost all of the immigrants coming to Canada from Europe after 1928 arrived at Pier 21 in the port of Halifax. Between 1928 and 1971 more than 1.5 million immigrants first set foot in Canada at this pier. Upon arriving, immigrants were inspected for signs of illness. If no illnesses were detected, they received papers granting them the status of "landed immigrant." Then they purchased train tickets from one of the railways, and if they were lucky to have money left over they might buy a few basic food items such as cheese, bread, and canned meat. Finally they boarded the trains that would take them to a new and (they hoped) better life than the one they had left behind.

Many found the land of opportunity that was promised to them, but others faced a harsh reality of broken promises. Young children and adults were often used as cheap labour, working as servants or factory workers. The work was tough, the hours long, the pay small, and the conditions poor. This was the Canada that many immigrants who came through Pier 21 experienced. But many of them persevered by whatever means they could and made a life for themselves in the young country. The character, courage, and determination of the people arriving at Pier 21 were essential aspects of the foundation of the developing Canadian nation.

Shovelling Out the Poor

While discrimination against immigrants was evident in the 1920s, hostility toward them increased as the Depression deepened. Labour groups believed that because immigrants would work for less pay, they were stealing jobs away from Canadian-born workers. The truth, however, is that immigrants suffered more than Canadian-born workers did. Immigrants were often refused any type of relief, and the government began to deport them from Canada. They could be deported for various reasons, including any physical or mental disability, infectious disease, and unemployment. This was called "shovelling out the unemployed," and it happened all across the country to people who were out of work through no fault of their own. Recent immigrants were usually the first people laid off by employers and were therefore more vulnerable to the deportation laws.

Surviving in the 1930s

The 1930s were dark times for many other Canadians. Some people found it hard to say anything good about these years, which were sometimes called "the years of despair." Said one survivor who was asked to talk about the Great Depression: "The Dirty Thirties! Might say I never took a backward step in my life until that Depression whipped me, took away my wife, my home, a section of good land back in Saskatchewan. Left me with nothing. Write that down."

Other Canadians responded to the Depression with humour and swapped Depression jokes, like this one about a farmer in the notorious "dustbowl" of Saskatchewan: "In a high wind, a farmer went to

Canadian Pacific Steamships continued to try to attract immigrants to Canada. Why would Canadian Pacific benefit from immigrants coming to Canada? What does this poster say about the type of immigrants it wanted?

the bank to get a loan on his property. The banker said, 'I'd kinda like to see your land.' Just then, a big gust hit the side of the bank, and the farmer answered, 'Well, open up your window, cuz here she comes.'" Although, in many ways, the Depression brought people closer together, more often it created deep divisions in Canadian society.

Recreation

Many other Canadians looked for ways to escape the worries of the Depression years — at least for a while. Many made do with homemade entertainment. They played sandlot baseball in the summer and football in the fall. Curling became a favourite winter pastime. At school, children played games of curling with jam tins filled with frozen mud and looped with wire handles. There were old-fashioned pleasures like horse races, picnics, swimming, and berry picking, as well as sleighrides, school plays, and church socials to keep people entertained.

Above all there were the "talkies" — motion pictures complete with sound. Canadians who could find the 25¢ to 50¢ for a ticket could see Alberta-born actress Fay Wray swinging in the hairy grasp of King Kong or a young Judy Garland skipping down the yellow brick road in *The Wizard of Oz*. At the end of this era, *Gone With the Wind*, released in late 1939 and starring Clark Gable and Vivien Leigh, became the world's most-watched movie.

The Best of Times, The Worst of Times

Life in Canada in the 1920s and 1930s was characterized by dramatic technological change and equally dramatic economic and social ups and downs. The widespread use of radio, telephones, and automobiles, as well as the beginnings of the air age and a wide array of new consumer products, improved communication among Canadians and changed forever the way they lived. This generation of Canadians experienced the economic and cultural peak of the Jazz Age as well as the deep despair of the worst economic depression of the century. Immigrants were welcomed and offered opportunities to begin a new life, but they were also frequently the first victims of the Great Depression. Women, Black Canadians, and Aboriginal people found new ways to organize, express, and support themselves, but as the 1930s ended, their struggles to find a genuine and secure place in Canadian society continued.

Web Connections

http://www.school.mcgrawhill.ca/resources

Go to the Web site above to find out more about Pier 21. Go to *History Resources*, then to *Canada: A Nation Unfolding, Ontario Edition*, to find out where to go next.

chapter review

CHAPTER SUMMARY

In this chapter we have seen

- how artists like the members of the Group of Seven and institutions like the Canadian Broadcasting Corporation helped establish a distinctive Canadian culture

- how technological changes such as the radio, the telephone, movies, and the automobile brought about great social and cultural changes

- how people lived during the excitement of the Jazz Age and the gloom of the Great Depression

- how women, new immigrants, Black Canadians, and Aboriginal peoples dealt with the challenges they faced during the 1920s and 1930s

UNDERSTANDING HISTORICAL FACTS

1. Identify the following people, places, and events, and explain their historical significance.

Group of Seven	Combine
Ted Rogers	Chautauqua
Mary Pickford	*I'm Alone*
"Bobbie" Rosenfeld	Pier 21

2. Why are the 1920s and early 1930s considered the "Golden Age of Sports" for Canadian women?

3. Design a poster to advertise a Canadian Chautauqua. Think of reasons why the Chautauqua appealed to so many people, and include these elements in your poster.

4. What evidence of emerging activism among social groups can be found in the 1920s and 1930s?

5. Create a visual time line that shows the major events in Canadian society during the 1920s and 1930s. Choose at least six events and include a drawing or photograph that captures each date.

EXPRESSING YOUR OPINION

1. Write a newspaper editorial on one of the following topics in which you argue for a particular course of action, and give as many supporting reasons as possible for taking this course of action. Your arguments should reflect the conditions that existed at the time.
   a) the proper role of government in protecting and promoting Canadian culture
   b) discrimination in Canada — where it is and what to do about it

2. Compose a dialogue between a government official who really believes that residential schools are the best thing for Aboriginal people and an Aboriginal person who does not.

3. Why was the Canadian Broadcasting Corporation created? Is there still a need today for a government-funded radio and television corporation to ensure quality Canadian programs?

4. Considering the scandals that occurred during Prohibition, which method is a more effective way to deal with the problems brought on by excessive drinking: regulating alcohol or imposing an outright ban?

WORKING WITH THE EVIDENCE

1. In 1923, Foster Hewitt first exclaimed "He shoots! He scores!" Nearly seven decades later, the first hockey game broadcast in Cree took place in Québec. Why could the play-by-play announcers not use Hewitt's famous line in their broadcast?

2. During the 1920s many slang terms were used. How many of these slang terms can you translate?

swanky	horse feathers	giggle water
cheaters	high hat	heebie jeebie

Canada's Growing Autonomy

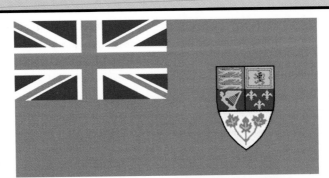

After World War I Canada began to pull away from the imperialist ties that bound it tightly to Britian. At the same time, its relationship with the United States was growing stronger. How autonomous do you think Canada could ever really be?

INQUIRING INTO THE PAST

- **What were the main reasons for Canada to want increased independence from Britain in the 1920s?**
- **Why would Canadians not want to become involved in crises outside of Canada in the 1920s and 1930s?**
- **In what ways would closer ties between Canada and the United States influence Canadians?**

KEY TERMS

Autonomy

Direct Investment

Foreign Policy

High Commissioner

Imperial Conference

Portfolio Investment

Sovereignty

TIMELINE

1919 ▶
Canada becomes a member of the League of Nations

1922 ▶
Canada refuses Imperial demands at Chanak

1926 ▶
Imperial Conference recognizes Canada's autonomy

1931 ▶
Statute of Westminster formally recognizes Canada's independence

Canadians came out of World War I with a greater national self-confidence and a deeper understanding of the effects of war. Canada's record of wartime bravery had much to do with its march to political **autonomy** in the 1920s. Mackenzie King, Prime Minister during most of the 1920s and 1930s, saw an important connection between achieving autonomy from Britain and maintaining national unity. He made both of these his main goals during his years as Prime Minister.

At the same time that Canada was gradually achieving independence from Britain, it was developing closer economic and cultural ties to the United States. Although most Canadians enjoyed this growing influence, there were some concerns, especially in the area of public broadcasting, about its long-term effects. Close economic ties meant that whatever happened to the American economy would happen to Canada's as well. The 1920s and 1930s revealed both the positive and negative effects of this relationship.

The Growth of Canada's Autonomy

After the war both Canada and its new Prime Minister had had enough of European conflicts. In the early 1920s Mackenzie King was intent on keeping Canada out of any future wars on the other side of the Atlantic. King wanted Canada to free itself from British foreign policy and to determine its own relations with other nations. He had, after all, seen at first-hand the divisions within Canada that had resulted from its past involvement in British foreign affairs.

As a member of the Liberal Party, King had watched Sir Wilfrid Laurier try, and fail, to steer a middle way through the Boer War and naval issues. The strong pro- and anti-British sentiments about these issues in Canada were partly responsible for Laurier's defeat in the election of 1911. The results of the 1921 election reinforced King's conclusion that Canada's involvement in foreign affairs was politically dangerous. The Conservative Party, now led by Arthur Meighen, had introduced conscription in World War I under Robert Borden and had paid a terrible price. In Québec, where anti-con-

scription riots had broken out, Meighen's Conservatives had won only three of sixty-five seats. For most of the next two decades both King and the majority of Canadians were in agreement: neither wanted anything to do with foreign involvements.

King knew that the best way to stay clear of foreign entanglements was for Canada to become a completely autonomous country. Only by being truly independent could Canada control its own foreign policy. In this area, World War I had paved the way. Canada's great contributions and sacrifices had gained it a separate seat at the Paris Peace Conference and an ability to sign the various peace treaties independently. Canada's participation also led to membership in the new League of Nations. Although membership in the league would cause King problems in the future, in the early 1920s it provided a foundation upon which he could build Canada's independence from Britain.

The Chanak Affair

The first test of Mackenzie King's goals came in 1922. As part of the peace treaty agreements after World War I, Britain had agreed to keep some troops in Chanak, a village in Turkey. Their task was to keep the Dardenelles, straits that linked the Black Sea to the Mediterranean Sea, a neutral territory. In 1922, however, the small British garrison was threatened by Turkish forces under the nationalist leader Mustapha Kemal.

Britain called upon its empire to help it protect the straits. A delay in telegram service meant that King read about Britain's request for help in the same place that other Canadians did — the morning paper! After consulting with his Cabinet, King informed British Prime Minister Lloyd George that he would not think of sending troops to Chanak without first consulting Canada's Parliament. And he had no intention, yet, of calling it into session. In doing this, King was announcing that Canada would no longer automatically commit to fight at Britain's side whenever the British demanded it. He was more aware of war-weary Canadians than was Conservative leader Arthur Meighen, who stated that Canada's response should have been, "Ready, aye Ready; we stand by you." By the time the issue

With the horrors of World War I fresh in their minds, many Canadians had no desire to send troops to help Britain in the Chanak affair. How does this cartoon, from the Québec newspaper *Le Soleil*, show this feeling?

had been debated in the House of Commons, the threat at Chanak had passed. Nevertheless, King had made his point: Parliament would decide the role that Canada would play in external affairs.

King suspected that the British were using Chanak to see how much support there was in the empire for a common Imperial foreign policy — a policy that Britain would, of course, control. His suspicions were confirmed in 1923, when he attended an Imperial Conference, a meeting of all the member countries of the British Empire. There, Britain indeed tried to persuade delegates to stay united in support of British foreign policy. But King reminded Britain that Canada was a self-governing country. He insisted that "the decision of Canada on any important issue, domestic or foreign, we believe should be made by the people of Canada." The British foreign secretary was deeply unhappy with the Canadian Prime Minister's insistence on Canadian indepen-

dence, but King held his ground. Canada was to be autonomous in its foreign (external) policy as well as in its domestic (internal) policy.

The Balfour Declaration

Mackenzie King wanted a formal declaration of autonomy for Canada, and he received it at another **Imperial Conference** in 1926. Here, nations such as Canada, Australia, New Zealand, and South Africa, which had been settled largely by people from Britain and Europe, were to become self-governing nations, "equal in status" to each other and "freely associated" with Britain in the new "Commonwealth of Nations." For these countries a formal report that became known as the Balfour Declaration marked the end of old-style British imperialism and the beginning of an association of equal nations, bound together by common interests and loyalty to the British monarch. Britain continued, however, to control those countries in Africa and Asia in which the local populations were, in its judgement, not yet ready for independence.

Mackenzie King (second from right) at the Imperial Conference, 1926. Standing with him are (left to right) Peter Larkin, Canada's high commissioner to Britain; Ernest Lapointe, minister of justice and King's Québec lieutenant; and Vincent Massey, Canada's ambassador to the United States.

technology

DR. FREDRICK BANTING

Frederick Banting, a boy from rural Ontario who barely scraped through medical school, was by the age of thirty-one Canada's favourite son and an international celebrity. Banting rose to prominence through his experimentation and discovery of insulin in 1922. Together with Dr. Charles Best, Dr. J.J.R. McLeod, and Dr. J.B. Collip, Banting's experiments with insulin became a life-saving therapy for people suffering from diabetes mellitus.

For this discovery, Banting shared the Nobel Prize for Medicine in 1923 with colleague J.J.R. McLeod. He went on to receive the Starr Gold Medal from the University of Toronto, the George Armstrong Peters Award, the Reeve Prize, and the Charles Mickle Fellowship Award. The University of Toronto appointed Banting as its first full professor of medical research, and a grateful Canadian government set him up as the

The "Flame of Hope."

head of his own research institute.

Prior to his success with the insulin experiments at the University of Toronto, Banting had served as a doctor in Flanders during World War I and later attempted to set up a general practice in London, Ontario. He was intensely patriotic and devoted himself to the war effort after the outbreak of World War II. He was killed during his fiftieth year, in a plane crash in Newfoundland, while en route to England on a mission in 1941.

At the Sir Frederick Banting Square in London, Ontario, a "Flame of Hope" was lit in 1989 as a tribute to Dr. Banting and to those who have lost their lives to diabetes. It is also a reminder that insulin is only a control for diabetes. Only when a cure is found will the Flame of Hope be extinguished.

CONTRIBUTED BY JANE MCGAUGHEY. JANE WAS A STUDENT AT KINGSTON COLLEGIATE VOCATIONAL INSTITUTE, AND IS NOW AT THE UNIVERSITY OF TORONTO.

The King–Byng Affair

Despite the Balfour Declaration, "old-style British imperialism," at least in Mackenzie King's mind, was not quite dead. In June 1926 King's Liberals held a minority of seats in Parliament and therefore tried to form a minority government relying on support from the recently founded Progressive Party to stay in power. Support from the Progressives, however, decreased as evidence emerged that government officials, perhaps even a Cabinet minister, had been involved in illegal liquor smuggling. King tried to avoid a full debate on these charges in the House of Commons by going to the Governor General, Lord Byng, to ask that the Parliament be dissolved and elections held.

King hoped to win a majority of seats in a quick election to be held before the public knew the full extent of the liquor smuggling scandal. Previous governors general had almost automatically accepted these requests in the past. But to King's amazement and anger, Lord Byng, who had been appointed by the British government, refused the Prime Minister's request.

Lord Byng believed that the Conservative leader, Arthur Meighen, should be given an opportunity to form the government and save Canadian taxpayers the expense of a second election in two years. To King this was another example of British interference in Canadian affairs. However, Meighen's attempt to form a minority government failed within a few weeks. The Conservatives lost the

METHODS OF HISTORICAL INQUIRY

WORKING WITH PRIMARY DOCUMENTS

Sources of historical information can be divided into two groups – primary sources and secondary sources. A primary source is virtually anything that originates from the particular time and place that is the focus of investigation. It can be anything from a letter or diary entry, to a painting, song, or an actual building. A secondary source, on the other hand, is a historian's interpretation of events based on primary sources written after the time period of investigation. Most sources in your library are secondary sources.

Depending on the area and time period of study, primary sources can be either easy or difficult to find. The earlier the time period of study, the more difficult it can become to find primary sources, as artifacts and documents become lost or are destroyed over the years. When a primary source is found, the researcher must evaluate it for its historical worth.

EVALUATING PRIMARY SOURCES

1. Limitation of Information
The strength of each source lies in its direct connection with the area of investigation. But it is important to keep in mind that each source is also limited in what is reveals. For example, if the area of study was Toronto's architecture in the 1920s, the historian would have to look at many types of primary sources (buildings) to come to an accurate and well-balanced conclusion. Architects who designed and built Toronto's impressive Union Station and its neighbouring buildings in the late 1920s clearly intended to make a statement to travellers coming into the city. But not all the buildings being constructed at this time were in the same style, so one could not make a conclusion on Toronto's architecture based on the Union Station buildings alone.

ACTIVITY
Each of the following photographs were taken in Canada in the 1930s. They are therefore primary

sources which seem to portray conditions at that time. After examining the photographs, answer the questions below.

  a) List the conclusions about the conditions of the time period that are suggested by the contents of the photographs.

  b) List any reservations you would have about supporting the validity of these conclusions along with the reasons for your reservations.

  c) List the information about the time period that you believe you can be reliably stated based on each of the photographs. Be prepared to explain your statements.

  d) Suggest how you would go about confirming or denying the validity of the conditions presented in these photographs as reflective of life in the 1930s.

2. Bias

Just as we learned about detecting bias in the Methods of Historical Inquiry in Unit 2, the historian must be alert to the biases in primary sources. It is important to remember that every sources reflects a bias – the particular perspective, point of view, or experience of the person(s) involved in the source.

ACTIVITY

The following is an excerpt from a letter by Agnes Macphail on the subject of marriage in the 1930's. Read the excerpt and then answer the questions below.

I love children and I have always had dear men friends; it was a deep sorrow to me that I couldn't do all that I expect women to do, to be a wife and mother, but also an untrammelled [unrestricted] active person finding outlet for her ability in the fields of learning, agriculture, industry, business, the arts, or government. I was poor and had I married, the man would not have been rich or even comfortable in a financial sense. In addition, I have never enjoyed housework. I can do it if I must, but it gives me so sense of fulfillment. This I regret, but so it is.

  a) Who is Agnes Macphail? Would her views on marriage be typical of the average woman?

  b) What biases are present in this excerpt?

  c) Could the researcher obtain an accurate conclusion on women's view of marriage in the 1930's from this excerpt?

  d) Suggest what further investigation should be done to achieve a well-balanced conclusion.

3. Credibility of Sources

Along with bias, the historian must also question the credibility, or reliability of the primary source. Who created the source? Did they intend on people seeing what they were writing or creating? Were they trying to express a specific point of view? Were they actually at the time and place of the event in question? For example, if a researcher is looking at a painting of a battle scene from World War II, the following questions should be asked:

1. Who was the artist?

2. What was the purpose of the painting? Was the painting drawn to drum up support for more volunteers? What effect would this have on the artist's painting?

3. Was the artist actually on the battlefront to draw the scene, or was the painting drawn from what the artist imagined the battlefront to look like?

Using primary sources is a very exciting process in the study of history, but just like other types of sources, they must be examined and evaluated with caution. Armed with the right questions, you will make good use of the primary sources that you find.

Lord Byng was a British army officer who commanded the Canadian Corps during its victory at Vimy Ridge in World War I. He was Governor General of Canada from 1921 to 1926.

clear by the repetition of the phrases that had been used earlier in the Balfour Report of 1926: Canada was an "autonomous community ... equal in status" to Britain and the nations were "in no way subordinate one to another in any aspect of their domestic or external affairs." Some direct political links remained between the Canadian and British governments. For example, the British Parliament still had to formally amend the Canadian Constitution (the British North America Act), mainly because the federal and provincial governments in Canada could not agree on how to do it. Britain's Judicial Committee of the Privy Council remained the highest court of appeal for Canadians until 1949. Nevertheless, the Statute of Westminster marked a major milestone on Canada's road to **sovereignty**.

Web Connections

http://www.school.mcgrawhill.ca/resources

Go to the Web site above to find out more about the Statute of Westminster and other Canadian Constitutional documents. Go to *History Resources*, then to *Canada: A Nation Unfolding, Ontario Edition* to find out where to go next.

support they required from the Progressives and were also forced to request an election. This time, Lord Byng granted the request. King, furious that an appointed British official was determining when Canadian elections could be held, made Canadian nationalism the focus of his election campaign. He won the election with a majority government and immediately set out to restrict the powers of the Governor General. A Canadian **high commissioner** (or ambassador) was established in London, England, and a British ambassador in Ottawa so that a representative of the Canadian government, not the Governor General, became the channel of communication with the British government. Soon, Canada and the United States also exchanged representatives and Canada established diplomatic relations with France and Japan. All that remained was for Britain to formally recognize full Canadian independence.

The Statute of Westminster

In 1931 the British Parliament passed the Statute of Westminster, which gave Canada and other British Commonwealth countries complete control over their relations with other nations. This was made

Canada and European Conflicts in the 1930s

Even as war threatened to overwhelm Europe again in the last half of the 1930s, Mackenzie King set out to keep Canada free of foreign commitments. When Italian fascist dictator Benito Mussolini invaded Ethiopia in 1935, King would have nothing to do with any possible actions by the League of Nations to control Mussolini. When civil war broke out in Spain in 1936, King refused any involvement, although 1600 Canadians risked their lives — and hundreds of these volunteers lost them — in support of the Spanish republic against the fascist leader, Francisco Franco. The maintenance of Canadian national unity was more important to King, and his policy of "no **foreign policy**" allowed Canadians to deal with their own problems, rather than issues in other nations.

the arts

CANADIAN MUSIC BETWEEN TWO WARS

In the period between World Wars I and II, Canada moved toward a national consciousness of the arts. Canadian music, however, retained either a French or an English orientation. Composers from French Canada usually studied in Paris, whereas English Canadian composers either came from England or went there to study music. The two best-known Canadian composers representing these two groups between the wars were Healey Willan and Claude Champagne.

HEALEY WILLAN

Healey Willan was born in London, England, in 1880 and came to Canada in 1913 to teach at the Toronto Conservatory of Music. In addition to being a teacher, Willan was an organist and choir director at several churches. In 1921, he became the director of music at Toronto's Church of St. Mary Magdalene, a position he held until shortly before his death in 1968. During his forty-seven years at St. Mary Magdalene, he composed many pieces for organ and for choir in the late English Romantic tradition. Willan's compositions, which total more than eight hundred, have been performed around the world, making him Canada's best-known composer of the twentieth century.

CLAUDE CHAMPAGNE

Claude Champagne was born in 1891 in Montréal and began composing music without formal instruction. His compositions were so well received that Alfred Laliberté, a well-known Montréal music teacher, raised money to send Champagne to Paris to study. On his return to Canada, Champagne worked as a teacher and administrator at McGill University and at the Conservatoire de musique du Québec à Montréal. Much of his inspiration came from French Canadian folk music, adding a distinctive Canadian quality to the twentieth-century French style. He died in Montréal in 1965.

Closer Canadian–American Relations

At the same time that Canada was moving away from Britain's control, it was coming increasingly under the influence of the United States. The proportions of other nations' investment in Canada became much smaller, as the following table shows.

FOREIGN INVESTMENT IN CANADA, 1900–1930 (PERCENT)

Country	1900	1910	1920	1930
Britain	85	76	51	36
United States	13	20	45	61
Other	2	4	4	3

Source: *Historical Atlas of Canada.* Vol. 3. *Addressing the Twentieth Century* (Toronto: University of Toronto Press; 1990), plate 3.

Not only did these years see increasing American investment in Canada, but also a different type of investment. Most British investment had acted as a loan does: the British lenders earned a portion of the profits, but the ownership of the investment remained in Canada. This is known as **portfolio investment**. However, most American investment in the 1920s was in the outright ownership of Canadian businesses. This is known as **direct investment**, and it resulted in a loss of Canadian control of Canadian business.

Another result of direct investment was an increasing number of "branch plants," American manufacturing and commercial firms that were located in Canada to avoid the import tariffs that were part of the National Policy. American investors also bought huge tracts of land for the timber and mineral rights that came with them. By 1930, over 30 percent of Canada's pulp and paper industry, and 40 percent of the mining industry, was American-owned. Few Canadians seemed to care that this might undermine Canada's newly won independence, as provinces competed for vast sums of development money from their southern neighbour. The United States replaced Britain, not only as Canada's main source of foreign investment, but also as its main trading partner.

New Independence?

The 1920s and 1930s saw Canada become a more North American nation. The country weakened both its economic and political ties to Britain and increased its ability to act independently. At the same time, it developed closer economic and cultural ties with the United States. Whether these ties would undermine Canada's newly gained political independence was not clear as the 1930s ended.

chapter review

CHAPTER SUMMARY

In this chapter we have seen

- how several factors, including war weariness, concern for national unity, and the role of Mackenzie King, contributed to Canada's growing autonomy

- how Canada joined the League of Nations but did not play an active role in the new world organization because of domestic concerns

- how the United States replaced Britain both as the main source of foreign investment in Canada and as Canada's main trading partner

UNDERSTANDING HISTORICAL FACTS

1. Identify these people, places, and events, and explain their historical significance.

   Chanak   Balfour Declaration
   Lord Byng   Statute of Westminster

2. Identify Mackenzie King's two main political goals in the 1920s, and explain how the two were connected.

3. Explain how the 1926 "King–Byng affair" demonstrates Mackenzie King's ability to avoid political defeat.

4. In your own words, explain the difference between "direct" and "portfolio" investment.

EXPRESSING YOUR OPINION

1. Mackenzie King kept a diary. Imagine that you are King, and write a diary entry in which you explain why you want Canada to be able to make its own foreign policy and do not want it to get involved in foreign affairs.

2. Was Lord Byng right in his election decisions in 1926, or was Mackenzie King right to make Byng's action a national issue?

3. Should Canadians have been concerned about the growing American influence on the everyday lives of Canadians? Why or why not?

WORKING WITH THE EVIDENCE

1. In the mid-1930s England's King Edward VIII met and fell in love with an American woman named Mrs. Wallis Simpson. He was forced to make a choice between the throne and the woman he loved. King Edward chose to abdicate (give up his throne) in order to marry Mrs. Simpson. Why was he forced to make this choice?

2. Two Canadians met for lunch at the local Chinese Restaurant in Shelburne, Ontario, before attending the Fiddlefest. One of them was the father of the other one's son. How was this possible?

unit review

BRINGING THE PAST INTO FOCUS

REVIEWING THE FACTS

1. Create a photo essay that shows how technology influenced the way Canadians lived in the 1920s and 1930s.

2. It has been stated that during the 1920s and 1930s Canada became a "modern industrial nation." The characteristics of such a nation include:
   - an increase in the number of manufacturing establishments
   - an increase in industrial production
   - the development of the resources needed to support this production
   - an increase in urbanization
   - an increase in the labour supply
   - technological innovation
   - growing international trade
   - an increase in investment
   - new, and often larger, corporations

   Using evidence from this unit, to what extent would you agree or disagree with this statement? Give specific examples to support your statement.

3. What challenges did women encounter in the 1920s and 1930s? How did they deal with these obstacles? Write a newspaper article entitled "Meeting the Challenges" that discusses the ways in which women responded to various challenges in those two decades.

4. Create a two-column chart like the following one to show how the Canadian government dealt, or failed to deal, with the economic, social, and cultural changes of the 1920s and 1930s. Consider the following issues: the regional disparities in the Maritimes and the Prairies; the growing influence of American culture; unemployment in the Depression; and conditions among the Aboriginal peoples.

CONDITION/PROBLEM	GOVERNMENT ACTION

5. Throughout the 1920s Mackenzie King strove to establish Canadian autonomy. Although he was quite successful in gaining greater independence from Britain, the United States came to have an increasingly greater influence on Canada. Discuss this issue by referring to entertainment, investments, and politics.

MAKING CONNECTIONS

At the bottom of this page are a number of terms central to understanding Canada in the 1920s and 1930s. The terms have been organized under four headings: International (world), National (Canada), Regional, and Personal. Select any three terms, and show how these terms are connected with the others.

INTERNATIONAL	NATIONAL	REGIONAL	PERSONAL
Statute of Westminster	On-to-Ottawa Trek	Dust Bowl	Bennett Buggies
Prohibition	Bennett's "New Deal"	Maritime Rights Movement	Pogey
Privy Council	Pier 21	CCF	"Shovelling Out the Poor"
Stock-market Crash	Persons Case	Chautauqua	Relief Camps

HISTORICALLY SPEAKING

1. During the 1920s and 1930s Canada was flooded with American movies and radio programs. At the same time a new sense of national unity and pride could be seen in the art of the Group of Seven and as a result of the work done by the CBC and the NFB. Do you think the 1920s and 1930s were decades of growth for Canadian culture, or were they a period when Canada began to lose its unique identity to Americanization? Explain your answer.

2. Prepare a script for a radio broadcast entitled, "The 1920s and 1930s: A View from (one of Canada's regions)." Choose the Maritimes, the Prairies, or one of the Central Canadian provinces. Use historical evidence from this unit for the basis of the script.

3. Some people suggest that as a result of new technology, Canadians' lives were being completely changed or transformed during these years — that a technological revolution was taking place. Make a list of significant new inventions that came into use at this time. For each one, suggest how it changed peoples' lives and whether it seems to have affected a few, many, or most Canadians. Based on your examples, to what extent would you agree that a technological revolution was taking place?

4. Create a report card on how well the Mackenzie King and R.B. Bennett governments dealt with the following challenges: differences in regional development, economic depression, foreign cultural domination, and poverty. Describe what was done or not done; indicate whether it had a positive or negative result; and evaluate that result as "good," "satisfactory," or "unsatisfactory."

PERSPECTIVES

1. Write a poem or song that captures both the despair felt by the Aboriginal peoples in the 1920s and 1930s and the determination for cultural survival that would lead to Aboriginal activism. You may want to illustrate the poem or song and put your work on display for others to see.

2. During the 1920s and 1930s many groups of people suffered discrimination at all levels. Using the information in this unit, write a paragraph on how each of the following people would respond to the following questions: "Did you experience discrimination during these years? If so, in what ways?"
   a) a woman
   b) a young Black Canadian
   c) an Aboriginal teenager
   d) a new immigrant

3. Do some research to find out what life was like in the relief camps. Imagine that you are one of the young men working in the camps. Write a letter to a friend, describing your experiences in the camp and your hopes for the future.

Democracy at the Crossroads: Canadians in World War II

> "Keep it in mind during the days ahead that war does inexplicable things to people, and no man can guess how it is going to affect him until he has a really stiff dose of it.... The most unfortunate ones after any war are not those with missing limbs; they are the ones who have had their spiritual feet knocked out from under them."
>
> —FROM FARLEY MOWAT'S *AND NO BIRDS SANG*

TIMELINE

SEPTEMBER 10, 1939 ▶
Canada enters
World War II

AUGUST 1942 ▶
Canadians suffer
heavy losses in the
Battle of Dieppe

The Great War, as the conflict between 1914 and 1918 came to be known, failed to be "the war to end all wars." A mere twenty years later, the world would once again be embroiled in a devastating war. Throughout the 1930s, Canada — like Britain and the United States — had hoped to avoid being drawn into another deadly conflict. This reluctance would allow Italy, Germany, and Japan to aggressively expand their military forces and their borders. In 1939, the Western powers took a stand against fascism, and thus began World War II.

By the war's end, Canada would once again have played a crucial role in the Allied victory. During the war, Canada would supply both soldiers and vital supplies to the war effort. But Canada's participation would again come with a price: thousands of soldiers would die in battle, the conscription issue would again test Canadian unity, and wartime paranoia would lead to the denial of basic human rights for some Canadians.

LET'S INVESTIGATE

1. How did the Canadian government deal with the challenges of managing the wartime economy differently than it had in World War I?

2. How did the role of women in World War II differ from their role in World War I?

3. What contributions did various ethno-cultural groups make to the war effort?

4. How did Canadian soldiers contribute to battles such as Dieppe, Hong Kong, Ortona, and Normandy?

5. How did new technological developments alter the nature of warfare, and how were these developments adapted to civilian use in the post-war era?

6. How did the outcome of World War II influence global politics after 1945?

APRIL 1945
Jewish survivors liberated from Nazi concentration camps

AUGUST 6, 1945
World's first atomic-bomb attack destroys Hiroshima

The first Canadian soldiers to go overseas in World War II left Halifax on December 18, 1939. How would the experience of World War I have changed volunteers' views of warfare?

INQUIRING INTO THE PAST

- Why did fascism become popular in some European countries in the 1920s and 1930s?
- Why did Western nations allow Adolf Hitler to violate terms of the Treaty of Versailles?
- How did Canada respond to Germany's treatment of its Jewish citizens?
- How did Nazi Germany use new military technology to revolutionize warfare?

KEY TERMS

Allied Powers

Anti-Semitism

Appeasement

Axis Powers

Dictatorship

Fascism

Kristallnacht

Nazism

TIMELINE

JANUARY 30, 1933 ▶
Hitler assumes power as German Chancellor

SEPTEMBER 29, 1938 ▶
Munich Agreement is signed

SEPTEMBER 1, 1939 ▶
Germany invades Poland

SEPTEMBER 10, 1939 ▶
Canada declares war on Germany

By the end of World War I most European nations were ruled by democratic governments. Monarchs such as Kaiser Wilhelm of Germany were replaced by elected parliamentary governments as a condition of the Treaty of Versailles. For millions of Germans, democratic government was accompanied by a crippling economic depression and a sense of national humiliation resulting from the terms of the peace agreement. Across Europe, as people struggled to recover from the devastation of the war, many began to question traditional political and economic systems. They began to consider the new fascist and communist parties that were springing up across Europe, and by the 1930s Germany, Italy, Spain, and the Soviet Union were ruled by ruthless dictators.

Canada was also influenced by the age of extreme politics; some Canadians embraced the new ideas of fascism and communism openly, while others were too preoccupied with surviving the Great Depression to be concerned about events in Europe. As the 1930s drew to a close, however, the entire world would again take notice of Europe. Once more, the world verged on the brink of total war.

An Age of Extreme Politics: The Rise of Fascism and Communism

Fascist Italy

In 1919 a new political movement emerged in Italy under the leadership of Benito Mussolini. This movement, known as **fascism**, was a revolt against democratic values, including equality and individual freedom. Followers of the fascist ideology believed that democracy weakened the state by placing too much emphasis on the individual. Central to fascism was the belief in the state above all else. Human lives only had value and meaning in so far as they served the needs of the state. Mussolini erased the line between public life and private life when he declared: "For the fascist, the state is all-embracing; outside it no human or spiritual values exist." Mussolini's rise to power was fast and bloody.

In 1922, black-shirted Italian fascists marched on Rome and destroyed Italy's stumbling democratic government. Mussolini took for himself the name of "Il Duce" ("the leader"). The fascists immediately banned opposing political parties and workers' unions and censored newspapers to stop freedom of expression. By controlling the media, Mussolini was able to spread propaganda glorifying the Fascist Party, the Italian state, and Il Duce. For those who were reluctant to support the new dictator, a secret police force was set up to terrorize people into obeying Mussolini and his fascist followers. The world's first "totalitarian **dictatorship**" had taken root; all aspects of life were now controlled and monitored by the government.

Germany after World War I: Inflation, Depression, and Political Unrest

The Treaty of Versailles had imposed harsh conditions on Germany to keep the German nation from rising up again. As well as placing severe restrictions on the German armed forces, the treaty forced Germany to pay huge sums of money to countries such as France and Belgium, which had suffered enormous damage during the war. To meet the financial obligations imposed by the treaty, Germany printed huge amounts of currency. This action devalued the German mark (Germany's currency) and led to rampant inflation. The result was that by the early 1920s Germany's economy was in tatters and spiralling inflation destroyed the wealth of the German middle classes. A loaf of bread, which cost two marks in 1918, cost about *six million* marks in 1924. Desperate families fled to the countryside to try to scrounge enough to eat from the forests and fields, while anxious farmers took up rifles to force them away. The cities turned violent as starving people roamed the streets, looking for work and food. What could be done to lift Germany from ruin?

Adolf Hitler and the Rise of Nazi Germany

The person who profited most from Germany's desperate search for solutions was Adolf Hitler. A master at public speaking, Hitler said out loud what many Germans secretly thought and wanted. He promised to tear up the hated Treaty of Versailles, restore Germany to greatness, create a mighty German army, and see that German lands and peoples inside the borders of nations created by the peace treaty — Austria, Czechoslovakia, and Poland — would be returned to German rule. The victors of World War I would feel the weight of a new German empire.

Adolf Hitler was born in Austria in 1889. He left school early and drifted from job to job until the outbreak of World War I. During the war, Hitler served in the German army on the Western Front. He was one of the few enlisted men (non-officers) to be awarded the Iron Cross, first class, for bravery under fire. After Germany's defeat, he dedicated himself to restoring the German nation to military glory. Hitler went to Munich, where he took control of a small right-wing political group, built up its membership, and changed its name to the National Socialist German Workers Party — later known to the world as the Nazis.

In November 1923, Hitler tried to seize control of the government in the German province of Bavaria as the first step in taking over the German democratic republic. However, the "Beer Hall Putsch" (armed revolt) failed and Hitler was jailed. But the putsch won him nationwide attention. To make the most of his new fame, Hitler wrote *Mein Kampf* ("My Struggle") in prison. The book was a rambling mixture of personal stories and threats against "enemies" of the German people.

In *Mein Kampf*, Hitler set out the goals that rallied the German nation. He claimed that "Aryans" (Caucasians of pure German descent) were a master race destined to rule over other races such as the Jews and Slavs of Eastern Europe, especially Poles, Czechs, and Russians. Hitler also called for more *Lebensraum* ("living space") for the German people to support a growing German population, and demanded *Anschluss*—the unification of Austria and Germany. He planned to extend German rule over the lands held by the Poles, Czechs, and Russians. The conquest of Eastern Europe was to be achieved by unleashing a new and all-powerful German army. Hitler claimed he would lead the German nation to greatness. Within a few short years, Hitler's appealing promises had won him much support. In 1933, Hitler was elected Chancellor of Germany and took for himself the title of "der Führer" ("the leader"). Shortly after being elected, Hitler disbanded the

Using his powerful speaking skills, Adolf Hitler espoused his racist ideas and his plans to restore Germany's greatness. Could a leader such as Hitler have been successful in prosperous times?

Reichstag (the German Parliament). This marked the end of the German democratic republic and the start of the Nazi "Reich."

Anti-Semitism and the Holocaust

The most horrifying legacy of the Nazi regime was its deliberate effort to eliminate Europe's Jewish population. During the reign of Adolf Hitler, negative selection, whereby unwanted members of a society were weeded out, became official policy in Germany. The largest group targeted by the Nazis were the Jews. For centuries, their religion and culture had set Jews apart from other Europeans. This often made them convenient scapegoats in difficult times, such as the years following World War I.

The persecution of German Jews began in 1933. At first, Jewish citizens were removed from jobs in government, teaching, and the media. They were banned from entering many shops and public sports grounds. They were forced into separate Jewish schools, placed under a nightly curfew, and forbidden to marry non-Jews. They were attacked on the streets by Nazi supporters, and their homes and businesses were vandalized. Later, many Jews were systematically rounded up and taken to concentration camps. Germans who spoke up for their Jewish friends and neighbours were also subject to violence. Hitler would stop at nothing to destroy his "enemies," and Hitler's will was law — the only law.

Fascism, Nazism, and Anti-Semitism in Canada

Fascist movements were not limited to Europe; they soon arrived on Canadian shores. Italian government representatives in Montreal and Toronto planted fascists in the cities' Italian communities to win support for fascist aggression in the Mediterranean. The German consulate also began to plant Nazi ideas among some German people in Canada. The movement was most active in Saskatchewan, with its large German-speaking population, and in Winnipeg.

Canada also had its own fascist organizations. As fascism took hold across Europe, Canadian-born Nazi groups in Winnipeg, Toronto, and Montreal grew bolder and stepped into public view. The Nazi leader in Québec, Adrien Arcand, was even given financial support by R.B. Bennett's federal Conservative Party. The Winnipeg-based Canadian Nationalist Party took to wearing badges showing a swastika (the emblem adopted by the Nazi Party) surrounded by maple leaves and topped with a

beaver. Canadian Nazis published newspapers full of Nazi slogans. They dressed up in matching shirts and paraded in city streets, shouting slogans against "foreigners" and Jews. Occasionally, riots broke out in Toronto, Winnipeg, and Montreal as fascist and anti-fascist marchers clashed.

Some Canadians were attracted to fascism because it seemed to offer a way out of the Great Depression. Hitler appeared to be turning the German economy around and putting people back to work. Some Canadian Nazis hoped for the same economic transformation in Canada. But sympathy with Hitler's **anti-Semitism** — his deep-seated hatred of Jews — was the bedrock of most of the fascist groups in Canada.

Discrimination toward Jews occurred in many areas of Canada. There were hiring restrictions for Jews in businesses, the civil service, and other professions. In some cities, Jews were forbidden to buy property or to join certain clubs and organizations. Occasionally, in Winnipeg, Toronto, and Montreal, violence broke out between Jews and anti-Semites. Even as Nazi violence toward Jews in Europe increased — which caused thousands of Jews from Germany, Austria, and Czechoslovakia to flee as refugees by the summer of 1938 — few Canadians were willing to let them come to Canada.

When 907 Jews fled Nazi Germany in May 1939 aboard the ship *St. Louis*, they hoped to find safety

To some Canadians, Adolf Hitler's style of politics was appealing. These young men, known as "blueshirts," are giving the Nazi salute at a rally in Montreal in the 1930s.

in Cuba. Much to their dismay, their visas were rejected by the Cuban government and by every other Latin American country. Desperate for a refuge, the Jews aboard the *St. Louis* turned to Canada and the United States, only to find their pleas again rejected. Frederick Blair, director of the Canadian Immigration Branch, claimed that no country could "open its doors wide enough to take in the hundreds of thousands of Jewish people who want to leave Europe; the line must be drawn somewhere." Eventually, the passengers aboard the *St. Louis* had to return to Europe, where many died in Nazi death camps. By 1945 Canada had accepted a mere 4000 Jewish immigrants, while Britain had taken in 85 000 and the United States, 240 000. Canada did not have a good record of providing a safe haven for European Jews.

The Soviet Union: The Rise of Joseph Stalin

While fascism was making tremendous gains in Central Europe, Joseph Stalin was tightening his grip on the Soviet Union. The old Russian Empire, led by a succession of czars, could not survive the pressures of World War I. With war underway in 1917 and food shortages plaguing Russia, communist revolutionaries, led by Vladimir I. Lenin, overthrew the last Russian Czar, Nicholas II, and established the world's first communist government. The central aim of communism was to create a classless society in which all members shared equally in the distribution of resources. Eliminating private property and placing

the means of production (farms, factories, mines, and so on) in the hands of a government was supposed to eliminate the gulf between rich and poor, which characterized modern industrial societies. When Lenin died in 1924, Joseph Stalin secured enough support in the Communist Party to ensure his victory in the leadership struggle that followed.

Immediately after coming to power, Stalin implemented a series of five-year plans designed to rapidly industrialize the Soviet economy. Within ten years, the Soviet Union underwent an industrial revolution that took smaller countries many decades to attain. But the costs were extremely high: anyone who opposed Stalin's plans to industrialize the Soviet Union was dealt with harshly. When Ukrainian farmers resisted surrendering their land to the government, Stalin sent up to three million people to forced-labour camps in Siberia and seized their crops, creating a famine. Stalin referred to his actions as "a policy of liquidating the kulaks [Ukrainian farmers] as a class." In the end, Stalin's "terror famine" led to the deaths of an estimated seven million people.

Like dictators in fascist countries, Stalin also established a totalitarian state that tolerated no opposition to his rule. He was so suspicious of others that he carried out the "Great Terror" from 1935 to 1938, in which all those suspected of working against Stalin were eliminated. Laws ordered the death penalty for people who were found to have withheld information about others engaged in acts against Stalin. The laws even extended to children

This Jewish refugee ship is leaving Canada en route to Israel after World War II. Can you read the banner on the side of the ship?

Joseph Stalin was the ruthless dictator of the Soviet Union from 1924 until his death in 1953.

as young as twelve who did not report the crimes of their parents. In three years, the Great Terror claimed one million victims.

By the mid-1930s the communist government of the Soviet Union was on a collision course with the new fascist government of Germany. The underlying principles of fascism insisted on the surrendering of individual rights and freedoms for the good of the state, whereas communism sought to ensure the welfare of all workers. These two extreme ideologies, both focused on world conquest, viewed each other with tremendous suspicion. It would only be a matter of time before the new age of extreme politics would pit the fascist forces against their arch-rivals, the communists.

Planting the Seeds of War

The Rome–Berlin Axis

Mussolini's aim was to build a new Italian empire that would circle the Mediterranean Sea. In newspapers and radio broadcasts, on movie screens and street posters, Italians were bombarded with fascist war slogans such as "A minute on the battlefield is worth a lifetime of peace!" and "Believe! Obey! Fight!" In 1936, the Italian army marched into Africa and seized Abyssinia (now Ethiopia). Italy also formed close ties with Hitler's Germany, a relationship that was formalized in an agreement in

1936 known as the Rome–Berlin Axis. At that time, Hitler was preparing to invade Austria, and Mussolini promised not to interfere with Hitler's plans for attack. In return, Hitler promised to limit future German empire-building to northern and central Europe, leaving Mussolini free to build an Italian empire in southern Europe.

German Rearmament and the Militarization of the Rhineland

In March 1935, Hitler began to show his contempt for the treaty terms that limited German military strength. He revealed the existence of a German air force and announced plans for military conscription and a thirty-six-division army. Publicly, Hitler claimed that Germany was building up its armed forces to gain military "equality" with the strongest European nations. Secretly, he was aiming for armed superiority. Once Germany had enough troops and weapons to tip the balance of power in Europe in its favour, Hitler could ignore the Treaty of Versailles completely. For the next few years, he told his cabinet, it must be "everything for the armed forces."

Adolf Hitler (right) leader of Nazi Germany, and Benito Mussolini (centre) leader of fascist Italy, were two of the most prominent dictators of the 1920s and 1930s. Why did some nations reject democracy and choose to support the rise of dictators?

By March 1936 Hitler was ready for the next step. He marched his troops into the Rhineland, an area bordering France in which the Treaty of Versailles had ordered Germany to have no military presence. Hitler was careful to tell his soldiers to make the occupation seem as peaceful as possible because he did not want to stir up European fears about an immediate invasion. Anti-aircraft guns and Luftwaffe fighter squadrons were moved in, but no tanks and no bombers were visible; they would come later. For now, Hitler wanted the military buildup to look as if peacetime soldiers were simply taking up defensive posts in their own country. On the day that Nazi troops marched into the Rhineland, Hitler declared to the world, "We have no territorial demands to make in Europe. Germany will never break the peace."

The Policy of Appeasement

The new British Prime Minister, Neville Chamberlain, came to power in 1937 under the threat of a potentially devastating war and the reality of the worst economic depression in memory. Like most European leaders, Chamberlain had neither the economic luxury nor the desire to be drawn into a costly war over what were considered remote areas of Europe. Memories of World War I were still fresh, and Chamberlain was unwilling to oppose Hitler for fear of another "Great War." He hoped that diplomacy could save the fragile peace. Chamberlain favoured a policy of **appeasement**. He believed that Hitler was a reasonable leader and that some German demands, such as a reduction in war reparations payments and a German military presence in the Rhineland, were

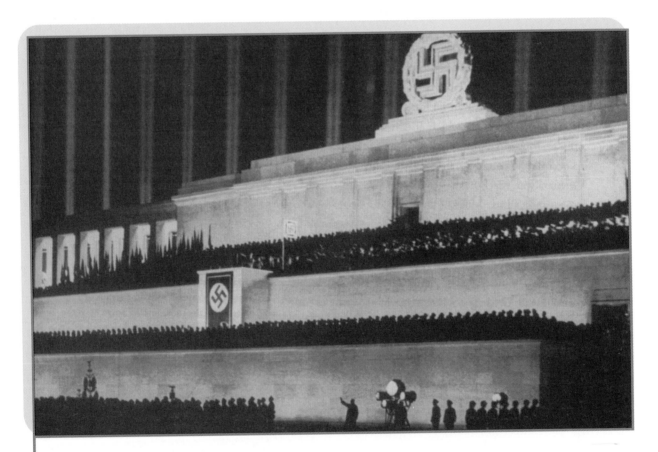

Rallies such as the Nuremberg Rally were used by the Nazis to generate enthusiasm and loyalty among the German people. Why is this type of propaganda such a powerful tool?

Canadian profiles

DR. NORMAN BETHUNE

The name of Norman Bethune is unfamiliar to many Canadians, yet in China he is one of the nation's most respected heroes. Born in Gravenhurst, Ontario, in 1890 and educated at the University of Toronto, Bethune's travels took him to Detroit, Montreal, Spain, and finally to China.

Bethune's determination to contribute to society could be seen throughout his adult life. As a young man, he served as a stretcher bearer in World War I. After being severely wounded in the leg by shrapnel at the second battle of Ypres, Bethune was sent home to Canada, where he finished his medical studies. He then returned to active duty as a lieutenant-surgeon aboard HMS *Pegasus* in the North Sea.

Following the war, Bethune accepted a position at Montreal's Royal Victoria Hospital. When the Spanish Civil War broke out in 1937, Bethune, like many others who were committed to the defence of democracy, travelled to Spain. There he was greatly disturbed to see the number of soldiers who died on stretchers from loss of blood. Determined to stem the loss of life, Bethune designed the first mobile blood-transfusion service, a service that has since saved thousands of lives.

After a brief return to Canada, Bethune moved on to China to provide medical support to the Chinese revolutionaries led by Mao Zedong. Bethune turned his attention to the development of a mobile medical team, which would get medical care out to the soldiers in the field rather than waiting for the soldiers to reach the medical centres. Bethune's idea would develop into the Mobile Army Surgical Hospitals (M.A.S.H.) Units. As well as serving on the battlefield, Bethune also worked endlessly to provide a wide range of medical care to Chinese peasants.

In October 1939, while completing an operation, Norman Bethune suffered a minor cut on his finger. A few days later, infection caused by blood poisoning set in. On November 12, 1939, Bethune died. Despite spending less than two years in China, he acquired hero status, rarely given to foreigners. Today, the name Norman Bethune is better known among the Chinese than that of almost any other Canadian.

ACTIVITY

The Royal Canadian Mint has decided to issue a series of commemorative coins that capture the exploits of Canadian heroes, and you have been asked to design the Dr. Norman Bethune Memorial Coin. What would your design look like? Remember to draw both sides of the coin.

reasonable. The British Prime Minister wanted Hitler to tell the world exactly what Germany wanted. Then, through diplomatic negotiations, Germany's needs could be satisfied (or "appeased") and the Wehrmacht (army) could be kept safely inside German borders. Chamberlain was convinced that Hitler was a man who kept his promises.

Canada's Prime Minister, Mackenzie King, also supported appeasement. In 1937, Mackenzie King travelled to London, Paris, and Berlin to seek a peaceful settlement of the European conflict. In Berlin, he met and talked with the Führer himself. Hitler made a favourable impression on Mackenzie King. Following their meeting, Mackenzie King noted in his diary that Hitler was a sincere man who had no intention to provoke a war. He agreed with Chamberlain that the Nazi dictator could soon be appeased.

Mackenzie King had what he believed were good reasons for supporting appeasement. The Canadian Prime Minister felt that Germany had been treated too harshly following World War I and that adjustments had to be made. Many Canadians backed King's views. The *Winnipeg Tribune* argued that "a Germany with her self-respect restored may be the means of dispelling the war clouds hanging so ominously over Europe." Furthermore, although Mackenzie King might not like Hitler's heavy-handed tactics, the Führer was not the only ruthless dictator in Europe. In the Soviet Union, Joseph Stalin was killing hundreds of thousands of generals, intellectuals, politicians, and ordinary citizens who opposed him. Nazis and communists were deadly enemies, and a strong Nazi Germany might keep the Soviet Union from spreading communism across Europe. Above all, Mackenzie King was unwilling to push for a strong stand against Germany for fear that Canada might be drawn into another world war. "No sacrifice can be too great," he wrote in his diary, "which can save war."

The Invasion of Austria

The first sacrifice made for the sake of peace was Austria, a new democratic state that had been carved out of the old Austro-Hungarian Empire by the Treaty of Versailles. Austria's people were German-speaking, a fact that gave Hitler all the excuse he needed for Anschluss, or the "union" of the German peoples of Austria and Germany in a "Greater Germany." No European nation was willing to risk war to stop Hitler from moving into Austria.

Austria's Chancellor was left with no choice; his country was too small to fight the Nazis alone. When Germany invaded Austria on March 12, 1938, it met no resistance. Without losing a single soldier, the German army rolled into Vienna and seized control of the government. The next day a beaming Hitler proclaimed the *Anschluss*. He was triumphant; a quiet Austrian surrender meant that the Nazi invasion could be described as the reunion of peoples unhappily kept apart by the Treaty of Versailles.

Prime Minister Mackenzie King met with Adolf Hitler on June 29, 1937. During the meeting King told Hitler that he hoped nothing would prevent the work of his regime from continuing. Why did foreign leaders praise Hitler despite his blatant defiance of the Treaty of Versailles?

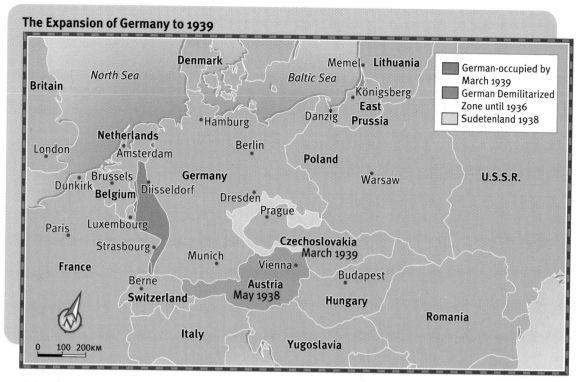

The Expansion of Germany to 1939

Legend:
- German-occupied by March 1939
- German Demilitarized Zone until 1936
- Sudetenland 1938

Britain · North Sea · Denmark · Memel · Lithuania · Baltic Sea · Königsberg · East Prussia · Danzig · London · Netherlands · Amsterdam · Hamburg · Berlin · Poland · Warsaw · U.S.S.R. · Brussels · Germany · Düsseldorf · Dunkirk · Belgium · Dresden · Prague · Paris · Luxembourg · Czechoslovakia March 1939 · Strasbourg · Munich · Vienna · Budapest · France · Berne · Austria May 1938 · Hungary · Switzerland · Romania · Italy · Yugoslavia

0 100 200KM

Before the outbreak of war in September 1939, Germany had already begun to expand its borders. What was the strategic significance of the areas acquired by Germany?

Czechoslovakia and the Munich Agreement

Hitler's next target was Czechoslovakia, another nation created by the peace treaty of 1919. Since the twelfth century, Germans had been migrating to the Sudetenland, now a region of Czechoslovakia. Although the Sudetenland had never belonged to Germany, Hitler saw that he could use the excuse of "liberating" the German-speaking Sudetenlanders to seize Czechoslovakia. Once again, Britain and France were unwilling to risk all-out war with Nazi Germany over troubles in a small Central European nation. In a radio broadcast on September 27, 1938, Neville Chamberlain spoke to the British nation: "How horrible, fantastic, incredible it is that we should be digging trenches and trying on gas masks here because of a quarrel in a far-away country between people of whom we know nothing. If we have to fight, it must be on larger issues than that."

The leaders of Italy, France, and England met with Hitler in Munich in September 1938 to decide Czechoslovakia's fate. Neither the Soviet Union nor the Czechs were asked to attend. The four men struck a bargain: Hitler could have the Sudetenland — one third of Czechoslovakia — but he must stop all demands for more territory. Hitler solemnly agreed to the terms, and, delighted, Chamberlain returned to London to announce the agreement reached in Munich. "I believe it is peace for our time," he declared to cheering crowds. Chamberlain genuinely believed that the crisis had passed. Czechoslovakia was forced to accept Hitler's demands to give up territory to the Nazis or fight it out alone. Another small democracy was cast away to appease Hitler. In Canada, the Munich Agreement was greeted with relief because Canadians believed the threat of war had passed. Convinced that peace would last, the Canadian government made no plans to increase its small defence budget.

Germany's Aggression Increases

Less than two months after the signing of the Munich Agreement, the optimism for peace was shattered. On the night of November 10, 1938,

METHODS OF HISTORICAL INQUIRY

MAKING SENSE OF POLITICAL CARTOONS

Political cartooning has provided Canadians with satirical and often hilarious views of the issues of the day. Much like written editorials, political cartoons convey a point of view about a significant contemporary event, individual, or issue. As a primary source, political cartoons can provide valuable glimpses into the past. Fully appreciating the power of political cartoons requires a careful dissection of their components. The following simple steps can assist the reader to understand and interpret political cartoons from the past.

STEP ONE: ESTABLISH A KNOWLEDGE BASE

As historical documents, political cartoons cannot be properly understood until their context is established. When you see a political cartoon in the editorial pages of a daily newspaper, it will often make immediate sense because it addresses an issue currently in the news. A cartoon from a 1942 newspaper will not be easily understood unless the reader understands the historical events to which the cartoon is responding. Before attempting to interpret any political cartoon, be sure that you have a general understanding of the issue, event, or individual portrayed.

STEP TWO: IDENTIFY THE ISSUE

Often, knowing the general historical background is not enough to fully appreciate the message and point of view of the cartoon. While the historical context is a crucial starting point, identifying the issue is also critical to understanding political cartoons. For example, a general understanding of the World War II era would help make it obvious that the accompanying political cartoon addresses the battle over conscription. But what particular issue is being addressed? A closer look reveals that the cartoonist is making a comment on Prime Minister Mackenzie King's reluctance to make a final decision on conscription. Fully appreciating this cartoon requires an understanding of both the historical context and the particular issue.

STEP THREE: DETERMINE THE DEVICES USED BY THE CARTOONIST

When analyzing a political cartoon, determine which of the following devices the cartoonist has used:

- *Caricature*: This is the most commonly used technique of the political cartoonist. As a form of visual satire, a caricature exaggerates or distorts an individual's physical characteristics so that the character becomes easily recognizable or an aspect of the character is revealed.

- *Analogy*: Often cartoonists will choose to express their viewpoint by using an analogy rather than a literal portrayal. An analogy draws on historical, literary, or cultural references to draw parallels with the issue or event. For example, showing a prime minister as a captain of a sinking ship could be used as an analogy to the declining popularity of a governing political party.

- *Symbols*: Cartoonists sometimes use symbols to capture an idea or a trait. For example, a skull conveys the idea of death, whereas a dove or an olive branch suggests peace. Animals can also be used as symbols. A lion may suggest courage, whereas a donkey may express stubbornness. Sometimes cartoonists will use size as a symbol; for example, showing an individual as being much larger than others in the cartoon can symbolize power, strength, or status. Sometimes cartoonists rely on stereotypes to communicate ideas. Workers may be shown as ragged and thin, while business leaders are often shown as fat and wealthy.

- *Facial Expressions and Gestures*: Cartoonists can capture a wide range of emotions and ideas by drawing on a vast pool of expressions, created through winks, smiles, scowls, and gestures, created by the suggestion of movements of hands, arms, legs, and so on.
- *Words*: Most cartoons rely on a combination of visual images and words to convey a viewpoint. Words can be used in captions, titles, labels on characters or items in the cartoon, or as a dialogue between characters in the cartoon.

Step Four: Identify the Cartoonist's Bias

Earlier, in Unit 2 of this text, you learned about detecting bias, which was defined as a slanted or prejudiced attitude that can prevent people from presenting evidence clearly and truthfully. Political cartoonists present a point of view that has often been shaped by many influences. They tend to portray issues in extremes: bad is very bad, and good is very good. Often, issues are exaggerated and facts may be distorted. The cartoonist hopes to sway the viewer's opinion through emotion and generally portrays negative aspects of the person, event, or issue to discredit the opposing point of view. When examining a political cartoon, watch for these biases:

- *national/regional/local bias*—where was the cartoonist born, and where does he or she live?
- *political bias*—is the cartoonist a supporter of a particular political viewpoint or cause?
- *religious bias*—are the views of the cartoonist influenced by religious views?
- *racial/ethnic bias*—has the cartoonist's racial or ethnic background shaped the cartoon's viewpoint?
- *economic bias*—has the cartoonist's perspective been influenced by his or her economic status?
- *gender bias*—is there evidence of gender bias in the cartoon?

- *personal values*—does the cartoon reflect the personal morals and values of the cartoonist?

You are now ready to interpret historical political cartoons. Good luck!

Activity

For the political cartoon shown, complete the following activity.

1. In one paragraph, explain the historical context and the issue addressed by the cartoon. Review the chapters in this unit to help with this step.
2. List and describe the ways in which the cartoonist uses the devices listed in Step Three.
3. Identify and explain any biases you find in the cartoon.
4. Write a one-paragraph summary of the cartoon in which you clearly explain the cartoonist's main message and your opinion of the effectiveness of the cartoon.

ADAPTED FROM CHARLES AND CYNTHIA HOU, *THE ART OF DECODING POLITICAL CARTOONS: A TEACHER'S GUIDE* (VANCOUVER: MOODY'S LOOKOUT PRESS, 1998).

Jewish synagogues and businesses in Germany were ransacked and looted with the support of the German police. The day following *Kristallnacht* ("night of broken glass"), twenty thousand Jews were arrested and sent to concentration camps at Dachau and Buchenwald in Germany. In Toronto, thousands of people gathered at Maple Leaf Gardens to protest against the treatment of Jews in Germany. The *Toronto Daily Star* reported,

> *Race, creed and class were forgotten yesterday as Toronto, with one voice, protested the martyrdom of German Jews at Nazi hands. More than 16,000 persons thronged the Maple Leaf Gardens to attend a memorial service for the victims of persecution and oppression; and thousands more were turned away because of lack of accommodation....*

Six months after the Munich Agreement, Hitler dismantled the delicate peace even further by attacking Czechoslovakia. By March 15, 1939, he stood in the President's Palace in Prague, proclaiming the end of Czech independence. Even Chamberlain now realized that Hitler was bent on world conquest and that nothing short of war would stop him. Britain was determined to draw the line at Poland, but Hitler was just as determined to invade that nation. The Nazi propaganda machine began pouring out demands for "justice," including the return of the "Polish Corridor," which gave Poland access to the sea and split Germany in half. But first Hitler had to ensure that the Soviet Union would not side with the Poles when the Wehrmacht started to roll into Poland.

The Nazi–Soviet Pact

Hitler hated communism, and Stalin hated **Nazism** just as fiercely, so it seemed unlikely that Germany and the Soviet Union could come to an agreement on Poland. But in 1939 the two nations shocked the world by signing the Nazi–Soviet Pact, in which they promised not to go to war against each other and secretly agreed to divide Poland between them.

Stalin probably knew that the pact would eventually fall apart, but he believed that Hitler would first attack Western Europe. Nothing suited him better than a war between his enemies, the democratic and fascist countries of Europe. While both sides exhausted themselves in long, hard trench warfare, the Soviet Union would have plenty of time to build up its army and prepare for an inevitable war with Germany.

Hitler also knew that the pact was only temporary, but he did not want to fight a war on two fronts at once. First he would conquer Western Europe and then turn his guns on the Soviet Union. For Hitler, the Nazi–Soviet Pact kept the Soviet Union quiet while he used his armies elsewhere. Once the pact was signed, Hitler was free to take Poland. At the crack of dawn on September 1, 1939, the German Wehrmacht rolled across the German–Polish border. There was no official declaration of war. The uneasy peace ended with a barrage of German gunfire.

War Returns to Europe

Within two days of Germany invading Poland, Britain and France declared war on Germany, and Europe was once again engulfed in war. Would Canada step to Britain's side in the coming conflict?

Angered by the murder of a German citizen by a Jewish youth in Paris, France, Germany erupted into a night of anti-Jewish violence that destroyed thousands of Jewish homes, businesses, and synagogues.

This map shows the territory that Germany lost as a result of World War I. Was Germany's anger over the loss of the "Polish Corridor" a legitimate grievance?

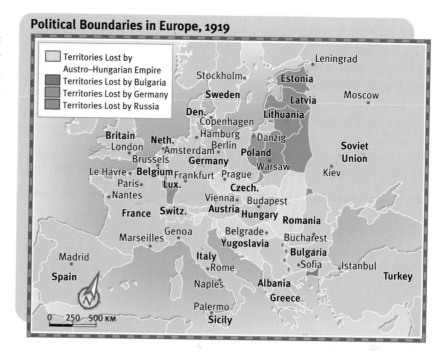

Political Boundaries in Europe, 1919

Territories Lost by Austro–Hungarian Empire
Territories Lost by Bulgaria
Territories Lost by Germany
Territories Lost by Russia

0 250 500 KM

Unlike the situation in 1914, when Canada's colonial status placed matters related to foreign affairs in British hands, Canada's participation in World War II would be an entirely Canadian decision. Prime Minister Mackenzie King hastily recalled Parliament for an emergency debate and vote. Support for the war effort was almost unanimous. Only the leader of the CCF, J.S. Woodsworth, who was a pacifist, opposed the armed conflict. Canada's answer was delayed but never in doubt. On September 10, 1939, a popular 1930s tune was playing on the airwaves when the Canadian Broadcasting Corporation interrupted its programming for a special announcement: Canada had formally declared war on Germany.

This time, there was none of the wild enthusiasm that had swept Canadians into the streets at the declaration of war back in 1914. Canadians sat quietly at home and braced for the bloody ordeal ahead: it was the second time in twenty years that war had come to their doorsteps. Almost every family had a loved one or neighbour buried in French or Belgian fields. Every Canadian town and city had its share of war survivors injured in body or mind as daily reminders of the horrors of war.

Posters like this one reflect Canada's confidence that Adolf Hitler would eventually be defeated. What does this poster tell you about the role the air force had come to play by World War II?

leisure

WORLD WAR II AND LIFE AT HOME

During World War II almost every aspect of life, at home and abroad, was influenced by the war effort. Still, life went on in Canada, and people made valiant efforts to enjoy themselves.

DANCE

A popular dance craze during the 1940s was jitterbugging. This was a very fast dance, generally performed to swing music. Often the jitterbug saw the male throwing his female partner over his shoulder. Another popular dance was the boogie woogie, which was performed to boogie woogie music — a style of blues-jazz on piano that is marked by persistent bass rhythm.

FASHION

"Zoot sooters" were groups of young males, including teenagers, who chose to rebel against wartime clothing restrictions by wearing what were thought, at the time, to be outrageous costumes called zoot suits. Zoot suits featured long, draped jackets with padded shoulders and high-waisted, tapering trousers. Many zoot sooters wore brightly coloured shirts, huge bow ties, wide-brimmed hats, and yellow pointed shoes. A long chain looped to one of the suit pockets. Zoot sooters were considered by some, especially people in the services, to be anti-social, and they were banned from some establishments.

SPORTS

While many athletes, such as members of the Toronto Maple Leafs, served in the forces, numerous sport leagues and teams continued to play, and Canadian fans cheered for their home teams.

Blitzkrieg and the Attack on Poland

The technological advances that had revolutionized warfare in 1914 would continue to be the single most important factor in determining success in the war that was about to begin. During the six years leading up to the start of World War II, Hitler had rebuilt the German armed forces. The new German army was equipped with the latest in military weaponry and had devised a plan of attack that made effective use of the new technology. In Germany's invasion of Poland, the world had its first chilling encounter with the blitzkrieg, a revolutionary style of hard, fast warfare based on surprise attack. The key to its success was close co-operation between German panzer (tank) divisions and the dive-bombing aircraft of the Luftwaffe (air force). First a wave of panzers crashed without warning through weak spots in the enemy line and pushed forward as fast and far as possible. Overhead, German warplanes knifed out of the air to dive-bomb enemy units. The effect of the sudden and massive attack was to spread confusion and panic among enemy troops.

Meanwhile, selected sabotage troops, using parachutes or gliders, dropped behind Polish lines to destroy key transport and communication sites. Then the main body of infantry, in motorized transport, skirted around pockets of heavy resistance to swoop deep into lightly defended areas at the rear of enemy lines. In the lead were motorcycle troops armed with machine guns in sidecars, scouting the country ahead to report on enemy positions.

The effect of the blitzkrieg was shattering. The German army struck at Poland from three directions at once — north, west, and south — and moved with astonishing speed toward the Polish capital of Warsaw. The Polish defenders were stunned by the pace of the attack and the sheer number of German aircraft, tanks, and guns levelled against them. A bewildered Polish High Command lost contact with its armies and could not rally a defence. The Poles bravely fought back, but their army relied on cavalry troops and heavy, outdated equipment, while the Germans had the very latest and best equipment. In less than a month, the Germans had defeated an army of over 700 000 Poles and lost only 14 000 soldiers.

The "Phony War"

Although many of the **Allied powers**, including Canada, had declared war on Germany by early September 1939, the first seven months of the war on the Western Front saw both sides locked in a war of nerves, during which no shots were fired. The "sitzkrieg," or "phony war" as it was sometimes called, held Western Europe in a strange calm throughout the fall and winter of 1939–1940.

While the bulk of the German army was thrown against Poland, a much smaller German force sat tight along the French border, hoping the fighting would be delayed until the armies then in the east could join them. On the other side of the border, British and French troops stood glaring at them. The French had invested much in a defensive strategy designed to block German advances. They were not, however, prepared to go on the offensive. Britain, meanwhile, continued to be wary of committing soldiers and resources to conflicts outside its borders. Both sides waited out the winter, anxious for what the spring would hold.

Tensions in the Pacific

Europe was not the only region in the world poised on the brink of war in 1939. In Asia, Japan was continuing an aggressive campaign to expand its empire and extend its sphere of influence. The United States' policy of high tariffs to protect the American economy had had a crippling effect on the Japanese economy and had strengthened Japan's determination to drive Western powers out of the Pacific and to establish itself as the dominant power in the region. First on Japan's list was the conquest of China. In 1932 the Japanese successfully invaded the region of Manchuria. Later, in 1936, shortly after allying themselves with Nazi Germany, the Japanese launched a campaign to conquer much of China. The Western world was horrified by the savagery carried out during this undeclared war. The citizens of the city of Nanking were subjected to rape, torture, and murder after their defeat. It is estimated that 200 000 Chinese were slaughtered after the city fell to the Japanese. Western powers, including Britain, the United States, and Canada, protested against Japan's aggression by severing diplomatic ties and banning the shipment of war materials and oil to Japan. Expecting further Japanese aggression, the United States threatened to retaliate and began to prepare for the possibility of war in the Pacific.

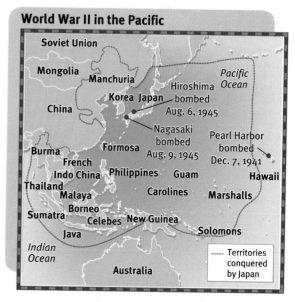

In 1936, Japan launched a campaign to conquer much of China and establish itself as the dominant power of the region.

Japanese troops arrived in China in 1932. Following their victory in Manchuria, the Japanese military took control by assassinating the Japanese Prime Minister and other politicians. Japan was firmly set on a military course.

A Reluctant Return to War

The return to war created interesting alliances. Germany, Italy, and Japan and the areas swallowed up by Hitler prior to 1939 formed the **Axis powers**. Opposing the fascist forces were the Allied powers, which initially included Britain and its Commonwealth, France, and Poland. In time, the Allied forces would be bolstered by the entry of the Soviet Union and the United States into the war. Ironically, the world's greatest capitalist and greatest communist powers would join forces against fascist aggression.

The years between the two world wars were a restless period for the Western world. While some nations, including Canada, Britain, and the United States, were determined to avoid another war at all costs, Germany sought to reverse the humiliation of the Treaty of Versailles and aggressively prepared for war. Canada's Prime Minister, Mackenzie King, was among many politicians who believed that war could be avoided through negotiation. Unfortunately, by the time leaders of the major Western powers realized that Hitler could not be trusted, it was too late. The Nazi army was prepared to engage in a fierce war. In 1939 Canada and the Allied powers reluctantly returned to the battle-fields of Europe.

Web Connections

http://www.school.mcgrawhill.ca/resources

Go to the above Web site to find out more about Canada and World War II. Go to *History Resources*, then to *Canada: A Nation Unfolding*, *Ontario Edition* to find out where to go next.

chapter review

CHAPTER SUMMARY

In this chapter we have seen

- how the years following World War I saw the rise of extreme political forces in countries such as Italy, Germany, and Russia

- that the Canadian government hoped to avoid returning to war and believed that a policy of appeasement would be successful

- that fascism and anti-Semitism had a following in Canada

- that Canada failed to provide sufficient support to Jews fleeing persecution in Nazi Germany

UNDERSTANDING HISTORICAL FACTS

1. Identify each of these people, places, and events, and explain their historical significance.

Adolf Hitler	Norman Bethune
Munich Agreement	*Mein Kampf*
Kristallnacht	*St. Louis*
Joseph Stalin	Nazi–Soviet Pact
Neville Chamberlain	anti-Semitism

2. Describe the treatment of German Jews under the Nazi regime.

3. Create a time line of the events that laid the foundations for the Holocaust, beginning with the publication of *Mein Kampf*.

4. What evidence in this chapter suggests that while some Canadians shared the anti-Semitic beliefs of Nazi Germany, others were disgusted by how Jews were being treated?

5. How did the blitzkrieg revolutionize warfare?

EXPRESSING YOUR OPINION

1. Some historians have described the two world wars as a ten-year European civil war with a twenty-year lull in the middle. Considering the issues and events surrounding the outbreak of World War II, would you agree or disagree that this war was the product of unresolved issues from World War I? Explain.

2. Canada, like many other nations, chose not to act when Hitler gathered strength in the 1930s. Considering Hitler's actions prior to the invasion of Poland, should Canada have taken an earlier and firmer stand against Nazi Germany? Why or why not?

3. Hitler has been described as perhaps the greatest gambler in history for the risks he took and his ability to bluff his opponents. Is this an accurate title? Defend your answer by using concrete examples.

4. When people are facing persecution, such as the Jews in Nazi Germany did, do other countries have a moral obligation to help them? Should Canada have opened its doors to Jews fleeing Nazi Germany?

5. During the inter-war years, the extreme political ideologies of fascism and communism dominated Europe. Which of the two systems would you have most feared living under? Give reasons for your answer.

WORKING WITH THE EVIDENCE

1. Joseph Stalin and Adolf Hitler were arch-rivals who viewed each other with suspicion and mistrust. One thing both men had in common was a desire to conquer Europe and, later, the world. In August 1939 the two enemies agreed to sign a pact. Why would each leader believe that an agreement with his country's greatest enemy would be in its best interest?

2. Hitler appears to have been committed to going to war at some point. How might events have differed if Chamberlain had refused to consent to the Munich Agreement? Would Hitler have invaded the Sudetenland? Would war have broken out in 1938? Sketch out a hypothetical time line based on Chamberlain's rejection of Hitler's demand for part of Czechoslovakia. Your time line should include at least five events.

Canada's Role in the Defeat of Fascism

Charles Comfort's painting *Dieppe Raid* captures the intense fighting faced by Canadian soldiers in their ill-fated attack on the French coast in August 1942.

INQUIRING INTO THE PAST

- By 1939 there had been significant changes in the make-up of the Canadian military. What was the nature of these changes?
- Why does controversy continue to surround the Battle of Dieppe?
- How did Canada contribute to the Normandy invasion, and why was its success crucial to the eventual defeat of Nazi Germany?
- What was the Holocaust, and why can it be considered a war within a war?

KEY TERMS

Brigades

Destroyers

Genocide

Panzers

TIMELINE

DECEMBER 1941 ▶
Canadians defeated at the Battle of Hong Kong

AUGUST 19, 1942 ▶
Canadians suffer heavy casualties at the Battle of Dieppe

DECEMBER 27, 1943 ▶
Canadians victorious at the Battle of Ortona

APRIL 1945 ▶
Liberation of the Netherlands by Canadians

Only a generation after enduring the bloodiest war in human history, Canada's Parliament voted to declare war on Germany. Most Canadians reluctantly agreed that Canada should go to war, and by the end of the first month of war seventy thousand people had signed up for armed service. By the end of the war, more than one million Canadian men and women would serve with the armed services and 42 042 Canadians would lose their lives.

Blitzkrieg across Western Europe

The calm in Western Europe was shattered in April 1940, when the German blitzkrieg struck Denmark and Norway. Canadian troops were immediately ordered to Scotland to board a ship for Norway. The next day, however, the order was changed and British troops took their place. The Canadians were spared the sting of a quick and overwhelming defeat. By May, Norway and Denmark had fallen to the Nazis, and the German Wehrmacht had conquered the Netherlands and Belgium and pushed

German and Italian Expansion by 1940

By 1940, fascist forces had conquered much of the Mediterranean Region.

These soldiers were among the 340 000 rescued from the beaches of France in "the Miracle of Dunkirk." How might the war have unfolded if cloud cover had not prevented the Luftwaffe from attacking?

into France as far as Amiens. On May 21 the **panzers** reached the English Channel. Retreating British forces were trapped in the French coastal town of Dunkirk. Hitler ordered the Wehrmacht to pull back and give the Luftwaffe the honour of striking the final blow. Fortunately, a dense fog pinned the German aircraft to the ground and gave British forces time to plan an escape. The delay would prove to be Hitler's first major mistake. In the meantime, however, the new British Prime Minister, Winston Churchill, warned the British House of Commons to prepare for disaster.

The Miracle of Dunkirk

Some historians believe that only "the Miracle of Dunkirk" prevented Hitler from winning the war before the end of May 1940. A call went out for boats to help the British troops escape Dunkirk. Almost nine hundred boats of all sizes — sightseeing boats, river ferries, fishing boats, and pleasure boats — joined up with heavy British **destroyers**. The makeshift fleet sailed across the English Channel in the fog to ferry soldiers back to Britain. It was expected that only ten thousand men could be saved, but the rescue effort succeeded beyond all hopes. When it ended, 340 000 soldiers had been rescued from certain destruction by the German Wehrmacht.

Meanwhile, France faced disaster. The French army, once considered the most powerful in the world, had collapsed. On June 14, 1940, the Nazis marched into an undefended Paris, and three days later France surrendered. In revenge for Germany's treatment after World War I, Hitler forced France to sign the surrender in the same railcar in which Germany had accepted defeat in 1918. Hitler was now master of Europe from Poland to the Atlantic Ocean.

Now only Britain and its Commonwealth allies were left to prevent a complete Nazi takeover of Europe. No one doubted that Hitler would let loose a savage attack against Britain. When France fell to the Nazis, a French general predicted that Britain would collapse in three weeks. Britain had only the Royal Navy, the effective but small Royal Air Force, and a few infantry divisions, including the well-equipped Canadian division, to fight off the German attack.

The surprising success of the German army in Europe raised immediate concerns for Canada. If Britain fell, Canada also faced disaster because the Canadian economy depended on selling goods to Britain. Even more frightening was the threat of a Nazi invasion of North America. Canada had counted on the British navy to protect its vulnerable eastern coast. The only remaining hope was for American protection. Both Mackenzie King and U.S. President Franklin Delano Roosevelt were concerned about protecting North America from Hitler.

The time had come for Canada to mobilize all its resources for the war against Hitler. Canadians pinned on lapel buttons that said, "Chin up, there'll always be an England" and got ready to do their part. Across Canada, factories, farms, volunteer organizations, and families prepared to support the war effort. At the same time thousands of Canadians enlisted for service overseas.

The Changing Face of the Canadian Military

There is considerable justification for referring to World War I as "the White Man's War." Certainly at the outset of that war there seemed to be little room for ethnic minorities or women in the military. By 1939, however, there had been a significant shift in attitudes in Canada that allowed for the active participation of visible minorities and women in the Canadian armed forces.

Unlike the case in World War I, the Canadian army during World War II had no segregated units. By 1939 it had become unacceptable to separate soldiers by race or ethnicity. Instead, Canadians of many ethnic backgrounds, including second-generation German Canadians and a few Japanese Canadians, formed a significant part of the Canadian army. Among Canada's increasingly diverse population, many visible minorities showed a strong desire to serve in defence of their country, Canada. From the outset of World War II, visible minorities were generally welcomed into the military in full combat roles and in several cases were promoted to officer rank. Gerry Carter, a Black Canadian from Saint John, New Brunswick, had the distinction of being Canada's youngest officer when, in 1943, at the age of eighteen, he was commissioned as a pilot officer.

Although the blatant racism of World War I had vanished, racism on an individual basis persisted. Many Japanese Canadians tried to enlist in the armed forces, but most were turned away. Some sol-

Aboriginal peoples, such as Sergeant Thomas Prince (centre) played an important part in the Canadian military during World War II.

diers had to endure racial slurs from fellow soldiers and at times were made to feel unwelcome in leisure activities.

Aboriginal Canadians were in a unique situation in Canada. In 1939 Aboriginal people still did not have the rights or responsibilities of citizenship, yet many chose to volunteer to serve overseas. Unlike the situation they faced in World War I, Aboriginal volunteers experienced no initial opposition to their enlistment. In fact, during World War II, recruiting parties campaigned on Aboriginal reserves. Why would Aboriginal Canadians eagerly volunteer to fight in a war on another continent against an enemy they knew very little about? The reasons varied widely. Some felt a strong sense of loyalty to Canada and the Crown because their ancestors had signed agreements with Queen Victoria. Some, like many other Canadians, wanted to assist in the defeat of tyranny and oppression. For others, the war was simply a way to travel or finally receive a paycheque after years of poverty and unemployment.

Another group for whom World War II was to be dramatically different from World War I were Ukrainian Canadians. Whereas between 1914 and 1918 they were deemed "enemy aliens" and often interned in camps, Ukrainian Canadians in World War II were welcomed into the Canadian military. By the end of the war up to fifty thousand Ukrainian Canadian men and women had served in the Canadian forces. World War II was a defining period for the Ukrainian Canadian community and helped to shape its identity in Canada.

Women in the Services

World War II also proved to be a turning point for Canadian women. For the first time, they were allowed to enlist in the Canadian military and to take on a wide range of jobs, although combat roles were never given consideration. Nurses had been a part of Canadian military tradition since the Boer War. About 2800 Canadian women had served as nurses in World War I, and many served again as nurses in World War II. The armed forces initially resisted recruiting women for other services, however. Many Canadian women nevertheless prepared themselves for a more active part in the war. At first they joined unofficial women's service groups, where they learned how to drive and fix trucks, read maps, operate wireless equipment, and give first aid. One group, the Canadian Auxiliary Territorial Service (CATS), was started by a columnist who worked for the *Toronto Daily Star*. Soon more than three thousand women were singing the CATS theme song:

> *We will fight for the might*
> *that we know is right*
> *And even Mussolini knows*
> *that CATS can fight…*

Many women in voluntary organizations lobbied for acceptance into official military service. Their request was ignored until military personnel shortages became critical and Britain suggested sending over members of its Women's Auxiliary Force to work at air training schools. In July 1941 the Canadian government established the Women's Division of the RCAF — the Canadian Women's Auxiliary Air Force (CWAAF). In August 1941 the Canadian Women's Army Corps (CWAC) was established, and in 1942 the Women's Royal Canadian Naval Service (WRENS) was begun. The air force was the first to realize that women had a place in uniform. By 1945 more than 17 400 women had served with CWAAF, more than 21 500 had joined CWAC, and 7100 had signed up with WRCNS.

This poster encouraged Canadians to play a role in the war. What do each of the caps represent? How many of the caps are meant to be worn by women?

Women's roles in the armed forces also expanded during the war years. For example, the number of trades for women in the air force grew from eleven to fifty by February 1943, including jobs as armourers, mechanics, fitters, and welders. And, by May 1944, selected groups of CWACs were being sent to combat areas in Europe, although women did not perform combat roles for several more decades.

Although only twenty years separated the end of World War I and the beginning of World War II, significant changes in racial and gender attitudes had

Women carried on the vital task of caring for the wounded, a tradition started by Florence Nightingale a century earlier. These Nursing Sisters cared for the wounded at a Canadian General Hospital in France, after the landing at Normandy.

Women occupied many more roles in World War II than in World War I. Here, members of the Women's Royal Canadian Naval Service are on board the HMCS *Sudbury* in Halifax.

led to a dramatic change in the composition of the Canadian military. This trend has continued, as women and visible minorities are increasingly prominent in the Canadian armed forces.

Canadians and the European War

In June 1940 only the British Commonwealth stood between the powerful German Wehrmacht and the British coast. Adolf Hitler had conquered almost all of Europe. All that remained outside his grasp were the British Isles to the west and the Soviet Union to the east. Hitler had already drawn up a plan for the invasion of Britain under the code-name Operation Sea Lion. It called for the landing of twenty-five divisions along the south coast of England and a quick thrust forward to take London. But the panzer (tank) divisions that were the key to the German invasion forces, as well as the infantry troops and motorized equipment that rolled in behind them, could reach Britain only by ship. To ensure the safe transport of troops and equipment across the English Channel, Germany would first need to destroy the Royal Air Force and seize control of the air.

The Battle of Britain

On July 10, 1940, Hitler ordered a savage air attack on British ships in the English Channel. The Battle of Britain had begun. By mid-August, nearly two thousand German aircraft swarmed the skies over Britain. The British air force was only about half the size of the German Luftwaffe. The future of the British people, and perhaps of North Americans as well, depended on the success of a few fighter pilots. At first the Luftwaffe was devastatingly successful, knocking out airfields and supply factories with ruthless efficiency. The Royal Air Force (RAF) could do little to counter the German attack.

A turning point in Nazi strategy occurred on September 7, when two night-flying Luftwaffe planes bombed London. Germany feared that the coming winter would delay a land invasion of Britain, and the decision was made to shift the Battle of Britain to a new phase. This phase would attempt to break the will of the people by targeting civilians.

In response, British Prime Minister Churchill ordered bombing raids on Berlin. Hitler was outraged, and at a mass rally in Berlin he promised Germans that the British would suffer for the raids: "We will raze their cities to the ground." However, the Luftwaffe's continuous attacks on British cities allowed the RAF to anticipate German attacks and to be ready and waiting. The German attacks peaked on September 15, 1940, when more than one thousand Luftwaffe bombers and nearly seven hundred fighters flew over London in a daring all-out daylight raid. RAF Spitfires and Hurricanes climbed high to meet them, and the sky over London was streaked with vapour trails from aerial combat.

The Luftwaffe's losses that day were heavy enough to convince the Germans that their tactics were not working. Germany had failed to seize air supremacy over the English Channel, and Operation Sea Lion was abandoned. By May 1941

The bombing of civilian targets such as London became a horrifying aspect of World War II. Why were the bombings referred to as "terror bombings"? Can they be justified as a necessary part of war?

Hitler had redeployed the Luftwaffe to the Balkans, and later it was assigned to the Russian front. For Britain, the worst was over.

Canada's Contributions to the War in the Air

Canadians were often in the thick of the air war, both in the Battle of Britain and afterward in Europe, Africa, and the Pacific. A quarter of a million Canadians served in the RAF and the Royal Canadian Air Force (RCAF) as pilots, air crews, ground crews, transport crews, and flight instructors. By the end of the war, 17 101 members of the RCAF had died in battle. The RCAF fatalities were equal to the number of Canadian infantry deaths in Europe. The casualty figures show how important war in the air had become.

Canadians flew all kinds of airplanes during the war, and the fighting was often vicious. Some flyers provided air cover for infantry or armoured divisions in North Africa. When the Luftwaffe's daylight raids over England had almost stopped, RAF and RCAF fighter and bomber squadrons began to make raids on German-occupied France. Canadian bomber units attacked German air bases, gun positions, rail and road traffic, and military headquarters in France.

Although Canadian bomber crews were not in the centre of public attention, their work was dangerous and their casualty rates terrifyingly high. Canadian bomber units became experts at night-bombing techniques against targets. On their night missions, their job was to fly "blind" in the darkness to bomb targets deep inside Germany.

By mid-1943 Canadian crews flying Lancaster and Halifax bombers were dropping huge loads of high explosives on German factories and steel mills in the Ruhr. They also rained destruction on German civilians in the cities of Hamburg, Frankfurt, and Berlin. On July 24, 1943, eight hundred bombers destroyed the port of Hamburg. Three days later, a second wave of bombing and an intense heat wave touched off a terrible firestorm that killed almost fifty thousand German men, women, and children. A week later, the bombers struck the ruins of Hamburg for a third time.

Hitler denounced the attacks on Hamburg and other German cities as "terror bombing." Although Germany had begun the bombing of civilian targets in raids on Warsaw, Rotterdam, London, and Coventry, the Allies responded with deadly efficiency. Hitler was forced to pull the Luftwaffe back to protect German cities and industrial sites from Allied bombing raids. By mid-1944, the Allies ruled the skies over Europe. The Luftwaffe was in full retreat.

Canadian World War II flying ace George Beurling records another of his hits on the side of his plane.

Germany's Invasion of the Soviet Union

On June 22, 1941, Hitler took the biggest gamble of the war by launching a massive attack on the Soviet Union. Code-named Operation Barbarossa, the blitzkrieg ended the Nazi–Soviet Pact, and the Soviet Union suddenly found itself in the Allied camp. Hitler was sure that the blitzkrieg would bring the Soviet Union to its knees within months, but he badly miscalculated. He underestimated the Soviets' will to resist and counted on capturing Moscow and most of the Soviet army before winter set in.

In Operation Barbarossa, the Nazis used the blitzkrieg on a much larger scale than ever before. At first the Soviets were unable to stop the German forces and suffered more than one million casualties — more than double the German casualty toll. But, even though the tactics of blitzkrieg were successful, the massive size of the Soviet Union meant that a quick victory was almost impossible. The Soviet army could keep retreating into an almost unlimited country.

By late fall 1941, the Wehrmacht had reached the outskirts of Moscow. It had, however, expected to reach Moscow well before winter and was unprepared for temperatures as low as –50°C. It was so cold that German soldiers sometimes found their soup frozen solid before they had time to eat it. They had no warm winter clothing and no anti-freeze or oils suitable for the cold-weather operation of their tanks and transport vehicles. As a result, they suffered terribly in the bitter Russian winter. Meanwhile tough, warmly clothed Siberian

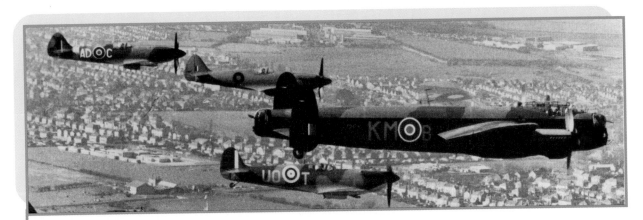

Airplanes such as the Lancaster bomber (seen here followed by two Spitfires and a Hurricane) would play a crucial role in the eventual defeat of Nazi Germany. Many of the Lancasters were built in Canada.

troops had been brought in to defend Moscow. They were ready for winter fighting and stopped the Wehrmacht only fifty kilometres from the city.

Hitler's gamble had failed. The Soviet army, though bloodied, fought back. A quick, decisive victory had escaped the German troops. They were locked into a long, hard war against a Soviet army that had huge reserves of soldiers.

The War in the Pacific

At about the same time that Operation Barbarossa ground to a halt in the Russian winter, U.S. naval ships were anchored in the Hawaiian waters of Pearl Harbor. Japan's aggressive campaign to establish a Pacific empire and the crippling effects of import tariffs (taxes) imposed by the United States had brought relations between Japan and the Western nations to a breaking point. In response the United States had stationed its naval fleet in Hawaii in case war broke out in the Pacific Ocean. Britain had also decided to strengthen its forces in the region, but few troops could be spared from the defence of the British Isles. Britain asked Canada to help by sending Canadian soldiers to the British colony of Hong Kong, on the south coast of China. By early December 1941, two Canadian **brigades** had settled into the British garrison at Hong Kong.

The Attack on Pearl Harbor

Meanwhile, the United States tried to hammer out a peace treaty with Japan. What no one in the West knew was that the Japanese had already decided to make war on the United States and Britain three months earlier. The peace talks were meant to keep the Allies off guard while Japan prepared for the attack. Japan aimed to conquer the West's resource-rich colonies in East Asia and the Pacific.

The only major barrier to a Japanese victory in the East was the U.S. fleet at Pearl Harbor, which was out of reach of a Japanese land-based attack. Japanese Admiral Isoroku Yamamoto planned a surprise attack using fighter planes launched from Japanese aircraft carriers. Attacks on the U.S. base in the Philippines and the British colonies of Malaya and Hong Kong were also planned for the same date — December 7, 1941.

At 8 a.m. the first wave of Japanese war planes appeared in the sky over Pearl Harbor and began bombing their targets. Japan had not declared war on the United States, and no one in Hawaii expected an attack. When the surprise attack ended less than two hours later, almost nothing was left of the American Pacific fleet. Eighteen warships and 349 aircraft were lost or damaged, and 3581 American combatants and 103 civilians were killed or injured.

The United States Enters the War

Americans were shocked and horrified by the surprise attack on Pearl Harbor. The United States immediately declared war on Japan, adding a crucial ally to the fight against fascism and Japanese expansion. In 1941, the United States was the richest nation in the world. With the world's largest steel industry and a population ten times larger than Canada's, it could invest enormous amounts of money, arms, and personnel into the war effort. It would take time for the Americans to mobilize for war, but once they did, the Allies could begin planning to liberate Europe. Meanwhile, Canada and the other Allied nations still faced a bloody struggle in Europe and the Far East.

The Canadians at Hong Kong

Just a few hours after the attack on Pearl Harbor, Japan began its invasion of Hong Kong. What the Canadians in Hong Kong did not know was that before the attack on Pearl Harbor, more than fifty thousand Japanese soldiers had been massed within fifty kilometres of Hong Kong for an invasion. They were well equipped and hardened by four years of fighting, having been part of the force that invaded China in 1937. The Japanese plans for conquering Hong Kong had been laid out more than a year before under the code-name Hana-Saku — "flowers in bloom, flowers in bloom."

The Canadian soldiers, by comparison, were unready for battle. The troops were classified as C Force: "in need of refresher training or

Eighteen warships and 349 aircraft were lost or damaged, and nearly 3700 American combatants and civilians were killed or injured when the Japanese attacked Pearl Harbor. This attack brought the United States into the war. What important resources would the Americans bring to the Allied war effort?

insufficiently trained and not recommended for operations." Almost 30 percent of the Canadian soldiers had never fired a shot in rifle practice. The raw Canadian troops joined a small Commonwealth defence force that totalled no more than fourteen thousand people, including nurses and civilian volunteers. Although the Canadians were garrisoned on the Chinese mainland, their job was to defend positions on the nearby island of Hong Kong.

On December 8, 1941 (December 7, across the international date line in Canada), Japan launched its attack on Hong Kong. Less than two weeks later, Canadian troops heard the first wailing of air raid sirens. The Japanese air force destroyed docks, military barracks, gun emplacements, and the five old RAF airplanes on the British airfield. Now the defenders had no protection in the air. They also had no help from the sea: the U.S. fleet had been crippled at Pearl Harbor, and the two great British warships, *Prince of Wales* and *Repulse*, were sunk by the Japanese off Malaya.

The defence forces on the Chinese mainland were far too small and had too few guns to withstand the Japanese attack. The troops were ordered to retreat across the water to Hong Kong Island, and

Japan nearly succeeded in gaining control of the entire Pacific region. Do you think that Australia would have been the next nation to be invaded by Japan?

many Canadian soldiers believed that Hong Kong would never be captured. But, as darkness closed in on December 18, 1941, thousands of Japanese troops began crossing the strait to Hong Kong Island in collapsible boats and sampans (small, flat-bottomed boats propelled by two oars). On December 19 the Winnipeg Grenadiers, looking down into a place called Happy Valley, were startled to see hundreds of bushes advancing up the hill toward them. Japanese soldiers, using bushes as camouflage, were on the attack. The Canadians were outnumbered by ten to one, and on Christmas Day 1941 Hong Kong officially surrendered.

When the invasion ended, every Canadian soldier in Hong Kong had either been killed or captured by the Japanese. For the next three and a half years, Canadian prisoners of war were crowded into barracks and used as slave labour. Some were put to work building landing strips; others worked in shipyards near Tokyo; and yet others worked in coal mines in northern Japan.

The prisoners were given only a single serving of plain rice three times a day. Those who fell ill from exhaustion, malnutrition, or diseases such as pneumonia, diphtheria, or cholera had little chance of survival. Red Cross packages destined for the camps were seized and sold on the black market. Medicines were also withheld, leaving camp doctors powerless

These Canadian soldiers survived the harsh conditions of the Japanese prisoner-of-war camps. Should they be awarded compensation from the Japanese government for the way in which they were treated?

to help the sick. As a result of the appalling conditions, the death rate in Japanese prisoner-of-war camps was six times higher than in German camps.

During the summer of 1945, all surviving Canadian prisoners of war were sent to work in coal mines, and an order was given that if Japan were invaded, all prisoners were to be executed. Fortunately, this order was later cancelled.

The War in Europe: 1942–1945

The first two years of the war had been a stunning success for Nazi Germany and an utter disaster for the Allied forces. Fortunately, the tide of war was about to turn in favour of the Allies. But before it did, Canada suffered another tragedy on the battlefield — the Battle of Dieppe.

The Battle of Dieppe

In August 1942 five thousand Canadian troops stationed in England were picked for a raid on the French port of Dieppe. They had been trained in England for almost three years. Along with another thousand British commandos (troops specially trained for hit and run raids) and American Rangers, the Canadians were to attack the strongly defended port. The raid on Dieppe was launched to find out what was needed to make a full-scale Allied invasion across the English Channel a success. It was also intended to draw German forces away from the Russian front.

The defeat of Canadian soldiers occurred almost before the attack began. Well-placed German defence forces fired down on the landing craft from high cliffs above the beaches. Many Canadians were killed as they charged down the ramps of the landing crafts. The few who made it onto the beaches were killed as they raced for cover. Only a few soldiers made it into the town of Dieppe, where they took on the German defenders in close combat.

The casualty toll in those few bleak hours at Dieppe recalled the mass deaths of World War I. The Canadian magazine *Saturday Night* called Dieppe "another Passchendaele." Of the 5000 Canadians who sailed for Dieppe, almost 1000 died and more than 500 were wounded. Almost 2000 Canadians were captured and became prisoners of war.

In recent years considerable historical debate has swirled around the Battle of Dieppe. It has been suggested that the raid on Dieppe was intended to respond to Stalin's demands for an attack from the West to help take pressure off the Soviet Union by drawing off German troops. If this was the case, many Canadians were sacrificed to appease Stalin. Questions have also been raised about the value of the attack as compared with the very high cost in human lives. Should soldiers have been sent in on a mission with so little hope of success? How crucial were the insights gained from this attack to the success of the Normandy invasion two years later? Could such an attack be justified by the long-term gains? These difficult questions must be considered in the context of the war rather than in the comfort of hindsight.

The Shifting Tides of War

Despite the tragedy at Dieppe, the war began to shift in favour of the Allies. Big American armies were taking the field against the Axis powers in North Africa (where Italy and Germany had invaded Egypt), and the Soviet army was holding off the German Wehrmacht. After six months of fierce fighting at Stalingrad, the Soviets managed to

The Dieppe raid ended in disaster. Here, several of the nearly one thousand Canadian soldiers who died lie among the silenced tanks and landing craft of the Calgary Regiment.

encircle the German forces and cut off their supply lines. Now the tables were turned. In North Africa British General Bernard Montgomery had scored a major victory at El Alamein, Egypt. His troops defeated the Afrika Korps of the famous German general, Erwin Rommel, known as "the Desert Fox." At the same time, the Allies made landings at Algeria and Morocco and began moving east across North Africa. These events marked important successes for the Allies.

Canadians in Sicily and the Italian Campaign

By the summer of 1943 the Canadian soldiers who had not been involved in the Dieppe raid had been in Britain for almost three and a half years, waiting for a chance to fight. On June 26, the word came at last: they were told to pack up their bedrolls and get ready to move out. The Canadians were headed for Sicily, the island just off the toe of the Italian "boot." There they would join the British Eighth Army under the hero of El Alamein, General Montgomery. The battle plan was to invade Sicily and trap German and Italian soldiers between the British Eighth Army, at the northeastern tip of the island, and the U.S. Seventh Army, which would land on the eastern shores, before the Axis armies could escape to Italy. From Sicily, it was a short jump onto the Italian mainland. The next step was to attack Italy, the weakest of the Axis powers.

Sicily fell fairly quickly, and many Italian soldiers were captured. The Allied "trap" had closed too slowly, however, and tens of thousands of German troops escaped to Italy. The Allies were now ready to invade the Italian mainland. Canadians were part of the Allied forces that moved from Sicily to the toe of the Italian boot. They landed on September 3, 1943, and began moving up the Italian peninsula. Fresh Canadian troops from Britain also joined in the attack.

Mussolini enjoyed the support of Italians only so long as the war was fought away from home. Once their homeland was invaded, Italians quickly turned against Mussolini. When he responded to a summons to appear before King Victor Emmanuel he was deposed as Prime Minister and imprisoned. By the end of September 1943 Italy had surrendered to the

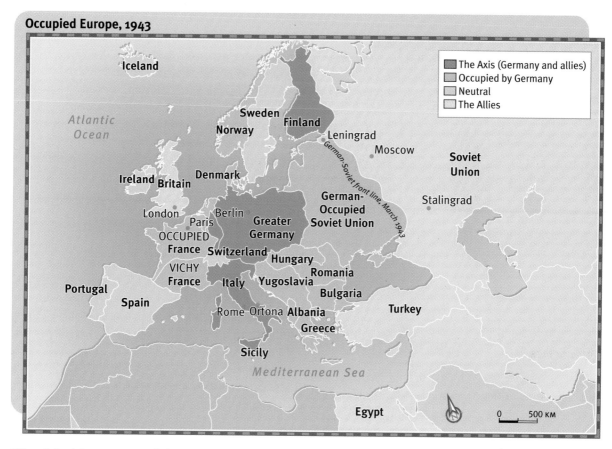

Occupied Europe, 1943

Legend:
- The Axis (Germany and allies)
- Occupied by Germany
- Neutral
- The Allies

Iceland

Atlantic Ocean

Sweden
Norway
Finland
Leningrad
Moscow
Soviet Union

German-Soviet front line, March 1943

Ireland Britain Denmark

German-Occupied Soviet Union

Stalingrad

London
Paris Berlin Greater Germany
OCCUPIED France Switzerland
VICHY France Hungary
Italy Romania
Portugal Yugoslavia
Spain Bulgaria
Rome Ortona Albania Turkey
Greece
Sicily

Mediterranean Sea

Egypt

0   500 KM

Although the Axis powers controlled most of Europe, 1943 was the year the Allies began to strike back, marking the beginning of the end for Nazi Germany. Which battles would be the main turning points in the war?

Allies. This did little to end the Italian campaign, as the German army stepped up its efforts against the invading Allied forces. At one point German soldiers staged a daring rescue of Mussolini, who then set up an "Italian Social Republic" in northern Italy. Mussolini's return did little more than lead to a civil war in the north, which ended in his capture and execution. The founder of fascism faced an ignoble end as his body was hung upside down with piano wire in a town square.

The mountainous Italian countryside was nightmare terrain for the Allied troops. The German defenders had fortified a line of hilltops and mountain peaks that ran the length of Italy. The soldiers of the Wehrmacht were also experienced fighters. As a result, it cost the Allies far more in men and equipment to capture German positions than it cost the Germans to defend them. But the Allies were slowly gaining ground; by the late autumn of 1943 the Canadians had moved 650 kilometres up

the central mountains of Italy. The Allies were on their way to Rome. The Germans, however, ensured that there was no safe way to get there.

The Canadians at Ortona

As December approached, the Allies found that their route toward Rome was blocked at Ortona, an ancient town situated on cliffs above the Adriatic Sea. The Canadian forces were ordered to capture Ortona. The Germans had blown up all bridges in the area, and the steep countryside gave them the advantage as they were firmly entrenched in hilltop fortifications. The German defenders were the first-rate 90th Light Panzer Grenadier Division, famed for their tough fighting in North Africa.

The Canadian losses were high; since crossing the Moro River, the 1st Canadian Division had lost 2339 soldiers. Sixteen thousand more had to be evacuated because of sickness or battle fatigue.

The Princess Patricia's Canadian Light Infantry, shown here marching through Valguarnera, Sicily, were part of the Canadian force that captured Sicily. Why was success in Sicily an important step in the defeat of the Axis powers?

Despite the heavy costs of the battle, the Canadians faced Germany's elite troops and were triumphant. On December 27 they captured Ortona. The town fell to a regiment from Edmonton, and for weeks afterward a sign stood in Ortona that read, "A West Canadian Town." The struggle for Ortona became one of the best-known battles fought by Canadians during World War II.

By December, 27, 1943, the Canadians had defeated the Germans at Ortona. Here, a Canadian tank of the Three Rivers Regiment moves through the main square of the city. Ortona is remembered as one of the great achievements of the Canadian military in World War II.

In the spring and summer of 1944 the Canadian forces were assigned to fight in the centre of the Italian peninsula. They played an important role in breaking the line of German defences. By June 1944 the Allies had succeeded in capturing Rome. Canadian forces continued to fight in Italy until February 1945, when all Canadian troops were reunited in northwestern Europe as the 1st Canadian Army.

D-Day and the Normandy Invasion

Two days after capturing Rome, the Allied forces invaded France. The lessons of Dieppe were taken to heart in planning the invasion. Massive air and naval firepower and better communications from ship to shore were put in place. New versions of the Sherman tank, called "Funnies," were built. They could wade through water, bulldoze obstacles, explode mines, and throw bursts of flame. Allied soldiers worked hard to prepare for action. By early June, more than thirty thousand Canadians were ready to do their part on "D-Day," the day scheduled for the Allied invasion of Europe. The invasion plan called for five divisions to land along an eighty-kilometre front. American forces were to attack at the western end of Normandy Beach, and British and Canadian troops were to land farther to the east. The 3rd Canadian Division was to land with the first wave of attackers in an area called Juno Beach. The sky above Juno Beach was to be protected by RAF bombers, many of which were flown by Canadian bomber crews. The invasion force also included 171 air squadrons to knock out the German Luftwaffe and destroy enemy tanks. More than seven thousand Allied ships of all descriptions — navy landing craft, destroyers, cruisers, corvettes, frigates, torpedo boats, and minesweepers — were also scheduled for the invasion.

D-Day Begins

It took enormous care and good luck to keep the massive invasion plans secret, but the Allies had done it. As dawn broke on June 6, 1944, surprised German defenders looked out to see a huge flotilla

In June 1944, Canadians joined the Americans and the British in launching the Normandy invasion. This photo shows soldiers struggling ashore in an attempt to establish a beachhead.

of ships sweeping toward the French coast. "As far as your eye could see, there were ships," said one sailor aboard the Canadian minesweeper *Canso*. "I always said that if you could jump a hundred yards at a clip you could get back to England without even wetting your feet. That's how many ships were involved."

The invasion did not go perfectly because some of the German positions had not been knocked out by the massive Allied air and sea bombardments. Many soldiers had to scramble for cover across exposed beaches raked with artillery fire. The landing of the 3rd Canadian Division was delayed by reefs and choppy seas for an hour and a half. By the time the Canadian forces touched down on Juno Beach, the enemy was ready for them. The worst trouble, however, occurred in the American sector at Omaha Beach. American forces were at the mercy of German defenders who fired down at them from high ground. Casualties were heavy, and the Americans lost 7500 soldiers.

Despite the heavy setbacks, the invasion was considered a success. By the end of D-Day more than 155 000 soldiers, 6000 vehicles, and 3600 tonnes of supplies had been landed in France. The fighting on the beaches had destroyed the defending German division, and Allied forces moved inland. The Canadians had pushed to within five kilometres of the city of

Caen, farther inland than any other Allied troops. Canadian losses were also lower than had been feared. Still, almost a thousand Canadian soldiers were killed, wounded, or captured that day.

Germany was now fighting the land war on three fronts: the Soviet Union, Italy, and France. On the Eastern Front, the Soviet Union continued to drive Germany back. In Italy, the Allies were pressing north. A new invasion through France would almost certainly mean the defeat of Germany.

Preparing for the End of War and a New Europe

With the defeat of Germany all but certain, the three main leaders of the Allied forces, Britain's Winston Churchill, the Soviet Union's Joseph Stalin, and the United States' Franklin Delano Roosevelt met in February 1945 to the discuss the fate of a defeated Germany and lay the foundations for post-war Europe. The conference, held at Yalta, in the Crimea, resulted in several key decisions. First, after it was defeated, Germany was to be demilitarized (stripped of any military forces) and denazified (the Nazi party was to be disbanded). Furthermore, post-war Germany was to be divided into four zones of occupation. Britain, France, the United States, and the Soviet Union would each occupy one of the zones. The other major development to come out of the Yalta Conference was an agreement to create a new organization to replace the failed League of Nations. This new organization would come to be known as the United Nations. It would be one of the dominant organizations to shape the post-war world. But on the battlegrounds, meanwhile, the war raged on.

The Drive into Germany

As the Allies drove toward the Rhine River, Hitler made a last attempt to hold off the inevitable defeat. He extended the age limits for armed service to include all German males between sixteen and fifty years of age. As a result, he managed to get 750 000 soldiers and three thousand tanks to push back the advancing Allied forces. But Germany's last desperate gamble failed, and the remains of the Wehrmacht were forced to retreat. Although this last assault made

no difference to Germany's fate, it probably changed the map of post-war Europe. The attack delayed the Western Allies' advance for six or eight weeks and gave the Soviet Union time to move across Eastern Europe and seize territory during its drive toward Berlin.

By the end of March 1945 the Allies had crossed the Rhine River from the west and invaded Germany. By April 30 the first Soviet troops were picking their way through the rubble of Berlin. Some troops were already within blocks of the bomb-proof bunker, deep under the chancellery building (government office), where Hitler had gone into hiding. Hitler and his companion, Eva Braun, carried out a suicide pact. Their bodies were later carried out of the bunker, doused with gasoline, and set ablaze. Immediately following Hitler's death, Grand Admiral Karl Donitz became head of the Third Reich, as set out in Hitler's will. On May 7, 1945, Donitz surrendered the German army to the invading Allied forces. This day is referred to as VE (Victory in Europe) Day.

Jubilant crowds poured into the streets of Delden, the Netherlands, to welcome the 3rd Canadian Division and celebrate their liberation, on April 13, 1945. To this day, Canadians are extended a warm welcome by the Dutch.

The Movement of Allied Forces, 1944–1945

As the end of the war in Europe neared, the German army was pushed out of Eastern Europe by the Soviet Union and out of Western Europe by a coalition of nations, including Britain, Canada, and the United States.

The Liberation of the Netherlands

There are few places in the world where Canadians are made to feel more welcome than in the Netherlands. Suffering under the brutal Nazi regime for five years, the Dutch were barely avoiding starvation, surviving on as little as 320 calories per day, while many Dutch men were being used as slave labour. The task of liberating the Dutch fell to the Canadians under the leadership of General Harry Crerar. While the bulk of the Allied forces pressed on toward Berlin, the Canadian army was to sweep into the Netherlands, clearing out any remaining German forces.

Although the eventual outcome of the war was no longer in doubt, the Canadian soldiers still faced some difficult opposition. Through the months of April and May 1945, Canadians struggled to free the Dutch. The two large Canadian cemeteries at Groesbeek and Holten serve as reminders of the sacrifices made by Canadian soldiers in the liberation of the Netherlands. The spring of 1945 is remembered by the Dutch as the "Sweetest of Springs." Triumph and tragedy mingled together during their spring of liberation. Canadian soldiers were welcomed with kisses and flowers by the grateful Dutch in 1945; and in 1995, when Canadian veterans returned to the towns they liberated, they were once again greeted with adoration by the children and grandchildren of those they had liberated fifty years earlier. Nor have the Dutch forgotten those who died in the struggle to liberate their homeland. Today, Dutch school children still make annual trips to the Canadian cemeteries in the Netherlands to lay flowers on the graves of the brave young men who died so that they could enjoy their freedom.

The Holocaust: The War Within a War

While Germany waged war against the Allied countries, it was also carrying out another, more sinister war against European Jews. The aim of this war was the total annihilation of the Jews. Before this **genocide** was stopped, six million Jews, including two million children, would perish.

The Nazi Persecution of the Jews

Anti-Semitism — hatred of Jews — was a key element in Nazism. Hitler blamed the Jews for Germany's failures, and Nazis persecuted Jewish Germans mercilessly throughout the 1930s, despite the fact that Jews had lived in Germany for centuries and had become part of the life of the community.

When World War II began, the persecution of Jews moved into a new and terrible phase. When Germany invaded Poland in 1939, almost three million Jews fell into Nazi hands. When it conquered Denmark, Norway, the Netherlands, and France, hundreds of thousands more fell under Nazi control. Jews were forced to leave their homes and were crowded into slums called ghettos. Often, several families shared a single room. The Nazis also forced the Jews to wear the yellow Star of David and to work as labourers for the Nazi regime. Food was in such short supply and living conditions so brutal in the ghettos that thousands of Jews died of starvation and disease.

The "Final Solution"

When the Wehrmacht marched into the Soviet Union in 1941, the Nazis began to work on another solution to the "Jewish problem." The Wehrmacht was followed by special SS (Schutzstaffel) "action squads." These Nazi death squads began the mass execution of Jews during the winter of 1941–1942, when half a million people were shot to death. The slaughter of Russian Jews sealed the fate of European Jews and began one of the most frightful episodes in history. In January 1942, top SS officials met in the Berlin suburb of Wannsee to work out the details of the Endlosung, "the final solution of the Jewish problem." They prepared a plan for secretly murdering eleven million Jews in Europe.

After the Wannsee Conference the Nazis began to step up the construction of huge gas chambers at specially constructed death camps. The ghettos of Europe served as holding places until enough death camps were ready. Then "consignments of Jews" were rounded up by ghetto police and delivered to the SS for shipment to Nazi death camps at Auschwitz, Treblinka, Sobibor, and elsewhere.

As the Nazis were driven out of Western and Eastern Europe, the full extent of the atrocities committed in death camps and concentration camps came to light. This man, standing in the mud at Auschwitz, shows the effects of the deprivation that victims of the Holocaust suffered. Millions died in these camps. They were executed, gassed, starved, or simply worked to death.

The death camps were run by the SS units known as "Death's Head Brigades." When the deported Jews arrived at the camps, they were separated into two groups. Those who could work were kept alive as slave labour. Those who were unable to work — mostly the elderly, mothers, and children — were immediately killed in the gas chambers. One prisoner described what he saw on his first day in a work camp: "We're at a gravel-pit, prisoners in striped clothing are shoveling gravel. Emaciated. Covered with wounds from blows. A Capo (supervisor) shouts and beats the prisoners with the handle of a shovel. Actually they're walking skeletons. Will we one day look like this, too?" This hard labour under conditions of great cruelty was intended to result in death. Slave labour was called "productive annihilation."

To prevent resistance, prisoners were tricked into believing that they were getting ready for deportation. Treblinka, for example, had a fake front that resembled a large railway station. Signs directed new arrivals to onward trains, and the station even featured a painted clock. In some camps, the gas chambers were disguised as shower rooms. Some prisoners, after being told that they were being sent to Canada, were ordered to place all their belongings in a "Canada Room." Then they were herded into the deadly "shower rooms." In Auschwitz, about two thousand people at a time could be gassed. When the gas chamber was full of adults, small children were shoved in over their heads. Then, deadly Zyklon-B gas was released into the sealed chamber.

Word of the secret slaughter began to filter out of the death camps. In August 1942, the *Montreal Star* ran a news story with the headline: "Nazi Slaughterhouse — Germans Massacre Million Jews in Extermination Drive." But news about the atrocities being committed against the Jews prompted little immediate reaction. Not until 1944, when news of the mass killings at Auschwitz reached England and the United States, did plans for serious action begin to take shape. Meanwhile, the Jews in Warsaw and other European ghettos bravely fought back, even though they were far outnumbered and mostly unarmed. It took the Nazis months of fighting to put down the resistance in Warsaw. They finally destroyed the Warsaw ghetto by systematically blowing up houses.

Web Connections

http://www.school.mcgrawhill.ca/resources

Go to the above Web site to find out more about the life of Anne Frank, a young Jewish girl, during the Holocaust. Go to *History Resources*, then to *Canada: A Nation Unfolding, Ontario Edition*, to find out where to go next.

The Horror That Was the Holocaust

The aftermath of war revealed the horrors of the Nazi regime. Canadians had heard rumours and read reports of Nazi concentration camps, but many had believed that these stories were only war propaganda. What the Allies found when they arrived at the concentration camps was indescribable: piles of corpses, mass graves, camp survivors so starved that they looked like walking skeletons. Millions of people had been murdered and had died of disease or starvation in the camps. They included political prisoners, communists, certain religious groups such as Jehovah's Witnesses, homosexuals, prisoners of war, resistance fighters, and ethnic groups such as Gypsies and Poles. But the single largest group was European Jews. Six million Jews were murdered by the Nazis in mass murders that came to be called the Holocaust — the attempted extermination of the Jews.

It is estimated that by the end of the war, almost two thirds of the Jews of Europe had lost their lives. Only about one million people survived the Nazi death camps. When the first photographs of death-camp survivors were published, the world was horrified. How could a thing like this happen?

The horror of the Holocaust remains with us today. Despite what the world should have learned about humanity's capacity to commit unspeakable crimes, the Holocaust has not been the final genocide. Mass exterminations have occurred since, in Cambodia and Uganda in the 1970s, and in Rwanda, Bosnia, and Kosovo in the 1990s. The question remains, how can we prevent genocide from ever happening again?

Belsen Camp, The Compound for Women by Leslie Cole captures the horrors that greeted the first British soldiers to arrive at Bergen Belsen. These emaciated women are startled to see soldiers in British uniforms.

The Atomic Bomb and Victory in the Pacific

By 1944 the United States had retaken New Guinea, the Solomon Islands, and the Philippines from Japan. By early 1945 the British Commonwealth forces, with the support of China, had retaken Burma. The Japanese fleet was almost destroyed, and a circle was slowly closing around the Japanese army. But the Japanese were digging in and fighting a tough defensive war from tunnels and prepared positions. When American forces invaded Okinawa in March 1945, the 100 000 Japanese soldiers fought almost to the last person. Japanese pilots flew suicide missions called kamikaze attacks. They deliberately crashed aircraft crammed with dynamite into U.S. warships, killing themselves as well as many U.S. sailors.

Some U.S. military leaders believed that Japan was too proud to surrender. To invade Japan, they argued, would mean huge military and civilian casualties. But the United States had a terrifying new instrument of war — the atomic bomb. American President Harry Truman believed that the atomic bomb could force Japan to surrender without an invasion that might cost half a million American lives.

the arts

LOST ART OF AUSCHWITZ

Auschwitz is perhaps the most infamous of the Nazi death camps. Here, between May 1940 and January 1945, nearly two million people were murdered, 90 percent of them Jews. As in all concentration camps, having a specialized skill was often the key to saving one's life or at least delaying death. Physicians, architects, engineers, mechanics, tailors, musicians, dentists, barbers, carpenters, shoemakers, and artists were all pressed into service by the Nazis. Artists in the concentration camps were forced to create propaganda art, such as posters celebrating Hitler's birthday, or to paint swastikas and eagles on captured tanks.

Many of the artists placed themselves at great risk by secretly painting images of their lives in the camps. Some of these paintings, hidden from the eyes of their Nazis captors, have been uncovered since the end of World War II. Included in the art that has been uncovered are murals depicting the work done in the penal company, prisoners in a rock quarry, washroom decorations, and slogans.

Ballerina Block 18, basement Main Camp

The secret art of the inmates of Auschwitz served a dual function; it kept their spirits alive and became a record of life in the camps. The famous artist Pablo Picasso wrote, "Painting is an instrument of war to be waged against brutality and darkness." Such was the purpose of the "lost" art of Auschwitz.

The Penal Company "Königsgraben" Birkenau, Block 1

Making the Atomic Bomb

The American government had earlier decided to work on the invention of an atomic bomb by forming the top-secret Manhattan Project. Working under tight security, a group of scientists led by the brilliant physicist Robert Oppenheimer attempted to solve a wide range of problems relating to the atomic bomb. Their aim was to have the bomb ready by mid-1945. It was a race against time, because Nazi Germany was thought to be working on the same problems.

Dropping the Atomic Bomb

By July 1945 word had reached President Truman that the atomic bomb was ready. On July 26, he called for Japan to surrender or accept "prompt and utter destruction." He promised that if Japan surrendered, its economy, culture, and traditions would remain unchanged. Japanese Prime Minister Kantaro Suzuki replied that his government would *mokusatsu* the Allied demand — "kill it with silence." Truman and his military advisers decided against a demonstration of the bomb's awful powers to scare the Japanese into surrender. Instead, Truman decided to drop the bomb on a Japanese city.

On August 6, 1945, an American B-29 bomber, the *Enola Gay*, flew over Hiroshima, Japan's sev-

enth-largest city. The *Enola Gay* carried an atomic bomb called "Little Boy." At 8:15 a.m. the United States dropped "Little Boy" on Hiroshima. It was the first nuclear bomb ever used in war. More than 70 000 people were killed and 61 000 injured; 20 000 of the dead and missing were schoolchildren. Only 10 percent of the Japanese who had been within five hundred metres of the centre of the blast lived through the day. Some people in the streets were vaporized. Only their shadows remained, imprinted on walls. Others were scorched by radiation burns, killed by flying debris, or buried in the rubble of collapsed buildings. Many survivors of the first day later died of radiation sickness from deadly gamma rays. In later years, survivors had a higher risk of cancer and other diseases. The not-yet-born children and grandchildren of the atomic-bomb victims were also at risk from birth defects.

Again the United States issued an ultimatum, and again no reply was given. Three days later, on August 9, 1945, a second nuclear bomb, called "Fat Man," was dropped on the Japanese city of Nagasaki. Another forty thousand people were killed. That night, Emperor Hirohito told the Japanese military that "the time has come when we must bear the unbearable." Japan agreed to unconditional surrender on August 10, 1945, a day remembered as VJ (Victory over Japan) Day. The surrender was signed aboard the U.S. battleship *Missouri* in Tokyo Bay. World War II was over at last.

The Nightmare Draws to a Close

Canadians greeted the news that Japan had surrendered with wild enthusiasm. Prime Minister Mackenzie King declared VJ Day a national holiday. In August 1945, Canadians were in no mood to question the morality of how the war was won. After six brutal years of war, they were simply glad that peace had returned. The moral dilemmas would rest with those who had designed and used the bomb. Later, as the nations with nuclear weapons grew and Cold War tensions intensified, Canadians would reflect on the path the world had taken. But for now, most Canadians were content to just savour victory.

Although the use of nuclear bombs brought a quick end to the war, it left the cities of Hiroshima and Nagasaki in ruins. This photograph shows the centre of Hiroshima several weeks after the bombing.

technology

CANADA'S ROLE IN DEVELOPING THE ATOMIC BOMB

On August 6, 1945, the world was forever changed. On this day, the Japanese city of Hiroshima was obliterated by the world's first atomic bomb. Three days later a second Japanese city, Nagasaki, faced the same fate. About 110 000 people were killed and an additional 110 000 injured by the two bombs, known as "Little Boy" and "Fat Man." The bombing had the desired result – Japan was forced to surrender, and the war was over. The nuclear age had begun.

Research into nuclear capabilities had been underway for several years before the 1930s, but the rise to power of Adolf Hitler and the re-arming of Nazi Germany stepped up research into harnessing nuclear power for war. The race to develop the nuclear bomb, officially known as the Manhattan Project, became the largest research project the world had ever seen. Requiring a staff of more than 200 000, the development of atomic weapons absorbed more funds than NASA later spent to reach the moon.

Most Canadians are unaware of the crucial role Canada played in the development of the atomic bombs that destroyed Hiroshima and Nagasaki. From the outset of the Manhattan Project, the Canadian government co-operated with the British and American governments to ensure that the Allies would develop the nuclear bomb before the Axis powers.

A key ingredient of an atomic bomb is uranium, a heavy radioactive metallic element. The Nazi conquest of Europe had the result that all European uranium refineries were under Nazi control. Only one uranium refinery was left for the Allies to use — the Eldorado Refinery in Port Hope, Ontario. It was here that all the uranium used in the Manhattan project was refined. Much of the uranium came from mines on the shores of Great Bear Lake in the Northwest Territories, and the heavy water used in the development of the plutonium bomb (Fat Man) was supplied by the Consolidated Mining and Smelting Co. in Trail, British Columbia.

Canada's role in the development of the atomic bomb extended well beyond supplying raw materials. Canada provided a safe working environment, far from the battlefields, for British scientists working on the Manhattan Project. Also, Canadian scientists played a crucial role in the project from its beginning. They discovered uranium 235 (the basic element of the atom bomb), helped to create the first chain reaction using uranium 235, and discovered how to purify uranium 235. They also were part of the team working in New Mexico in 1945, which assembled the core of the first plutonium bomb.

Some Canadians were unwitting participants in the development of the atomic bomb. Men of the Sahtugot'ine people, a nomadic group of Aboriginal people who lived near Great Bear Lake, were hired as transporters for the uranium. Despite warnings from federal-government scientists about the dangers of radioactive substances, the Sahtugot'ine were allowed to carry tonnes of uranium without being provided with any protective clothing and were not warned about the dangers they faced. The men, covered in uranium dust, brought the radioactive material into their tents, thereby unknowingly contaminating their families.

The long-term effects of their work in transporting the uranium have been devastating for the Sahtugot'ine community. Gina Bayha, from Deline, N.W.T., noted: "Men from my grandmother's generation regularly lived into their nineties or one hundreds. But we hardly have any men past the age of sixty-five. They all died of cancer." In August 1998, representatives of the Sahtugot'ine travelled to Hiroshima, Japan, to meet with survivors of the nuclear bombing. There they apologized for the indirect role they played in the destruction of the cities of Hiroshima and Nagasaki in 1945.

Some Canadians celebrate the country's role in the atomic bomb as a great technological accomplishment; many others are ashamed of Canada's contribution to the development of weapons of mass destruction. Whatever their opinion, it is important for Canadians to understand Canada's role in the birth of the nuclear age.

chapter review

CHAPTER SUMMARY

In this chapter we have seen

- that the make-up of the Canadian military had changed significantly since World War I

- that Canadians played a vital role in defeating Nazi Germany in battles such as Ortona, and Normandy

- how the entry of the United States and the Soviet Union tipped the balance in favour of the Allied powers over the Axis powers

- how racism and intolerance led to the mass slaughter of Jews in the Holocaust

UNDERSTANDING HISTORICAL FACTS

1. Identify each of the following people, places, and events, and explain their historical significance.

Operation Sea Lion	Holocaust
Miracle of Dunkirk	Manhattan Project
Pearl Harbor	Operation Barbarossa
Battle of Hong Kong	Battle of Ortona
Battle of Dieppe	D-Day

2. What happened to Canadian soldiers at the Battle of Dieppe?

3. Using a sketch of the Normandy coast and the beaches, illustrate the plan of attack for the D-Day landing. To what degree did the D-Day landing go as planned?

4. Describe the treatment of the Jews and other inmates of the Nazi concentration camps.

EXPRESSING YOUR OPINION

1. Why are many Canadian veterans still bitter about the decision to send Canadian troops to Hong Kong in 1941?

2. Hitler's attack on the Soviet Union proved to be a crucial factor in the defeat of Nazi Germany. Was Operation Barbarossa a miscalculated gamble, or could it have been a success? Discuss with a classmate.

3. Select three events from the war that you consider to be crucial to its outcome. Rank the events in order of importance, and justify your ranking.

4. Could more have been done to prevent the atrocities committed against the Jews during the Holocaust? Prepare a list of options that governments might use to prevent future atrocities against their own or other citizens. Compare your options with a classmate's.

5. Can the use of weapons of mass destruction, such as the atomic bomb, ever be justified? Has the development of nuclear weapons made the prospect of lasting world peace more or less likely? Explain your answer.

WORKING WITH THE EVIDENCE

1. During World War II there was a footbridge over a ravine separating Germany from Switzerland. It was guarded by one German soldier who was ordered to shoot anyone attempting to leave Germany and to turn back anyone arriving from Switzerland without proper papers. The German soldier sat on the German side of the bridge in sentry post and came out to check the bridge every three minutes.

A woman desperate to get out of Germany knew she could not sneak past the guard and make it across the bridge in less than six minutes. There was no place to hide on the bridge, and the German soldier never missed checking the bridge at three-minute intervals. He saw everyone who crossed the bridge and accepted no bribes of any kind. How did the woman make it safely across the bridge without being shot?

Canadian workers played a vital role in Canada's war effort. Frederick B. Taylor's painting *Applying the Tracks* shows Canadian Pacific Railway workers in Montreal straining to fit the tracks on a Valentine tank.

INQUIRING INTO THE PAST

- **Why did groups such as Mennonites and Hutterites oppose Canada's participation in World War II?**
- **Why were Japanese Canadians perceived as a threat by many Canadians?**
- **How did the government's handling of the war effort and the economy during the war years differ from its efforts in World War I?**
- **How did Canada's handling of the issue of conscription in World War II differ from its handling of the same issue in World War I?**

KEY TERMS

Conscientious objectors

Convoys

Plebiscite

Total War

Zombies

TIMELINE

NOVEMBER 1941 ▶	**SUMMER 1942** ▶	**OCTOBER 1942** ▶	**NOVEMBER 1944** ▶
Wage and price controls take effect to control inflation	All Japanese Canadians are removed from the West Coast	SS *Caribou* sunk by German U-boats	Conscription takes effect

These young children anxiously awaited the arrival of King George VI and Queen Elizabeth. Would a royal visit generate as much interest today?

On May 17, 1939, King George VI and Queen Elizabeth landed at Québec City for a whirl-wind tour of the Canadian provinces. It was the first time that a British monarch had set foot in Canada. Everywhere the royal couple appeared, crowds gathered to cheer. But the royal visit had a special — and disturbing — significance. The King had come to rally the support of his loyal British subjects. Hitler was on the move, and Britain might soon need every bit of help it could get from Canada.

In 1939 more than half of all Canadians were of British (English, Welsh, Scottish, or Irish) origin, while another third were French Canadians. A growing number of English Canadians were starting to call themselves simply "Canadians," but ties to Britain remained strong. Still, Prime Minister Mackenzie King, like many Canadians, was unhappy about Canada going to war. Canadians had enough problems at home. "The idea that every twenty years this country should automatically and as a matter of course take part in a war overseas," the Prime Minister had grumbled, "seems to many a nightmare and sheer madness." Mackenzie King never questioned that Canada would step to Britain's side. However, he was deter-mined to keep Canada's commitment as moderate as possible. On September 10, 1939, Mackenzie King asked Parliament to vote on Canada's entry into World War II. The decision to go to war received nearly unanimous support. Another generation of Canadians would soon be off to Europe to fight in the bloody conflict of World War II.

Opposition to the War

For most Canadians, Adolf Hitler and the Nazis embodied all that was evil. Nonetheless, not all Canadians supported Canada's participation in another European war. Many Canadian communists actively campaigned against Canada's involvement until the Soviet Union was drawn into the war in 1941. In Québec, anti-war sentiment remained high. Some urged Canada to declare a "friendly neutrality," which would keep Canada out of the war but still supply food and other essential materials to Britain, France, and Poland.

Pacificists and Conscientious Objectors

As was the case in World War I, some Canadians refused to support Canada's participation in war for ethical reasons: they believed that using force to settle disputes was wrong. Those who oppose war

This propaganda poster suggested the possibility of Canada being invaded if the Nazis were not stopped in Europe. Do you think it would have been effective in mobilizing support for the war effort?

LICK THEM *over there!*

COME ON CANADA !

Canadian voices

MENNONITES

My grandmother was an Old Order Mennonite. When she was growing up, she wore plain dresses and a muslin prayer cap on her head, and she rode in a horse and buggy. Many Mennonites today still wear and practise these same things. I am a Mennonite. I wear jeans and T-shirts, have short hair, and drive a red car. Many Mennonites live this way too. So, what makes us all Mennonites?

One thing that has set the Mennonite people and religion apart since their beginning in the sixteenth century has been their stance on non-resistance. We believe in and seek peace. But what does non-resistance mean in a country, such as Canada, that has gone to war?

Canadian Mennonites were preparing for the worst as it became inevitable that the world was going to war once again. In March of 1939, six months before the war began, representatives from seven different groups of Mennonites, as well as two other peace-seeking churches, met for a conference in Chicago. This began a long discussion on the role Mennonites felt they should play in war.

Although the Mennonite leaders at the time were united in deciding against participation in combatant military service, they differed in their opinions about what to do in its place. Some

Mennonites wanted to wait and see what the Canadian government would do, since Mennonites had been granted exemption from military service in World War I. Most Mennonites, however, knew that they would need to have some offer of service in case exemption would no longer be allowed. Many began to think about how they and their young people could serve Canada in non-violent and productive ways.

There were many discussions and debates about alternative service, within the Mennonite community and between Mennonites and the government. The result was that Mennonite men of conscription age were exempted from military service because they objected to it for "reasons of conscience." However, Mennonites played a vital role by working in agriculture and industry to provide important goods such as food items overseas.

I am Mennonite. This means a lot of different things to me, but perhaps most clearly, it means that I seek to follow the way of peace. It is easy to try and blend into the crowd, and to do as others do, but in hearing of my ancestors who refused to back down from their beliefs, I am encouraged that I, too, can work productively for peace.

CONTRIBUTED BY ALISSA BENDER. MS. BENDER WAS RAISED IN A MENNONITE FAMILY IN WATERLOO, ONTARIO. SHE IS CURRENTLY A STUDENT AT WILFRID LAURIER UNIVERSITY.

of any kind are referred to as pacifists. During World War II, Canadians whose beliefs would be compromised by participating in war could be registered as **conscientious objectors**.

Pacifism was central to the religious beliefs of several groups in Canada in 1939. Among the pacifist religious groups were Mennonites, Hutterites, and Doukhobors. Nationalist sentiment ran high during wartime, so refusing to support the war effort was often seen as "un-Canadian" and led to hostility toward these groups. This hostility was

compounded by other factors, such as the German heritage of the Mennonites and Hutterites. During and after the war the level of hostility toward these groups would vary, depending on how each pacifist group reacted to the war. The Mennonite community was the most widely accepted group. Mennonites responded to charges of pro-Germanism by voluntarily reducing the number of religious services they held and suspending their German-language schools. Those who registered as conscientious objectors worked on farms and in factories to support the war effort. As well, nearly half of the young Mennonite men eligible for service abandoned their pacifist convictions and joined the armed forces.

In contrast, Hutterites, who lived on large communes in Alberta, remained isolated from most Canadians. Their German heritage and isolation from public life led to suspicions about Hutterites, especially since many Canadians saw the war as a defence of individualism and democracy. Doukhobors, although not German-speaking, had developed an unfavourable reputation as a result of the actions of a radical sect in British Columbia known as the Sons of Freedom. Throughout the 1930s the Sons of Freedom were often featured in the press for their participation in nude parades and for bombing and burning their own property to demonstrate their faith. Now, with war at hand, this religious group, about which Canadians knew little, was viewed with suspicion and hostility. Columnist Richard Needham of the *Calgary Herald* captured the reaction of Canadians to these groups when he wrote: "the Mennonites are really playing a much fuller part in the war than the isolationist Hutterites or the stubborn Doukhobors."

The British Commonwealth Air Training Plan

Prime Minister Mackenzie King was hopeful that Canada's major contribution to the war would be the British Commonwealth Air Training Plan (BCATP), which was announced on December 17, 1939. Under the plan, air crews were to be brought to Canada from all over the Commonwealth for training as pilots, navigators, air gunners, bombardiers, and wireless operators. Canada provided airfields, aircraft, and basic services, far out of range of the German Luftwaffe, while Britain supplied instructors. The program turned out more than 130 000 graduates, including 50 000 pilots. Almost 73 000 of the graduates were Canadians.

Canada's role in the training of pilots such as these proved to be a critical factor in the outcome of the war.

War Comes to Canada's Shores: The East Coast

Soon after the outbreak of war, Mackenzie King's hopes for a limited Canadian role began to fade. The horrifying series of victories by Germany and its allies across Europe and Africa frightened Canadians. Soon the shadow of the European war had fallen across Canada's eastern seacoast.

Halifax was the centre for Canadian naval operations in the North Atlantic and a base for British and Allied shipping. Day after day **convoys** of ships, including merchant vessels loaded with vital troops and supplies such as guns, tanks, shells, and foodstuffs, docked in Halifax Harbour and then headed out to make a run across the North Atlantic to Europe.

The Battle of the Atlantic and the Battle of the St. Lawrence

Germany realized that supplies sent from Canada were crucial to Britain's survival, so it did everything in its power to interrupt supply lines. In what became known as the Battle of the Atlantic, convoy

Convoys such as this one made Bedford Basin in Halifax a bee-hive of activity during the war. Why did Halifax's role in the war effort attract attention from the Germans, and how might the Germans have attempted to disrupt the supplies being shipped from Halifax?

By the summer of 1942 fact and fiction were beginning to blur. While Canadian government propaganda led the public to believe Canada was winning the Battle of the Atlantic, German U-Boats were becoming increasingly daring. Initially they had restricted their activity to the coastal waters around Newfoundland and Nova Scotia, but now attacks were made on ships in the St. Lawrence River. On August 27, 1942, the American ship *Chatham* was sunk in the St. Lawrence, the first time an attack had taken place in Canadian waters. During the summer and fall of 1942, German U-boats sank twenty-one ships in the St. Lawrence and claimed 259 lives while sustaining no casualties of their own. The most callous attack occurred on October 13, when the passenger ferry SS *Caribou*, en route from Port aux Basques, Newfoundland, to Sydney, Nova Scotia, was sunk by a single torpedo. One hundred and thirty-seven civilians died from the attack. The Battle of the St. Lawrence awakened Canadians to the reality of **total war**.

Newfoundland's Role in the War

The island of Newfoundland was still a British colony in 1939, but for the first time the co-operation between Canada and Newfoundland was close. Newfoundland was key to the defence of North America, but it lacked the money and personnel to ward off a German attack, which was a very real threat: U-boats were often seen prowling off the coast of Newfoundland. To guard St. John's harbour against a torpedo attack, a net was strung across the narrows that link the harbour with the Atlantic Ocean. During the Battle of the Atlantic, at least two German torpedoes were caught in this net.

With Newfoundland's consent, Canadian troops were stationed on the island, and Royal Canadian Air Force (RCAF) aircraft flew out of airports at Gander and at Goose Bay, Labrador. Canadian forces were joined by Newfoundland troops, including two infantry battalions (army units consisting of foot soldiers), two anti-aircraft regiments, three coastal batteries (collection of heavy guns), and a number of administrative and service units.

ships were mined or torpedoed by German vessels, often within hearing distance of Halifax. Most deadly was the German U-boat (short for *Unterseebooten*, "undersea boat" or submarine). U-boat teams called "wolf packs" broke through the convoy escort ships to pick off merchant ships one after the other. By the end of the war U-boats had sent 175 Allied ships, 500 merchant ships (with millions of tonnes of cargo), and 50 000 seamen to the bottom of the Atlantic Ocean. In response to these attacks Canada began to quickly produce "corvettes," small ships that provided some protection for merchant ships carrying vital supplies across the Atlantic.

In and around Halifax, navy "plotters" tracked ship movements, including those of the silent and dangerous U-boats, in the North Atlantic. Many of the plotters were from the Women's Royal Canadian Naval Service (WRCNS). One WRCNS plotter later said, "Most Canadians had no idea just how close those German U-boats got — way up the St. Lawrence."

Canadian profiles

BRIDGET "BRIDE" FITZPATRICK AND THE DISASTER ON THE SS *CARIBOU*

It is only now that Newfoundlanders realize how near the war is to us; Wednesday marks a sad day in our history for the SS Caribou *was sunk about 15 miles off Port aux Basques. Many people have someone dear that was on this ship. Wednesday was a dismal day at school. Both teachers tried to show pupils how great a disaster this sinking was to Newfoundland.*

From a Newfoundland teacher's diary, October 1942

Bride Fitzpatrick was among those who perished when the passenger and car ferry SS *Caribou* was sunk by a German U-boat. The memory of that dreadful evening, one day after Thanksgiving, lives on in the memories of most Newfoundlanders. To this day a picture of the ill-fated ship hangs on the walls of many Newfoundland homes, and surviving relatives of Bride Fitzpatrick fondly remember her heroism of that evening and the zest with which she lived her life.

Bridget "Bride" Fitzpatrick was raised in the small Newfoundland village of Bay Roberts. As the only female crew member of the SS *Caribou*, Fitzpatrick had earned a reputation for her spunky character. On a June crossing between Port aux Basques, Newfoundland, and North Sydney, Nova Scotia, it was reported that a light had appeared on the deck. Fitzpatrick tracked down the source of the light and sternly reprimanded an American passenger, reminding him that lights on the deck were an invitation to be attacked by a German U-boat.

The very disaster she sought to avoid on that June evening would eventually claim the lives of Bride Fitzpatrick and 136 others. During the Battle of the Atlantic, German U-boats prowled around the Gulf of St. Lawrence hoping to disrupt the convoys of ships carrying supplies to Britain. Unfortunately, civilians were often among the victims of the Battle of the Atlantic.

The attack on the *Caribou* came in the early morning hours of October 14, 1942. As the *Caribou* approached Port aux Basques, it came into the sights of the German U-boat *U-69*. Taking deadly aim, the *U-69* unleashed a single torpedo, which hit the *Caribou*. Hundreds of terror-stricken passengers scrambled to flee the sinking ferry. The crew of the *Caribou* valiantly struggled to ensure as many passengers as possible found their way to safety. Among those working feverishly was Bride Fitzpatrick. As the life rafts became full, she gave up her seat in the lifeboat to a mother and young child. The next morning, her lifeless body was found floating in the water twenty-five kilometres due west of Grand Bay, Newfoundland.

The sinking of the SS *Caribou* was of little strategic significance to the war, but it was emotionally devastating to Newfoundland. Many of the tightly knit communities that dot the Newfoundland shoreline lost someone when the *Caribou* went down. The sinking of the *Caribou* was World War II's greatest blow to Newfoundland, but the memories of the heroic victims, such as Bridget "Bride" Fitzpatrick, live on.

ACTIVITY

In the days following the sinking of the SS *Caribou*, newspapers across Canada reported on what was called "the blackest Maritime tragedy in the history of naval warfare off Canada's coast." The *Ottawa Journal* stated: "The nauseating brutishness of the Nazi soul [was] revealed again in the murder of defenceless women and children." Assume that you worked for a Canadian newspaper during World War II. Write a news story reporting on the sinking of the *Caribou*.

Concerned about a possible Japanese invasion, the Canadian government built coastal-defence gun installations like this one at Alert Head, British Columbia.

The War in the Pacific and on Canada's West Coast

Times were also tense along the coast of British Columbia. In the Far East, Japan had invaded large parts of China. The U.S. and British naval fleets in the Pacific had been crippled by Japanese surprise attacks in December 1941. Three months later the Japanese swept across the Philippines, Malaya, Burma, and Singapore, and they were headed south toward Indonesia and Australia.

The opening of a new war zone in the Pacific frightened Canadians on the West Coast. The suddenness of the Japanese attacks, the number of their targets, and the ease of their victories made Western Canadians fear that the next Japanese target might be British Columbia. For days after the attacks on Pearl Harbor and Hong Kong, Vancouver enforced a blackout at night. School children were drilled to respond to a gas attack, and nervous adults tried to prepare for an invasion. As it turned out, the only direct Japanese attack on Canada was a submarine shelling of a Vancouver Island lighthouse in June 1942. However, the Japanese did occupy the Aleutian Islands off Alaska in mid-1942; they were later pushed off by a combined Canadian and American force.

The Internment of Japanese Canadians

In the early 1940s about 22 000 people of Japanese descent lived in British Columbia. The first Japanese immigrants had come to work on the railways and in mines and lumber camps. Later, many settled on the coast, where they bought fishing boats or plots of land. Most earned their living from fishing, market gardening, and small business. Their hard work was paying off, and some Japanese Canadians were beginning to prosper. However, their success was resented by many British Columbians.

Even before the war, Japanese Canadians had been targets of anti-Asian rioting and were treated as second-class citizens. They were denied the right to vote, teach, or take jobs in the civil service and other professions. Japan's attacks on Pearl Harbor and Hong Kong opened the floodgates of long-standing racial hostility against Japanese Canadians. They were suddenly seen by many as spies and enemy aliens bent on helping Japan to destroy Canada.

In Vancouver the RCMP had been keeping a close eye on Japanese Canadian residents since 1938. It concluded that this community was loyal to Canada. Japanese Canadians had been patriotic supporters of Red Cross work and Victory Bond drives, and many were eager to fight for Canada. No sign of treason or treachery was uncovered at that time — or at any time later.

Thousands of Japanese Canadians such as these people were sent to internment camps in British Columbia and northern Ontario. How can we safeguard against such injustices in the future?

On its own, Mackenzie King's government would not have taken harsh measures against Japanese Canadians on the West Coast. But anti-Japanese feeling was running high in British Columbia. Rumours sprang up about a Japanese invasion, and the stories grew wilder as they passed from one person to the next. Newspapers, patriotic societies, service clubs, and town and city councils targeted people of Japanese descent. In a letter to her brother, Muriel Kitagawa, a twenty-nine-year-old Japanese Canadian, pointed out the irony of Canadians' actions.

> Strange how these protesters are much more vehement against the Canadian-born Japanese than they are against German-born Germans, who might have a real loyalty to their land of birth, as we have for Canada. I guess it is just because we look different. Anyway, it all boils down to racial antagonism, which the democracies are fighting against.

Ottawa eventually gave in to mounting public pressure. At first, only male Japanese nationals — men without Canadian citizenship — were rounded up and taken to internment camps well away from the coast. Soon, however, the Japanese conquest of British-held Singapore hit the headlines. The news fuelled racist feelings, and British Columbians pressed Ottawa even harder to remove all Japanese from coastal areas. Under the War Measures Act and the Defence of Canada Regulations, the internment order was extended to everyone of Japanese descent — Canadian citizen or not.

Soon, Japanese Canadians were herded onto eastbound trains. Most were sent to internment camps in the interior of British Columbia. Others were sent east of the Rocky Mountains, to sugar-beet farms in Alberta, or farther east to Manitoba and Ontario. The government also placed about seventy Japanese Canadians it considered dangerous behind barbed wire in northern Ontario.

The Japanese Canadians interned in British Columbia lived in shacks or makeshift houses measuring about four metres by eight metres. Some shacks had no running water or electricity, and none were built for the bitter mountain winters. Often families were broken up and the father was sent to one camp while the mother and children went to a different one. The men were put to work building roads such as the Trans-Canada Highway and cutting trees.

When the Japanese Canadians were interned, they had to leave most of their belongings behind in the "safekeeping" of a government agent called the Custodian of Enemy Property. But the authorities auctioned off all this property, including fishing boats, cars, houses, shops, and personal belongings, to others.

The shameful treatment did not stop at the war's end. After the war, Ottawa passed a law to deport Japanese Canadians, and almost four thousand were sent to Japan before the law was repealed in 1947. Many had never been to Japan before. For several years after the war, Japanese Canadians had to report to the RCMP if they travelled more than eighty kilometres from home. By 1949, however, Japanese Canadians had gained the right to vote in federal and provincial elections. The Canadian government did not formally apologize for the wartime injustices until 1988, when Brian Mulroney's government offered $20 000 to every survivor of the Japanese internment.

A Japanese Canadian internment camp. Can you suggest a more just way in which the government could have addressed the security concerns of some Canadians?

Japanese Canadians: An Alternative View

Most often, when discussing Japanese Canadians and World War II, the focus is on their internment,

Canadian Voices

PERSONAL REFLECTIONS ON THE WORLD WAR II INTERNMENT OF JAPANESE CANADIANS

*How is one to talk to a woman, a mother who is
also a stranger
because the son does not know who or what she is?
Tell me, Mother,
who are you? What is it to be a Japanese?*
    John Okada, *No-No Boy*

In John Okada's 1957 novel *No-No Boy*, a young Japanese man named Ichiro watches his mother work and longs to bridge the gap of silence that exists between them. At times, I too felt that the silences, the words not spoken, the stories not told, separated me needlessly from my mother and father. Like Ichiro, I seek to bridge that silence.

I grew up in a loving, working-class Japanese Canadian family. I am a Sansei — third-generation Japanese Canadian. My parents were both born in British Columbia. They were Nisei — second-generation Japanese Canadians. Both sets of grandparents, Issei, grew up in the Fukuoka prefecture of Japan and immigrated to Canada in the late 1800s. My father's father was a printer employed by one of Vancouver's Japanese-language newspapers. My *ba-chan* (grandmother) was a fastidious homemaker who made everything from scratch — from curtains to soap to pickles to saki. My mother's family owned a berry farm in Haney, British Columbia. On this farm, they raised five children, all of whom laboured on the land, daily, before and after school, and throughout the summer months. Seasonally, to earn cash, my *ba-chan* also worked in a nearby fish factory. Although they must have encountered racism in its ugly, unmasked forms, my grandparents eked out an existence, drawing strength from the West Coast's small but cohesive Japanese Canadian community.

This is the history I learned in the 1960s and 1970s growing up in a White neighbourhood of Toronto. By adulthood, I could see that there were gaps in my family's history — silences. In my family, the silence revolved around the internment of Japanese Canadians during World War II. The experience of internment taught my parents that being of Japanese descent was bad, shameful and brought with it harsh penalties.

During World War II, both my parents were sent to internment camps. My mother, then a teenager, remembers hurriedly burying clothes, dishes, pots, and pans, giving her pet dog to neighbours — all within an allotted twenty-four hours before being rounded up by the RCMP. She can still see and smell her family's stop at Hastings Park, where horse stables had been turned into a "relocation centre" for those of Japanese descent during the war. Most vividly she recalls her train voyage from British Columbia to Ontario. At the war's end, the federal government prohibited Japanese Canadians from returning to what remained of their homes on the West Coast. Encouraged by government officials, she found a position as a live-in domestic servant with a wealthy family in the affluent Toronto neighbourhood of Rosedale. After this, she faced endless days of polishing silver, vacuuming expensive oriental carpets, and feeding and minding the three children of a respected lawyer and his homemaker wife. My mother remains a domestic worker to this day.

My father's experience during the internment was different. When he heard about the decisions of the federal government, my father openly resisted. Angry and hurt that he was considered a threat to his country of birth, he refused to leave the only home he knew. The RCMP picked him up on the streets of Vancouver, not even permitting him to notify his parents of his whereabouts. For resisting, they put him in a prisoner-of-war camp in Petawawa, Ontario. He remembers having to wear a white top with a red circle on the back. During the war, the government used his labour, first in Petawawa, then on various road camps throughout Ontario. After the war, like my mother, he had nothing to return to. He eventually ended up in Toronto where, for the remainder of his life, he put in endless hours earning a living as a taxi cab driver. My father died before the Canadian government made a formal apology to the Japanese Canadian community. He did not receive any financial compensation for the economic losses suffered to himself or his family during the war.

Clearly, the forces of racism shaped their lives.

Both my mother and father worked hard to shield me from these forces, for years upholding a wall of silence around their wartime experiences. I now am a parent myself. I have a four-year old daughter, a Yonsei (fourth-generation) of mixed race. She tells me that she wants to learn to speak Japanese. In her imaginary play, she speaks of living in Japan. When she is older and asks about my family's past, I will tell her these stories, to be sure the silence is forever broken.

CONTRIBUTED BY PAMELA SUGIMAN. DR. SUGIMAN IS AN ASSOCIATE PROFESSOR OF SOCIOLOGY AT MCMASTER UNIVERSITY IN HAMILTON, ONTARIO.

racism, and their general mistreatment by fellow Canadians. However, a valuable contribution was made by many Japanese Canadians during the war years. As a result of the War Measures Act, all Japanese Canadians had been removed from coastal British Columbia, but not all were placed in internment camps. More than 2600 were relocated to southern Alberta, where they provided vital labour in the sugar beet fields. The chronic shortage of manual labour resulting from the war threatened the harvest of sugar beets. For Japanese Canadians, the options of working for a wage and keeping their families intact were much preferable to internment camps. Following the war several of these families remained in southern Alberta, where they have made important contributions to their communities.

Central Canada: Retooling to Support the War

Once the Nazis had occupied most of Europe and the Japanese were driving swiftly across the Far East, Canadians began to talk about "total war" — using everything possible for the war effort. By the end of 1941, industries across the nation were working overtime to produce war materials. Unemployment vanished. In fact, competition for workers had become so stiff that the government created a National Selective Service (NSS) to direct Canadian workers to the industries where their labour was most needed. If workers took jobs without NSS approval, they could be fined $500 and jailed for a year. The economy, crippled by the Great Depression, was up and running again.

The biggest change occurred in Canadian manufacturing. Hamilton steel mills, Toronto munitions plants, and Montreal aircraft factories began to run shifts around the clock, seven days a week. Although production remained largely concentrated in the industrial heartland of southern Ontario and Québec, several new plants were established across Canada. Winnipeg, for example, became a major supplier of munitions and communication technology, while a Boeing aircraft factory and new shipbuilding facilities appeared in Vancouver.

Canadians also started making many items that they had once bought abroad. For the first time, Canadians produced diesel engines, synthetic rubber, roller bearings, electronic equipment, and high-octane gasoline and other products. The minister in charge of industrial production, C.D. Howe, predicted, "Never again will there be any doubt that Canada can manufacture anything that can be manufactured elsewhere." He was right. Many new industries survived into peacetime and became a permanent part of the Canadian economy.

Resurgent Prairie Farms: Meeting the Agricultural Demand of the War Years

While the industries of Central Canada produced products at a rapid pace, the farms of Western Canada also joined in the "total war" effort. After years of drought, the weather co-operated and the Prairies turned green at last. Farmers began harvesting bumper crops, for which they earned reasonable profits. In 1942, high school and university students from the East and Aboriginal people from the North headed into Saskatchewan to help harvest a record-breaking crop of wheat. Hungry Britons were desperate for food, and the soldiers overseas had to be fed. Canadian farmers began to produce a wider range of products to meet the new demand, including pork, beef, dairy products, flax, and oil seeds. These vital contributions to the war came from a diversity of ethnocultural groups.

Aboriginal Contributions to the War Effort

During the war years the contributions of Canada's Aboriginal peoples took many forms. Despite widespread poverty, Aboriginal people donated over $23 000. In some cases Aboriginal bands donated the $5 that each member received from the federal government as treaty money. In other cases, money was raised through the sale of moccasins and furs. In addition to the money donated, support for the war effort came in the form of knitted socks and mufflers and other garments.

Aboriginal people also supported the war effort by expanding the amount of reserve land under cultivation. Under the "Greater Production Campaign," the government supported Aboriginal farmers by providing seed, cattle, poultry, goats, and fruit trees. As a result, a steady increase in foodstuffs was recorded during the war years. Aboriginal people who did not enlist in the army or find employment on farms found work on railways and in packing plants, factories, and lumber mills. Over two hundred Aboriginal men who had been rejected for military service were relocated from the West to Ontario, where they worked in munitions factories and forests. While meeting with Aboriginal leaders in Regina, Mackenzie King expressed gratitude for their loyalty to the Crown and stated that he was proud to see "the complete unity in the Dominion's war effort."

Women's Contributions to the War Effort

The war effort opened many new doors for women, at least for the duration of the war. Men going overseas left job vacancies behind, so the federal government began actively recruiting women into the labour force. "Women! Back Them Up — To Bring Them Back," said one government campaign poster urging women to take jobs in munitions work. "Roll Up Your Sleeves for Victory!" shouted another poster.

Many factories, such as this Inglis plant in Toronto, were converted to munitions or weapons factories. These workers played a critical role in supplying the Allied forces with weapons.

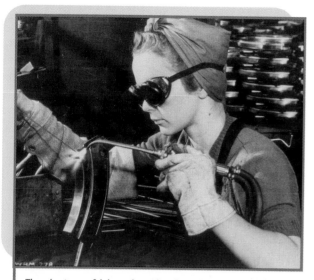

The shortage of labour brought about by the war opened up numerous opportunities for women in new fields. Many women were employed in heavy industries, building weapons and machinery. Nicknames for women working in factories included "Rosie the Riveter" and "the Bren Girl." Can you explain these nicknames?

At first, the government campaign targeted single women, but by September 1942, labour shortages were so acute that all women between the ages of twenty and twenty-four were required to sign up with the National Selective Service. Later, the government campaigned for married women to take jobs, and near the end of the war women with children were targeted for the labour force. With federal help, Ontario and Quebec set up a few day-care centres to free mothers for war work. By 1944, almost one million women had taken jobs across Canada.

Women in Industry

At the peak of wartime production, 30 percent of workers in aircraft plants — 25 000 — were women, more than 260 000 women had jobs in munitions plants and there were 4000 female workers in shipbuilding and 4000 in construction. They assembled radio tubes and Bren guns (submachine guns) and worked at spot welding, auto assembly, riveting, and meat packing. The female war worker, wearing trousers and a bandana wrapped around her head to keep long hair out of machinery, became a kind of national heroine. Sometimes nicknamed "the Bren

Girl" or "Rosie the Riveter," the female war worker appeared on billboards almost as often as the Canadian soldier did.

Women were still paid less than men for doing the same jobs — although the differences between men's and women's wages were smaller than before — and women almost always had male bosses. Many still worked in traditionally female jobs, but a sizable number took on jobs usually done by men. The divisions between "women's work" and "men's work" were beginning to blur.

Women in Agriculture

Many young men and some women left the farms for service overseas or better-paying jobs in war industries. As a result, the burden of agricultural

Finding reliable day care was a major challenge for women entering the workforce during the war. This Mi'kmaq woman's solution was to carry her child with her to the Pictou, Nova Scotia, shipyards where she worked.

production often fell to the more than 800 000 women who chose to stay on the farms. Women had always done their share of farm labour, but in the war years they often had to work double-time to compensate for missing husbands and farm workers. One farm wife managed to do the heavy farm work, service the equipment, run the house, look after the children, and still have time for hunting and curling. When her husband came back from the war, she handed him the bank book. "There is more money in there," she proudly told him, "than we ever had in our lives."

The Changing Role of Government

War often has the effect of jolting governments out of traditional roles. In both world wars, the Canadian government adopted a more active role in the day-to-day functioning of society. And in both cases, the changes in the role of government in the lives of Canadians would become permanent features of post-war Canadian society.

The Wartime Economy and Government Controls

Prime Minister Mackenzie King was determined to manage an efficient, orderly, and honest war effort.

He put a group of cabinet ministers in charge of the shift to a wartime economy and the minister of munitions and supplies, C.D. Howe, in charge of the war production effort. Britain desperately needed all kinds of supplies, and Howe obtained contract after contract for guns, tanks, trucks, uniforms, ships, and much more.

But many of Howe's contracts were for products that Canada had never made. He turned to top businesspeople across Canada for help in meeting wartime production demands. He asked them to take a "holiday" from work and to become civil servants until the war ended. They became known as "dollar-a-year men" for the token salary paid by the government. (Many companies continued to pay their employees' salaries while they worked for Howe's department.) Canadian factories that had been making refrigerators were switched over to producing tank tracks or Bren guns. Railway shops started making tanks. Automobile makers stopped making cars and began producing army trucks.

Soon Canada was geared up for war production. By 1944, Canadians were building four thousand trucks and 450 armoured vehicles a week. "When you consider that pre-war Canadian industry had never made a tank, a combat airplane, or a modern high-caliber rapid-fire gun," the American magazine *Fortune* marvelled, "the speed with which industry was organized and production started ranks as an industrial miracle."

This photograph represents the daily production of trucks at the Ford Motor Company in Windsor during World War II. Canada would produce more than 815 000 military vehicles by the end of the war.

Widening Government Controls Over Industry

C.D. Howe's Department of Munitions and Supplies was given new powers over private enterprise. It could tell businesses what to produce, where to sell their products, and even when to deliver them. If a business refused to co-operate, the department could take over the plant and schedule production itself.

New Crown corporations (government-owned corporations) were created by Howe's department whenever private enterprise could not supply a specific demand. By the end of the war, there were twenty-eight Crown corporations, producing everything from wood (Veneer Log Supply Limited) to synthetic rubber (Polymer Corporation). One Crown corporation, Eldorado Mining and Refining in Port Hope, Ontario, secretly processed uranium for the U.S. atomic bombs that were dropped on Japan in 1945. Never before had a Canadian government taken such wide-ranging control over private enterprise.

The Hyde Park Declaration

One of the most important Crown corporations was War Supplies Limited. This corporation sprang from a meeting between Prime Minister Mackenzie King and his friend, U.S. President Franklin Delano Roosevelt, at Roosevelt's family estate in Hyde Park, New York. Mackenzie King explained that Canada, in trying to help Britain, would soon be in financial difficulty if it did not balance the trade deficit with the United States. As the war escalated, Canada increasingly relied on American supplies to fuel the factories. This led to a huge trade deficit with the United States. However, if the United States bought products from Canadian industries worth roughly as much as the products that Canada was buying in the United States, King said, Canada's problem would disappear. Roosevelt liked Mackenzie King's proposal, and the two leaders signed an agreement known as the Hyde Park Declaration. More than $1 billion worth of Canadian goods were eventually sold to the United States. The declaration marked the beginning of a new era of close economic ties between the two nations.

Managing the Wartime Economy: The Problem of Inflation

The booming wartime economy brought Canadians new prosperity. More people were working, and they had more money in their pockets than ever before. But most of Canada's resources were going into wartime production, with the result that fewer consumer goods were on store shelves. Mackenzie King's financial advisers were worried that with "so many dollars chasing so few goods," prices would rise quickly. The result would be a crippling inflation. It had happened in World War I, and Mackenzie King was determined that it would not happen again.

A Nova Scotia lawyer, James Ilsley, was put in charge of Canada's financial affairs. Ilsley kept inflation under control through the use of large tax increases, forced savings, and the sale of Victory Bonds. By restricting the amount of money Canadians had in their pockets, the government left them with less money to spend on consumer items. In limiting the demand for these items, the government managed to keep the general increase in prices (inflation) under control. In 1938 Ottawa had collected just $42 million from personal income taxes, but by 1943 it took in $815 million. Ilsley also mounted nine huge publicity campaigns for War Loans and Victory Loans. Celebrities — including child movie star Shirley Temple and the five-year-old Dionne quintuplets — were used to make public appeals for Victory Bonds. Posters and magazine advertisements with slogans like "The Men Are Ready... Only YOU Can Give Them Wings" appeared everywhere. The publicity effort was a stunning success, producing $8.8 billion for the war effort.

Web Connections

http://www.school.mcgrawhill.ca/resources

Go to the above Web site to find out more about how posters were used to gain public support for the war. Go to *History Resources*, then to *Canada: A Nation Unfolding, Ontario Edition*, to find out where to go next.

Rationing became a part of everyday life during the war years. Closely study the sign in the window and consider that meat was limited to one kilogram per person per week. How would you have adjusted your diet in response to rationing?

Wage and Price Controls and Rationing

Despite Ilsley's efforts, prices were going up by 1941. Mackenzie King's government worried that explosive inflation lay ahead. In November 1941 the Wartime Prices and Trade Board (WPTB), a government agency that regulated the supply of key commodities and food rationing, took the revolutionary step of freezing all prices and wages to prevent inflation. The WPTB also decided who could buy scarce goods. Consumers who wanted to buy items such as electric stoves, typewriters, or rubber tires first had to get a permit from the WPTB. The permits went to people who showed that their use of an item contributed most to the war effort.

Food rationing was also introduced in 1942, and quotas (limits) were placed on a number of everyday commodities. Canadians were limited to 250 grams of sugar, 250 grams of butter, 30 grams of tea, 115 grams of coffee, and 1 kilogram of meat per person per week. More than eleven million ration books were handed out, and ration coupons became a part of Canadian life. The WPTB preached: "Use It Up, Wear It Out, Make It Do, and Do Without." Women's groups taught classes on how to cook nourishing home meals with few supplies. They also ran huge salvage campaigns under

the motto, "Dig In and Dig Out the Scrap." They salvaged paper, rags, iron, aluminum, edible fats, bottles, and even meat bones for aircraft glue and milkweed for life preservers. But rationing was more of a nuisance than a real hardship. In European eyes, Canadians still lived in a land of plenty. Even Americans faced tighter rationing than Canadians did.

The Fight Over Conscription

Canada had been torn apart in World War I by the bitter fight between French and English Canadians over conscription. Mackenzie King was determined to avoid another disastrous conscription battle. He took Canada into World War II with the solemn pledge that no Canadians would be conscripted and forced to fight against their will. French Canadians accepted Canada's declaration of war on the understanding that they would never be conscripted to fight in Europe.

Celebrities often lent their support to the war effort. Here, Prime Minister Mackenzie King and actor Shirley Temple kick off the 7th Victory Loan Drive on Parliament Hill in October 1944.

But Hitler's victories in Europe soon had many English Canadians thinking about conscription. Pressure mounted, and Mackenzie King reacted with the National Resources Mobilization Act (NRMA). In his words, it let the government "call out every man in Canada for military training for the defence of Canada." Under the NRMA, men could be conscripted and trained as soldiers, but only for home defence within the borders of Canada. The NRMA conscripts could not be sent overseas to fight.

A growing number of English Canadians came to see the men conscripted for home duty in the NRMA as less than patriotic because they refused to fight in Europe, and these conscripts were soon nicknamed "**Zombies.**" The term appears to have been borrowed from Hollywood films in which people without souls had only an outer appearance of existence. Similarly, those who were conscripted by the NRMA but had refused to volunteer were seen to have only the outward appearance of support for the war effort. English Canadians mistakenly believed that most of the "Zombies" were French Canadians and grumbled that they should not be allowed to "sit comfortably" in Canada while the battle raged in Europe.

The army tried all kinds of threats and promises to get the NRMA men to "go active." Its tactics were sometimes harsh, and many "Zombies" finally agreed to active service. But a tough core of NRMA conscripts, fully trained for service, steadily refused to go to war. The conscription issue was becoming a political "hot potato" for Mackenzie King, who was locked into his pledge against conscription. Public support began to swing to the Conservative Party. The architect of conscription in World War I, Arthur Meighen, was asked to come back as the Conservative Party leader. He agreed, and it began to look as if the Liberal Party might be beaten on the conscription issue just as it had been in World War I.

Then Mackenzie King had an idea. He would hold a **plebiscite**, a federal referendum open to all Canadian voters. He would ask Canadians whether or not they favoured releasing his government from its earlier pledge against conscription. On April 27, 1942, almost four million Canadians went to the

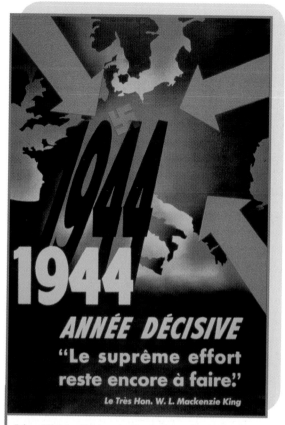

Prime Minister Mackenzie King had promised, "Not necessarily conscription, but conscription if necessary." By 1944 the war had dragged on for five years, and finally a possible end was in sight. This poster encouraged a supreme effort from all Canadians for what was called the "decisive year." Would you have supported conscription in 1944?

polls to vote. The plebiscite passed, and King was freed from his promise. Once again Canada was divided into warring camps over conscription, and so was Mackenzie King's government. Quebeckers were outraged at what they saw as his betrayal.

Mackenzie King was now free to bring in conscription, but he was in no hurry to do it. He feared that conscription might trigger massive civil disorder in Québec. He had once told a group of Liberal members of Parliament that if conscription were brought in, "we would have to enlarge our jails and use our tanks and rifles against our own people." Mackenzie King summed up his position in the famous motto: "Not necessarily conscription, but conscription if necessary."

For a while, voluntary enlistments kept pace with the demand for new recruits. But after a time the flow of volunteers slowed, and the invasions of Italy and France began taking their toll of Canadian soldiers. The Canadian forces lost 23 000 soldiers in Italy and France, most of them in the infantry. By 1944, the infantry replacement pools were drained.

Seeing that the last hope for volunteers had disappeared, Mackenzie King did an about-face on conscription. He agreed to conscript 16 000 for active duty, and about 12 000 NRMA conscripts were sent overseas. By the time they arrived in Europe, however, the war was winding down. Fewer than 2500 conscripts reached the front, where 69 were killed in action. Mackenzie King faced some political hostility for his switch to conscription. There were brief riots in Montreal, and a brigade of NRMA men in British Columbia commandeered their training camp and refused to move out. But Mackenzie King had secured the support of his young justice minister from Québec, Louis St. Laurent, before announcing conscription. St. Laurent was a well-respected French Canadian politician whose presence helped soften public opinion in Québec. In fact, Mackenzie King credited St. Laurent with saving both his government and Confederation.

The conscription crisis had once again divided the nation, and a bitter Québec would not forget its treatment at the hands of English Canada. But in the election of 1945, Mackenzie King's Liberal Party still looked better to Québec than the other parties did. The Liberal government was returned to power. Québec was quiet, if not happy. The transition to peacetime went smoothly, and a more prosperous Canada looked forward to a new era of peace and security.

The Good, the Bad, and the Ugly

Canadians from coast to coast had risen to the challenge of yet another world war. Lessons learned from World War I proved invaluable in meeting the challenge. By war's end, Canadians could reflect back with a certain pride in the unity demonstrated and the hurdles overcome. Some mistakes had been made, some people had been mistreated, and conscription had once again reared its head. Yet in the end Canada had not only played a vital role in supporting the war in Europe and the Pacific, but had shown considerable unity. War had exposed the good, the bad, and the ugly in Canada.

chapter review

CHAPTER SUMMARY

In this chapter we have seen

- that although most Canadians supported the war effort, some opposed armed conflict
- that fear of enemies from within led to the denial of some Canadians' basic rights
- how the Canadian government organized the economy to meet the demands of war without causing crippling inflation
- how support for the war effort came from all regions and many different groups in Canada
- that the issue of conscription once again threatened national unity

UNDERSTANDING HISTORICAL FACTS

1. Identify each of the following people, places, and events, and explain their historical significance.

Battle of the Atlantic	SS *Caribou*
Japanese Internment	National Selective Service
C.D. Howe	Hyde Park Declaration
The Bren Girl	War Measures Act
National Resources Mobilization Act	Wartime Prices and Trade Board

2. Create a mind-map that highlights the various ways in which Canada and Canadians contributed to the war effort. At the centre of your mind-map place "Canada's Contributions to the War Effort."

3. Explain why the British Commonwealth Air Training Plan was critical to the Allied war effort.

4. Create a chart that illustrates the ways in which the government's role in World War II differed from its role in World War I.

5. Describe how the role of women in Canadian society evolved during World War I and World War II.

EXPRESSING YOUR OPINION

1. Explain what the phrase "Not necessarily conscription, but conscription if necessary" means. Why do you think Mackenzie King used this phrase?

2. Few today believe that the actions of the Canadian government toward Japanese Canadians were justified. What can we do to ensure the security of Canada without violating basic human rights?

3. Select the most effective propaganda poster that appears in this chapter and explain its appeal. Select an issue from World War II and create your own poster that could have been used to support the war effort or the view of a group opposed to government actions.

4. Should Canadians have the right to decide whether or not they want to participate in war in any manner, or should all Canadians be required to make some kind of contribution to the war effort? Defend your answer.

5. The Canadian government continues to play a much more direct and active role in the economy than it had prior to the war. Do you believe that this was a positive or negative development? Explain your answer.

WORKING WITH THE EVIDENCE

1. Multi-lane highways, which would become a common feature of post–World War II cities, were first created by the Nazis in the late 1930s. Their interest was not in easing traffic congestion or improving the efficiency of automobile travel. Why did the Nazis invent the superhighways?

2. Frank Fender is an avid collector of hubcaps for cars. After years of collecting he has gathered hubcaps for every year between 1920 and 1999, except for the years 1942, 1943, 1944, and 1945. Why has he been unable to find hubcaps for these years?

The Consequences of War for Canada and the World

These Canadian soldiers arrived home at Halifax on June 30, 1945, bringing with them some war trophies. What kinds of challenges would these returning soldiers face in their adjustment to civilian life?

INQUIRING INTO THE PAST

- **What impact did World War II have on Canada's economy and society?**
- **Which countries emerged from the war as the new superpowers?**
- **How would wartime technology be adapted to peacetime uses?**
- **What were the primary goals of the United Nations when it was created?**

KEY TERMS

Civil war

Cold War

Containment

Espionage

Gulags

Middle Power

Satellite States

Superpowers

TIMELINE

APRIL 1945 ▶
United Nations holds its first meeting

JULY 1945 ▶
Canadian government begins to pay family allowances

SEPTEMBER 1945 ▶
Gouzenko affair reveals spies in Canada

APRIL 1949 ▶
North Atlantic Treaty Organization (NATO) is created

Peace returned in 1945, but at a terrible price. Nuclear weapons had unleashed a frightening power that had the potential to destroy the human race. This new threat and horrible danger darkened prospects for the future. Even many of the people who helped to create the atomic bomb were deeply troubled by the morality of creating such a terrifying weapon. Robert Oppenheimer, the director of the laboratory that built the first atomic bomb, once said to U.S. President Harry Truman, "I have blood on my hands." But he also later said that he believed that developing atomic weapons made achieving peace "more hopeful ... because it intensifies the urgency of our hopes — in frank words, because we are scared."

The coming of peace was, however, a joy and relief for Canadians. World War II veterans returned to a nation more prosperous than the one they had left. They looked forward to settling down and rebuilding their lives in peacetime. Many Canadians were also proud of Canada's achievements in the war: Canada had built the world's third-largest navy and fourth-largest air force. It had become an important partner of Britain and the United States and had shared in major wartime projects. Canadians began to believe that their nation could play a bigger role on the world stage.

The World in 1945

While North America enjoyed its new prosperity, many other places still had much rebuilding to do. Europe was a wasteland of ruined cities and devastated countrysides. European governments were in disorder, and their economies were badly damaged. Food was in short supply, and millions of people were on the brink of starvation. France had been badly weakened by the German occupation during the war. Britain had been sapped of its economic strength by the enormous costs of the war. Despite massive aid from Canada and the United States, Britain would take years to become part of the world economy again.

Following the agreement among the Allies that emerged from the Yalta Conference, defeated Germany had been carved up into four occupation zones by the major Allied powers — the United States, France, Britain, and the Soviet Union. Germany's capital, Berlin, now deep in the Soviet zone, was also divided into occupation zones. Although Germany remained an independent nation, all important decisions about its future were made by the occupying Allies. The nations of Europe under Soviet control would have a very limited version of democracy put

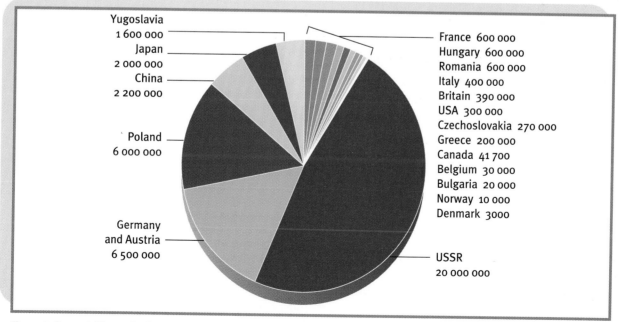

Yugoslavia 1 600 000
Japan 2 000 000
China 2 200 000
Poland 6 000 000
Germany and Austria 6 500 000
France 600 000
Hungary 600 000
Romania 600 000
Italy 400 000
Britain 390 000
USA 300 000
Czechoslovakia 270 000
Greece 200 000
Canada 41 700
Belgium 30 000
Bulgaria 20 000
Norway 10 000
Denmark 3000
USSR 20 000 000

The cost of war: civilian and military deaths, 1939–1945.

The devastation caused by World War II left much of Europe in rubble. Try to imagine the challenges that cities must have faced as they tried to rebuild.

into place; although elections would be held, only members of the Communist Party would be allowed to run for office. Until the late 1980s, countries in the Soviet zone would be ruled by communist governments with close ties to Moscow.

On the other side of the world, Japan had accepted defeat after the U.S. atomic bomb blasts in Hiroshima and Nagasaki and accepted a U.S. occupation force. China was a huge but crippled giant. Not only had it suffered under wartime occupation by the Japanese, but the **civil war** between the Nationalists, led by Chiang Kai-shek, and communist rebels, led by Mao Zedong, that had ravaged China since the 1920s returned in full force after the war.

The New Superpowers: The Soviet Union and the United States

Even though Britain and France had been badly weakened by the war, both nations were still considered major powers because they had been great world powers before the war. Although China was a poor and struggling nation after the war, it was also considered a major power because of its great size and huge population. The two most important new **superpowers**, however, were the Soviet Union and the United States.

The Soviet Union had also been devastated in the war, but because of its large area, population, and wealth of natural resources, it was undeniably a world power. Most importantly, it led the world in military might. After the war, the Soviet Union still had armed

Zones of Influence in Europe, 1945–1949

West Germany (1949)

East Germany (1949)

Berlin

Poland 1948

Soviet Union

Czechoslovakia 1948

Vienna

Austria

Hungary 1948

Romania 1948

Yugoslavia 1945

Bulgaria 1947

Albania

- States that became Communist, with date of takeover
- Allied control zones: British, American, French and Soviet, shown by flags
- Cities divided into Allied control zones
- The "Iron Curtain"
- Divisions between Allied control zones

0   250   500 KM

One of the results of World War II was the division of Europe along Eastern (communist) and Western (democratic) lines.

Canadian profiles

FARLEY MOWAT'S WORLD WAR II EXPERIENCES

Like many young men in 1939, Farley Mowat envisioned war as a great romantic adventure. When he sailed for England in July 1942, Mowat was eager to see action. The horrors he encountered on the battlefield quickly shattered any illusions he held. As part of the Canadian force that landed at Sicily and drove north through Italy, Mowat was engaged in bloody, fierce fighting.

Since returning to Canada, Farley Mowat has become one of Canada's best-known authors and has written classics such as *Lost In the Barrens* and *Never Cry Wolf*. The excerpts below are taken from his book *And No Birds Sang*, which has been described as his finest work. In this gripping war story, Mowat tells of his own experiences and the reality of war. As you read these excerpts, reflect on Mowat's message to the reader. Do you think Mowat would support another war? If so, under what circumstances? If not, why not?

[A note to his parents before leaving Canada]
Thank heavens, this is it! It's worth two years of waiting. A couple of months' battle training with the Regiment and then, praise be, we'll get a show to try our talents on…. Apart from you two, I don't in the least regret leaving Canada even though there is the chance I may not see it again. If we get a damn good lick in at the Hun, it'll be worth it….

[Recollections of a battle]
One…dash took me close to a hut whose partly collapsed stone walls still seemed capable of providing some protection, and the banshee screech of Moaning Minnie rockets sent me scuttling frantically toward this ruin. I reached it just as the bombs exploded a few score yards away. The blast flung me through the empty doorway with such violence that I sprawled full-length on top of a prone human figure who emitted a horrid gurgling belch. It was an unconscious protest, for he and two of his three companions — gray-clad paratroopers — were dead, their bodies mired in the muck and goat manure on the floor. The fourth man—dimly seen in that dim place — was sitting upright in a corner of the little unroofed room and his eyes met mine as I struggled to my hands and knees.

In that instant I was so convinced I had had it— that he would shoot me where I knelt—that I did not even try to reach for the carbine slung across my back. I remained transfixed for what seemed an interminable time, then in an unconscious reflex effort to cheat death, I flung myself sideways and rolled to my feet. I was lurching through the doorway when his thin voice reached me.

"Vasser…haff…you…vasser?"

I checked my rush and swung up against the outer wall, knowing then that I was safe, that he posed no threat. And I felt an inexplicable sense of recognition, almost as if I had heard his voice before. Cautiously I peered back through the doorway.

His left hand was clasping the shattered stump where his right arm had been severed just below the elbow. Dark gore was still gouting between his fingers and spreading in a black pool about his outthrust legs. Most dreadful was a great gash in his side from which protruded a glistening dark mass which must have been his liver. Above this wreckage, his eyes were large and luminous in a young man's face, pallid to the point of translucency.

"Vasser…please giff…vasser."

Reluctantly I shook my head. "Sorry, chum, I've got none. Nein vasser. Only rum, and that's no good for you."

The eyes, so vividly alive in the dying body, pleaded with me. Oh, hell, I thought, he's going anyway. What harm!

I held the water bottle to his lips and he swallowed in deep, spasmodic gulps until I took it back and drank from it myself. And so…and so the two of us got drunk together. And in a little while he died….

The blanket that screened the shattered cellar door was thrust aside and a party of stretcher-bearers pushed in among us. Al Park lay on one of the stretchers. He was alive, though barely so…unconscious, with a bullet in his head.

As I looked down at his faded, empty face under its crown of crimson bandages, I began to weep.

I wonder now…were my tears for Alex and Al and all the others who had gone and who were yet to go?

Or was I weeping for myself…and those who would remain?

forces of up to six million soldiers, fifty thousand tanks, and twenty thousand aircraft. Its army occupied Central and Eastern Europe as well as Manchuria and North Korea in East Asia.

The only nation that could equal the Soviet Union in military strength was the United States. Like Canada, the United States had not suffered bombing or invasion during the war. It had been able to build up powerful armed forces, and its sole possession of the atomic bomb was enough to keep its potential enemies in line. The United States had also taken over Britain's role as the world's greatest imperial power. American military bases and colonies were scattered across the Pacific Ocean, the Caribbean Sea, and Latin America. Above all, the United States was the richest country in the world. With a huge budget for both foreign aid and arms, its presence was felt in almost every corner of the globe in the post-war years.

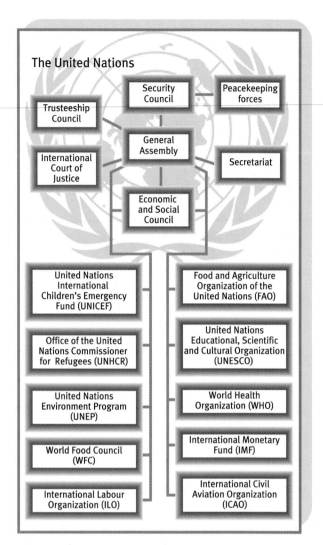

The United Nations

- Security Council
- Peacekeeping forces
- Trusteeship Council
- General Assembly
- International Court of Justice
- Secretariat
- Economic and Social Council

- United Nations International Children's Emergency Fund (UNICEF)
- Food and Agriculture Organization of the United Nations (FAO)
- Office of the United Nations Commissioner for Refugees (UNHCR)
- United Nations Educational, Scientific and Cultural Organization (UNESCO)
- United Nations Environment Program (UNEP)
- World Health Organization (WHO)
- World Food Council (WFC)
- International Monetary Fund (IMF)
- International Labour Organization (ILO)
- International Civil Aviation Organization (ICAO)

This colourful poster was made for the United Nations by the famous American artist Norman Rockwell. It reads: "Do Unto Others As You Would Have Them Do Unto You." What do the picture and the statement tell you about the goals of the United Nations?

The United Nations

In 1945 the so-called "Big Five" nations — the Soviet Union, the United States, Britain, France, and China — decided to attempt to shape a peaceful future for the world. The major Allied powers had started preparing for peace even before the war ended. In the fall of 1944, officials from the United States, Britain, the Soviet Union, and China gathered at Dumbarton Oaks, a mansion in Washington, D.C. There they laid plans for a new international organization called the United Nations (U.N.). The United Nations was intended to provide a place where nations could meet to find peaceful solutions to world conflicts.

Although most details of the U.N. Charter were worked out at Dumbarton Oaks, the new organization was not born until after the war. In April 1945,

Lester Pearson, who would later become Prime Minister of Canada, addresses an international meeting in San Francisco in 1945. The formal charter of the United Nations was drafted during this conference.

delegates from fifty-one nations gathered in San Francisco to formally establish the United Nations. The opening words of the charter set out the U.N.'s most important goal. It reads, "We the peoples of the United Nations, determined to save succeeding generations from the scourge of war, which twice in our lifetime has brought untold sorrow to mankind...do hereby establish an international organization to be known as the United Nations." Some of the most important goals cited in the U.N. Charter are:

- to keep world peace and prevent the outbreak of new wars;
- to help advance justice and law throughout the world;
- to defend human rights and help promote equality among different individuals and groups around the globe; and
- to encourage friendly relations among nations.

Canada as a Middle Power

Canada's Prime Minister Mackenzie King was among the world leaders who attended the United Nations conference in San Francisco. Although Canada was not one of the "Big Five," it was only one rung down on the international ladder and had become a major **middle power**. With its booming economy, undamaged industries, and sizable armed forces, Canada was one of the most prosperous countries in the world in 1945. By the end of the war, more than one million Canadians were in uniform. Canada had also been an important wartime ally of Britain and the United States.

For perhaps the first time, Canada was too important to be overlooked by the major powers. Mackenzie King wanted to ensure that smaller nations like Canada would not be forced into future wars by the Big Five. His voice was heard at the U.N. conference. As a result of Canadian efforts, the U.N. Charter was changed so that any country asked to contribute troops or money to U.N. security operations had to be consulted about those operations first. Mackenzie King also wanted special powers for middle-power countries like Canada, Australia, New Zealand, and the Netherlands, but only the Security Council members received special powers. All other member-nations were treated equally and given one vote each in the U.N. General Assembly.

The Origins of the Cold War

The search for world peace was seriously threatened by growing tension between the two new superpowers after World War II. For the first time in history, competing superpowers were ideologically opposed. Whereas the Soviet Union sought to implement communism wherever possible, the United States committed itself to promoting American-style democracy, free elections, and free-market economies. In a major speech in 1947, U.S. President Harry Truman set out the guiding principles of what would come to be known as the Truman Doctrine:

At the present moment in world history nearly every nation must choose between alternative ways of life ... one way of life is based upon the will of the majority.... The second way of life is based upon the will of a minority forcibly imposed upon the majority.... I believe that it must be the policy of the United States to support free peoples who are resisting attempted subjugation by armed minorities or by outside pressures.

This speech would shape American foreign policy in the post-war years.

Over the next few years the hostility between the United States and the Soviet Union deepened, and once again other nations began lining up with one side or the other. The term **"Cold War"** was first used in 1947 to describe this power struggle, which was being fought by every means short of all-out warfare. Both sides feared a nuclear war. So, instead of waging a "hot" war with troops and weapons, the Cold War was fought with propaganda, **espionage,** economic and political pressures, and limited military aggression. The Soviets and Americans used these tactics to win the support of uncommitted nations. Above all, the Cold War was fought with the scare tactics of an arms race: each side raced to stockpile larger, more destructive weapons in order to frighten its enemies.

Canada and the Beginning of East–West Hostilities

One of the early warning signals of growing post-war hostilities occurred on Canadian soil. On September 5, 1945, a young clerk with the Soviet Embassy in Ottawa, Igor Gouzenko, walked out of the embassy carrying 109 top-secret documents. He announced to authorities that he had evidence that the Soviet Union was running a spy ring of civil servants and military officers in Canada. Gouzenko claimed that the Soviets were trying to collect secret information about political activities, troop movements, and scientific secrets. He said that the Soviets were especially interested in getting information about the atomic bomb, which Canada had worked on with Britain and the United States. Gouzenko also claimed that the Soviets had set up spy rings in Britain and the United States.

At first, Gouzenko's claims were ignored. It was only when Soviet embassy officials broke down the door of the apartment where Gouzenko hid with his family that the government finally took notice. The Royal Canadian Mounted Police questioned Gouzenko for five hours and then placed him in protective custody. Soon, a shocked Mackenzie King was told the news of Gouzenko's defection and his claims about the Soviet Union's

international spy ring. Mackenzie King immediately warned President Truman and the British Prime Minister Clement Attlee.

Growing East–West Conflict

The Gouzenko spy story made headlines around the world. Many Canadians were as shocked as Mackenzie King was to find out that the Soviet Union was trying to steal military secrets from its former wartime allies. But many other Canadians had remained deeply suspicious of communism and communist intentions. The Soviet leader, Joseph Stalin, brutally repressed anyone in the Soviet Union who did not support his rule both before and after World War II. Stalin's secret police arrested Soviet citizens suspected of opposing him. Some were executed, and others were sent to horrifying labour camps called **gulags**.

The Soviet army came to occupy large areas of Eastern Europe in 1944 and 1945. When World War II ended, Soviet troops stayed in Romania, Bulgaria, Hungary, Poland, East Germany, and Czechoslovakia. News was leaking out that in these countries, too, personal freedoms were being taken away and that one-party communist governments were being set up. The Soviet takeovers in Eastern

This is how Igor Gouzenko was known to the world after he exposed a Soviet spy ring operating in Canada. Why was it necessary that his identity be kept a secret?

Europe peaked with the overthrow of a social-democratic government in Czechoslovakia in 1948. These countries were sometimes called Soviet **satellite states** because their communist governments were directly linked to Moscow.

Communism was also beginning to gain ground in Western Europe. During the war, communists had often been at the heart of European resistance movements. They had worked underground to fight the Nazis in occupied countries, and many became national heroes. By the late 1940s, communist parties were firmly established in Italy, France, and elsewhere. Italian and French communist parties staged huge strikes and demonstrations. Many people in Western Europe viewed the resulting economic and political turmoil as a communist attempt to shut down the Western European economy and create social chaos. They worried that Stalin would become another Hitler and try to extend the Soviet Union's power and influence across Europe and around the globe.

Canada's new Prime Minister, Louis St. Laurent, was one of the leaders of the Western nations who feared the Soviet Union. In 1948 St. Laurent made impassioned pleas to put a stop to the spread of communism. "For us there is no escape in isolation or indifference," he said. "Recent events have brought home to all of us the increasing threat to our democracy of the rising tide of communism." The only nation strong enough to oppose the Soviet Union was the United States. Canadian diplomats worried that the United States might retreat from its commitments in Europe now that the war was over. They wanted the Americans to stand fast against further Soviet expansion.

Many Americans shared St. Laurent's suspicions and fears. They were also prepared to take on a greatly expanded international role. American officials were already crafting a new foreign policy aimed at opposing the Soviet Union. The new American foreign policy, based on the Truman Doctrine, was built on a policy of **containment**. It aimed at "containing," or halting, the spread of communism in Europe and around the world. This would be accomplished in a variety of ways, from providing economic aid to countries to giving military support to anti-communist forces.

The North Atlantic Treaty Organization

Even though Canada encouraged the United States to oppose the Soviet Union, it still wanted to avoid being drawn into future U.S. wars without consultation. Canadian diplomats decided to propose an alliance of democratic nations in the North Atlantic region. They hoped that the new alliance would give Canada greater participation in the shaping of American defence policy.

Although Canadian hopes for having major influence on American military policy were never realized, Canada did persuade the United States to join Canada, Britain, France, and eight other nations in signing a treaty in 1949. The treaty contained clauses about trade and cultural exchanges among member nations, but it was primarily a pact to create an organization for mutual defence, the North Atlantic Treaty Organization (NATO). Each member-nation agreed to contribute army, navy, and air force units to a new NATO defence force. The combined strength of the NATO alliance membership was intended to discourage the Soviet Union from any attempted takeover of Western Europe.

Web Connections

http://www.school.mcgrawhill.ca/resources

Go to the above Web site to find out more about the North Atlantic Treaty Organization. Go to *History Resources*, then to *Canada: A Nation Unfolding, Ontario Edition*, to find out where to go next.

The Warsaw Pact

The Soviet Union was upset by the new Western alliance. It argued that NATO was not needed because the Soviet Union was not a threat to Western Europe. On the contrary, it claimed, the Soviet Union had twice been invaded by Western European powers in the twentieth century. It was only interested in protecting itself from yet another invasion from the West. The Soviets also pointed to expanding U.S. power as an attempt by the United States to extend its influence around the globe. The Soviet Union reacted by organizing its own defence alliance, the Warsaw Pact, in 1955. The Soviet satellite countries of Eastern Europe agreed to defend each other and the Soviet Union if any Warsaw Pact member was attacked.

Now the two sides, East and West, had squared off across a line running from the Baltic Sea in the north to the Adriatic Sea in the south. On the Eastern side stood the communist countries under the control of the Soviet Union. On the Western side was the coalition of nations under the leadership of the United States. Winston Churchill had declared in 1946 that "an iron curtain had descended on Europe." The two new alliances — NATO and the Warsaw Pact — deepened the rift between East and West. The Cold War grew colder.

Canada and the Marshall Plan

One of the first skirmishes of the Cold War was an economic fight over the recovery of Western European nations. While Britain and the United States wanted to see their war-torn allies back on their feet again, it was in the best interests of the Soviet Union to prevent an economic recovery of the American allies in Western Europe. Not only would communism be more appealing in economically desperate countries, but a weak Western Europe would ensure that the Soviet Union and its allies held the upper hand in post-war Europe.

In 1948 U.S. Secretary of State George Marshall proposed a European recovery plan that came to be known as the Marshall Plan. Canada had already loaned huge sums of money to Britain. Now it joined in the Marshall Plan and shipped $706 million in food, equipment, and raw materials to Europe. Between 1948 and 1953 Canada and the United States jointly contributed $13.5 billion in European economic aid, most of it from the United States. Western Europe made an amazing recovery, far beyond the expectations of the people who had helped to engineer it. Within a decade, stability and prosperity had returned to Western Europe, including the former Axis powers, especially Germany.

After examining this photograph of a French farmer admiring his new tractor, speculate as to how the Marshall Plan affected both his life and the life of his family.

The Changing Nature of Canadian Society

Few events in Canadian history have shaped society to the extent that World War II did. After suffering from a decade-long economic depression and six years of war, Canadians adopted a new outlook on life and on the nature of the society in which they wished to live. Following the apparent failure of free-market economics (in which governments played a limited role) and the sacrifices made by many during the war years, Canadians developed a sense that they had a right to a high quality of life. Before the war, a good job, quality health care, an affordable house, pensions, and child care had been considered personal goals; after the war they came to be seen as rights that accompanied Canadian citizenship.

Government Intervention at the End of the War

Massive government intervention in the wartime Canadian economy seemed to have paid off. Canada had managed to keep inflation in check without slowing down the economy. In fact, the nation's record of keeping inflation under control was the best in the world. The expanding web of government regulations during the war, including

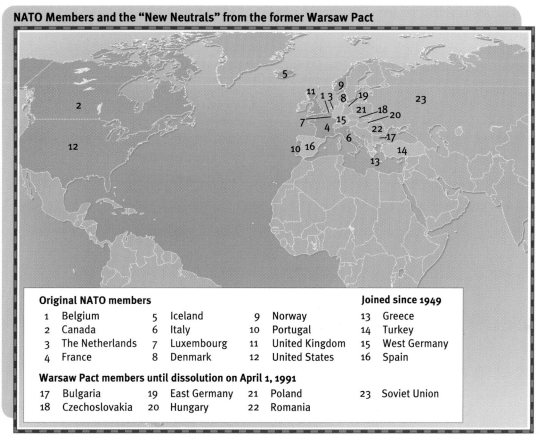

NATO Members and the "New Neutrals" from the former Warsaw Pact

Original NATO members

1	Belgium	5	Iceland
2	Canada	6	Italy
3	The Netherlands	7	Luxembourg
4	France	8	Denmark

9	Norway
10	Portugal
11	United Kingdom
12	United States

Joined since 1949

13	Greece
14	Turkey
15	West Germany
16	Spain

Warsaw Pact members until dissolution on April 1, 1991

17	Bulgaria	19	East Germany	21	Poland
18	Czechoslovakia	20	Hungary	22	Romania

23	Soviet Union

NATO was originally developed as an organization for mutual defence to discourage the expansion of the Soviet Union. Following the end of the Cold War, NATO was restructured to allow it to participate in security issues for all of Europe. In March 1999, the former Warsaw Pact members, the Czech Republlic, Hungary, and Poland joined NATO.

National Selective Service rules (which had directed workers to areas where labour was most needed), rationing, and wage-and-price controls, had severely limited Canadians' freedom of action. But the scarce goods had been shared fairly equally among Canadians, and many workers enjoyed a higher standard of living. As the war came to an end, however, Canadians feared a return to the Great Depression. Many began to think that the federal government should continue to direct the economy. Mackenzie King's government had already provided for Unemployment Insurance in 1940 and family allowance — a monthly payment for food and clothing for children — in 1945.

Many important steps in the development of the welfare state occurred in the immediate post-war years. Mackenzie King's Liberal government increased veterans' benefits and addressed a severe housing shortage by promoting home-building. It also brought in programs to help industries shift to peacetime production and to secure export sales, and it increased federal aid to health care. King's new programs were popular, and his government was re-elected in 1945. These programs were the beginning of a whole new involvement of the federal government in social and economic affairs.

Mackenzie King had planned to carry social reform much further much faster than he was able to. Shortly after being re-elected in 1945, he hosted a Dominion–Provincial Conference on Reconstruction. At the conference, the federal government unveiled its Green Book, a set of proposals that called for a comprehensive set of national programs that would look after the old, the sick, and the unemployed.

PHOTO ESSAY

VICTIMS OF WAR

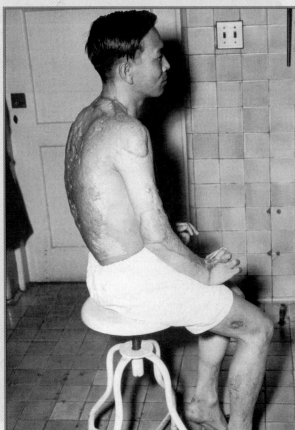

Survivor of atomic bombing of Hiroshima.

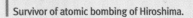

Holocaust survivors.

A European city at the end of the war.

Canadian prisoners of war.

Saying goodbye to a fallen comrade.

Japanese Canadian children being removed from their West Coast homes.

Looking for affordable housing while father is at war.

Army chaplain giving fallen soldier last rites.

To finance these new commitments, the federal government argued that it needed exclusive control over income and corporate taxes and succession duties. The provinces, however, said that they could not meet their obligations without having a share of these major sources of tax revenue. After nine fruitless months of negotiations, talks broke off. Added pressure from pro-business forces such as the Canadian Chamber of Commerce forced the federal government to scale back its ambitious initiatives. In time, however, the social reform envisaged in the Green Book would come about. The Great Depression and World War II provided the impetus for change.

Charting a Course for the Future

With both the Great Depression and the war now fading into the past, Canadians looked to the future with an optimism they had seldom felt before. They had risen to the challenges of difficult times and in the process had reinvented their nation. By the late 1940s Canada was well on its way to becoming a vibrant multicultural society. An expanding economy and a rising population laid the foundations for a prosperity Canadians had never known. Building on its international reputation, Canada ventured into the world to become a major player in international trade and international peacekeeping. Prosperity, security, and an expanding social safety net soon made Canada the envy of the world and among the most desirable places to live.

chapter review

CHAPTER SUMMARY

In this chapter we have seen

- that a Cold War between the new superpowers — the United States and the Soviet Union — developed after the war

- that Canada emerged from the war as an important middle power and played a significant role in international affairs

- how Canada helped devastated European nations to rebuild their economies

- how the Canadian government came to play an increasing role in the lives of Canadians

UNDERSTANDING HISTORICAL FACTS

1. Identify these people, places, and events, and explain their historical significance.

United Nations	Igor Gouzenko
Lester Pearson	Cold War
Louis St. Laurent	Marshall Plan
Warsaw Pact	North Atlantic Treaty
Iron Curtain	Organization (NATO)

2. Compare Canada's strength with that of the world's other leading nations following World War II. Why was Canada referred to as a "middle power"?

3. Why is the "Gouzenko affair" considered to have signalled the beginning of the Cold War?

4. What actions on the part of the Soviet Union prompted Western nations to fear communist expansion? How did they react?

5. What was the Truman Doctrine, and how did it help to shape American foreign policy in the years following World War II?

EXPRESSING YOUR OPINION

1. Imagine that you are one of Mackenzie King's top advisers at the time Harry Truman delivers the speech spelling out the principles that became known as the Truman Doctrine. What advice would you give the Prime Minister regarding the future of Canadian foreign policy? Consider the following issues. (a) Should Canada support the American commitment to protecting "free people" and opposing the spread of communism? (b) Should Canada support the use of military force to oppose communism?

2. Despite their incredible destructive powers, nuclear weapons are considered by many people to have been the key to a lasting peace over the past five decades. Create two webs that compare the costs or dangers and the benefits of nuclear weapons.

3. When a country is abusing the human rights of its own citizens, should the United Nations have the right to send in troops to end the abuse? Describe the type of situations in which the United Nations should send forces into a country to protect that country's citizens.

4. After years of economic depression and war, Canadians came to expect a more active role from their government and seemed to assume that a decent standard of living was a right, not a privilege. As a result, governments in Canada came to play a much larger role than they did before the 1930s. In your notes, prepare a two-column chart. Complete the chart by listing the areas in which you believe government should and should not be involved. Consider health, education, children, roads, unemployment, and housing.

WORKING WITH THE EVIDENCE

1. When the four major powers divided post-war Europe into areas of influence, they agreed to hold democratic elections within a few years. By 1950 East Germany was renamed the German People's Democratic Republic and the Soviet Union claimed that the government was democratically elected. Yet, it was a communist country. How could the claim be justified?

unit review

BRINGING THE PAST INTO FOCUS

REVIEWING THE FACTS

1. Unlike World War I, during which the horrors of war remained a distant fear, World War II brought the threat of war to Canadian shores. On a map of the world, indicate, using appropriate symbols, the potential threats to Canada that existed during World War II. Your map should indicate Japanese expansion in Asia and the South Pacific, marine and military activity on Canada's east and west coasts, and the Japanese balloon attacks on Western Canada.

2. Create an illustrated time line that traces the key events of World War II from the outbreak of war in September 1939 to the end of the war in August 1945. Your time line should include at least eight dates. Be sure to incorporate at least five illustrations or photographs that capture the key battles, people, or events.

3. Prime Minister William Lyon Mackenzie King made Canadian independence a priority throughout his political career. How did he promote Canadian independence during World War II?

4. How was Canada's contribution to World War II similar to and different from its contribution in World War I? In responding, consider Canada's military, technological, and economic contributions. Use a chart to organize its contributions to the two wars.

5. The years between 1939 and 1945 showed the darkest side of humanity. Complete the chart below to illustrate the inhuman treatment of peoples during the war.

6. During an age of extreme intolerance that saw people tortured and killed due to their race and religion, what evidence is there that Canada was becoming a more tolerant nation? Consider the composition of the Canadian military, the changing role of women, and the treatment of minorities in answering this question. Does the refusal of Canada to admit Jews fleeing Europe and its treatment of Japanese Canadians suggest Canada was not becoming more tolerant?

HISTORICALLY SPEAKING

Respond to any two of the following questions. Be sure to prepare your response carefully and to use historical evidence in supporting your position.

1. The failure of the Western powers and the League of Nations to stop the rise of Nazi Germany and the persecution of the Jews has often been seen as one of the great failures of the twentieth century. Canada's foreign policy in the inter-war years reflected support for the policy of appeasement and the desire to avoid another costly war. Was appeasement a valid option, or should a firm stand have been taken against Hitler's aggression? Avoid relying on hindsight in responding to this question.

2. To what degree did the outbreak of war provide a solution to the economic depression that Canadian governments had failed to solve? Examine Canadian employment rates, gross national product, the value of exports, and average incomes for the years before, during, and immediately after the war. (You will need to do some additional research to answer this question.) Use bar graphs and line graphs to illustrate the differences in these areas.

GROUP	NATURE OF TREATMENT	PERPERTRATORS
European Jews	*[handwritten]*	*[handwritten]*
Canadian Soldiers in Hong Kong	*[handwritten]*	*[handwritten]*
Japanese Canadians	*[handwritten]*	*[handwritten]*

3. After the first year of war it appeared that Hitler would have little trouble in conquering all of Europe and establishing the dominance of the Third Reich. Yet, by 1943, the Third Reich was showing signs of weakness and the seemingly invincible Nazi army was in retreat. What were the key turning points in the war that allowed for the Allied forces to stage a comeback? Which of the factors resulted from mistakes made by the Nazi army or leadership? Which factors can be attributed to the planning and resources of the Allied powers?

4. As a military strategist, would you have recommended dropping atomic bombs on both Hiroshima and Nagasaki? To answer this question, consider the costs of an invasion of Japan in both dollars and lives. If you agree with the use of the atomic bomb, how long after using the first bomb would you wait for a Japanese surrender? Would you consider the use of a second bomb on Nagasaki, to establish post-war control over Japan and to block the expansion of the Soviet Union into Japan?

MAKING CONNECTIONS

When looking at the eventual outcome of World War II, we can see that several events could have "gone the other way" and that the consequences would have been profound. For each of the counter-factual scenarios presented below, sketch out how you believe the war (and perhaps the post-war world) might have unfolded.

Policy of Appeasement	Appalled and frightened by the re-arming of Germany, and Hitler's violations of the Treaty of Versailles, leading Western powers decide to take a stand against Germany over the intended invasions of Austria (Anschluss). Hitler faces the prospect of war in early 1938 against the united forces of the British commonwealth, France, and the United States.
Dunkirk	The fog lifts, allowing for a devastating attack by the German Luftwaffe and preventing the escape of Allied forces from the beaches of France.
Battle of Britain/ Operation Sea Lion	During the air raids designed to knock out the British air force, no German aircraft stray off course. Instead, they successfully destroy British aircraft factories, and oil tanks, virtually grounding the Royal Air Force. This lays the foundation for the Nazis to attempt the invasion of Britain.

PERSPECTIVES

1. Imagine that you are a Jewish Canadian with relatives living in Germany and other parts of Europe. You are concerned about the plight of your family overseas and have decided to express your concerns to the federal government. Write one-paragraph responses to the following developments.

   a) Word of *Kristallnacht* reaches Canada.

   b) Information about the Nazi death camps is reported in Canadian newspapers.

2. For you, as a member of the Mennonite community, pacifism has always been an important part of your religious and moral beliefs. Yet, you are troubled by the prospect that fascist dictators may succeed in conquering much of the free world. Do you go against your beliefs and your community to fight against evil? Explain your decision.

3. World War I pitted colonial empires against each other. As a French Canadian, you saw no reason to fight in a European war over issues that had little to do with Canada and even less to do with French Canadians. Now, twenty years later, the world is once again at war. Given the causes of the war and the threats to Canada, what is your attitude toward enlisting in the army and to the government's possible use of conscription?

4. Throughout the war, you and women that you know have accepted roles never before filled by women. From work in factories and farms to military roles, women have filled vital gaps, allowing for Canada's tremendous success during the war years. Now the war is drawing to a close. What do you expect for women in the post-war years? Will there be significant change, or will women return to their pre-war roles in society?

Expo 67

"Canadians can ... make Canada a better and better country for all its citizens to live in, while ... [helping] to heal the world of its grievous wounds."

—FROM MARGARET McWILLIAMS'S *THIS NEW CANADA*, 1948

TIMELINE

1945
Baby boom begins

1956
Canadian peace-keeping born as a result of Suez Crisis

The Canada of 1945 and the Canada of 1968 had many things in common. The nation still enjoyed its connection to Britain; it continued to welcome immigrants and refugees; its population and economy continued to prosper with new technologies and industries; the United States was its most important trading partner; and Canada continued to expand its international role as a referee and peacekeeper. But the differences! Between 1945 and 1968 Canada's population doubled; the remote Canadian North became a focal point for resource exploration and national defence outposts; Aboriginal peoples began to assert their rights and land claims; women began to question their role in society; French Canadians began to fight the dominance of English Canadian culture; and Canadians began to demand the protection of the Canadian economy and culture from overwhelming American ownership and influence. By the time Canada celebrated its one-hundredth birthday in 1967, it was proud to proclaim both its multicultural heritage and its international role.

LET'S INVESTIGATE

1. In what ways did Canada participate in promoting global peace and security after World War II?
2. What events drastically changed demographic patterns in Canada?
3. Why did Québec nationalism grow after World War II? How did this affect French–English relations?
4. How did the government become more involved in the lives of Canadians?
5. How did the beliefs and values of Canadians change between the 1950s and the 1960s? Why did they change?

1961
Jean Lesage begins
Quiet Revolution in
Québec

►

1965
Canada gets new
flag

►

►

The 1960s brought about many social changes that made life very different from the 1950s. What changes do these two pictures suggest came about for many Canadian women?

INQUIRING INTO THE PAST

- **How did a second wave of immigration change Canadian society? Who was part of this wave?**
- **What was "the baby boom" and what impact did it have on Canada during the 1950s and 1960s? How long would this impact last?**
- **What types of American influences were changing Canadian culture?**
- **Would all groups of people share in Canada's post-war prosperity? Who would be left out?**

KEY TERMS

Baby Boom

Counterculture

Generation Gap

Hippies

La Survivance

Suburbia

Youth Generation

TIMELINE

1945 ▶
Baby Boom begins

1949 ▶
Massey Commission recommends strengthening Canadian arts programs to combat dominance of American culture

1962 ▶
Black-Canadian town of Africville, Nova Scotia, is bulldozed

1967 ▶
Royal Commission on the Status of Women begins its study

Between 1945 and 1968 Canada experienced significant changes. With the war now over and the economy booming, it once again became the land of hopes and dreams. Canadians were ready to live the good life, and a wave of optimism swept across the country. Houses, cars, television, rock 'n' roll, and hippies all became part of Canadian society. But would their effects on Canada all be positive? Would all Canadians share in this prosperity?

Canada's Growing Population

In the years following World War II Canada experienced a population boom like it had never seen before. This was the result of two major factors: a second large wave of immigration, and the **baby boom**.

Moving to Canada

Immigration boomed after World War II, and almost 1.5 million people came to Canada between 1945 and 1957. About 20 percent of the new arrivals between 1945 and 1955 came from Britain. Many were war brides who were brought to Canada by their Canadian soldier husbands. About forty-eight thousand war brides came to Canada after the war. Other immigrants were skilled tradespeople who left Britain to find work because their factories either had suffered heavy war damage or had been shut down when war production stopped. Most other immigrants came from the Netherlands, Germany, Poland, Hungary, southern Italy, and Ukraine.

Many immigrants were *"displaced persons"* who had been living in refugee camps throughout Europe. These refugees could not return to their homelands because their homes had been destroyed or because civil wars and unrest made it too dangerous for them to go back. Most immigrants came to Canada looking for a new and better life, and they were willing to work long and hard for it.

Most of the newcomers settled in cities, especially Toronto, Montréal, and Vancouver. The Italian community in Toronto had 140 000 people by the end of the 1950s, and displays of pasta,

In the years immediately following the end of war, thousands of war brides, mostly from England and the Netherlands, arrived in Canada. What challenges would women such as those pictured here face in adjusting to life in Canada?

Why would immigrants such as this Jewish family see Canada as the land of new hope?

The Baby Boom

The large post-war wave of immigration to Canada also coincided with a population increase that is known as the "baby boom." With the war behind them and good economic times at hand, more young couples than usual decided to get married and start families. Between the years 1945 and 1965, there was a huge increase in the number of babies being born. In fact, at the peak of the baby boom in 1959, 20 percent of all women in their twenties had babies, and this led to a rapid increase in Canada's population. The average family had three to four children. As the baby boomers grew up, the sheer size of their age group would continue to affect Canadian society in different ways. In the 1950s and 1960s, this population boom led to one of the most well-known characteristics of Canadian life — **suburbia**.

imported cheeses, and other Mediterranean delicacies became familiar sights in Toronto stores. German immigrants set up shops along Robson Street in Vancouver, and Viennese pastries, Bavarian sausages, and German-language newspapers attracted the eye of passing shoppers.

By the end of the 1950s Canada's immigration picture had changed. Western Europe had largely recovered from its war losses, and new opportunities were available at home for many skilled Europeans. The decline in their desire to emigrate coincided with a severe economic recession that swept through North America. When the economic climate improved in the early 1960s, many Canadian industries began again to seek skilled workers who had technical and professional training. Because fewer Europeans were asking to come to Canada, Canada began accepting more immigrants from countries of the Third World, especially from Commonwealth countries . The largest number came from South Asia, followed by the Caribbean, Latin America, and Africa. In addition, many new refugees were welcomed to Canada. Like their European predecessors, these immigrants were excited and optimistic about their opportunities to work for a new beginning. Unfortunately many Canadians resented these new "visible minorities," and old prejudices and discriminations were revived wherever the newcomers settled.

Web Connections

http://www.school.mcgrawhill.ca/resources

Go to the above Web site to find out more about the immigration boom to Canada after World War II. Go to *History Resources*, then to *Canada: A Nation Unfolding, Ontario Edition*, to find out where to go next.

Life in the 1950s

Suburbia

After the war Canadians wanted their own homes, where they could raise their new families. In the early 1900s the development of streetcar systems had led to the appearance of suburbs around a few larger cities. The cancellations of these systems, the Great Depression, and World War II curtailed any further suburban expansion until the baby boom created an overwhelming demand for new homes. To meet the demand, more than 1.1 million new housing units were built, and as a result the 1950s became the first

An unmistakable sign of the prosperity of the 1950s was the growth in subdivisions. Don Mills, Ontario, was Canada's first planned subdivision. Why did families love them and critics hate them?

decade of "urban sprawl." Many of the new houses were built in subdivisions that were springing up almost overnight on the outskirts of Canadian cities. Farms and pastures disappeared beneath dozens of new "planned communities" that were designed to provide affordable single-family houses for the stampede of first-time homebuyers.

Suburban streets were lined with lookalike split-level bungalows, complete with a picture window, carport or garage, and newly seeded front lawn. At least fifty thousand Canadians a year took out mortgages for their first homes. Although many

critics wrote about the negative side of suburban life — its blandness, conformity, and materialism — for many Canadians in the 1950s, a home in the suburbs was a dream come true.

The Automobile

Life in the new suburbs was made possible by the automobile and paved roads. In 1949, Canada had only sixteen thousand kilometres of paved roads. But car owners were demanding more roads, like the impressive new four-lane Queen Elizabeth Way that linked Toronto and Hamilton. The federal government had also started work on the Trans-Canada Highway in 1949. The new cross-Canada link symbolized the importance of the automobile. During the 1950s and 1960s Ontario began and expanded its east–west Highway 401 and, north of Toronto, Highway 400 systems. By 1970 these superhighways had replaced the railways as the principal routes for passenger travel throughout Canada.

But the car was more than a means of transportation. Canadians fell in love with the "chrome boats" being churned out by Chrysler, Ford, and General Motors in Windsor, Oakville, and Oshawa. The bigger, faster, and fancier these cars were, the better. Many teenagers spent months customizing old cars to turn them into fantastic "road machines."

Canada's love affair with the automobile reached a new high during the 1950s. Each year new models of cars, many with whitewall tires and plenty of chrome, were put on the market.

Rock concerts become a major social event for teenagers in the 1950s.

Teenagers

The baby boom created an age-group bulge in the population, and during the 1950s thousands of Canadian baby boomers became teenagers. Although adolescence is not new, the unprecedented number of teenagers created new issues and demands for Canadians. In the 1950s many communities began to develop arenas, recreational facilities, and organizations for the growing numbers of young people. Even though many teenagers joined sports teams and marching bands, they also enjoyed hanging out at shopping centres, drive-in movie theatres, and restaurants. Wherever they gathered, they listened to tunes of the latest rock 'n' roll sensations, including Elvis Presley, Chuck Berry, and Ottawa's Paul Anka. Rock 'n' roll became a subculture for the youth of North America. In the 1950s adolescence was recognized for the first time as a distinct stage in a person's growth. As marketers discovered the enormous disposable income of teenagers, they began to cater to them in music, movies, books, and automobile marketing.

Educational Reform

As the baby boomers started to enter the school system, changes occurred to the traditional classroom. In the 1950s many Canadian students were still expected to obey strict dress codes, enter and leave schools by separate boys' and girls' doors, and sit in neat rows in the classroom and face the teacher. As attitudes began to change in the 1960s, however, students and many teachers began to demand a different kind of education. Many wanted school to be a relaxed place, where students could learn at their own pace and in their own way, without the threat of failure. In some schools, formal teaching methods, dress and discipline codes, compulsory courses, strict timetables, and, sometimes, grades, tests, and examinations became a thing of the past.

Life in the 1960s

The Counterculture

The period called "the Sixties" actually extended from the 1960s into the early 1970s. And, continuing from the 1950s, the **"youth generation"** — the two million baby boomers born between the late 1940s and mid-1960s — took centre stage in Canada. Many young Canadians led lives in ways that were little different from those of their parents, but some young people became known as **"hippies"** and "revolutionaries." They rejected whatever they saw as part of "the Establishment" — especially the police, the government, and big business. They wanted "liberation" — personal freedom and social change. The word **"counterculture"** came into being, representing the new cultural standards among youth that ran counter to (against) the values of their parents' generation. Tie-dyed T-shirts, old jeans, sandals or bare feet, and long, flowing hair became the unisex style of the 1960s.

Many young people gathered in Canada's hippie districts, such as Fourth Avenue in Vancouver and Yorkville in Toronto. They danced to the music of Janis Joplin, Jimi Hendrix, the Doors, the Rolling Stones, and the Beatles. They also listened to

Canadian youth

A REVOLUTION IN EDUCATION: THE HALL-DENNIS REPORT

The decade of the 1960s was characterized by a return to post-war prosperity and optimism. The children of the baby boom were entering school, and post-war technology would shortly alter the kinds of careers youth would enter upon graduation. To meet the new challenges in education, the Ontario government commissioned a report that would identify and suggest a framework to meet these challenges. Published in 1968, *For the Love of Learning* (often referred to as the Hall-Dennis Report after the co-chairs, Justice Emmet Hall and Lloyd Dennis) brought in a revolution in learning for Ontario school children. Following is a brief extract from the opening pages of *For the Love of Learning*. Has the spirit of this report survived in our education system of today?

THE TRUTH SHALL MAKE YOU FREE

The underlying aim of education is to further man's unending search for truth. Once he possesses the means to truth, all else is within his grasp. Wisdom and understanding, sensitivity, compassion, and responsibility, as well as intellectual honesty and personal integrity, will be his guides in adolescence and his companions in maturity.

This is the message that must find its way into the minds and hearts of all Ontario children. This is the key to open all doors. It is the instrument which will break the shackles of ignorance, of doubt, and of frustration; that will take all who respond to its call out of their poverty, their slums, and their despair; that will spur the talented to great heights of achievement and provide every child with the experience of success; that will give mobility to the crippled; that will illuminate the dark world of the blind and bring the deaf into communion with the hearing; that will carry solace to the disordered of mind, imagery to the slow of wit, and peace to the emotionally disturbed; that will make all men brothers, equal in dignity if not in ability; and that
will not tolerate disparity of race, colour, or creed.

We stand today in the dawn of our second century and assess the field of future education. Surrounded by the greatest array of learning paraphernalia we have ever seen, and immersed in new knowledge, we must not lose sight of the human needs that the new dawn brings. We are at once the heirs of the past and the stewards of the future, and while we take pride in our inheritance, we can ill afford to bury our talents in the soils of satisfaction. We have in our hands means of change for human betterment that few people of the world enjoy. We must find a way to their application that will germinate the seeds of a more fruitful way of life, not only for the people of Ontario but for all Canadians; and hopefully the harvest will make its contribution to all mankind.

A principle which has dominated our thinking is that money and effort spent on education is money and effort well spent; an investment in human resources that will pay handsome dividends not only in terms of economics but in human happiness and well-being. It is an investment in which all young people of Ontario must have the opportunity to participate.

The child's right to the best education available is now universally recognized. It is an entrenched right which no one would dare to challenge. It is now beyond question that all our young people must be better educated and more fully and competently trained if Canada and Ontario are to survive in this highly competitive age of electronics, specialization, and automation.

ACTIVITY

As a student in the Ontario school system, do you feel you are receiving the quality of education you deserve and will need to be successful after graduation? Write a personal critique of the education system you have experienced so far. Compare your assessment of today's schools with your parents' recollections of their school experiences. What progress, if any, has been made?

EXCERPT FROM *LIVING AND LEARNING* (TORONTO: PUBLICATIONS OFFICE, ONTARIO DEPARTMENT OF EDUCATION, 1968), PAGE 9.

A "flower child" photographed in a Canadian city in the late 1960s. Long hair and "granny glasses" marked the typical hippie of the Sixties.

Canadian musicians who became famous, such as Joni Mitchell, the Band, Neil Young, Buffy Sainte-Marie, the Guess Who, and Gordon Lightfoot. Drugs such as marijuana, LSD, amphetamines, and barbiturates were part of the hippie culture. Young people talked and wrote more openly about sex, and censorship was challenged.

There was, however, a negative side to "liberation." Drugs and alcohol ruined many young lives. The "free speech" that was championed by youth lifted old-fashioned censorship, but it also paved the way for more disturbing forms of expression, such as brutal pornography. The negative aspects of the counterculture offended so many older Canadians that the term **"generation gap"** came into the language. Few people were completely untouched by what one writer called the "youthquake." The Sixties made deep and lasting changes in Canadian values.

Social and Political Protest

The 1960s were also a decade of social and political protest, and hundreds of young Canadians waved

banners and wore buttons with the new slogans of the Sixties, such as "Flower Power," "Power to the People," and "Peace." Both the rise of the nuclear arms race and the war in Vietnam became a major focus for their protests. In Southeast Asia, troops from communist North Vietnam were helping South Vietnamese guerrilla fighters to overthrow the American-backed government of South Vietnam. Fearful of the spread of communism, the United States sent over troops to help the government of South Vietnam. The war escalated sharply in the mid-1960s; by 1967 there were almost half a million American troops in Vietnam. It was a brutal and destructive war, and for the first time television brought the full horrors of war home to the watching world. Political protests by young Canadians against the Vietnam War and nuclear war became a part of everyday life in the 1960s and the early 1970s.

Countering the Influence of American Culture

During the 1950s and 1960s the rising tide of American culture turned into a flood, and American radio and television programs, movies, books, and magazines poured into Canada. At the same time, the Canadian government reduced

Aboriginal artist Buffy Saint-Marie gained international attention in the 1960s. Can you name other popular Aboriginal musicians?

During the 1960s, protests such as this one in Edmonton, 1967, were highly critical of the United States' participation in the Vietnam War. Are protests an effective way to achieve goals? What issues would prompt you to join a protest?

funding for the Canadian Broadcasting Corporation (CBC) and the National Film Board (NFB). The combination of these two factors led many Canadians to become worried about the increasing influence of the United States on Canadian culture.

In terms of popularity, American motion pictures far outpaced Canadian films. In music, although some Canadian artists and bands such as Paul Anka, the Diamonds, Joni Mitchell, Neil Young, and Buffy Sainte-Marie found success with American audiences, Canadian demands for popular music by American artists such as Elvis Presley, Jerry Lee Lewis, Bob Dylan, Janis Joplin, and Jimi Hendrix almost silenced Canadian artists. American television broadcasts swept across Canada in the 1950s, and only *Hockey Night in Canada* could compete with American programs like *I Love Lucy* and the *Ed Sullivan Show*.

The Massey Commission

As early as 1949 the Canadian government established the Massey Commission (headed by Vincent Massey) to investigate the Canadian development of the arts. The Massey Commission called for increased government support for the CBC and the NFB, as well as the establishment of a federal agency to provide funds and support for the arts in Canada. Six years later the government created the Canada Council to do such a job. Canadian arts organizations such as the Stratford Shakespearean Festival, Niagara-on-the-Lake's Shaw Festival, and many symphony orchestras began to flourish with

Many Canadian actors began their careers on stage at the Stratford Festival Theatre performing in Shakespearean plays. Both Lorne Greene, left, and William Shatner, right, went on to become major Hollywood stars.Why do Canadian actors often move to the United States?

PHOTO ESSAY

IMAGES OF A NEW CANADA

Canada's love affair with the automobile.

Barbara Ann Scott wins Canada its first Olympic gold medal for figure skating.

Newfoundland joins Confederation.

Television in the home.

Air transportation.

National Film Board.

Suburbia.

the help of the Canada Council.

Both French Canadian and English Canadian literature gained prominence after World War II. In Québec, novelists such as Gabrielle Roy and Roger Lemelin wrote about urban Québec, and Yves Thériault gained international recognition for his novel about the Inuit, *Agaguk*. English Canadian authors gained recognition for such works as Mordecai Richler's *The Apprenticeship of Duddy Kratvitz*, W.O. Mitchell's *Who Has Seen the Wind*, and Margaret Laurence's *The Stone Angel*. Other authors, such as Robertson Davies, Morley Callaghan, Hugh MacLennan, Margaret Atwood, and Alice Munro, also gained national and international recognition.

Exclusion and Discontent in the Land of Plenty

Unfortunately, sizable minorities of Canadians were excluded from the post-war prosperity. Visible minorities such as Black and Asian Canadians and Aboriginal peoples had been isolated in separate cultural enclaves that offered little or no opportunity to experience the economic prosperity that some considered to be the "Good Life." Others, such as women and people with disabilities — more "invisible," but just as isolated — felt alienated from traditional policies, programs, leaders, and lifestyles. By the late 1950s and 1960s, these minorities recognized the need for change, equity, and social justice and were prepared to work for their causes.

Black Canadians

Long-established Black Canadian communities were often isolated from the prosperity and opportunities that graced the Canadian majority. Among visible minorities, Black Canadians often faced the most openly racist discrimination. Despite being a sizable force, Black Canadians faced discrimination on all angles, including employment, schooling, and even where they could live. This desperate state of affairs gained international attention in 1961, when the city of Halifax decided to demolish Africville.

Since the 1850s the community of Africville had been home to Halifax's Black population and had existed as part of the capital city. But Africville was ignored by city councillors; it was not even given the basic necessities, such as public water, sewage, or garbage collection services. In 1962, anxious to create new industrial space for big industries, Halifax City Council removed the four hundred citizens of Africville and bulldozed the community, without even consulting its residents. Although some received compensation for their property, the disrespect shown toward the residents of Africville was horrifying. Black Canadians did, however, form organizations to confront the discrimination. The NSAACP (Nova Scotia Association for the Advancement of Coloured People) was one of the earliest Black Canadian organizations, and in 1968 the BUF (Black United Front) was formed to push for change.

Discrimination was also evident in many Ontario communities. In 1949 the Ontario Court of Appeal upheld a clause in property deeds that prevented Jews and Black people from buying property in Beach O'Pines, near Sarnia. In Dresden, Ontario, the city maintained segregated commercial services, and it was not until 1967 that Essex County abolished Ontario's last racially segregated school system. Although many of the segregated services ended in the late 1960s, the racist attitudes toward Black Canadians often remained.

Asian Canadians

Although most Chinese Canadians had long been excluded from mainstream jobs, many prospered in the service industries that were open to them. In the larger cities of Vancouver, Toronto, and Montréal, segregated communities, called "Chinatowns" had been established for a long time. In the 1960s many of these were broken up by urban renewal projects and punitive by-laws. Nearly half of Toronto's Chinatown was bulldozed in the 1960s to make way for the new city hall.

South Asians from Pakistan and India also endured discrimination from mainstream Canadians. Although many had received advanced schooling and training in their native lands, Canadian officials would not recognize their achievements and relegated them to unskilled labour and ghetto-like living

Canadian voices

AFRICVILLE

Africville was a small Black Canadian community in the north end of Halifax. It was first settled in the early 1800s, and later Black American refugees of the War of 1812 settled in Africville. Although a part of Halifax, Africville was ignored by the city. The community was excluded from receiving most city services such as paved roads or running water, and the city dump was relocated near the community.

In 1962 the city took away the land in Africville to expand the urban development of Halifax. The community was not consulted, and the average settlement given to Africville residents for their property was five hundred dollars each. The town was bulldozed in 1962.

Today Africville is commemorated by a park built by the City of Halifax on the former community site. Some residents still protest the forced destruction of their community and have asked to be resettled there. The following poem was written by David Woods, in memory of the fallen community.

Africville

The tracks of the CP Railway lines
Glow white and hard against the blackness that is now
Africville.
It survives here – Mythic symbols of this new land,
The iron will of modern men and modern ambitions
Leaving other dreamed worlds behind.

Two hundred years of history – Suddenly bulldozed,
Thrown into garbage heaps.
A death – Putrid and anonymous,
You think of slaves in their slow torture,
Their heavy chains,
Their lockjaw and pneumonia.
Their unmarked graves.

Was it the bulldozing of Seaview Baptist Church?
Or Deacon Jones' collapse?
Or Pa Carvery's lonely defiance?

Or was it Mom Sooks?
Laura Howe? Stan Dixon?
They were nervous, beautiful faces lined up at City Hall –
Signing away more than they could understand.

The confused mess we agreed to
Because we did not know –
Could not know –
The pure conviction of our enemies,
The mixed hues of our betrayers,
The evil that had laid tracks all across this land.

I move through the heaps of garbage –
In search of the place where my house once stood,
It lies here – a pile of old photographs, charred wood.
In the distance a city goes on –
The busy traffic presses across the new bridge,
A church bell gathers a smiling congregation.
A careful subdivision goes up
But Africville –
Its church bulldozed, its children scattered
Its soul betrayed
Sits in the stink welter of these broken images,
Crying in the silent eyes and hidden voices –
Buried under centuries of garbage and pain.

CONTRIBUTED BY DAVID WOODS. HE IS A WRITER AND ARTIST FROM DARTMOUTH, NOVA SCOTIA.

PLEASE BOIL THIS WATER BEFORE DRINKING AND COOKING

Basic services such as clean water were not provided to the residents of Africville.

Humour in History

Johnny Wayne (1918–1990) and Frank Shuster (born 1916) formed the popular Canadian comedy team Wayne and Shuster. They made their first appearance on Canadian television in 1952. In 1958 they made their first of a record sixty-seven appearances on the highly popular U.S. program, *The Ed Sullivan Show*. Despite being one of Canada's first successful television comedy exports, Wayne and Shuster chose to live and work in Canada. The following television script is an excerpt from one of their famous skits.

"Shakespearean Baseball Game"
by Wayne and Shuster

(Orchestra: *fanfare*.)

(Zoom in Super: THE ROYAL WAYNE AND SHUSTER FESTIVAL PLAYERS)

ANNOUNCER (*voice-over*): The Royal Wayne and Shuster Players present...

(Zoom in : A COMEDY OF HITS, RUNS, AND ERRORS)...

ANNOUNCER: A comedy of hits, runs, and errors.

(*Dissolve to dugout set empty. Two umpires enter from either side. Orchestra: fanfare.*)

First: Hail, Bernardo...

Second: I give you greetings, Antonio. Thou hast the line-ups?

First: Aye ... The batting orders duly signed by managers both.

Second: 'Tis well ... what o'clock is it?

First: 'Tis at the stroke of two.

(*Music: short modal fanfare.*)

Second: Hark ... The players come. To our appointed places. Shall we go? You at first and I behind the plate.

First: 'Tis done. (*He turns and second and takes his arm.*)

Second: This game depends on how you make your call. Farewell until you hear me cry Play Ball.

(*They exit. Music: big fanfare to herald entrance of baseball team. They enter Stratford style, with flourish.*)

Frank: My excellent good friends, may fortune smile upon our enterprises today. As manager of this most valiant club,
I swear by all that's holy in our game,
I shall not rest until the pennant over Stratford flies....
[Later, Frank and Johnny debate whether or not to televise the game.]

Johnny: TV or not TV, that is not the question....

---

conditions. South Asian women often had to accept the lowest-paying and most difficult jobs in factories in the large cities of Montréal, Toronto, and Vancouver. South Asians also made up the majority of the farm labour force in British Columbia's Fraser Delta, where, unprotected, they harvested crops that had been sprayed with pesticides and lived in converted barns that had no running water or electricity.

Aboriginal Peoples

Perhaps Canada's Aboriginal peoples were the most excluded from the post-war prosperity. Many lived either on small, scattered reserves or in large cities

such as Vancouver, Edmonton, Winnipeg, and Toronto, where unskilled work was easier to find. Grim statistics on lifespan, income, unemployment, family breakdown, law-breaking, and suicide showed how difficult and painful life was for many Aboriginal people. Their lives were still regulated by the Department of Indian Affairs, which controlled Aboriginals' access to financing, education, and social services such as hospitals and community programs.

Conditions were similarly difficult for the Inuit. The construction of the DEW (Distant Early Warning) Line, north of the Arctic Circle, resulted in huge changes in the lives of the Inuit. On the positive side, government money poured into the North, bringing dozens of airports and regular air service, as well as better harbours and water transportation. The federal government began to take full responsibility for the education, health, and welfare of the Inuit. Better transportation services meant that doctors and nurses could reach isolated areas, and health care slowly began to improve for the Inuit. Education also improved as the government spent $20 million on new classrooms for northern communities. The number of Inuit children with access to schooling shot up from 18 percent in 1957 to 66 percent by 1963. But this increase in government intervention in the lives of the Inuit had a price: traditional Inuit patterns of life were severely disrupted.

The Inuit people had lived a nomadic lifestyle, moving from place to place while hunting, fishing, and trapping. But the federal government encouraged them to move into permanent settlements, where it could more conveniently provide government services. Many Inuit gave up their traditional practices for a completely foreign way of life in the new, permanent communities. Inuit people had little say in the planning and building that was going on in their homeland. Even the benefits disrupted their ways of life. Education was provided in the English language, so the textbooks were written for city school children in the south. The teachers knew little or nothing about the language and culture of their Inuit students. The result was a generation of partly educated young people who no longer easily fit into either Inuit or White culture.

Some Inuit groups were relocated to remote Arctic areas by the federal government despite their protests. For example, Inuit from Port Harrison in northern Québec were relocated to Grise Fiord on Ellesmere Island, where, they were told, game was much more plentiful. But government documents later revealed that the Arctic had become vital for strategic defence purposes in the 1950s. The Canadian government wanted to have Canadian Inuit living on Ellesmere Island as proof that the land belonged to Canada.

By 1970 relations between White people and Inuit were strained in many Arctic settlements. Some Inuit had found jobs in the settlements as unskilled labourers, but they usually earned less money than White workers doing the same job.

ANTHONY JENKINS/The Globe and MAIL

This cartoon depicts the Inuit claim that they were used as human flagpoles by the federal government in order to assert Canadian sovereignty in the Arctic. Is this an accurate assessment of the situation?

Others did not find work at all. The Inuit lived in much poorer housing than their White neighbours from the south and were often treated as social inferiors by the White community. Like the Aboriginal people in southern Canada, in the next decades the Inuit made efforts to preserve their culture from disintegration.

Women: "The Second Wave"

Since women had played such an important part in the labour force during World War II many believed that their participation in the workforce would continue. When the soldiers came home, however, attitudes toward women at work began to change. As marriage rates soared and the baby boom began, traditional views about the woman's place in the home began to be reinforced. Emphasis was placed on the importance of the woman as wife and mother. The government introduced new policies to encourage women to stay at home, including closing down child day-care centres that had been opened during the war and renewing rules that did not allow women to hold positions in the civil service. Employment opportunities that did exist for women still remained in the traditional occupations of teaching, office work, and nursing. By 1960, however, many women began to question their roles in society. Many began to wonder why their needs were second to that of the family, and why so many opportunities were open only to men.

A second wave of feminism began to rise during the 1960s. The first wave of feminism, during the late nineteenth and early twentieth centuries, had focused on the right to vote. The second wave, which became known as the women's liberation movement, wanted overall social and economic reforms such as equal-pay legislation, paid maternity leave, and the removal of occupational barriers in the workplace. Women also began to have more control over whether and when they would have children. The availability of better contraceptive methods, including the birth-control pill, which became available in Canada in 1966, gave women more control over their bodies. Within the movement, a more forceful, outspoken wing arose. Known as radical feminists, they believed that society had been entirely arranged for the benefit of men and that the only way to gain power was to take it from men.

The second wave, especially the radical feminists, met opposition from both men and women. Many people feared that altering the position of women in society would threaten the structure of the traditional family. Also, because the movement was led largely by White middle-class women, those who were not part of the mainstream often felt that they were not being represented.

Royal Commission on the Status of Women

Despite the opposition, the second wave of the women's movement began to change Canadians' view of women in society. In 1966, thirty women's groups formed the Committee on Equality for Women. They believed that a royal commission on the status of women was needed to address the concerns of Canadian women.

In 1967 the Royal Commission on the Status of Women, headed by Toronto journalist and broadcaster Florence Bird, began touring the country. Its job was to examine the status of women and to recommend "what steps might be taken by the federal government to ensure equal opportunities with men in all aspects of Canadian society." The commission discovered that

- in 1970 only 3.9 percent of managers were women
- although eight of ten provinces had equal-pay laws, women were still paid less than men for doing the same work
- two thirds of all welfare recipients were women

When the commission's report came out in 1970, it included 167 recommendations to ensure equality of opportunity between men and women. Some of the key recommendations were that

- "gender" and "marital status" be prohibited as grounds for discrimination by employers
- training programs offered by the federal government be made more open to women
- the federal government name more women judges to all courts within its jurisdiction
- more qualified women from each province be appointed to the Senate as seats became vacant, until a more equitable balance between men and women was achieved
- employed women be granted eighteen weeks of unemployment benefits for maternity leave.

As a result, the commission helped to establish an agenda of reform for women's-rights groups in the 1970s.

In the 1960s women began to question their role in society and fight for equal rights.

French Canadians

Québec had long been committed to "**la survivance**," the survival of its own language and traditions. Its survival strategy was to retain the French language, the Roman Catholic faith, the traditional values of Québec rural life, and obedience to authority, especially the authority of church leaders. But, during the 1950s, the support for "la survivance" began to crumble as it became obvious that such a strategy was not benefiting French Canadians economically. The economic conditions of French Canadians were not as bad as those of Black Canadians or the Aboriginal peoples; a strong economy meant that many of them were enjoying a new prosperity. A closer look, however, reveals that there were significant obstacles for Quebeckers.

By 1961 almost half a million young Quebeckers had moved from rural areas to urban centres in search of work. They found that many of Québec's industries were run by English-speaking businessmen, and employment favoured those who could speak English. In many areas, such as Montréal, English Canadians earned up to 50 percent more than their fellow French Canadians. Outside Québec the barriers for French Canadians were even higher because of their relatively small number. Speaking French began to be seen as a hindrance to getting employment. Another problem was that for French Canadians outside Québec, there was little government support for schooling in languages other than English. By the 1960s Quebeckers realized that the rural French Canada of farm and parish church was gone forever. They wanted to bring the economy, the government, and education into the twentieth century. Their wish to move forward would result in the Quiet Revolution.

A Time of Change

Through the 1950s and 1960s, Canadians experienced radical changes in their lifestyles. More than ever before, Canadians owned homes and cars, youth was king, and television brought the world into the Canadian home. But not everyone received an equal piece of the pie of prosperity, and Canadian culture began to be alarmingly influenced by its southern neighbour. By the end of the 1960s, many of those who faced discrimination began to form organizations and protest for change, and Canada began to set up organizations to protect its culture. Each of these groups would have some success, but their fights were far from over.

chapter review

CHAPTER SUMMARY

In this chapter we have seen

- how a second wave of immigration and the baby boom made a lasting impact on Canadian society

- how the Canadian government set up institutions to deal with and counter the growing influence of American culture

- how visible and invisible minorities such as Black Canadians, Asian Canadians, Aboriginal peoples, and French Canadians, as well as women, faced discrimination and fought for change.

UNDERSTANDING HISTORICAL FACTS

1. Identify these people, places, and events, and explain their historical significance

Africville	Counterculture
Baby Boom	Massey Commission
Hall-Dennis Report	Suburbia
Royal Commission on the Status of Women	Inuit on Ellesmere Island

2. What did the Canadian government do to counter the influences of American culture and promote a common Canadian identity?

3. How did the views of many women about themselves change between the 1950s and 1960s? What steps did they take to change the public's view of women?

4. What kinds of demands did the baby boom make on Canadian industry and society in the 1950s and 1960s? Create a web using the baby boom as your starting point. Consider such aspects as housing, schools, service sectors, and culture.

5. What was the "youth generation," and how did it make such an impact on Canadian society?

EXPRESSING YOUR OPINION

1. Aboriginal leader Harold Cardinal stated that the federal government seemed to think that the "only good Indian is a non-Indian." What did he mean by this, and what evidence in this chapter supports his feelings? Assume you are an Inuit teenager during the 1950s. Write a poem, or a letter to Parliament, that expresses your concerns over the federal government's treatment of the Inuit.

2. During the 1950s and 1960s the "youth generation" became a dominant part of society. Are teenagers a distinct cultural group, or are they just a creation of advertisers and social critics? Explain your answer.

3. The second wave of the women's movement was met with opposition from many people, even some women. Why would some women be against it?

4. What did the concepts of "la survivance" and "maîtres chez nous" mean? Were they in opposition to each other, or did they work together to strengthen Québec's goal to be a distinct society?

WORKING WITH THE EVIDENCE

1. The peace symbol was a common sight in the 1960s. What are the origins of this symbol?

Canada's Coming of Age

INQUIRING INTO THE PAST

- Why would the federal government's efforts to create national programs such as medicare result in conflict with provincial governments?
- What actions at various levels did governments take to protect Canadians from a return to the hardships experienced in the Great Depression?
- Why did Newfoundland enter Confederation with Canada in 1949?
- How did television influence the nature of politics in Canada?

KEY TERMS

Canadian Bill of Rights

Canada Assistance Plan

Medicare

Trudeaumania

Social Safety Net

Louis St. Laurent, John Diefenbaker, Lester Pearson, and Pierre Trudeau dominated Canadian politics

TIMELINE

1948
Louis St. Laurent succeeds Mackenzie King as prime minister

▶

1957
John Diefenbaker and the Progressive Conservatives come to power

▶

1960
Québec Liberals defeat the Union Nationale

▶

1968
Trudeau becomes Prime Minister

▶

irecting Canada in the post-war years required vision and commitment from governments at all levels. Although conflicts over jurisdiction were constant, political leaders from all parties and all levels of government seemed to share in the dream of a renewed Canada, in which all Canadians shared in the national prosperity.

From the late 1940s to the mid 1950s, Canada appeared to be a strongly united nation under a common vision and the direction of a wise and kindly federal government. In 1957, however, the Canadian economy fell into a deep recession that lasted into the early 1960s. One result was that, throughout the 1960s, relations between the federal and provincial governments became more difficult. By 1968 Canada's national unity seemed to be shattering, and many Canadians began to fear that the nation would disintegrate.

The Post-war Era: King and St. Laurent

During the twenty-two years from the re-election of Mackenzie King in 1935 to the 1957 federal election, Canada's government was dominated by the Liberal Party. In 1948, the ailing Mackenzie King personally picked his minister of external affairs, Louis St. Laurent, to succeed him as Prime Minister. St. Laurent's dignity, personal decency, and courage had made him popular with Canadians. He was nicknamed "Uncle Louis" in the press because he was "like everyone's favourite uncle." Most Canadians expected him to stay in office for a long time.

Newfoundland Enters Confederation

A 1945 school-room map showed Canada and Newfoundland as separate political bodies within the British Commonwealth. In 1897 Newfoundland had chosen to keep its ties to Britain and rejected joining Confederation with Canada. By 1945, however, economic conditions in Newfoundland had become desperate. The

In front of a photo of their Liberal ancestor, Sir Wilfrid Laurier, MacKenzie King (right) and future leader Louis St. Laurent are seen at the Liberal leadership convention.

Newfoundland fish and lumber industries had not recovered from the Depression, and post-war Britain could not afford financial subsidies to its colony. The United States, however, was interested in the strategic military and economic potential of Newfoundland and Labrador.

Joey Smallwood, a Newfoundland broadcaster and politician, almost single-handedly created a wave of popular support for his plan to bring Newfoundland into Canada's Confederation. As Newfoundland's economy continued to spiral downward, Smallwood argued that joining Canada would bring in badly needed money for schools, hospitals, and roads. But many Newfoundlanders did not want to join Confederation. A referendum was held, and the "confederates" narrowly won (78 323 votes for to 71 334 against). Newfoundland became Canada's tenth province on March 31, 1949.

Joey Smallwood led the campaign for Newfoundland to enter Confederation. Here, he signs the documents that join the British colony with Canada. Why do you think many Newfoundlanders did not want to join Confederation?

The Liberal Reign Comes to an End

When St. Laurent's government announced that the contract to build a pipeline to carry oil and natural gas from Alberta to Eastern Canada — and a loan of $80 million — had been awarded to a company that was 83 percent American-owned, many Canadians were outraged. Why, they asked, should the contract and government money go to an American company? Why not a Canadian one? There was a storm of controversy over the trans-Canada pipeline bill in Parliament. The Liberal government managed to push the bill through by cutting off debate and forcing a vote. But its reputation was shattered by what many Canadians saw as arrogant tactics in Parliament. At the same time, a new voice and style emerged on the federal scene from Western Canada, and it began to attract the attention of Canadians.

The Diefenbaker Era

The new Progressive Conservative leader, John Diefenbaker, made rousing speeches against the "American pipeline buccaneers." He promised to free Canada from American influence. The small-town Saskatchewan lawyer was a passionate and gifted speaker and seemed to bring a new spark and energy to dreary Canadian politics. By contrast, St. Laurent appeared tired and worn down by years in public life. The 1957 election was the first time in Canada that a national campaign was televised, and many Canadians noticed striking differences between the two leaders in their TV appearances. In the end, the Conservatives narrowly won a minority government. A year later, Lester Pearson became the new Liberal leader, taking over from Louis St. Laurent. Another election was called in 1958, and once again Diefenbaker proved to be a spell-binding campaigner with passionate promises of a "new vision" for Canada. His Progressive Conservatives won a landslide victory over the more quietly spoken Pearson and the Liberals.

The Progressive Conservatives believed that Ottawa should ensure the well-being, prosperity, and rights of all Canadians. "All Canadians should share in the nation's general economic advance," Diefenbaker told Canadian voters. "There should be no permanent 'haves or have nots' in Canada." Diefenbaker's government raised old-age pensions and set up a winter-works program to create construction jobs in order to encourage a year-round construction industry. It also brought in government crop subsidies, set up a government farm-loan program, and negotiated a huge sale of wheat to China in 1960, which sold off a 19.9-million-tonne backlog of wheat. The Diefenbaker government also helped to pay for provincial job-creation projects in the Atlantic provinces, such as small fish-packing, textile, and hardboard plants in Nova Scotia. Unfortunately, the economic recession that swept through North America at the end of the 1950s was greater than the government's policies. Unemployment and hard times continued across Canada into the 1960s.

Diefenbaker's Northern Vision

In the 1958 federal-election campaign, Diefenbaker outlined his "vision" for Canada's North. He wanted to unlock the rich resources of the Canadian Shield and the Arctic. "I see a new Canada," Diefenbaker declared, "a Canada of the North." Included in his plans were massive oil and

the arts

GUY LOMBARDO AND HIS ROYAL CANADIANS

As the world watches the New Year's celebrations from Times Square in New York each year, at the stroke of midnight we hear the strains of the Robert Burns ballad, "Auld Lang Syne," played by a big band called The Royal Canadians. This tradition, which has become such an important part of the annual New Year's celebration, is rooted in the lives of three brothers, born in London, Ontario.

The Lombardo brothers, Guy, Carmen, and Lebert, were born in the early years of the twentieth century. All of this Italian Canadian family's seven children studied music. When the boys were teenagers, their father formed the Lombardo Brothers Concert Company, which played at socials and parties around London.

In 1923 the Lombardo brothers and their band left Ontario to "conquer the world" in the United States. In order to sound more distinctive, in 1924 the band changed its name to Guy Lombardo and His Royal Canadians. They went on to great success in Chicago, finally settling in New York in 1929. There they were the house band at the Roosevelt Grill, a popular Manhattan restaurant. Throughout World War II, in what has come to be known as the "The Big Band Era," Guy Lombardo and His Royal Canadians (often referred to as "the sweetest orchestra this side of heaven") played in a number of popular movies and became well known for their recordings.

Even after World War II the band's success continued. In 1964 the Royal Canadians staged the biggest New Year's Eve party ever held in North America. They hired New York's Grand Central Station for the night of December 31 and held a charity benefit for two thousand guests. Naturally, at midnight they played their signature tune, "Auld Lang Syne."

Guy Lombardo continued to work until his death in 1977. The band had been a New York Institution for over four decades. The Royal Canadians continue to tour and perform under the leadership of Lebert Lombardo's son, Bill.

ACTIVITY

Why did the Lombardo brothers take their band to the United States in 1923? Would they do things differently today? Make a list of other artists or groups who have left Canada to work in the United States.

In 1957 a powerful and emotional speaker, John Diefenbaker, moved Canadians to follow his vision of a united Canada. How has television changed the style of political speech-making?

mineral explorations, huge programs of building "roads to resources," new townsites for the North, and increased government services for the Yukon and Northwest Territories. From 1958 to 1963, more was achieved in the Canadian North than ever before in the nation's history. But the achievements fell far short of Diefenbaker's campaign promises. During the recession, markets for resources grew smaller, while the costs of development were higher than expected. Despite all the building and subsidies, only one new gold mine and one new tungsten mine came into operation, while two uranium mines shut down. Unfortunately, Diefenbaker's "Northern Vision" did not fulfil Canada's great economic "destiny" and, unintentionally, it created serious problems of adjustment for Canada's Aboriginal peoples.

Building a United Canada

As a son of German immigrants, John Diefenbaker firmly believed in a national unity based on equality for all Canadians, regardless of race or creed. He called it a policy of "unhyphenated Canadianism." Once in office, Diefenbaker appointed an Aboriginal person to the Senate and named a member of Parliament of Ukrainian descent as his minister of labour. He also brought the first woman into the cabinet: Ellen Fairclough was appointed secretary of state. Diefenbaker's proudest achievement, however, was passing the **Canadian Bill of Rights** in 1960. The full title of the bill was "An Act for the Recognition and Protection of Human Rights and Fundamental Freedoms." It was intended to provide certain legal protections, such as the freedoms of speech, religion, the press, and the right to equal protection before the law. However, like his other programs, this new bill was limited. It was a federal statute — not a constitutional guarantee of human rights — and it could be changed or abandoned at will by Parliament. It did not apply to areas under provincial authority, and it could be ignored by the provinces. Nonetheless, the Canadian Bill of Rights did prompt some provinces to pass similar human-rights acts in the 1960s and clearly showed that Canada was committed to certain fundamental human rights. It set a precedent for the later constitutional guarantees of human rights in the Canadian Charter of Rights and Freedoms of 1982.

The Pearson Years

By 1963 Diefenbaker's charm had worn thin, and his government and Canada were suffering from the deep recession that limited the achievement of his "new vision." The quietly assertive but not-very-imposing Lester Pearson and his Liberals defeated the Progressive Conservatives but only managed to win a minority government. Despite this, Pearson governed Canada for four productive years. The recession that had plagued Canada

John Diefenbaker considered the passing of the Canadian Bill of Rights in 1960 one of his proudest moments in office. Why is a bill of rights an important piece of legislation?

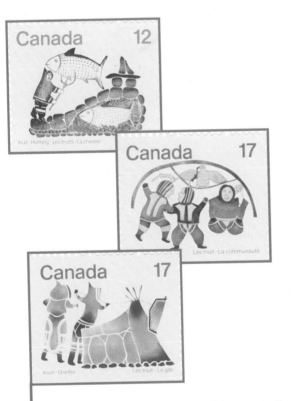

This series of stamps, issued by Canada Post, celebrate aspects of traditions and community life among the Inuit. Was Diefenbaker's "Northern Vision" a positive influence on the people and environment of Canada's North?

between 1957 and the early 1960s led to a doubling of the unemployment rate, causing the unemployment insurance fund to nearly disappear and creating a high demand for social assistance across Canada. The drastic situation compelled the Pearson government to institute several new welfare and employment programs.

Building the "Social Safety Net"

By 1966 a **Canada Pension Plan** for seniors and low-cost loan programs for post-secondary students had been set up. As well, the **Canada Assistance Plan** provided equal access to welfare for all Canadians. Under the Canada Assistance Plan, the federal government agreed to share with the provinces the costs of a whole range of programs, including child care, health care for the needy, employment projects, and aid for disadvantaged groups such as widows and people with disabilities.

Medicare was perhaps the most important new federal social program proposed by the Pearson government. It was patterned on a bold new plan pioneered by the New Democratic Party government in Saskatchewan in 1962. The federal government offered to share with each province the costs of a medical plan that would pay for all necessary medical services for the people of that province. Finally introduced in 1968, medicare freed Canadians from the nightmare of costly and unexpected medical bills.

The federal government also took action to ensure that the housing needs of lower-income Canadians were being addressed. The federal and provincial governments built more public-housing facilities throughout the 1960s. Spurred on by the memories of the Great Depression and a return to prosperity by the mid-1960s, the Pearson Liberals took government involvement in Canadian society to new heights while weaving a **social safety net** that would become the envy of the world.

Keeping Canada United

During his years as Prime Minister, Lester Pearson also tried to find solutions to ease French–English tensions. One of these solutions was a new national flag. At the time Canada's flag, called the Red Ensign, included Britain's Union Jack. Many French Canadians objected to that flag because the Red Ensign was a British symbol and ignored the fact that the French were also one of Canada's founding peoples. But changing the Red Ensign also alienated many English Canadians, who felt that this would be a rejection of the English heritage in Canada. Pearson pushed for a new, distinctive flag that represented all Canadians and hoped that it would help unite the country. After viewing over two thousand choices, the Red Ensign was replaced by the red-and-white maple leaf flag in February 1965.

Pearson's government also set up the Royal Commission on Bilingualism and Biculturalism in 1963 to seek advice about working out "an equal partnership between the two founding races." The commission told Canadians that French must be on equal footing with English in Canada and that the federal government must operate in both languages. It also warned Canadians that Quebeckers needed to be assured that all of Canada was their homeland. If they failed to do so, the country would separate along French–English lines.

Out With the Old, In With the New

American politics were beginning to have an influence on Canada during the 1960s. Tired of old-style political leaders, many Canadians admired the charisma, wit, and determination of the handsome young American president, John F. Kennedy. He seemed to embody the optimism and mood of the 1960s. Kennedy was certainly suited to the new style of politics: his good looks, attractive young family, and powerful presence on camera ensured his success in the new age of politics. As Canada's centennial approached and optimism was again peaking, many Canadians were ready for a new, modern style in their Prime Minister. In 1967, many of them believed that they had found it in the new federal Liberal leader, Pierre Trudeau.

Web Connections

http://www.school.mcgrawhill.ca/resources

Go to the above Web site to find out more about Lester Pearson. Go to *History Resources*, then to *Canada: A Nation Unfolding, Ontario Edition,* to find out where to go next.

The Beginning of Trudeaumania

Modern political charisma hit Canada with the rise of Pierre Trudeau — a new kind of Canadian politician. Throughout his eighteen years in office, Trudeau would remain somewhat of an enigma. He was loved by many, despised by others, but few

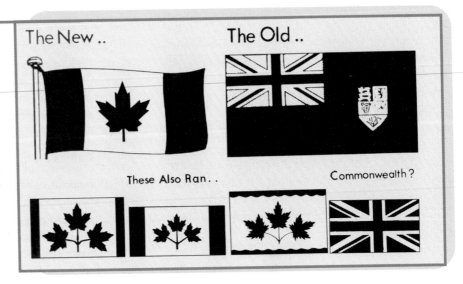

The New ..

The Old ..

These Also Ran ..

Commonwealth ?

In an attempt to better reflect Canada's growing multicultural heritage, the Red Ensign (top right) was replaced by the present Canadian flag. Four of the more than two thousand designs that were submitted are also seen here. Did Canada make the right choice? Do you think this flag represents all Canadians?

could claim indifference. Although he was nearly fifty years old when he first took office, he did not look or act like a middle-aged politician. The bachelor millionaire dressed casually, drove fast sports cars, and charmed women. He clowned for the press and tossed off quotable comments that made instant headlines. He slid down banisters and pirouetted for the cameras. Trudeau was a newcomer to federal politics in 1968. He won a seat as a member of Parliament in 1965 and became the justice minister in Pearson's cabinet in 1967.

As justice minister, Trudeau gained a reputation as a social reformer. With his remark that the "state has no place in the bedrooms of the nation," Trudeau eased federal laws about divorce, homosexuality, and abortion. His reforms found favour with many young people who were protesting against old social conventions. As a French Canadian strongly opposed to Québec separatism, Trudeau also won the admiration of many English Canadians. During the Liberal leadership convention, he gradually won over those who had wanted a more traditional leadership style and succeeded Pearson as Prime Minister.

In the federal-election campaign of 1968, Pierre Trudeau became an instant celebrity across Canada. His enormous popular appeal reminded people of "Beatlemania," and it was quickly called **Trudeaumania**. The Conservatives, on the other hand, had endured a publicly nasty leadership race. Ultimately, they selected Robert Stanfield, a very capable and successful Nova Scotia businessman and former premier. Unfortunately, he was of the "old school," and the media made vicious fun of his appearance and slow, measured words. The 1968 election was no contest; Trudeau seemed to be the right politician for the 1960s, and the Liberals won the election with ease.

National Dreams, Regional Realities

From 1945 to 1968, King, St. Laurent, Diefenbaker, Pearson, and Trudeau led the federal government to play an increasingly important role in the everyday lives of Canadians. By attempting to share the riches of the wealthier provinces with the less prosperous provinces and by establishing a safety net of social programs, Ottawa hoped that regional and individual inequalities would be diminished. These leaders hoped that Canadian citizens and provinces would be proud members of Canada and that a strong feeling of unity would result. But a closer look shows that despite these national dreams, some provinces resented and resisted federal involvement in provincial matters. In both the West and Québec, provincial governments fought against being controlled by Ottawa.

From 1968 to his retirement in 1984, Pierre Trudeau dominated Canadian politics. Shown here playing baseball, Trudeau brought a flair to the Prime Minister's office, making him popular with many Canadians.

Balancing National Goals and Regional Interests

To provide a unified response to the crises of the Great Depression and World War II, the federal government began to assume planning and taxation powers that were provincial responsibilities, according to the British North America Act. In 1945 the Liberal government of Mackenzie King proposed to widen federal powers to direct the economy to benefit all the Canadian regions. These plans received heavy criticisms from many provincial leaders because they felt their powers to direct their own provinces were being stripped away. A compromise solution, called "tax rental," was adopted in 1947 that allowed both an increased federal tax base and an assertion of provincial rights. In 1957 this system was modified to introduce "equalization grants." These grants would share the prosperity of the wealthier provinces, such as Ontario, Alberta, and British Columbia, with the less prosperous regions, such as Saskatchewan and the Maritime provinces. Today's issues of national unity were founded partially in

the debates of how the post-war prosperity pie would be sliced — and by whom.

Growing Western Alienation

Since the time of John A. Macdonald's National Policy, the West has felt that the policies of the federal government have served the interests of Central Canada, often at the expense of the Western provinces. One of the results of a growing sense of Western alienation has been a periodic rejection of the main political parties and widespread support for regional protest parties. Several of the regional parties, such as the Social Credit Party, the Co-operative Commonwealth Federation (CCF), and, later, the Reform Party, eventually gained national prominence.

Although the traditional Liberal and Progressive Conservative parties controlled Manitoba's provincial government, they were minor players in the other three Western provinces. Saskatchewan was the home of both the provincial and national CCF party. Its constitution, the Regina Manifesto, written in 1933 in the depths of the Great Depression, emphasized the CCF's concern for social democracy and regional needs. Under the leadership of Tommy Douglas, the CCF (which became the New

Tommy Douglas led the CCF government in Saskatchewan from 1944 to 1961 and was then chosen as the first leader of the federal New Democratic Party. When Douglas was young he almost had to have his leg amputated because his family could not obtain proper medical care. How do you think this situation influenced the policies that he proposed?

the arts

ROCH CARRIER'S *THE HOCKEY SWEATER*

Roch Carrier is one of Québec's best-known writers. Many of his novels and short stories have been translated into English and have become widely known across Canada. "The Hockey Sweater" is a light-hearted story about a young French Canadian boy who faces a terrible dilemma when Eaton's mistakenly sends him a Toronto Maple Leafs sweater instead of a Montreal Canadiens sweater. As you read this story, consider how it reflects French–English relations and what aspects of French Canadian culture you can detect in it.

The winters of my childhood were long, long seasons. We lived in three places — the school, the church and the skating-rink — but our real life was on the skating-rink. Real battles were won on the skating-rink. Real strength appeared on the skating-rink. The real leaders showed themselves on the skating-rink. School was a sort of punishment. Parents always want to punish children and school is their most natural way of punishing us. However, school was also a quiet place where we could prepare for the next hockey game, lay out our next strategies. As for church, we found there the tranquillity of God: there we forgot school and dreamed about the next hockey game. Through our daydreams it might happen that we would recite a prayer: we would ask God to help us play as well as Maurice Richard.

We all wore the same uniform as he, the red, white and blue uniform of the Montreal Canadiens, the best hockey team in the world; we all combed our hair in the same style as Maurice Richard, and to keep it in place we used a sort of glue — a great deal of glue. We laced our skates like Maurice Richard, we taped our sticks like Maurice Richard. We cut all his pictures out of the papers. Truly, we knew everything about him.

On the ice, when the referee blew his whistle the two teams would rush at the puck; we were five Maurice Richards taking it away from five other Maurice Richards; we were ten players, all of us wearing with the same blazing enthusiasm the uniform of the Montreal Canadiens. On our backs, we all wore the famous number 9.

One day, my Montreal Canadiens sweater had become too small; then it got torn and had holes in it. My mother said: "If you wear that old sweater people are going to think we're poor!" Then she did what she did whenever we needed new clothes. She started to leaf through the catalogue the Eaton company sent us in the mail every year. My mother was proud. She didn't want to buy our clothes at the general store; the only things that were good enough for us were the latest styles from Eaton's catalogue. My mother didn't like the order forms included with the catalogue; they were written in English and she didn't understand a word of it. To order my hockey sweater, she did as she usually did; she took out her writing paper and wrote in her gentle schoolteacher's hand: "Cher Monsieur Eaton, Would you be kind enough to send me a Canadiens' sweater for my son who is ten years old and a little too tall for his age and Docteur Robitaille thinks he's a little too thin? I'm sending you three dollars and please send me what's left if there's anything left. I hope your wrapping will be better than last time."

Monsieur Eaton was quick to answer my mother's letter. Two weeks later we received the sweater. That day I had one of the greatest disappointments of my life! I would even say that on that day I experienced a very great sorrow. Instead of the red, white and blue Montreal Canadiens sweater, Monsieur Eaton had sent us a blue and white sweater with a maple leaf on the front — the sweater of the Toronto Maple Leafs. I'd always worn the red, white and blue Montreal Canadiens sweater; all my friends wore the red, white and blue sweater; never had anyone in my village ever worn the Toronto sweater, never had we even seen a Toronto Maple Leafs sweater. Besides, the Toronto team was regularly trounced by the triumphant Canadiens. With tears in my eyes, I found the strength to say:

"I'll never wear that uniform."

"My boy, first you're going to try it on! If you make up your mind about things before you try, my boy, you won't go very far in this life."

My mother had pulled the blue and white Toronto Maple Leafs sweater over my shoulders and already my arms were inside the sleeves. She pulled the sweater down and carefully smoothed the creases in the abominable maple leaf on which, right in the middle of my chest, were written the words "Toronto Maple Leafs." I wept.

"I'll never wear it."

"Why not? This sweater fits you... like a glove."

"Maurice Richard would never put it on his back."

"You aren't Maurice Richard. Anyway, it isn't what's on your back that counts, it's what you've got inside your head."

"You'll never put it in my head to wear a Toronto Maple Leafs sweater."

My mother sighed in despair and explained to me:

"If you don't keep this sweater which fits you perfectly I'll have to write to Monsieur Eaton and explain that you don't want to wear the Toronto sweater. Monsieur Eaton's an Anglais; he'll be insulted because he likes the Maple Leafs. And if he's insulted do you think he'll be in a hurry to answer us? Spring will be here and you won't have played a single game, just because you didn't want to wear that perfectly nice blue sweater."

So I was obliged to wear the Maple Leafs sweater. When I arrived on the rink, all the Maurice Richards in red, white and blue came up, one by one, to take a look. When the referee blew his whistle I went to take my usual position. The captain came and warned me I'd be better to stay on the forward line. A few minutes later the second line was called; I jumped onto the ice. The Maple Leafs sweater weighed on my shoulders like a mountain. That captain came and told me to wait; he'd need me later, on defense. By the third period I still hadn't played; one of the defensemen was hit in the nose with a stick and it was bleeding. I jumped on the ice: my moment had come! The referee blew his whistle; he gave me a penalty. He claimed I'd jumped on the ice when there were already five players. That was too much! It was unfair! It was persecution! It was because of my blue sweater! I struck my stick against the ice so hard it broke. Relieved, I bent down to pick up the debris. As I straightened up I saw the young vicar, on skates, before me.

"My child," he said, "just because you're wearing a new Toronto Maple Leafs sweater unlike the others, it doesn't mean you're going to make the laws around here. A proper young man doesn't lose his temper. Now take off your skates and go to the church and ask God to forgive you."

Wearing my Maple Leafs sweater I went to the church, where I prayed to God; I asked him to send, as quickly as possible, moths that would eat up my Toronto Maple Leafs sweater.

SOURCE: ROCH CARRIER, *THE HOCKEY SWEATER AND OTHER STORIES* (TORONTO: HOUSE OF ANANSI PRESS, 1979), PP. 77-81.

Democratic Party in 1961) dominated Saskatchewan's politics throughout the 1940s, 1950s, and 1960s and created Canada's first public-health-care system in 1962.

Alberta was another province controlled by a non-traditional political party. With its roots also in the Depression, the Social Credit government, led in the 1950s and 1960s by Ernest Manning, followed a very conservative approach to social programs. The Social Credit Party also had a large popular following in British Columbia. Dominated by the eccentric and outgoing W.A.C. Bennett, Social Credit controlled B.C. politics. From 1945 to 1970 Western Canada's politics were controlled by parties that both wanted money from Ottawa and objected to controls from a federal government located in Central Canada.

"The Great Darkness": The Duplessis Years in Québec

Determined to protect the distinctiveness of French Canadian culture, including religion and language, Québec also resisted the growing intrusion of the federal government into areas of provincial juris-

Maurice Duplessis' reign in Québec became known as the "la Grande Noirceur" – the Great Darkness. How would you have protected Québec's "la survivance"?

diction. Maurice Duplessis, leader of the Union Nationale and premier of Québec for almost all the years between 1936 and 1959, was dedicated to preserving the importance of the province's Roman Catholic faith and French language, often by shutting out the outside world. Duplessis believed that Québec had to avoid English influence on its society by refusing federal programs that affected Québec life. For example, he refused sizable federal grants for health care and education because he saw them as threats to the traditional Québec society.

But Duplessis saw no problem in encouraging mostly English-speaking businesspeople, especially Americans, to establish industries in Québec. He offered businesses special privileges and tax breaks. American and English Canadian money built the hydro-electric power dams and factories that appeared alongside the French Canadian churches on the St. Lawrence River. Young French Canadians left family farms to work in the new peacetime industries. By 1961, half a million people had left the Québec countryside farms to work in the new industries. They were mostly poorly paid, and they had to work hard to make ends meet.

Québec workers soon became angry at their working conditions, and the 1940s and 1950s were marked by bitter labour disputes. The Union Nationale, however, discouraged union activity and sided with the mostly English-speaking owners against the mostly French Canadian workers when strikes occurred. In the 1949 strike at Asbestos, Québec, Duplessis ordered the provincial police to break up the picket lines and arrest the strike leaders.

For Quebeckers committed to social change, Duplessis's policies began to be seen as old-fashioned and restrictive. They were tired of the old ways and the old authorities. The Roman Catholic church was slowly losing its authority in public matters, and Québec was becoming a secular (non-religious) society. The province was also becoming more urban and industrialized, and Quebeckers realized that the rural French Canada of farm and parish church was gone. They wanted to bring the economy, the government, and education into the twentieth century. Young intellectuals, including the young lawyer and journalist Pierre Trudeau, began to publish anti–Union Nationale publications, such as the magazine *Cité Libre*. They called for a more modern Québec and began to call Duplessis's regime "la Grande Noirceur" — the Great Darkness.

The Quiet Revolution

In 1960 the Québec Liberals won a narrow victory over the Union Nationale, which was in disarray after Duplessis's death and scandals of widespread corruption had tainted the party. Immediately, the new Liberal government, under the leadership of Premier Jean Lesage, began a rapid but non-violent process of reform and modernization known as "The Quiet Revolution" (La Révolution Tranquille). "Il faut que ça change!" ("Things must change!"), shouted Lesage. Many who had seen themselves as Canadien(ne)s now called themselves Québécois. While they wanted to remain within Canada, they also demanded a new, equal partnership as one of Canada's two founding nations.

The Lesage government made sweeping changes. It created a professional civil service to counter the Union Nationale's habit of giving government jobs and money to its political supporters. It modernized an outdated educational system that was run by the Roman Catholic church. Previously, most French Canadians did not continue their education after elementary school, and little preparation for careers in science or business was provided in the high schools. But by the end of the decade, the now-government-controlled school system had grown by more than 500 000 students and over forty thousand students were attending two new colleges.

Lesage took French Canadian nationalism a step further by pressing the federal government for "special status" for Québec. He felt that Québec needed more provincial powers than other provinces to protect its French language and culture. He demanded that federal money be handed over to the Lesage government and proposed that it, in turn, would use the money for its own range of health, education, and social-security programs. The federal government, in response, promised greater recognition of French Canadians and allowed Québec to run its own pension, student-loan, and medical-insurance plans. A few radicals and urban intellectuals wanted to bring even greater

Jean Lesage, premier of Quebec from 1960 to 1966, was famous for his slogan "Maîtres chez nous." What did this phrase mean to French Canadians? Does it still apply today?

change for the province, including separation from Confederation. In the mid to late 1960s, a very extreme group, the Front de Libération du Québec (FLQ), carried out terrorist bombings and violent raids to bring attention to their separatist claims.

Nationalism and the Quiet Revolution

There was a strong element of French Canadian nationalism in the Quiet Revolution. Its slogan became "Maîtres chez nous" — "Masters in our own house." While the nationalists did not seek independence for Québec, they did want more French Canadian control inside their own province. English-speakers were a relatively small percentage of the population, but they controlled the commercial life in Québec. Of the fifty largest corporations in Québec, only three were French Canadian. The government wanted to reverse this trend, and the Québec people overwhelmingly agreed with its aims. In 1962 eleven private power companies were taken over, and Hydro-Québec was born. The working language of Hydro-Québec was French, and the construction of new facilities was planned and carried out by French Canadian managers and engineers. The success of Hydro-Québec gave French Canadians a new confidence.

"Vive le Québec libre!"

In the late 1960s one event signalled future troubles between French and English Canada. In 1967 the President of France, Charles de Gaulle, had been invited to take part of the world exposition that was taking place in Montreal. On July 24, 1967, de Gaulle stepped onto the balcony of Montreal's City Hall to say a few words to a jubilant Expo crowd gathered in the square. At the end of this speech, de Gaulle raised his hands into a "V" for "Victory." Then he spoke the words that jolted a nation: "Vive le Québec libre!" — "Long live free Québec!"

The four words had a threatening meaning for many Canadians. "Vive le Québec libre!" had been scrawled on a wall near the Canadian National Railways building in Montréal, where a fire bomb had gone off in March 1963. It was the first attack by the FLQ. Under the slogan "Independence or death," the FLQ bombed several areas where English

Canadians lived or owned businesses. While most French Canadians disliked their violent tactics, a growing number felt that Québec had been badly treated by English Canada since Confederation. During Expo '67, some even put tags on their licence plates that read "100 ans d'injustice" ("100 years of injustice"). The words "Vive le Québec libre!" signalled the troubling times ahead.

Toward a New Canada

The years between 1945 and 1968 provided Canadians with a fabulously prosperous standard of living. At the same time, most Canadians accepted that all citizens, regardless of heritage and ancestry, deserved the protection of a national social services "safety net." Yet, by the end of the 1960s, many Canadians could no longer accept the political and economic structures that had provided their prosperity and security. Throughout these years, long-established antagonisms — federal versus provincial, region versus region, English–French — continued to grow bigger and to frustrate those Canadians who were hoping for unity at last.

When French President Charles de Gaulle spoke in Montréal in 1967, his words, "Vive le Québec libre," excited many separatists. Should a foreign leader offer words of encouragement to separatists in Canada?

chapter review

CHAPTER SUMMARY

In this chapter we have seen

- that Canadians' sense of pride swelled in the decades following World War II

- how the federal government became a major provider of social services in all regions of Canada

- that despite common visions for Canada, regional differences also continued to develop

UNDERSTANDING HISTORICAL FACTS

1. Identify these people, places, and events, and explain their historical significance.

   John Diefenbaker   Canadian Bill of Rights

   Maurice Duplessis   Lester Pearson

   Pierre Trudeau   Quiet Revolution

2. What was the Quiet Revolution? Why did it occur?

3. Create a chart comparing the benefits and the costs of the massive building programs undertaken by Canadian governments.

4. Create a web showing the variety of ways in which the federal government became involved in the lives of Canadians between 1945 and 1970.

5. On a blank map of Canada, list the regional concerns and issues raised in this chapter about each of the pertinent areas of Canada. Around Ottawa, list the national initiatives of the federal government. Finally, select a region other than Ontario, and explain why you feel this region was being ignored or well served by the federal government.

EXPRESSING YOUR OPINION

1. Should all federal parties alternate their leaders between English and French Canadians, as the Liberal party does? Explain your answer.

2. Did Canada's social safety net, which was developed in the 1960s, create more problems than it could answer? Do you agree that a portion of the wealth generated by middle- and upper-income earners should be directed through taxation to maintaining social programs that benefit low-income earners? Why or why not?

3. "Spindoctors" work with politicians to improve their image or to portray issues in a positive manner. In other words, they put a positive spin on things. The role of spindoctors has become especially important in an age of television. Play spindoctor to one of the politicians discussed in this chapter. If a photograph of the politician is not included in this chapter, try to find a picture in the library. Your challenge is to "make over" the politician so that he or she will appeal to voters of today. This will require working with that person's physical appearance (hair, glasses, clothes) and policies.

WORKING WITH THE EVIDENCE

1. In 1959 a new product, which could be described as "the motorcycle of the North," was introduced to the world. This single-track-driven machine would transform life for the Inuit and Arctic communities. What was the name given to this product? Who invented it?

During the 1950s and 1960s, Canada's north became a busy area for resource development. How would this affect Canada's northern regions?

INQUIRING INTO THE PAST

- **How would post-war prosperity affect Canadians?**
- **Did the economic boom of the 1950s and 1960s occur in all regions of Canada? What regions were left out? Why?**
- **How did mass-marketing change the nature of selling goods in Canada? What new means did advertisers use to promote their products?**
- **What were the advantages and disadvantages of growing American participation in the Canadian economy?**

KEY TERMS

Branch Plants

Consumerism

Mass Marketing

TIMELINE

OCTOBER 1958 ▶	1959 ▶	1960 ▶	1965 ▶
Springhill mine disaster in Nova Scotia kills 74 miners	St. Lawrence Seaway is completed	Three out of four Canadian households own a television set	Auto Pact signed between Canada and the United States

"My, how you've grown!" Anyone looking at Canada in the 1950s would have been astonished to see how fast the country was growing up. Canada's economy was expanding by leaps and bounds. Ordinary Canadians were earning more money, and the middle class was swelling. More money meant more buying power, and Canadians went on a national shopping spree. They began buying more consumer goods than their parents had ever dreamed of owning. This consumer spending helped fuel the expansion of Canadian industries. New resources were discovered and mined in Canada's northern regions, bringing prosperity to many provinces. New trade agreements and joint projects with the United States tied the Canadian economy closer to the United States' economy. One writer called it the decade when Canadians "learned to lived with bigness."

The Consumer Revolution

North American industries had switched from wartime to peacetime production with ease. The techniques of mass production suddenly made consumer goods available in North America at affordable prices. Refrigerators, radios, and even automobiles were now within the reach of average income earners. Wartime savings and fatter peacetime paycheques meant that people had more money to spend.

The average take-home pay of Canadians grew rapidly after the war. Canadians enjoyed the second-highest living standard in the world. For example, only three other cities in the world bought more Cadillacs per capita than did Toronto. Canadian shoppers earned their 1950s label as "consumers" by rushing to buy the new mass-produced goods that tumbled off the production lines. **Consumerism** had arrived.

New Products and Mass Marketing

Wartime technology also helped to set off an explosive increase in peacetime technological inventions. These included the long-playing record, the digital computer, nylon, cellophane, jet airplanes, antihis-

tamines, aerosol spray cans, and electric typewriters. All kinds of specialized products, new gadgets, and games also found their way onto store shelves. Canadian consumers were tempted by a dazzling array of products, including ballpoint pens, frozen TV dinners, "home permanents" for hair, hula hoops, electric can openers, and Scrabble games. But the most important product was television. Millions of the little boxes found their way into Canadian living rooms in the 1950s, and family life was revolutionized. Family conversations, eating habits, humour, political attitudes, personal styles, and social values were all influenced by television.

The 1950s also saw the introduction of **mass marketing**. Manufacturers began to spend huge sums of money on advertising campaigns to convince Canadian consumers to pick their products over rival brands, which were often called "Brand X" in television commercials. Canadians were blitzed

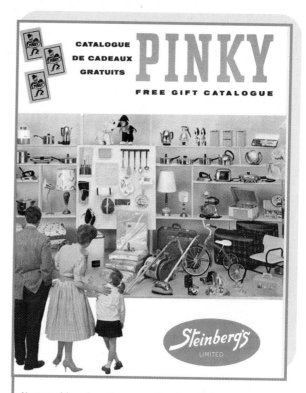

CATALOGUE DE CADEAUX GRATUITS PINKY FREE GIFT CATALOGUE

Steinberg's LIMITED

New wealth and a wide range of products led to new methods of marketing. Stamps, received when purchasing goods, could be cashed in for a number of gifts, such as those shown on the cover of the Pinky Gift Catalogue. Can you think of instances in which this kind of marketing is still used?

technology

TELEVISION AND CANADIAN SOCIETY

Few technological innovations have affected society as television has. Many people claimed that the introduction of television sets into Canadian homes weakened community organizations, reduced significantly the amount of conversation between family members, and distracted children from reading and their homework. Yet, despite the dire warnings of some, the "idiot box," as the television was called by its critics, did not ruin Canadian society. In fact, in many ways the television age contributed to a cultural boom in North America and placed information at everyone's fingertips.

Although television was first pioneered in Britain in 1926, the Depression and World War II delayed its development. By the early 1950s, television was beginning to make its way into North America. In 1952 the Canadian Broadcasting Corporation (CBC), which had been established during the 1930s to ensure quality Canadian radio programming, began broadcasting television programs. Its goal was to provide Canadian programs that would serve the interests of national unity. A year earlier, the Massey Commission had argued in favour of government controlling television rather than following the American approach, which placed broadcasting in the hands of business.

Despite the best efforts of the CBC and the Massey Commission, Canadians fell in love with American television programs. A

The introduction of television drew thousands away from the movie theatres and into their living rooms. In an attempt to win back the crowds, 3-D movies were introduced. Using a pair of cardboard and tinted celluloid glasses, viewers were given an experience billed as "more sensational than real life."

generation of Canadians and Americans grew up sharing a fascination with programs such as *I Love Lucy*, *Howdy Doody*, and *Your Hit Parade*. Television introduced many new American stars and heroes — including Davy Crockett, Ed Sullivan, and Elvis Presley — to Canadians. Although Canadian broadcasters did not have the money to compete with American programs, several successful Canadian programs hit the airwaves in the 1950s, including *Front Page Challenge*, *Tugboat Annie*, and *Hockey Night in Canada*.

Many Canadians had grave reservations about what the coming of the television age would mean to Canadian society. They feared that American-dominated television would undermine the Canadian identity by blurring the distinctions between Canadians and Americans. There was also a fear that Canada's youth would cease to excel in school and would spend too much time in front of the television, becoming passive receivers of information.

Today the number of channels available to many Canadians is virtually limitless. To what degree have the fears of television's early critics been realized? How do you balance your television viewing with other activities in your life? What, if anything, should be done to ensure that quality Canadian programs continue to be available to Canadians?

with media advertisements for brand-name products ranging from Kleenex facial tissues to Kellogg's corn flakes. Vance Packard, author of the 1957 bestseller *The Hidden Persuaders*, argued that advertisers were unfairly manipulating consumers by using new psychological techniques to trigger consumers' unconscious fears and wishes to persuade them to buy advertised products. But mass advertising continued to grow in the 1950s, and so did consumer sales.

An Era of Growth?

After World War II many of Canada's provinces experienced a boom in prosperity. While consumer demands for new products and gadgets helped fuel the economic growth, much of the growth was powered by the booming sales of natural resources that were being discovered in Canada's northern areas. Because of the rush of exploration and mining that followed these discoveries, the Canadian North was sometimes called the "last great frontier." But in a land as large as Canada, not all areas shared equally in the booming times.

The Atlantic Provinces

Although the war had brought some economic opportunities to the Atlantic economies, the post-war years were not as prosperous there as in the rest of Canada. The coal and steel industries, which had been part of the backbone of the Maritime economy, collapsed due to falling demand and cheaper sources of raw materials in Central Canada and the United States. This collapse pushed thousands of workers either to find new jobs or leave the Atlantic provinces altogether. During the 1950s more than eighty thousand people left the region to find work elsewhere. In 1956 and 1958 Nova Scotia's faltering mining industry received a further blow when two explosions in the coal mines in Springhill killed more than one hundred miners. For many people, these two disasters symbolized the desperate and worsening conditions for Atlantic Canada amidst the post-war boom. Many of the family incomes in the Maritimes were nearly one third less than family incomes in other provinces.

A massive explosion in the Springhill mine in Nova Scotia killed seventy-four miners in 1958.

In an attempt to help the floundering economy, the federal government introduced several plans during the 1960s. In 1962 the Atlantic Development Board was set up to found new projects and to improve the area by building new roads and railway lines. The Nova Scotia fishing industry received grants to offset declining world prices and demands for its fish. In Cape Breton, coal mining and steel production were heavily subsidized by federal grants. Many new industries, including a luxury-automobile factory in New Brunswick, an oil refinery in Newfoundland, and a heavy-water plant in Nova Scotia, were set up by the federal government. But few of these businesses took root, and most were bankrupt within a few years.

Québec

Québec's economy faired much better than that of the Maritime provinces. After World War II, Maurice Duplessis's government aggressively sought investment in Québec's industries from businesses in the United States and Ontario, and "outside" money poured into the province. Québec's economy expanded in all areas, especially in the development of its natural resources. The province became a main supplier of raw materials to the United States, selling such resources as iron ore, nickel, copper, lead, aluminum, and asbestos.

Agricultural employment, however, continued to decline in Québec. Thousands of farmers headed for the cities to seek the better wages and benefits that industrial and service-sector jobs could offer. In 1935 about 25 percent of Quebeckers lived on farms, but by 1961 this had dwindled to 11 percent. As the number of farmers decreased, the remaining farms increased in size. This trend ended any lingering myths of Québec being a rural, agricultural province.

Ontario

Ontario was a big winner in Canada's post-war prosperity. The influx of people from other provinces and from other countries into Ontario created a great demand for items such as food, housing, cars, and roads, which in turn created many job opportunities. In mineral-rich Ontario, an explosion of mining ventures saw discoveries of zinc, nickel, copper, and other valuable minerals. The wartime development of atomic energy had sparked a new peacetime demand for the uranium needed to produce atomic energy. After uranium was discovered at Elliot Lake, Ontario, in 1954, eleven mines went into production, and the Consolidated Denison mine became the world's biggest uranium mine. In Sudbury the mining company Inco made the Ontario city a major world producer of nickel. Other mining centres, such as Kirkland Lake and Timmins, continued to expand their output of raw materials. As a result, by 1960 Ontario was producing almost 60 percent of Canada's metal output. The demand for lumber, pulp, and paper also helped expand northern Ontario's forest industry.

In southern Ontario, farmers generally prospered as the demand increased for their fruit, vegetable, and dairy products. Further developments in hydro-electric generating plants and nuclear-power plants completed the process of electrifying all of Ontario by the mid 1950s. In the booming "Golden Horseshoe" from St. Catharines to Oshawa, thousands of Ontario's family farms were sold and transformed into subdivisions, schools, and shopping centres.

The completion of the St. Lawrence Seaway in 1959 opened the formerly isolated Great Lakes cities to ocean-going ships. Port Arthur and Fort William (now amalgamated into Thunder Bay) continued to grow as the Great Lakes' eastern terminus for the shipment of grain, minerals, and forest products. Sarnia expanded its role as a leading petroleum-processing centre when the trans-Canada pipeline was completed in 1959. The steel industries in Hamilton, using newly discovered iron ores, expanded to meet the orders placed by construction and manufacturing industries. Toronto continued to increase its role as the centre for many manufacturing industries as well as business and commercial head offices.

Ontario's tourist and resort centres also enjoyed the post-war prosperity. Resort communities such as Grand Bend, Wasaga Beach, the Muskokas, Bala, Picton, and Killaloe became summer destinations for vacationers. Private and provincial parks such as Algonquin Park drew increasing numbers of campers, who happily endured black flies and mosquitoes to enjoy the beauty of the province's lakes and forests. More and more Crown lands were sold in Ontario's near north to meet the demand for cottage properties. Winter sports expanded with the development of ski resorts at Collingwood and with the growth of interest in snowmobiling and nordic skiing.

The Prairies

Natural resources also brought some wealth to the Prairie provinces. One late afternoon in the winter of 1947, a jet of oil, gas, and mud spewed fifteen metres into the Alberta sky. Oil — "black gold" — had been discovered at Leduc, Alberta, near Edmonton. Imperial Oil's fabulous strike at Leduc set off an oil and natural gas boom in Alberta, and the exploration and production of oil provided many jobs. The main market that Alberta oil needed was Central Canada. But Central Canada had easy access to cheap American oil and gas, and there was no easy way to get Alberta oil to this large market. Recognizing this problem, the Canadian government built the trans-Canada pipeline, which was completed in 1959. This huge pipeline was built to carry Alberta gas and oil to Central Canadian markets. Although it helped the Western oil industry, the real boom for the oil-rich provinces would not come until the 1970s.

Other minerals, such as potash, gave Saskatchewan a limited economic boost. Next to Elliot Lake, Ontario, one of the biggest uranium

Oil, discovered in Alberta in 1947, brought billions of dollars into the Canadian economy and made Alberta one of Canada's wealthiest provinces, especially after the trans-Canada pipeline was built.

British Columbia

During the 1950s and 1960s British Columbia's economy attracted more and more people. Fort St. John, in the province's northeast, became another Canadian centre for a spree of oil and gas exploration. The discovery of aluminum near the central coast also provided a big boost to the West Coast economy. The number of workers taking advantage of the new aluminum-related jobs was so large that the Aluminium Company of Canada (Alcan) built the first suburban-style community in the wilderness up the coast from Vancouver, complete with schools, a shopping mall, and a sports centre. This new town of Kitimat housed workers for the aluminum company's huge hydro-electric and smelting projects. Other jobs also emerged as the provincial government sponsored huge hydro-electric power projects along the Columbia and Peace Rivers.

Other factors also helped the British Columbia economy to grow. The Okanagan Valley attracted attention as an excellent area for orchard crops such as, cherries, apples, plums, and peaches. Forestry products also became an important export to the rest of Canada and the world. Vancouver and Prince Rupert benefited from being at the western ends of the two transcontinental railways. The export business provided many jobs, as goods were passed from railway cars to ships in these two cities. Like Ontario, British Columbia also became a major tourist destination for Canadians and foreigners. The many mountain ranges gave rise to new ski resorts such as Whistler, in the Coast Mountains.

mines was discovered and led to the opening of the Eldorado mine and the founding of Uranium City.

Despite these discoveries, most prairie farmers and rural communities missed out on the post-war economic boom. The recession of 1960–1963 hit Western farmers particularly hard. A worldwide overproduction of wheat resulted in falling prices, as the supply of wheat outweighed the demand. Even though the government attempted to help by financing farms to produce other types of crops, more and more farmers left the Prairie provinces for more prosperous regions.

Vancouver's high-rise buildings were typical of Canada's urban boom in the 1960s. What would people living in such large cities expect from their governments?

Organized Labour Speaks Out

When work is scarce, employees often feel that they cannot risk losing their jobs by demanding higher wages or better working conditions. When times are good, however, and jobs are plentiful, workers are able to make more demands on their employers. As the post-war economic boom occurred, it also created a rise in the organized-labour movement. During the 1950s and 1960s strikes became regular occurrences in Canada's growing industries. Wages, health-care benefits, and working conditions became major issues in contract disputes. As the movement spread, most Canadian unions joined with the Canadian Labour Congress, which had been formed in 1955 to co-ordinate labour action. As union membership grew, members increasingly looked for a stronger political voice. As a result, in 1961 the Canadian Labour Congress joined with the Co-operative Commonwealth Federation (CCF) to create the New Democratic Party (NDP).

Canadian–American Economic Relations

Britain had always been an important trading partner for Canada. But after World War II its economy had faltered, and trade relations between Canada and Britain dropped off. Meanwhile the American economy was booming. Canada was right next door, and many Canadian industries found it easy to sell their products on the American market. Canadian consumers and industries were also eager to buy American goods. The two countries became each other's most important trading partners.

The St. Lawrence Seaway

The construction of the St. Lawrence Seaway symbolized the expanding economic relations between Canada and the United States. The seaway was a massive construction project that would enable large, ocean-going freighters to sail past the dangerous rapids of the St. Lawrence River and into the Great Lakes. The two nations had been discussing

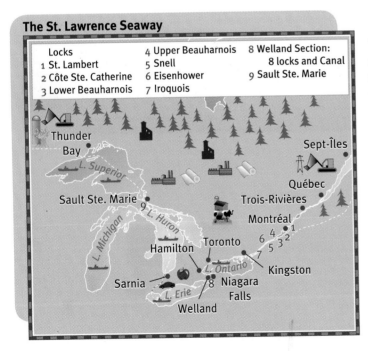

The St. Lawrence Seaway

Locks	4 Upper Beauharnois	8 Welland Section:
1 St. Lambert	5 Snell	8 locks and Canal
2 Côte Ste. Catherine	6 Eisenhower	9 Sault Ste. Marie
3 Lower Beauharnois	7 Iroquois	

The St. Lawrence Seaway allows ships to travel 3700 kilometres into the industrial heartland of North America. Entire towns were moved, and roads and railways were rerouted to allow the seaway to be built. How would the seaway help Canadian industries to prosper?

the building of a seaway for decades, but without any result. In 1949, however, the Canadian government decided to build the seaway, with or without American help. In 1954 the United States agreed to take part in the project. Each country agreed to pay for the portions of the seaway inside its own territory.

The St. Lawrence Seaway was planned, designed, and largely built by Canadians. The size of the project was staggering. Huge rapids were dynamited, whole towns were flooded, and 6500 people were relocated in new homes elsewhere. Railways and highways were rerouted around the new flood zones. Seven new locks were built, five of them by Canada. The seaway was officially opened in a joint ceremony in June 1959, with Queen Elizabeth II representing Canada and President Dwight Eisenhower representing the United States. One Canadian observer commented that the new St. Lawrence Seaway "was like a huge economic zipper knitting these [two] countries together."

Web Connections

http://www.school.mcgrawhill.ca/resources

Go to the above Web site to find out more about the St. Lawrence Seaway system. Go to *History Resources*, then to *Canada: A Nation Unfolding, Ontario Edition*, to find out where to go next.

The Auto Pact

Another agreement signed in 1965 — the Auto Pact — also tied the Canadian and American economies more closely together. By the mid-1960s, Canadians had become upset by a growing trade imbalance with the United States: Canada was spending more money to buy American goods than it was making by selling Canadian goods to the United States. The biggest trade deficit existed in automobiles and automobile parts. For example, in 1962, while Canada exported $62 mil-

lion worth of "automotives" to the United States, it imported $642 million worth from the United States. The Canadian government argued that Canadians needed a new deal in the cross-border automotive industry. Although Canadians bought more than 7 percent of the cars produced by America's "Big Three" automobile manufacturers — Ford, Chrysler, and General Motors — the Big Three plants in Oakville, Windsor, and Oshawa, Ontario, produced only 4 percent of these manufacturers' cars.

The Canadian government wanted the number of cars bought and produced in Canada to be equalized. Talks with the United States began in July 1964, and by January 1965 the Auto Pact was signed. The pact guaranteed free trade in automobiles between the two countries. The automobile manufacturers could locate their plants wherever they wanted and sell their cars duty-free in either country. The only major qualification was that the Big Three manufacturers had to build one car in Canada for every car they sold in Canada. The pact also put a tax on cars imported from Japan, Germany, and Britain. The Auto Pact brought real benefits to Canada, but it also tied the Canadian economy even more closely to the U.S. economy.

The auto industry is a vital part of the Canadian economy, especially in Ontario and Québec. Plants such as this one employ thousands of workers.

METHODS OF HISTORICAL INQUIRY

ORAL HISTORY: INVESTIGATING BY ASKING AND LISTENING

Have you ever heard your parents, grandparents, or a relative talk about what life was like when they were your age? Have you listened to someone tell you about their experiences in another country? Without even knowing it, you were listening to oral history.

Oral history is a way of recording or just listening to people's experiences through spoken words. In many cultures, such as the Aboriginal peoples, oral history is a way of passing down that ethnic group's history from generation to generation. Immigrants also rely on oral history to pass information and stories about their family and original homeland to their children and relatives as a way of keeping their history alive.

Oral history can be as simple as listening to stories and past experiences by someone you know. Or it can be a more formal process of obtaining information for research purposes. Oral history can be used as a technique by historians to create a primary source by interviewing and recording a person's memories about a particular time or event. Their memories can help students and historians to better understand what actually happened. Without oral history, the experiences of everyday people — their triumphs, joys, sorrows, and mistakes — would most likely be missed and remain silent.

Just like writing an essay or completing a project, conducting a good oral history interview takes time and preparation. The best results come from work that is well researched, planned, and prepared in advance.

PREPARING FOR THE INTERVIEW

Here are a few steps to follow as you get ready for your oral history project:

1) **Understanding the topic.** Once your topic has been decided, the first thing to do is to find out what traditional historians and sources have said about the topic. You can find this information in texts, resource books, and on the Internet. While it is not necessary to know all of the details, a solid knowledge of the topic is essential for effective questioning during the interview.

2) **Determining what you want to find out.** What information do you hope to learn by conducting an oral history interview? Determining what you want to find out will help you focus on what questions you want to ask the person you are interviewing.

3) **Writing good questions.** The success of your interview will largely depend on the type of questions you ask. Writing good questions involves some trial-and-error work. General questions — such as "what was it like in the 1960s?" — are usually not very effective and show a lack of preparation. A better question brings in some specifics to help to focus the answer — such as "what were some of the fascinating things happening in Halifax in the 1960s?" Try to avoid questions that can be answered with either one word or yes/no. For example, asking "Why did you participate in anti-nuclear protests?" will result in a much more detailed answer than if you asked, "Did you participate in anti-nuclear protests because you were angry with the government?"

4) **Choosing who you are going to interview.** Your topic of research will dictate whom you can interview. A contemporary topic allows you a much wider scope of people to choose to interview, whereas you may be very limited in choice if your topic is for example, related to World War II. Always start by asking your friends, family, relatives, and community members for ideas of who you might talk to. Chances are, there may be someone in close that you can interview!

5) **Making the appointment.** Once you have a lead on someone to talk to, phone the person to see if they would be interested in doing the interview. Introduce yourself, explain why you are calling, and tell them why you think they would be able to help you in your research. If they agree, make an

appointment to go see them at a time that is convenient for both of you. Whether it is a friend of the family or someone you have never met, remember to be professional in your attitude. You might want to offer them a copy of your questions in advance so that they can prepare. Depending on the subject, memories can be painful and complex, so it is important to be courteous and sensitive to your subjects at all times.

DOING THE INTERVIEW

You have done the research, written the questions, and made the appointment. Now it is time for the actual interview.

1) **Taking Notes.** There are essentially three different methods of recording the conversation during an interview:

a) **Pen and Paper:** Taking notes during an interview involves the least amount of advance preparation. However, it does not leave you free to concentrate on what the person is saying, as you will be busy trying to write everything down. When you are interviewing, make quick notes about what is said, but do not interrupt to get proper spelling or dates – that can come later.

b) **Tape recorder:** Using a tape recorder allows you more freedom to participate in the interview, knowing that your conversation is being recorded for your use later. Before you start, you must ask your subject if he or she would mind being recorded. Be sure to practise and test the sound quality before the real interview begins, and if possible, position the tape recorder so it is not directly in the subject's face so they do not feel uncomfortable.

c) **Video:** Like a tape recorder, a video taping of your interview allows you to make general notes and participate in the conversation. Also like a tape recorder, you must obtain permission from the subject to videotape the interview. Remember that your subject may feel uncomfortable in front of a video camera.

2) **Don't Panic!** Pauses in the conversation, while natural, can be awkward. But do not jump in with your next question right away. A gentle pause often signals to the subject that you are interested to hear

more, and may lead the subject to further expand his or her story. On the other hand, if the pause becomes too long, move on to your next question.

3) **Length of the Interview:** How long an interview session lasts depends on how well things are going. Be sure to give your subject time to talk, but do not stay too long. If at the end of your session you still have more questions or need clarification on some facts, ask your subject if you could meet for a second time, or do a follow-up phone call.

4) **Preparing the Transcripts:** When the interview sessions are over, you need to prepare a transcript or summary of what was said. It is polite and a good idea to have your subject read over your notes on your conversation before you put them in finished form. It is also nice to show your subjects how you are going to tell their experiences that they have shared with you.

You now have created a valuable, unique, oral history document that you can use as direct quotes, paraphrases, or in other ways for presentations, essays, or stories.

ANALYZING ORAL HISTORY SOURCES

As with any other type of historical source, oral histories should be carefully examined. As you conduct your own interview, or as you read another source of oral history, you must consider the following:

1) **What is the interviewer trying to find out?** Because the interview is often conducted with the intention of finding out specific information, the questions asked can sometimes be very narrow in focus, and can omit important information.

2) **What are the biases of the interviewee?** Just as an author may have certain biases that we must be aware of, we also need to be concerned with the biases of the subject. Are these biases preventing the subject from giving a truthful answer? Are facts being ignored or omitted because of these biases?

Be sure to keep your ears wide open. You will start to notice how much oral history you are hearing everyday!

American Investment in Canada

After World War II Canada found that it had many of the natural resources that the United States needed to keep its economy in high gear. The Americans needed oil, and Alberta's newly discovered Leduc oil field gave them what they needed. They bought aluminum from Kitimat, B.C., and uranium from northern Saskatchewan and Elliot Lake, Ontario. They also bought nickel, natural gas, and a host of new chemical products.

Resource development has always been risky. For instance, Imperial Oil spent $23 million and drilled 133 dry wells before it struck "black gold" at Leduc in 1947. Most often, it was American rather than Canadian investors who were willing to take risks. Because American companies invested money in Canadian resources, they also collected most of the profits. Still, the growth of American-backed industries helped Canada to prosper. New industries meant more jobs and a higher standard of living for many Canadians.

It is not surprising that many Canadians welcomed the flow of American money into Canada in the 1950s. But in 1957 the Gordon commission — the Royal Commission on Canada's Economic Prospects — published its findings on the foreign ownership of Canadian industries and resources. The commission's report denounced the huge scale of foreign — especially American — ownership of Canada's industries and resources. Critics noted that Canadian **"branch plants"** were under American direction and funnelled most of their profits to investors back in the United States. By 1967, 81 percent of the $34.7 billion worth of foreign investment in Canada came from American sources. Public opinion shifted: a 1967 poll showed that two thirds of Canadians wanted the federal government to control American investment in Canada. Several other government reports, including the Watkins Report of 1968, raised concerns about the extent of the foreign ownership of Canadian firms.

Canada's "Big" Economy

The 1950s and 1960s brought an incredible growth in economic well-being for most Canadians. These were the years of optimism, as Canadians — both governments and private citizens — worked to create economic and material prosperity. American investment in Canadian resources was welcomed, but what consequences would this have for Canadian businesses? There can be no question that, from 1945 to 1970, "big" was a good word to describe Canada's economy. But it is also important to remember that not all Canadians shared in these years of economic good times.

chapter review

CHAPTER SUMMARY

In this chapter we have seen

- how post-war prosperity contributed to a consumer revolution in North America

- how mass-marketing changed the nature of retailing in Canada

- that the economic boom of the 1950s and 1960s was not equally enjoyed by all regions of Canada

- how closer economic ties to the United States both contributed to Canadian prosperity and raised concerns among many Canadians

UNDERSTANDING HISTORICAL FACTS

1. Identify these people, places, and events, and explain their historical significance.

   Auto Pact
   Trans-Canada
      pipeline
   Atlantic Development
      Board

   St. Lawrence Seaway
   Canadian Labour
      Congress
   Gordon Commission

2. Of all the new products to hit the market in the 1950s, none had the widespread impact of television on the culture and daily lives of Canadians. Create a web with television at the centre to show the ways in which television has changed life in Canada.

3. Create a chart that includes each of the following regions: the Atlantic provinces, Québec, Ontario, the Prairies, British Columbia. Describe the economic growth of each of the regions and indicate, using a symbol, whether the region shared in the prosperity or remained economically stagnant.

4. Since the creation of the Auto Pact, the automobile industry has been an essential component of the economy of Central Canada. Create a web with automobiles in the centre that shows the related industries that depend on the vitality of the automobile industry.

5. Using the information in this chapter, list the industries and cities that would have been served by the St. Lawrence Seaway.

EXPRESSING YOUR OPINION

1. During the 1950s and 1960s some regions of Canada enjoyed great economic prosperity while others remained economically stagnant. Is the federal government obligated to balance the wealth of the nation between the regions? If so, how should the federal government encourage economic growth in areas that are not prospering?

2. Do you agree with labour's view that in a time of high profits for corporations, workers should receive a share of the wealth in the form of higher wages and improved benefits? Why or why not?

3. Since 1945, American investment in Canada has grown immensely. Do you believe this investment has had a positive or negative effect on Canada? Consider both economic growth and the social implications of American ownership of industries (including oil and gas), cultural industries (publishing, film, and music), and manufacturing. Should the government encourage or discourage further American investment in the Canadian economy?

WORKING WITH THE EVIDENCE

1. Nikita is told to have her date home to Atikokan, Ontario, by midnight on Saturday night. The couple are attending a party in Thunder Bay. At 10:30 p.m. they leave the party and drive back to Atikokan, which is approximately two hundred kilometres from Thunder Bay. Nikita does not exceed the speed limit yet still manages to have her date home on time. How is this possible?

Canada's Entry onto the World Stage

UNEF 1 598

One of Canada's most important contributions to post World War II world security has been its peacekeeping program. Do you think this has affected the way people characterize Canadians?

INQUIRING INTO THE PAST

- **How did the nuclear-arms race and the spread of communism affect the Cold War?**
- **How would jet bombers and guided missiles change Canada's position in the world?**
- **How might Canadians and the world benefit from Canada's peacekeeping and foreign-aid programs?**
- **Why would Canada want to develop a distinctive foreign policy?**

KEY TERMS

Ballistic Missiles

McCarthyism

Middle Power

TIMELINE

1949
The Soviet Union acquires nuclear weapons

1956
Lester Pearson develops the plan for a United Nations peacekeeping force

1962
The Cuban Missile Crisis brings the world to the brink of all-out nuclear war

1968
Prime Minister Pierre Trudeau begins a complete review of Canada's foreign policy

Building on wartime economic growth, most Canadians — whatever their origin — saw the future as a time of opportunity for themselves and their children. The discovery of valuable new resources and the boom in new industries made the promise of prosperity seem very real. But as much as Canada changed between 1945 and 1968, the world stage also changed. This resulted in many challenges to older ideas and practices. The positive ways in which Canadians responded to these challenges showed Canada's new strength, pride, and willingness to be a world leader.

Caught in the Crossfire: Canada and the Cold War

In the years immediately after World War II a fierce power struggle developed between the two superpowers, the United States and the Soviet Union. From 1945 to 1949 this conflict — the "Cold War" — was centred in Europe, as the citizens of the war-devastated nations struggled to restore political stability and democracy and to revive their shattered economies. Canadians helped to support their efforts by contributing economic aid through the Marshall Plan to rebuild these economies. Canada also joined the North Atlantic Treaty Organization (NATO), a military alliance aimed at protecting Western Europe from a Soviet invasion. However, in 1949 two events changed and widened the scope of the Cold War. One result of these events was that Canada became more firmly located in a middle ground between determined rivals.

The Cold War Intensifies

The first event to intensify the Cold War occurred on August 29, 1949, when the Soviet Union detonated an atomic bomb at a test site in Siberia. Soviet propaganda portrayed the successful test as evidence of the strength and promise of communism. The military balance had now changed drastically, because the Western monopoly on nuclear weapons had been shattered: both sides in the Cold War possessed unprecedented destructive power.

Immediately a new arms race began to develop vastly more powerful thermonuclear weapons, or hydrogen bombs. In 1952 the United States detonated the world's first hydrogen bomb on a small island in the south Pacific. However, the Americans' lead was short-lived. In 1953 the Soviet Union detonated its own thermonuclear device. For the next forty years both sides rushed to amass huge stockpiles of more powerful bombs.

The possession of the hydrogen bomb by both the United States and the Soviet Union escalated the arms race.

The second event occurred on October 1, 1949, when the Chinese communists, led by Mao Zedong, won a long, bitter civil war against Chinese Nationalists. The war had ravaged China since the 1930s. In Beijing, Mao Zedong declared the establishment of a new communist regime, the People's Republic of China. The defeated Nationalists fled to the island of Taiwan, where they continued to claim to be the legitimate Chinese government. Western nations were shocked at the defeat of their wartime ally, the Nationalist Chinese government. To combat the much-feared spread of communism, the United States demanded that its NATO allies not recognize the communist government in Beijing. Most nations complied until the late 1960s.

The United States also demanded that the Taiwan government continue to officially represent China in all United Nations councils. From 1949 to the present day, American economic and military aid has poured into the small island republic to help it resist attacks from mainland China. The Cold War meanwhile spread to Asia as communists worldwide, especially in the Soviet Union, loudly supported the claims of Mao Zedong's government. Eventually, in the 1970s, the People's Republic of China gained international acceptance as China's official government. However, bitter diplomatic, economic, and small-scale military battles between the two rival Chinese governments still rage today.

Anti-Communism in Canada

Canada's Gouzenko affair confirmed anti-communist fears in North America. In the United States the anti-communist investigations were led by Senator Joseph McCarthy and his "Red Scare" hysteria from 1950 to 1954.

Although the excesses of **McCarthyism** in the United States did not occur in Canada, the Red Scare was very real and had severe consequences for some people. The Royal Canadian Mounted Police responded to anti-communist sentiments by carrying out illegal and secret inquiries. People wishing to immigrate to Canada who were believed to be communists or sympathizers were denied entry. Known communists were often deported from Canada or denied even the opportunity to visit. Eventually, Joseph McCarthy's excessive and unsubstantiated claims against communists worked against him, and his "Red-baiting" campaign was broken. However, the damage he caused to American lives, liberty, and government policies were immense both at home and abroad.

The Quest for Global Stability

Since the end of World War II, nations have avoided conflict on a global scale. Nonetheless, in the past fifty years, hundreds of regional wars have been fought, claiming millions of lives and causing immeasurable damage. Throughout this period

Princess Patricia's Canadian Light Infantry in Korea, 1951. Why was the war in Korea such a devastating experience for both Koreans and United Nations forces?

Canada has emerged as a leading nation in the struggle to bring about global peace and stability. Since the Korean War in 1950, Canadians have taken leading roles in the search for sustainable peace around the world.

The Korean War

After World War II Japanese-held Korea was divided into two parts. North Korea was occupied by troops from the Soviet Union, and South Korea was occupied by U.S. troops. It was intended that the country would eventually be peacefully reunited as a single, independent nation. However, in June 1950, 100 000 North Korean troops armed with Soviet weapons invaded South Korea. Many Americans saw this invasion as another example of international communist aggression. The United States asked the United Nations (U.N.) Security Council to meet in a special session to discuss the Korean situation. The Soviets were boycotting the Security Council at the time to protest against the exclusion of the Peoples' Republic of China from the U.N. In their absence, the United States demanded that the U.N. come to the military defence of South Korea. The Security Council quickly voted to send U.N. forces, under American command, to defend South Korea. Although fourteen U.N. member-nations sent troops to take part, the U.N. fighting forces were overwhelmingly American.

At first, Canada sent three navy destroyers and an air-transport squadron to join the forces, but it later sent ground troops as well. In the three long, bloody years of fighting, 22 000 Canadians fought in Korea. More than 1000 Canadians were wounded, and more than 300 were killed before the war ended. Although the shooting stopped on July 27, 1953, Korea remained a divided country.

Web Connections

http://www.school.mcgrawhill.ca/resources

Go to the above Web site to find out more about Canadians in the Korean War. Go to *History Resources*, then to *Canada: A Nation Unfolding, Ontario Edition*, to find out where to go next.

Egypt and the Suez Crisis: The Birth of U.N. peacekeeping

Shortly after a truce was reached in Korea, the idea of Canada being a **"middle power"** mediator became a reality. Many African nations began to seek more independence from their European colonial overlords after World War II. In 1952, a new, nationalistic government took power in Egypt. It was determined to create an independent and modern nation that would control its own resources, such as the Suez Canal.

In 1956 Egyptian President Gamal Abdal Nasser seized the Suez Canal from British and French control. Britain and France saw Nasser's action as threatening their links to vital Asian resources and markets, so a few months later they joined Israel in an attack on Egypt. Their objective was to take back the Suez Canal.

The invasion caused an international diplomatic uproar. The Soviet Union sided with Egypt and demanded the withdrawal of the invading armies. Fighting around Suez was stepped up, and the world

edged closer to a major war. At that point Lester Pearson, Canada's acting minister of external affairs, stepped forward to defuse the explosive situation. He went to the United Nations and suggested creating a United Nations Emergency Force (UNEF) in the Suez to "keep the borders at peace while a political settlement is being worked out." The idea was eagerly accepted by the United Nations. In just a few days, all battle forces were withdrawn from the combat zone and replaced by blue-helmeted U.N. peacekeeping units. The fighting had been stopped, peace had been restored in the Suez, and the United Nations had proven its worth. In recognition of his efforts for world peace, Lester Pearson was awarded the Nobel Peace Prize in 1957.

After the Suez Crisis, Canada continued its peacekeeping and mediating role. From 1960 to 1964, Canadian troops and citizens were active in U.N. peace programs in Zaire, a newly independent African nation now known as Congo. When violence between Turkish and Greek inhabitants of the island of Cyprus threatened to widen into war in 1964, Canada volunteered to send peacekeepers. The Canadian troops in their now-familiar blue helmets managed to create a line of separation between the two sides. This "green line" was respected by all sides throughout the U.N. peace-

Why do peacekeepers wear blue helmets or berets and ride in white vehicles?

Suez Canal

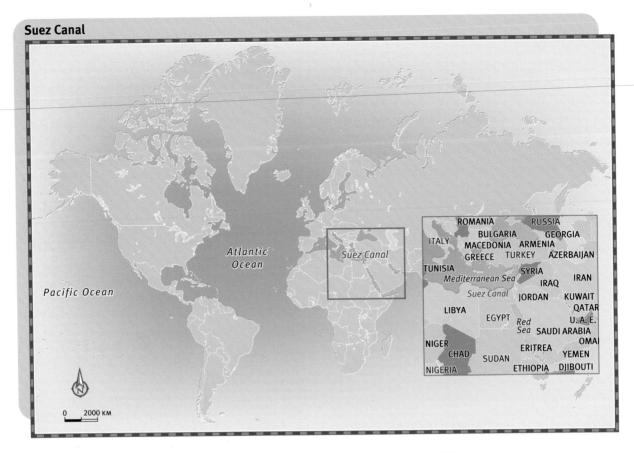

Why was the Suez Canal geographically important to the economic prosperity of many countries?

keepers' stay in Cyprus. Canada also participated in U.N. commissions of investigation in Vietnam, Yemen, and Kashmir. When war broke out again in 1967 between Israel and its Arab neighbours, Canada once again volunteered peacekeepers. Canada has been part of every U.N. peacekeeping mission since 1956.

The Nuclear-Arms Race Goes Ballistic

When the Soviet Union detonated nuclear bombs in 1949 and 1953, the race for nuclear supremacy was on. By the mid-1950s the American and Soviet militaries had amassed huge stockpiles of newer, larger, and far more devastating hydrogen bombs. The leaders on both sides threatened to unleash their nuclear arsenals. To deliver their bombs, both

sides developed huge fleets of long-range bombers as well as air-defence systems against these bombers. Across North America, governments and individuals were in a frenzy to build bomb shelters in remote areas, under large buildings, and even in home basements. In 1956 an American strategist created a terrifying name and acronym for the stalemate that these huge stockpiles had created: Mutually Assured Destruction, or MAD.

Throughout the 1950s Canada and the United States co-operated to build a system of radar stations, called the Distant Early Warning (DEW) line, and jet-fighter bases in the Canadian North to detect and intercept flights of Soviet bombers. A larger system called the North American Air Defence (NORAD) system was established in 1957 to co-ordinate these defence programs. In the same year the Cold War took another ominous turn. The Soviet Union used a ballistic rocket to launch the

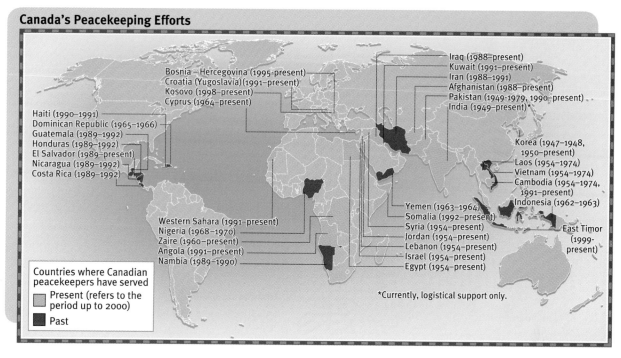

Canada's Peacekeeping Efforts

Canada's involvement in peacekeeping missions.

first human-made earth satellite, *Sputnik*. *Sputnik* proved that the Soviets could use missiles to send nuclear warheads deep into the American heartland. The United States scrambled to keep pace with the Soviets. Both the Soviet and American militaries worked feverishly to produce bigger **ballistic missiles** to carry even larger, deadlier payloads. The world did not have long to wait for the first superpower confrontation that might actually result in the total destruction of life on earth.

The Cuban Missile Crisis

In 1959 Cuban communist forces, led by Fidel Castro, successfully overthrew the pro-American government of Cuba. Castro welcomed the economic aid and military support that the Soviet Union sent to Cuba, located only 150 kilometres south of the United States. From 1959 to 1962 relations between the United States and Cuba and its ally, the Soviet Union, steadily worsened. Then, in October 1962, the United States discovered that Soviet missiles with atomic warheads were being installed in Cuba. The world held its breath as the two leaders, U.S. President John F. Kennedy and the Soviet Union's Nikita Khrushchev, exchanged stern warnings and threats of all-out nuclear war. American and some Canadian air force units were put on "red alert," ready to launch attacks if the Soviet supply ships going to Cuba did not turn back. Fortunately, the Cuban Missile Crisis ended suddenly, when the Soviets agreed to remove the missiles. Although the immediate tensions eased, everyone — on all sides of the Iron Curtain — knew that the age of the potential total destruction of life had arrived.

The Development of an Independent Canadian Foreign Policy

Throughout late 1940s and 1950s Canada and the United States continued to co-operate in their foreign-policy objectives, especially the American anti-

What message is this cartoon attempting to convey about the arms race? Do you think the cartoon is overly pessimistic, or is it realistic?

The Battle over Bomarc Missiles

By the mid-1950s Canadians felt they could safeguard themselves from a Soviet nuclear-bomber attack only through joint air defence with the United States. Prime Minister John Diefenbaker had reluctantly agreed to join the NORAD system and to share in building the DEW line in the North. He also accepted U.S. Bomarc-B missiles for Canada, a battery of American-made "Honest John" missiles for the Canadian army in Europe, and CF-140 jetfighters for the Canadian NATO squadrons. But these weapons were effective only when armed with nuclear warheads. Diefenbaker's decisions seemed to commit Canada to a strong role in NORAD and NATO defence and to the use of nuclear weapons.

But the Prime Minister backed away from accepting American nuclear weapons to arm the missiles and aircraft of the Canadian armed forces. There had been a recent upsurge of protest against nuclear weapons in Canada. The Co-operative Commonwealth Federation (CCF), the Liberal Party, women's groups, and many intellectuals raised a storm of protest against "nukes."

communist drive. Canada's active membership in NATO and NORAD supported American military and foreign-policy decisions. Its participation in U.N. peacekeeping in Egypt and Lebanon, which pacified potentially explosive situations, also seemed to support American foreign-policy decisions. By the end of the 1950s, however, considerable strains had developed in the uneven partnership. American pressure, which led to the cancellation of the Avro Arrow jet and the installation of American Bomarc missiles on Canadian soil, rankled Canadian nationalists. Increasingly, Canadian journalists broke with the American policy of criticizing communist governments. In 1959 the Canadian newspaper *The Globe and Mail* accepted China's offer to become the first Western newspaper allowed into the People's Republic. Despite American displeasure, Ottawa gave diplomatic recognition to Castro's communist government, and Canadian companies continued to be active in Cuba.

Despite this picture of friendliness, John Kennedy and John Diefenbaker did not get along. How did Canada's position on Cuba affect the leaders' relationship?

technology

THE AVRO ARROW

As the Cold War intensified in the 1950s, Canada became increasingly concerned with the possibility of a Soviet attack. To guard against an attack, Canada required modern supersonic aircraft. The CF-100 Canucks, which had been in use since 1953, were slow and outdated despite their reliability. As early as 1949, the Canadian government had backed the A.V. Roe Company in the ambitious project of developing one of the world's fastest supersonic jets: the Avro Arrow.

The jet developed by the A.V. Roe company was a twin-engine, all-weather interceptor jet and was reputed to be the fastest and most advanced interceptor of its time. Reports from test pilots praised the speed and handling of the Arrow. Despite this acclaim, the Avro Arrow project was cancelled on February 20, 1959, which led to the loss of fourteen thousand jobs. Many of those who lost their jobs were top scientists and engineers who then left Canada to find employment in the American space program.

Why would the government give up on a jet with so much potential? The answer to this perplexing question could have been the high costs of the project. When the Arrow was proposed, it was estimated that each aircraft would cost $2 million to produce. At this cost, Canada could expect international sales and planned to make about six hundred planes. However, during the development of the Avro Arrow, costs skyrocketed by over 600 percent, to $12.5 million per plane. Therefore, the government was not successful at selling the Arrows to foreign buyers because the price had become too high. It decided to scrap the Avro Arrow and opted to buy F-101 Voodoo fighters from the United States.

The government, led by Prime Minister John Diefenbaker, received a great deal of criticism for this decision. The loss of jobs, as well as the renewed reliance on American military technology and the blow to Canada's aerospace industry, did not sit well with Canadians. What advice would you have given Prime Minister Diefenbaker? Should the project have been shelved or continued?

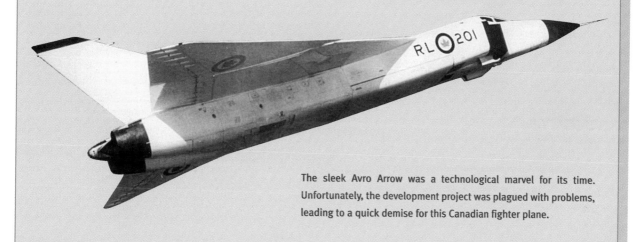

The sleek Avro Arrow was a technological marvel for its time. Unfortunately, the development project was plagued with problems, leading to a quick demise for this Canadian fighter plane.

An America Bomarc-B missile in North Bay, Ontario. Since Canada relied on the United States for its military strength, do you think it had an obligation to accept the U.S. missiles?

Diefenbaker told U.S. President Kennedy that "in view of public opinion in Canada it would be impossible politically at [the] moment ... to accept nuclear weapons."

It was not the last time Diefenbaker turned a cold shoulder to the American President. During the 1962 Cuban Missile Crisis, American NORAD aircraft were put on immediate alert for a possible Soviet nuclear attack over the Canadian Arctic. Kennedy counted on Canadian military support in the looming conflict, but Diefenbaker delayed putting Canada's NORAD aircraft on the alert until just before the crisis ended.

The Americans were enraged at Diefenbaker's lack of enthusiasm for their plans, as were many Canadians who supported Kennedy's action. By the end of 1962 it was time for a debate about Canada's defence commitments and nuclear weapons. The newly founded New Democratic Party (formerly the CCF) was firmly against nuclear weapons for Canada. But Liberal Party leader Lester Pearson, who had also opposed nuclear weapons, changed his mind and supported the acceptance of nuclear warheads. Prime Minister Diefenbaker was still undecided, and in a speech to the House of Commons he waffled, making statements that could be taken as either for nuclear weapons or against them. As a result, the Diefenbaker government was brought down by a non-confidence vote in Parliament in February 1963 on the question of nuclear weapons. When the Liberals came to power, Prime Minister Lester Pearson quietly accepted the obsolete nuclear weapons.

Conflicting Views on Vietnam

Lester Pearson also encountered occasional rough spots in his relations with American leaders, especially during a head-to-head conflict with U.S. President Lyndon Johnson over American involvement in the increasingly bloody and unpopular war in Vietnam. In a speech at Temple University in Philadelphia in April 1965, Pearson gently prompted the Americans to "rethink their position" on bombing raids over North Vietnam and President Johnson was outraged. The matter was smoothed over, but tensions still remained as more and more Canadians began to speak out against American military actions in Vietnam. American protesters and "draft dodgers" — young men who fled compulsory military service — were welcomed in Canada. Canadian officials refused all American efforts to force the return of draft dodgers to the United States. These incidents reminded Canadians how difficult it sometimes was for their nation to keep an independent stance in foreign policy and still maintain friendly relations with the United States.

By the 1960s, Canadians had become very aware of the dangers of a nuclear arms race. Would you have joined an antinuclear rally such as this one? Why or why not?

Defining a New Foreign Policy

In 1968 Canada's new Prime Minister, Pierre Trudeau, called for a complete review of Canada's foreign policy. He began by reducing Canada's defence spending and freezing Canada's contribution to NATO. Reacting to the huge increases in American military involvement in the Vietnam war, Trudeau also wanted to loosen Canada's ties with the United States. He became the first Western leader to visit the United States' arch-enemy, Fidel Castro. As part of the visit, government officials established wider trade and tourist connections for Canada and Cuba. Trudeau also worked to create more profitable links with other nations, such as the members of the European Economic Community.

Trudeau also signalled a new direction in Canada's foreign policy by breaking with the long-standing U.S. policy that rejected the Chinese Communist Party's claim to be the official government. In 1970 Canada officially recognized the People's Republic of China and supported its admission into the United Nations. Canada began to seek out new and wider trading relationships with China, Japan, and the other Asian countries of the Pacific Rim. Trudeau also made a "goodwill" tour to the Soviet Union to promote cultural exchanges and new trade partnerships with the Warsaw Pact nations of Eastern Europe.

Canada's Membership in International Organizations

As part of its Cold War defence commitments, Canada's armed forces actively participated in military exercises and exchanges with its NATO allies. Throughout the 1950s and 1960s Canada continued to station battle-ready troops in Germany. In addition, northern Canada, because of its similarity to the geography and climate of the Soviet Union, became an important NATO military training ground. The Canadian navy, army, and air force played important roles in war-game simulations designed to prepare for an anticipated world war. Likewise, Canadian and American forces worked together to expand the NORAD warning and defence systems in Canada's North. Canada also gradually extended its mediating role in other directions that were not focused on war. Since 1931 the Canadian government has been active in an organization of former British colonies now called the Commonwealth.

Canada and other prosperous Commonwealth nations, such as Britain, Australia, and New Zealand, have helped to establish aid and development programs for less prosperous members. In the 1950s Canada contributed to the Colombo Plan, which provided extensive aid to Commonwealth nations in Asia. Canadians helped to build factories, power-generating plants, and irrigation projects in Pakistan, India, and Sri Lanka. Cultural exchanges, festivals, and major sports competitions have become other important links between members of the Commonwealth.

Since 1931, when the British Empire was replaced by the British Commonwealth, meetings have been hosted by the ruling monarch and attended by the heads of state from former British colonies. How can countries such as Canada benefit from close relations with other Commonwealth nations?

Since the mid-1960s Canada has also developed links with an organization of French-speaking nations called La Francophonie. Beginning very modestly, Canadian funding to aid programs, especially to those for the French-speaking nations of West Africa, has grown steadily to become a sizable part of Canada's foreign-aid budget.

Canadian Foreign-Aid Programs

Although some of the new nations that emerged after World War II are stable and self-sufficient, many are unstable and desperately poor. These countries lack economic resources; their trade and industries are not developed; and they are experiencing huge population explosions. Their people are often poorly educated and lack job training. Some do not even have such basics as food, housing, clothing, clean water, and medical care. Over the years Canadians have worked to reduce world poverty and to help bring improved economic development. As early as the 1950s thousands of young Canadians volunteered to work abroad in Third World development programs. Private organizations such as Canadian University Service Overseas (CUSO) and World University Services of Canada (WUSC) helped bring money and technology to many less developed nations.

In the 1950s the Canadian government's spending on foreign aid was very modest. For example, in 1957 Canada spent only $50 million on foreign aid. However, Canada's foreign aid increased in the 1960s, after Lester Pearson became Prime Minister. It also expanded to include new areas. Canada began to send food to famine-stricken countries, make low-interest loans for economic development projects, and offer scholarships and technical assistance to the people of the Third World. In 1968 Canada set up the Canadian International Development Agency (CIDA), which co-ordinates all Canadian aid projects from both government and non-governmental sources.

Non-governmental organizations, sometimes called NGOs, are private groups that sponsor aid programs. NGOs receive some money from CIDA, but much of their funding comes from private citizens. Well-known NGOs include the Canadian Red Cross Society, CARE Canada, Oxfam Canada, the Unitarian Service Committee of Canada, and the Canadian Save the Children Fund.

As part of its continuing effort to help Third World nations, the Canadian government funds the Canadian Industrial Development Agency (CIDA), which works abroad to learn from and assist developing countries.

Canada Takes Its Place on the World Stage

Between 1945 and 1970 Canada emerged as a major player on the world stage. Canadians actively participated in all of the councils and agencies of the United Nations. The concept and practice of "peacekeeping" came from Canada, and Canadian forces participated in all such U.N. missions. Canadians were deeply involved in the issues and conflicts that surrounded the Cold War. In the 1960s, as Canada became more multicultural and more determined to limit American cultural and economic influences inside its borders, a new direction was needed. Moving away from close ties to American attitudes and policies, Canada developed its own distinctive foreign policy. As a result, Canada increased its commitment to be an international mediator, to aid the development of less prosperous nations, and to assert human rights worldwide.

Canadian contributions

EXPO 67

In 1962, when the Soviet Union cancelled its plans to host the 1967 world exhibition, Montréal's mayor, Jean Drapeau, proposed that his city be the site. Drapeau made a presentation to the Bureau International des Expositions (BIE). The BIE awarded the 1967 exhibition to Canada — the first such exhibition to be held in North America.

Expo 67 was a three-way partnership, with 50 percent participation by the federal government, 37.5 percent by the Québec government, and 12.5 percent by the city of Montréal. The three governments met to choose a central theme and develop a philosophy for Expo. "Man and His World" evolved as the theme to show the full range of activities of contemporary humanity.

The next decision was the choice of a site. Many proposals were studied, and eventually it was decided that Ile Ste-Hélène, an island in the centre of the St. Lawrence River, would be enlarged, and a new island, Ile Notre-Dame, would be created. Together, these islands would be the location for Expo 67. Landfill from the bottom of the St. Lawrence and from the excavations for a new subway line to serve Expo was used to create Ile Notre-Dame and to enlarge Ile Ste-Hélène.

Countries that participated in Expo 67 either built their own pavilions or combined with other nations to create regional pavilions. Altogether there were 120 governments at Expo, housed in sixty pavilions. In addition, thousands of private exhibitors and sponsors co-operated in setting up displays in fifty-three private pavilions. When it was all over on October 27, 1967, more than fifty million people had paid the admission to Expo —almost double the number of people the exhibition had planned to accommodate.

What was Expo 67? It was an international world fair. It was a spectacular exhibition of art, music, architecture, food, language, colour, people, literature, sculpture, history, high technology, and politics. In fact, it was everything related to "Man and His World." Above all, it was a magnificent way to celebrate and honour Canada on its one-hundredth birthday.

In short, Expo 67 was the most successful world fair ever, judging by the number of people who visited the site, by the number of participating countries, and by the praise lavished on the fair by those who visited Montréal in that fabulous time between April and October of 1967. What an incredible way to celebrate our centennial year!

CONTRIBUTED BY RICHARD B. GIBB. RICHARD GIBB VISITED EXPO 67 IN HIS YOUTH. TODAY HE IS A RETIRED HISTORY TEACHER LIVING NEAR FEVERSHAM, ONTARIO.

chapter review

CHAPTER SUMMARY

In this chapter we have seen

- how the escalation of the Cold War led to a nuclear-arms race

- how Canada began its long and acclaimed participation in United Nations peacekeeping missions in 1956

- that in the 1960s Canada developed its own foreign policy and an independent position as a mediating "middle power" in world affairs

- that Canada steadily increased its relief and aid programs to many less prosperous countries during the 1960s

UNDERSTANDING HISTORICAL FACTS

1. Identify these people, places, and events, and explain their historical significance.

NORAD	M.A.D.
La Francophonie	Commonwealth
Suez Canal	Avro Arrow
Cuban Missile Crisis	Foreign Policy
McCarthyism	DEW Line

2. Using a cause-and-effect diagram, show how the detonation of the Soviet Union's nuclear weapons affected the Cold War balance of power.

3. Explain why the victory of the Chinese communists was so important to the two superpowers in 1949 and to emerging nations worldwide.

4. Imagine you are part of the selection committee that awards the Nobel Peace Prize. Having considered the major events and people of the past year (1957), you believe the award should go to Canada's Lester Pearson. Write a one-page defence of your selection, highlighting his work, especially his concept of peacekeeping.

5. Describe the primary goals of Canada's foreign policy in the post-war years. List and describe four examples of Canada's foreign policy in action before 1970.

6. Define what it means for Canada to be considered a "middle power."

EXPRESSING YOUR OPINION

1. If nuclear weapons had not been invented, do you believe a major war between the United States and the Soviet Union would have erupted in the decades following World War II? Defend your answer. What do you believe to have been the cause of the tension between these two superpowers?

2. As a middle power, what role should Canada play to ensure world peace and economic stability? Should Canada play a primarily military or non-military role in world affairs? Defend your answer.

3. Are prosperous countries morally obligated to assist poorer countries? What are the possible consequences (for both the rich and poor countries) if wealthy countries refuse to assist poor countries?

4. The two decades following World War II have often been referred to as Canada's "golden age" of foreign policy. Is this an accurate statement? Defend your answer.

WORKING WITH THE EVIDENCE

1. During the 1960s and 1970s it was common for Canadian aid workers to travel to African nations and help in the digging of wells to provide water for drinking, irrigation, and other uses. Despite the best intentions, many efforts of the aid workers have led to worse problems than those they intended to solve. Why is this?

unit review

BRINGING THE PAST INTO FOCUS

REVIEWING THE FACTS

1. Between 1945 and 1968 three prime ministers dominated Canadian politics: Louis St. Laurent, John Diefenbaker, and Lester Pearson. Prepare a character profile or draw and label a caricature of each of these prime ministers in which you highlight elements of their background, their character, their major achievements, and their significant failures. If you choose to write a profile, use subheadings to focus the reader's attention. If you choose to draw a caricature, be sure to include items that symbolize character traits.

2. Imagine that two friends, and English-speaking resident of Québec and a French-speaking Québecois, are at Expo 67 when French Prime Minister Charles du Gaulle exclaims "Vive le Québec libre!" Create the conversation that may have occurred between the two friends following du Gualle's statement.

3. Create a collage which illustrates the differences between teenagers of the 1950s and the 1960s. Include such items as photos, news articles, sheet music, album covers, and advertisements. Once you have completed your collage, write 300 words explaining which decade you would have preferred to be a teenager.

4. Copy and complete the following chart into your notes.

THE INFLUENCE OF THE UNITED STATES ON POST-WAR CANADA

AREA OF INFLUENCE	POSITIVE EFFECTS	NEGATIVE EFFECTS
Music	*sample text*	*sample text*
Television	*sample text*	*sample text*
Foreign Policy	*sample text*	*sample text*
Economy	*sample text*	*sample text*

5. Explain how development in technology including telecommunications, impacted on the lives of Canadians in the 1950s and the 1960s and how new innovations led to economic change in this period.

HISTORICALLY SPEAKING

1. Explain how post-war immigration patterns in Canada differed from earlier immigration movements to Canada in the twentieth century. Using one of the groups of immigrants that came to Canada during the twenty years following World War II, show how the diversification of Canada's population was enriched society as a result of the contributions of new Canadians.

2. Some historians believe that during the 1960s, Canadians ignored issues about racism because they believed they did not face the same problems as in the United States, where issues of racism often turned into violence. Is their evidence to suggest that racism was a problem which needed to be addressed in Canada but was being ignored? Provide evidence to support your answer.

3. Why do you think this unit was given the title "A Nation Matures"? Is this a suitable title for Canadian history in the decades following World War II? Defend your answer by using examples of economic growth, international involvement, and the creation of a social safety net.

MAKING CONNECTIONS

Below is a list of key events, trends, or issues from the 1950s and 1960s. Select one term from three of the categories and explain what connection can be made between each of the three terms.

PERSPECTIVES

1. The Cold War and the threat of nuclear annihilation led to deep divisions within North American society. Some believed the best route to sustainable peace was through strength. These people support the building of nuclear bombs. Others opposed nuclear weapons, seeking peace through cooperation and disarmament. Write one paragraph defending the build up of nuclear weapons as the best means to a stable peace and a second paragraph arguing for the destruction of nuclear arms.

2. During the 1960s songs such as "Times are a Changin'" by Bob Dylan and "My Generation" by The Who claimed that the youth of North America were not understood by their parents generation because they did not share the same values. This was often referred to as a "generation gap". Re-create a conversation that may have occurred between a 1960s Canadian teenager and their parents. Try to capture the essence of the counter-culture and the clash in values between the two generations.

3. The 1960s were a prosperous decade. Jobs were plentiful, new social programs made life easier and Canadians seemed to have a great deal of money to spend on new consumer goods. But not all Canadians would remember the 1960s in such positive terms. Pick two different perspectives from the list below, and write a paragraph to finish the statement: "I remember the 1960s..."

Aboriginal Peoples	Black Canadians
Women	Asian Canadians
Teenagers	Labourers

4. Which group or groups of Canadians do you believe benefitted the most from changes in technology, especially in telecommunications during the 1950s and 1960s? Which group or groups benefitted the least and/or suffered from technological change during this period? Explain your answer using examples.

INTERNATIONAL	NATIONAL	REGIONAL	PERSONAL
Baby Boom	Foreign Policy	Great Darkness	Automobile
Cold War	St. Lawrence Seaway	Suburbia	Television
American Relations	D.E.W. Line	Africville	Residential Schools
Cuban Missile Crisis	Social Safety Net	Western Alienation	Anti-nuclear protest

Contemporary Canada, 1968–2000

"What we continue to create, today, began 450 years ago as a political project, when the French first met with the Aboriginal people. It is an old experiment, complex and, in worldly terms, largely successful. Stumbling through darkness and racing through light, we have persisted in the creation of a Canadian civilization."

— GOVERNOR GENERAL ADRIENNE CLARKSON

TIMELINE

1970
October Crisis erupts as a result of Front de Libération du Québec kidnappings ►

1982
The Canada Act is passed, bringing Canada's constitution home from Britain ►

During the last few decades of the twentieth century Canada earned a reputation as a world leader in many fields. Several times during the 1990s Canada was ranked the best place in the world to live by the United Nations. Yet, throughout this period of apparent unparalleled success, child poverty was rampant, the homeless problem grew steadily worse, and Canadians were constantly searching for a unifying identity. As Canada became home to millions of immigrants from around the world, the search for a single expression of Canadian identity grew more and more difficult. Throughout the chapters of this unit you will explore Canada's triumphs and challenges from 1968 to the present. You will become aware of government efforts to promote Canadian culture, and you will grapple with issues such as official multiculturalism. As well, this unit will introduce you to the origins of the term "global village" and increase your awareness of the role that technology has and will play in defining where and how we live and work.

LET'S INVESTIGATE

1. What is meant by the term "global village"? How has technology contributed to the development of a global village?

2. How has the Canadian economy changed in the past few decades?

3. What changes have occurred in the ways in which Canada's Aboriginal peoples are treated?

4. How has Canada's changing ethnic make-up both strengthened and resulted in a questioning of the Canadian identity?

1992
The North American Free Trade Agreement creates a trading bloc including Canada, the United States, and Mexico

2000
Canadian government announces large budget surpluses for the first time in decades

Canada and the World, 1968–2000

From 1985 to 1987, Canadian paraplegic Rick Hansen travelled over 40,000 kilometres in 34 countries for his Man In Motion World Tour. The tour (pictured here on the Great Wall of China) raised millions of dollars and world interest in spinal chord research.

INQUIRING INTO THE PAST

- **Why did the superpowers enter a period of disarmament?**
- **What are the primary objectives of Canada's foreign policy?**
- **How did Prime Ministers Trudeau and Mulroney differ in their relationships with the United States?**
- **How are science and technology altering the way in which Canada does business with the world?**

KEY TERMS

Acid rain

Détente

Disarmament

Global village

Proxy wars

TIMELINE

LATE 1960S–EARLY 1970S
Cold War enters era of détente

▶

1983
Pierre Trudeau embarks on a global peace crusade

▶

1988
Agreement on Arctic Co-operation soothes tensions between the United States and Canada over sovereignty in the Arctic

▶

2000
United Nations Biosafety Protocol to regulate the sale of genetically modified foods is negotiated in Montréal

▶

Consider the rapid pace of change in Canada over the past half century. Today, Canadians not only export goods to the four corners of the earth but also consume products from around the world. As players in an increasingly interconnected world, Canadians are involved in treaties and agreements designed to ensure peace, protect the environment, and promote fair trade practices. World War II and the Cold War that followed took the world to the brink of destruction. After the thawing of the Cold War in the late 1980s, Canada and the world were able to turn their attention to global solutions.

Détente and the End of the Cold War

After the Cuban missile crisis the superpowers realized the dangers of a nuclear standoff. They had stepped to the brink of nuclear war once and did not want to risk it again. In the late 1960s and early 1970s the Cold War began to thaw and a new era of **détente** — a relaxing of tensions — began. A direct "hotline" was set up between Moscow and Washington, D.C., so that a nuclear war would not be sparked by a misunderstanding between the superpowers.

The United States and the Soviet Union also signed a nuclear-test-ban treaty in 1963. This treaty was the first step in a new policy of co-operation and restraint. A series of arms-limitations talks began, aimed at **disarmament** — putting a stop to the arms race and reducing the stockpiles of Soviet and American nuclear weapons. As a result of these discussions the United States and the Soviet Union had signed two strategic-arms-limitation treaties by 1979 to set limits on specific types of nuclear arms.

The treaties were an important step in the march to world peace, but they did not bring an end to the Cold War. Rather than risk direct confrontation, the two nuclear superpowers resorted to lending military support to other countries engaged in struggles between communism and democratic capitalism. In this way the United States and the Soviet Union continued to oppose each other in "**proxy wars**" throughout Asia, Africa, and Latin America.

Vietnam, a divided nation in Southeast Asia, was probably the most hotly contested area. In the north-ern part of the country, Viet Cong rebels, supported by China and the Soviet Union, fought "a war of liberation" against French imperial rule. When France pulled out of Vietnam, the United States stepped in. Americans feared that if Vietnam came under communist domination, then all of Southeast Asia would fall into "the Soviet camp." At first the United States tried to help the Vietnamese government by sending military advisers, but it soon became obvious that this aid was insufficient. Eventually American troops were dispatched to Vietnam as well. By the end of the 1960s both sides were involved in a long, drawn-out war that did not end until 1975.

Foreign aid was also used as a weapon in the proxy wars. Southeast Asia was a major recipient of aid from the superpowers and their allies. Both the United States and the Soviet Union gave India, a

Sports also became an extension of the Cold War. When the Canada–USSR hockey series was announced, it became the Cold War on ice. Here, Canadian Paul Henderson scores the winning goal that made Canada victorious. This became one of the most memorable goals in hockey history.

neutral nation, billions of dollars in aid. Canada contributed $35 million for the Colombo Plan, an aid program to assist the Commonwealth countries of Asia. Canadians approved of the aid for humanitarian reasons, but their support was also part of a policy to fight communism. Prime Minister Lester Pearson warned that "if Southeast and South Asia are not to be conquered by communism, we of the free democratic world must demonstrate that it is we and not the Russians who stand for national liberation and economic and social progress."

In 1979 the Cold War heated up again, when the Soviet Union placed 350 missiles in Eastern Europe. In response, the United States announced plans to place Cruise missiles in Western Europe. That same year, the Soviet Union invaded neighbouring Afghanistan. In protest, Canada, the United States, and other Western nations boycotted the 1980 Moscow Olympic Games. (The Soviet Union struck back by boycotting the 1984 Los Angeles Olympics.) In 1981 U.S. President Ronald Reagan began loud verbal attacks on the Soviet Union, which he dubbed "the evil empire." He also spoke about ways of "winning" a nuclear war and announced a $180 billion increase in defence spending. Later he proposed the expensive Strategic Defence Initiative (SDI), nicknamed "Star Wars," a space-based technology intended to destroy Soviet missiles attacking the United States.

The Cold War Ends

Then, a completely unexpected series of events took place in Eastern Europe. The Soviet Union was in turmoil in the late 1980s. Mikhail Gorbachev, the new leader of the Soviet Union, attempted to make badly needed reforms under the slogans of *perestroika* — meaning "restructuring," or economic reform — and *glasnost* — meaning, in Gorbachev's words, "openness in public affairs, in every sector of life." The reforms were intended to shift the Soviet Union's economic and political systems toward those in the West.

As part of his reforms Gorbachev loosened the Soviet hold over Warsaw Pact nations. In autumn of 1989 the "Iron Curtain" from the Balkans to the

In 1989 the Berlin Wall, which separated East Berlin from West Berlin, was torn down. Why do you think Berliners from both sides of the wall attacked it with such vigour?

Baltic collapsed. The Soviet Union made no effort to prevent the collapse, and to the surprise of a watching world the Berlin Wall, which had divided the German capital of Berlin, was torn down in 1989. Communist control in East Germany (known as the German Democratic Republic) melted away, and the territory was reunified with democratically governed West Germany (known as the German Federal Republic).

Many other Warsaw Pact countries — Poland, Czechoslovakia, and the Baltic states — also began to replace communist rule with democratic government and to sever their ties with the Soviet Union. By December 1991 the Soviet Union itself had broken into fifteen smaller states, including Russia, Ukraine, Georgia, Moldova, and Tajikistan. With the collapse of the Soviet Union, the Cold War came to an end.

Canadian Foreign Policy, 1968–2000

In 1968 Lester Pearson retired as Canada's Prime Minister. His experience as an active diplomat after World War II convinced him that Canada should play an active role in international affairs. But as a middle power Canada could not hope to have the same influence as bigger nations such as the United States, Britain, France, and the Soviet Union. Instead, Canada could act as "a helpful fixer." Canadian diplomats worked quietly behind the scenes at the United Nations (U.N.) to defuse international tensions, such as occurred in the Suez Crisis in 1956.

But when Pearson's successor, Pierre Elliott Trudeau, became Prime Minister the international situation had changed. In the new, expanded U.N., Canadian diplomats no longer enjoyed the kind of influence they formerly had. The Third World nations who criticized superpower domination were just as suspicious of the superpowers' allies, including Canada. Since the Cold War had started to thaw in the 1960s, there was less public concern about the Soviet threat.

Shortly after being elected to power, Trudeau called for a fresh look at Canada's foreign policy. The government's agenda was set out in a document, *Foreign Policy for Canadians*, which contained three goals. These included fostering economic growth and protecting Canadian sovereignty. Although working for international peace and security was important, Canadian national interests should be kept in mind. As one historian said, "For Trudeau, Canada would no longer be the world's boy scout."

Peacekeeping has remained an important part of Canada's foreign policy.

Nuclear Arms and Defence

After completing a review of Canadian defence policy, Prime Minister Trudeau decided to slash Canada's defence spending and freeze its contribution to the North Atlantic Treaty Organization (NATO). Canada's nuclear arms were gradually eliminated. Between 1970 and 1972 the Honest John nuclear missiles were removed from Canadian NATO bases in Europe. The CF-104 airplanes in Germany were stripped of nuclear missiles and rearmed with conventional (non-nuclear) rockets. Some Canadians were unhappy with the government's policy, as were Canada's NATO allies.

While the government was phasing out its nuclear armaments in NATO, it was also dismantling Bomarc missile sites in northern Canada that were part of the North American Aerospace Defence Command (NORAD). In 1984, CF-18 Hornets armed with conventional (non-nuclear) weapons replaced the aging Voodoos bought by the Diefenbaker government. By July 1984, just before the end of Trudeau's term of office, the last nuclear warheads had been removed from Canadian soil.

Canada was not, however, completely nuclear-free. The Canadian government still allowed U.S. ships with nuclear-arms capacity to sail into Canadian ports, and the Canadian defence industry was still closely tied to that of the United States. Canadian companies continued to accept million-dollar defence contracts for developing, building, and testing nuclear parts from missile launchers to guidance systems.

Despite the defence cuts, Canada's commitment to peacekeeping remained important. In 1975, 1500 Canadians were on duty in various regions of the world. They were part of the largest peacekeeping force contributed by any nation.

Canada and the Third World

The world's colonial regions had been exploited for their resources for hundreds of years, and many of them were very poor after they were granted independence from their colonial past. During the 1950s and 1960s Canada had aided Third World nations, both for humanitarian reasons and to fight

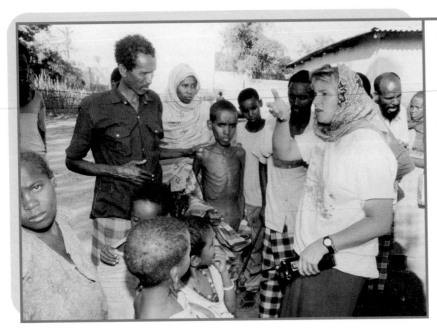

Many Canadians work overseas to help raise living standards in other parts of the world. Here, a Canadian nurse describes to a father in Somalia the importance of drinking plenty of liquids to avoid dehydration.

communism. Under Prime Minister Trudeau, Canadian foreign aid continued to be important and Canadian spending on aid rose. Trudeau was convinced that "in the long run the overwhelming threat to Canada will not come from foreign investments ... or even foreign nuclear weapons. It will come instead from the two thirds of the people of the world who are falling farther and farther behind in their search for a decent standard of living."

Before the 1970s most Canadian aid still went to the English-speaking countries of the Commonwealth. But during Trudeau's years as Prime Minister, Canada widened the scope of its foreign aid to include former French colonies. Trudeau wanted to be certain that Canada's policy abroad matched its new commitment to the French language and francophone culture at home. Between 1960 and 1968 the twenty-one French-speaking nations of Africa received only $300 000 in Canadian technical aid, but in 1973 they received $80 million — one fifth of the total Canadian International Development Agency (CIDA) budget. Next to France, Canada became the biggest donor of aid to French-speaking African nations.

Operating with money from CIDA, Canada has also helped Third World countries through Canadian Universities Service Overseas (CUSO). Since 1961 over ten thousand skilled Canadians have been placed in countries ranging from Bangladesh to Bolivia. Initially, most of the volunteers were recent university graduates who were placed in teaching positions, but it is now much more common for CUSO to receive requests for agriculturalists, foresters, mining experts, and tradespeople.

Canadian–American Relations Under Trudeau

Canada's relationship with the United States has always been important. During the Pearson years, the phrase "special relationship" was used to describe Canadian–American relations. Ottawa accepted American leadership in foreign policy and did not hinder American investment. The American State Department spoke up for Canada whenever legislation came up in Congress that threatened Canada's interests. Disagreements were to be resolved behind the scenes, through "quiet diplomacy," not public confrontation.

As the 1970s approached, however, Canadians were less willing to accept American leadership. Public-opinion polls showed that many Canadians were worried about the high level of American investment in Canada. The United States was bogged down in an unpopular war in Vietnam; race riots in American cities were common and

Canadian profiles

MARSHALL McLUHAN: PROPHET OF THE INFORMATION AGE

Students never knew what to expect when Professor Marshall McLuhan walked into class at the University of Toronto, except for one thing — they would not be bored. Born in Edmonton, Alberta, in 1911, Marshall McLuhan was one of the world's leading theorists of communication. He is best known for creating the phrases "the medium is the message" and "**global village.**"

What did he mean by "the medium is the message"? This was McLuhan's way of explaining that the way information is recorded and transmitted often determines the character of a culture and has a greater influence on people than does the information itself. McLuhan was focusing on the impact of the computer and technology on humanity. The way people use computers to record and transmit information has had a greater impact on them than has the infor-

mation they are transmitting via computer.

Stop for a minute and think about the power of Internet technology. As early as the 1960s, long before the Internet was being used by masses of people, McLuhan realized that the linking of electronic information would turn the world into a "global village." Geographic and language barriers have in many cases disappeared with the development of the Internet. Was McLuhan correct in theorizing that technology would create a "global village?"

For his theories and foresight, Marshall McLuhan is regarded as one of the intellectual giants of the twentieth century.

---

tarnished the image of American society. Meanwhile Expo '67 had stimulated a sense of nationalism and desire for independence in the minds of many Canadians. On his first trip to Washington, Prime Minister Trudeau told a press conference that he did not want Canada to be a "mirror image" of the United States. It was a speech very much in tune with the Canadian national mood.

An occasion to test the new independent Canadian stand soon came up. In 1969 the *Manhattan*, an American oil supertanker, steamed through the Northwest Passage to see if oil could be transported safely through Arctic waters. The voyage gave rise to fears about environmental pollution in Arctic waters. In response Parliament passed the Arctic Waters Pollution Act, which set a sixty-five-kilometre pollution zone under Canadian control.

In the following year Canada further tested its new independence by breaking with official U.S. policy on the communist People's Republic of China. The communists, led by Mao Zedong, had taken over the government of mainland China in 1949. The United States was hostile toward the new communist government and continued to support the exiled government in Taiwan. But Canada broke rank with the Americans by officially recognizing the People's Republic of China. It also supported communist China's membership in the United Nations.

American Reactions

In the early 1980s the mood in the United States had changed. Ronald Reagan, who became President in January 1981, pledged to "make

Canadian Prime Minister Pierre Elliott Trudeau helped to promote Canada on the international stage. Here he meets with Chinese leader Chou En-Lai.

Trudeau's Peace Crusade

By 1983, when Pierre Trudeau had been in office for nearly sixteen years, the Cold War heated up again. That year, a Korean Air Lines passenger jet was shot down when it flew into Soviet airspace. As a "war of words" flared up between the Soviet Union and the United States, Trudeau became alarmed at the prospect of a renewed Cold War. He drew up a series of proposals to end hostilities and travelled to many European capitals, Commonwealth countries, and China to seek support for his suggestions. He also contacted officials in the Soviet Union and the United States.

There was not much response from the two superpowers. The Soviet Union was in the midst of a leadership change, and President Reagan was suspicious of Trudeau. Though the impact of Trudeau's crusade was minimal, it received support from the Canadian public as well as from opposition-party leaders Brian Mulroney and Ed Broadbent.

Mulroney and Canadian–American Issues

Pierre Trudeau's defence alliance with the United States was reluctant, and personal relations between Trudeau and Reagan were chilly. But when the new Progressive Conservative leader, Brian Mulroney, swept into office not long after Trudeau retired, Canada–U.S. relations warmed. Though he also came from Québec and also was a lawyer, Mulroney's background was different from that of Trudeau. He had been an executive for an American iron ore company and was sympathetic to business interests. His first order of business as prime minister was closer friendship with the United States. On September 24, 1984, he told an American journalist, "Good relations, super relations, with the United States will be the cornerstone of our foreign policy."

On Saint Patrick's Day, 1985, President Reagan flew to Québec City for talks with Prime Minister Mulroney. Both leaders were of Irish descent, and they ended their first day at a gala concert by singing "When Irish Eyes Are Smiling." Their talks were quickly nicknamed the "Shamrock Summit." They announced a number of agreements, includ-

America strong again" by rebuilding U.S. military power. The Reagan government pressed Canada to take a more active defence role because Americans felt that Canadians were taking a "free ride" on the American defence system. Reagan wanted to test Cruise missiles in the Canadian North. Since North American defence was linked to NATO, Canada's NATO allies also supported Cruise missile testing.

When news of the proposed tests became public, Canadians raised a storm of protest. "Refuse the Cruise" signs sprang up all across the nation. Despite the massive anti-nuclear protest and his personal dislike of nuclear arms, Trudeau felt that his government could not say no. In explaining the government's decision he said that as a good NATO ally, Canada had to do its part to strengthen NATO defence. In 1983 Canada and the United States signed a five-year agreement that allowed the United States to make up to six tests a year of unarmed Cruise missiles in Canadian air space. The first Cruise missile test took place at the Primrose Lake test range, near Cold Lake, Alberta, in March 1984.

In the late 1970s the testing of Cruise missiles in Canadian air space became a controversial issue. Many Canadians joined in demonstrations because they were determined to keep Cruise missiles out of Canada.

ing new defence arrangements and more joint ventures in space like the very successful Canadarm for the American space-shuttle program.

Although Mulroney believed that friendship with the United States produced direct benefits for Canada, he did not always follow the American lead. He did not, for example, accept Reagan's invitation to take part in the Strategic Defence Initiative (SDI), or "Star Wars," but he left the door open for Canadian companies to accept SDI defence contracts.

After the Cold War

In the last years of Brian Mulroney's period in office, the Cold War came to an end. Dramatic changes in Eastern Europe had brought a sense of hope to a world desperately weary of the Cold War. But it was not long before new conflicts shattered such dreams. In 1990 a war broke out in the Persian Gulf after Iraq invaded Kuwait, whose rich oil fields were important to the West. The United Nations condemned the invasion and sent in a force that succeeding in driving back the Iraqis.

Crisis in the Balkans

Another major crisis area was the Balkans, where Yugoslavia collapsed into violent ethnic warfare. After the death of Yugoslav leader Joseph Tito, no strong leader emerged to take his place. Economic and financial problems created difficulties for his successors, who exploited national and ethnic differences to gain power. In 1991, two of Yugoslavia's six republics — Slovenia and Croatia — declared their independence and were quickly recognized as autonomous states by the United Nations.

Next to declare its independence was Bosnia, where 40 percent of the population was Muslim. The Bosnian declaration of independence prompted a furious response from the region's Serb minority, and in 1992 Bosnia emerged as the main theatre of war. After three years of intense fighting the warring factions agreed to accept the Dayton Accords, which were negotiated with the aid of American diplomats. Under the Dayton Accords, Bosnia was split into a Muslim–Croat region and a Serb republic, and a single central government was

Prime Minister Brian Mulroney developed a close friendship with U.S. President Ronald Reagan. What potential benefits and dangers could result from close ties between the Canadian and American governments?

Innovations such as the Canadarm showcase the talent of Canadian scientists. Can you think of other examples that have shown Canada to be a world leader in technological developments?

established in Sarajevo. Despite the settlement, only the presence of a U.N. peacekeeping force (including a Canadian contingent) prevented a resurgence of violence.

Jean Chrétien Becomes Prime Minister

By the time the Dayton Accords had been signed, Brian Mulroney was no longer in office. He resigned in 1993 and was succeeded briefly by Kim Campbell. After an election in September in which Campbell's Conservatives were defeated, the Liberals formed a new government under the leadership of Jean Chrétien. The Chrétien government consulted a wide range of groups and individual Canadians for their views on the shape of Canadian foreign policy. Peacekeeping, foreign aid, open markets, human rights, and an active Canadian role in international affairs emerged as priorities.

It soon became clear that the Liberal government's foreign policy was ruled by an economic agenda. Roy McLaren, minister of international trade, declared bluntly: "Foreign policy is trade policy." The prime minister led trade missions —

nicknamed "Team Canada" — to Asia and Latin America. In *Canada and the World*, a document that spelled out the foreign-policy objectives of the Liberal government, foreign aid was presented as a way to connect Canada to some of the world's fastest-growing markets.

The Chrétien government took a strong position on land mines. For decades, land mines have maimed and killed civilians long after wars have ended. After much international lobbying and debate, a Land Mines Treaty was adopted by most nations in 1998. This treaty not only banned the future use of land mines but also committed countries to a timetable for removing land mines left over from past conflicts. Foreign Affairs Minister Lloyd Axworthy succeeded in establishing a deadline for participating nations to ratify the treaty.

Balancing National Interests and Global Concerns

The belief that a nation's actions inside its own borders are of no concern to the rest of the world is no longer valid. Most governments have come to realize that international agreements are essential, especially those concerning the environment: pollution knows no borders. Over the past few decades Canada has participated in drafting a number of global agreements.

Canadian Sovereignty in the Arctic: The Polar Sea Affair

In 1985 environmental issues once again stirred up trouble between the United States and Canada. The U.S. Coast Guard ship *Polar Sea* planned to sail from Greenland to Alaska. As a courtesy, the U.S. Coast Guard had told Canadian officials about its plans, but the Americans did not feel they needed Canada's permission to make the voyage. Americans viewed the Northwest Passage through the Arctic as an international waterway. On the other hand, the Canadian government claimed that the Northwest Passage belonged to Canada and that foreign ships needed permission to sail through Canadian waters.

The U.S. Coast Guard Ship *Polar Sea* planned to sail through the Northwest Passage without asking Canada for permission. Why would Canada consider this an unfriendly act?

News of the *Polar Sea* voyage prompted an unexpected public outcry in Canada. Opposition leader Jean Chrétien accused Prime Minister Mulroney of selling out Canadian interests. Mulroney's first action was to give the U.S. Coast Guard permission for the *Polar Sea* voyage, even though it had not asked for permission. Then he warned the Americans that failing to recognize the Arctic as Canadian territory was "an unfriendly act." He declared: "It is ours. We assert sovereignty over it." In addition to making strong public statements, his government also began talks with the United States on the Arctic. These talks resulted in the Agreement on Arctic Co-operation in 1988. The United States agreed to get prior permission every time a U.S. government-owned or -operated ship wanted to sail in the Arctic.

Working Toward Global Solutions to Global Problems

By the mid-1960s Canadians were beginning to realize the state of the environment was an issue that transcended national boundaries and that international agreements would be necessary for environmental improvements. Canadians became more aware of polluted air and water, the destruction of forests and farmlands, and threats to wildlife. Not only were cars and factories emitting poisonous gases into the air, but the Great Lakes were dying: fish and other marine life could not survive in their badly polluted waters. In northern Ontario, pulp mills poisoned the English–Wabegoon River system, making it impossible for Ojibwa fishers and tourist operators to make a living. Even in the Arctic, massive doses of mercury and other contaminants were found in whales, seals, and polar bears, threatening the health of the animals and of the Inuit who hunted them for meat.

Acid Rain: Canada–U.S. Negotiations

Until the 1990s Canadian lakes and forests were being poisoned by **acid rain**, a deadly shower of sulphuric and nitrous oxides produced by industries and automobiles across North America. Winds often carried the pollutants hundreds of kilometres from their source before they fell to earth in dust, rain, or snow. Because of wind patterns, more than half the acid rain in Canada came from the United States — much of it from the steel mills of Pennsylvania and Ohio. But acid rain was not just a Canadian problem; Canadian polluters also contributed.

Canada needed the United States' help to solve the acid rain problem. Prime Minister Mulroney had told President Reagan at their first meeting in 1984 that acid rain was his "number one priority." However, the Reagan government strongly resisted efforts to promote U.S. action on acid rain. Although Canadian environmental lobbyists and the Canadian government continued to urge the United States to take action, not until George Bush became President did the U.S. government decide to act. In 1990 the U.S. Congress passed a new law to control acid rain. In March 1991 President Bush conceded that pressure from Mulroney had played a key role in the passage of the law.

Environmental Action

As awareness of environmental problems grew, so did the desire to take action. Dozens of environmental groups formed from coast to coast, including the Vancouver-born Greenpeace, the Society for Pollution and Environmental Control, and Pollution Probe. These environmental activists were successful in capturing public attention, and in the 1970s governments began taking steps to clean up

PHOTO ESSAY

SYMBOLS OF CANADA

...AND OFTEN THE BEAVER WILL USE ITS BROAD, FLAT TAIL TO THUMP OUT ALARM SIGNALS...

ACID RAIN

U.S.A. CANADA

Acid rain, which is killing Canadian lakes and forests, is a problem that must be jointly addressed by Canadians and Americans. Why can Canada not solve the problem without the co-operation of the United States?

the environment. In 1971 the federal government established the Department of the Environment, and most provincial governments set up similar ministries. They set emission standards for clean air and water, and industries were forced to reduce their harmful emissions. Those who failed to comply could be taken to court and fined. Efforts were also made to control the use and disposal of poisonous chemicals and to clean up polluted rivers, lakes, and landfill sites. Parks were created to preserve fragile ecosystems. In Ontario an Environmental Bill of Rights was passed in 1994. This Act gave individual citizens the right to force the government to inquire into the activities of suspected polluters.

Web Connections

http://www.school.mcgrawhill.ca/resources

Go to the Web site above to find out more about Greenpeace Canada. Go to *History Resources*, then to *Canada: A Nation Unfolding, Ontario Edition* to find out where to go next.

International Action

Dealing with the many forms of environmental pollution required co-operation between nations. Along with other nations, Canada took part in a variety of world environmental conferences and agreements, including the:

- 1972 United Nations Conference on Human Environment in Stockholm, Sweden, which prepared a declaration of environmental rights and a list of suggestions for environmental protection
- 1987 Montréal Protocol, signed by 163 countries, which placed restrictions on the use of CFCs (chlorofluorocarbons, used in air conditioners and refrigerators) and set a schedule for the eventual phasing out of the use of CFCs and other chemicals that destroy the ozone layer
- 1992 Rio Summit in Brazil, which developed international agreements to protect the global environment
- 1997 Kyoto Protocol, which set a target of a 5 percent reduction in world air pollution by 2012

Another area of increasing concern is genetically modified foods. Delegates at a United Nations–sponsored meeting in Montreal in January 2000 negotiated the United Nations Biosafety Protocol to regulate the trade in genetically altered foods. Under the agreement, nations retain the right to block the import of genetically modified foods if there is scientific evidence of a risk to consumers' health or the environment.

Thinking Globally, Acting Locally

In the 1980s many Canadians reconsidered their own lifestyles and became "green activists." They began composting garbage and recycling cans, bottles, and paper. Many stopped buying products manufactured by known polluters, started using unleaded gasoline, and bought pesticide-free fruits and vegetables. They continued to press governments at all levels to take stronger stands on important environmental issues. As a result, governments began to respond. For example, CFCs and leaded gasoline were banned, and curbside "blue box" recycling programs were started in many communities.

Despite these measures, cleaning up the environment has not been easily accomplished, either in Canada or elsewhere in the world. Clearly, much work remains to be done.

chapter review

CHAPTER SUMMARY

In this chapter we have seen

- how new technologies are creating new challenges in an interconnected world

- many ways in which Canada has provided assistance to countries around the world

- how the thawing of the Cold War has led to dramatic changes in many parts of the world

- the central goals of Canadian foreign policy

UNDERSTANDING HISTORICAL FACTS

1. Identify these people, places, and events, and explain their significance.

Marshall McLuhan	Pierre Trudeau
La Francophonie	CIDA
"Shamrock Summit"	Polar Sea Affair
Department of the Environment	

2. Create a web that illustrates how Canada is a part of the "global village."

3. Tensions during the Cold War rose and subsided several times. Create a line graph that illustrates the swings in the Cold War. Label each of the events that led to peaks and valleys in international tensions.

4. Recreate the following chart in your notes. Complete the chart by selecting four ways in which Canada has provided assistance to other countries.

EXPRESSING YOUR OPINION

1. Three goals central to Canadian foreign policy are fostering economic growth, protecting Canadian sovereignty, and promoting international peace and security. If you were Canada's foreign-affairs minister, how would you prioritize these goals? Describe one strategy you would pursue to support each of the foreign-policy goals.

2. Create a chart in your notes that lists the benefits and dangers of closer ties between Canada and the United States. After you complete the chart, explain why, if you were Canada's Prime Minister, you would or would not favour developing closer ties with the United States.

3. As the world becomes more connected through environmental concerns and the globalization of the economy, international summits leading to multinational agreements become increasingly common. Do you feel a world government with real authority will some day become a reality? Write a 250-word editorial or prepare a political cartoon that reflects the benefits or dangers of a world government.

WORKING WITH THE EVIDENCE

1. Imagine that you are given the challenge of designing a symbol for use at international events that captures the essence of Canada in the twenty-first century. What would your symbol look like? You can either describe or draw the symbol.

2. In the 1988 election more Canadians voted against the Free Trade Agreement with the United States than for it. Despite this, Brian Mulroney and the Progressive Conservative Party could legitimately claim to have the majority they needed to pass the agreement in Parliament. How could this be so?

NAME OF PROGRAM/ ORGANIZATION	DESCRIPTION OF THE TYPE OF ASSISTANCE PROVIDED	AREAS OF THE WORLD RECEIVING ASSISTANCE
Ginpure Tut Rudoyunonie 4 two two	*Ginpure Tut Rudoyunonie 4 two two*	*Ginpure Tut Rudoyunonie 4 two two*
Ginpure Tut Rudoyunonie 4 two two	*Ginpure Tut Rudoyunonie 4 two two*	*Ginpure Tut Rudoyunonie 4 two two*

23 The Canadian Economy, 1968–2000

One of the dominant events in Canada's contemporary economic history was the North American Free Trade Agreement (shown being signed here) that created a trading bloc including Canada, the United States, and Mexico. Why do you think some Canadians supported the agreement, while other Canadians objected to it?

INQUIRING INTO THE PAST

- **What are the drawbacks and benefits of foreign investment in Canada?**
- **Why did efforts to control the price of gas and oil in Canada please some regions and anger others?**
- **What benefits have resulted from free-trade agreements? What drawbacks have accompanied free trade?**
- **How should the Canadian government use its budget surpluses to benefit Canadians?**

KEY TERMS

GATT

National Debt

"Nixon Shock"

Stagflation

TIMELINE

1971 ▶
Foreign Investment Review Agency is created to monitor takeovers of Canadian companies

1980 ▶
National Energy Program is created to regulate the price and supply of oil and gas in Canada

1992 ▶
North American Free Trade Agreement creates a trading bloc including Canada, the United States, and Mexico

2000 ▶
Finance Minister Paul Martin unveils budget with first federal tax cuts for Canadians in decades

Whereas Canadians in 1900 were mainly involved in primary industries (such as farming, mining, and forestry) and secondary industries (manufacturing), today they are increasingly employed in the service industry. Today's workforce is also dramatically different from that of a century ago. Women are far more active in a wide range of paid employment, and the education level of the Canadian workforce has risen dramatically.

Other changes, both in the nation and in the world, have significantly affected the Canadian economy. The development of computers and satellite technology coincided with other changes in the world economy. A freer international financial system took shape after World War II. Large multinational companies, based in the United States and in Europe, expanded into other parts of the globe. They succeeded in globalizing the production of goods, investments, and services throughout the world. National borders became almost meaningless. By the 1990s many multinational companies had more power than many nation-states.

The Challenges of the 1970s

The buoyant economy of the 1960s became turbulent in the 1970s. A variety of national and international crises put serious strains on the Canadian economy, resulting in high unemployment, rising prices, and, by the end of the decade, interest rates of nearly 20 percent. The election of a separatist government in Québec in 1976 frightened foreign investors, leading to a significant decline in the value of the Canadian dollar from nearly on par with the U.S. dollar to about $0.70 (U.S.).

The OPEC Oil Crisis

The interconnectedness of global economies became very apparent in the fall of 1973. During the Arab–Israeli War of October 1973 many Western countries, including Canada and the United States, supported Israel. Following the war the oil cartel known as the Organization of Petroleum Exporting

Countries (OPEC) retaliated by placing an embargo on oil shipments to all countries that had supported Israel. Two months later OPEC decided to drastically increase the price of oil, from $4 to $16 a barrel. The effect of quadrupling oil prices on the Canadian economy was dramatic.

For Eastern and Central Canada, which relied heavily on oil and gas to heat homes and fuel industries, the rise in oil prices meant higher prices for many goods. Factories increased prices to offset higher costs, and consumers paid higher prices to heat their homes and drive their cars. One of the spinoffs of the rise in gas prices was a shift away from the large "gas guzzlers" typical of the early 1970s to smaller, more fuel-efficient cars. OPEC's actions had quite different effects on the oil-rich Prairie provinces of Alberta and Saskatchewan. Alberta, especially, rejoiced at the higher prices for gas and oil. This was the beginning of great prosperity for the West.

The National Energy Program

After Canada had endured several years of volatile oil prices and uncertain supply from abroad, the Canadian government decided to protect Canadians from the whims of the global economy. It created the National Energy Program (NEP) in 1980 to ensure Canada's future oil supply, control oil prices, and achieve 50 percent Canadian ownership of the oil industry by 1990. The NEP gave Canadian oil and gas companies special grants and special terms for northern exploration. Plans were made to build pipelines to bring Western crude oil to the East. It also gave the federal government a bigger share of oil and gas revenues. American oil companies were shocked and angry, but oil producers in Alberta and Saskatchewan were also outraged as the NEP established a fixed, made-in-Canada price for oil. Westerners viewed the NEP as a clear example of Central Canada's domination over the other regions, and they bitterly fought against it. Outside the West, however, Canadianizing the petroleum industry was very popular.

Petro-Canada was established in the 1970s by the Liberal government of Pierre Trudeau. It was intended to ensure a strong Canadian presence in the oil and gas industry. Should the government be involved in efforts to ensure Canadian ownership of essential resources?

The Big Squeeze: Stagflation

In the 1970s the huge increase in oil prices and the decline in the value of the Canadian dollar were among several factors that contributed to stubbornly high inflation throughout much of the decade. High inflation was coupled with high rates of unemployment, leading to an economic condition referred to as **stagflation**. An economy battling recession, high unemployment, rising interest rates, and high inflation is difficult to stimulate. Canadians would have to look for innovative solutions to turn around the economy.

American Participation in the Canadian Economy

Many Canadians welcomed the flow of American money into Canada in the 1950s. But by 1967, 81 percent of the $34.7 billion worth of foreign investment in Canada was from American sources. Public opinion shifted: a 1967 poll showed that two thirds of Canadians wanted their government to control American investment in Canada. Several government reports, including the Watkins Report of 1968 and the Grey Report of 1971, raised concerns about the extent of the foreign ownership of Canadian firms.

The Foreign Investment Review Agency and Investment Canada

In 1971 the Trudeau government created the Foreign Investment Review Agency (FIRA) to ensure that any foreign investment in or takeover of Canadian companies resulted in important benefits for Canada, such as job creation or increased exports. The FIRA could block any foreign investment that was not in the best interests of Canada, especially in cultural industries such as magazines and newspapers. But the

American participation in the Canadian economy can be seen almost everywhere. Could the Canadian economy survive without American participation?

FIRA had little effect on the flow of foreign investment. Americans owned about 25 percent of all shares of Canadian corporations (except financial institutions) when the FIRA was set up. Ten years later they owned the same proportion. By 1982 the FIRA was approving nine out of ten applications for foreign takeovers of Canadian companies.

The FIRA was scrapped by the Mulroney government in 1984 and replaced by Investment Canada. Investment Canada's role was more limited; it reviewed takeovers of Canadian companies only if a company's selling price exceeded $5 million. Investment Canada kept the power to review all takeovers in cultural industries, but its main goal was to welcome American investment. During his first major speech in the United States, Prime Minister Brian Mulroney told the Economic Club in New York that "Canada is open for business again."

Securing Markets for Canadian Products

Making investments in Canada was not the only way in which the United States played a major role in the Canadian economy. Seventy percent of all Canada's exports went to the United States. Canada was also the biggest customer for American goods. Any change in American economic policy sent major shock waves through the Canadian economy. In a famous comment, Pierre Trudeau described Canada's uncomfortable dependence on the U.S. economy: "Living next to you is in some ways like sleeping with an elephant: no matter how friendly and even-tempered the beast, one is affected by every twitch and grunt."

Just a few months after Trudeau's comment, the elephant twitched and Canadian businesspeople trembled. In 1971 U.S. President Richard Nixon ordered a 10 percent tariff on goods imported into the United States. This came to be known as the **Nixon shock**. As a result, Canadian-made goods cost more in the United States, and Canadian businesses faced the prospect of losing $300 million in exports. Although worldwide pressure forced the United States to cancel the 10 percent tariff a few months later, Canadians were shocked to discover how economically dependent they were on the United States and how badly they could be hurt by changes in American economic policy.

The Third Option

After the "Nixon shock," Canada had three choices: it could maintain its present relationship with the United States, move toward even closer relations, or try to create a more independent Canadian economy. Trudeau's government chose the third option. Canada began to look for new trading partners around the world as a way of lessening its dependence on the United States.

During the 1970s, Canada tried to forge new trade links in Europe, Asia, and Africa, but by the mid-1980s it looked as if the only important market willing to take Canadian goods was the United States. The United States, however, was thinking about creating its own trade barriers to keep out goods from other nations.

Ottawa began to worry that Canada would be locked out of global markets, including the American market. Trudeau seriously considered developing closer trade ties with the United States. In September 1985 the Royal Commission on the Economic Union and Development Prospects for Canada called for a "leap of faith" into free trade with the United States. By this time Prime Minister Trudeau had retired, and it would be up to Brian Mulroney and the Progressive Conservatives to steer Canada into free trade.

Making the "Leap of Faith" into Free Trade

Once he was in office, Prime Minister Mulroney proposed a full-fledged free-trade deal between Canada and the United States. Because of **GATT** (General Agreement on Tariffs and Trade) negotiations since World War II, about 80 percent of the tariff barriers that had existed between the United States and Canada in 1935 had been removed. The Free Trade Agreement (FTA) gave Canada and the United States open access to each other's markets for most goods, and committed the two countries to dropping cross-border tariffs by the end of 1998. It also dealt with other trade concerns, including energy, the movement of people for business purposes, investment, and financial services. Free trade became the issue of

the arts

THE CHORAL MUSIC OF R. MURRAY SHAFER

Murray Schafer (born in Sarnia, Ontario in 1933) is one of the few Canadian choral composers to enjoy a truly international reputation. Schafer regards the human voice as the most flexible of instruments, able to produce an amazing variety of sounds that he calls *choric textures*. As a result, Schafer decided that the sounds he wanted to hear could not be specified with traditional music notation. He describes his choric textures, many of which look more like visual art than music, with terms such as chaos, combustion, confusion, cloud, block, slab, wedge, and contour.

Schafer has taught in universities in Newfoundland and British Columbia and has authored a number of books on his views regarding music and sound in general. He has won national and international awards not only for his compositions, but also for his work in education and visual arts.

"Miniwaka or the moments of water," which was composed by Schafer, is a choral piece that describes the various states of water. The text consists of words for water, rain, stream, river, fog, and ocean in the languages of the Dakota, Wappo, Crow, Chinook, Achumawi, Otchipwe, Salish, Natick, Klamath and Luiseno Aboriginal Peoples. The piece depicts the transformation of water from rain, to streams, to quiet lakes, to broad rivers, to the ocean.

This excerpt from "Miniwanka" is Schafer's musical depiction of a waterfall. Can you tell from looking at Schafer's graphic musical score how the music will sound?

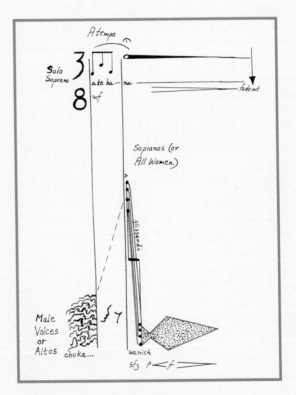

© European American Music Corp.

"DUTCH" DOOR POLICY

FREE TRADE

TO CANADA

STEEL SALES

DAIRY

TO U.S.A.   KEEP OUT!

SALES   U.S. SALES   PATENT DRUGS   CULTURE

Carefully examine this cartoon. What impact is the cartoon suggesting the Free Trade Agreement would have on Canada? Is there any evidence so far to suggest that these fears are justified?

the 1988 federal election, just as it had been in the 1911 election. Arguments for and against free trade raged across the country. In the election the Progressive Conservatives won a majority government, and the FTA became law on January 1, 1989.

From FTA to NAFTA

Shortly after the FTA came into effect, Mexico wanted to become a close trading partner of Canada and the United States. In 1992, after another round of trade talks, the leaders of Mexico, the United States, and Canada signed the North American Free Trade Agreement (NAFTA), which included Mexico in the free-trade region created by the FTA. It created a large free-trade bloc linking 370 million people in three countries, with 31 percent of the world's wealth, into a single trade region. Again Canadian public opinion became polarized over free trade. Opponents of the deal claimed that the United States would be the main winner, because American employers would take advantage of cheap Mexican labour and Canadian raw materials. Despite opposition, however, NAFTA came into effect in 1993.

Evaluating the Leap of Faith

What was the outcome of free trade, ten years later? Was the "leap of faith" justified? The results were uncertain. Statistics from 1998 showed an increase in Canadian exports to the United States. The greatest increase in exports was from Ontario, followed by Québec and Alberta. It should be noted, however, that the surge in exports was also due to a low Canadian dollar. Except in Ontario and Québec, where automotive parts were the major export, the exports continued to be from the resource sector. In other words, a longstanding pattern in Canadian economic history remained the same. There was an increase in north–south trade for all regions, integrating the Canadian economy more closely into that of the United States. Only Prince Edward Island exported more to the rest of Canada than it did abroad. Manufacturing increased, though not as much as the FTA's supporters expected. Nor was it clear that the NAFTA led to an increase in the number of jobs; wages had not risen as a result of the agreement.

NAFTA may also limit a country's power to protect its environment. A controversial provision in the agreement allows a company to sue if it loses

CANADA

U.I.C./CUTS PLANT CLOSURES
CHILDCARE HEALTHCARE
SOCIAL PROGRAMS JOB LOSS

NAFTA

Many Canadians were worried that NAFTA would not only lead to job losses but that it would put Canada's social programs in jeopardy. Why would they think this?

METHODS OF HISTORICAL INQUIRY

UNDERSTANDING HISTORICAL VIEWPOINTS

History is the study of change over time. It is as much the creation of the historian who writes it as it is a recounting of historical facts. Two historians writing about the same event or about the same historical period often arrive at different conclusions. This can result from different interpretations of the same historical documents or from the selection of different documents. Historians' viewpoints are the product of several influences. They may view history from a particular perspective, such as that of social history, political history, or economic history. Their views may also be shaped by their personal experiences. Someone who was raised and educated in southern Ontario may write history with an Ontario bias. Many Québec historians view Canadian historical events very differently from their English counterparts.

Until recently, much of Canada's history was written from a political or economic perspective and often with a Central Canadian bias. Since the 1970s the historical viewpoints of Canadian historians have greatly expanded. In today's universities students can study women's history, labour history, Aboriginal history, Black Canadian history, immigrant history, and many other fields of history. As a result, the study of Canadian history has been greatly enriched. With more viewpoints being represented, the story of more Canadians is being told.

When reading historical accounts, students must be aware that historians interpret the past. The documents historians select reveals a bias, as does the emphasis they place on historical events. When carrying out historical research, it is important to read more than one source to understand the different historical viewpoints. When writing history, be careful to scrutinize your sources, whether they are primary or secondary accounts. In the end you must reconstruct the past on the basis of the evidence you have found and the interpretation of the evidence that makes sense to you.

ACTIVITY

Consider how two historians' views of the impact of free trade might differ if they approached the study of the past from two different perspectives. Select the perspectives from the web below.

Environmental Perspective

Labour Perspective

Impact of Free Trade on Canada

Business Perspective

The Arts Perspective

Robotic technology has dramatically changed the way automobiles are produced in Canada. What are the benefits of robotic manufacturing? What are the disadvantages?

business because of environmental legislation. When the Canadian government banned the use of MMT, a gasoline additive, the Ethyl Corporation of Virginia sued for damages. Rather than proceed with the lawsuit, Ottawa paid the company $19 million and agreed to withdraw the ban on MMT. This action raised the possibility that a country might not be able to pass laws relating to environmental and health issues.

An Economy Transformed by Technology

Canada's economy has undergone significant transformations in the past one hundred years. A visitor travelling across Canada in 1900 would have noticed that most Canadians earned their living harvesting the country's bounty, whether from the sea, the forest, or the fields. Only a few major centres in southern Ontario and Québec had any significant manufacturing activity. By the 1950s, however, manufacturing had come to play a significant role in the Canadian economy. Today only about one quarter of employed Canadians earn their living from either primary or secondary indus-

tries. Astonishingly, nearly three quarters of Canadians are now employed in service industries, such as communications, sales, and health and education services. The creation of a post-industrial economy owed a great deal to the technology developed in the decades following World War II. Computers, fibre optics, and genetic engineering were among the many technologies that became available by the 1960s. All had tremendous potential for changing people's lives, work, and leisure activities. Key among them was the computer. Combined with space satellites orbiting the earth, computers could process and transmit vast amounts of information instantly.

New technologies made some workers more productive and eliminated some other workers' jobs. Farms, mines, the forestry industries, and factories were able to operate with fewer employees. Robotics at plants such as the Honda car factory in Alliston, Ontario, allowed fewer workers to produce more high-quality products at competitive prices. Industries such as banking replaced many workers with computers known as automatic teller machines (ATMs). Bell Canada laid off hundreds of operators when it automated its long-distance services, and e-commerce has allowed retailers to sell goods with fewer employees.

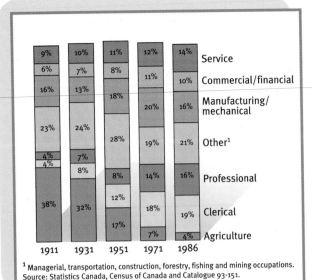

	1911	1931	1951	1971	1986	
Service	9%	10%	11%	12%	14%	
Commercial/financial	6%	7%	8%	11%	10%	
Manufacturing/mechanical	16%	13%	18%	20%	16%	
Other[1]	23%	24%	28%	19%	21%	
Professional	4% / 4%	7% / 8%	8%	14%	16%	
Clerical	38%	32%	12%	18%	19%	
Agriculture			17%	7%	4%	

[1] Managerial, transportation, construction, forestry, fishing and mining occupations.
Source: Statistics Canada, Census of Canada and Catalogue 93-151.

What does this chart tell about the changes in Canada's work force since 1911?

The impact of the computer age on Canada's economy has been profound. Whether those changes are seen as positive or negative often depends on individual circumstance. Not only have restructuring and downsizing resulted in job losses for many workers, but the increasing number of consumer goods are not always available to those with lower incomes. The gap between rich and poor has widened. On the other hand, some people welcome the freedom the computer age has brought to the job market: the revolutions in computers and telecommunications allow them to work from home while being connected to the office by a modem.

The Canadian Economy in the Year 2000

Will Canada thrive in the global economy of the twenty-first century? It seems to be poised to enjoy great prosperity in the decade ahead. The 1990s were unquestionably years of challenge and change. By the end of the decade nearly every province in Canada had balanced budgets and the federal government was predicting a $95 billion surplus over a five-year period. Here is a quick look at the economies of the regions of Canada at the dawn of the twenty-first century.

The Atlantic Provinces

Traditionally the Maritime economy has been heavily reliant on primary industries, including coal mining in Cape Breton, forestry in New Brunswick, farming in Prince Edward Island, and fishing throughout. During the 1990s global and environmental factors shook the foundations of the East Coast while recent discoveries and new technologies breathed life into a sluggish economy.

In 1992 the collapse of the cod fishery as a result of overfishing placed the livelihood of thousands of Newfoundland and Labrador families in jeopardy. All across the province, families moved away from their fishing villages in search of employment. Yet, despite this apparent blow to the economy, Newfoundland and Labrador rebounded with the fastest-growing provincial economy in 1999. The future holds much promise for this province: the Hibernia oil field created thousands of jobs and provided a large influx of revenue to the provincial government. Also, once it is developed, Voisey's Bay in Labrador may become a major producer of nickel.

The other Atlantic provinces were also hurt by the collapse of the fisheries and saw their

Located in eighty metres of water, 315 kilometres east southeast of St. John's, Newfoundland, the Hibernia oil field is a massive structure built upon a submarine oil field. A huge employer, Hibernia also brings a boost to Newfoundland's economy by accounting for about 12 percent of Canada's total oil production.

economies boosted by new developments. All across the Maritimes, the traditional economy based on the bounty from the sea was supplemented by new industries, especially service industries such as tourism. The construction of the Confederation Bridge created a fixed link between Prince Edward Island and mainland Canada, allowed for a more efficient flow of goods to and from the island, and increased tourism. New Brunswick was very successful at luring several companies to the provinces by offering low corporate taxes. Companies such as Federal Express found it quite advantageous to move their call-centres to New Brunswick from Ontario.

Central Canada

Ontario and Québec have long been considered the economic engine of Canada. The heaviest concentrations of population, industries, and wealth are clustered in and around Toronto and Montréal. The uncertainty created by the rise of the separatist movement in Québec led to a mass exodus of corporate head offices from Montréal to Toronto in

Despite Ontario's growing economy, many sectors of the province's workforce, such as education and health care, received funding cuts. Over a two-year period, labourers participated in "Days of Action" strikes against the Harris government to protest against the cuts.

the 1980s. This limited the economic growth of Québec over the past few decades. Ontario, however, entered the twenty-first century on an economic boom led by the service sector and high-technology industries. Ottawa clearly reflected this trend. No longer was the federal government the largest employer in the city. The largest source of jobs in Ottawa in the year 2000 was the high-tech industry.

Despite the boom in the Ontario economy, not everyone felt they were sharing in the new wealth. A study released in January 2000 revealed that despite a series of tax cuts implemented by the Ontario Progressive Conservative government under Premier Mike Harris, most Ontario families were earning less than they were a decade ago. Only the most wealthy seemed to be reaping the benefits of the robust economy. Often in times of economic prosperity there is little labour unrest. Yet Ontario saw more labour strife in the final few years of the 1990s than it had in the recessionary years of the 1980s. This had much to do with government employees, health-care workers, and educators feeling the effects of large reductions in spending. As well, many unionized workers believed that increased profits for industry should be reflected in their pay.

In the late 1990s the labour movement decided to take a stand against changes to labour laws and against what it considered massive cuts to the social fabric of the province. Over a two-year period a series of rotating one-day strikes attempted to paralyze cities across Ontario to send a message to the Harris government. Dubbed the "Days of Action," these protests attracted both large crowds of supporters and the wrath of many critics.

The Prairie Provinces

Blessed by an abundance of oil and natural gas, Alberta and Saskatchewan had a relatively secure source of income in the closing decades of the twentieth century. Yet beneath the apparent prosperity brought by the oil industry was a major threat to life on the Prairies: the death of the family farm. For many years prairie farmers struggled to earn a decent living from their land. Then, in the 1990s, the federal government began to reduce or

Life on the Prairies received an environmental blow during the 1997 Red River flood in Manitoba that drove 28,000 people from their homes. What other environmental disasters have hit Canada in the last few decades?

eliminate subsidies such as the Crowsnest freight rate, which subsidized the shipment of wheat. Many Western farmers felt they were being sacrificed so that urban Canadians could continue to enjoy low food costs.

Given the federal government's reluctance to provide assistance to aid in the survival of family farms on the Prairies, farmers were angered at its suggestion of providing support to NHL franchises. Industry Minister John Manly was forced to retract his proposals after he unveiled a plan to assist Canadian NHL teams. Hindered by a cold climate and a short growing season, farmers are now having

to contend with shrinking support from both the federal and provincial governments. Can the family farm survive and thrive in the new century?

British Columbia

In 1986 Vancouver hosted a party and invited the world. The party was Expo '86, the World's Fair. A consequence of the fair and the showcasing of British Columbia was a large influx of people from both within and outside Canada. Many visitors fell in love with Vancouver and the natural beauty of the province. Shortly after Expo '86, many Hong Kong families began to move to Vancouver or invest their money in the British Columbia economy. Fearing the consequences of Hong Kong being handed back to communist China in 1997, many wanted to find a safe haven for their assets. The infusion of people and money into the British Columbia economy created a huge economic boom. The prices of houses skyrocketed, thousands of jobs were created, and British Columbia, especially the Lower Mainland around Vancouver, enjoyed several years of prosperity.

Bordering on the Pacific Rim, British Columbia's economy was largely dependent on the economies of Japan, Korea, and other Asian countries. When some investors began to return their money to Hong Kong after realizing that the communist takeover would not threaten their assets, Vancouver's booming economy slowed considerably. Other areas of the province also encountered difficulties. The forestry industry was forced to battle with American interests opposed to Canada exporting softwood lumber, while salmon fishing, like cod fishing on the East Coast, was placed in jeopardy by overfishing. Despite the setbacks of the late 1990s, however, British Columbia remains one of Canada's wealthy provinces.

HOW FARMERS SHOULD DRESS WHEN SEEKING AID FROM OTTAWA..

While eliminating subsidies to Prairie farmers, the federal government voiced support for providing assistance to Canadian NHL teams. What point is this cartoon trying to make?

Web Connections

http://www.school.mcgrawhill.ca/resources

Go to the Web site above to find out statistics on Canada's economy, geography, demography, and more. Go to *History Resources*, then to *Canada: A Nation Unfolding, Ontario Edition* to find out where to go next.

Canada's Social Programs, 1968–2000

Canada's economic growth after 1963 gave the federal government more money to expand existing welfare programs and add new ones. The social safety net that had been sewn together bit by bit was more or less complete by the end of the Pearson years. The aid provided by the various social programs did not narrow the gap between the wealthy and poor Canadians, but it did protect Canadians from the insecurities of the modern industrial world.

When Pierre Trudeau campaigned in 1968 he put forth the idea of a *Just Society* — a society where individual rights, enshrined in a law, would be protected. There would also be protection for regions and social groups who had not shared in the material wealth enjoyed by others. Canadians were intrigued by Trudeau's image. Once he was in office, however, they saw a new side of Trudeau; he seemed arrogant and uncaring. Many people in the regions outside Central Canada, especially those in the West, felt that their problems were ignored by the Trudeau government. His popularity slipped badly over the next four years.

To prevent defeat in Parliament and win political support across the country, Trudeau committed his government to spending freely and passing popular legislation, including plans for increased unemployment insurance benefits, pensions, and family allowances. Schemes for rural and regional economic development were also heavily funded. By the end of the 1970s the federal government was spending half a billion dollars a year under its regional economic expansion program.

Safety Net versus National Debt

Unfortunately, the expected tax revenues necessary for these expenditures did not materialize. The government paid for these programs through borrowing. High interest rates meant that debt payments had increased. In 1978 the federal government debt was growing so quickly that the auditor general warned Canadians that the government "has lost or is close to losing effective control of the public purse." The business community was especially vocal in insisting on the need to cut back on government spending. Giving way to pressure from business, Trudeau argued that the only way to cut the huge federal deficit was to slash government spending.

But Canadians were unhappy about cutting funds for families, old-age pensioners, and the unemployed — especially in a time of high unemployment. Joe Clark's Progressive Conservative Party defeated the Trudeau Liberal government in 1979. In their first budget the Conservatives imposed a four-cent a litre gasoline tax. Proceeds from the tax would have gone to pay down the deficit, but the plan was wildly unpopular with Canadians. The opposition parties combined to defeat the budget and force an unexpected election in 1980. To the astonishment of many Canadians, Trudeau was returned to power.

Under Trudeau it became evident that a different approach to social welfare was taking form. Gone was the idea that people were entitled to help in times of difficulty. There was a greater emphasis on people taking responsibility for their own well-being.

Brian Mulroney's Conservative government came to power in 1984. Although it had promised to safeguard Canada's social safety net as a "sacred trust," it had also inherited a huge **national debt**. The Conservatives argued that because of the size of the national debt, Canada could not afford to pay well-off Canadians benefits such as family allowances and old-age pensions. In 1989 the Mulroney government "taxed back" some social welfare payments from wealthier recipients, and in 1992 it did away with family allowances and replaced them with an income supplement for

Having a budget surplus for the first time in decades, Liberal Finance Minister Paul Martin declared a national budget in February 2000 that injected money into the health-care system and social programs. Many critics said it was too little, too late.

working families. The principle of universality that had been the basis for social welfare programs was undermined; it looked to some observers as if Canada's social welfare system was being taken apart bit by bit.

The position of the following Liberal government under Jean Chrétien was made clear in its 1994 report, *Improving Social Security in Canada*. The report acknowledged that Canada's social welfare programs were a defining part of the Canadian identity and affirmed the duty "to give our children the best possible start in life" and enable all Canadians and their families "live with dignity."

At the same time the Chrétien government was committed to reducing the deficit. The Canada Assistance Plan was replaced with a reduced block payment to the provinces, who could spend it as they wished. As a result, there were cutbacks in many services. In medical care, provinces moved toward the privatization of services and user fees. The responsibility to care for sick and elderly people was increasingly shifted onto families.

Meanwhile the gap between rich and poor widened, and by the end of the decade the numbers of Canadian children living in poverty had increased. It is perhaps surprising that despite the changes in the social safety net, Canada still ranked the highest on the United Nations Human Development Index in 1999.

The Need for Balance

Canada left the twentieth century much like it had entered it: on a wave of prosperity and optimism. In 1900 a largely rural and agricultural country was on its way to becoming an urbanized and industrialized society. Today a similar transformation is occurring as Canada reinvents itself as a post-industrial economy. The ways in which Canadians earn their living may be rapidly changing, but the fundamental challenges of the twenty-first century are strikingly similar to those of the twentieth century. How does Canada ensure that the prosperity of the country is divided so as to provide all Canadians with the necessities of life? How will Canada prepare its youth to play a meaningful role in the new economy? And how can the seemingly insatiable demands of a consumer-driven economy be balanced with an increasingly endangered natural environment? Perhaps the most crucial difference in the new century will be the degree to which the answers to these questions must be considered in a global context.

chapter review

CHAPTER SUMMARY

In this chapter we have seen

- how international events such as OPEC's raising of oil prices can have a dramatic impact on Canada

- that Prime Ministers Trudeau and Mulroney held very different views on the dangers and benefits of American participation in the Canadian economy

- that Canadians were divided over the issue of the free-trade agreements with the United States and Mexico and remain divided over the effects of NAFTA

- how budgetary surpluses are leading to lower taxes in Canada and debates on how the surplus should be spent to benefit Canadians

UNDERSTANDING HISTORICAL FACTS

1. Identify these people, places, and events, and explain their significance.

OPEC	National Energy Program
FIRA	FTA/NAFTA
Investment Canada	Hibernia
Jean Chrétien	"Days of Action" strikes
Expo '86	Nixon shock

2. What evidence supports Pierre Trudeau's statement: "Living next door to you [United States] is in some ways like sleeping with an elephant: no matter how friendly and even tempered the beast, one is affected by every twitch and grunt."

3. Following the "Nixon shock," Canada considered three options for economic development. What were the three options, and which did Canada choose?

4. Using pictures, symbols, or diagrams, prepare an economic map of Canada that highlights the major sources of revenue for each of the nation's regions. Use labels if necessary for clarity.

5. Canada is recognized internationally for its social safety net, which helps provide Canadians with a high standard of living. Recreate the following chart in your notes, and for each of the prime ministers, write a brief description of how his government affected Canada's social safety net. (Did it help to expand, dismantle, or repair the social safety net?)

PIERRE TRUDEAU	BRIAN MULRONEY	JEAN CHRÉTIEN

EXPRESSING YOUR OPINION

1. After carefully considering the nature of the Canadian economy (what we produce, where we sell our products, and so on) weigh the benefits and dangers of Canadian free trade with the United States and Mexico. If a referendum on free trade were held, would you support the continuation of NAFTA or vote to remove Canada from the free-trade agreement? Explain your answer.

2. In the 1990s a debate emerged over whether governments should slash spending on social programs in order to reduce taxes or protect social programs. When provincial governments and the federal government began to have surplus budgets, the debate intensified. Should the surplus be used to pay down the debt, reduce taxes, or support social programs (such as health, education, and welfare)? As finance minister, how would you use a $10 billion surplus?

WORKING WITH THE EVIDENCE

1. A Canadian manufacturer received an order for ten thousand premium hockey skates from an American sporting-goods franchise before the 1988 free-trade deal came into effect. The existing tariff made exporting the skates unprofitable. How did the manufacturer legally ship the hockey skates to the United States without paying the tariff?

Canada: A Community of Communities

Some observers of Canadian politics believe that Canada is a fragile country that could break into cultural parts. Do you agree with this view?

INQUIRING INTO THE PAST

- How has Québec's separatist movement led to constitutional change and political strife over the past several decades?
- How have Canada's regions, women's groups, and Aboriginal peoples made their voices heard in constitutional reform?
- What were the primary objectives of the Reform Party? Why has Preston Manning created a new party to unite Progressive Conservatives and Reformers?
- How have changes to the Indian Act and land-claim negotiations begun to address the injustices suffered by Canada's Aboriginal peoples for many decades?

KEY TERMS

Referendum

Repatriate

War Measures Act

TIMELINE

1970 ▶
Pierre Trudeau invokes the War Measures Act in response to kidnappings by the Front de Libération du Québec

1982 ▶
Queen Elizabeth II signs the Canada Act, bringing Canada's constitution home

1992 ▶
Canadians reject constitutional reform in a country-wide referendum on the Charlottetown Accord

1999 ▶
The federal government introduces the Clarity Act, which requires a clear question for any future referendums on separation

The four colonies that came together in Confederation were all distinct societies, and disputes erupted regularly between Ottawa and the provinces over the years. As Canada expanded to ten provinces and now three territories, the grounds for conflict multiplied. Conflicts arose over how power was to be divided, over resources and how they were to be shared, and over language and religion. At times the nation seemed on the brink of breaking up.

The Three Prime Ministers from Québec

Since 1968 the prime ministership of Canada has been dominated by Quebeckers. Ironically, of the three prime ministers from Québec who have served since 1968, the two Liberal leaders, Pierre Trudeau and Jean Chrétien, were often accused of betraying their home province and enjoyed greater popularity outside Québec. When the Progressive Conservative Prime Minister from Québec, Brian Mulroney, failed to deliver the constitutional amendments he promised, several of his Québec members of Parliament abandoned the party and created a separatist federal political party called the Bloc Québécois. Whatever their successes or failures, these three men governed Canada through decades of tumultuous change. Each left his mark on the social and economic fabric of Canada.

Pierre Trudeau

Pierre Trudeau brought a flare and style to the Prime Minister's office that Canadians had never seen. He combined great intellect and wit with a social conscience. During his years in office (1968–79 and 1980–84), he helped to liberalize divorce laws, strengthen Canada's social programs, and expand Canada's role in the world. Throughout his tenure he was passionate in his defence of Canada; he considered regional divisions dangerous and opposed special treatment for Québec. Trudeau defended his beliefs by arguing that to grant Quebeckers special status within

Canada was to suggest that they were less able to protect their own interest than other Canadians were. To his critics he responded that as a proud Quebecker he believed he did require special treatment. Since leaving office in 1984, Trudeau has seldom spoken in public. However, when the Meech Lake Accord threatened to grant special status to Québec, his was one of the voices that rang out, not against Québec, but in favour of a united Canada in which all Canadians share the same protections.

Brian Mulroney

Brian Mulroney brought a very different style to Canadian politics; his government brought about a very businesslike attitude to government. During his nine years in office (1984–1993), Mulroney did not shy away from controversy. He attempted to tackle the huge national debt that Canada had amassed since the 1960s. When his government began to take away family allowances and old-age pensions from the wealthy, a heated debate was ignited: were social programs a right of all Canadians, or should they only be available to less well-off Canadians? Despite his efforts to deal with the yearly deficit, by the end of the Mulroney era Canada's deficit was nearly $40 billion and its national debt was approaching $600 billion. The Mulroney government also triggered passionate debates across Canada when it negotiated a free-trade deal with the United States, introduced the hated Goods and Services Tax (GST) to replace a hidden manufacturing tax, and made efforts to amend the Constitution to appease Québec. Despite his government winning back-to-back

Brian Mulroney became the most disliked prime minister in Canadian history. Why do you think this is so?

majorities in 1984 and 1988, when Mulroney left office his popularity among Canadians was the lowest of that of any Prime Minister in Canadian history. In the election that followed his resignation, his Progressive Conservative Party was reduced from a majority government to only two seats in Parliament.

Jean Chrétien

Jean Chrétien's political career stretches back to the 1960s. Throughout the Trudeau years he served as a Cabinet minister responsible for several portfolios, including justice and finance. Referring to himself as "the little guy from Shawinigan," Chrétien had the good fortune to become Prime Minister in 1993, as Canada was heading into an economic boom. The previous Progressive Conservative government had faced the brunt of the debate over issues such as free trade and the GST. Despite his vocal opposition to both these issues, once he was elected, Chrétien claimed the Liberal government could not reverse the policies. His finance minister, Paul Martin, engineered drastic cuts to government spending, many of which took the form of cuts in transfer payments to the provinces. These cuts and a booming economy allowed the Liberal government to erase Canada's deficit. By 1999 Canada enjoyed yearly surpluses projected to be $92 billion over five years. For the first time in decades, the debate in Canada shifted from where to slash spending to where to spend the surplus.

Once in power, Prime Minister Jean Chrétien decided not to reverse the Progressive Conservative's agreements on free trade and the GST. Why do you think he did this when he had opposed both of these issues before coming to power?

Federalism or Separatism? Protecting the Rights of Franco-Canadians

Too often the debate over the preservation of French Canadian culture in Canada has ignored the significant Franco-Canadian population outside of Québec. Many provinces, including New Brunswick, Ontario, Manitoba, and Alberta, have a large French-speaking population. Over the past 140 years almost each of these provinces has ruled against the French language at some point. For example, in New Brunswick in 1871 Catholic schools were closed and the teaching of French in public schools was outlawed, and in 1916 the teaching of French was forbidden at all levels. As recently as 1930, Saskatchewan barred the teaching of French even outside school hours. For over a century Franco-Canadians have struggled to ensure the protection of their culture.

The Federalist Answer for Québec: Bilingualism

To protect their culture and their position as one of the founding groups of Canada, Quebeckers began to demand equal treatment. Determined not to give Québec a special status, Prime Minister Pierre Trudeau's answer was official bilingualism: Canada was to become a nation with two official languages, English and French. Trudeau believed that Canada's future as a unified nation depended on bilingualism and on equal opportunities for Canadians who spoke either language.

In 1969 Trudeau's government passed the Official Languages Act, which gave all Canadians the legal right to deal with the federal government and the courts in either French or English, and the packaging of all products was required to be labelled in both French and English. Provinces also began to offer more French-language education, sometimes known as "French immersion programs." But in Québec the policy of bilingualism was not enough to settle the growing separatist feeling.

During the October Crisis of 1970, members of the Canadian armed forces could be seen on the streets of Montréal dressed in full battle fatigues. Why is this an unusual scene for Canada?

The Rise of Québec Separatism

The Quiet Revolution awakened a new kind of Québécois nationalism. No longer were the French Canadians of Québec willing to accept being treated as second-class citizens in their own province. By the late 1960s radical groups whose aim was to secure Québec's independence began to resort to terrorist acts to press their demands. Following a wave of bombings, terrorism in Québec reached its peak with the kidnappings of a prominent Québec politician and a British diplomat.

The October Crisis of 1970

On the morning of October 5, 1970, four men from the Front de Libération du Québec (FLQ) abducted the British trade commissioner, James Cross, at gunpoint from his Montréal home. The FLQ kidnappers demanded $500 000 in ransom money, transportation to Cuba in return for their hostage, and the release of what they called "political prisoners" — FLQ members jailed for terrorist bombings. They also demanded that the FLQ manifesto (declaration of beliefs) be read over national television networks. Five days later another FLQ group staged a second kidnapping. This time the kidnap-

pers seized Québec cabinet minister Pierre Laporte in front of his house.

At first many Quebeckers had some sympathy for the FLQ, but when Pierre Laporte's dead body was found in the trunk of a car on the St. Hubert air base on October 17, the mood in Québec shifted. Many people who had once sympathized with the FLQ were horrified by the violent murder.

After consultations with the federal government, Québec Premier Robert Bourassa agreed to broadcast the FLQ manifesto and give the kidnappers safe passage out of Canada in return for Cross's release. But Bourassa refused to release the FLQ terrorists who were in prison. As the crisis deepened, Bourassa turned to the federal government to request help in the massive search for James Cross. Prime Minister Trudeau sent in Canadian troops and, for the first time in peacetime, brought the **War Measures Act** into force, taking away the civil rights of Canadians. Membership in the FLQ became a criminal offence, and the government banned political rallies. The Act also allowed police to arrest, question, and detain suspects, without charging them, for up to ninety days.

Trudeau argued that invoking the War Measures Act was justified because the FLQ kidnappings were the beginning of a widespread conspiracy to overthrow the government. Police swept across Québec, conducted thousands of searches, and arrested more than four hundred people. Two months later the RCMP and the Québec police discovered that James Cross was being held hostage in a house in north Montréal. In return for his release, his captors and their families were allowed to go to Cuba. A total of twenty-three people were brought to trial and sentenced to prison for terrorist acts during the October Crisis.

Québec and the Language Question

The October Crisis put a stop to separatist terrorism, but other issues remained unresolved. One concerned language, particularly the role of the French language and culture in Canada. Protecting the French language in Québec was a growing concern for many Quebeckers. Before World War II the birth rate in Québec had been the highest in Canada, but in the 1960s it suddenly plunged, and by the end of the decade it was the lowest in Canada. In addition, immigration had skyrocketed in the post-war years and many newcomers had settled in Montréal. Most of these new immigrants chose to send their children to English-language schools because English was the language of North America.

Under the double impact of declining birth rates and increasing immigration, French-speakers began to fear for the survival of their language and culture in Québec. There were only six million French-speakers among 280 million English-speakers. Many feared that Trudeau's policy of official bilingualism was not enough to protect the French language. One solution was to make French the official language of Québec and to ensure that newcomers became part of the French-speaking community. To encourage this, the Official Languages Act, known as Bill 22, was passed in Québec in 1974. The Act made French the official language of Québec, brought in new measures to strengthen the use of French in the workplace, and sharply limited parents' right to choose the language in which their children would be educated. Only children who passed a test showing that they knew English were allowed to enrol in English-language schools. This meant that most children of recent immigrants had to attend French-language schools. Bill 22 sparked a bitter language battle, but the Québec government defended the law as necessary for the survival of the French language.

By 1976, however, the Bourassa government was faltering. The Québec Liberals had been damaged by rumours of scandal and corruption. Quebeckers were deeply troubled by Québec's economic woes, but the Bourassa government had no ready answers. Quebeckers began to look elsewhere for political leadership, especially to the newly formed Parti Québécois (P.Q.) and its leader, René Lévesque. The P.Q. was a non-violent separatist party dedicated to winning independence for the province through peaceful political means. Lévesque and the Parti Québécois seemed to be the best choice.

When Réné Lévesque came to power as the leader of the Parti Québécois, he told a cheering crowd: "Now we have to build this country of Québec!" What did he mean by this? Do you think his supporters wanted a change in government or independence from Canada?

The Parti Québécois and Bill 101

On November 15, 1976, English Canada woke up with a shock. The Parti Québécois had swept into power in Québec, winning 41 percent of the popular vote and 71 of the 110 seats in the Québec National Assembly. "Now we have to build this country of Québec," René Lévesque told a cheering crowd. The P.Q. had promised to win independence for Québec; its election seemed to spell the end of Confederation.

The P.Q. government passed a new and even stronger language law in 1977 to replace Bill 22. The Charter of the French Language, known as Bill 101, placed strong restrictions on the use of English in Québec. The French language was to be used by the government, the courts, and businesses in the

During the 1980 sovereignty-association referendum, "yes" and "no" sides divided the population of Québec. How would you have voted? Why?

Many Canadians outside Québec felt that Bill 101, which made French the only official language in Québec, violated the rights of non-francophones in the province. Do you think Bill 101 was necessary for the survival of French culture? What is this protester trying to say Bill 101 will do?

The Referendum on Sovereignty-Association

During the 1976 election campaign, René Lévesque had promised voters a **referendum** on independence. Four years later the P.Q. was ready to hold the long-promised referendum. Polls showed that only a minority of French Canadians wanted outright independence from Canada, so Lévesque proposed a vote on something less than full independence, called "sovereignty-association." Sovereignty-association meant that Québec would be a "sovereign," or independent, state. In particular, Québec would control its own taxes, its industrial and social policies, and its citizenship and immigration laws. But it would keep close economic ties with the rest of Canada.

May 20, 1980, was Referendum Day in Québec. Almost 90 percent of the province's eligible voters went to the polls. Almost 60 percent of them voted "no" to sovereignty-association. The referendum defeat was a major setback for the Parti Québécois.

The Constitutional Crisis

After his re-election in 1980, Pierre Trudeau began a process of "constitutional renewal." The key part of Canada's Constitution, the British North America (BNA) Act, had served Canada for more than a century. The BNA Act had remained under the jurisdiction of the British Parliament at the request of the Canadian government. Attempts had been made to **repatriate**, or bring home, the BNA Act, but they had all met with failure, partly because the provinces could not agree on an amending formula.

After the Québec referendum Trudeau was more determined than ever to see constitutional change. In particular, he wanted a formula under which any constitutional amendment could be approved if the federal government and a certain number of provincial governments agreed to it. He also wanted to add a written charter of rights and freedoms to the Constitution. In particular, he wanted a charter guarantee of the right of all Canadians to be educated in English or French. These were measures that Québec had opposed in the past.

province. Under Bill 101, commercial signs had to be in French only. The bill also drastically limited access to English schools. Most children whose families came from outside Québec were denied the right to education in English. Only children who had at least one parent who had gone to an English school in Québec (the "Québec Clause") or who were already enrolled in English schools themselves could be taught in English. But children of recent immigrants were forced to go to French-language schools. It seemed that the rights of newcomers to Québec had been taken away to ensure the survival of the French language. Lévesque believed it was necessary for Québec's immigrants to be French-speakers if the French culture was to survive.

Bill 101 outraged many people in Québec's English-speaking and immigrant communities. The head offices of many English-speaking corporations had already been relocating from Montréal to Toronto and Calgary. After Bill 101 even more English-speaking corporations shifted their head offices to English Canada. The dissidents formed a group called Alliance Quebec to challenge the new law in court.

leisure

A NEW ERA FOR THE LEAFS

As a seven-year-old boy, I was overwhelmed at the prospect of going to my first game at Maple Leaf Gardens. I can still smell the popcorn and hear the low roar of the crowd. That night I was in the full glory of a boy watching his first hockey game. My father and I sat at the edge of our seats watching the "blue and white" — the Toronto Maple Leafs. Little did I know that one day I'd be wearing those colours.

That night is vividly etched in my mind. Perhaps it was watching the sixteen thousand eager fans cheer for their favourite team. I remember after that game my dream was to one day play hockey at Maple Leaf Gardens. Coming from Greek immigrant parents who knew very little about hockey made it a long shot. But after I laced up my first pair of ice skates, I couldn't think of anything else.

Throughout the years I played with all my heart. I broke a few junior scoring records along the way, but never got drafted into the National Hockey League (NHL). I finally made the NHL as a walk-on — and with a lot of luck and hard work, I managed to stay in. Although I played nine years in the NHL and won a Stanley Cup with the New York Rangers in 1994, nothing could compare to the feelings of returning home to Toronto, wearing a Leafs jersey, and playing in Maple Leaf Gardens when I was traded to Toronto.

In its sixty-eight years, Maple Leaf Gardens has hosted some of the greatest hockey players in history. Bobby Orr, "Rocket" Richard, and Gordie Howe thrilled fans with their Hall of Fame talent. Thousands of fans watched Darryl Sittler score ten points in a single game — still an NHL record. And Wayne Gretzky considers the finest hockey performance of his career the seventh game of the 1993 playoff series in Toronto.

It was inevitable that a new arena would eventually replace the Gardens. Newer facilities were

Closing ceremonies at Maple Leaf Gardens.

needed that could hold bigger crowds. The Air Canada Centre (ACC) was the answer. Home to both the Toronto Maple Leafs and the Toronto Raptors, the ACC has restaurants, courtside lounges, and even televisions in the restrooms so you don't miss any of the action! Like the Maple Leaf Gardens in the 1930s, the ACC sets a new standard for modern sports and entertainment facilities. However, the mystique of Maple Leaf Gardens can never be duplicated. It represents a time when hockey was the passion of Canada, when there weren't million-dollar contracts, and the only reason you played was for the love of the game.

On February 13, 1999, I participated in the farewell ceremony to this hockey shrine. Hockey heroes and legends such as Red Horner, Johnny Bower, Frank Mahovlich, and Darryl Sittler walked down a red carpet and bid farewell to an emotional crowd. And I, Nick Kypreos, received one of my greatest honours. I walked down the length of ice at Maple Leaf Gardens, hearing the roar of the crowd for the last time. I looked around and thought that somewhere in the stands sits a young boy with a big dream. I joined my childhood heroes at centre ice and waved goodbye to an era. But in many ways, I waved goodbye to a friend.

CONTRIBUTED BY NICK KYPREOS. MR. KYPREOS PLAYED IN THE NATIONAL HOCKEY LEAGUE FROM 1989 TO 1998. HE IS NOW A HOCKEY ANALYST WITH CTV SPORTSNET.

Trudeau proposed his constitutional changes in a meeting of all the "first ministers" (provincial premiers and the prime minister) in September 1980. But only two provinces, Ontario and New Brunswick, supported him. Trudeau then announced that the federal government would carry out its plans for constitutional change with or without the support of the provinces. The Progressive Conservative opposition managed to block Trudeau's plans and forced him to agree to postpone further action until the Supreme Court of Canada ruled on the validity of his initiatives.

The Supreme Court declared that the federal government had the legal right to patriate the Constitution. However, for the government to act on its own would violate a long-standing Canadian political tradition of consultation between the provincial and federal levels of government. Both sides realized that they would have to work hard to hammer out a new agreement.

The ten provincial premiers met with Prime Minister Trudeau for one last conference in Ottawa in early November 1981. After several exhausting days of negotiation, they had still not reached an agreement. But after midnight on November 5, all the premiers except Lévesque were awakened and called together to look at a last-minute compromise proposal.

Lévesque woke up the next morning to discover that the Prime Minister and the other nine premiers had reached an agreement. Trudeau announced to the press that a compromise — a new constitutional package, including an amending formula and a written charter of rights and freedoms — had been found. Québec felt betrayed. Constitutional change had been promised as a way of meeting Québec's needs; now the rest of Canada was forcing a Constitution on Québec that it had not accepted.

Québec was not the only source of opposition. When discussions over repatriation began in 1978, Aboriginal peoples had not been represented. This they found unacceptable. Women also lobbied hard for changes. The National Action Committee on the Status of Women lobbied hard for constitutional guarantees of equality. They succeeded in persuading the government to include provisions for equality rights (sections 15 and 28) in the

Charter of Rights and Freedoms, which was a key part of the proposed Constitution. After these and other changes had been made, the bill was passed in Parliament on December 2, 1981. Then Canada formally asked Britain to pass the requested legislation, and Canada's new Constitution was ready for patriation.

April 17, 1982, was patriation day. Queen Elizabeth II signed the Constitution on the steps of the Parliament buildings in Ottawa. Prime Minister Trudeau was at her side. At the stroke of a pen, Canada's Constitution had come home at last, complete with an amending formula and a new Charter of Rights and Freedoms. Only one province, Québec, stayed away from the patriation ceremony. On that day in Québec, flags were lowered to half-mast, and René Lévesque led a protest march through the streets of Montréal.

The Meech Lake Accord

Québec would not agree to sign the Constitution until five years later. The P.Q. was out of power in Québec, and the Liberals had returned to govern the province under the leadership of Robert

While the rest of Canada celebrated the signing of the new Constitution by Queen Elizabeth II and Pierre Trudeau, Quebeckers felt bitter about not having their needs addressed.

Bourassa. When the Progressive Conservatives came to power in Ottawa, Canada's new Prime Minister, Brian Mulroney, promised "national reconciliation." He wanted to end the bitterness between Québec and the rest of Canada over the Constitution. In April 1987 he invited the ten provincial premiers to a conference at a private retreat at Meech Lake, in the hills outside Hull, Québec. His aim was to find a new constitutional agreement that satisfied every province, including Québec. To the amazement of most observers, the provinces managed to reach an agreement. The Meech Lake Accord included five major points.

- Québec was recognized as a "distinct society."
- Three of the nine Supreme Court of Canada judges were to be from Québec.
- Constitutional amendments about the structure or powers of the government (for example, changing the structure of the Senate or the Supreme Court, or creating new provinces) required the agreement of all ten provinces.
- Provinces could "opt out" of new federal programs and establish their own matching programs with federal money.
- Québec had control of its own immigration policy in the province.

Holding a feather for spiritual strength, Aboriginal MLA Elijah Harper voted against the Meech Lake Accord. In doing so, the accord failed. Why did many Aboriginal people not agree with the accord?

All ten premiers signed the Meech Lake Accord in 1987. Prime Minister Mulroney declared that the agreement was a way of welcoming "Québec back into the Canadian family." The House of Commons passed the accord with support from all three political parties, and Québec was the first province to ratify it. This set in motion a three-year constitutional clock. All the other provincial legislatures also had to ratify the Meech Lake Accord by June 23, 1990, or the agreement would be void.

Between 1987 and 1990, however, conditions in Canada changed. There was a loud outcry against the Meech Lake Accord in many parts of the country. Some English Canadians were outraged by Bourassa's Bill 178, which had sharply restricted the right to English-language signs. Women's groups in English-speaking Canada were concerned that the "distinct society" clause might take away Québec women's constitutional rights under the Charter of Rights and Freedoms, although women's groups in Québec did not share this view and supported the accord. Aboriginal leaders were angry that their demands for Aboriginal rights had not been fully met. In addition, New Brunswick, Manitoba, and Newfoundland had elected new governments. Their premiers had not been at the Meech Lake meeting, and they were therefore not necessarily committed to the accord. Time was running out.

Mulroney and the ten provincial premiers met in Ottawa in June 1990 in a last, desperate effort to save the accord. After a week they emerged with a compromise, but it still had to be ratified by New Brunswick, Newfoundland, and Manitoba. As the deadline drew near, the first two provinces ratified the accord. In the Manitoba legislature, however, Elijah Harper, an Aboriginal member of the legislature, voted against it. With the defeat of the Meech Lake Accord, the second attempt to give Québec a place in the Canadian Constitution ended in failure. "This is a sad day for Canada," said Prime Minister Mulroney. The failure of Meech Lake was a sharp setback for Québec and the Mulroney government.

The Charlottetown Proposal

The Meech Lake Accord came to be known as the "Québec round" of negotiations. It had focused on meeting Québec's needs and getting the province's signature on the Canadian Constitution. Part of the reason that Meech Lake died, however, was that other groups — including Native peoples, the smaller provinces, and people concerned with social and economic rights — had felt left out. They wanted their concerns taken into account in any new constitutional deal. The death of Meech Lake marked the birth of the "Canada round" of negotiations a few months later. Québec had decided to put together a new set of proposals for constitutional change. If the rest of Canada did not come up with acceptable counter-proposals, then Québec would hold a referendum on independence by October 1992.

The "Canada round" was a series of public forums and commissions at the federal and provincial levels. In addition, dozens of other conferences were organized by special-interest groups. The aim of all these conferences was to consult the public on the new constitutional package. Then Ottawa, the ten provinces, the two territories, and leaders of four major Aboriginal groups met in Charlottetown and reached an agreement on August 28, 1992. The outcome was a proposal called the Charlottetown Accord.

The Charlottetown Accord proposed sweeping changes to Canada's Constitution. Among its proposals were Aboriginal self-government, Senate reform, a new division of federal–provincial powers, and a social and economic union that defined Canada's commitment to programs such as universal health care, workers' rights, and environmental protection. It also included the "Canada Clause," which set out the principles and values on which the country was founded, including the statement that Québec was a "distinct society." The 1982 Constitution Act contained a "Canada clause" that superseded the Québec clause in Bill 101. The Canada clause allowed children with at least one parent schooled in English anywhere in Canada to go to English schools.

Québec had planned to hold a second provincial referendum on sovereignty, but it decided to hold a referendum on the Charlottetown Accord. Ottawa then decided that all Canadians would vote on the Charlottetown proposal in a national referendum. The question for voters was: "Do you agree that the

The independence movement remains very strong in Québec. In fact, the defeat of the Charlottetown Accord fuelled the separatist movement. Why would the defeat have had this effect?

Constitution of Canada should be renewed on the basis of the agreement reached on August 28, 1992?"

All three major political parties supported the "yes" vote. But in the last weeks before the October referendum, there was a groundswell of popular feeling against the accord. The "no" vote was led by a new Western political party — the Reform Party — as well as other special-interest groups, including the National Action Committee on the Status of Women. The Assembly of First Nations (AFN) chiefs also refused to support the "yes" campaign of AFN leader Ovide Mercredi, who had helped craft new constitutional guarantees concerning Aboriginal self-government. Some Aboriginal leaders were suspicious of the guarantees and were unwilling to support them.

Other people joined the "no" side because they felt that the Charlottetown proposals gave too much to Québec or too little to their own regions. Almost every section of the agreement came under attack by some group. Many other Canadians were simply overwhelmed by the sheer size of the agreement. How could they possibly understand it all or make a reasonable choice? Should they vote for the whole package even if they did not agree with parts of it?

On October 26, 1992, the Charlottetown Accord went down to resounding defeat. It was approved by only four of the ten provinces: Newfoundland, New Brunswick, Prince Edward Island, and Ontario. Canadians were exhausted by the long constitutional battle. British Columbia Premier Michael Harcourt said, "We should put the Constitution on the back burner for a while and turn the burner off." He seems to have spoken for the whole nation. The first priority for most Canadians was surviving a deep recession that had sent the Canadian economy into a nosedive and put many Canadians out of work.

After Charlottetown

In 1993, newly elected Prime Minister Jean Chrétien, a French-speaking Quebecker, appealed to Canadians to "leave constitutional quarrels on the back burner." He feared that any future constitutional talks about Québec's role in Confederation would tear the nation apart for good. But Quebeckers had also elected fifty-four Bloc Québécois members to Parliament — enough for the Bloc to become the official opposition party. The federal Bloc Québécois, like the provincial Parti Québécois, was a political party dedicated to creating a separate Québec. Its status as the official opposition in Parliament gave the Bloc Québécois a new forum for making its demands heard across Canada.

The constitutional issue did not remain quiet for long. In the 1994 Québec provincial election the P.Q. promised to hold another referendum on the question of sovereignty. After an emotional campaign, the "no" side won with a very narrow margin of victory. Of the votes cast, 50.6 percent voted no; 49.4 percent voted yes. Only 54 000 votes separated the two sides.

The debates over constitutional change made clear that deep divisions existed in Canadian society and politics. Although the differences between Québec and the federal government attracted most of the attention, these were not the only divisions within Canadian society. Other regions and groups had their own visions of the ideal Canadian society. Of particular importance were the concerns of the West and of the Aboriginal peoples.

The next initiative to forge a national consensus came from the provincial premiers. In September 1997, nine provincial premiers (Quebec's Premier Lucien Bouchard refused to attend) met in Calgary in an attempt to lay the groundwork for a unity package that they hoped would be supported by a majority of Canadians inside and outside of Québec. The **Calgary Declaration**, as the agreement came to be known, suggested that Québec be recognized as a "unique society" and that the government and legislature of Québec had a role to play in preserving the unique character of the province. The agreement also stated that all Canadians were equal and that all provinces had equal status. Furthermore, any future constitutional amendments would apply equally to all provinces. The Calgary Declaration was endorsed by Prime Minister Jean Chrétien and the leader of the Reform Party, Preston Manning. Aboriginal leaders, however, were very disappointed that the agreement did not address Aboriginal concerns. Premier Bouchard rejected the Calgary Declaration, claiming that it was meaningless to suggest that Quebeckers were unique like all other Canadians. The Calgary Declaration did little to bring about any resolution to Canada's constitutional woes.

Québec Premier Lucien Bouchard rejected the Calgary Declaration on the grounds that it was meaningless to suggest that Quebeckers were unique like all other Canadians. Would you agree with him?

The federal government waded back into the constitutional quicksand late in 1999, when its intent to pass the **Clarity Act** was unveiled. This Act requires that, in any future referendums, Québec ask a clear question and win a clear majority; otherwise the Canadian government will not negotiate with the separatists. In past referendums the question asked of voters was so vague as to leave open room for many interpretations. Some voters believed they could be part of an independent Québec but still keep their Canadian citizenship, use Canadian currency, and continue to receive the benefits of trade agreements negotiated by Canada. With a clearly stated question, Québec voters in the future will have a clear sense of what to expect in the event of a yes vote.

"The West Wants In"

It would not be correct to think of Canada's three Prairie provinces as a single, uniform bloc. In addition to the Aboriginal peoples already living in the West, the people who settled the Prairies included immigrants from Britain, continental Europe, the United States, and Eastern Canada. Their economies differed: oil and gas were important in Alberta, grain and potash dominated in Saskatchewan, and a more diversified economy existed in Manitoba. Despite their differences, these three Western provinces were united in their opposition to Central Canada and the belief that Ottawa did not listen to them.

The 1969 Official Languages Act provoked resentment in the West. The intention was to make francophones feel at home in all parts of Canada, but in a largely multiethnic, unilingual West, bilingualism was seen as an insensitive policy that reflected the federal government's preoccupation with Québec. Although a majority of Canadians approved of the Act, 70 percent of Westerners opposed it.

Conflicts over resources such as natural gas and oil were another sore point. The Trudeau government launched the National Energy Program in 1980 to ensure that foreign interests wouldn't completely control Canada's oil and gas industry. The program was created to protect Canada's future oil supply, control oil prices, and achieve 50 percent Canadian ownership of the oil industry by 1990. But

it also gave the federal government a bigger share of oil and gas revenues. Alberta Premier Peter Lougheed condemned it as "an outright attempt to take over the resources" of his province. Many people in Alberta and Saskatchewan strongly agreed with him.

Unlike many people in Québec, Westerners did not want out of Confederation; the slogan "The West Wants In" was a more accurate reflection of their views. As was often the case in the past, regional dissatisfaction found an outlet in political protest. In 1987, a group called the Western Reform Association formed a new political party, the Reform Party, with Preston Manning as its leader. Reformers criticized the existing party system for being unresponsive to people's wishes. Too many decisions took place behind closed doors — the Meech Lake Accord was a primary example. Reformers advocated the use of referendums on major policies as one way of making the political process more democratic. In addition they criticized the official federal policies of bilingualism and multiculturalism. They also called for less government as well as cuts to social programs in order to reduce government deficits. In the 1993 federal election the party won fifty-two seats and came close to forming the official parliamentary opposition, a position that it finally gained in 1997.

On March 25, 2000, almost 92 percent of Reform Party members voted in favour of forming a new political party called Canadian Alliance. What did Preston Manning hope the new political party would achieve?

Canadian Alliance

As the Reform Party continued to try to widen its appeal across Canada, a movement was spearheaded by some Reform Party members and Preston Manning in 1998 to form a new national party, the Canadian Alliance (C.A.). The goal of the C.A. is to form an alliance of Reform Party members, disenchanted Progressive Conservatives, and others searching for a way to defeat the Chrétien Liberal government, in order to end one-party dominance in federal politics. Convinced that this was the only way to move forward, Preston Manning promised to resign if Reform members did not approve of the C.A.'s formation.

Acceptance at Last? Aboriginal Peoples in Canada

Aboriginal peoples have become the fastest-growing group in Canada as a result of having the highest birth rate in the country over the last fifty years. But respect and recognition have not gone hand in hand with their increasing population. It has taken years of struggling just to be accepted as one of the founding nations of Canada.

The "Just Society" and Canada's Aboriginal Peoples

In his 1968 election speech Pierre Trudeau pledged to make Canada a "Just Society" — a place where all Canadians were equals. Many people wondered if Trudeau's promise of the "Just Society" would bring relief to Canada's Aboriginal peoples, who had suffered decades of discrimination and hardship. In the 1960s many of them lived either on small, scattered reserves or in large cities such as Vancouver, Edmonton, Winnipeg, and Toronto, where unskilled work was easier to find. Grim statistics on their lifespan, income, unemployment, family breakdown, law-breaking, and suicide showed how difficult and painful life was for many Aboriginal people. In a speech at a centennial birthday party in Vancouver in 1967, Chief Dan George spoke of his sadness:

Oh Canada, how can I celebrate with you this Centenary, this hundred years? Shall I thank you for the reserves that are left to me of my beautiful forests? For the canned fish of my rivers? For the loss of my pride and authority, even among my own people? For the lack of my will to fight back?

But he still looked to the future with hope. He called for the rebuilding of the Aboriginal peoples into "the proudest segment of our society" over the next century.

Trudeau's Proposals

In the 1960s Aboriginal people's lives were still regulated by the federal Department of Indian Affairs under the Indian Act. Many of them felt badly treated by the department. In 1969 Prime Minister Trudeau proposed to do away with the Act as part of a policy to slowly reduce Aboriginal people's special legal status under the Act until Aboriginal Canadians had exactly the same rights as all other Canadians. But Trudeau found himself caught up in a whirlwind of controversy. Many Aboriginal people were deeply angered by a policy based on assimilating (absorbing) them into White culture. It seemed to them that Ottawa wanted Aboriginal people to disappear into the Canadian mainstream and to let their cultures fade away. In a book called *The Unjust Society* (1969), Aboriginal leader Harold Cardinal accused Trudeau of attempting to destroy the Aboriginal cultures. As Cardinal angrily put it, Ottawa seemed to think that the "only good Indian is a non-Indian." Aboriginal protests over the proposed cancellation of the Indian Act and treaty rights were so fierce that the measures were finally dropped.

The battle over the Indian Act marked a major turning point. Aboriginal groups saw that strong and unified political action had worked. Aboriginal leaders began building up new organizations to protect and increase special status for Aboriginal people. It was the beginning of a new activism. In the following decades Aboriginal communities began taking control of their own schools, health clinics, and child welfare agencies. Some communities even brought back traditional forms of self-government.

In 1970 Minister of Indian Affairs and future prime minister Jean Chrétien met with representatives from the Aboriginal Association of Alberta and other Aboriginal groups in Ottawa. The Aboriginal representatives banded together to protest the government's cancellation of the Indian Act. Why did they not want the Indian Act to be cancelled?

Land Claims

A major focus of the new activism in the 1970s was Aboriginal land claims. There were no formal treaties signed between Aboriginal bands and the British or Canadian governments in most of northern Québec, the Northwest Territories, and most of British Columbia. Aboriginal groups in these regions claimed that they had never surrendered their Aboriginal rights over their land because they had occupied Canada before the coming of the Europeans. The Nisga'a of northern British Columbia, for example, had been seeking title to their lands as early as the 1890s. But Aboriginal demands were put aside time after time.

By the 1970s the federal government realized that it had to consult with Aboriginal groups. It began funding Aboriginal organizations to defend their land claims. In 1973 the Supreme Court of Canada agreed that Aboriginal rights did exist, and the governments began a long, slow process of negotiating land-claim settlements. At stake were millions of dollars of government money in exchange for Aboriginal land given up to the government. In addition, Aboriginal bands were seeking rights over resources such as timber and minerals, as well as hunting, trapping, and fishing rights.

Claims based on Aboriginal title in regions where no treaties were signed are known as "comprehensive claims." The Québec government was the first to reach a comprehensive land-claims settlement. It wanted to open the way for the huge new James Bay hydro-electric project. In return for giving up their claim to 60 percent of northern Québec, the Cree and Inuit residents were given complete control of almost 14 000 square kilometres of land and the exclusive rights to hunt, trap, and fish in more than 155 000 square kilometres. Although many other Aboriginal groups spoke out against the settlement, it was a major milestone. It meant that in regions not covered by treaties, land-rights claims could be pursued by Aboriginal groups.

Other comprehensive land claims soon followed. The Inuit of the Western Arctic won a settlement package that included about 90 000 square kilometres of land, $45 million, and other benefits. The Inuit Tapirisat made a much larger claim in the Eastern Arctic. The Council of Yukon Indians also claimed 70 percent of the Yukon, and more than twenty Aboriginal groups made land claims covering most of the province of British Columbia.

Aboriginal Resistance: The Oka Standoff

In recent years Aboriginal groups have become increasingly militant in asserting their rights. During the summer of 1990 a land dispute in Oka, Québec, between town officials and Mohawks from nearby Kahnesatake turned into a seventy-eight-day standoff. The conflict arose over a proposed golf course that would have been built on land considered sacred by the Mohawks.

The standoff began after about one hundred Québec provincial police attempted to break through a barricade erected on the highway by Mohawk warriors. A gun battle ensued, and one police officer was killed by a stray bullet. In the following weeks, negotiations failed to convince

Canadian soldier Patrick Cloutier and Mohawk warrior Brad Laroque come to a tense face-to-face encounter at the Kahnesatake reserve at Oka. Why do you think these Mohawks became militant in asserting their rights?

the heavily armed warriors to take down the barricade. Finally, on September 26, 1990, the Mohawk warriors surrendered to police. The protestors considered the eleven-week standoff a success because they were able to raise the profile of Aboriginal issues throughout Canada.

The Creation of Nunavut

On April 1, 1999, the map of Canada was again redrawn to create a new territory — Nunavut. Meaning "our land" in Inuktitut, Nunavut covers an area larger than Newfoundland, Prince Edward Island, Nova Scotia, New Brunswick, and Québec combined. The Inuit, who make up 85 percent of Nunavut's population, had attempted to gain their own territory and self-government since the 1970s. Finally, in the 1993 Nunavut land-claim settlement, Ottawa agreed to hand over 350 000 square kilometres of land and 36 000 square kilometres of mineral rights to the Inuit.

The new Nunavut self-government is decentralized; government departments are set up throughout the territory. The new territory's government has gradually taken over responsibilities that were formerly assumed by the Government of the Northwest Territories. By 2009 the transfer of responsibilities will be complete. To help preserve Inuit culture, Inuit *Quajimajatugangit* — traditional Inuit knowledge — will play an important role in developing government policies. Inuktitut is the official language of the new government; it is hoped that this will help the language to survive at

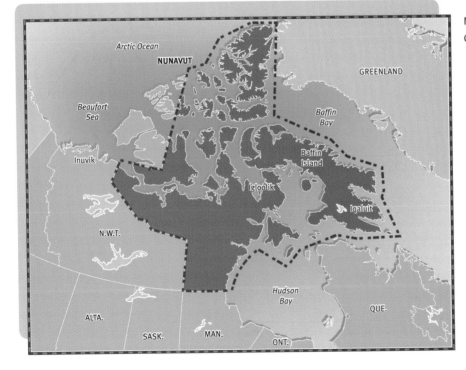

Nunavut covers one fifth of Canada's land mass.

The Nunavut flag contains the *inuksuk*, which symbolizes the stone monuments that guide the people on the land and mark sacred places, and the North Star, *Niqirtsuituq*, the traditional guide for navigation. The blue and gold colours symbolize the riches of land, sea, and sky, while red is a reference to Canada.

A Divided Canada?

The differences that divide Canada are in many ways rooted in its history. Canada's strong regional identities have produced regionally based federal political parties and vocal provincial premiers demanding more powers and, in some cases, even outright separation from Canada.

Feeling increasingly threatened by the English-speaking majority in Canada, French Canadians have become very politicized and at times militant in defending their language and culture. Aboriginal people have also faced a continuous struggle to have their rights recognized in the Constitution. Over the past few decades and into the twenty-first century, Canadian politics have been dominated by attempts to mend the rips that have at times divided the country.

Observers of Canadian politics since 1968 may assume that the nation is fragile and is in danger of coming apart. Closer reflection reveals that the strong regional voices are a clear measure of the success of Canada. Perhaps it is more accurate to see Canada as a country in which regional and political differences form the basis of peaceful and productive political debate.

a time when many young Inuit speak only English.

Although the formation of Nunavut finally allows the Inuit to control their own land and destiny, the future holds many struggles for the new territorial government. High unemployment, high suicide rates, and a high dropout rate in school are major problems facing Nunavut's relatively young population.

Web Connections

http://www.school.mcgrawhill.ca/resources

Go to the Web site above to find out more about Nunavut. Go to *History Resources*, then to *Canada: A Nation Unfolding, Ontario Edition*, to find out where to go next..

chapter review

CHAPTER SUMMARY

In this chapter we have seen

- how three prime ministers from Québec have dominated Canadian politics since 1968

- the effects of the Québec separatist movement on constitutional reform and on the relationship between French and English Canada

- that the West often feels that Central Canada has too much influence in determining the actions of the federal government

- that after decades of mistreatment, Canada's Aboriginal peoples are beginning to have a voice in Canada and are increasingly in charge of their own affairs

UNDERSTANDING HISTORICAL FACTS

1. Identify these people, places, and events, and explain their significance.

Bloc Québécois	Meech Lake Accord
October Crisis	Goods and Services Tax
Bill 101	René Lévesque
Elijah Harper	Charlottetown Accord
Clarity Act	Preston Manning

2. Create a visual time line using pictures or illustrations of major events that outline the development of the separatist movement in Québec from October 1970 to the present. Provide a brief caption that includes an adequate explanation for each date.

3. What restrictions did Bill 22 and Bill 101 place on English-speaking families in Québec? What were the goals of these bills?

4. Explain why the Meech Lake Accord was called the "Québec round" whereas the Charlottetown Accord was referred to as the "Canada round."

5. Who opposed the Charlottetown Accord? Why did they oppose it?

EXPRESSING YOUR OPINION

1. During his time as prime minister, Brian Mulroney ended the universality of social programs, introduced the GST, and negotiated free trade with the United States and Mexico. By the end of his time in office, he was one of the least-popular prime ministers in Canadian history. In the election that followed his resignation, his Progressive Conservative party was reduced to two seats in the House of Commons. Did Mulroney deserve the wrath of Canadians, or should he be praised for tackling difficult issues and making decisions that have benefited Canada in the long run? Support your answer with evidence.

2. In 1970 many Québec nationalists believed their language and culture were in danger and that the policies of the federal and provincial governments were not providing the necessary protection. Desperate for a solution, some turned to radical terrorist tactics, including bombing and kidnapping. Can actions such as these ever be justified? Should those who commit crimes to achieve political goals be treated differently from other criminals? Explain your answer.

3. Given the failure of both the Meech Lake Accord and the Charlottetown Accord, do you believe it is possible to create constitutional reforms that will be supported by all regions in Canada? Why or why not?

WORKING WITH THE EVIDENCE

1. Until the late 1970s Québec licence plates carried the slogan "La Belle Province." Since then they have read "Je me souviens." What is the significance of the new slogan to French Canadians?

The Search for Canada within an Emerging Global Community

INQUIRING INTO THE PAST

- How has technology changed the daily lives of Canadians in the past few decades? How has it affected education and health care?
- How has immigration changed the demographic make-up of Canada since 1968?
- How has Canadian culture been affected by immigration and American influences?
- Is there such a thing as a Canadian identity?

KEY TERMS

Ethnicity

Generation X

Melting Pot

Mosaic

Multiculturalism

Refugees

Canadian folk singer Murray McLaughlan suggested in a song that although the heart of Canada may be in the big businesses on Bay Street in Toronto, the soul lay outside the urban centres. What do you think he meant by this?

TIMELINE

1968 ►
Pierre Trudeau pledges to make Canada a "Just Society"

1978 ►
Canada passes a new Immigration Act that is more open and humane

1984 ►
Jeanne Sauvé becomes the first woman to serve as Canada's Governor General

1999 ►
Adrienne Clarkson, who arrived as a refugee from China in 1942, is appointed Governor General of Canada.

Several forces of change over the past thirty years have contributed to an increasingly close relationship between Canada and the world. Technological change has altered Canadians' homes and workplaces and brought the world to their doorstep. Demographic change has led to an ethnically diverse population, and social change has forced Canadians to reflect on their beliefs and values. As Marshall McLuhan's "global village" has emerged, Canada's view of itself as a transplanted British–French society and culture has changed. Since Canada has become a country of diverse ethnicity, the search for a uniquely Canadian identity has become more complex.

Technological Change in Contemporary Canada

Half a century ago many Canadians had no electricity or indoor plumbing in their homes, and most rural children still attended one-room school houses. Today, DVD players, microwaves, and computers that link Canadians to the world are common in many homes. Technology has transformed the lives of Canadians at home and in the workplace.

Technology and Daily Life

From the grocery-store checkout to the thermostat in most homes, computer technology is now a part of the lives of all Canadians. Dramatic declines in the prices of popular items such as VCRs, home computers, and cellular phones have made them affordable to a large number of Canadians. Access to the Internet has given Canadian youth a nearly inexhaustible source of information and the ability to communicate with others across Canada and around the world. Cellular phones and pagers allow parents to keep in touch with their teenage children, and the multi-channel television provides endless entertainment. The developments in technology, however, are not without drawbacks. Canadians spend too much time in front of the television, too many automobile accidents result from inattentive drivers using their cellular phones, and the Internet allows many groups or people to spread disturbing messages, images, and information.

Of major concern to many Canadians is how Canadian culture will be protected in the "high-tech" age. How can Canada protect its cultural identity in a world in which consumers will have endless choices? Will Canadians be interested in programs that are distinctly Canadian? Should government agencies attempt to regulate the Internet as they do radio and television? These are some of the difficult questions facing Canada in the twenty-first century.

Technology and Educational Reform

Rapid changes in technology have also affected Canadian schools. The new emphasis on information technology is evident in Ontario's schools. Libraries are now much more than a large collection of books, and are now likely to have many computers with CD-ROMs and Internet access. In many schools the shops in which students used to learn auto mechanics, woodworking, electricity,

To prepare students for the post industrial workplace, provinces have rewritten their curricula so that a strong emphasis on technological knowledge is central to the student's learning.

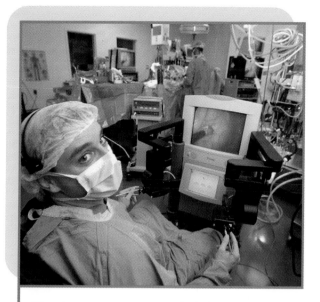

A Toronto surgeon uses a remote robotic device to operate on a man with a damaged spine. Canadians have been in the forefront of this non-invasive surgery.

and welding have either been replaced or supplemented with information technology courses. In these courses students work with video cameras, computer scanners, editing and mixing boards, and the latest software to create innovative products, from school newsletters to professional-looking videos of school events.

Technology and Health Care

Just as high technology is having a huge impact on Canada's education system, so too is health care being revolutionized by advances in technology. Breakthroughs in medical technology are giving cancer patients a greater chance of survival, making possible the transplanting of many organs, and even allowing infertile women to become pregnant. Some surgeries are now done by robotics, whereby the doctor guides the procedure from a computer terminal. Other Canadian doctors offer their services on-line to patients thousands of miles away, providing better medical service to remote parts of Canada. Scientists are predicting astounding changes to Canada's health-care system over the next twenty years. The changes include most medical consultations taking place by video calls or e-mail, damaged hearts being repaired with genetically engineered muscle cells, and cancer being stopped at an early stage by an immune system trained to kill cancer cells.

Some developments in medical technology have met with opposition. Many Canadians have concerns over the explosion in reproductive technology. Canada's first test-tube twins, Ian and Sean Cherry, were born on May 17, 1984. At the time most Canadians applauded the medical wizardry that allowed a previously infertile Noni Cherry to become pregnant. Today, however, the technology is beginning to raise concerns. Research being done at McGill University in Montréal may allow young women to have their eggs removed and frozen for use at a later date. What would the societal implications of this technology be? While the federal government considers passing laws to ban some practices related to reproduction, doctors and researchers oppose restrictions being placed on their research. Advances in medical technology may bring hope to many, yet they also give rise to difficult questions.

The Impact of Demographic Change

If technology has caused the most dramatic changes to the ways in which Canadians go about their daily lives, changes in demography (the make-up of Canada's population) have profoundly changed the face of Canada. A stroll through any of Canada's major cities reveals the diversity that now characterizes Canadian society.

Changing Patterns of Immigration

One of the most important factors in transforming Canadian culture was the change in immigration patterns. Immediately after World War II Canadian immigration policy favoured immigrants from the United Kingdom and Western Europe. Jewish and Black people were not welcomed, and immigrants from Eastern Europe were regarded with some suspicion. Asians were also rejected.

As the European economies recovered, fewer Europeans immigrated to Canada. Other sources

technology

DR. MARLENE RABINOVITCH:
CONTRIBUTING TO MEDICAL BREAKTHROUGHS

Dr. Marlene Rabinovitch graduated in medicine from Montréal's McGill University and went on to study pediatrics at the University of Colorado and pediatric cardiology at Harvard Medical School. Dr. Rabinovitch now heads the cardiovascular research program at Toronto's Hospital for Sick Children. Her research focuses on the complications of having a heart defect as a young child. Dr. Rabinovitch was interviewed about her work at the Hospital for Sick Children, particularly about her potentially life-saving research.

Dr. Rabinovich holds one of her success stories: 2 1/2-year-old Adam Pappas had transpositional heart surgery when he was six days old.

What does your job at the hospital involve?

Part of the time I do clinical work. This consists of taking care of children who have heart defects, in the hospital and at an out-patient clinic. I also serve as a consultant internationally for children who have heart defects, especially those with abnormal blood vessels in their lungs. Then, of course, I have my research.

Why is your research into the ductus so crucial?

First, the ductus is a blood vessel and it's absolutely critical in infants who have blockage of the valves in one of the heart's great vessels. The ductus must stay open, because if one of the valves is blocked, then it's used as a bypass channel to divert blood. In other words, if circulation to the lungs is blocked, then the ductus serves to bypass some blood that should go the rest of the body back into the lungs. If the valve that directs blood flow to the rest of the body, the aorta, is blocked, then this passage way needs to stay open to divert blood from the lungs back into the rest of the body. Another key reason for our interest in the ductus is that when it closes, it behaves much like a diseased blood vessel. So, by understanding the process that closes this vessel off, we have gained new insights into why blood vessels, like coronary arteries, begin to close off when they're injured.

How will your research help to correct heart defects in children?

We know how to target the genes that control the ductus. That would allow us to give the mother gene therapy treatment while the baby is still a fetus.
 The child would still need open-heart surgery. But we'd be able to perform that surgery when the child is older and the operation is much safer.

How will this affect babies' survival rates?

Performing numerous operations on very young infants is risky. In some cases, operations have as high a mortality rates as 50 percent. We could drop that to 5 percent if the research we're doing proves fruitful.

What do you find most satisfying about your work?

I enjoy the privilege of being part of the evolution in science that's allowing us to make major inroads into the treatment of children with heart disease.

In what other areas has the Hospital for Sick Children made significant medical research contributions?

They've shown leadership in the treatment of childhood cancers, metabolic diseases, cystic fibrosis, and neurological diseases. In pretty well every discipline, the hospital has shown innovation.

had to be found, and Canada began admitting more immigrants from Third World countries. After 1971 the majority of people immigrating to Canada came from Asia, followed by the Caribbean, Latin America, and Africa. Some of the immigrants found jobs in service industries, but others were professionals, technicians, and managers who were needed to fill Canada's need for highly trained workers.

Refugees

Canada had no specific provision for **refugees** — people fleeing danger, persecution, or death in their own country — in its immigration policy, but the government bent the rules occasionally to admit refugees. The Canadian government has allowed many groups of refugees into Canada over the last few decades. Canada took in 7000 Ugandans in 1972. It has also accepted more than 17 000 Chileans since 1973; 72 000 Vietnamese since 1975; and more than 10 000 Lebanese from 1976 to 1978. From 1980 to 1986 Canada accepted more than 130 000 refugees — more per capita than any other nation.

But Canadian immigration officials have been completely unprepared for the flood of refugees coming to Canadian shores and asking for asylum. Some are genuine refugees, some are not. There has been an increase in "queue jumpers" — would-be immigrants who come to Canada and falsely claim to be refugees in order to bypass thousands of other potential immigrants who are making legal applications from outside Canada. An unfortunate result of the refugee crisis has been a hardening of attitudes toward all refugees — even people who are genuinely fleeing repression in their own countries.

The Immigration Act of 1978

Changing needs in Canada as well as a more compassionate atmosphere led to a complete redrafting of the nation's immigration laws. After much public discussion and sometimes heated debate, Parliament passed a new Immigration Act in 1978. The new Act had three goals: promoting family reunion, upholding humanitarian values, and encouraging economic growth in Canada. It recognized three classes of immigrants: independent,

family, and refugee. The independent class included potential immigrants who satisfied the point system, which ranked applicants according to their education, skills, and resources; who were willing to be self-employed or set up businesses in Canada; or who had family members willing to sponsor them and help them get established. Over time, sponsored families became the largest group of immigrants admitted to the country.

The family class included close relatives of people who were citizens or permanent residents of Canada — husbands or wives, parents, grandparents, and unmarried children under the age of twenty-one. The refugee class applied to people who feared harm or had already suffered persecution in their own countries because of their religion, race, nationality, social identity, or political ideas. This was the first time that refugees were explicitly identified as a class.

Since the late 1970s Canada has absorbed between 200 000 and 250 000 immigrants annually. Of these immigrants, 60 percent have come from countries other than the United States or the European nations. Many recent immigrants are non-Whites, sometimes called "visible minorities." Many are well educated and highly skilled. Of the immigrants who came between 1981 and 1991, 17 percent had university degrees.

How does this Canadian family reflect its pride in its heritage?

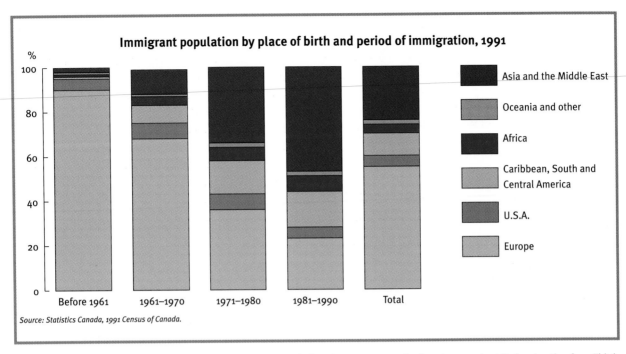

Immigrant population by place of birth and period of immigration, 1991

Legend:
- Asia and the Middle East
- Oceania and other
- Africa
- Caribbean, South and Central America
- U.S.A.
- Europe

Categories along x-axis: Before 1961, 1961–1970, 1971–1980, 1981–1990, Total

Source: Statistics Canada, 1991 Census of Canada.

This chart shows that since World War II, immigration to Canada from European countries has decreased, while immigration from Third World and Asian countries has increased. Why has this change occurred?

The Echo of the Baby Boom: Generation X

By the mid-1960s the baby boom had subsided. The introduction of the birth control pill in 1961 and a desire for smaller families led to a dramatic decline in Canada's birth rate. Boomers (those born during the baby boom) benefited from expanded college and university programs, new job opportunities, and numerous new consumer products aimed at meeting their every desire. By the 1970s job opportunities had begun to decrease, the economy took a downturn, and interest rates had shot up. The generation that followed the boomers would find life much more difficult, despite their being the best-educated generation in Canadian history. Good-paying jobs were less abundant, and promotions were even more rare as aging boomers held on to their comfortable jobs. By the 1980s governments were beginning to reduce funding for post-secondary education and to trim the size of their bureaucracies, which resulted in fewer white-collar jobs and less job security. The post–baby boom generation came to be known as **"Generation X"** after Vancouver author Douglas Coupland published his novel *Generation X*. This now-famous novel, set in the early 1990s, depicts the frustrations and disillusionment of several young people in their early twenties.

The Impact of Demographic Change on Aboriginal Communities

Aboriginal people are experiencing a boom in population growth. With fertility rates much higher than those in the rest of Canada and 62 percent of the more than 800 000 Aboriginal people under the age of twenty-nine, many feel confident about their role in the society of the twenty-first century. In Saskatchewan, Aboriginal people will represent more than 50 percent of the population by the year 2020. Healthier, better-educated, and more confident than earlier generations, many Aboriginal Canadians are beginning to make their mark in Canada. Musicians such as the members of Kashtin and Susan Aglukark, hockey stars such as Chris Simon, and CBC Newsworld anchor Carla Robinson are a few of the many who are providing positive role models for aboriginal youth. Aboriginal people are beginning to reclaim what had been lost over the past few hundred years.

Musician and singer Susan Aglukark is just one of many people who are providing positive role models for Aboriginal youth.

Shifting Sands: Women and Canadian Society

The "second wave" of the women's movement of the 1960s continued to gain momentum in the 1970s. This movement led to many changes in the position of women in Canadian society.

Breaking Through the Glass Ceiling

More women were beginning to work outside the home in the 1960s. The trend continued right into the 1990s. By 1971 more than a third of all married women were in the labour force. In 1981 the figure had risen to just under 50 percent, and in 1991 it had jumped to 69 percent. There were many reasons for women entering the outside workforce. In earlier days, marriage had been the great dividing line. Many women worked until they married, then they were expected to quit in order to raise families. But many families were finding that they needed a second income to maintain their standard of living. Unfortunately, despite the increased numbers of women in the workforce, very few have been able to reach the top jobs in their fields. This invisible barrier to the top of the job ladder is referred to as the "glass ceiling."

Women also wanted the choice of combining work and a family — or choosing a career over having a family. The new birth-control pill and other forms of contraception in the 1960s meant that women could postpone pregnancy and have fewer children. The 1960s saw the beginning of new patterns of family life. Since then, women have been marrying later or not at all. They have also been having children later in life, and having fewer children. More women return to work shortly after giving birth and combine work at home and on the job.

Women's Liberation

Many young women activists in the 1960s and 1970s began to push for "women's liberation" in a society dominated by men. Some used the counterculture ideas, slogans, and tactics of radical peace activists to press for changes in women's roles. The so-called "women's libbers" called for a revolution everywhere in society.

By 1969 women's liberation groups had sprung up all over Canada. The media was fascinated with their deliberately outrageous street demonstrations and the "new" issues of sexism and male domination. One of the best-known demonstrations was a

Quebecker Julie Payette is an accomplished musician, pilot, athlete, scholar, and astronaut. Would you consider her a role model just for young women, or for everyone?

Canadian voices

ME, A CANADIAN?

In the short essay below, Inuit author Alootook Ipellie describes why he is proud to call himself Canadian. As you read this essay, consider whether Canada's multicultural heritage hampers our national identity or helps to build a stronger nation.

Where I grew up there was no such place as Canada. I knew no Canada. I had never heard of it. My elders never mentioned Canada because they did not know Canada existed either. Later in life, I found out that I had been born in Canada, raised in Canada, and lived in Canada. Why did I not know about this place? Had the existence of Canada been censored in our land? I found the answers to these questions soon enough.

I was born in a small hunting camp on Baffin Island where my elders lived off the land. They had never heard anything about the outside world. Survival was a daily preoccupation when food was scarce, and they travelled from one hunting camp to the next in search of game. The Arctic was a hard land to live on but it was part of their lives and the only place they knew how to exist in. The land and the animals were sacred to them. Even if someone had told them they could lead easier lives in the cities and towns south of their land, they simply could not have survived there, or for a very short time only. Their upbringing had taught them to follow the traditions of their ancestors, and that was the only real life they knew. In earlier times, Canada did not exist for their ancestors although they walked on it every day.

I was brought up in the tradition of our ancestors. I suffered the hard days along with my elders when the hunters from our camp did not bring back any animals after being away for days at a time. And when food became plentiful, I rejoiced with my elders. Life went on like this in our part of the world from day to day, week to week, month to month, and year to year. Food meant survival. The land provided the food and this land happened to be Canada.

When I was about eight years old, I went to school for the first time. I did not know a word of English then.

Our teacher was a Qallunaaq (White) who spoke no Inuktitut, my mother tongue. She was more alien to me than I was to her. She had been sent to our land to teach and tell us about a whole new world we didn't know about. She taught us the language she spoke, and soon after that first year of school I heard her say the word "Canada" for the very first time. She then explained to us the history of Canada and how it began.

One thing I didn't understand at first was when she told me I was a resident of Canada and that I was a Canadian. Me, a Canadian? As long as I could remember I had been brought up as an Inuk first and foremost, and here was this teacher telling me otherwise. When she explained that I was an Inuk as well as a Canadian, I relaxed.

As I grew up and learned more about Canada and what it stood for, I became proud to be called a Canadian. Canada, I found out, respected my freedom to express myself through speech and civil liberties. This was important to me then and is today.

Canada is one of the few countries in the world that can say it has living in it a group of people who, through sheer determination and will to live, have survived for thousands of years on a land that tried to starve them out during its many fierce winters and brought them face to face with death and the possibility of extinction almost every day. Their survival speaks of hearts of steel.

The history of the Inuit is so long it surpasses human memory, although we do have some idea of where they came from. As the original people of Canada, they are in one sense "hosts" to all the nationalities who have settled in Canada and become Canadian citizens. Since Canada respects the cultural heritage of the Inuit and the freedom they enjoy, to live as they please, the Inuit have accepted the invitation to be called Canadians. By choosing to accept one another and live side by side, both benefit. Brother to brother, sister to sister, they are stronger today.

Without this sense of belonging to one another, we cannot hope to have a strong Canada.

SOURCE: ALOOTOOK IPELLIE IS EDITOR OF *INUIT TODAY* AND AN AUTHOR AND ARTIST FROM BAFFIN ISLAND AND OTTAWA.

New Democratic Party Member of Parliament Michelle Dockrill holds her son while debating an issue in Parliament. Have women achieved equality with men?

picket of the 1969 Toronto Miss Winter Bikini Contest. Female protesters paraded a mannequin marked off like a butcher's meat chart to protest the "sale" of women's bodies.

Women's liberationists wanted equal treatment with men and refused to be defined by their gender or marital status. Many rejected the symbols of "feminized" women, such as dresses, nylons, and high heels. Instead, many chose to wear unisex jeans and T-shirts and refused to use makeup. They called themselves Ms. instead of Miss or Mrs., and many kept their own last names when they married. At first, many Canadians dismissed talk of "sexism" and "male chauvinism" and the need for "women's liberation." But the feminist movement forced people to take a fresh look at women's roles in society and to change their thinking about men and women. Many ideas considered extreme in the 1960s — such as using the title "Ms." — are accepted without comment today.

Government Reactions to the Women's Liberation Movement

After the Royal Commission on the Status of Women issued its report and recommendations in 1970, sev-

eral changes were instituted by the government. In 1971, Prime Minister Pierre Trudeau appointed a first minister responsible for the status of women. Two years later, the Federal Advisory Council on the Status of Women was created. Its job was to educate the public and advise the government on important women's issues. At the same time, a federal women's program began giving grants, resource materials, and advice to women's groups across Canada. The Trudeau government also began appointing more women to key government jobs to set an example. Jeanne Sauvé became Speaker of the House of Commons in 1978 and Canada's Governor General in 1984. Other women became cabinet ministers and superior court judges.

The creation of the Canadian Human Rights Commission in 1977 was a major breakthrough for women. It prohibited discrimination on the basis of sex. It also provided for "equal pay for work of equal value." Men and women doing jobs that demanded similar skills, effort, responsibility, and working conditions were to be paid the same wage. In 1985, publicly owned corporations were told to establish plans to end discrimination against women, visible minorities, and people with disabilities in their companies.

In the same year the Indian Act was changed to end discrimination against Aboriginal women. Until then, Aboriginal men who married non-Aboriginal women were considered **Status Indians**, that is, Aboriginal people officially registered as band members. They have rights to use lands on the band's reserve and access to federal programs providing housing, education, and other benefits. But Aboriginal women who married non-Aboriginal men and their children lost their "Indian" status. The Act was changed so that, in future, status would no longer be gained or lost through marriage.

The Struggle Continues

In the 1990s many women looked back on the changes since the 1960s with a mixture of satisfaction and frustration. Many gains had been made. Political leaders talked more about major women's issues, and more women were entering politics. Audrey McLaughlin of the NDP became the first

Canadian voices

WHO AM I?

Who are you? Without using your name, what would you say? Would you talk about your personality? Your hobbies? Or would you discuss your friends and family? Would the grades you received on your last set of exams or your appearance factor into your self-description? Which aspects of yourself would you broadcast to the world; which ones would you keep to yourself? In the new millennium, we are kept so busy that sometimes the most important question of all gets left by the wayside: Who am I?

From waking to the sound of my alarm clock until the time I go to sleep, I am bombarded with the burden of choice. Do I want to look as if I stepped out from a GAP ad? Or should I wear Tommy Hilfiger? Should I eat Lucky Charms or Shredded Wheat? Yet in the grand scheme of things, my attire and breakfast cereal choices mean little. Who am I?

Do I want to become a lawyer or a painter; an architect or an actor? Is there any way to know that the profession I choose when I am in my late teens will satisfy me for the rest of my working years? As modern-day teens, we shoulder the burden of choice.

We have attained a standard of living in which the basic necessities of survival are regularly taken for granted. Education is widely accessible, giving each and every one of us the potential to become something good in this competitive world. We should capitalize on our good fortune to be living in an era when what we will become, what we will make of ourselves, is up to us. There is every reason to welcome the new millennium.

CONTRIBUTED BY AMANDA STEIMAN. MS. STEIMAN WAS A STUDENT AT VAUGHAN SECONDARY SCHOOL IN ONTARIO, AND IS NOW ATTENDING YORK UNIVERSITY IN NORTH YORK, ONTARIO.

woman to be the national leader of a major political party. Kim Campbell became Canada's first female Prime Minister when Brian Mulroney resigned and she was elected by her party as national leader of the Progressive Conservatives. More women are taking office as members of provincial legislatures, mayors, and city councillors. Although women are still not fully represented in politics, their numbers are growing.

Public attitudes toward men's and women's roles were also changing. The old notion that men and women had different jobs, family duties, and even recreational activities was dying. Between 1986 and 1991, the number of female lawyers jumped by 71 percent, and that of female economists by 65 percent. The number of female architects, engineers, and community planners doubled. Women's sports again started to make headlines, and women sportscasters report sports highlights on radio and TV. In a recent public-opinion poll, three out of four people agreed that the women's movement had a positive effect on Canadian society.

But much remains to be done. Women represented 45 percent of all workers in Canada in 1991, but almost a third were still working in low-paid, low-status jobs. Women accounted for two thirds of workers earning minimum wage. Job discrimination is still a fact of life for Canadian women; many women are still not welcomed in jobs formerly considered "men's work." Real equality for women still lies in the future.

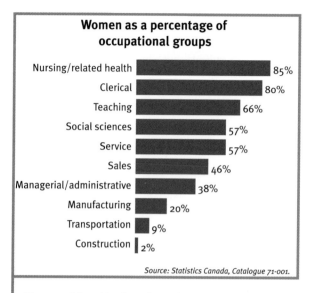

Women as a percentage of occupational groups

Occupational group	Percentage
Nursing/related health	85%
Clerical	80%
Teaching	66%
Social sciences	57%
Service	57%
Sales	46%
Managerial/administrative	38%
Manufacturing	20%
Transportation	9%
Construction	2%

Source: Statistics Canada, Catalogue 71-001.

After examining this chart, have the types of jobs that are largely occupied by women changed since 1900?

Searching for a Uniquely Canadian Identity

On the CTV program *W-5* broadcast on January 31, 1995, participants made the following statements.

"There isn't any one Canadian identity. Canada has no national culture." *Diane Finestone, federal Cabinet minister.*

"Can someone define to me what's a Canadian value?" *Cham-Yah Yuen, Chinese Parents' Association, Richmond, B. C.*

A couple of generations earlier, such comments would have been unthinkable. There *was* a Canadian culture. It was British and French in its origins and was based on respect for parliamentary government, loyalty to the monarchy, and pride in the Union Jack flag. High school students in Ontario took a full-year course in British history. July 1 was known as Dominion Day, and "God Save the Queen" was often sung as Canada's unofficial anthem. Foster Hewitt's voice announced *Hockey Night in Canada* every Saturday night, and the CBC's programming showcased Canadian issues and performers.

French Canada had a place in this culture, though it was small. To English Canadians, Catholic Québec was a slightly backward province. Aboriginal peoples were almost invisible on their reserves and were destined to be assimilated into White culture. Although the contribution of people from non-British backgrounds to Canadian society was acknowledged, they too were expected to blend into the dominant English-speaking culture.

But during the 1960s and 1970s the foundations for the British-centred view of Canadian identity began to change. The Quiet Revolution transformed Québec into a modern secular society, in which the role of the church diminished. Aboriginal peoples began to redefine their various identities and challenged policies that had pushed them toward assimilation. The arrival of immigrants whose origins were not Western European or American further transformed Canadian society. To some it seemed as if there were no longer any defining features of what it meant to be Canadian.

The Policy of Multiculturalism

In Canada's centennial year, 1967, the Royal Commission on Bilingualism and Biculturalism outlined a new vision of Canadian society. Its report recommended that Canada have two official languages — French and English. It also said, however, that Canada should be officially a nation of many cultures. A "multicultural nation" meant that the heritage of all Canada's ethnic groups would be respected and valued. As a multicultural liaison officer later described it, **multiculturalism** was accepting "all the goodness and all the values people have brought here."

Trudeau and the "Just Society"

In 1971 the government of Prime Minister Pierre Trudeau accepted the royal commission's recommendations. Trudeau proclaimed a policy of "multiculturalism within a bilingual framework." His announcement was in keeping with his 1968 pledge to make Canada a "Just Society" — a place where all Canadians were equals. Trudeau saw an emphasis on multiculturalism as a way of challeng-

racism fight

Don't be a wall... be a window

"You can be the answer and the solution."
Amber Selk, 15, from Lethbridge, Alberta created this poster.

What could you change within your own school community to create better racial relations among all peoples?

ing nationalist feelings in Québec, which were running high in the aftermath of the FLQ crisis. His policy pleased many non-British, non-French groups who had felt like second-class citizens in the formerly "bicultural" Canada. It was a formal recognition that Canada was not an American-style **"melting pot,"** in which people were expected to give up their ethnic identities in favour of the dominant culture. Instead Canada was a **"mosaic,"** where people from many ethnic groups lived side by side while participating in Canadian society.

Funding was made available to support various cultural activities, such as preparing ethnic histories and providing heritage language programs. Important new laws supporting multiculturalism were passed over the next decade. The Citizenship Act of 1977 did away with special treatment for British subjects seeking Canadian citizenship. The Canadian Human Rights Act of 1977 outlawed discrimination against members of racial or ethnic groups. Most important of all, the Constitution Act of 1982 contained two new clauses protecting individual and group rights in the Canadian Charter of Rights and Freedoms. One clause pro-

tected individuals from laws that discriminated on the basis of "race, national or ethnic origin, colour, religion, sex, age, or mental and physical disability." Another clause stated that the Charter should be interpreted so as to preserve and enhance "the multicultural heritage of Canadians." When the Progressive Conservative government came into power, it passed a revised Multiculturalism Act in 1988. As a result, more funds were available to promote minority cultures and fight discrimination.

The post-war waves of immigration changed Canadian society. City life, especially in Montréal, Toronto, and Vancouver, has become more varied and interesting. Ethnic foods have transformed the Canadian diet. Chinese has replaced Italian as the third most common language after English and French. People from non-English and non-French backgrounds have moved into more prominent roles in political life. A generation after Vincent Massey became the first Canadian-born Governor General, Ramon Hnatyshyn, whose family had migrated from Ukraine, was chosen as the Queen's representative. And in 1999, Adrienne Clarkson, who had been a Chinese refugee, was appointed to the post of Governor General.

All Canadian.

These children, from a variety of ethnic backgrounds, are holding a Canadian flag made of numerous flags from other countries. How does this photograph capture the true essence of Canada?

Canadian contributions

GUARDING CANADIANS FROM HATE CRIMES

One of the more unpleasant characteristics of Canadian history has been discrimination against some Canadians based on race, religion, ethnicity, or gender. Despite the passage of anti-discriminatory laws after World War Two, Canadians continue to be subjected to the distribution of materials that promote hatred against identifiable groups.

Hate literature that targeted Black Canadians, Aboriginal Peoples, Catholics, and especially Jews became widespread in the early 1960s. The volume of the material grew to such a degree that by 1965 it prompted the Canadian government to create a committee on hate propaganda. In 1970, its report led to passage of legislation that forbade the advocacy of genocide, the incitement of hatred, and group defamation. Since then, the law has been used infrequently, but with some success. A notable example was the charge against James Keegstra, a high school teacher from Alberta, who taught that Jews were responsible for revolutions and global conflicts in a secret conspiracy to control the world. When the case was taken to the Supreme Court of Canada, it upheld the conviction as constitutional in 1993. This set the stage of legislation that punishes those whose crimes are motivated by hate. It has been used in recent years against extreme right wing groups, including those convicted in the murder of a Sikh man in Vancouver in 1998.

In the aftermath to World War Two, hundreds of thousands of Europeans immigrated to Canada. These included people suspected of participating in the murder of civilians during the war. Most of the victims were Jews. Although Canadian immigration authorities were alerted to this possibility, many suspects slipped through the net. Despite public concern, little was done for four decades. Finally, in 1985 the government created a commission headed by Justice Jules Dêschenes to investigate the issue. Its report in 1987 led to legislation against war criminals. This had little effect, however, as the Justice Department found it difficult to find credible evidence and witnesses half a century after the war. As a result, the legislation was changed in 1997. Suspects found guilty of having falsified information about their activities during the war at the time of their application for admission to Canada were to be denaturalized. That meant that they were stripped of their Canadian citizenship, and were liable for deportation to a country from which they had emigrated. Currently, three people have been charged under this act.

Canada's participation in World War Two, the growth of public awareness of the Holocaust, and the publicity given to post-war mass murders and genocides has spurred Canadians to demand that the promotion of hatred and the admission of war criminals are not to be tolerated. This development is welcome and is in contrast to Canada's past history, which was marked by open discrimination against many of its citizens.

CONTRIBUTED BY DR. FRANKLIN BIALYSTOK. DR. BIALYSTOK IS A HISTORIAN SPECIALIZING IN THE HISTORY OF THE HOLOCAUST, AND CANADIAN IMMIGRATION AN ETHNICITY. HE IS A MEMBER OF THE CANADIAN JEWISH CONGRESS.

Questioning Multiculturalism in the 1990s

A tolerant attitude toward newcomers and support for multicultural ideals came more easily during times of prosperity. By the beginning of the 1990s, however, Canadian attitudes began to change. In 1991 the Spicer commission found that many Canadians were angry about the policy of multiculturalism. Surveys taken in 1993 and in 1995 found that Canadians believed that immigrants to Canada should accept Canadian values.

Some of the anger spilled over into criticisms of the immigration system. Too many people were taking advantage of the "family class" system by sponsoring an endless string of distant relatives.

Pardeep Singh Nagra of Brampton, Ontario, was initially barred from boxing by the Canadian Amateur Boxing Association unless he shaved off his beard. Nagra successfully challenged the ruling on the grounds that his beard was of religious significance.

Canada's generous attitude toward refugees provoked hostility. It seemed that Canadians were no longer as tolerant as they had been. Why had people's attitudes changed? The recession of the early 1990s meant that less money was available for social services. Some complained that too much was being spent on helping newcomers adjust to Canada. As unemployment figures rose, some believed it was foolish to welcome immigrants who would compete for jobs.

One problem is that the meaning of multiculturalism had shifted. Supporting multiculturalism was not a problem if the policy was limited to subsidizing folklore festivals, the writing of immigrant histories, or even providing heritage language instruction. But does support for multiculturalism require a tolerance of practices and values that are at variance with Canadian laws? Does multiculturalism lead to a fragmentation of Canadian culture? These questions are connected with the debate over Canadian culture and identity.

Web Connections

http://www.school.mcgrawhill.ca/resources

Go to the Web site above to find out more about multiculturalism. Go to *History Resources*, then to *Canada: A Nation Unfolding, Ontario Edition*, to find out where to go next.

What Is Culture?

Sometimes the word "culture" is used to refer to art, classical music, ballet, and literature. In this sense, culture focuses on the paintings of Emily Carr, the recordings of pianist Glenn Gould, or Alice Munro's short stories. These are examples of "*high* culture." At the other end of the scale is *popular* culture. The music of the Tragically Hip would be one such example; others include films such as *Wayne's World*, and the popular television series *Anne of Green Gables* and *Traders*.

But art in whatever form is only part of culture. In addition to including art, culture encompasses "knowledge, belief, morals, law, customs and any other abilities and habits acquired by a person as a member of society." This much broader definition refers to the whole way of life of a people.

Regional differences also complicate the task of defining a culture. Each part of Canada has a unique historical experience, population mix, and geography. Some of the differences are reflected in the foods people eat, the ways in which they make their living, and the works of their artists and writers. Aboriginal peoples and Black Canadians add yet another set of dimensions to Canadian culture. But neither of these groups is a single, homogeneous community. Language, customs, and history distinguish Mohawks from Cree, Nisga'a, and Inuit. A similar point can be made about the Black Canadian community. Some of its members are descendants of slaves who arrived at the time of the American Revolution or on the Underground Railway in the years before the outbreak of the American Civil War; they differ in many ways from recent arrivals from the Caribbean.

The Americanization of Canadian Culture

Canadian author Robertson Davies once described Canada as the "attic" of the North American continent: upstairs was the unimportant little nation of Canada, and downstairs was the giant American superpower. Even though Canada occupies an enormous part of North America, Davies is not the only Canadian who sees this country as a small and unrecognized nation perched atop the huge United States.

Canadian contributions

CANADIAN SOVEREIGNTY: CARVING OUT A UNIQUE IDENTITY

Throughout the late twentieth century the world has increasingly become a global village. Advanced telecommunications allow television and radio programs to be beamed into Canada from the United States. With the development of affordable and powerful satellite dishes, more and more Canadians are tuning in to American programs and listening to American music. Also, the increasingly multicultural nature of Canada has led some people to question Canada's national identity. Although sovereignty usually refers specifically to legal issues, in recent years it has also come to be used in relation to a country's ability to control its economy and cultural development.

Canadian Music Industry: The enormous American market allows for millions of dollars to be poured into the American music industry. With a limited market, Canadian musicians must struggle to establish a name for themselves. In 1971 the Canadian government set up CanCon, which is a body of regulations that requires that radio stations play a minimum of 30 percent Canadian music. Some feel that Canadian musicians should have to achieve success solely on their merit and should not be supported by regulations that force Canadians to listen to Canadian music. How important do you think content regulations are in promoting the Canadian music industry? Does the support for Canadian musicians help to preserve Canadian sovereignty?

Canadian Broadcasting Corporation: The Canadian Broadcasting Corporation (CBC) was set up in 1936 with its mandate being to develop and promote Canadian culture on radio and later television. The federal government has helped the CBC to produce such programs as "Traders" and "DaVinci's Inquest," as well as documentaries such as "The Fifth Estate" and "Undercurrents," and comedy programs such as "Air Farce" and "This Hour Has 22 Minutes."

Aside from producing Canadian-made programs, the CBC imports a large number of hit programs from the United States. Some feel the CBC should receive much less funding and should generate more revenue by showing the programs the public wants to see regardless of whether they are Canadian or American. Costs could be lowered by importing American programs, since it is far more expensive to produce episodes of Canadian programs than it is to buy existing American shows. Others feel that the CBC should be given more funding and show exclusively Canadian programs. Should the CBC's mandate be to earn a profit or to develop Canadian programs and promote Canadian culture? How does support for the CBC help to ensure Canadian sovereignty?

National Film Board: Created in 1939, the National Film Board of Canada (NFB) has produced films that reflect the social and cultural life of Canada. The founder of the NFB, John Grierson, wanted to make the NFB the "eyes of Canada" and hoped that through its work, it would "through the use of cinema, see Canada and see it whole: its people and its purpose."

Initially, the NFB produced propaganda films to support Canada's war effort during World War II. Two series, Canada Carries On, and World in Action was seen by millions each month in Canada to gather support for the war effort. After the war, the NFB started to produce animation films, and it has become a world leader in the art of animation.

The NFB now has more than 9,000 titles, won nine Oscars, and an honorary Oscar in recognition of its fiftieth anniversary and its dedicated commitment to originate artistic, creative, and technological activity and excellence in every area of filmmaking.

The NFB has played a major part in Canada's visual heritage, but budget cuts in recent years have forced the NFB to cut back on its production of Canadian films.

Humour in History

For the past several decades, comedy has been a major Canadian export. Toronto's Second City comedy theatre has spawned the careers of Dan Aykroyd, John Candy, Rick Moranis, Dave Thomas, Catherine O'Hara, and Martin Short. Canadian-bred comedians Jim Carey and Mike Myers have also enjoyed phenomenal box-office success with their off-beat characters.

During the early 1980s, *SCTV* (Second City Television) was a popular and critically acclaimed Canadian comedy show. A favourite skit involved actors Dave Thomas and Rick Moranis as Canadian characters Bob and Doug McKenzie. In his book *SCTV Behind the Scenes*, Dave Thomas tells how the sketch idea was born.

> Bob and Doug McKenzie were an accidental creation of the Canadian Broadcasting Corporation. The CBC show was two minutes longer than the American syndicated show because it had less commercial content. So the CBC asked for two minutes of distinctive Canadian programming. Andrew (the executive producer) had the hideous job of coming in and telling us this ... Rick and I railed at him. "What do you want us to do? Throw up a map of Canada and sit there wearing tuques and parkas?"

Bob and Doug McKenzie: typical Canadians?

> Andrew sat back, smiled, and said, "Yeah, and if you could have a Mountie in that would be great too."
> Not long after, we were back on the set in front of a Canadian map, wearing tuques and parkas, frying back bacon, with a Mountie mug sitting in front of us...

The "Great White North" sketches became immensely popular across North America, and the duo even made a movie about their misadventures. Soon Canadians, and even some Americans, were using the lingo of these "typical" Canadians— "Take off, eh!"

After the centennial celebrations of 1967, Canadians looked to the federal government to stem the tide of American culture flooding over Canada. In 1968 the government created the Canadian Radio–Television Commission (CRTC) to control radio and television licensing. The CRTC announced in 1970 that radio and TV stations would have to broadcast a certain percentage of Canadian content or risk losing their licences. For example, 30 percent of all music played on the radio had to be Canadian. Radio stations turned to Canadian singers like Anne Murray and Gordon Lightfoot and groups like Rush and Bachman–Turner Overdrive to meet the new "Canadian content" rules. Sixty percent of prime-time TV productions had to be made in Canada, and no more than 30 percent of programming could come from any other country. Soon television series like *The Beachcombers* and *King of Kensington*, which featured Canadian actors, writers, and producers, turned up on Canadians' TV sets.

The federal government also spent millions of dollars to build a Canadian feature-film industry. In the 1970s films like *Goin' Down the Road*, *Kamouraska*, *Mon Oncle Antoine*, and *Why Shoot the Teacher?* gave Canadians a chance to see their own country on the big screen. Canadian book publishers were given special loans and grants to help them promote the sale of Canadian books. More Canadian history and literature courses were offered in public schools. Canadian-studies programs were established in universities, and the Department of Immigration severely restricted the

Canadian voices

INDO-CANADIANS

"How come you people wear red dots on your forehead?"

"You don't eat meat?! Why not?"

"Why do you worship an elephant?"

Growing up Indian in Canada in the 1980s — it was certainly a challenge sometimes. East Indian, that is. It didn't seem to matter that I was born in Canada — downtown Toronto, to be exact.

However, I did experience the best and, sometimes, the worst of many worlds. Where I grew up, in Oak Ridges, Ontario, I was the only visible-minority person until I entered the eleventh grade. I became the object of all inquiries relating to non-Western subjects. But this experience also offered the opportunity to show how proud I was of my culture. I never hesitated to spend time explaining the real reason why Indian women wear a bindi — that beautiful mark on their forehead that was originally a symbol of gratefulness for the God-given gift of intelligence. Nor did I balk at questions about Indian politics or religion. I was flattered and honoured that people wanted to know.

But I know many young people who were not so comfortable with these questions. How do you explain to your friends why you are not allowed to go to the dance on Saturday night or your older sister had an arranged marriage? These questions are difficult and awkward to answer at an age when you are neither sure of the answers nor of whether you believe in the principles behind them. Often it was far easier to simply stay out later, lie about your sister's marriage, or eat that hamburger at McDonald's even though you had been raised as a vegetarian.

Growing up in Canada in the 1980s has also offered tremendous positive pressures. The various Indian communities around the Toronto area have become very concerned with maintaining their cultures. There are numerous classes teaching Indian languages. Various societies have been formed to maintain a sense of community, to carry on and explain important traditions, to give young people a chance to meet others who share a similar background and belief system.

Indifference and tolerance seem to have made way for acceptance and understanding. In the new millennium, the struggle seems to focus on the identity of young people who were born in Canada but whose parents were born in India. Are we Indian? Are we Canadian? Which traditions do we believe in? Which traditions have we made the effort to understand before rejecting them? In what form or shape will our culture be maintained? How will we create our own history, our own identity not merely as Canadians, but as Canadians with a difference? These are the challenges that face us in the new millennium.

CONTRIBUTED BY USHA JAMES. MS. JAMES GREW UP NEAR TORONTO AND IS NOW A TEACHER IN YORK REGION, ONTARIO.

Toronto's Deborah Cox has achieved international success, and has been called the new "Queen of rhythm and blues." Like many Canadian performers, she had to go to the United States to get recognition. Why do you think this is so?

hiring of foreign professors — mostly American — for Canadian university positions. It was hoped that these measures would help promote a distinctive Canadian culture.

So, Is "Canadian' an Ethnicity?

In an increasingly diverse country, being Canadian can sometimes become lost among all the ethnicities used to define the communities that make up Canada's population. Italian Canadians, Indo-Canadians, African Canadians, and Japanese Canadians, for example, are often defined by what distinguishes their **ethnicity** from other Canadians. Seldom are the characteristics of being "Canadian" discussed.

So what are the characteristics all Canadians share regardless of their ancestry? How can we define Canadianism? Living in a world made increasingly smaller by technology, in a country populated by people who have come from all over the world, the search for the Canadian identity remains elusive.

The End Is the Beginning

Your journey through Canadian history in the twentieth century is about to draw to a close. Just as the end of the twentieth century marked the beginning of the twenty-first century, so to the end of this journey marks the beginning of your travels into the future. Through the pages of this book you have learned about the exploits of a great many Canadians and have shared in the challenges and triumphs of Canada over the past one hundred years. The road to the twenty-first century was not always a smooth one. At times Canada encountered roadblocks, such as wars and economic downturns. At other times the nation veered down paths it would later wish to forget, such as the internment of Ukrainian and Japanese Canadians in World Wars I and II and the harsh treatment of Aboriginal young people in residential schools.

Nonetheless, Canadians persevered and built a nation to be proud of. Many challenges lie ahead for a nation that is envied around the world. Soon it will be your turn to take up the leadership of Canada, to safeguard the ideals that Canadians treasure and to erase the barriers that still prevent many Canadians from sharing in the abundant wealth of the nation. Use your knowledge of the past wisely. It can act as a guiding light to the future.

chapter review

CHAPTER SUMMARY

In this chapter, we have seen

- How technology has changed and will continue to change the lives of Canadians, especially in healthcare, education, and access to information.

- How immigration has changed the demographic makeup of Canada.

- That Canada is becoming a multicultural nation.

- That Canadians are struggling to find a Canadian identity.

UNDERSTANDING HISTORICAL FACTS

1. Identify these people, places, and events, and explain their significance.

Generation X	Canadian Human Rights Act
Multiculturalism	Adrienne Clarkson
CRTC	Canadian
"Glass Ceiling"	"Just Society"

2. List as many ways as you can of the ways in which the federal, provincial, and municipal governments promote and encourage the development of a distinctly Canadian culture and identity. Begin with the fact that you are required to take this course.

3. In the past, population growth in and around urban centres such as Vancouver often displaced Aboriginal peoples to make room for new housing developments. This trend is now being reversed. Explain how present trends in population growth are affecting Aboriginal communities.

4. Women have seen rapid and dramatic change in their roles in Canadian society since 1968. Capture the essence of this change by describing "a day in the life" of a woman aged twenty-five in 1968, and a woman aged twenty-five in 2000.

EXPRESSING YOUR OPINION

1. Discuss with your teacher, parents, or friends of your family what school was like when they were students. Then create a web to show the changes that have occurred in Canada's schools as a result of technology. Finally, write a paragraph that describes how you think education will be different twenty years from now.

2. How should Canada's policy toward refugees differ from its policy regarding other immigrants? Should those whose lives are in danger be accepted immediately and then questioned when they are safe? How should Canada treat those who are found to have falsely claimed refugee status?

3. Do you believe that content regulations (a set percentage of music on radio and programs on television that must be of Canadian origin) help to support and promote Canadian culture? Defend your answer.

4. Despite achieving legal and political equality, women continue to struggle for economic and social equality. What issues to you believe should be the primary focus of the women's movement today?

WORKING WITH THE EVIDENCE

1. One of the most unique Canadian phrases, often repeated on CBC television and radio, is: "Program X will be seen at 10:00 p.m., 10:30 in Newfoundland." Why does the CBC say this?

unit review
BRINGING THE PAST INTO FOCUS

REVIEWING THE FACTS

1. Is technology improving the standard of living for Canadians? Consider the impact of technology on the workplace, home, and leisure time. What are the costs and benefits of changes in technology for Canadians?

2. List three ways in which the federal government has attempted to promote a common Canadian identity. For each of the ways listed, provide a brief two- or three-sentence assessment of how effective each attempt has been.

3. What evidence can you find in this unit that Canada is a country made up of distinct regions with very different needs and views on many issues? Are there issues on which a majority of Canadians from all regions agree? Explain your answer.

4. Imagine that you are a visitor to Canada in 1970. Thirty years later you make a return visit. Prepare a list of five things you would notice that have changed in Canada in the thirty years since your last visit.

MAKING CONNECTIONS

Rating the performance of Canada's Prime Ministers requires an understanding of what you consider to be the essential elements of good leadership. Recreate the chart below. Once you have created and completed the chart, use it to guide your assessment of the leadership provided by Prime Ministers Trudeau, Mulroney, and Chrétien. Write one or two paragraphs defending one of these politicians as the best prime minister of the late twentieth century.

HISTORICALLY SPEAKING

5. The 1980s and 1990s saw the end of communism in Eastern Europe, the rapid growth of multinational corporations, and an explosion of computer technology that revolutionized banking and business around the world. Discuss three new challenges for the government of Canada that resulted from these changes.

6. Several Canadians have enjoyed significant success in the entertainment field: Mike Myers, Jim Carey, Sarah McLachlan, Celine Dion, Deborah Cox, and The Barenaked Ladies. To what degree do these performers reflect Canadian culture and identity? Do others who enjoy less commercial success reflect more about the Canadian identity? Defend your answer.

7. One of the most hotly debated topics in the past few decades has been Canada's relationship with the United States. Many Canadians feel that closer ties with the United States would threaten Canada's social programs, health-care system, and cultural industries. Do you agree that close ties with the United States involve threats to Canada? Or are close ties with the United States essential to the health of Canada? Defend your answer.

8. Do the events of the past thirty years suggest that Canada is becoming more a more tolerant and compassionate country? Consider the treatment of Aboriginal peoples, refugees, and the homeless; the Canadian Human Rights Code and the Charter of Rights and Freedoms; and Canada's social safety net.

	PIERRE TRUDEAU	**BRIAN MULRONEY**	**JEAN CHRÉTIEN**
Leadership Trait #1	*[handwriting]*	*[handwriting]*	*[handwriting]*
Leadership Trait #2	*[handwriting]*	*[handwriting]*	*[handwriting]*
Leadership Trait #3	*[handwriting]*	*[handwriting]*	*[handwriting]*

PERSPECTIVES

9. The photo essay in this unit captures several symbols of Canada. Create your own photo essay on the theme "The Many Faces of Canada." Use photographs from home, magazines, the Internet, or illustrations that you draw yourself. Be sure to stop and consider the many faces that make up Canada before you begin your project.

10. Imagine you are asked to chair a meeting of provincial representatives regarding the Constitution. For each of the following regions, provide in point-form what you believe would be that region's primary concerns or demands.

   British Columbia   Prairie Provinces
   Ontario   Québec
   Atlantic Provinces   Nunavut

11. Refer to the opening quotation by Wilfrid Laurier in Unit 1: "As the nineteenth century was that of the United States, so, I think the twentieth century shall be filled by Canada." Write five hundred words on how this statement might be viewed today from one of the following perspectives:

   Aboriginal Canadian   Black Canadian
   Asian Canadian   Canadian Woman

Glossary

Acid Rain A deadly shower of sulphuric and nitrous oxides resulting from atmospheric emissions from industries and automobiles.

Alliances Agreements or treaties between nations to co-operate for specific purposes.

Allied Powers In World War II, the anti-fascist forces, initially Britain and its Commonwealth, France, and Poland; the Allies later included the United States and the Soviet Union.

Anti-Semitism Prejudice against or hostility toward Jews.

Appeasement The policy of making concessions in order to maintain peace.

Armistice An agreement to stop fighting while a peace settlement is negotiated.

Artillery Barrage A heavy firing of mounted guns and cannons, intended to slow enemy action or to allow troops to advance with fewer casualties.

Assassination A murder carried out for political purposes.

Assimilation The absorption of a nation's various ethnicities and cultures into the majority culture.

Autonomy A nation's political independence from another nation's interference in its domestic affairs.

Axis Powers In World War II, Germany, Italy, Japan, and their allies.

Baby Boom The huge increase in the number of babies born in Canada from about 1945 to 1965.

Ballistic Missiles Rockets with warheads (bombs) attached to them.

Battalions Units of the armed forces that form part of a regiment.

Blind Pig A place where liquor can be bought illegally.

Bootlegging The illegal sale of alcoholic beverages.

Branch Plants Businesses operating in and employing the people of one country but owned and controlled by the people of another country.

Brigades Large bodies of troops, usually consisting of several regiments, battalions, or squadrons.

British Empire Britain and its many colonies around the world.

Business Cycle An economic cycle of alternating upswings and downturns.

Canada Assistance Plan A plan under which the federal government agreed to share with the provinces the costs of a range of programs, including child care, health care for the needy, employment projects, and aid for disadvantaged groups such as widows and people with disabilities.

Canadian Bill of Rights An Act passed by Parliament in 1960 that provided legal protections for freedom of speech, religion, the press, and assembly, and for equal treatment before the law.

Civil War A war between two or more groups within a single nation.

Colonies Areas that are first occupied and then governed by people from a foreign country.

Communism The economic theory that all property, business, and industry should be owned and managed by the state.

Compromise An agreement in which each side makes concessions.

Conscientious Objectors People who refuse to participate in military service because of their moral or religious beliefs.

Consolidated Companies Businesses that have merged in order to strengthen their position in the economy.

Consumerism The belief that a continuing increase in the consumption of goods is good for the economy and hence for the culture.

Containment An American foreign policy during the Cold War, aimed at halting the spread of communism around the world.

Continentalists People who believe that the various nations of a continent, especially North America, should be more interdependent and perhaps form a single nation.

Convoys Groups of merchant ships that are protected from enemy attack by naval escort ships or air force planes.

Counterculture The standards and values of a mostly younger generation who have rejected the cultural norms of established society.

Cultural Mosaic A multicultural society in which immigrants and their descendants are encouraged to preserve their cultural heritage. The term is often contrasted with "melting pot," in which immigrants are encouraged to abandon their cultural distinctiveness in favour of the culture of their new country.

Culture The customs, traditions, and whole way of life of a group of people.

Demobilization The disbandment of armed troops.

Depopulation The drastic reduction of population as a result of war, disease, famine, or emigration.

Destroyers Small but well-armed warships used both to defend allied ships and to attack enemy ships.

Détente A relaxation in tensions between nations.

Dictatorship Government by a single leader or group that tolerates no opposition.

Diplomacy The management of relations between various nations.

Direct Investment A form of investment in which investors establish a business and thereby hold control over it.

Disarmament A nation's reduction of its stockpiles of weapons and armed forces.

Discrimination An unjust difference in the way that people are treated.

Dominion A self-governing nation within the British Commonwealth.

Drought A long period of dry weather.

Enemy Alien A term used during wartime to describe anyone who had not yet gained Canadian citizenship and who was a former citizen of a country at war with Canada.

Espionage The use of spies to obtain military, political, or scientific secrets from other nations.

Ethnicity The cultural characteristics that define a person's sense of identification with a larger group.

Expansionism The policy of extending influence over other lands or countries by either taking territory by force or increasing economic control.

Fascism A system of government that is based on strongly centralized powers and permits no opposition or criticism.

Foreign Policy A nation's policy toward other nations.

Free Trade Unrestricted exporting and importing, not subject to customs, duties, or tariffs.

GATT The General Agreement on Tariffs and Trade, established by Canada and twenty-two other nations in 1948, to encourage a reduction in tariffs and other international trade barriers. GATT negotiations are continuous and have resulted in the organization being largely superseded by the World Trade Organization (WTO), which has more than 130 member nations.

Generation Gap Differences between the personal attitudes and social values of a generation of teenagers and young adults and the values of their parents' generation.

Generation X A term to describe the post–baby boom generation, coined by Vancouver's Douglas Coupland in his novel of the same name.

Genocide The mass murder of an ethnic, racial, or religious group.

Global Village A term coined by Canadian communications specialist Marshall McLuhan to describe a world in which electronic communications have reduced the geographic and language barriers between nations and given people all over the world a sense of belonging to the same group.

Great Depression The period of economic depression, marked by a severe decline in business activity, that began in 1929 and lasted through most of the 1930s.

Gulags Soviet labour camps set up by Joseph Stalin for political prisoners.

Handpick Mining Mining done with hand tools.

High Commissioner A nation's ambassador established in another country.

Hippies Young people in the 1960s who held countercultural values and attempted to avoid pursuing middle-class ideals.

Imperial Conference A meeting of member nations of the British Empire.

Imperialism A nation's extension of its authority over other lands by political, economic, or military means.

Industrial Revolution The great shift from agriculture to manufacturing that occurred in Europe and North America from about 1750 to 1850.

Industrialization The process of industry attaining an important position in a region's economy.

Internment Camps Wartime camps set up in Canada to house people considered to be enemy aliens.

Jazz Age One description of the 1920s, when jazz was tremendously popular and regarded as a revolutionary form of music.

Jubilee Celebrations The celebrations held in 1901 to commemorate Queen Victoria's sixty years of rule over the British Empire.

Kristallnacht "The night of broken glass," November 10, 1938, when German Jews were attacked and Jewish synagogues and businesses in Germany were ransacked and looted.

La Survivance The survival of Québec's language and traditions.

Labour Unions An organization formed to protect workers from unfair exploitation and promote their common interests.

Laissez-faire A French term ("let it be") for the policy of strictly limiting government control and direction of trade, business, or industry.

Market Value The present selling price of an item.

Mass Marketing The use of a marketing program to sell goods that appeal to the average consumer to a large number of people.

Mass Production The efficient manufacture of products in large numbers, usually accomplished by using assembly lines.

McCarthyism The "Red Scare" that accompanied the anti-communist investigations led by U.S. Senator Joseph McCarthy in the early 1950s.

Mechanization The increasing use of machines to perform tasks.

Medicare A government-sponsored medical-care plan that pays for all necessary medical services.

Melting Pot A society in which people are encouraged to gradually abandon their various ethnic identities in becoming part of the majority culture.

Middle Power A nation (like Canada) that takes advantage of its diplomatic expertise and lack of military strength to play a role in mediating conflicts between major world powers.

Militarism The policy of continually building up armaments and armed forces or of threatening armed aggression.

Mosaic A society in which people are encouraged to celebrate their original ethnic identities as part of their participation in the larger society.

Multiculturalism A federal government policy aimed at promoting the heritages of all Canada's ethnic groups.

Munitions Weapons such as guns and ammunition used for the purpose of war.

National Debt The debt incurred by a nation's government as a result of its borrowing to pay for its programs.

National Policy A policy for developing Canada that contained three proposals: a protective tariff to protect Canadian manufacturers (a tax added to the price of American goods), the completion of a national railway to move settlers and manufactured goods to the West and move wheat to the East, and large-scale settlement of the West to serve as Canada's breadbasket and to provide markets for the industries of Central Canada.

Nationalism Devotion to the interest of a nation, sometimes leading to putting the interests of the nation above everything else.

Nationaliste In Canada, a person who believes that Québec's unique francophone culture should be expressed in a national rather than merely a provincial political status.

Naval Blockade The use of ships to block off a route or a port to prevent maritime trade.

Nazism The totalitarian and racist doctrines of Germany's National Socialist Party under its dictator, Adolf Hitler.

Neutrality An official refusal to take sides in international disputes.

Nixon Shock The imposition of a 10 percent tariff on Canadian goods being imported into the United States, imposed by U.S. President Richard Nixon in 1971.

No-Man's Land A belt of unoccupied land between the trenches of opposing forces in war.

On-to-Ottawa Trek A 1935 march of unemployed Canadian workers to Ottawa to demand "work with wages."

Pacifist People who oppose war on moral grounds.

Pandemic A worldwide epidemic.

Panzers Heavily armoured German tanks.

Parapets Defensive walls or barriers of earth or stone built in front of a trench.

Patriotism Love of one's country.

Pensions Allowances paid regularly by governments or businesses to certain groups such as the elderly and people with disabilities to help them obtain the necessities of life.

Plebiscite A vote on a public issue.

Pogey Slang term for government relief vouchers in the 1930s.

Portfolio Investment A form of investment in which investors purchase shares in but do not control a business.

Potlatch A traditional community ceremony practised by some Pacific Northwest Aboriginal peoples.

Privy Council A British council that was the highest court of appeal for Canadian legal cases until 1949.

Progress Advancement and improvement.

Prohibition The banning of certain activities or products, such as liquor.

Proxy Wars Wars between nations that are not fought within their borders but in the territories of other nations, often by supporting various factions in those other nations' wars.

Racism A belief in the innate superiority of one race to another race.

Reciprocity A Canada–United States trade agreement allowing a large number of goods to cross the border without a tariff.

Reconnaissance A survey of enemy territory to gather military information about such things as the enemy's strength and position.

Red Menace The much-feared and exaggerated threat of communist revolution in North America from the 1920s to the 1950s.

Referendum The putting of a question of general importance to a direct vote of citizens for their approval or rejection.

Refugees People fleeing danger, persecution, or death in their home country as a result of government action or war.

Regina Manifesto A 1933 statement of the political aims of the Co-operative Commonwealth Federation.

Reparations Money paid by a defeated nation as compensation for damages to civilians and property during war.

Repatriate To return a person or thing to its own country; to bring legislation under the authority of the country to which the law applies, as Canada did with its Constitution.

Reserves In Canada, areas set aside for Aboriginal peoples by the federal government as compensation for the loss of their traditional territories.

Residential Schools Government-established schools in which Canadian Aboriginal children were forced to abandon their traditional culture and assimilate into the dominant European culture.

Ross rifle A Canadian-made rifle used by Canadian troops in the early years of World War I.

Sanatoriums Institutions in which people with long-term, serious illnesses can receive medical treatment.

Satellite States During the Cold War, countries whose governments were directly linked to the Soviet Union.

Secondary Manufacturing The making of products from processed, or secondary, materials rather than from primary, or raw, materials.

Segregation A separation of one group of people from other groups in public places.

Service Industries Businesses that perform economic activities other than manufacturing.

Service Sector The part of the economy that engages in activities other than manufacturing.

Shell Shock A serious nervous disorder resulting from prolonged exposure to sustained artillery fire.

Shrapnel Sharp-edged metal fragments released from an exploding shell.

Social Credit A British economic theory that held that a depressed economy was the result of people not having spending money.

Social Gospel The belief that the meaning of Christianity is to be found in changing society, not only in "saving souls."

Social Reformers People who work to make society more just, equitable, and fair for all but avoid advocating revolution because they regard it as too extreme and perhaps counterproductive.

Social Safety Net A network of government programs, including medicare, the Canada Pension Plan, the Canada Assistance Plan, and employment insurance, that help to ensure that Canadians' basic needs are met.

Social Welfare Programs and services to ensure that people have access to basic necessities such as food, shelter, and medical care.

Sodbusters Canadian pioneers who first ploughed the prairie soil for farming.

Sovereignty Self-government; a nation's power to set its own policies and be free from foreign interference in its domestic affairs.

Spinoff Industries Businesses that are created to provide the services or products required by other industries.

Stagflation A stagnant economy resulting from high inflation in times of high unemployment.

Stock Market A place where bonds and stocks, or shares of corporate capital, are bought and sold.

Storm Troops Armed forces trained for sudden and efficient assault.

Strikebreakers People hired to replace striking employees and thereby weaken the impact of a strike.

Subsidies Financial aid provided to businesses and other organizations.

Suburbia Large urban subdivisions that were made possible by efficient public transit as well as the popularity of the automobile and that became a major feature of North American life after World War II.

Suffrage The right to vote in elections.

Suffragists People who advocate women's right to vote.

Sun Dance A traditional ceremony of some prairie Aboriginal peoples.

Superpowers Nations that have great power over most others as a result of their military superiority.

Total War A war fought with no limits put on the resources used to achieve victory.

Transcontinental Railways Railways that span the continent from coast to coast.

Transients Homeless people who roam in search of work, shelter, and food.

Trench Foot A medical condition resulting from having wet feet for a long period; feet swell up to twice their normal size and go numb; gangrene may result.

Trench Warfare Armed combat conducted from trenches dug to provide protection in open areas.

Trudeaumania The enormous popular support for the charismatic Pierre Trudeau in the late 1960s.

Turtle Island Another name for North America, in the traditions of some of its Aboriginal peoples.

U-Boats Short term for *Unterseebooten*, "undersea boat": German submarines used to deadly effect in World War I.

Underground Railway The network of anti-slavery activists that helped slaves from the United States escape into Canada.

Union Nationale A Québec political party, headed by Maurice Duplessis, that held power in the province for most years from 1936 to 1959.

Victoria Cross The British Commonwealth's highest military honour.

War Measures Act A law passed in 1914 giving the federal government sweeping emergency powers in times of war, invasion, or rebellion; the Act severely limits the freedoms of Canadians.

World War A war that, even though it may begin in one region, spreads to involve many nations around the world, often as a result of international alliances that existed before the war began.

Xenophobia A fear of other cultures or of people from other countries.

Youth Generation In the late 1960s, the two million "baby boomers" born between the late 1940s and mid-1960s.

Zombies A slang term coined during World War II to describe men who were conscripted for home defence within the borders of Canada; so called because they were thought to display limited support for the war effort.

Credits

Cover

Front Cover, clockwise from top left: UN photo/159289/J. Isaac, Glenbow Archives/NA-863-4, http://www.inac.gc.ca/nunavut/kit/flag.pdf, Canapress/Paul Chiasson, NASA, NAC/PA-001332; **Back Cover, clockwise from top right**: Musée-J. Armand Bombardier, CP Picture Archive, Tak Toyota/NAC/C-046350, Duncan Cameron/NAC/PA-170161, Thunder Bay Finnish Canadian Historical Society Collection (MG8), Chancellor Paterson Library Archives, Lakehead University

Photo Credits

page vi Canadian War Museum, *Stretcher Bearer Party* by Cyril Henry Barraud/CN#8021; NAC/C-033446; NAC/PA-001332; NAC/PA-000880; Canadian War Museum, Armistice Day by George Reid/CN#8685; NAC/PA-005122; **page vii** NAC; NAC/PA-001891; NAC/PA-001017; "K-K-K-Katy" words and music by Geoffrey O-Hara, copyright © 1918 (renewed 1946) Leo Feist, Inc., Warner Bros. Publications Inc.; **page viii** NAC/C-080027; NAC/PA-001305, The Toronto Star Syndicate, H.G. Aitman/DND/NA/PA-108174, NAC/PA-001355; DND/EKS 1360, DND/PL 20839, Department of Defense, Canadian Forces photograph/IHC88-12-2; Ken Bell/DND/NAC/PA-132838; **page ix** DND/NAC/PA-003747; William Rider, DND/NAC/PA-002156; NAC/PA-002279; **Page 2** © Canada Post Corporation, 1898. Reproduced with Permission; **page 3** CP Picture Archive/Tom Hanson; **page 6** Benjamin West/*The Death of General Wolfe*/Acc # 8007/National Gallery of Canada, Ottawa; **page 8** NAC/C-011053; **page 9** Stone/Rosemary Calvert; **page 10** Artist, Henry Bishop/Book: "Out of Past: Into the Future"; **page 11** NAC/C-003693; **page 12** NAC/C-014115; **page 14 top** Glenbow Archives/NA-470-1, **bottom left** NAC/C-002616, **bottom right** Manitoba Archives/N7968; **page 15 bottom left**

NAC/C-027360, **bottom right** Glenbow Archives/NC-6-1746; **page 16** NAC/C-0052819; **page 18 top** City of Toronto Archives/SC 244-342, **bottom** NAC/C-000932; **page 19** NAC/C-002616; **page 21** E.A. Hegg/NAC/C-005142; **page 23** NAC/PA-110154; **page 24** NAC/C-030620; **page 26** Dick Hemingway; **page 27** Dick Hemingway; **page 29** Provincial Archives of Alberta/E. Brown Collection/B4113; **page 30 left** Toronto Library Board/Canadian Annual Review, 1909, **right** Toronto Library Board/Canadian Annual Review, 1909; **page 31** Manitoba Archives/N7968; **page 32 left** William Molson Macpherson Collection/NAC/PA-062200; **page 32** William H. Gibson/NAC/PA-059895; **page 33** Used with permission of Sears Canada Inc.; **page 34** National Gallery of Canada/Gift of Gordon C. Edwards, Ottawa, 1923, in memory of Senator and Mrs. W.C. Edwards; **page 35 top left, top right and bottom left** Garfield Newman; **page 37** Glenbow Archives, NA-263-1; **page 39** Multicultural History Society of Ontario; **page 40** Provincial Archives of Alberta/B2738; **page 41** Provincial Archives of Alberta/B1004; **page 44** Archives of the United Church of Canada; **page 45** Archives, Eaton's of Canada Ltd., with permission of Sears Canada Inc.; **page 46** NAC/PA-0093160; **page 47 left** Provincial Archives of Alberta/B4678, **right** Provincial Archives of Manitoba/N2438; **page 48** Archives, Eaton's of Canada Ltd., With permission of Sears Canada Inc.; **page 48 top right all images** Archives, Eaton's of Canada Ltd., With permission of Sears Canada Inc., **bottom left all images** Thomas Fisher Rare Book Library, found in MacLean's, January 1912; **page 49** Glenbow Archives/NA-5055-1; **page 50** Clarence Gagnon 1881-1942/*Harvesting* 1928-1933/mixed media on paper/21.2 x 18.9 cm/Gift of Col. R.S. McLaughlin/McMichael Canadian Art Collection/1969.4.27; **page 51** NAC/C-058596; **page 52** NAC/PA-013012; **page 54** The Vancouver Daily Province, March 1912/Courtesy of the Province; **page 55** Glenbow Archives, NC-6-1746; **page 56** Provincial Archives of New Brunswick/P338-200; **page 58** Toronto Reference Library; **page 59** Reprinted with the permission of The Globe and Mail; **page 60** © Canada Post Corporation, 1898. Reproduced with Permission; **page 61** NAC/C-006097; **page 62 clockwise from top right** NAC/PA-031580, Anglican Church of Canada/P7517-464, NAC/PA-066579, Glenbow

Agency; **page 397** CP Picture Archive/Tom Hanson; **page 400 top left** Government of Canada, **bottom right** Ministry of Culture, Tourism, and Recreation; **page 402** CP Picture Archive/Kevin Frayer; **page 406** CP Picture Archive/Mike Pinder

Text Credits

Page 23 From *Literary Lapses* by Stephen Leacock, Toronto: McClelland & Stewart, 1989, © 1957; **page 79** From *Canada: A Nation Unfolding*, 1/e by Garfield Newman and Diane Eaton, Whitby: McGraw-Hill Ryerson Limited, 1996; **page 81** From *Canada: A Nation Unfolding*, 1/e by Garfield Newman and Diane Eaton, Whitby: McGraw-Hill Ryerson Limited, 1996; **page 84** "K-K-K-Katy" words and music by Geoffrey O'Hara, copyright © 1918 (renewed 1946) Leo Feist, Inc., Warner Bros. Publications Inc.; **page 90** George Borden; **page 100** From The *Halifax Explosion* compiled and edited by Graham Metson, Toronto: McGraw-Hill Ryerson Limited, 1978.; **page 107** From *Canada: A Nation Unfolding*, 1/e by Garfield Newman and Diane Eaton, Whitby: McGraw-Hill Ryerson Limited, 1996; **page 112** From *Generals die in bed* by Charles Yale Harrison, Waterdown, Ontario: Potlatch Publications, 1999, © 1974; **page 120** From *Letters From Home*, by John Macfie, © 1990; **page 126-127** *Maclean's*, January 1919, p. 89; **page 129** From *Canada: A Nation Unfolding*, 1/e by Garfield Newman and Diane Eaton, Whitby: McGraw-Hill Ryerson Limited, 1996; **page 147** From *Historical Atlas of Canada*, Vol. III, U of T Press, 1990, Plate 16; **page 147** From *Historical Atlas of Canada*, Vol III, U of T Press, 1990, Plate 16; **page 156** From *Next-Year Country: Voices of Prairie People* by Barry Broadfoot. Copyright © 1988 by Barry Broadfoot. Used by written permission, McClelland & Stewart, Inc. *The Canadian Publishers*; **page 168** From *Why Shoot the Teacher?* by Max Braithwaite, 1975, © 1965, McClelland & Stewart Inc. *The Canadian Publishers*; **page 216-217** Adapted from *The Art of Decoding Political Cartoons: A Teacher's Guide* by Charles and Cynthia Hou, Vancouver: Moody's Lookout Press, 1998; **page 221** From *Canada: A Nation Unfolding*, 1/e by Garfield Newman and Diane Eaton, Whitby: McGraw-Hill Ryerson Limited, 1996; **page 267** From *And No Birds Sang* by Farley Mowat, Toronto: McClelland & Stewart, © 1979, with permission of Farley Mowat Limited; **page 268** From *Canada: A Nation Unfolding*, 1/e by Garfield Newman and Diane Eaton, Whitby: McGraw-Hill Ryerson Limited, 1996; **page 273** From *Canada: A Nation Unfolding*, 1/e by Garfield Newman and Diane Eaton, Whitby: McGraw-Hill Ryerson Limited, 1996; **page 287** From *Living and Learning*, Toronto: Publications Ontario, Department of Education, 1968, page 9.; **page 292** David Woods; **page 294** The Johnny Wayne Estate and Frank Shuster Enterprises Limited; **page 308-309** From *The Hockey Sweater and Other Stories*, by Roch Carrier, translated by Sheila Fischman, Toronto: House of Anansi Press, 1979, pp. 77-81; **page 331** Steven Fick/*Canadian Geographic*, Nov/Dec 1992; **page 362** European American Music Corp.; **page 366** Statistics Canada, Census of Canada and Catalogue 93-151; **page 394** Statistics Canada, 1991 Census of Canada; **page 396** From *My Canada*, edited by Glenn Keith Cowan, Toronto: Irwin Publishing, 1984; **page 399** Statistics Canada, Catalogue 71-001; **page 404** From *SCTV: Behind the Scenes* by Dave Thomas, Toronto: McClelland & Stewart, 1996.

Index